Glimpses of Fifty Years

Yours for Home Protection,

Frances E. Willard.

Jan. 30, 1889.

GLIMPSES OF FIFTY YEARS

The Autobiography

OF

AN AMERICAN WOMAN

BY

FRANCES E. WILLARD.

Source Book Press

Library of Congress Catalogue Card No. 71-134197
ISBN 0-87681-079-2
Source Book Press, a Division of Collectors Editions Ltd.,
185 Madison Avenue, New York, N.Y. 10016
Unabridged republication of the 1889 Chicago edition: First printing 1970
Manufactured in the United States of America

GLIMPSES OF FIFTY YEARS.

The Autobiography

OF

AN AMERICAN WOMAN

BY

FRANCES E. WILLARD.

WRITTEN BY ORDER OF THE NATIONAL WOMAN'S CHRISTIAN TEMPERANCE UNION.

INTRODUCTION BY HANNAH WHITALL SMITH.

"Nothing makes life dreary but lack of motive."

PUBLISHED BY THE

Woman's Temperance Publication Association.

H. J. SMITH & CO.

CHICAGO, PHILADELPHIA, KANSAS CITY, OAKLAND, CAL.

General Agents for United States, Canada, Australia, Sandwich Islands.

EXPLANATORY.

We wish it distinctly understood that Miss Willard's responsibility for this book ended when she furnished her manuscript.

She repeatedly requested that but one picture of herself be given. This, however, would leave her out of official groups where she is the central figure, and to preserve the unity of these, also as illustrative of altogether different phases of her life, we have arranged the pictures as we believed the interests of the book and the preference of the public warranted us in doing.

It should also be stated that Miss Willard wrote twelve hundred pages that had to be cut down to seven hundred, and in so doing, scores of names, facts and allusions, all of which she was especially desirous to have in this book, had to be omitted. To this omission the author has kindly agreed, having written rapidly ana without calculating for the space required by this overplus of manuscript.

WOMAN'S TEMPERANCE PUBLICATION ASSOCIATION.

Chicago, Feb. 22, 1889.

Dedicatory.

THERE IS ONE

"Face that duly as the sun,
Rose up for me since life begun;"

ONE ROYAL HEART THAT NEVER FAILED ME YET.

TO MOTHER,

AS A BIRTHDAY GIFT,

ON

JANUARY 3, 1889,

THE EIGHTY-FIFTH ANNIVERSARY OF HER UNDAUNTED LIFE,

I DEDICATE

HER ELDEST DAUGHTER'S SELF-TOLD STORY.

THOU, under Satan's fierce control,
Shall Heaven on thee its rest bestow?
I know not, but I know a soul
That might have fall'n as darkly low.

"I judge thee not, what depths of ill
Soe'er thy feet have found or trod;
I know a spirit and a will
As weak, but for the help of God.

"Shalt thou with full day-lab'rers stand,
Who hardly canst have pruned one vine?
I know not, but I know a hand
With an infirmity like thine.

"Shalt thou, who hadst with scoffers part,
E'er wear the crown the Christian wears?
I know not, but I know a heart
As flinty, but for tears and prayers.

"Have mercy, O thou Crucified!
For even while I name Thy name,
I know a tongue that might have lied,
Like Peter's, and am filled with shame."

Introduction.

I have been asked by the publishers of this Autobiography to write the Introduction. I am very glad to be asked. There is no woman in the world whose book I would rather introduce than that of my friend and co-worker, Frances E. Willard. From the first hour of my acquaintance with her, now more than sixteen years ago, she has been to me the embodiment of all that is lovely, and good, and womanly, and strong, and noble and tender, in human nature. She has been my queen among women, and I have felt it to be one of the greatest privileges of my life to call her my friend. I have been inspired by her genius, I have been cheered by her sympathy, I have been taught by her wisdom, I have been led onward and upward by her enthusiastic faith. We have met on almost every point of human interest, and have been together in joy and in sorrow, in success and in apparent failure; she has been a member of my household for weeks together, and I have seen her tried by prosperity and flattery, by misunderstanding and evil report; and always and everywhere she has been the same simple-hearted, fair-minded Christian woman, whose one sole aim has been to do the will of God as far as she knew it, and to bear whatever of apparent ill He may have permitted to come upon her, with cheerful submission, as being His loving discipline for the purpose of making her what, above all, she longs to be, a partaker of His holiness.

In regard to her public work she has seemed to me one of God's best gifts to the American women of the nineteenth century, for she has done more to enlarge our sympathies, widen our outlook, and develop our gifts, than any man, or any other woman of her time. Every movement for the uplifting of humanity has found in her a cordial friend and active helper. Every field of inquiry or investigation has shared in her quick, intelligent sympathy, and she has been essentially American in this, that she is always receptive of new ideas, without being frightened at their newness. One saying of hers is eminently characteristic—that we have no more need to be afraid of the step just ahead of us than we have to be afraid of the one just behind us; and, acting on this, she has always given all new suggestions a candid and fair-minded consideration, and has kept in the forefront of every right movement, whether in the world of ideas or the world of things. I have called her to myself, many times, our "see-er," because, like all seers, she seems to have an insight into things not visible to the eyes of most. We who know her best have so much confidence, born of experience, in these insights of hers, that I am not sure but that something once said about us laughingly is, after all, pretty nearly the truth: that "if Frances Willard should push a plank out into the ocean, and should beckon the white ribbon women to follow her out to the end of it, they would all go without a question." The reason is that we have discovered that her planks always turn out to be bridges across to delectable islands which she has discerned while yet they were invisible to us.

How such a woman came to be, is told us in this book, and it is a story that will, I believe, be an example and an inspiration to thousands of her fellow-women, who will learn here the vast possibilities of a pure and holy womanhood, consecrated to God and to the service of humanity.

How this story came to be told is as follows: As president for nearly ten years of the great organization called the National Woman's Christian Temperance Union, numbering more than two hundred thousand women, scattered all over the United States, from Maine to Texas, and from Florida to Alaska, Frances E. Willard has won a love and loyalty that no other woman, I think, has ever before possessed. It was natural that the many members of this widespread organization, who could not see their leader, should desire to read the story of her life, and for some time she has been besieged with requests to write her own biography. At the annual W. C. T. U. Convention held in Nashville, Tenn., in 1887, these desires voiced themselves in the following resolution, unanimously adopted by the whole convention:

Resolved, That in view of the fact that the year 1889 will be the fifteenth of the organization of the National Woman's Christian Temperance Union, and also that in the same year our beloved president, Miss Frances

E. Willard, enters upon the fiftieth year of her strong and beautiful life, we, the Woman's Christian Temperance Union delegates, in National Convention assembled, do request Miss Willard to prepare for publication an autobiography, together with the history of the Woman's Christian Temperance Union from its birth to 1889, with a collection of her addresses on various themes.

Miss Willard was at first averse to the plan, and put off yielding to it as long as possible. But the white ribbon women do not generally give up an idea when once originated, and since *they* had so often walked in unknown paths at *her* bidding, she felt herself, at last, bound to walk in this path at *their* bidding. Hence this book.

Furthermore, the women wanted a *true* story, not a story that, out of a conventional modesty, would tell only half the truth, in the fear of being thought egotistic and full of self. Their idea is admirably expressed in these words of Emerson, "Say honestly and simply that which your own experience has given you and you will give to the world something new, valuable and lasting." Having taken, for a rarity, the authority into their own hands, they have insisted upon having the work done in their own way, and have required their leader to tell them all about herself, her work, her life, the very inmost of her being, without fear or favor, because only thus could she give them what they desired.

Whoever reads this book, therefore, must remember that it has been written by request of and for the women of whom Miss Willard is the well beloved leader, the white ribbon women of America; if others see it, that is their own good fortune. It is a home book, written for her great family circle, and to be read around the evening lamp by critics who love the writer, and who want to learn from her experience how to live better and stronger lives. It is a woman's book, warm, sympathetic, offhand; it is an object-lesson in American living and American development, and as such can not fail to interest all those who think American women worthy of a little study. It begins in the West of forty years ago, picturing a pioneer farm and the unique, out-of-door life of adventurous young Western boys and girls. It tells of a free-spirited mother, who sympathized with her children rather than governed them, and who, although she would have liked her daughter to learn house work, yet did not force her into it, because she had the rare good sense to know that it was far better to help her child to do the best in her own line than to force her to do a half-best in any other line, and also because she believed every natural gift to be God-given and meant for divine uses in serving the world, and therefore worthy of respect and of development. We have in the story of this mother and daughter a glimpse into the relation between parents and children such as it ought always to be, not one of arbitrary control on the one hand and slavish submission on the other, but one of coöperation, or partnership, in which each should try to help the other to do and be their best, and should each realize the sacred duty of leaving one another free to follow, without hindrance, the path which they should feel called upon to pursue. It is no small thing to have laid open before us the methods of a grand and truly typical mother, one who had not the help of the usual environment, one who made herself her children's world. Were there more such mothers as Mrs. Willard, there would be more such daughters as hers.

The father in this story, while more reserved, and consequently less manifestly sympathetic than the mother, was a noble and gifted man, of sterling goodness, and great power in the lives of his children, to whom he was most devotedly attached. There is also a sweet young sister who brightened the family life for "nineteen beautiful years," and then left them for the home above, leaving with her latest breath a legacy of infinite value to her sister Frances in the simple words, "Tell everybody to be good."

There is a brother, too; a young man of great promise, endowed with rare genius, and of a most lovable nature, who left the world before he had had time to do more than make a passing mark on the annals of his own day, leaving behind him, however, a gentle widow, whose life and work have been and still are of great value to her family and the work of the Lord.

The book contains a history of the Woman's Crusade against the liquor traffic in 1874, and of what we are accustomed to call "its sober second thought"—the Woman's Christian Temperance Union, that great organization which Mary A. Livermore says is "so grand in its aims, so superb in its equipment, so phenomenal in its growth, and has done so much for woman as well as for temperance, that it challenges the attention of Christendom, and excites the hope of all who are interested in the welfare of humanity."

Those who read between the lines of this book can not fail to see how largely the evolution of this mighty organization has been the work of its gentle, yet magnetic leader, whose wonderful administrative talent and superb tact, have given her an almost unparalleled success in controlling and guiding one of the greatest movements of modern times. Yet with all this success, Miss Willard is, I believe, truly humble minded. When calls come from every direction, and some seem to feel indignant, and others accuse her of one thing, and still others of another, and they fit her out with motives, knowing nothing whatever about the facts in the case, she writes after this fashion : "Am badgered to death and am not worried a hair—what do you make o' that? I fancy the explanation is that, unless I am an awfully deceived woman, I am desirous of doing God's will, and so the clamor on this footstool is like the humming of ''skeeters' outside the curtain. It rather lulls me into quiet." No one could realize more deeply than she does the truth that, "Except the Lord build the city, they labor in vain that build it," and she has always sought to commit her work and her ways to the keeping of the Divine Master, in a simple, child-like faith that He would lead her in the way she should go, and would make all her paths straight before her. That this faith has been answered to a remarkable degree the book before us will clearly show.

The beautiful illustrations of the book are entirely the work of the Woman's Temperance Publication Association, which is bringing it out. Miss Willard would not have felt willing in her own name to send forth such personal pictures for the public gaze, but she was obliged to yield in this, as in all else concerning the book, to the wishes and judgment of the white ribbon women, who, for once, have got the upper-hand of their leader, and greatly enjoy making her do their bidding. The W. T. P. A. took the whole responsibility of the illustrations, and has prepared this part of the volume in an unusually original and artistic manner.

Altogether, we of the W. C. T. U. of the United States look upon this book as a most creditable witness to the value of our organization and to the successful working of the Woman's

Temperance Publication Association, which is one of our most promising children.

I would like to tell a little story in conclusion. There is a creature in the sea called the Octopus, with a very small body but with immense arms covered with suckers, radiating from every side, that stretch themselves out to indefinite length to draw in all sorts of prey. Miss Willard seems to have the same characteristic of being able to reach out mental or spiritual arms to indefinite lengths, whereby to draw in everything and everybody that seem likely to help on the cause she has at heart. Hence I, who have felt the grip of those arms of hers, have come to call her in our private moments, "My beloved Octopus," and myself her contented victim.

What future histories will need to be written concerning the coming years of the life here portrayed, no one can tell. But of this I am sure, that the same Divine Hand that has led her hitherto will still lead, and will bring her in triumph to life's close, for the motto of her heart continues more and more to be, "This God shall be our God, even unto death."

Hannah Whitall Smith

44 Grosvenor Road, Westminster Embankment,
London, S. W., England.

Prefatory.

Whether for good or ill, I have set down with absolute fidelity these recollections of myself. The wise ones tell us that we change utterly once in every seven years, so that from the vantage-ground of life's serene meridian, I have looked back upon the seven persons whom I know most about: the welcome child, the romping girl, the happy student, the roving teacher, the tireless traveler, the temperance organizer, and lastly, the politician and advocate of woman's rights! Since all these are sweetly dead and gone, why should not their biographies and epitaphs, perchance their eulogies, be written by their best informed and most indulgent critic?

A thousand homes in as many different towns, have kindly cherished me in my many pilgrimages. The fathers in those homes treated me with high respect, the mothers with sacred tenderness; the lads and lasses with heartiest kindness, the blessed little children loved me for their mothers' sake.

To them all, my heart goes out with unspeakable good will and gratitude. Perhaps the honest record of my fifty years may give them pleasure; perhaps it may do good. At all events they asked for it—at least their leaders did, in the great, genial meeting that we had down South in 1887—so I have put it into black and white, not as I would, but as I could, and here it is.

1889. Frances E. Willard

Illustrations.

FRONTISPIECE.—Steel Engraving, Miss Willard.

PHOTOGRAVURES, PAGE

The Office—Rest Cottage, - - - - - - 128
Kate A. Jackson, - - - - - - - - 288
Anna A. Gordon—"My little Organist," - - - - 384
"The Den"—Miss Willard's Workshop, - - - - 544
The Parlor—Rest Cottage, - - - - - - - 656

REPRODUCTIONS FROM PHOTOGRAPHS AND AQUARELLES.

I. A Welcome Child—Early Sports, - - - - 1
II. A Romping Girl—Forest Home, - - - - - 14
III. A Happy Student, - - - - - - - 71
IV. A Roving Teacher—Evanston College for Ladies, - 132
V. A Tireless Traveler, - - - - - - 244
VI. A Temperance Advocate and Organizer—Illinois Petition for Home Protection, 175,000 Names, - - - 331
VII. A Woman in Politics, - - - - - - 374
Silhouettes, - - - - - - - - - 492
Homes—Birthplace, the Oberlin Residence, Forest Home, Swampscott, Rest Cottage, - - - - - - 8
Churches—Churchville, Ogden, Janesville, Evanston, - 48
The Hill and Willard Homesteads, - - - - - 64
School-buildings (Student-life)—Forest Home, Milwaukee Female College, Northwestern Female College, - - 96
Family Group—"My Four," - - - - - - 160
School-buildings (Teacher-life)—Harlem, Pittsburgh, Lima, - 176
School-buildings (Teacher-life)—From Public School to Northwestern University, Evanston, - - - - - 208
Bas-relief—Miss Willard, - - - - - - - 344
Bas-relief—Madame Willard, - - - - - - 345
Officers of the National W. C. T. U., - - - - - 408
Officers of the World's W. C. T. U., - - - - - 432
The First Composition—Fac-simile, - - - - - 496

Editors of *Our Day*, - - - - - - - - 512
Officers National Council of Women, - - - - - 592
Picturesque Evanston (looking toward Rest Cottage)—Rest Cottage Playground, - - - - - - 624

LITHOGRAPHS.

W. C. T. U. Banners.—Ohio, Massachusetts, New York, The National, The World's, etc., - - - - - - 456
The Children's Page.—Father Mathew Medal, Silver Cup, Roman Cameo, "Old Faithful," etc. - - - - - 680

PEN AND INK SKETCHES.

Seal of National W. C. T. U., - - - - - - x
Ships of the Prairie, - - - - - - - 46
Sampler, - - - - - - - - 61
The Master's Desk, - - - - - - - 98
Pansies, - - - - - - - - 132
"It won't come right," - - - - - - 145
Silver Goblet, - - - - - - - - 189
Old Oaken Bucket, - - - - - - - 197
Roll of Honor, - - - - - - - - 225
College Cottage, - - - - - - - 244
"Shall we ever go anywhere?" - - - - - 252
En route in Montana, - - - - - - 330
Beer Mug from Saloon in Hillsboro, - - - - - 341
W. C. T. U. Coffee Cart, - - - - - - 355
National W. C. T. U. Gavel, - - - - - - 381
Portland (Or.) W. C. T. U. Shield, - - - - - 409
White Cross and White Shield Emblem, - - - - 429
World's W. C. T. U. Emblem, - - - - - - 436
White Rose, - - - - - - - - 453
Metropolitan Opera House, - - - - - - 468
Bourbon Jug Water-cooler (New Orleans Exposition), - - - 478
Chicago Post Placard, - - - - - - - 514
John B. Gough's Gift of Tea Set, - - - - - 654
Mother's Scrap Books, - - - - - - - 665
"Old Rye," - - - - - - - - 685
Music—"May de Lord," - - - - - - - 694
Vale, - - - - - - - - - 698
Willard Farm, - - - - - - - Appendix
Willard Coat-of-Arms, - - - - - - - "

Table of Contents.

INTRODUCTORY MATTER. - - - - - - - iii–xi

I. A WELCOME CHILD.

A LITTLE PILGRIM. - - - - - - - - 1–14

Heredity—Early childhood days—Almost named for Queen Victoria—Not handsome, to say the least—Childish sports.

II. A ROMPING GIRL.

CHAPTER I. MY APPRENTICESHIP TO NATURE. - - - - 15–46

Near to Nature's heart—Fort City—Girlish sports—Outdoor life—Spring-time at Forest Home—Boy comrades—The forest monarch.

CHAPTER II. THE ARTISTS' CLUB. - - - - - 47–61

Mother's Eastern visit—Amateur painters and hunters—Home incidents—President Finney.

CHAPTER III. LITTLE BOATS SET OUT FROM SHORE. - 62–72

First break in the home-circle—Another Eastern visit—Prize cup—Young ladyhood—Freedom and rebellion—Good-by to Forest Home.

III. A HAPPY STUDENT.

CHAPTER I. DELIGHTFUL DAYS AT SCHOOL. - - 73–98

Mother's teachings—Early school-days—First flight from home—Aunt Sarah—Milwaukee Female College—School honors.

CHAPTER II. COLLEGE DAYS. - - - - - - 99–123

Northwestern Female College—The grammar party—A student of Emerson—Inquirer, not infidel—"There is a God"—Faith for doubt.

CHAPTER III. FIRST YEAR OUT OF SCHOOL. - - 124–132

Life at home—The Civil war—Neglected and forgotten—Solemn vows.

IV. A ROVING TEACHER.

CHAPTER I. DISTRICT SCHOOL, NO. 1. - - - 133–145

Starting out—New responsibilities—Summer studies—Sabbath away from home—A lonesome school-ma'am.

CHAPTER II. KANKAKEE ACADEMY, - - - 146–161

Tell your age—A sense of right and justice—Mesmerism—Lincoln—Home again.

CHAPTER III. THE PUBLIC SCHOOLS IN HARLEM AND IN EVANSTON. - - - - - - - - 162–168

Our first war meeting—Evanston public school—Nineteen beautiful years ended—"Tell everybody to be good"—A change.

CHAPTER IV. "PRECEPTRESS OF THE NATURAL SCIENCES." 169–174

Northwestern Female College—One day's work—Teacher and pupil—"The slaves are free."

CHAPTER V. PITTSBURGH FEMALE COLLEGE. - - 175-184
First day at Pittsburgh—A botanical outing—A wordless secret—One year ago—War rumors.

CHAPTER VI. THE GROVE SCHOOL AND THE BUILDING OF HECK HALL. - - - - - - - - 185-189
The Bank of Character—Word studies—Heck Hall.

CHAPTER VII. GENESEE WESLEYAN SEMINARY. - - 190-197
First days at Lima—A chapter in Methodist history—A European trip in prospect.

CHAPTER VIII. EVANSTON COLLEGE FOR WOMEN. - 198-205
Something new—Bishop E. O. Haven—The women's Fourth of July—The new college building.

CHAPTER IX. SELF-GOVERNMENT FOR GIRLS. - - 206-225
Original plans—Roll of Honor—The Self-governed—The Good-behavior Club—Art and composition classes—The first Woman's Commencement—The Chicago fire.

CHAPTER X. WHY I LEFT THE UNIVERSITY. - - 226-244
Puzzling questions—Union of University and College—New methods—Resignation of position—Reports of committees—Trial and triumph—After fifteen years.

V. THE TIRELESS TRAVELER.

EARLY JOURNEYINGS. - - - - - - - 245-330
My benefactors—Itinerary—The Giant's Causeway—The Garden of Eden—St. Bernard—Paris—Ecumenical Council—Pyramids—Palestine—Car-window jottings at home.

VI. A TEMPERANCE ADVOCATE AND ORGANIZER.

CHAPTER I. ON THE THRESHOLD. - - - - - 331-341
First Crusade days—A turning-point in life—Early speeches.

CHAPTER II. THE OPENING WAY. - - - - - 342-355
Odd faith test—Secretary State W. C. T. U.—Secretary National W. C. T. U.—Woman's ballot.

CHAPTER III. MOODY'S BOSTON MEETINGS—OLIVER'S DEATH. 356-367
Bible talks—A change of plan—A "free lance"—The great petition—Brother's death.

CHAPTER IV. CONSERVATIVES AND LIBERALS. - - 368-374
President National W. C. T. U.—Mrs. Hayes' Picture—Southern trip.

VII. A WOMAN IN POLITICS.

CHAPTER I. THE HOME PROTECTION PARTY. - - 375-381
Temperance in politics—Extracts from speeches—A secession that did not secede.

CHAPTER II. NATIONAL CONVENTIONS. - - - 382-402
Our temperance round-up—World's W. C. T. U.—Memorial to National Conventions—Nomination of Governor St. John—"Home Protection" as a name.

CHAPTER III. THE ST. LOUIS CONVENTION. - - 403-409
Gospel politics—The famous resolution—Call to prayer—Protest and reply.

CHAPTER IV. WOMEN IN COUNCIL. - - - 410-417
Pageants of the New Crusade—Mrs. Margaret Bright Lucas—Address to Labor Organizations—Nashville Convention.

CHAPTER V. WHITE CROSS AND WHITE SHIELD. - - 418-42

Pall Mall Gazette disclosures—The White Cross League—Efficient help from the Knights of Labor—Mrs. Laura Ormiston Chant.

CHAPTER VI. THE WORLD'S W. C. T. U. - - 430-436

Mrs. Mary Clement Leavitt—The work in England and Canada—The world's petition.

CHAPTER VII. THE GREATEST PARTY. - - - 437-453

The "catnip tea" resolution—The Indianapolis Convention—Nomination of Fisk and Brooks—The Blue and the Gray—Prohibition platform—The suffrage debate—The white rose.

CHAPTER VIII. THE NEW YORK CONVENTION (1888). - 454-468

Metropolitan Opera House—Protests and memorials—Distinguished guests—Advancement "all along the line"—Ecclesiastical emancipation of women—W. C. T. U. deaconesses.

CHAPTER IX. AIMS AND METHODS OF THE W. C. T. U. 469-478

Crusade annals—Evolution—Organization—One in Christ Jesus.

CHAPTER X. MISCELLANEOUS INCIDENTS OF TEMPERANCE WORK. - - - - - - 479-492

Pledges broken and fulfilled—Mrs. Judge Thompson—Convention episodes.—Dr. Bushnell's pulpit—Temperance women are total abstainers.

SILHOUETTES.

WHAT I HAVE DONE AND SUFFERED AS A PEN-HOLDER, - 493
PEOPLE I HAVE MET, - - - - 515
WOMEN SPEAKERS—FIRST PUBLIC LECTURE, - - - 569
NATIONAL COUNCIL OF WOMEN, - - - - - 590
MY OPINION OF MEN, - - - - - - - 597
GENERAL CONFERENCES, - - - - - - 615
GOD AND MY HEART, - - - - - - 622
THE GOSPEL OF HEALTH, - - - - - - - 631
MIND-CURE, - - - - - - - - - 636
COMPANIONSHIP, - - - - - - - - 637
DEMERITS, - - - - - - - - - 646
MY HOLIDAYS, - - - - - - - - 650
MOTHER, - - - - - - - - - 655
FATHER, - - - - - - - - 666
BITS FROM MY NOTE-BOOK, - - - - - - - 671
INTROSPECTIVE, - - - - - - - - 686
FINALLY, - - - - - - - - - 695
ANCESTRY, - - - - - - - - - Appendix.

I

A Welcome Child.

"Keep near to thy childhood, for in going from it thou art going from the gods."

GLIMPSES OF FIFTY YEARS:

THE AUTOBIOGRAPHY OF AN AMERICAN WOMAN.

A LITTLE PILGRIM.

Mother was nearly thirty-five when I was born, the fourth of her five children, one of whom, the first, had passed away in infancy, and the third at the age of fourteen months. This little girl, Caroline Elizabeth, mother has always spoken of as the most promising child she ever bore, or, for that matter, ever saw. "She was a vision of delight," with deep blue eyes and dark brown hair; a disposition without flaw, her nerves being so well encased and her little spirit so perfectly equipoised that she would sit or lie in her cradle cooing to herself by the hour, and when she rode, the beauty of the world outdoors seemed so well apprehended by this seraphic child that her little hands were constantly outstretched and her sweet eyes were full of light and comprehension, while her silvery voice took on such an ecstasy as was remarked by all who knew her. My little sister passed to heaven just as she began to speak the language of this world. My mother's first great grief then broke her heart, and as I came less than one year afterward, the deep questionings and quivering pathos of her spirit had their effect on mine. She lived much with her books, especially the Bible and the poets, in this chastened interval. Many a time has she said to me, "Frank, above all things else thank heaven you were *a welcome child*, for I had prayed so often that another little girl might come into our home for us to love." She says she hoped this also for my brother's sake, who was five years my senior and then her only child. During this year she often went to singing-school and there saw a young woman with fair complexion, auburn hair and blue eyes, moving about among the people to take their names. Mother says she liked the quiet, intelligent and rapid way in which the work was done, and in her heart earnestly wished that the little one whose coming was her constant thought, might be a girl, and might grow up to be such a young woman as the one she watched with thoughtful and observant eyes.

And that is all I choose to tell of my heredity.

It has been my good fortune to have an accomplished stenographer always within call the last few years, and since my mother's hand is not so steady as it once was, she often has a sitting with Miss Mitchell, who takes down her words of reminiscence and of wisdom. This serves to give needed variety to my mother's life, and also to preserve very many facts otherwise lost.

Some notes here follow in reply to questions asked her by an interested friend.

"What do you recall about your daughter's birth?"

"It occurred at eleven o'clock, Thursday morning, September 28, 1839, in our quiet home on the principal street of Churchville, Monroe County, N. Y., fourteen miles west of Rochester. Dr. Lillie, a refined and unusually gifted physician and a great friend of my husband's, presided at her advent. I remember saying, 'Is it a little girl?' and my unspeakable joy on learning that my long prayer was answered. 'Why did you not tell her without being asked?' said Frank's Aunt Elizabeth, who was present, and Dr. Lillie answered, 'Because I did n't choose to please her well enough,' which was meant as a piquant little remark to enliven me the more, for he well knew how eager were my empty arms to clasp another girl-baby to my breast. Every morning the lonesome little brother would run down-stairs without waiting to dress, and exclaim, 'Ma, is the baby dead?' he so much feared it, as the sweet one had died the year before, and when he found that Frank lived on, he still would come when he awoke and say, 'Ma, is the baby well?'

"The principal family in Churchville was that of Deacon Hall, the merchant of the village. They were Presbyterians, and it used to be said that the Deacon extended one, two, three or four fingers of his hand to those who came as customers, according to his estimation of their social status. Mrs. Hall was a lovely woman, a sort of 'Lady Bountiful.' Living just across the street from them, we were among the very few families that were admitted to the charmed circle of their home. It was considered a distinguished honor. Mrs. Hall was with me when Frank made her first appearance, and took such a fancy to her that she used to come across the street every morning for six weeks to give the little baby her bath, and look after her generally. The family consisted of five sons, four daughters and two relatives, cousins, I think they were, of Mrs. Hall, Miss Ruth Rogers and her brother Joshua. Miss Rogers afterward married Elisha Harmon, a staunch young farmer and miller some few miles away, and became the mother of Mrs. Folsom, who is now President Cleveland's mother-in-law. Miss Rogers was a handsome, well-poised, vigorous young woman, whom I remember to have thought specially agreeable and promising. She entered heartily into all the work and amusements of her cousins and was greatly beloved by them. Her granddaughter, Mrs. Cleveland, no doubt owes to her many of the fine qualities with which she is endowed. Deacon Hall's family were conservative in manner, and we could but appreciate the cordial welcome they gave us when we removed to the village. When Frank's eldest sister, Caroline Elizabeth, died less than a year before Frank was born, and my heart was well-nigh broken, I prized beyond all words their active sympathy; they neglected nothing in their power to do, that could palliate that fearful blow or stimulate my hopes. The family all, both young and old, evinced much anxiety for me and for the baby's safety and welfare."

"What sort of a looking baby was Frances Elizabeth, anyhow?" pursued the questioner, whereupon, after the fashion of mothers since the world began, this answer came: "Very pretty, with sunny hair, blue eyes, delicate features, fair complexion, long waist, short limbs. She was called the doll-baby of the village."

"Was she brought up by hand?" Answer: "Yes, she was,

as we used to say in the old-fashioned phrase, a bottle baby, or one 'brought up by hand' after the first four weeks, on account of my not being strong. But I ought to add for her present reputation's sake, she had no affinity for the bottle—putting it away when ten months old with no regret. She suffered very much from teething, more than any other of my children, being of an organism remarkably susceptible to physical pain. She always slept with both hands on my face. She was a very affectionate little creature. She could talk some time before she could walk, speaking quite wisely at fourteen months, but not walking until twenty-four months old. As a little girl she was very confiding and fond of her childish friends, even beyond what one expects to see at that period.

"Her father used to say when walking to and fro with her at night, her vigorous lungs in full action, sending forth screams that could be heard in the remotest part of the house, 'I declare, this young one ought to amount to something, she gives trouble enough!' He was very kind as a care-taker of the children, sharing with me far more than husbands usually do, or did in those days, the work of bringing up our little ones. He would get up at night, heat the milk for the crying baby, and do his best to reconcile her to the hard bit of ivory now replaced by the gutta-percha tube.

"She dearly loved her brother Oliver and sister Mary, who were ever ready to enter into her plans for pastime. They were very much to one another always. She was mentally precocious, but physically delicate beyond any other of my children. She was inventive and original in her amusements. This last used particularly to impress me. She early manifested an exceeding fondness for books. She believed in herself, and in her teachers. Her bias toward certain studies and pursuits was very marked. Even in the privacy of her own room she was often in a sort of ecstasy of aspiration. In her childhood, and always, she strongly repelled occupations not to her taste, but was eager to grapple with principles, philosophies, and philanthropies, and unwearyingly industrious along her favorite lines. I wonder sometimes that I had the wit to let her do what she preferred instead of obliging her to take up housework as did all the other girls of our acquaintance. She was an untrained vine rambling whithersoever she would. When she was two years old we removed from Churchville, to Oberlin, Ohio, her Aunt Sarah going with us. I held Frank all the way. It was a tiresome journey, for we went by carriage. She often put her little arms around my neck, laid her head upon my shoulder and said, 'Mamma, *sissy's dress aches!*' It rejoices me to believe that she intuitively recognized the fact that it is not one's real self that is ever tired, but only this dress of mortality that aches sometimes.

"She used to see the students rehearsing their speeches and would get up an amusing imitation of them, when but three years old. Many a time I have seen her standing on the well-curb or on top of the gate-post imitating the gestures of some bright young sophomore who stood there, 'laying it off' for her amusement. She was very fond of playing outdoors, indoor amusements seeming irksome to her always. Her brother was her favorite comrade, and his sturdy little playmates among the boys would sometimes call her 'Tomboy,' which she resented very much and I did for her.

"Once she ran away when about three years old, going through the fields and creeping under the fences, so that when, after a great fright, she was discovered, her brother said it was pitiful to see the little creature's bravery combined with her panting fatigue, for she did her utmost not to be overtaken.

"She used often to go with me to church where President Finney usually preached. She said his great light eyes, white eyebrows, and vigorous manner were to her like a combination of thunder and lightning; lightning in his look, thunder in his voice. I am sure her impressionable spirit became somewhat frightened by the thought of Christianity as administered by that great orator, who was very much given to rehearsing in our hearing the pains and penalties of the condemned."

So much for mother's memories of my babyhood and early years at dear old Oberlin.

The first religious teaching that I can call to mind is the learning of this sweet prayer of every little child:

> "Now I lay me down to sleep,
> I pray the Lord my soul to keep,
> If I should die before I wake,
> I pray the Lord my soul to take,
> And this I ask for Jesus' sake."

Mother taught me that before I can remember, but it seems to me I can recall, though it may be but the memory of a memory, her sitting with a little Testament in hand and telling me it was God's message to us, and that instinctively within my spirit rose the thought and utterance, "How do you know?" I was not one who naturally took things for granted. It was intuitive with me to seek for causes and for reasons. My faith faculty was not naturally strong, and yet when I say so, it almost seems as if I did injustice to my gift in that regard. Mother was surprised at my inquiries and called me playfully, in talking with her friends, her "little infidel." But I have always thought my infidelity was of that harmless kind quite curiously illustrated by an incident in my brother Oliver's four years' old period. At that date, we did not have family prayers, though I have no recollection of such a graceless time in our family history. When my parents took my brother to my mother's home, her father, who was a most devout and earnest man, had prayers both night and morning, and little Ollie, as she called him, said to her one day, looking up with his blue eyes, so full of questions always, "Mamma, what does gran'sir say to the chair when he gets down on his legs?" The simple fact was he proposed to investigate a phenomenon with which he was not familiar, and this he had a most undoubted right to do.

All through my childhood I was docile toward the supernatural, wondering about it, with great sighs in my little breast, but I think I should not have feared it so much if a man who died next door to us had not been "laid out" in such a chilly shroud, and had not been so repellent in death. At least, I know that the first fright my spirit got was when my father lifted me up, a child not five years old, and held me quite close down to see what was inside that coffin. I never had a blow that struck so deep as did that sight; I never had a burn that seared so, nor a pain that tingled like it. Young as I was, something in me akin to a high dignity, resented this rude introduction to what then seemed the "King of Terrors." I never said it, but I always felt I had received an injury, suffered a wrong. On pleasant summer days, out in the bright, sunshiny weather, thoughts "too deep for tears" have come to me when I remembered seeing *that*. It seems to me that we intrude upon the royal little heart of childhood when we thrust upon it such a cruel blow. Always since then, in spite of all my faith and the fervors I have known religiously, there is about the thought of death the clammy horror stamped upon me when I saw that face. So I mused much why these things were, and could but wonder, if we had a God so kind, why He should make us fair and sweet as children, bright and happy in youth, serene and strong in middle-life and then send us away like that! I have often heard good people say they "thought it necessary to take their children early to a funeral," but why they must do this I can not see. If the first sight of death could be some sweet and lovely face, such as I have sometimes beheld since then, the impression on childhood's plastic little nature would surely be far more in keeping with what we believe death really is.

The years went on, and while my sister Mary was always willing, at least, I was strongly averse when "they came to talk religion," as I was wont to call it. I would sit silent and let them have their say, but seldom answered save in monosyllables, in case I must. We could not often go to church because we lived three miles away and the minister had to "preach around" at different appointments. Nor did we have much Sunday-school instruction. I am ashamed that what we had I can not specially recall, except that I learned by heart many chapters in the four Gospels, the first scripture that I ever committed to memory being what mother says is the first she ever learned, "In the beginning was the Word." We always had for Sunday reading the little *Sunday-school Advocate*, so well known to Methodist Sunday-school children, and the *Myrtle*, a pretty juvenile paper, the organ of the Free-Will Baptist Sunday-schools. Besides this, we took any number of books, sometimes five at once, out of the Sunday-school library, and nothing was more familiar to me than those words upon the title page, "Revised by D. P. Kidder." We afterward became acquainted with this honored son of the church when we came to live in Evanston. The things I loved to read, however, in all these books and papers, were stories of adventure, when I could get them—which was seldom—historical facts, dialogues about nature, of which there were many, and anything that taught me what sort of a world was this of which I had become a resident. "The Slave's Friend," that earliest book of all my reading, stamped upon me the purpose to help humanity, the sense of brotherhood, of all nations as really one, and of God as the equal Father of all races. This, perhaps, was a better sort of religion than some Sunday-school books would have given. It occurs to me that I have not estimated at its true value that nugget of a little fanatical volume published for children by the Anti-slavery Society. Some one gave me the "Life of Nathan Dickerman," whose charming face as represented in the frontispiece attracted me immensely, and I think it was for its sake I read the book through. He was a dear boy, a little saint, and I grieved over his death. The "Children's Pilgrim's Progress" was a charm, the sweetest book of all my childhood, and while I loved Christiana and the boys and Mercy, how like a personal Providence grew on my fancy the character of Greatheart! Feeling as I do even now, the impress of those earliest books, I grieve sadly to have missed the helpfulness and sweetness of nature I might have learned from "Little Lord Fauntleroy." Happy children of the present, do not fail to read it, every one!

After all, the best religion of a theoretical kind came to us in our Sunday hour of song. I early learned to play on the melodeon, as it was called, but had no fancy for the piano, and I remember how much meaning, sweet and solemn, we used to find in the deep tones of the instrument and of my father's voice as we sang the hymns we loved.

My first appearance on any stage was in Oberlin, Ohio, at the age of three or four, when my father used to stand me up on a chair and have me sing for guests in my queer little voice, especially after a dinner, as I remember, and the song was always this:

"They called me blue-eyed Mary when friends and fortune smiled,
But oh, how fortunes vary! I now am sorrow's child;
Kind sir, then take these posies, they're fading like my youth,
But never, like these roses, shall wither Mary's truth."

When mother stood me up on a chair to speak, it was a more warlike "piece." Father would have something feminine, or else nothing at all; but mother would let me select what I liked, and this is a specimen of my choice at the age of ten years:

"O sacred Truth! thy triumph ceased a while,
And Hope, thy sister, ceased like thee to smile,

"FOREST HOME"
SWAMPSCOTT, EVANSTON
"REST COTTAGE" EVANSTON
MISS WILLARD'S BIRTHPLACE
THE OBERLIN RESIDENCE

When leagued oppression poured to Northern wars
Her whiskered pandours and her fierce hussars.
Tumultuous horror brooded o'er the van,
Presaging wrath to Poland—and to man!
Warsaw's last champion from her heights surveyed
Wide o'er the fields a waste of ruin laid—
'Oh, Heaven!' he cried, 'my bleeding country save!
Is there no hand on high to shield the brave?
Yet, though destruction sweep these lovely plains,
Rise, fellowmen! our country yet remains!
By that dread name, we wave the sword on high,
And swear for her to live!—with her to die!'

* * * * * *

In vain, alas! in vain, ye gallant few,
From rank to rank your volleyed thunders flew;
Hope, for a season, bade the world farewell,
And Freedom shrieked, as Kosciusko fell!"

I can recall the stirring of my little heart as the drama of the brief poem proceeded, and how almost impossible it was for me to hold my voice steady so as to give the closing lines. Mother taught me how to speak it, where to put in the volume of sound and the soft, repressed utterance, and as for the pathos I knew where to put that in myself.

In 1868, at Warsaw, the capital of Poland, I stood beside the monument of Kosciusko, and while my tourist comrades read about it in their guide-books, I repeated softly to myself the poem I had learned on the Wisconsin prairies, and looked up with worshipful glance at the statue of the hero for whom my heart ached and my eyes filled with tears when I was but a child.

I came very near being named for Queen Victoria! Indeed, my mother was quite bent upon it. The youthful sovereign had recently come to her throne, and the papers were full of accounts of her earnest Christian character, while the highest expectations were cherished of what she would accomplish for humanity. But my father said it would look as if we, who were the most democratic people in the world, were catering to the popular idea, and, what was worse, regarded royalty with favor, so mother did not have her wish, but was well pleased with the name Frances Elizabeth Caroline, which she and father, in council with my score of uncles, aunts and cousins, concocted after much consultation. Frances was a "fancy name," so father said. Frances

Burney, the English writer, and Frances Osgood, the American poet, were names that had attracted his attention, and he bestowed their Christian name upon what was then his only daughter. Elizabeth was for my mother's third sister, described in "Nineteen Beautiful Years" as one of the truest women that ever breathed, brave, delicate, and with a piquant speech and manner. Her life was sorrowful by reason of an unhappy marriage, and her death in the prime of her years was a release. Caroline (so stands my third name in the old family Bible) was my father's youngest sister, of whom it may justly be said,

> "None knew her but to love her,
> None named her but to praise."

Blithe as the birds, refreshing as the showers of spring, she led a rarely happy life. After the death of her noble husband, Hosea Town, she and her brother, Zophar Willard (he being a widower by reason of my mother's second sister's death), shared the same house, and, having a competence of this world's goods, were generous helpers of every worthy cause.

My mother had much care about our manners, for we saw nothing of society, and she knew that we were missing real advantages, while at the same time we were escaping real dangers. Of course we did not learn to dance, but mother had a whole system of calisthenics that she learned at Oberlin, which she used to put us through unmercifully, as I thought, since I preferred capering at my own sweet will, out-of-doors. There was a little verse that she would sing in her sweet voice and have us "take steps" to the time; but the droll part was that the verse was out of a missionary hymn. And this is as near as I ever came to dancing school! I only remember this:

> "Bounding billows, cease thy motion,
> Bear me not so swiftly o'er!
> Cease thy motion, foaming ocean,
> I will tempt thy rage no more.
> For I go where duty leads me,
> Far across the billowy deep,
> Where no friend or foe can heed me,
> Where no wife for me shall weep."

What a spectacle was that! Mother teaching her children dancing steps to words like these. She had a copy of Lord

Chesterfield's letters to his son, and we read it over and over again. We used to try and carry out its ceremonial, to some extent, when we had our make-believe banquets and Fourth of Julys.

Our Mary carried conscientiousness to the point of morbidity. I remember one day when I was working in my little garden south of Forest Home, that Mary came around there, standing up and looking so tear-stained and discontented, and said, "Frank, I have done so and so; don't you think it was wrong?" and what she did was so infinitesimal as not to be worth the thinking of, much less repeating. The poor little thing went on and told me so many things, that I, who had no such "conscientious streak," as I used to call it, in me, said to her that I was tired of this; that I should have a talk with mother; that it was moral unhealthfulness, and that she never would be strong and happy if she did not give it up. I was the day-book of her ill-desert, and mother was the ledger. The books were posted every night. This was when Mary was about ten years of age. She afterward outgrew the morbid part and only retained the beautiful and lofty sense of duty in which she excelled all other persons whom I have ever known.

We have all heard the story of that philosophical boy who, when looking at a misshapen tree, said "Somebody must have stepped upon it when it was a little fellow."

In but one particular did a calamity of this sort befall me as a child, and that related to my personal appearance. Soothed, praised and left at liberty by my mother, that home deity of a sensitive child, all happy hopes were mine, save one—I was n't the least bit good-looking! To make this fact more patent and pronounced, my younger sister was remarkably attractive. She was plump, and I was thin; she had abundant, pretty hair of brown; and mine, when a little girl, was rather sparse and positively red, though my dear mother would never permit me or anybody else to say so. When in those early days at Oberlin, some hateful boy would call out "Red head" as I passed, or when my quick temper had vented itself upon my brother in some spiteful way, and he used the same opprobrious epithet, I would run at once to mother and tell her with rebellious tears of this outrageous treatment. Her beautiful hand would smooth my hated hair with a tenderness so magical that under it the scanty strands seemed, for the moment, turned to gold, as the kindest of all voices said, "Don't mind those boys, Frankie, the poor things don't know what they are saying; you get your hair from your Grandfather Hill; his was quite bright-colored (she never would say "*red*") when he was a little boy, but it was a lovely gold-brown when he grew up; and so will yours be. I wish you could have seen your Grandpa Hill's queue, a thick braid smartly tied up with a black ribbon. I never saw a handsomer head of hair. We children cried when the fashion changed and father's queue had to be cut off. You are like him, every way, and he was the noblest-looking man in all the country round."

Sweet ingenuity of mother-love! How quickly it comforted my heart and so transformed my thoughts that I forgot myself and saw before me only the brave figure of my Grandpa Hill! But there were not wanting other witnesses who took sides with my mirror rather than with my mother. Our first dear music teacher, Mary King, of Milwaukee, a blind lady who had graduated from the Institute for the Blind, in New York, married an Englishman who worked for us, and he told me repeatedly that it was a great pity for a girl to be so "plain looking" as I, especially when she had a younger sister so attractive. One of two distant relatives, a girl near my own age, said on slight acquaintance, "Are n't you sorry to be homely, Frank?" and the other declared "to my very face" that I was "the drawn image of Mrs. B.," who was the farthest from good looks of anybody, because while, like myself, she had regular features, her eyes were pale, her complexion was lifeless, and her hair the color of old hay. But when I bemoaned myself to mother and Mary, of whom I could no more have been jealous than the left hand can be of the right, mother would say, "Come, now, Frank, this is getting a little monotonous. I think you wrong your Heavenly Father who has fitted you out so well," and then she would analyze each feature and put upon it the stamp of her approval, while my genial-hearted sister would echo every word and say, "Besides, you have father's nice figure and the small hands and feet of both houses, so, as mother says, it is downright sin for you to berate yourself in this way." Dear hearts! If they could but have waved a fairy wand over my head, so often bowed because of this one grief, how soon they would have endowed me with Diana's beauty and been far happier so than to have gained it for themselves.

In my teens I became a devoted student of Emerson and took this verse as a motto:

"I pray the prayer of Plato old,
Oh, make me beautiful within,
And may mine eyes the good behold,
In everything save sin."

"The mind hath features as the body hath"—mother used to din that thought into my ears; "Handsome is that handsome does," was my father's frequent proverb; "Never mind, Frank, if you are n't the handsomest girl in the school, I hear them say you are the smartest," were my brother's cheery words, and so that magic tie of home love and loyalty helped me along until the homeliest of mother's children slowly outgrew the pang of being so.

When I was thirty-five I made my first temperance speech away from home—Evanston and Chicago counting as home ever since I was eighteen. It was in Portland, Maine, September 14, 1874, and years afterward a friend sent me the letter that follows, written by a mother to her children, without a thought that it would ever meet my eye. What I have just revealed about my greatest personal disadvantage will make it easier to estimate the grateful rejoicing with which I read these lines:

"Last night I attended a temperance meeting in the elegant Baptist church here. I counted eighteen bouquets of flowers, besides a handsome hanging-basket over the pulpit. Though very large, the church was literally packed. The speakers were men and women. Miss Frances Willard, late Dean of the Woman's College in Northwestern University, made the speech of the evening. Her language was remarkable for simplicity and eloquence. She told the story of her first awakening to the need of women's work, in the great 'Temperance Crusade.' There was a pathos in some of the pictures which she drew that caused even the men to weep. Having been Principal of a Ladies' School, she was very refined and highly cultivated. She has a straight, elegant figure, an oval face, a wealth of light brown hair, and a clear, bell-like voice made her a very effective speaker. She is the first woman I ever heard in public. Four others spoke. All wore their bonnets."

Now, though I knew this dear lady must have sat far back, so that she did n't even note my eye-glasses, I thanked God and took courage as I read her no doubt honestly-intentioned lines.

My mother's greatest friend and solace was Mrs. Hodge, wife of the Yale College graduate and Oberlin College tutor in Latin, who, for his children's sake, taught our district school in 1854. Our homes were about a mile apart and their "cheek by jowl conferences," as my father playfully called them, occurred perhaps once a fortnight and related to their two favorite themes, "How to be Christians ourselves," and "How to train our little ones." Mr. and Mrs. Hodge had decided literary gifts and were well versed in the best English authors. To her I went, by my mother's advice, to read my compositions in verse and prose. She was kind but not enthusiastic. From her unsparing criticisms I went swiftly home to mother to get my spiritual strength renewed. But I think now that Mrs. Hodge, who under favoring fortunes would have been a successful literary woman, took a wise view of the situation. "Frank will have a long youth," was one of her oracular remarks to my mother; "she matures so slowly in body and mind. At fifteen years old she has the physique of a girl of twelve years, and though in some things very acute, she has the crudeness of penmanship, pastime and manner that belong to childhood. When I hear the large words she uses, and then see her down in the mud playing marbles with my little boys, I can only explain the incongruity on the hypothesis that she patterned her talk after that of her parents and her play after her own childish fancy."

II.

A Romping Girl.

FOREST HOME.

"EVERY PLACE IS HAUNTED, AND NONE SO MUCH AS THE ONE WHERE WE LIVED IN OUR YOUTH."

CHAPTER I.

MY APPRENTICESHIP TO NATURE.

"These as they change, Almighty Father, these
Are but the varied God; the rolling year
Is full of Thee; forth in the pleasing spring
Thy beauty walks, thy tenderness and love."

—*Thomson's Seasons.*

The above lines from a book early and often read by me, express what, from my earliest recollection, has been to me the constant, universal voice that speaks from Nature's heart. I loved the poets because they uttered the wonder and the worship of which my soul was full; my mother's memory was stored with their words of inspiration, and from her lips I learned much of Coleridge, Cowper, Thomson, and other great interpreters. I have never elsewhere heard Wordsworth's "Intimations of Immortality" repeated with the delicate appreciation that was in her voice when she once more rendered it for me recently, on the verge of her eighty-fifth year.

How often looking up into the heavens from the wide prairies of our farm, I repeated, almost with tears, what she had taught me from Joseph Addison:

"The spacious firmament on high
And all the blue ethereal sky
With spangled heavens, a shining frame,
Their Great Original proclaim;
The unwearied sun from day to day
Doth his Creator's power display,
And publishes to every land
The work of an Almighty hand."

"Earth, with her thousand voices, praises God," has always been a truth upspringing like a prayer out of my heart, and turning bitter things to sweet.

My mother says that her own mother, an unschooled but a God-smitten nature, who knew nothing of the poets, loved to walk the woods and fields alone, and to go forth under the open sky at night, praising with voice of rapture, the great and blessed Spirit who had made the universe so beautiful.

My father had a heart that beat closer to Nature's own, than mother's, even: she felt the moral aspects of birds and woods and sky; he loved them simply for themselves. He felt at one with them; their sweet, shy secrets seemed to be open to him. The ways of birds and butterflies, the habits of gophers, squirrels, and ants—he seemed to know about them as a faun might, and he taught us, Sunday and every day, to learn them; to know the various herbs and what their uses were; to notice different grasses and learn their names; to tell the names of curious wild flowers. When he found something new to him in any floral line, he brought it home as a great curiosity to "study up." As a gardener and pomologist, he had few equals, and, later on, he was for years president of the State Agricultural and Horticultural Society. He always carried his little spy-glass, folded two-foot measure, and pocket thermometer, teaching us how to use them. He carried a tape-line, too, and was fond of measuring the girth of trees, and he taught us to make a thorough study of the weather as well as of the woods.

All these observations were made at "Forest Home" a farm in Wisconsin where we lived from my seventh to my nineteenth year, a farm that we made out of the woods and prairies, little by little, putting up all the buildings and stocking it so well that it became the prize farm of Rock county.

The way of it was this: after four years of hard study in Oberlin College, my father's health, which never was strong, showed symptoms of a decline, and he decided to go West. There was no railroad and so we put our household goods into white-covered wagons, of which father drove one; my brother Oliver, twelve years old, another; and my mother the third. In front of her, on father's writing-desk, sat my little sister and I, aged seven and four. The big Newfoundland dog, Fido, trotted behind this procession. When we reached Chicago we found so many mud holes with big signs up, "No bottom here," that father said he "would n't be hired to live in such a place." When we saw the great Lake Michigan, we little girls were afraid. Oliver brought us pretty pebbles with wave-ripples marked on them, and I threw them away, saying they "made me hear the roaring of that awful sea." Once the horse that mother drove went down in the quicksand almost to the ears, and men had to come with rails from the fences and pry him out. We never traveled on Sunday, and it took us over three weeks to reach our destination, and after living in Janesville, the county-seat, a few weeks, while the house on the farm was building, we moved into it before it had any windows or much of any roof. But it was beautiful June weather, and we children thought the whole affair a sort of joke and "as good as a picnic." The cook-stove was set up out-of-doors, and the shavings and bits of shingles made nice playthings. Oliver built a play-house for his sisters, with a make-believe oven where we could have a real fire, and also a make-believe stable for Fido, who was our make-believe horse. Father's tenants, who lived in a log-house by the beautiful Rock river near by, brought us fish and game, and vegetables from their garden. There were calves, pigs and chickens to play with, and we children, who had always lived in town, thought there was never anything half so delightful as this new home in the edge of the fine groves of oak and hickory that lined the river, and looking out on the prairie that stretched away toward the east until it met the sky.

As years passed on, we learned to love it more and more, and never thought of being lonesome; though, except the tenants, we had no neighbors within a mile and never went anywhere in general or saw anybody in particular. We had no toys except what we made for ourselves, but as father had a nice "kit" of carpenter's tools, we learned to use them, and made carts, sleds, stilts, cross-guns, bows and arrows, "darts," and I don't know what besides, for our amusement. Oliver was very kind to his sisters and let us do anything we liked that he did. He was not one of those selfish, mannish boys, who think they know everything and their sisters nothing, and who say, "You're only a girl, you can't go with me," but when he was in the fields plowing he would let us ride on the beam or on the horse's back; and when he went hunting I often insisted on going along, and he never made fun of me but would even let me load the gun, and I can

2

also testify that he made not the slightest objection to my carrying the game!

Once when we had lived on the farm several years, a bright girl came from Janesville to spend a week with us. Her name was Flora Comfort, and she was our pastor's daughter. She told us "She should think we would get lonesome, away down there in the woods." To this remark we took great exceptions, for we had begun to think that "Forest Home" was the "hub of the universe," and to pity everybody who did n't have the pleasure of living there. So I spoke up and said, "If we ought to have a city here, we will have one. It won't take long to show you how that is done. You town people depend on others for your good times, but, as mother is always saying, we have to depend on our own resources, and I propose now that we set at work and have a town of our own."

This proposition met with great favor. We told father of it when he came home from Janesville, whither he went on business almost daily, and he said, "All right, go ahead."

So a consultation was held in "The Studio," as I called a room fitted up in the attic, where my sister and I were wont to mould in clay, making all sorts of utensils as well as what we were pleased to call "statues," of whose general effect the less said the better. There we consulted long and loudly about the plan of a city, and who should be the officers, who edit the paper, how the streets should be named, and many other subjects of equal import. At last little Mary grew tired and went to sleep on the old "settee," while Oliver, Flora and I held high discourse, the burden of which was a name for the new city and how it should be governed. We decided at once that it should have no saloons, no billiard halls, and that it would not need a jail. Oliver was a great wit, and amused himself by introducing outdoor antics into this dignified assembly, much to my disgust, and I kept telling him that if he dropped the make-believe for a minute he would spoil it all, whereupon he picked up a bit of light-colored clay from my work-bench, and, taking off a piece, flattened it out and clapped it across my nose, saying, "Why, Frank, what a nice impression I could get from this."

"Mr. Willard," I replied sternly, "you forget the proprieties of the occasion; you are not now my brother Oliver, but a gentleman acting with me in an official capacity."

A loud ha! ha! from the gentleman interrupted "the proprieties" still more — waked little Mary and caused the dog Fido to set up a howl of annoyance.

"Have n't you made any plan yet? Am I to have an office?" murmured little Mary from among her pillows.

"Little girls should be quiet when statesmen are in conversation," said Oliver in a deep voice. Mary, being of an amiable disposition, was easily consoled by the cooky that I placed in her hand, and munched it contentedly, while Oliver, Flora and I continued to talk of the "resources of the corporation." Then the debate proceeded until at my suggestion we decided upon "Fort City" as the appropriate name, because we could thus combine the idea of adventure with that of life in town. At ten o'clock, father tapped on the door as a signal that young persons of our size would do well to seek "tired Nature's sweet restorer."

"Rome was not built in a day," neither was Fort City. We studied carefully the pages of father's favorite *Janesville Gazette*, and copied out names for the streets. Mother said of course the road in front of the house must be Broadway, because that was the most famous street in America. So we put up a shingle painted white, on which, from a pasteboard where our ingenious father had cut the word in large letters, we painted the name black and plain as print. The "by-road" at right angles, that led to the river, we called Market Street, because it ran along past the barn, the cow-yard, granary, etc. The barn was "Warehouse of J. F. Willard," the cow-yard, "City Market," the well, "City Fountain," the hen-house, "Mrs. Willard's Family Supply Store;" the granary was "City Elevator," and the pig-pen, "City Stock-Yards." We had a "Board of Trade," and "bought, sold and got gain," the question of money having been at last decided in favor of specie payments in little round bits of tin, representing silver; while some handsome yellow leather, that father brought us, was cut into circles representing gold, and stamped to stand for any sum from one to fifty dollars. But I insisted that we "must have bank notes or there was no use in pretending to be bankers," so the city treasurer finally issued some handsome bills painted by Mary on paper that had been nicely pasted over small strips of cloth.

A good deal of work was done on the highways, for we were dear lovers of old Mother Earth, and in the twinkling of an eye would leave the editor's sanctum where we had been laboriously printing *The Fort City Tribune*, and taking the fire-shovel, one would begin spading the street up to a higher level, while the other would fit bricks and pebbles into a queer mosaic to make it more like the pavements of the town. A few minutes later, perhaps, we would be walking on the ridge of the house, with an old rake handle for our "balance-pole," then crawling in at a dormer window, we would scurry down the back stairs and have a shooting match out by the well, with bow and arrows. For Oliver and Loren, a boy who worked for us, had declared that "the girls" liked the city part of this great "make-believe" too well, and did n't seem to remember that this was, after all, only a city in a fort, of which the fort part was by far the most important. The boys insisted that it was high time to have an attack by Indians, and that if we girls did n't agree to it they "would n't play city" any more.

Now the fact was that we girls did not at all object to a skirmish with the redskins, but we had played that often, while this game of the city was new. It was agreed, therefore, that when corn-husking was over there should be a regular Indian invasion.

I will give a few specimens of our laws, copying them from the very book in which they were first written by me, a wee pamphlet bound in yellow paper:

LAWS OF FORT CITY.—VOL. I.

(BY AUTHORITY.)

I. OFFICER'S LAWS.

1. The officers shall be elected once a month by ballot.

They shall consist of a Mayor, Secretary, Treasurer, Tax-gatherer and Postmaster.

The duty of the mayor shall be to preside at all meetings of the officers. His word during the meetings of the officers shall be perfect law. If any of the officers shall refuse to obey him, he shall immediately turn himself into a constable, serve a writ of attachment on said officer, and the officer shall pay to the mayor, a fine of fifty dollars ; one third of the same fine shall be paid to the mayor by any officer who, on rising to speak in any of the meetings, does not make a bow to the mayor. The mayor shall wear a badge at all meetings of the society, and whenever he goes on a visit to any of the officers; also to concerts, shows, lectures, or other performances of a public nature. If anybody besides the mayor takes it upon himself or herself to wear a badge, he or she shall pay to the mayor fifty dollars for the first offense, and fifty more for every time after the first. Before he does anything else the mayor shall be sworn in by the secretary in the following manner:

"I promise faithfully to discharge the duties of my office for one month to the very best of my ability; this I promise on my sacred honor."

He shall stand up and hold up his right hand, and repeat this after the secretary, and then sign his name to it, and the secretary shall keep the paper, but the mayor may keep the secretary's oath.

II. GENERAL LAWS.

1. No officer shall go into any other officer's room without permission from the owner, or forfeit fifty dollars for the first offense, and an additional ten for each future offense. For the second he shall pay the fine just mentioned and shall have his hands tied behind him and be kept in the city pound for five minutes in total darkness. If an officer goes into another's room and the other does not see him, he need not pay any fine nor be put in the pound; or if the owner of the room be absent from the city this law has no effect. A person may also go into another's room provided they are sent there by any person whom they *must* obey, but they must never try to get sent in.

2. Mrs. Mary T. Willard shall, on all occasions, act as judge in law cases as to which side has gained the day.

3. If any person has seen or heard of a thing he wishes to have, he shall have it for all of any officer of this city: that is, after he has said, *I speak for that thing*, or something of that sort. After that, if any officer or signer of this book tries to get it away, or persuade the owner not to give it to the one who spoke first, said person shall be fined two hundred dollars for the first offense and twice as much for every future offense. Since it may not always be some *thing* that the speaker wants, the law is, that supposing it is to go a walking, or a riding, or read some book or paper then in the hands of another, whatever it is, it is secured to the one who speaks for it first, if he can get it, for all any one else, except the owner. If, sometimes, two speak for a thing at a time, the mayor shall decide who shall have it, only we promise never to speak for a thing that is unfair or unreasonable, or that we know we can not get.

4. If any of the officers find any of the others' things, he shall immediately return it without asking or expecting any pay, and show himself or herself a polite gentleman or lady.

Oliver wished to hasten our Indian fight and so proposed that we girls should help him husk the corn, which we were glad to do for the outdoor's fun of it. We were fitted out with "husking-pins"—bits of hard wood whittled to a point and fastened to the right middle finger by a piece of leather. With this the tough husk was torn open and the ear of corn wrenched from the stalk. I took a little cricket and seated myself beside a big "shock" of corn, resolved to run a race with Oliver as to who should husk the most that day, with the understanding that Mary should be allowed to get the stalk of corn ready and pass it along to me. She was also to take care of the tassel that topped out each ear, for they were sold as skeins of silk in mother's handsome dry-goods store.

The dog prowled about, carrying an ear of corn from one of the rival heaps to another, following a rabbit scent, or bow-wowing on general principles as best suited his notions.

"Now, as to that Indian raid," sang out Oliver from beside his little stack of corn, "I will head the attack from out-of-doors, and Fido shall be with me. You may stay in the house and have Loren to help you. Mary can look on, but must not be in the fight; that's a fair divide."

"No," said I, "let it be this way: you and Loren and the dog may club together out-of-doors. Mother, Mary and I will defend the fort inside, and I'd like to see you 'effect an entrance,' as the war books call it."

"Well, I'm surprised at you for being so risky," he replied. "I warn you that you give all the fighting force to us at the start, and if your defense does n't turn out a minus quantity, I miss my guess."

"Very well, you'll miss it," was my vainglorious answer, and so the great attack was planned.

It was about four o'clock of the brief winter day. Snow covered the ground, and the recent beginning of a thaw followed by a sudden freeze had made a solid, slippery crust, which I thought to be a disadvantage to the boys in their attack. Every door and window of the large,. rambling farm-house was carefully fastened. Mother had got her baking out of the way, and the loaves of her toothsome "salt-rising" bread reposed upon the kitchen table. The fat Maltese cat, "Trudge," purred on the hearth, all unconscious of approaching hostilities.

Tired though she was, mother entered heartily into the project of the hour. Bridget was gone for a week's visit at her brother-in-law's, otherwise the women would have had a force unfairly strong. Mother had the brain of a statesman and the courage of a major-general, but it was always her plan to put her children forward, and then to help them by her quiet counsel. So I was leader of the forces inside the "Fort." I arrayed myself in an old coat of Oliver's, upon which Mary had sewed some gilt paper epaulets, and I fastened a hickory sword at my side. But all this was simply a dumb show. "Pump the milk-pail full of water and have the dipper handy," was my "general order number one." "Let Mary keep up a bright outlook. She's not to fight, but she can watch out for the enemy, as Rebecca did when she helped Ivanhoe," was number two. "Let's have a bit of spare-rib ready with which to coax the dog away from those two horrid Injuns," was number three.

"Now, mother, you keep a sharp lookout at the front door. Take the broom for your weapon, and whenever you see a head, hit it."

"What do you propose to do?" asked mother, laughing, while Mary jumped up and down with glee, and flattened her audacious little nose against the window pane, saying in mock alarm, "The booger-man will catch you if you don't watch out!" I explained as soberly as if mother and I had not talked over the whole plan the day before. "It is my part to generalissimo the forces, watch the back door and have this garden syringe ready to give those red rascals a shower bath if they dare to show their heads."

It was now getting dark and not a sign of life was to be seen. We could hear the sheep bleating in their fold behind the barn and the gossip of the hen-house was faintly borne to our keen ears, as our beloved "Cochin Chinas," "Polands" and "Brahmapootras" clambered to their roosts. It was almost milking time and yet no attack was made; no bark of Fido betrayed the wily foe. *Where were those boys?*

Suddenly we heard a war-whoop and a pow-wow that were enough to make one's blood run cold. Mary shrieked in fright, but pluckily held her post, while I muttered, "We shall need a gag for the spy after this!"

Mother, convulsed with laughter, raised her broom with threatening attitude, and called out, "I will die at my post!"

I charged the syringe and placed it over a chair-back, ready to swing in whatever direction was most available. Another Indian screech, and the cellar door that opened into the kitchen fell flat (the boys had taken out all the screws but one); the dog came tearing in, but received such a deluge of water that he ran howling under the table, while the cat, fat and all, flew to the top of the sink and hissed defiance at the invaders from her safe perch. Oliver, with waving feather and face red with war-paint, dashed up to me, and with a terrific whoop, knocked the water apparatus from my hand, and waved his wooden scalp-knife, while Mary jumped on the table and set up a wail of disappointment to think I had been beaten; but mother claimed that the fort's garrison was not altogether defeated, because, with her broom, she had chased Loren down cellar, and, clapping the door into its place, was at that moment literally "holding the fort" against him. The struggle, like many of which we read in more ambitious records, was "short, sharp and decisive," for Loren returned to the attack, and, having Oliver to help him from within, soon succeeded in forcing the door, in spite of my fierce deluge down my brother's spine, and mother's vigorous flourishes impartially distributed among the two boys and their four-footed ally.

When the Indians were finally victorious, and sat by in flaming red shirts, worn over their usual garments, and with wooden tomahawks of frightful size, while their waving roosters' feathers stuck out above their heads (though Oliver's were somewhat lopped by reason of the water), mother said, "You know right well that in the open field we are a match for you. This taking of the fort has been done by your miserable Indian strategy."

"Yes, indeed," we girls chimed in, "you had to come sneaking around so that we had n't a fair chance."

"Of course we did," smiled Oliver; "that's what we're for. You see, I had been reading in 'Western Scenes' about some Indians that came *under the snow*, so Loren and I just dug our way under the solid crust to the cellar window, which we had already loosened, and burst in the door, that we had fixed to our liking, and what could you do after that?"

Sure enough, the boys had won, "Indian fashion," and nobody could complain.

"I don't like such plays," said Mary, sitting on mother's lap; "do you?" patting her cheek.

"Why, no. I like the city better than the fort," replied mother. "But we did this to give the boys a frolic, and as they got the better of us, they won't want another such game very soon."

"The trouble is," said I, not feeling very much elated just then, "the trouble is, not that we were outfought, but that we were outwitted. The next time you want an Indian fight, boys, we'll be ready for you at all points."

But the discussion of the battle ended abruptly when mother reminded the flushed combatants of the time, and soon besiegers and besieged were busy in removing all traces of the conflict. Oliver began the peaceful work of mending the door and fastening the cellar window, while we quickly set all things in order in the kitchen. Loren, after taking off his Indian "toggery," sped out into the darkness to do his evening chores, whistling merrily as he went, and long before the early bed-time came, all the inhabitants of Fort City had settled down to the peaceful ways of civilized life.*

In all our plays (and we "kept a hotel," among the rest, in a regular "shanty" play-house that was built for us by a carpenter when the big barn was going up), Mary was mine hostess, and I mine host. Mother did not talk to us as girls, but simply as human beings, and it never occurred to me that I ought to "know house-work" and do it. Mary took to it kindly by nature; I did not, and each one had her way. Mother never said, "You must cook, you must sweep, you must sew," but she studied what we liked to do and kept us at it with no trying at all. There never was a busier girl than I and what I did was mostly useful. I knew all the carpenter's tools and handled them: made carts and sleds, cross-guns and whip-handles; indeed, all the toys that were used at Forest Home we children manufactured. But a needle and a dishcloth I could not abide — chiefly, perhaps, because I was bound to live out-of-doors. This was so from the beginning, and perhaps it had something to do with our noble mother's willingness to live out in the country away from everybody but her own. Anyhow, her three children were far

*Several "Indian stories" are "bunched" in this sketch.

better amused because left to amuse themselves. I pity the poor little things that have so many toys all "brand new" from the store, and get no chance to use their own wits at invention and to develop their own best gifts. "Fort City" taught Oliver and his sisters a better way.

What to do on Sunday with these restless spirits was a serious question, for father and mother had the old Puritan training. It was in their birth and bones that the Sabbath was a day holy unto the Lord. This feeling was even stronger in my father, perhaps, because his father was the son of Elder Elijah Willard, of Dublin, N. H., for forty years pastor in that parish, a good man and a righteous, who trained his children strictly in faith and practice. Perhaps, also, the lawyer-like character of his mind had something to do with his greater severity in holding us to the white line of what he deemed our duty. For himself, he would not shave or black his boots; he would not read or write a letter; he would not so much as look in the dictionary for a word upon the Sabbath day. He said, "The children must have habits." This was the most frequent phrase he used about their training. He never said "good habits," so that I grew up with the idea that there were no habits except good ones! He said, "You must draw your lines and set your stakes, for if you don't you will be just nobody." So he decided that no calls or visits should be received on Sunday, which was easy enough to observe, as there was nobody to come but the birds, and nowhere to go except to the fields and pasture. He also said that no books or papers should be read except those of a strictly religious nature. Mother did not interfere with all this by any word, but we felt a difference, and had a sense of greater "elbow room" with her. A little incident illustrates her tact. In the early years of our farm life, one New Year's eve came on Saturday and our small presents were given and put away without waiting for morning, because father thought it would n't be right to have them on Sunday. One can hardly imagine the bottled-up condition of children in such a case. Fortunately for Oliver, he had a Sunday book, "Austin's Voice to Youth," and little Mary had a child's edition of Pilgrim's Progress, so they could get at work on their presents. But, alas for poor me! My prayer and dream had been for months, "some pictures to look at on Sunday," and I had a slate, instead.

To be sure I had devoutly desired a slate, for I had imagined any amount of things that could be written and drawn upon it, but the rule of the house did not permit such a week-day article to come into use upon the Sabbath. At last I hit upon a plan, and going to mother,—I did not dare suggest even this to the revered "Squire," as the farmers called my father—I said, in a pleading voice, "May n't I have my new slate if I'll promise not to draw anything but *meetin' houses?*" (That's what they called churches in those days.) Mother laughed in spite of herself at this bit of childish ingenuity, and said, "Yes, you may, my little girl, and mamma will make you a pattern to go by." So there was peace and quiet, while mother, who had much skill with her pencil, made a "meeting house," and I was the envy of my brother and sister, who had before thought themselves the favored ones.

This is a handy place in which to mention that, though we were all good at it, the premium coaxer of the family was little Mary. Whenever the others wanted a master-stroke in this line, they sent her as their ambassador at court. Mother disliked to let us be exposed to the damp, changeable days when winter was just giving way to spring, and as we loved "outdoors" better than any other place, we would send Mary, who, climbing on mother's knee and stroking her face with her soft little hands, would murmur in the sweetest of voices, "Dear, nice, good, pretty, beautiful mamma, it's warm and cool and comf'table, and won't you *please* let us go out and play?" After which speech and performance mamma generally did.

But to return to the Forest Home Sunday. In the early days, before the new bridge across Rock river, we were four miles from church, and as we cast in our fortunes with the Methodists (though mother was a Congregationalist), we were "on a circuit," and the minister came only once a fortnight or once a month. Then we were dressed in our Sunday best, the big wagon was brought out with Jack and Gray, and family and farm hands bundled in—the latter to be dropped at the Catholic church. But my parents soon decided not to leave the house alone, for prairie fires sometimes crept unpleasantly near, cattle broke into fields or garden, and there was no dinner when we got home. In those days such a being as a "tramp" had not been heard of, and in our twelve years of isolation on this farm, not one theft, much less any fright or danger, befell us brave pioneers. Once a drunken man came in to warm himself; once we found behind a straw-stack signs of men having slept there, and some slices of bread hidden under the stack; sometimes men stopped to ask about the "river road to Beloit," or how far it was to Janesville, but that was all. The present records of fright and peril to our country folks seem strange and pitiful to one who remembers how safe and peaceful was their lot long time ago.

We made this plan at Forest Home: One Sunday father should "hold the fort," the next, mother, and the third, Oliver. Whoever did this had to get the dinner ready, and as both father and son were famous cooks, the plan worked well. Indeed, to see my brother brandish the carving-fork in air as we approached on our return from church, and to inhale the rich aroma of his roast chicken, nice home-raised vegetables and steaming coffee, was an event. Sunday dinner was to us the central point of the day, and served to keep it in fragrant memory, notwithstanding its many deprivations.

For us it was all very well, under the peculiar circumstances, but I do not approve of a Sunday dinner that deprives working people of their rest and their opportunity to go to church.

Careful as he was, from training and long habit, about what we should read upon the Sabbath day, father was quite easy-going when we could once get him out-of-doors. He would whistle to the dogs—for when we came to have a thousand sheep we kept three of them—and off we would go together to the pasture, father, we girls and the dogs, leaving Oliver lying upon his face on the front piazza, reading his beloved "D'Aubigne's History of the Reformation," and mother with the big family Bible on her lap. As we wended our way down by the grassy bank of the broad, tree-shaded river, I liked to lag behind and "skip" a stone, in which art I was something of an adept. But Mary would wave her hand for me to "Come on," and I would smilingly desist. I liked to clip a fresh twig from the alders, or to make a "whistle" with my jack-knife, but father said, "Frances, you know I don't allow you to keep up your carpenter work on Sunday." Whereupon I answered with a queer pucker about the lips, that would have been a smile, only it did n't dare to, "But, father, can't I whittle if I'll promise that I won't *make* anything?" and he agreed to that. He would even cut a chip from the gnarled old cedar tree, and, after smoothing it, give it to us, and say, "Did you ever smell anything more wholesome?" I liked this so much that even now the odor of red cedar, though but in a lead pencil's handle, brings back to me the river, softly flowing, the sentinel trees, my father's manly figure marching at the head, Mary and me walking demurely after, in the path the cows had worn.

On Sunday afternoon, almost the only leisure time she had, mother would walk a little while with us children in the orchard, taking scissors along with her, and clipping a sprig of caraway or fennel for "the girls," or a bunch of sweet-smelling pinks for Oliver, from the pretty little beds in the heart of the orchard, where no one was privileged to go except with mother. Here she talked to us of God's great beauty in the thoughts He works out for us to learn about Him by; she taught us tenderness toward every little sweet-faced flower and piping bird; she made us see the shapes of clouds, and what resemblances they bore to things upon the earth; she made us love the Heart that is at Nature's heart. Thus it could not be said of us, as of poor Peter Bell,

> "In vain through every changeful year
> Did Nature lead him as before;
> A primrose by the river's brim,
> A yellow primrose was to him,
> But it was nothing more."

Father did not "talk religion," as we called it, very much, nor did our mother. They had family prayers always, with Scott's "Practical Observations" at the close of the Bible reading. They always had a blessing at the table, and if father did not ask it, mother did. They did not insist that the children read the Bible for themselves, and I was very shy about it, the tendency of my mind to doubt and question revealing itself even then; when, at a very early age, the Testament was specially read to me on Sunday, I had asked, "How do you know God sent it?" And if the family Bible was sometimes open before me, I would say with a toss of the head, when mother expressed pleasure at the sight, "I'm looking at the births and deaths," or, "I'm only reading the Apocrypha." My mother had the good sense never to seem shocked by this bit of bravado, but patted the busy little head with her kind, steady hand, saying, "My little girl will be a missionary, yet." She knew these symptoms were not of ugliness, but just the prancing about of a mettlesome steed before it settled to life's long and difficult race. She knew the more she argued and reproved, the worse the case would be, so she just lived the gospel right along and taught its precepts and *prayed much.*

We seldom had the opportunity to attend church on Sabbath evening, but our song service at home was, as already mentioned, an inspiration and delight. My father had a fine bass voice and mother a tender, well-trained soprano. There were no "Gospel Hymns," but in the *Mother's Assistant*—a family magazine that they subscribed to for some years—were sweet songs of Christian faith, and the old Methodist hymn-book with its "Guide me, O Thou Great Jehovah," and Kirke White's "The Star of Bethlehem," used just about to break my heart in the sweet summer twilights, though I would n't have had anybody know, save Mary. Fair and bright, in spite of occasional shadows, seemed those years of childhood; still fairer and brighter they seem now.

Father made us big paper hats, shaped like cornucopias, trimmed with peacock feathers and painted with "Injun fights," by ingenious sister Mary. Then mother sewed for us belts of bright red flannel, in which were stuck wooden swords, bunches of arrows, etc., as we marched away on hunting expeditions. Father was so careful of his girls and so much afraid that harm would come to us if we went horseback riding, that I determined to have a steed of my own, contrived a saddle, and trained a favorite heifer, "Dime," to act in that capacity. "She can do it if she has a mind to," was my unvarying reply to all the ingenious objections of Oliver, who said that a creature which chewed the cud and divided the hoof was never meant for riding purposes. He also claimed that Dime did her part when she gave milk, and ought not to be put through at this rate. But I took the ground that "cows were a lazy set, and because they never had worked was no reason why they should n't begin now. Up in Lapland they made a great many uses of the deer that people did n't where we live, and he was all the better and more famous animal as a result of it. So, since father would n't let me ride a horse, I would make Dime the best trained and most accomplished cow in the pasture; and Dime would like it, too, if they'd only let her alone." So with much extra feeding and caressing, and no end of curry-combing to make her coat shine, I brought Dime up to a high degree of civilization. She would "moo" whenever I appeared, and follow me about like a dog; she would submit to being led by a bridle, which Loren, always willing to help, had made out of an old pair of reins; she was gradually broken to harness and would draw the hand-sleds of us girls; but the crowning success was when she "got wonted" (which really meant when she willed) to the saddle, and though I had many an inglorious tumble before the summit of my hopes was reached, I found myself, at last, in possession of an outlandish steed, whose every motion threatened a catastrophe, and whose awkwardness was such that her trainer never gave a public exhibition of the animal's powers, but used to ride out of sight down in the big ravine, and only when the boys were busy in the field. Jack and Gray were the chief farm horses, and to see Oliver and Loren mount these, and go tearing over the prairies like wild Indians, was my despair. This was the one pleasure of farm life that was denied the girls, but when I was fifteen, father declared, at mother's earnest request, that "the girls might now ride the horses whenever their mother thought best." Many a time did she take her stand in the road and watch us while we galloped "to the ravine" near "Bluff Wood," the Hodge homestead, and back again. To offset my "trained cow," Mary had a goat for which panniers (side-pockets) had been made, in one of which a nice, toothsome lunch was often placed, which Bridget took great pleasure in providing, and in the other, our sketching materials. A sheep-bell was tied on the goat's neck and to see us with our tall caps, red belts, and cross-guns on shoulder, wending our way to the groves along the river bank, while the dog Fido scoured the bushes for gophers, often returning to walk in the procession, was the delight of mother's heart, for well she knew how pleasant and how healthful all this was to her two girls. Mary wore the official badge of "Provider," for the practical part of the expedition was in her charge. This badge was a bit of carved pine, like a small cane, painted in many colors and decorated with a ribbon.

The one who wore it had the "say," about what the lunch should be, and where and when it should be eaten; also whether Fido had behaved well enough to go along, and many other questions not needful to repeat. When the time came, a nice white tablecloth was spread, and some of mother's light, sweet bread, with butter that fairly smelled of violets, and nice sugar strewn over it, was set in order, with a piece of pumpkin pie and a few hickory nuts. Our drink was water, bright from the crystal spring up the bank, and we brought it in a bottle and drank it through a clean-cut straw. We asked a blessing at the table, and acted like grown folks, so far as we could. This generally closed the expedition, but before eating we would fish, chiefly for "minnies" (or minnow fish), and we usually had several of these little swimmers in dishes at home, which was a pity, for they died after a few days. We did not mean to be unkind to animals, for mother had taught us better, but we did n't think, sometimes. One of the first bits of verse mother ever repeated and explained to us was this, from her favorite poet, Cowper:

> "I would not rank among my list of friends,
> Though graced with polished manners and fine sense,
> Yet wanting sensibility, *the man*
> *Who needlessly sets foot upon a worm.*"

Then there were other beautiful lines on the same subject, by Wordsworth, I think, which closed with

> "This lesson, shepherd, let us two divide,
> Taught both by what life shows and what conceals,
> Never to blend our pleasure or our pride
> *With sorrow of the meanest thing that feels.*"

We used to shoot at a mark with arrows and became very good at hitting, so much so that at my request, Mary, whose trust in her sister was perfect, stood up by a post with an auger-hole in it, and let me fire away and put an arrow through the hole when her sweet blue eye was just beside it. But this was wrong, and when we rushed in "to tell mother," she did n't smile, but made us promise "never, no, never," to do such a thing again.

Down by the river bank, Mary took her pencil and made sketches, such as they were, while I delighted to lie stretched out upon the grass, look up into the blue sky and "think my thoughts." Sometimes I would reach out my hand appealingly toward heaven, and say to her: "See there! could *you* resist a hand that so much wanted to clasp your own? Of course you could n't, and God can not, either. I believe that, though I do not see that He reaches down to me." And lovely, trusting Mary answered: "I know He does, for mother says so."

One day when we girls were thus having our good times down by the river, the three Hodge boys came along, hunting for birds' nests. "But you must n't carry any away!" said Mary, greatly stirred. "You may climb the trees and look, if you want to see the eggs or little ones, but you can't hurt a birdie, big or little, in *our* pasture." The boys said their mother told them the same thing, and they only wanted to "look." So Mary and I showed them under the leafy covert some of the brown thrush's housekeeping, and the robin's, too, and then we told them that since they were such kind boys, and did n't want to kill the pretty creatures God had made, and since they had just come West and did n't know all the ways we had out here, we would help them to "drown out a gopher," and they might have it if they wanted to.

John was delighted; Rupert's eyes fairly danced, but thoughtful Jamie, "the preacher," as they called him, said, "But why do you drown out a gopher? Is that a kind thing to do?"

"Well, it is this way," explained the Western prairie girls; "the gopher digs up the corn and spoils the crop. Many a time we've dropped corn into the hills for Oliver or father till we've tired ourselves out getting it under ground, and along would come this black-striped yellow-coat and eat up our crop before it was started. So father said it was our plain duty to catch as many as we could, and we've set traps and tried all sorts of ways, but the one the boys like best is drowning out. Father told us that the poet Cowper, who writes so well about kindness to animals, says 'Our rights are paramount and must extinguish theirs;' that is, when they spoil our work, we are obliged to spoil them, for the general good."

The boys thought there was common sense in this, and I led the way to a hole in the ground about as large around as an ear of corn, where Fido had been clawing for some time. "The way we do is to pour water into the hole, stand there with a big stick or a shovel, and when the gopher comes crawling up, Fido snatches him by the throat, and the poor, drenched thing does n't have long to suffer, you may be sure,'' said Mary. So John went to the house for a couple of pails and he and Rupert brought water from the river, Jamie and we watched at the hole, one with a shovel and the others with sticks, and the dog was wild with importance and delight. Pretty soon the poor, wet gopher crawled to the front, his mouth open, and his long teeth in full view. "Whack" went the shovel, but "snap" went old Fido's jaws, and the "happy corn-fields," as I said, claimed the destroyer so unwelcome here. "What! you don't think that gophers will have another life?" said preacher Jamie, quite shocked by the idea.

"I only know that mother says John Wesley thought the birds would go to heaven, and the Indians think that,

> 'Transported to that equal sky,
> Their faithful dogs shall bear them company,' "

was my reply. "It is a thing that nobody can tell anything about, but I like to think the fact of life predicts the fact of immortality."

"Did n't mother put that into your head?" asked Mary as we wended our way home.

I said I guessed so, for she always answered all my questions and told me so much that I hardly knew where her thoughts ended and mine began.

Sometimes in winter I would set a "figure-four trap" down in the grove south of "Fort City," where I caught many a plump quail. The trap was nothing but a rough box, held up on the edge by three sticks, fitted together like the figure 4, and having fastened to the cross bar of the figure a few grains of wheat. When the little "more wheat" singing quails pecked away at the stick to knock off these grains, the whole thing fell down and they were prisoners. I used to put on an old coat of father's, and some droll little boots my brother had outgrown, and, perching a soft hat on my head, wend my way over the snow's hard crust to see my trap. But I never killed a quail. I would bring them home and hand them over to Loren, who soon set them free into the heavenly bird-land. Then Bridget would pick, stuff and cook the quails, putting in flavored bread crumbs and such delicious "summer savory" as never was tasted before or since, and browning the delicious game to a turn. All this we considered a right and proper thing to do, because quails could be eaten, and so were useful and were not killed for mere sport. But Mary, whose heart was pitiful as an angel's, used to wish that "folks could get along without meat, and not kill the creatures with such bright, kind eyes as calves have, and lambs, and little birdies," and her older sister, who was given to "branching out," would tell her she "presumed that time would come, and hoped it might. Anything that you could imagine was apt to happen some day."

"Father's Room" was a sort of literary refuge to all concerned. Here were his tall book-case and his desk that locked up, with which latter no mortal ever interfered for the good reason that its black, velvet-lined interior was never seen save when "the Squire" was seated there at work. He would sit for days making out the tax list of the (real) town, writing his speech for the fair, or his "History of Rock County," and we would be near him, at work with brush, or pen, or pencil, never speaking a word to each other or to him. All other rooms in the house were full of life and talk and music, but "Father's" was a place of privilege conditioned upon quiet; therein we children were on our best of good behavior, and even the cat, of which he was very fond, ceased to be frisky when admitted to the room which its owner called his "*sanctum sanctorum.*"

My father did not believe in medicine—I mean, not as most people do. He thought every family ought to pay so much a year to the doctor, and then deduct for every day's illness. He said this would soon make all the M. D.'s careful students of how to keep folks well, instead of how to get them well when by their own carelessness they had fallen sick. He used to say that God had but about half a dozen laws of health, and if people would only study these and obey them, they would have a happy, well-to-do life. He thought it was wonderful how easy our Heavenly Father has made it for us in this world, if we will "only take hold of it by the right handle." Just as He made but one law in the Garden of Eden—so easy to remember—and in all other things Adam and Eve could act of their own free will, so in the new Garden of Eden that we called Forest Home, and in the great world, there were few things to do, and then all would have health. He did n't say "*good* health," for he was not one of those who ever said, "I *enjoy bad* health!" In the first place, it was n't enjoyable, and in the next, there was no kind of health but *good*, since the word itself meant wholeness or holiness,—a perfect state, as compared with the imperfect state of being sick.

In Oberlin he had been much attached to Dr. Jennings, a cold-water physician who had written a book on right living, which father read more than anything else except his Bible and A. J. Downing's *Horticulturist.* If we had sore throats, a cold water compress was put on; when I stepped on a nail, and might easily have had locked-jaw, mother lifted me into the kitchen "sink" and pumped water over the aching member; when on a summer morning Oliver's leg was broken by an ugly ox, his mother sat beside him, attending to the cold-water bandage by night and day for a week. And yet, in the twelve years of our farm life, "The Happy Five" (as I was wont to call them) knew almost nothing about sickness. Our golden rules were these, worthy to be framed beside the entrance door of every home:

"GOLDEN RULES OF HEALTH."

Simple food, mostly of vegetables, fish and fowls.

Plenty of sleep, with very early hours for retiring.

Flannel clothing next the skin all the year round; feet kept warm, head cool, and nothing worn tight.

Just as much exercise as possible, only let fresh air and sunshine go together.

No tea or coffee for the children, no alcoholic drink or tobacco for anybody.

Tell the truth and mind your parents.

"But yet, Fort City must have a doctor, or else, you see, it would n't *be* a city," I pleaded one day. So, being told to "go ahead," I collected a lot of spools, whittled the projecting part off the smaller end of each, and made a stopper for it, plugged the other end with a bit of wood, and so had a fine outfit of bottles, which were labeled with all the outrageous names of drugs that mother or I could think of, only the real contents (fortunately) were sugar, starch, salt, flour, pepper, etc., from the store-room. Mary made for me a large assortment of powder papers, cut in different sizes; surgical instruments were shaped from bits of tin, with handles of wood; a tin watch was used in counting the pulse, and poor Mary, stretched out on two chairs, obligingly "made believe sick." The following extract from the journal that I dutifully kept through all those years, will give the outcome of my medical experience:

> Sister was sick, and I brought out all my little bottles of sugar, salt and flour. Besides these medicines, I dosed her with pimento pills, and poulticed her with cabbage leaves, but she grew no better quite fast, so mother called another doctor. Dear me, if I were my brother, instead of being only a girl, we'd soon see whether I've talent for medicine or not.

But the "other doctor" was purely imaginary, for Mary jumped up and ran off with Oliver after the cows, telling me that I could "try my skill on the calves or the cat next time," and the young M. D. got quite a lesson from her mother on the value of moderation in medicine and all other undertakings.

I have said but little about winter-time at Forest Home. The truth is, it seemed to us that when the lovely summer and beautiful autumn days were gone, they never would come back. And though we made sleds and went coasting, took care of our scores of pets, set our figure-four traps for quails, and played "Fort City" with great zest, it remains true that we greeted the return of spring with such keen delight as city children can not know. The first flower—who should find and bring it home to mother? That was a question of the highest interest, and little Mary was quite as likely as the older ones to win this beautiful distinction. The hill-side behind the house, the "Big Ravine," and "Whale's-back," near the Hodge homestead, were the favorite hiding-places of the "March flower," "wind flower," or "anemone," that hardy pioneer which ventured first to spread its tiny sail and catch the favoring breeze. Next came the buttercups, then the violets, and, later on, the crow's-foot geranium, shooting star, wiid lady's slipper, wild rose and lily, and a hundred sweet, shy flowers with unknown names. But the spring sounds were more to me than the spring posies.

Like all rural people, our family rose at day-break in spring, in winter long before that time. Father went to his desk; Oliver, Loren, and the "hired hands" went to the cow-yard to milk, or to the barn to feed the horses; Mary and I cared for our special pets, the turkeys, chickens, and pea-fowls, the rabbits, goats, calves, colts and dogs, while mother and Bridget got the breakfast. But when the witchery of spring-time came, we girls would take turns about waking each other, and first of all in the house would steal away to our best-beloved "Outdoors." It seemed to us that we learned secrets then, such as dear old Mother Nature did not tell to most folks.

We sought the quiet dells in the "north pasture," where a sort of wild mint grew, with smell so fresh and sweet as can't be told, and where were mosses lovelier than the velvet of the Queen's throne. We put our ears to the ground, as Indians do, and heard sounds afar off, or thought we did, which answered just as well. Voices came to us as we listened, through the woods and from the prairie near by, that thrilled our hearts with joy. The jay, the bluebird and the robin made music vastly sweeter than any we ever heard elsewhere or afterward. But the "prairie-chickens" had organized the special orchestra that we listened to with most delight in the fair spring days. It was a peculiar strain, not a song at all, as everybody knows, but a far-off, mellow, rolling sound, a sort of drumbeat, rising and falling, circling through the air and along the ground, "so near, and yet so far," it seemed to us like a breath from Nature's very lips. Perhaps it came so gently and with such boundless welcome to our hearts, because it was the rarest, surest harbinger of spring. Now the lambs would soon be playing in the pastures; now the oriole would soon be flashing through the trees, the thrush singing in the fields, and the quail's sweet note, "more wheat," would cheer the farmer at his toil; the river would soon mirror the boughs that would bend over it in their rich summer green, for winter was over and gone, fresh spring rain was often on the roof, and the deep heavens grew warm and blue. All these things were in the far-off, curious notes of the prairie-chickens that we never saw, but only listened to with smiling faces, while girls and chickens, after their own fashion, thanked God that spring had come once more.

In the earlier years at Forest Home, prairie fires were a gorgeous feature of the spring landscape. Only a few times did they come near enough to make us anxious. Returning from church one Sabbath noon with Oliver, mother saw one of her mile-away neighbors motioning to her vigorously,—a woman, by the way, who did n't believe in "going to meetings," for which reason, father would have nothing to do with her family outside of business. Oliver stopped the horses, and coming out to her gate Mrs. P. said, "You'd better be at home 'tending to your prairie fires ; the neighbors are fighting them for you, and trying to save your buildings."

Oliver whipped up his team, and away they flew down the river toward Forest Home. There they found father in his shirt-sleeves directing the forces that had already put the fire to rout. He had strolled out with Mary and me to "take an observation," as he called it, and had seen the fire bearing down in braggart style from Mr. Guernsey's prairie toward a log tenement house where one of our hired men was living. The house was closed, for all the family (Catholic) had gone to church. "Bring some pails, girls, and follow me," said father, as he ran toward this house, which was in danger.

"I know what he'll do," said I to Mary, as we armed ourselves with pails, and, whistling to the dogs, scampered away following father ; "of course, he must fight fire with fire, or else Ed Carey's house is gone."

It was a long run, through the orchard, across the Big Ravine and over a stretch of prairie, but we were not far behind our father. We found him "back-firing," as it was called ; that is, setting the grass burning all along between the fire and the house, and then, with a neighbor or two, beating it out again when the flame grew too strong. We brought water, thrashed away at the grass with sticks, and grew black in the face, not from work, but from the smoke and cinders. By the time Oliver and mother appeared on the scene, the crisis was over and we girls clambered into the democrat wagon, covered all over with dirt and glory, and both telling at once about the hair-breadth 'scape of Edward's house. But for the most part the prairie fires were among the pleasant features of spring, for they seldom did any harm. In burning over a new section of land, before breaking it up with the plow, men would fire it from each of the four sides and let it burn toward the center. The grass, so long, thick, and sometimes matted, made a bright, high wall of flame, sending up columns of smoke like a thousand locomotives blowing off steam at once. At night these fires, on the distant horizon, looked to us like a drove of racing, winged steeds; or they swept along, dancing, courtesying, now forward, now backward, like gay revelers; or they careered wildly, like unchained furies; but always they were beautiful, often grand, and sometimes terrible.

Another rich experience that came to my sister and me was following the "breaking plow" in spring. Just after the prairie fire had done its work and the great field was black with the carpet it had spread, came the huge plow, three times as large as that generally used, with which the virgin soil was to be turned upward to the sun. Nowadays in the far West, that keeps going farther every year, they use steam plows. Just think of a locomotive out in the boundless prairie, going so fast and far that one would n't dare tell how many miles it gets over in a day! But away back in the forties and fifties, so distant from these wonderful eighties in which we live, we thought that nothing could go beyond the huge plow, with steel "mould-board" so bright that you could see your face in it; "beam" so long that we two girls could sit upon it for a ride and have space for half a dozen more; formidable "colter"—a sharp, knife-like steel that went before the plowshare to cut the thick sod—and eight great, branch-horned oxen sturdily pulling all this, while one man held the plow by its strong, curving handles, and another cracked a whip with lash so long it reached the heads of the head oxen away at the front. As father generally held the plow, and Oliver, who was very kind to animals, the whip, Mary and I used to enjoy running along and balancing ourselves on the great black furrow, as it curved over from the polished mould-board and lay there smooth and even as a plank. Sometimes the plow would run against a snag in the shape of a big "red-root"; for, strange to say, the prairie soil, where no tree was in sight, had roots, sometimes as large as a man's arm, stretching along under ground. Then would come a cheery "Get up, Bill! Halloa there, Bright! Now's your time, Brindle!" The great whip would crack above their heads; the giant creatures would bend to the yoke; "snap" would go the red-root and smooth would turn the splendid furrow with home and school and civilization gleaming from its broad face, and happy children skipping, barefooted, along its new-laid floor. These were "great times" indeed! As the sun climbed higher and the day grew warm, we would go to the house, and compound a pail of "harvest drink," as father called it, who never permitted any kind of alcoholic liquor in his fields or at his barn-raisings. Water, molasses and ginger were its ingredients, and the thirsty toilers, taking it from a tin dipper, declared it "good enough to set before a king."

Later on, we girls were fitted out with bags of corn, of beans, onion, turnip or beet seed, which we tied around our waists, as, taking hoe in hand, we helped do the planting, not as work, but "just for fun," leaving off whenever we grew tired. We "rode the horse" for Oliver when he "cultivated corn"; held trees for father when he planted new ones, which he did by scores each spring; watched him at "grafting time" and learned about "scions" and "seedlings"; had our own little garden beds of flowers and vegetables, and thought no blossoms ever were so fair or dishes so toothsome as those raised by our own hands. Once when I was weeding onions with my father, I pulled out along with the grass, a good-sized snake by the tail, after which I was less diligent in that department of industry. The flower-garden was a delight to people for miles around, with its wealth of rare shrubs, roses, tulips and clambering vines which mother and her daughters trained over the rambling cottage until it looked like some great arbor. I had a seat in the tall black oak near the front gate, where I could read and write quite hidden from view. I had a box with lid and hinges, fastened beside me, where I kept my sketches and books, whence the "general public" was warned off by the words painted in large, black letters on a board nailed to the tree below: "THE EAGLE'S NEST, BEWARE!" Mary had her own smaller tree, near by, similarly fitted up.

Oliver thought all this was very well, but he liked to sit betimes on the roof of the house, in the deep shade, or to climb the steeple on the big barn, by the four flights of stairs, and "view the landscape o'er," a proceeding in which his sisters, not to be outdone, frequently imitated him. Indeed, Oliver was our forerunner in most of our outdoor-ish-ness, and but for his bright, tolerant spirit, our lives, so isolated as they were, would have missed much of the happiness of which they were stored full. For instance, one spring, Oliver had a freak of walking on stilts; when, behold, up went his sisters on stilts as high as his, and came stalking after him. He spun a top; out came two others. He played marbles with the Hodge boys; down went the girls and learned the mysteries of "mibs," and "alleys," and the rest of it. He played "quoits" with horseshoes; so did they. He played "prisoner's-base" with the boys; they started the same game immediately. He climbed trees; they followed after. He had a cross-gun; they got him and Loren to help fit them out in the same way, and I painted in capitals along the side of mine its name, "Defiance," while Mary put on hers, plain "Bang Up!" After awhile he had a real gun and shot muskrats, teal, and once a long-legged loon. We fired the gun by "special permit," with mother looking on, but were forbidden to go hunting and did n't care to, anyway. Once, however, Oliver "dared" me to walk around the pasture ahead of him and his double-barreled gun when it was loaded and both triggers lifted. This I did, which was most foolhardy, and we two "ne'er-do-weels," whose secret no one knew but Mary, came home to find her watching at the gate with tear-stained face, and felt so ashamed of ourselves that we never repeated the sin—for it was nothing less. Oliver was famous at milking cows; his sisters learned the art, sitting beside him on three-legged stools, but never carried it to such perfection as he, for they were very fond of milk and he could send a stream straight into their mouths, which was greater fun than merely playing a tuneful tattoo into a tin pail, so they never reached distinction in the latter art. They did, however, train the cat to sit on the cow's back through milking time. Oliver could harness a horse in just about three minutes; his sisters learned to do the same, and knew what "hames" and "tugs" and "hold-backs" were, as well as "fetlock," "hock," and "pastern."

There were just four things he liked that we were not allowed to share—hunting, boating, riding on horseback and "going swimming." But at this distance it looks to this narrator as if hunting was what he would better not have done at all, and for the rest, it was a pity that "our folks" were so afraid "the two forest nymphs" might drown, that they did n't let them learn how not to—which boating and swimming lessons would have helped teach; and as for horseback-riding, it is one of the most noble sports on earth for men and women both. We proved it so when (after the calf-taming episode) it was permitted us, by the intercession of our mother, who had been a fine rider in her younger years.

Happy the girls of the period who practice nearly every outdoor sport that is open to their brothers; wear gymnastic suits in school, flee to the country as soon as vacation comes, and have almost as blessed a time as we three children had in the old days at Forest Home. It is good for boys and girls to know the same things, so that the former shall not feel and act so overwise. A boy whose sister knows all about the harness, the boat, the gymnastic exercise, will be far more modest, genial and pleasant to have about. He will cease to be a tease and learn how to be a comrade, and this is a great gain to him, his sister, and his wife that is to be.

Here are some bits from journals kept along through the years. They are little more than hints at every-day affairs, but, simple as they sound, they give glimpses of real life among the pioneers.

From Mary's:

Frank said we might as well have a ship, if we did live on shore, so we took a hen-coop pointed at the top, put a big plank across it and stood up, one at each end, with an old rake handle apiece to steer with. Up and down we went, slow when it was a calm sea and fast when there was a storm, till the old hen clucked and the chickens all ran in, and we had a lively time. Frank was captain and I was mate. We made out charts of the sea and rules about how to navigate when it was good weather, and how when it was bad. We put up a sail made of an old sheet, and had great fun till I fell off and hurt me.

To-day Frank gave me half her dog, Frisk, that she bought lately, and for her pay I made a promise which mother witnessed, and here it is:

"I, Mary Willard, promise never to touch anything lying or being upon Frank Willard's stand and writing-desk which father gave her. I promise never to ask, either by speaking, writing or signing, or in any other way, any person or body to take off or put on anything on said stand and desk without special permission from said F. W. I promise never to touch anything which may be in something upon her stand and desk. I promise never to put anything on it or in anything on it. I promise, if I am writing or doing anything else at her desk, to go away the minute she tells me. If I break this promise I will let the said F. W. come into my room and go to my trunk, or go into any place where I keep my things, and take anything of mine she likes. All this I promise unless entirely different arrangements are made. These things I promise upon my most sacred honor."

Mother says Frank liked to walk on top of the fence, and to chop wood with a broken ax handle, and to get Oliver's hat while he was doing his sums, and put it on her head and go out to the barn.

I've made a picture of the house Frank was born in—mother helped, of course; she always does. I was born in Oberlin, and that's a nicer town than Frank's. I remember Mr. Bronson and Mr. Frost—they were students in Oberlin, and boarded at our house. I guess it's the very first thing I do remember—how they made us little rag dolls and drew ink faces on them, and we really thought they were nice; but we should n't now, I know, for my doll Anna is as big as a real little girl, and father painted her with real paint and mother fastened on real hair, and I made her clothes just like mine; but she is a rag doll all the same, only she's good, and not proud like a wax doll.

Mr. Carver and Miss Sherburn went with us from Oberlin to Wisconsin. They were both good Christians, and Mr. C. often led in prayer at family worship; but when he killed our puppies (though father told him to) I thought he was a sort of awful man.

From mine:

I once thought I would like to be Queen Victoria's Maid of Honor; then I wanted to go and live in Cuba; next I made up my mind that I would be an artist; next, that I would be a mighty hunter of the prairies. But now I suppose I am to be a music teacher—"simply that and nothing more."

When it rained and filled the stove so full of water, standing right out on the ground, that mother could n't even boil the kettle for tea, we did n't think it very funny. Mother had n't any money to get us Christmas presents; father was sick in bed with ague, and yet we hung up our stockings, and Oliver put his boot strap over the front door knob. So mother stirred around and got two false curls she used to wear when it was the fashion to wear them on a comb, and put one in my stocking and one in Mary's, with little sea-shells that she had kept for many years, also an artificial flower apiece; to Oliver she gave a shell and Pollock's "Course of Time." We had n't a hired man, and mother and Ollie went out in the woods and dragged in branches of trees to burn. We girls thought it great fun, but father called it his "Blue Christmas." Next day Oliver went to town and hired a good, honest, Yankee fellow, whose name was John Lockwood. Then we had Lewis Zeader, Thomas Gorry and his wife, and so on; never after that having to go it alone. I like farm life; "God made the country and man made the town"—"them's my sentiments."

I tried my hand at poetry. Here is a specimen written on an occasion that afflicted me—almost to tears. A noble black oak that grew near one of the dormer-windows of Forest Home was heard straining and cracking in a high wind one night. It was found to be so much injured that the order was given next day to cut it down. This was a sort of tragedy, for father had taught us to regard the trees as creatures almost human, and he guarded those about the house and in the pastures as if they had been household pets. So when "old Blackie" was cut down, Mary and I were greatly wrought upon, and I penciled my thoughts as follows:

TO AN OLD OAK.

RECENTLY FELLED AT FOREST HOME.

And so, old Monarch of the Forest, thou hast fallen!
Supinely on the ground thy giant limbs are laid;
No more thou'lt rear aloft thy kingly head,
No more at eventide the chirping jay
Shall seek a shelter 'mid thy boughs or 'mong them play.
No more the evening breeze shall through thy branches sigh,
For thou art dead. Ah, e'en to *thee*
How fearful 'twas to die!
Perhaps, ages ago,—for 'mong the centuries thou hast grown on,—
Some swarthy warrior of a race long past,
Some giant chieftain of an early day,
Beneath thy shade has rested from the chase,
And to thy gnarled trunk told some wild revenge,
Or gentle tale of love.
And in the dusk of the primeval times,
Some fair young maid, perchance, to thee complained
Of vows unkept, or, in a happier mood,
With smile as innocent as e'er maid wore,
Has told to thee some simple happiness,
Scarce worth the telling, save that in her path
Joys were the flowers that by the weeds of care
Were overwhelmed.
Around thy base the forest children played
In days long passed away, and flowing now
In the dark River of Eternity.

The years but lately gone were waiting then to be;
Time quickly sped, these years that were to be
Came, hastened by, and are no more; with them,
Well pleased to go, my childish hours fled trait'rously,
Bearing to Shadeland holiest memories.
Telling of busy feet and happy heart,
Delighted eyes and all the unnumbered joys
Given us but once — in Childhood
Glorious were mine, old Tree!

Birds have sung for me, flowers bright have bloomed
That had not, had I ne'er been born to greet their beauty.
Skies wore their loveliest hues for me
Just as they do in turn for all that live,
And as they will for happy hearts to come.

E'en when the tiny nut that held thee first,
Dropt quietly into the rich, dark soil,
'Twas in the plan of the great God of all,
That thy bright leaves, thy green crest lifted high,
Thy sturdy trunk, and all thy noble form,
Should be, some day far distant, loved by me;
Should cause my eyes with joy to rest on thee,
And so increase earth's gifts of God to me.
Thou hast given this grace to many, thou hast granted it to me;
But none, perhaps, besides me shall extol thy memory.

Stern Death, remorseless enemy, spares nothing that we love;
Upon the cold, white snow to-night, lie boughs that waved above.
And I'm lonely, sad and silent, for I feel a friend is gone,
As 'mong thy great, dead boughs to-night,
I hear the strange wind moan.

Old Tree, hast thou a spirit? If so, we'll meet again!
I shall not give thee up yet, for I'll meet thee, Yonder—*when?*
Perchance thy leaves, etherealized, above me yet shall wave
When to bright Paradise I come, up from the gloomy grave!
So in this wistful, hopeful tone,
Farewell, old King of Forest Home.

SHIPS OF THE PRAIRIE.

CHAPTER II.

THE ARTISTS' CLUB.

In 1856 the greatest event occurred that we Forest Homers had chronicled since the famous "Founding of Fort City." Father's only brother, who had married mother's sister, came with his wife and our aunts Elizabeth and Caroline to "spy out the land" and "see how Josiah and his family had got along." It was an unheard of thing for this quartette of Vermont-New Yorkers to venture so far from home, and to our secret astonishment they evinced no love for the Great West. "Josiah was the only one that strayed," they said, and her sisters bemoaned mother's long loneliness even more than she did herself, whose isolation was, until her great bereavement came, the memorable misfortune of her life. But of all this her children knew practically nothing, so sunny was her spirit and so merged was her life in theirs. Our "nice uncle Zophar" was a revelation to us children. He was tall, like father, and had the same dignified ways, but was more caressing toward his nieces and had one of the kindest faces, and yet the firmest in the world. He was a Whig and father a Democrat, at the time of his visit, so there was no end of argument about Webster and Clay, and the principles they represented on the one hand, and the "grand old Jeffersonian doctrines" on the other. He was a Congregationalist and father a Methodist, so there was no end of talk about their differences in theology, and uncle Zophar liked to quote the line, "A church without a bishop and a state without a king." But the old stone church, where both of them had once belonged, the old stone school-house where they had been pupils, the old neighbors who had come with them from Vermont, on runners across the snow, about 1815, these were subjects of which we never tired, especially when the sparkle of aunt Caroline's fun and the bright recollections of aunts Abigail and Elizabeth were added to the conversation.

These things seemed more engrossing to us than all the wonders of the New West to them. When, in a few weeks, they returned to the old home near Rochester, N. Y., where nearly all our relatives of the last and present generations have remained, they insisted on taking mother with them, for they said, "Mary has had a hard time of it here on the farm, a steady pull of ten years, and she ought to have rest and a change."

After this lovely visit with our dear relatives it was very hard, not only to have them all go at once, but, most of all, to have them take our mother with them, who had never, that we could remember, spent a night away from us. A big carriage was hired to carry them to Belvidere, where they would take the cars; good-bys were said, with many falling tears, and away they went, leaving little Mary with her face all swollen from crying and her elder sister biting her lips very hard for fear she would follow suit, and so make a bad matter worse.

"You asked dear, beautiful mamma to bring you a box," sobbed Mary. "You thought about a box when she was going away off," and she cried aloud.

"Well, I was sorry enough to have her go," was my philosophic answer, "but since she had to leave us I thought I might as well have a little something when she came back." All the same, Oliver and Mary never ceased poking fun at me about that box, which after all I did not get!

And now it was my father's turn to play consoler to his bereft "young hopefuls," as he often called us. Well did he fulfill his new task. Instead of going to town almost every day he stayed at home most of the time, for he and mother never believed in putting their children in care of what he called "outside parties." He made each of us girls a tall, cone-shaped, paper cap, which Mary trimmed with peacock feathers and symbols of hunting, according to father's directions. He fitted us out with fresh arrows, taught us how to "fly a dart," made a wonderful kite and sent it up over the fields, imitated perpetual motion by the "saw-boy" that he carved with his "drawing knife," balanced with a stone, and set at work with a wooden saw. He went with us to watch the sheep, and to carry lunch to the men at work in the fields, took us out to ride when he had to go on "school business," went with us to visit the Whit-

CONGREGATIONAL CHURCH
CHURCHVILLE N.Y
OLD M.E. CHURCH EVANSTON
NEW M.E. CHURCH, EVANSTON
"THE OLD STONE CHURCH." OGDEN N.Y.
BUILT 1832
FIRST M. E. CHURCH,
JANESVILLE, WIS.

mans and our dear teacher, Miss Burdick,—now "married and settled" in Janesville as Mrs. Gabriel L. Knox—and good Mrs. Hannah Hunter, one of mother's best friends in town. He left us at Sutherland's book store while he did his errands, and that was our delight, for the very presence of books was a heart's ease, so that always, next to our own home, we felt at home where books were kept, for we knew the wisest and kindest men and women who had lived were there in thought. Mr. Sutherland was a dear friend of father's. My big "History of All Nations" had been bought from him in monthly parts, mother paying for it out of her "butter and egg money," that I might have it on my birthday. Mr. Sutherland would let us go about at pleasure among his handsome shelves and counters, in that cool and quiet place—"more like the woods than any other that we know," and "so different from those horrid stores where you buy dresses and gloves," I used to say.

That summer we had a new girl, Margaret Ryan, by name, for Bridget wanted rest. She was but eighteen years old, and great company for Mary and me. She was true and kind, very intelligent, and we became much attached to her and gave her piano lessons, read aloud to her while she was at her work, and never learned anything from her that was not good. So our memories of "Margie" were always pleasant. Mother was so considerate of her helpers that she seldom changed, but in our twelve years on the farm we had perhaps thirty or more men and women with us, at different times, some from Ireland, others from England, and a few from America, while of Germans and Norwegians there was a large representation. But Catholic or Protestant, Lutheran or Methodist, we found good hearts in all, and made common cause with every one, teaching them English, giving them writing lessons, and never receiving anything but loyalty and kindness in return. If the foreign population of this country was fairly represented at Forest Home, it is neither drunken, immoral nor irreligious, but warmly responds to every helpful word and deed, and can be Americanized if Americans will but be true to themselves and these new friends.

In the loneliness of mother's absence, I began to write more than ever, though I had kept a journal since I was twelve years old. Climbing to my high perch in the old oak tree, I would write down the day's proceedings, scribble sketches and verses, and I even began a novel entitled, "Rupert Melville and his Comrades: A Story of Adventure." Mary, too, kept a journal and competed for a prize in the "Children's Column" of *The Prairie Farmer.* I tried for the premium offered for the best poem at the County Fair, but it was won by Mrs. E. S. Kellogg, the Janesville poet. This did not, however, discourage me at all; I wrote the harder, took my essays to Mrs. Hodge, who had fine taste and was an uncommonly good writer herself, and made up my mind that "write I could and should and *would.*"

My novel was a standing joke in the family. I worked at it "off and on," but chiefly the former. I had so many characters that Oliver said "for the life of him he didn't see how I expected to get them all decently killed off inside of a thousand pages." Every day when my regular chores about the house were done, which took only an hour or two, I got at work and insisted on doing at least one page, from which it is plain that I had no great inspiration in my undertaking. Perhaps nobody appreciated it more than Lizzie Hawley, a bright young dressmaker from Janesville, to whom I was wont to read each chapter aloud, as fast as it was written. Sometimes, since, I have wondered if the main reason why Lizzie listened so dutifully was not that she had no choice in the matter; there was the reader, and there was the story, and the busy needlewoman could not get away.

Perhaps father's fitting us out with hunting implements during mother's absence had something to do with the writing of this story. It is more likely, however, that the irrepressible spirit of his two daughters, drove him to allowing them to hunt, for we seemed to have developed a passion in that direction stronger than ever, about those days. Especially was this true of me. I had got hold of a story book, "The Prairie Bird," another called "Wild Western Scenes," and a third, "The Green-Mountain Boys," and secretly devoured all three without leave or license. They had produced on my imagination the same effect that they would upon a boy's. Above all things in earth or sky I wanted to be, and meant to be, a mighty hunter. The country I loved, the town I hated and would none of it. "Fort City" and all its belongings were no longer to be thought of as an adequate "sphere."

Mary shared this enthusiasm in her own more quiet way. She had read with me, "Robinson Crusoe" and the "Swiss Family Robinson," to neither of which father objected, because they were not "miserable love stories," as he said—for at these he drew the line firmly and would not allow them in the house. But something artistic must be connected with all of Mary's plays, and I was strongly inclined that way, too, so we started two clubs, one called "The Artists," and the other, "The Rustic," for the purpose of combining our hunting and sketching ideas. From some carefully preserved documents the rules of these two are given:

LAWS OF THE ARTISTS' CLUB.

1. The officers shall be a president and secretary.

2. The meetings shall be held twice a week (unless unforeseen occurrences prevent), and shall be on Tuesday and Saturday afternoons or evenings, as the secretary shall direct.

3. The object of the meeting shall be the *mutual improvement* of the artists who attend. The occupations of the Club at these meetings shall be reading articles on art, reading compositions and making speeches upon the same subject (never on anything else), drawing, painting, modeling in clay, conversing, singing, and encouraging each other. The Club must always open with a song.

4. There shall be an exhibition held on the last day of each month, at which prizes shall be awarded to those artists whose works are the best. The person to decide upon this shall be Mrs. Willard, and Mr. Willard when she is away, and the meetings shall always be held up-stairs in the studio.

5. There shall be twenty honorary members. (Here follows a list of every uncle, aunt and cousin that we two girls were blessed with, and Miss Burdick from outside the family.)

6. There shall always be something good to eat and the president shall look after this matter, in return for which she shall have the seat of honor, and make the first speech, etc. She shall also get things ready when the Club goes on an excursion; shall see that the dog is haltered, and take a little food along for him as well as for the rest; shall get the gun ready and the box in which things are carried.

7. Because it is hard work, the members shall take turns once a week at being president.

8. If any member makes or repairs any article belonging to the Club, he shall be paid one half the value of the same by the other member.

9. If one member goes off alone, he shall prepare his own outfit, and let Margaret Ryan know of it so that folks need n't be scared.

We, the members of this Club, pledge ourselves to keep faithfully all these, our own laws.

FRANK WILLARD.
MARY E. WILLARD.

We fixed up a studio behind the dormer-windows, by taking old quilts and making a partition. We improvised an easel, though I had never seen one, and was forced to pattern it after pictures in books. We had benches, wooden mallets and chisels for working in clay. We pinned up all the engravings we could get on the quilt partition, and added our own rude drawings in pencil, pen and ink and water-colors. We copied drawings that father and mother had done in Oberlin, hung up our home-made flags, and arranged all the queer collection of "pretty stones," Indian arrow-heads, curious insects, etc., which we had inherited from Oliver, and gathered for ourselves. So we had quite a studio.

The very first thing we set about in the Art Club was designing a "Hunter's Costume." No doubt I had "Rupert Melville," the hero of my story, in mind, for I often declared that "if I could n't go West and be a real hunter, somebody should, and I'd see that he did."

We agreed that it must be "none of your soft, city clothes," but "must stand wear and tear, not take forever to put on, and be snake-proof." So I designed coat, trousers, hat and mittens of calfskin, and boots of cowhide. The original drawings of these, now in my possession, are in high colors, with emphatic directions for the manufacture.

It was natural that two amateur hunters who could design such a "coat of mail" should have their own opinions about rural sports, and the following copy of their plans casts some light upon that subject:

RULES AND REGULATIONS

OF THE

RUSTIC CLUB.

ORGANIZED THE THIRTY-FIRST DAY OF JULY, 1854.

God made the country,
Man made the town,
The country is our choice.

1. The object of this Club is to give its members the enjoyment of *hunting*, *fishing*, and *trapping*, with other rural pleasures, at once exciting and noble.

2. We, the members of this Club, hereby choose Fred as our dog, although once in a while we *may* take Carlo; he can go when he has sense enough.

3. The meetings shall be held (after a few days) every Wednesday and Saturday, at such times as shall be deemed convenient and proper. The first one shall be held in F.'s half of the studio, and the next in M.'s half, and so on.

4. The object of these meetings is to relate any anecdote that pertains to hunting, in any of its branches; tell what great things we have done ourselves, or that Oliver or Loren or the Hodge boys have, or Daniel Boone or anybody else.

5. For hunting purposes, the names of the founders of this Club shall be Bowman and Bonny, and, as we may get a good ways apart when we are out hunting, one of us will carry an old dipper handle to serve as a hunter's bugle, and the other a sheep bell for the same purpose, and we will have the following arrangement of

SIGNALS.

When Bowman gives—
Two blasts, that means, "Bonny, where are you?"
Three blasts, "Come here, *quick.*"
Four blasts, "Meet me at Robin Hood's tree."
Five blasts, "Meet me on the river bank."
Six blasts, "Let's go to the house."
Eight blasts, "Yes."
Ten blasts, "No."
Twelve blasts, "*Oh, do!*"

When Bonny gives—
One shake, "Bowman, where are you?"
Two shakes, "Come here, *quick.*"
Three shakes, "Meet me at the tree."
Four shakes, "Meet me on the river bank."
Five shakes, "Yes."
Six shakes, "Let's go home."
Ten shakes, "No."
Twelve shakes, "*Oh, do!*"

N. B.—Any signal repeated over and over means that you request compliance *very earnestly.*

[Signed] BOWMAN AND BONNY.

No doubt many of our ideas were gained from Charles Gifford, of Milwaukee, a nursery man by profession, and an amateur artist of rare abilities, who was father's friend and used to come in summer to shoot prairie-chickens. He had been educated at Brown University and Oberlin, and had traveled in Europe. His brother was S. R. Gifford, the famous landscape artist, whose pictures of Egyptian scenery are so generally known. Charles Gifford might have been as famous under equally good conditions. He was a remarkable man, and we looked upon him as a sort of prince, and when he sent by express a great book of engravings, with some of his own sketches and of his brother's, we thought it the red-letter day of all, in its beautiful happenings. (Happen comes from "haps" and so does "happiness.") He sent us Longfellow's "Evangeline"—the first long poem we ever read—and it was delighted in by all the club, and so impressed me that years after, with my first "school money" I bought a picture of Evangeline by Faed, and to this day keep it hanging on the walls of my room. We made a scrap-book of our drawings and such pictures as we could get, in feeble imitation of Mr. Gifford's elegant one.

Miss Helen Clough, of Janesville, was also an artist, and with her and her sister we held sweet counsel as to how shading was done and what could be accomplished in India ink, at which work Miss Clough was an adept.

Nothing pleased father so much as to have his two daughters sing for him when the day's work was done. He took great pride in our musical education, and spent much money upon it. His idea was that girls and women were to find their sphere in the home, and not elsewhere, and that the more accomplished they could be, the better. I did not take kindly to this, but lovely Mary did, and was her father's favorite beyond all competition, though he was very fond of all his children. Mary had a sweet, pure, soprano voice, and I a good, clear alto, hence we sang well together, and Mary was excellent at keeping the time, so she came to be the one who played the accompaniments. We would sing thirty songs in an evening, and often father furnished the bass, for he "read notes" and was a good singer. Mother was, too, and would help Mary on the "air" when not too busy with household duties. One of the most pathetic songs was "The Withered Tree":

> "I'll sing you a song, but not of love,
> For love's bright day is past with me,
> But one that shall more truthful prove,
> I'll sing you the song of the withered tree."

Folks used to laugh as the fresh, young voices sang these plaintive words, but I invariably answered, "It will come true with me; I'm sure of it."

For one thing I was always sorry—my voice was spoiled for

singing soprano, by beginning too early. My father's mother had the finest voice in the county, and it seemed as if her grand-daughter inherited a little of its power. I could go up very high on the octave and father delighted to hear me. One evening I was singing "Mary, mavourneen," when, at the highest note, my voice broke utterly and I almost cried outright. From that day I never could sing "air" with comfort or success, and I am fully convinced that parents ought not to urge the voices of their children, as it is almost sure to spoil them for singing at all.

Nothing pleased me in those days like Mrs. Hemans' song:

> "I dream of all things free;
> Of a gallant, gallant bark,
> That sweeps through storm and sea
> Like an arrow to its mark;
> Of a chief his warriors leading,
> Of an archer's greenwood tree;
> My heart in chains is bleeding,
> But I dream of all things free."

And this prairie song:

> O fly to the prairie, sweet maiden, with me,
> 'Tis as green and as wide and as wild as the sea.
> O'er its broad, silken bosom the summer winds glide,
> And waves the wild grass in its billowy pride.
> The fawns in the meadow fields fearlessly play;
> Away to the chase, lovely maiden, away!
>
> There comes incense pleasant on gales from the west,
> As bees from the prairie-rose fly to their rest.
> Hurrah for the prairie! no blight on its breeze,
> No mist from the mountains, no shadows from trees;
> It brings incense loaded on gales from the west,
> When bees from the prairie-rose fly to their rest.

As Mary grew older she developed wonderful sensitiveness of conscience, and although so much better than her sister, she used to come to me with every little act, and say, "Frank, do you think that is right?" and if I said, "O yes, that's all right, I'm sure," she would go away satisfied. But she would take me to task very plainly when I did wrong. One of the customs that grew out of this was started by my saying one night, as we two were snugly tucked away in bed in our own pretty little room, "Mary, would n't it be a good plan for us to ask each other's forgiveness the very last thing before we go to sleep, for any word or deed that was n't just sisterly and kind, and to thank each other for everything that was kind and sisterly?"

"Oh, yes, that's what I should be so glad of, not only to do this to you, Frank, but to everybody, if I could," the gentle girl exclaimed with joy. So it was agreed upon, and became a custom between us two, who were as one heart and soul in our mutual love and confidence, only we used, after awhile, instead of saying it all, to say, "for short," "I ask your forgiveness, and thank you," to which the answer was, "I freely forgive you, and welcome." And this we did until, after "nineteen beautiful years," the last night on earth came to her, and I "asked her forgiveness and thanked her" as of old, just before her sweet young spirit passed away to heaven.

Never was mortal welcomed home more lovingly than dear mother, when she came back to us after that summer's absence. To be sure, "father had made it splendid for us," so we told her, but then, the house had but one divinity, and as we knelt in prayer, that deep, motherly heart carried to the Heart that "mothers" all the world, its love, its trust and adoration. She did not bombard heaven with requests, as many do, but "she took a deal for granted," as Loren used to say.

"Thou hast done us only good," so she prayed who had been bereft of the tenderest of mothers, and had lost out of her arms her loveliest child; "Thou dost brood over us, as the mother bird broods over her helpless little ones," so she prayed, who had known much about "the slings and arrows of outrageous fortune"; "we are often tired of ourselves, but Thy heart is never weary of us; Thou hast made the world so lovely that we might love it, and Thou art preparing heaven for us every day, even as we, by Thy blessed help, O Christ, are trying to learn its language and its manners so that we shall feel at home when we reach heaven."

Mother's prayers and singing always made her children glad. In the wild thunder-storms of that new West, I was wont to hide my face upon her knee and say, "Sing 'Rock of Ages.'" Somehow I was never afraid while mother's soul was lifted up to God.

She questioned us about our manners, which, as she soon

perceived, had fallen away to some extent. She made us walk with books upon our heads so as to learn to carry ourselves well, and she went with us through the correct manner of giving and receiving introductions, though, to be sure, "there was nobody to be introduced," as Oliver said. "But there will be," replied mother, with her cheerful smile.

We had a habit of mindfulness that was inherited from our pioneer ancestors. It is said that people who have moved away from their early homes love them better than those who stay, because of the "home-ache," as the Germans call it, that comes to them so often. In Oregon, where for so long a time the pioneers were cut off from close association with the outside world, they have the reputation of being a very gentle sort of folk, extremely considerate as neighbors, and specially kind to animals. In the summer of 1883, when the Northern Pacific railroad reached them, one often heard such remarks as, "I'll go back to the old place in Massachusetts on the first through train east," or, "I'm just pining for a sight of the old school-house in Vermont. I'll make tracks for the cars, soon as ever they heave in sight, and will go to see my folks."

Well, as Wisconsin pioneers, we were very fond of old-time talk of places and of people, and were never more interested than when father and mother around the evening lamp would discourse of incidents in the past, somewhat after this fashion:

Mother: "I don't want our children ever to forget the story that they've heard so often about the patriotism of my grandfather, Nathaniel Thompson, of Holderness, New Hampshire."

"Hurrah for Grandfather Nathaniel—in whom there was no guile!" responded Oliver, looking up from Goldsmith's "History of England," while I said, "I'll make a note of that," and Mary began to draw her brave ancestor in Continental costume in the sketch-book before her.

"And *I* want my children always to remember," said father, "that their great-grandfather, Elijah Willard, was a Baptist minister forty years in the parish of Dublin, near Keene, New Hampshire; and that their ancestors helped to settle Concord, Mass., where Emerson, Hawthorne and other *literati* live. Some day I hope they'll go to visit Major Solomon Willard's old farm there."

"I don't believe I'm a worthy descendant of my great-grandfather, for I'm afraid of snakes and lightning, and most of all, of the dark," said I in a bewailing tone.

"Oh, that's all foolishness! you'll outgrow it, my daughter; it's only a case of nerves," said father, consolingly. "You were such another screamer when a baby that I used to say to myself, as I walked back and forth with you in the night season, 'This young one is in duty bound to amount to something sometime, to pay for all the trouble that she makes.'"

"Yes, and for the blood she pricked from her forefinger when Elizabeth Hield and mother tried to teach her to sew," remarked my brother, adding, "But she did make a 'sampler,' though, in silk, and I shall never be contented till it's framed and hung up as the eighth wonder of the world."

"Well, she did it, my son, and you know my motto is, 'Do it and be done with it,'" said mother, always ready to defend the weaker side.

"I wish Mrs. Marks and Julia would ever come to see us," said I, changing the subject; "she is *such* a good woman, and 'David Marks, the boy preacher,' was father's nearest friend when we lived in Oberlin."

"Yes, I have greatly missed Mrs. Marks," replied mother, quietly, bending over her "sewing-work," for she never complained of the loneliness from which she had so keenly suffered, except to stir the aspirations of her children. For this purpose she would sometimes say:

"I had many ambitions, but I've buried myself on this farm—disappearing from the world to reappear, I trust, in my children at some future day."

"So you shall, mother; see if you don't!" we used to shout in glee.

"But that means hard work—investing your time, instead of spending it; earnest ways, and living up to the old Scotch proverb, 'It's dogged as does it,'" mother would reply.

"Why is anybody afraid of the dark?" I asked, in one of these gatherings around the evening lamp.

"Because he does n't know and trust God enough," was the reply. "If you can just once get it into your heart as well as your head that the world lies in God's arms like a baby on its mother's breast, you'll never mind the dark again ; I don't ; I'm not afraid to go all over the house and into the cellar when it is dark as a pocket. I know I am infinitely safe always and everywhere."

"But, mother, I have lots of imagination, and I picture out things in the dark."

"Why not turn your power of picture-making to a better use and always keep in mind that you are really never in the dark at all—the bright, cheery, twinkling stars are glistening with their kind light upon your path every minute of the day and night. What if a few clouds get between—the stars are there all the same—fix your eyes on them and go ahead."

"I remember," said Mary, once on a time, "that Frank used to go without butter, and father gave her a cent a week for it, which I guess is the reason she liked it so well when she grew older. And I can say the pretty verses that Mrs. Hodge sent back when Frank carried the little pair of socks that mother had knit for John, one Christmas morning." Then she repeated these lines:

"I thank you, little Frankie,
You're very kind to me,
And by and by I promise
Your little friend to be.

"Your nice and pretty present
Keeps my little toes so warm,
And makes me good and pleasant
In all the winter storm.

"I'm such a little boy, you know,
And oh, how I would cry
If I should freeze my tiny toes,
But I sha'n't now—good-by."

"All the same, Frank never set a stitch in those socks," remarked my brother.

"That's a fact, but I gave them to her to give to Johnnie, and I had a right to, had n't I?" replied mother.

"Do you remember Ozias, the clerk in an Elyria store, who used to be so kind to us and give us pretty ribbons?" chipped in Mary; "he was as generous as nice Mr. Hamilton Richardson, in Janesville, who gave us the books of stories about Greece and Rome, and Mr. Elihu Washburn who brought us the pretty poetry books. Don't you remember our little book-case that Frank made out of an old box set on end, papered on the outside, and with shelves put across, where we kept our books, in the little cubby-place under the stairs, that we called our 'corner room,' and how it was as dark as night except when we had a lighted candle in it, and how Oliver bought us a pretty set of little wooden dishes that we used to set out on a stool, with a white handkerchief for table-cover; and then the handsome pewter dishes father gave us at Christmas, and how Frank made an X on her plates and cups, to tell them from mine? and the city that father got for us another time that was cut out of little blocks, and the big doll, Anna, and"—

"Do stop and take breath or you'll be struck of a heap," exclaimed Oliver, putting his fingers into his ears.

"Well, let's see if you can do any better at remembering than your sister," said his mother; "just put on your thinking-cap and try."

"Well, I can go back along the circle of years," said Oliver, "to that distant period when Prof. James Dascomb and Prof. George Whipple, of Oberlin College, came to see us in our pioneer house of one room, and clambered up to the garret on a ladder, telling next morning they never had such solid chunks of 'tired nature's sweet restorer, balmy sleep,' in all their lives before. I can remember President Finney's preaching in the Oberlin church, and how he moved about like a caged lion on that great platform, his light blue eyes blazing under those shaggy, white eyebrows, and how scared I was of my bad behavior when he preached."

"You don't mean that you behaved badly when he preached?" smartly put in his sister Frank.

"No interruptions, let Oliver spin on. I loved those days and I like him to recall them," said mother.

"And I remember how Frank, when four years old, took to her heels and ran away across lots, creeping through the fence, and frightening mother almost to death, and father, too, so that he went and looked into the well and cistern to see if she had tumbled in, while I raced around like a crazy Jack, and discovered the little minx running as if on a wager, breathing like a steamboat, and bound to keep on, so that I had to chase her up for dear life, and fairly carry her home in my arms to her heart-broken ma."

"Enough said under that head," I remarked, not looking up from my book, for this exploit was one I did n't glory in.

"That will do, for 'I remember,'" said mother, clipping the thread at the end of the seam in her sewing-work. "Suppose you go down, Loren" (for all the evening the boy had been a docile listener, while he carved a new cross-gun for little Mary), "and get us some of the apples that the children's Uncle Zophar sent from the old place."

SAMPLER.

CHAPTER III.

LITTLE BOATS SET OUT FROM SHORE.

The first great break in our lives was when Oliver went to Beloit, fourteen miles down the river, to finish his preparatory studies and enter college. He had rarely spent an evening away from home in all his life until he was eighteen. Busy with books and papers "around the evening lamp," sometimes "running a (writing) race" with me, going into the dining-room to teach Mike and other "farm hands" to read and write, cipher and spell, busy with his chores and sports and farm work, Oliver, with his perpetual good-humor, was a tremendous institution to have about, and the shadow was heavy when he first started out from dear old Forest Home into the world. He was to board at the home of Dr. Lathrop, who was Professor of Natural Science at Beloit, and whose wife was Rev. Dr. Clement's daughter and mother's cousin.

With his easy-going, happy nature and his dear love for the old place, my brother would have lived on contentedly all his days, I think, a well-to-do, industrious, and yet book-loving farmer. But mother gave her only son no rest. He was to go to college, carve out a future for himself, be a minister, perhaps, that was her dearest wish and father's for the most gifted of their children.

From the first, we had gone regularly to Beloit to "Commencement," that great day when the people gathered in the grove, and President Chapin, so stately and so handsome, sat in the midst on the gayly festooned platform, with noble looking Professor Emerson and the other "college dons" beside him. We had heard Horace White, now a famous journalist, in New York City, pronounce his graduation speech, and I hardly knew which most impressed my fancy, his address on "Aristocracy," or his lemon-colored gloves. We had rejoiced in the brass band on these occasions, and hummed its airs for a whole year afterward. And now "Ollie" was to go, and sometime he would be a part of all this pageant, but not the girls. This gave to me those "long, long thoughts" of which my cousin Morilla Hill had read to me in a classical book:

> "A boy's will is the wind's will,
> And the thoughts of youth are long, long thoughts."

(Only, when she read it, I always said "a *girl's* will.")

So the new suit of clothes was made, the trunk packed with every good and pleasant thing that we could think of, even to a little note from Mary, "just to surprise him when he's lonesome," and I made a pen-wiper for him—one of my very few achievements in that line. Mother put in his Bible, Watts "On the Mind," and Beecher's "Lectures to Young Men," and Bridget got up such a dinner of roast turkey as made him sigh at thought of how much too much he had eaten, as well as at thought of how much too little he should get in future of flavors from the bounteous old farm.

Father and he mounted the big wagon, stored with bed, stove, etc., for his room, and that precious new trunk; crack went the whip, round rolled the wheels, and Oliver was gone for aye!

"Does God want families to be broken up this way?" was my query, as I watched them from the front piazza until my brother's waving handkerchief was lost to view. "I don't believe He does, and it would be far better for Oliver and for me, too, if we had gone together."

"Or, better still, if we could all go together, and you three children still live on at home, until you had homes of your own," said mother gently, as we three women folks, feeling dreadfully left behind, wiped our eyes and went in to help Bridget clear away the dinner dishes.

Later, in one vacation time, Oliver went to yoke up his "steers," when one of them deliberately kicked him squarely below the knee, and he fell to the ground with a broken leg—the second in the family, for father had had the same mishap at the County Fair. Mike and Edward got a board, lifted him upon it, brought him in and laid him on his bed, while Bridget followed with her apron over her head, crying aloud, and his mother and sisters threw the harness upon Jack, and got him ready for Mike to drive to town to bring Dr. Chittenden. Our faces were white, but we did n't cry at all, and as for Oliver, he, who never had but this one accident, and was almost never ill, bore the long and painful visitation like a philosopher. Indeed, his good-nature never forsook him, but his jokes and quaint, original turns of expression, made bright and pleasant every place he entered. Carried to his room now, he lay there all through the heat of summer, his devoted mother, for the first few nights after the accident, never undressing, but remaining all night at his bedside, with her hand upon his, that he might not, by moving, hazard the successful knitting of the bone. She was the most famous nurse in all the region round about—so firm and gentle, with resources for every emergency, and such a heart, full of courage and good cheer, that I often said: "I have yet to hear my mother utter the first downcast word."

We girls read many books aloud to our brother that summer: "Don Quixote," "Gil Blas," the "Dunciad," "Gulliver's Travels," and others that he liked.

One autumn, when mother had gone East once more, this time to take care of Oliver, who had been at Oberlin in school and went down to Churchville, where all the "relatives" lived, because he fell ill, father told us on very short notice, to "pack our trunk and be ready, for he was going East to see the folks, and we might go along."

We girls had never been on the cars in our lives, except once, to attend the State Fair at Milwaukee and spend a day or two at "Rosebank," Charles Gifford's home; and no shriek of locomotive had disturbed the town of Janesville until ten years after we came to live near there. So it was with an indescribable twittering of heart and tongue that this great news was received. Bridget set at work to get up "such a lunch as would make your eyes glisten." Loren wondered how "we could bear to go off and leave the old place"; the Hodge children bemoaned our prospective absence; Professor and Mrs. Hodge helped us to plan and pack the new trunk father had brought us. My only thought was to get my pet manuscripts in, and Mary, while not forgetful of the nice new clothes that father had provided, was specially intent upon having her sketch-board and paints along.

Mike carried our happy trio to Afton, five miles down the river, where we took the train, and in less than a night and a

Hill Homestead.
Willard Home.

day the Westerners were at Churchville, a pretty little place, fourteen miles this side of Rochester, where lived nearly every relative we had in the world. Here we spent a wonderful fortnight, all our kindred gathering in the home of each for a "visit" lasting all day and well into the evening. The tables groaned under the multiplied good things that a Monroe county farm supplies, and young folks went by themselves for fun and frolic outdoors and in, while older ones talked of what had been, and rejoiced in all the good that was.

Father's smart, witty, old mother was living, as was mother's father, so mighty in prayer and exhortation. Most of our cousins had been to Oberlin, or else were going there to study, and among them all, the best and most gifted was Charlotte Gilman, about my age, and greatly loved and admired by her Western cousin for her gifts of heart and mind and pen—for Charlotte was looking forward to a literary career. We two girls had no end of talks, going off at every opportunity, with arms over each other's shoulders, to plan for what we meant to be and do, while Oliver, the young collegian, with his gay talk, kept his sturdy young men cousins, Willard, Wright, and James, in roars of laughter, as they all took care of the many horses at the barn, or led at "playing proverbs" with their bright young lady cousins, Mary, Emily and Sarah. Our Mary was the universal favorite, her chubby figure, smiling blue eyes, sweet voice, and loving spirit, winning everybody. She liked to keep pretty near her mother, whose absence she had so keenly felt. We went over to Uncle Aaron's and Aunt Rebecca's, and fell in love with our quiet, gentle Cousin Catharine; listened with reverence to the wise words of that born philosopher, our Uncle James; rode behind Uncle John's spanking team, and marveled at Aunt Hester Ann's immaculate housekeeping; doted on the two old homesteads where father and mother were brought up—so staid and roomy, so historic-looking in contrast to the West. We visited the old stone school-house, where our parents had been pupils, and went to meeting in the old stone church called "The House of God in Ogden," because it was a union of denominations, and could n't take the name of any.

We drove to Rochester to see the sights, and thought it the most beautiful of cities; listened with delight to a hundred stories of the olden time, and how father had started out early for himself, and mother had taught hereabouts "eleven summers and seven winters," beginning when she was but fifteen.

We lamented the absence of Cousin Morilla Hill, a graduate of Elmira Female College, who was our ideal of everything gifted and good; but take them for all in all, those four weeks when Aunt Caroline's home was ours and we went visiting to Uncle Zophar's, Uncle Calvin and Aunt Maria's, Aunt Church's, Aunt Hill's, Cousin John Hill's and all the rest, seemed to us like a merry-go-round that left us almost dizzy with delight. And when we took the train for home, waving good-bys from the platform to our dear kindred, and seeing the pretty village with bridge and creek, white church spires and fair fields, fade out of view, we two girls were for a little while quite inconsolable.

"When we went East" was the most important date in history from that time on for years. The world was wider than we had thought, and our security in the old home-nest was nevermore so great as it had been previous to this long flight.

During the quiet evenings at Forest Home we used often to compare views concerning East and West. Father had carried to New York a box of the rich, coal-black soil of the Forest Home farm, and told our cousin, Willard Robinson, that the Eastern soil in the fields and on the roads looked "light-complexioned, thin and poor." "Never you mind," retorted the sturdy young farmer, who was Oliver's favorite, "you must judge by the crops and the yield per acre. Yes, and the price, too; we can beat you on that, every time, and when it comes to wheat, we beat the world at that product, as you know."

The Westerners had to admit that there was no such variety of foliage in Wisconsin as in Monroe county, N. Y.; that stone fences were more solid than "sod and ditch," or "stake and rider," or "log on end," or "rail" fences, such as theirs; that the homes had a general look of thrift, snugness and well-to-do-ness not found on the prairies ("except ours," stoutly urged Oliver), and that "it was wonderfully nice to have a cellar full of apples." I ran a race on apple eating with my "York State" Cousin Sarah, and reached in one day a figure so high that it would hardly do to tell.

I admitted that the landscape at the East was more cozy, but urged that out West it was more "outdoorsy" and that it was better and bigger. But Cousin Lottie insisted, "You have n't any history West, except as you make it yourselves, while we have the old traditions of the early pioneers, the old stone schoolhouse and church; then, too, we have that beautiful graveyard where our dear great-grandmother lies, who was almost ninety-seven when she died, and ever so many others of 'the best and truest hearts that ever beat.'"

Silence was my only response to these assertions. True, I had seen no other cemetery, and I had a wonderful reverence for the past, but I told Oliver later, in confidence, that "when it came to mentioning the graveyard as a cheerful feature of the landscape, I was n't up to it." Poor, foolish young thing! So little did I know about transition, and that "there is no death." But when my heart well-nigh broke, later, at loss of the dearest and best, then I found out, as we all do.

In studies the Easterners were far ahead of Mary and me, but not of Oliver, which was a great help to his sisters' "family pride." Indeed, he had no superiors for scholarship, or writing and speaking gifts, in college.

As regards pets, our Eastern cousins had been forced to admit themselves outnumbered. "Simmie, the learned lamb"; "Sukey, the pig that drank lye and was cured by loppered milk"; "Stumpy, the chicken whose legs froze off, and which knew so much it could almost talk"; "Ranger, the dog that killed sheep, and had to be killed himself"; "Nig, the black goat"; "Trudge, the Maltese kitten," and "Roly-poly, the tame mouse," passed in review like a Noah's ark menagerie, and formed my special list, while Mary described the "peacock that never was suited except when seated on the ridge of the barn"; "our guinea-hens that took the prize"; "our Suffolk piggy-wiggies that can't be beat for cunningness."

"And then the folks!" said Oliver, "they're so big-hearted, so progressive, and willing to live and let live. I tell you, Horace Greeley has it right—'*Go West, young man, go West.*'" But the home farms were so fertile and handsome, the old places and traditions so dear that none of our New Yorkers ever followed this sage advice. Father and his family were the "rolling stones that gather no moss." "Who cares!" Oliver used to say;

"What we want is not moss, but momentum, and a rolling stone gets that."

Lord Chesterfield's "Letters on Politeness, Written to his Son," was a book read through and through at Forest Home. Mother talked much to her children about good manners, and insisted on our having "nice, considerate ways," as she called them, declaring that these were worth far more than money in the race of life.

Oliver brought home many books from college ; indeed, while there, he got together a library of about eight hundred volumes. The book-case in father's room had Shakspeare, which Oliver and I had each read before we were fifteen, and reviewed to suit ourselves as to our favorite plays ; also the English Reader, which we knew nearly by heart, and volumes of travel and biography; but, after all, there were not very many books we cared for. Newspapers and magazines were our chief reading until this wonderful library of Oliver's began to appear upon the scene. Here were cyclopedias, Bohn's translations of the classics, the English poets, essayists and historians. It was a perfect reveling place and revelation.

One day I noticed in the *Prairie Farmer* that the Illinois Agricultural Society had offered a prize for the best essay on the "Embellishment of a Country Home," and right away I said to my mother, "I'm going to compete." As usual, she encouraged me to "branch out" and so, pencil in hand (for I "could n't think at all except thus armed and equipped"), I began my formidable task. I had this in my favor, that my own home was a model, and that I had seen it grow from nothing to a bower of beauty. What little I could do at writing or anything else, I always did "upon the fly," my brother said, and it was true ; so the essay was soon ready and criticised by my four standbys, father inserting a characteristic sentence : "Plant trees, and do not fail, for health and beauty's sake, to plant the evergreen—the emblem of perpetual life." A few months after, a small box came through the postoffice, addressed to me. I had never before received anything in Uncle Sam's care that looked so ominous. Strings were cut, tissue papers removed, and behold ! there was a handsome silver medal with my name, and the words, "First prize for essay," and a lovely cup, besides, while under all was a note from "S. Francis, Secretary Illinois Agricultural Society," congratulating "a lady so young on an achievement so creditable." I was of an enthusiastic nature — that was evident from the way I went with a hop, skip and jump through every room in the house, singing out "Hurrah!" until Bridget in the kitchen, Mike in the garden, and rollicking old Carlo took up the strain, and the whole family laughed and shouted and rejoiced in my joy.

No girl went through a harder experience than I, when my free, out-of-door life had to cease, and the long skirts and clubbed-up hair spiked with hair-pins had to be endured. The half of that down-heartedness has never been told and never can be. I always believed that if I had been let alone and allowed as a woman, what I had had as a girl, a free life in the country, where a human being might grow, body and soul, as a tree grows, I would have been "ten times more of a person," every way. Mine was a nature hard to tame, and I cried long and loud when I found I could never again race and range about with freedom. I had delighted in my short hair and nice round hat, or comfortable "Shaker bonnet," but now I was to be "choked with ribbons" when I went into the open air the rest of my days. Something like the following was the "state of mind" that I revealed to my journal about this time:

This is my birthday and the date of my martyrdom. Mother insists that at last I *must* have my hair "done up woman-fashion." She says she can hardly forgive herself for letting me "run wild" so long. We've had a great time over it all, and here I sit like another Samson "shorn of my strength." That figure won't do, though, for the greatest trouble with me is that I never shall be shorn again. My "back" hair is twisted up like a cork-screw; I carry eighteen hair-pins; my head aches miserably; my feet are entangled in the skirt of my hateful new gown. I can never jump over a fence again, so long as I live. As for chasing the sheep, down in the shady pasture, it's out of the question, and to climb to my "Eagle's-nest" seat in the big burr-oak would ruin this new frock beyond repair. Altogether, I recognize the fact that my "occupation's gone."

Something else that had already happened, helped to stir up my spirit into a mighty unrest. This is the story as I told it to my journal:

This is election day and my brother is twenty-one years old. How proud he seemed as he dressed up in his best Sunday clothes and drove off in the big wagon with father and the hired men to vote for John C. Frémont, like the sensible "Free-soiler" that he is. My sister and I stood at the window and looked out after them. Somehow, I felt a lump in my throat, and then I could n't see their wagon any more, things got so blurred. I turned to Mary, and she, dear little innocent, seemed wonderfully sober, too. I said, "Would n't you like to vote as well as Oliver? Don't you and I love the country just as well as he, and does n't the country need our ballots?" Then she looked scared, but answered, in a minute, "'Course we do, and 'course we ought,—but don't you go ahead and say so, for then we would be called strong-minded."

These two great changes in my uneventful life made me so distressed in heart that I had half a mind to run away. But the trouble was, I had n't the faintest idea where to run to. Across the river, near Colonel Burdick's, lived Silas Hayner and several of his brothers, on their nice prairie farms. Sometimes Emily Scoville, Hannah Hayner, or some other of the active young women, would come over to help mother when there was more work than usual; and with Hannah, especially, I had fellowship, because, like myself, she was venturesome in disposition; could row a boat, or fire a gun, and liked to be always out-of-doors. She was older than I, and entered into all my plans. So we two foolish creatures planned to borrow father's revolver and go off on a wild-goose chase, crossing the river in a canoe and launching out to seek our fortunes. But the best part of the story is that we were never so silly as to take a step beyond the old home-roof, contenting ourselves with talking the matter over in girlish phrase, and very soon perceiving how mean and ungrateful such an act would be. Indeed, I told Mary and mother all about it, after a little while, and that ended the only really "wild" plan that I ever made, except another, not unlike it, in my first months at Evanston, which was also nothing but a plan.

"You must go to school, my child, and take a course of study; I wish it might be to Oberlin"—this was my mother's quiet comment on the confession. "Your mind is active; you are fond of books and thoughts, as well as of outdoors; we must provide them for you to make up for the loss of your girlish good times;" so, without any scolding, this Roman matron got her daughter's aspirations into another channel. To be busy doing something that is worthy to be done is the happiest thing in all this world for girl or boy, for old or young.

On the day I was eighteen, my mother made a birthday

cake, and I was in the highest possible glee. I even went so far as to write what Oliver called a "pome," which has passed into oblivion, but of which these lines linger in memory's whispering-gallery :

I AM EIGHTEEN.

The last year is passed ;
The last month, week, day, hour and moment.
For eighteen years, quelling all thoughts
And wishes of my own,
I've been obedient to the powers that were.
Not that the yoke was heavy to be borne
And grievous,
Do I glory that 'tis removed—
For lighter ne'er did parents fond
Impose on child.
It was a *silver* chain ;
But the bright adjective
Takes not away the *clanking* sound
That follows it.
There is a God – an uncreated Life
That dwells in mystery.
Him, as a part of his vast, boundless self,
I worship, scorning not, nor yet reluctantly
Paying my vows to the Most High.
And this command, by Him imposed,
"Children, obey your parents,"
I receive and honor, for He says :
"Obey them in the Lord,"
And He is Lord and God !
But now having thro' waitings long,
And hopings manifold,
Arrived here at the limit of minority,
I bid it now, and evermore, adieu,
And, sinful though it may be,
Weep not, nor sigh,
As it fades with the night.

* * * * * *

The clock has struck !
O ! heaven and earth, I'm free !
And here, beneath the watching stars, I feel
New inspiration. Breathing from afar
And resting on my spirit as it ne'er
Could rest before, comes joy profound.
And now I feel that I'm alone and free
To worship and obey Jehovah only.

Glorious thought! Maker and made,
Creator and created,
With no bonds intervening!
One free, to worship and obedience pay,
The other on His heaven-spanning throne,
Deigning to receive the homage of His child.
God will I worship then, henceforth,
And evermore;
'T is night, and men and angels sleep,
While I adore.

Toward evening, on this "freedom day," I took my seat quietly in mother's rocking-chair, and began to read Scott's "Ivanhoe." Father was opposed to story books, and on coming in he scanned this while his brow grew cloudy.

"I thought I told you not to read novels, Frances," he remarked, seriously.

"So you did, father, and in the main I've kept faith with you in this; but you forget what day it is."

"What day, indeed! I should like to know if the day has anything to do with the deed!"

"Indeed it has—I am eighteen—I am of age—I am now to do what *I* think right, and to read this fine historical story is, in my opinion, a right thing for me to do."

My father could hardly believe his ears. He was what they call "dumbfounded." At first he was inclined to take the book away, but that would do harm, he thought, instead of good, so he concluded to see this novel action from the funny side, and laughed heartily over the situation, Oliver doing the same, and both saying in one breath, "A chip of the old block."

After the visit East we began to be somewhat restive even in our blessed old nest, and gave our father little peace till he arranged to send us away to school, and so it came about that in the spring of 1858 we left our Forest Home forever. Looking back upon it in the sweet valley of memory and from the slow-climbed heights of years, my heart repeats with tender loyalty the words written by Alice Cary about her country home:

"Bright as the brightest sunshine,
The light of memory streams
'Round the old-fashioned homestead,
Where I dreamed my dream of dreams."

III.

The Happy Student.

"I WOULD STUDY, I WOULD KNOW, I WOULD ADMIRE FOREVER. THESE WORKS OF THOUGHT HAVE BEEN THE ENTERTAINMENTS OF THE HUMAN SPIRIT IN ALL AGES."

CHAPTER I.

DELIGHTFUL DAYS AT SCHOOL.

"I would study, I would know, I would admire forever. These works of thought have been the entertainment of the human spirits in all ages."

—*Emerson.*

A little group around my mother's knee studying a book and afterward going with her into my father's flower garden where she plucked rewards of merit for us in the shape of pinks and pansies, is my earliest memory as a student. Mary and Maria Thome, children of our own ages, and daughters of Professor Thome, of Oberlin College, were among the group, and my first impressions of study take me to that fragrant garden, where choice flowers circled around a handsome evergreen, snowdrops and snowball bushes brightened the scene, and upon all the diamond dewdrops glistened.

Soon after that we took our journey into a far country, five hundred miles overland in the white "ships of the prairie," and for two years I have no special recollection of books for my parents were very busy with the farm.

It is a curious fact that I remember distinctly the first time I ever wrote my name, doubtless for the reason that I was late in learning, probably nine years old. We had been kept diligently to the writing of pot-hooks, and other uninteresting forms, filling little copy-books with them as we sat around the table in the large, bright kitchen at Forest Home, with all the conveniences for the evening school that my mother maintained steadily for her children and the hired help alike, during the long, cold winter of 1848, while my father was at Madison, the capital of Wisconsin, sixty miles away, attending to his duties as a legislator.

A vaulting ambition entered my little head, and I said to my indulgent teacher, "Just write my own name for me in your nice hand, and see if I can not imitate it pretty well." So with great care, she wrote it out, and it looked beautiful to me, standing there at the head of a fresh sheet of foolscap paper. Mother's writing was very clear and even ; like her character, it had a certain grace and harmony. I used to think some of her capitals were pretty as a picture. How long I gazed upon that magical creation I can not tell, but it was imprinted so deeply on my memory that I could not forget the incident, and looking long and steadily upon the copy she had given me, I followed it so well, "the first time trying," that I have sometimes thought the first was the best autograph I ever wrote.

Thus, in a desultory fashion, our lessons proceeded until I was nearly twelve years old. About this time my father brought home from Janesville an elegant card announcing that a college-bred gentleman from the East was about to open a classical school in that town. Around the edge of the card were some Latin words that I did not understand, but my father taught me how to pronounce them and what they meant. They were as follows: *Scientia auctoritas est et labor vincit omnia*, and he told me they meant, "Knowledge is power and labor conquers all things." Very many times I said them over to myself, much more I thought about them, seriously determining that I would attain knowledge so far as in me lay, and that I would compass the results which labor can achieve for one who is in earnest. I know no other road out of the wilderness. It is the straight and narrow way, appointed in so much of kindness by Him who knows from the beginning what we often learn only at the end, viz., that traveling the road does us more good than all we gather on the way or find awaiting us when we achieve the goal.

As time passed on, mother became very much in earnest for us to go to school. But there was no school-house in our district, so she "put on her thinking-cap," as we were wont to say, and, as usual, something came of it. Once or twice she had met at church in Janesville, a new family from the East, by the name of Burdick. They had bought a large farm across Rock river, hardly a mile away "on a bee line," but as the river was usually too deep to ford, it was miles around by the town bridge.

Still carrying out our favorite play, the "Fort City Board of Education" was organized, with mother in the chair. The meeting was regularly opened by singing and prayer, and then mother stated the object of the assembly.

Oliver followed her, saying, "Mrs. Chairman, I agree with all that has been said, and so well said. If we young folks don't amount to something when we grow up, it won't be the fault of *materfamilias*."

"But," continued he, "I hardly see what we've got to make an institution of learning out of, here in Fort City. Father and mother know too much to go to school, and they have n't time to do the teaching. As for me, I've graduated, you know, from Fort City, and am a Janesvilleian. Loren is a hopeless case, devoted to his traps, and guns, and farm work. The girls have taught Mike to read and write, and that is all he wants to know in the way of 'book-learning.' Bridget would n't be bothered with even that much, when we offered to teach her. So the case narrows down to this: Frank and Mary are growing up in heathenish darkness."

As I "rose to a point of order" here, protesting that mother had taught us, and taught us well, thus far, and that we were not quite so ignorant as the speaker implied, Oliver hastened to qualify his statement.

"I mean," he continued, "that Frank and Mary ought now to have advantages greater than it is possible for you, Mrs. Chairman, in the limited time at your disposal, to bestow upon them. So I move that we found an academy for their special benefit."

This proposal met with unanimous approval, and the motion was carried with enthusiasm. So resolving ourselves into a "Committee of the Whole on Ways and Means," we began to canvass possibilities. Where could we have the academy? Who would be the teacher? These were vital questions to Mary and me, for mother was not more anxious for our education than were we ourselves. After much talk, pro and con, mother reminded us of our new neighbors, the Burdick family, and we at once appointed her our "envoy plenipotentiary," with full powers to do whatever could be done through them.

Col. Burdick had been agent for Van Rensselaer, the "patroon" of Central New York, and his only daughter, Rachel Burdick, a remarkably bright and winsome girl, had been permitted to go to school with the patroon's children and was now a young lady of rare accomplishments, to whom her father's Western farm seemed lonely, after spending her life thus far upon the Hudson's lovely banks, near Albany. Mother was charmed by Miss Burdick, and asked if she would not do her the favor to come and teach Mary and me, Oliver having already been two winters in the "Academy" at Janesville, walking in and out each day. Of course he was to go to college, but the fate of his sisters was more misty in those days. I looked upon him as a prince, and only wished, although I dared not say it, that I had been born to a boy's chances in the world—though I never really wished to be a boy, at least, I hope not. Miss Burdick agreed to come, and mother began more frequently than ever to get off "homilettes," as father called them, in the following strain:

"The dearest wish of my heart, except that my children shall be Christians, is that they shall be well educated. A good education will open the world to you as a knife opens an oyster. Riches will not do this, because riches have no power to brighten the intellect. An ox and a philosopher look out on the same world, and perhaps the ox has the stronger and handsomer eyes of the two, but the difference between the brains behind the eyes makes a difference between the two beings that is wider than all the seas. I want my children's brains to be full of the best thoughts that great minds have had in all centuries; I want stored away in your little heads the story of what the world was doing before you came—who were its poets, its painters and philosophers, its inventors and lawgivers. I want you to know what is in its noblest books, and what its men of science say about their study of the earth, the ocean and the stars. I want you taught to be careful and exact by your knowledge of figures; and, most of all, I want you to learn how to speak and write your own noble English tongue, for without the power of expression you are like an æolian harp when there is no breeze. Now your father and I have assisted you and taught you until Oliver has already a good start in school and Frank is twelve years old. My son takes the highest rank as a student, just as I expected; my elder daughter is devoted to books and keeps a journal—which is a good beginning, and my younger will follow on into all that I desire, and already goes beyond the others in artistic taste. I have the promise of bright Miss Burdick that she will come and teach you during the summer, and by that time I hope your father will have a school-house in this district. But for the present we will fit up the parlor and the Inman girls will study with you."

This announcement rejoiced us beyond measure, for these two girls, living a mile away, we greatly liked, though we had seldom seen them, as theirs was not a church-going family, and hence we were not allowed to visit at their home.

One Monday school began. Father had made a large, "cross-legged" pine table, with a place below for our books, and around this, in the bright, fragrant June morning, sat four girls, from eight to fourteen years of age, and at the head, Miss Burdick, our eighteen-year-old teacher.

This first day's schooling we had ever known we called "the greatest kind of fun." Indeed we preferred it to any other form of amusement, for the reason that mother had always cried it up as the choicest experience we could possibly know, and because we had fully entered into all the other plays within our reach. We had a zest for study that school-cloyed children can not dream of, and learned in a year what little ones are tormented into, now, during seven years. Effie and Mattie Inman lived over a mile down the river and had lately come from Pottsville, Pa. They were true, good girls, carefully reared by a Presbyterian mother who had died just before they moved West. I greatly admired my handsome, dark-eyed, curly-haired classmate, Effie, whose steady sweetness of temper was so surprising to one of my impetuous nature that I told my mother I had "just stepped on Effie's toes at recess to see if she would n't frown, and sure enough she did n't." My mother replied that I had better set about imitating Effie's lovely ways instead of carrying on any more experiments of that sort. Mattie was more like common clay, but was a talkative, impulsive little thing, who was to Mary very much such an offset as Effie proved to be to me. But Miss Burdick was a whole picture gallery and musical performance in herself to us untutored prairie girls. She had come from a city ; she knew the world—that great, big world we had only read about in books.

She was a lady in every utterance and motion. She had rippling brown hair, smiled a good deal, had a silvery little laugh, and a beautiful white hand. Her trim, graceful figure was very small, almost fairy-like. She knew any amount of songs, and taught them to her attentive quartette; she was skillful with the pencil, and we all learned to draw; though Mary and I, especially the former, had made some progress in this branch already. Straightway I fitted up some "sketch-boards," tacking stiff white cloth over pieces of pine planed thin, and tacking on another piece of cloth, with one side open for our paper, pencils and rubber, and out we went, after four o'clock P. M., to "sketch from nature." Of these sketches no extended account had best be given, but all the same we had "a splendid time."

Miss Burdick was a botanist, and knew the names of more flowers than we who had lived West so long. She taught us how to "analyze," and we ransacked woods and fields to bring her "specimens." Miss Burdick could recite poetry by the hour, and we gave her no rest until she had told us all she knew of Walter Scott, Wordsworth, Cowper, and the rest. She told us of the Hudson, and the old Knickerbockers, of Madam Emma Willard's school, of Washington Irving and his Sunnyside home, of the Catskills and Palisades, and the great, fascinating city beyond. To her I used to talk of what I meant to be, and the cheery, responsive words of my teacher were a delight. Miss Burdick encouraged me to write, corrected my compositions carefully, rehearsed me on "The Downfall of Poland," which was my favorite "piece," and chilled no tender bud of aspiration in my heart.

One of my duties was to "keep the observations," and Miss Burdick helped me in this. Father had agreed to be one of the fact-gatherers for the Smithsonian Institution at Washington, which sent out to trusty persons all over the country instructions for studying the weather. They were to notice three times a day the direction of the wind, the indications of thermometer, barometer and rain-gauge, shape of the clouds, etc., and once a month fill out a blank report, giving all these particulars. Father was so often absent in town or at the Institute for the Blind, that these observations had to be left in other hands. The "Signal Service" that has its bulletin in every morning paper and postoffice nowadays, and which is so great a help to the public in many ways, was built upon the foundation laid by these observers. I learned many valuable lessons in this work when I was but a girl, as I studied the clouds and found out which were "cirrus," "cirro-stratus," "nimbus," "cumulus," and so on.

We had winds on those prairies, sometimes, that came so near carrying off the house that father sat with Mary in his arms, I hid my face, as usual, in mother's lap, and all expected to be blown away. But though we had several terrific visitations of this sort, no harm ever reached any of us. Oliver used to say he believed the "Prince of the Power of the Air" got up those storms, and he did n't think it was fair to "lay them to the Lord."

For two summers Miss Burdick carried on her institution of four pupils, the second summer a few more coming in, and gave an elaborate "Exhibition" at the close, which seemed as great to us as the "Commencement Exercises" of the college where some of us graduated in 1858–59.

Father and Mr. Inman now bestirred themselves, for their daughters' sake, and a little school-house, belonging to the district, was built about a mile away. It was plain and inviting, that little bit of a building, standing under the trees on the river bank. No paint has ever brightened it, outside or in, from that day to the present. It looks like a natural growth; like a sort of big ground-nut. Inside, the pine desks were ranged around the wall, boys on one side, girls on the other, a slight platform with rude desk taking up the end nearest the door. But this school-house was a wonder in our eyes, a temple of learning, a telescope through which we were to take our first real peep at the world outside of home.

It was too far from "Fort City" for our "make-believes" to include it, and as we grew older we took life more as it really was, because there was so much more of it to take. I was about fourteen when the new school-house was built, and I regarded it as the great event of my life that I was now, at least, to become really "a scholar," go outside my own home and be "thrown upon my own resources," as father wisely called it. Miss Burdick's had been a sort of "play school," after all, for she was so young herself and made such a companion of me that the teacher had been lost in the friend.

Miss Burdick had listened to all the imaginings of which my head was full, about what I was to be and to do in the world—for I was fully persuaded in my own mind that something quite out of the common lot awaited me in the future; indeed, I was wont to tell this dear teacher that I "was born to a fate." Women were allowed to do so few things then, that my ideas were quite vague as to the what and the why, but I knew that I wanted to write, and that I would speak in public if I dared,—though I did n't say this last, not even to mother. And now here was to be a real school and a real, live graduate of Yale College was to be the teacher. Mr. Hodge became "Professor" to us children—he had been Tutor Hodge at Oberlin College—and we were eager for the intellectual fray.

"There will be lots of rules," remarked Oliver, wisely, the evening before school was to begin. He was at home for a brief vacation, and used many big words, among others, unique, which, just for fun, he pronounced in three syllables, and the example was followed by me, who gravely took up his methods as my standards.

"What if there are lots o' rules?" piped sweet-toned Mary, "we sha'n't break them, as some college boys do."

"No, indeed," said I; "it will be a pleasant change to us to have some rules and live up to them."

"Do you mean to say I have given you none all these years?" asked mother, looking up from her sewing.

"Well, you've had mighty few, mother, I can tell you that," said Oliver.

"But we had to mind, you know," chimed Mary.

"Yes, and we had a mind to," I declared.

"That may all be, Miss Biddlecome," replied my brother, who, with father, often called me by this odd name, "but when it comes to sitting beside your favorite Effie and never speaking a loud word for six hours per day, you won't enjoy it. A girl that has played Jehu to calves, reapers and plow-beams as long as you have, won't take kindly to sitting still all day, either, and I prophesy there'll be a riot, a rumpus, a row before the month is out."

"Wait till you see," I responded, with a vim, and the discussion ended.

It was a cold winter morning when school opened. We two girls had risen long before light, because we could n't sleep, and packed our little tin dinner-pail with bread and butter, apples, and some of mother's "fried cakes"—which had already won a reputation that has since expanded into fame. We emptied her old satchel that we might stuff it out with school-books; filled our inkstand, and made all our small preparations, wondering if it would ever be daylight, and if nine o'clock A. M. would ever come. We hardly tasted our breakfast, and were so uneasy that long before the time Loren yoked the big oxen to the long "bob-sled," and he and Oliver carried us to school. The doors were not yet open, so we sent to Professor Hodge's, which was near by, got the key, made the fire, and were the first to take poses-sion. Loren stayed as a scholar, looking as if he did not like the bargain. Oliver cracked the whip and "geed up" the oxen, saying, "Well, I hope you'll enjoy what you've got yourselves into;" and I shouted, "We've got a Yale graduate to teach us, and Beloit can't beat that."

Professor Hodge's children were out in force, and made up the majority. Effie and Mattie Inman were there, Pat O'Don-ahue and his sisters, from two miles over the prairie, and a few others. Loren was the big boy of the school, and behaved like a patriarch. Jamie Hodge had already asked to have his lessons measured off, had selected a desk with his brother John, and be-fore the hour for school had arrived he was studying away like a sage. Rupert Hodge, a blithe little fellow, was coasting down the hill with his sisters Annie and "Tottie," while Fred and Charley Hovey, new-comers and cousins of the Hodges, looked like little bread-and-butter cherubs with their red cheeks and flaxen hair. At last Professor Hodge appeared, in his long-tailed, blue coat with brass buttons, carrying an armful of school-books and a dinner-bell in his hand. He stood on the steps and rang that bell long, loud and merrily. My heart bounded, as I said, inside of it, so that nobody heard, "At last we are going to school all by ourselves, Mary and I, and are going to 'have ad-vantages' like other folks, just as mother said we should! O goody—goody—*goody!*"

Professor Hodge stepped upon the rough little platform, opened his pocket Testament and read the first chapter of Mark;

6

we sang "Jesus, lover of my soul," and then every head was reverently bowed, while in the simplest language the good man asked God's blessing on the children and their homes, on their lessons and their companionship as scholars. He was a tall man, with strong frame, large head covered with bushy hair, piercing blue eyes, pleasant smile, and deep, melodious voice. Accustomed to teach men, he bent himself gently to the task of pointing out A B C's to the youngest and setting copies for them all. He was a fine reader and his greatest pleasure seemed to be when his older pupils rendered to his satisfaction some gem from the English poets, in which he trained us carefully.

He was of English birth, and his first names, Nelson Wellington, united the last names of two heroes of whom he liked to talk. He was patient to a fault, and I was glad that in my mathematics, which I did not like, one so considerate took my difficult case in hand. He announced no rules, offered no prizes, but seemed to take it as a matter of course that we would all "behave." So passed the day—our first in the old school-house we learned to love in spite of—nay, perhaps the better *because* of, its ugliness. We had about four months of study with Professor Hodge, and later on, in the same place, six months with Mrs. Amelia Hovey, sister to Mrs. Hodge. This teacher was a delight to us. Her bright face, sparkling blue eyes, voice full of rising inflections, and her pride and pleasure in her pupils, made school just like a play-day. She was a charming singer and we delighted in her favorite song:

"Now to Heaven our prayer ascending,
God speed the right!
In a noble cause contending,
God speed the right!
Be that prayer again repeated,
Ne'er despairing, though defeated;
Truth our cause, what e'er delay it,
There's no power on earth can stay it,
God speed the right!
Pain nor toil nor trial heeding,
And in Heaven's own time succeeding,
God speed the right!"

These words used to ring out through the lonesome little school-house like a clarion call, while our teacher stood before us with an exaltation in her face that gave an uplift to each little heart as our fresh young voices sang,

"God speed the right!"

Mrs. Hovey's sunny nature and beautiful spirit of hope bent like a rainbow above those happy months at school, while her rare aptness to teach brought us on at railroad speed from title page to "finis" of a half-score of knotty text-books.

There was but one blur upon the pages of that happy time. One scholar, who has not before been mentioned, a girl older than I, said to me at recess, "You are the most ignorant girl I ever saw. I don't know what to make of it. Come with me around the corner of the school-house where no one will hear, and I will tell you things that will make your eyes open bigger than ever." Nothing could have vexed me more than to be called "ignorant," and nothing could have roused my interest like the chance to get that ignorance cured. "To know" had been my life's greatest desire from the beginning. I had carried a great many curious questions to my mother, such as every thoughtful child is sure to ask, and ask right early, too. The reply had always been, "Come to me when you are fifteen years old and I will tell you. You would not understand me now, if I should try to tell."

And here was this girl, a new scholar, who was laughing at me because I could not answer the very same questions—for she asked them as soon as she and I were alone. Then she went on to answer them with illustrations and anecdotes, riddles, puns and jokes, using many words that had to be explained to me, who had never heard their like before. My brother Oliver was a boy so wholesome and delicate that he had almost never said a word my mother did not know, and this strange vocabulary amazed and disconcerted me. I never talked with this coarse girl again upon these subjects, but afterward I felt so sorry to have talked at all. It was a rude awakening, one that comes to many a dear little innocent of not half my years, and is morally certain to come if a child goes to school at all. But it is inevitable that children should go and be brought up with other children, only the mother at home ought, I think, to take her little one into a very tender and sacred confidence, and in true, pure and loving words reply to every question the thoughtful little mind can ask. A boy and his mother, a girl and her mother, may, and ought to speak of anything that God has made. The "works of darkness" are evil; the secret words, the deeds previous to which some one says, "But you must never tell"—these are wicked and dangerous. Dear fathers and mothers who read between these lines, let me beg you to forewarn your little ones, and to tell them, upon the high level of your own pure thoughts and lives, what they are certain to learn sooner than you think, when they go with other children. There will always be some one to teach them naughty words and deeds, unless your lessons have come first. Happily for me, I was too well established before I heard these things to get harm out of them, but not one home in a thousand is so isolated as was mine. Besides, think of the pain and sense of loss that came to me from that one miserable interview!

Louise Alden was a friend made at this school, and greatly valued by us, especially by Mary, who was of nearly the same age. Our coasting down the hill was wonderful to see; our fishing with a crooked pin, small bait and less fish, in the mellow-voiced river; our climbing trees for toothsome hickory-nuts, beating the bush for mealy hazel-nuts, and scouring the pastures for sweet-smelling plums that grew wild; our play-houses, with dishes moulded from clay in my "china manufactory," and dolls for which I declined to make clothes—are not all these written in memory's "book of chronicles"? What times we used to have on "composition day," and at the "spelling school" on Friday afternoon, when I was at the head on one side and Effie on the other, or Pat O'Donahue and Johnny Hodge marshaled the forces. We "toed the line," and "went up head," and "spelled down," after the approved, old-fashioned style. Mother and Mrs. Hodge were "company" on such occasions, and were escorted to platform seats with much decorum by my sister. As school was so far away we stayed from 9 A. M. to 4 P. M., and made much of our dinners, setting them out on the teacher's desk and sharing our wholesome food with many a cheery speech and laughing reply as the noon hour, all too short, sped away. But, most of all, we were diligent to learn, for we were behind other scholars of our years, and were afraid, as we almost daily told our mother, that our "smart cousins down in York State would get so far ahead that we never could catch up."

Later, our family spent one winter in Janesville and we went to Mrs. Fonda's "Select School," where I especially doted on Cutler's Physiology, and proudly took turns at editing the school paper, while Mary drew maps so well as to astonish the natives, and painted in water-colors after school. Here our Aunt Sarah and Cousin Morilla, both teachers in Catharine Beecher's and Miss Mary Mortimer's "Female College" at Milwaukee, came to spend the holidays, and their wise and bookish conversation was a delight beyond words to us. Here we heard "Elder Knapp," the great revivalist, preach in the Baptist Church and our hearts were deeply exercised, but we did not come out as Christians. Still it never entered our minds not to pray, but the sweet and simple "Now I lay me down to sleep," quieted our young hearts at night, and every morning father's prayer found an echo in our own. But Oliver, always ready for every good word and work, went to the front with his beloved school-mate, William Henry Brace, the two boys yielding at once to mother's gentle invitation to "come out boldly on the Lord's side." Indeed, Oliver had been converted at twelve years of age, just before we left Oberlin, and later on he was immersed in our own Rock River and joined the church "on probation." When father went to the legislature at Madison, leaving the farm folks pretty lonesome, little Mary was sent by her brother and sister, to say to their mother that they intended to be Christians all the while pa was gone, and not make her any trouble, and they thought it would comfort her to know it. "And I do, too," added the dear, chubby-faced girl, who was not only born "a Sunday child," but always seemed to stay so.

Our episodes of school included a month or so of outing at the summer home of Rev. and Mrs. Peleg S. Whitman, accomplished Southerners, who had driven all the way from Georgia to Wisconsin in their own carriage on a health excursion. They were both teachers, having a ladies' school at home, and father meeting them at Janesville, invited them to spend some time at Forest Home, and bought an elegant piano of their selection, that Mrs. Whitman's masterly musical gifts and teaching might be enjoyed by his daughters. We had been taking music lessons for years from the teachers at the Wisconsin Institute for the Blind, a mile away, and were quite well advanced, but played only on the melodeon. My love for this instrument was so unbounded that when the piano was brought home I evinced but little pleasure and turned to my old pet so steadily that father saw no way but to sell it, which he did. When it was being boxed to be carried out of the house, mother found us two girls kissing the sweet-voiced old melodeon good-by, almost with tears.

From that time, although I still had lessons, I felt small interest in the study of music, but Mary's dainty hands took kindly to the piano, and she swiftly passed her sister, whose knowledge of "thorough bass" had been her despair until the instrument of wind and reeds gave place to the twanging wires and mysterious pedals of the piano. But when Mrs. Whitman sang some sweet Scotch ballad, or our favorite "Once more at home," to its accompaniment, I was almost as much delighted as my sister, and when she struck the martial notes of the "Battle of Prague" we, like the Queen of Sheba, "had no more spirit in us" for very wonder. I was passionately fond of martial music, but when Mrs. Whitman rendered the cries of the wounded and dying, both of us, to whom scenes of sorrow were unknown, wanted to "put our heads in mother's lap and cry."

Mrs. Whitman was a French scholar, and we were eager to learn, so it was agreed that we might go to Mr. and Mrs. Whitman for a few weeks' study.

"Let our birds try their wings a little before they fly far from the old home-nest," said father, who dearly loved to have us run to meet him when he came home from town, delighted himself with our singing, and was grieved to the heart at the thought that we must sometime leave him. So the greatest event of all our lives, thus far, was going six miles from home, to stay with the Whitmans in their pleasant rural retreat, and for the first time to spend a night out from under the old home roof. Father carried us over, one blithe summer day, with the trunk which we had packed so carefully, and as we saw him drive away, we had a most "all-overish feeling of lonesomeness," as I called it, while Mary actually had tears in her sweet blue eyes.

"For shame," I said to her in a low voice; "it's only six miles to Forest Home, and we are only away for a month. Just think how much more we shall *know* when we go back."

"Yes, but I want ma to tuck me up in bed and kiss me

good-night,'' she murmured, her red lips trembling as she turned away.

Mr. and Mrs. Whitman made it very pleasant for us with music, reading aloud, and a drive in the fields now and then. Ollendorff's French Method was placed in my hands, and I diligently conned those oldest of all questions, "*Avez vous faim? Avez vous soif?*" while Mary sketched from nature, grieved over English grammar and rejoiced to practice on the piano. We had never read novels, and stories were almost unknown to us, except the lovely story of "Outdoors," in four parts, with a new edition every year. "Pilgrim's Progress" we knew almost by heart, and Bible histories were familiar—more so from mother's lips than by our own reading, though we had regularly "read the Bible through" that year, at the rate of three chapters a day and five on Sunday, and received the promised Bibles, "all our own," as a reward. Miss Trumbull, a seamstress, who was also "a character," had told us "Children of the Abbey" and "Thaddeus of Warsaw," after which lengthened dissipations we could "hardly sleep a wink"—the first loss of sleep known to our happy and well-ordered lives. We had read many biographies of great men and much of the best in English poetry, besides Robert Ramble's "Stories of Greece," and Goldsmith's "History of Rome." We knew much of mythology, but, aside from "The Shoulder Knot," "Norman Leslie," a religious romance, and a few hunting stories, we were absolutely, blessedly ignorant of "novels." But our gifted teachers were readers of the best in fiction, and here I found "Jane Eyre," "Shirley," and "Villette," those wonderful books by the lonesome-hearted genius, Charlotte Bronté. These opened a new world, and to one less anchored to mother and home than I was, they might have done untold mischief. As it was, I read them all in feverish haste, closing with "Villette," in the midst of which I was, on a lovely summer evening just before twilight, when a long shadow fell across the threshold where I was sitting, unconscious of everything about me, and my father's tall form bent over me; he took the book from my hand, and as he saw the flush on my cheeks his brow was clouded.

"Never let my daughter see that book again, if you please, madam," he said to the lady of the house, who, not knowing his rules, had hardly noted my proceedings; the book was taken from me, and to this day I have never finished reading "Villette."

Of course I did not like this then, and was angry with my father, although I did not dare to say so. But I learned as years passed on how much I owed to the firm hand that held my impetuous nature from a too early knowledge of the unreal world of romance. Thanks to parental wisdom, I passed my childhood and my early girlhood in perfect quietness, simplicity and the holiness of nature's company.

But with the autumn these genial Southern friends flitted away to their beautiful Georgia, to escape the chill of the Wisconsin climate, and we went home enriched by their words of grace and graciousness, and instructed by their polished manners not less than by the books and music we had studied.

We still published, at intervals, the Fort City *Tribune*, for which mother was a frequent contributor, giving us once the following bit of verse she had composed especially for our paper, and which was intended to afford us some account of her own childhood in her beloved Vermont:

RAYS FROM THE PAST.

From distant years a gentle light
Is ever bright'ning up my way;
'Twill cheer me to eternal morn
By its sweet ray.

'Tis from life's dewy, radiant dawn,
That introduced my infant day,
From that sweet Eden, diamond-gemmed,
Where children play.

'Tis from my father's sheltered home,
That calm and love-illumined spot,
Where fragrant incense bathed my brow,
Not yet forgot.

'Tis from the bright and purling brook,
And from the towering elm-tree's shade,
And from the pure and holy joys
For young life made.

'Tis from the thorny brier bush,
With ripe and tempting raspberries hung,
Which we on slender threads of grass
For "Teacher" strung,

To dim her youthful vision bright,
To mystify her opening mind,
That to our many childish faults
She might be blind.

Dainty reflections, clear and bright,
Still gleam from the delicious past,
Cheering the traveler to her home—
That home, her last.

Oliver brought any amount of books from college and read them in vacation. He was now too much of a young man to help on the fortunes of Fort City any longer. The Hodge boys were busy with the farm, Bridget was less company for us than of old, and we girls turned to the blind pupils at the Institute as our base of supplies. We had a music teacher from there, whom we dearly loved. This was Mrs. Eliza King Walls, a graduate of the New York Institute, a beautiful woman and an accomplished player. It was an event when she came to give the weekly lessons, for she entered heartily into our plans and was an enthusiast as to our musical abilities. Her elder sister, Miss King, often came with her, and her lovely little girl, Mamie—the first "wee toddler" that we had known. I thought she was "enough better than a stupid doll,"—indeed, except "Doll Anna," I had never cared for these "wooden effigies," as I called them, but gave my wax doll to my sister, with some show of generosity, but no inward sense of sacrifice.

Mary was fond of every breathing creature—except snakes, spiders and mosquitoes—and she liked dolls because "they reminded her of humans," but upon little Mamie Walls she lavished her rich young heart in a manner beautiful to see. She brought out all her small store of pretty things and placed them at her disposal; spread a "playing place" for her on a big shawl under her favorite tree; toyed with her soft curls, hugged her tenderly, and even counted the days till her next music lesson, chiefly because "Mamie would come again."

But much as I loved Mrs. Walls and her baby, my favorite teacher was Mr. Frank Campbell—since then a well-known London musician, and famous as the only blind man who ever climbed Mt. Blanc; this he did to prove how mind may triumph over matter; his son walking ahead, and he setting his feet in the tracks thus made. He used to come to give us girls our lessons, over the rough country road, with its ups and downs, all alone, except for his faithful cane, which, we declared, "had brains, could almost talk and ought to vote."

He was a brilliant pianist—could play any piece of music, no matter how difficult, if but once read in his hearing, and was a most gifted as well as a most gentle-natured man. His wife was an invalid, and I thought it a high honor when I was permitted to write letters for him and to sit beside the sweet little lady who was so often ill. The other teachers at the Institute were frequent guests at Forest Home. Mr. P. Lane, of Mississippi, a blind man of much culture and strong character, was Principal, and a great friend of my father. Later on, Mr. William H. Churchman, of Indianapolis, also blind, held that position. He was often at Forest Home and was so fine a scholar that we never grew tired of listening to his conversation with our parents. We had been taught that "children should be seen, not heard," and never dreamed of speaking in the presence of our elders unless spoken to. This early habit, with my great sensitiveness and timidity, made me the shy one of the trio, so that my dread of going out into "company" was extreme. Oliver and Mary used often to joke me about this.

Mr. Churchman's daughter Anna was about my age, and was the most accomplished young person that we young folks had seen, except our cousin, Miss Abby Clement, of Vermont, who had come West with her father, Rev. Dr. Jonathan Clement, on a visit, and, spending a week at Forest Home, had so astonished us country girls by her knowledge of books and of the world, that we almost despaired of "ever being anybody," except as our ever cheery mother laughed at our fears. I used to think that if I could recite Bryant's "Thanatopsis" and Campbell's "Last Man" as Abby could, I would ask no more in this stage of existence. The blind girls, too, were a marvel to us Forest Homers. They were regular "lightning calculators" in mental arithmetic; they could read the raised letters in the great books printed for them; could trace with delicate finger-tips all the countries on the raised maps, and repeat poetry by the hour. They were not a bit sorrowful because they could not see, but when they came to spend an afternoon at Forest Home, would propose to play "Blind Man's Buff," and say, merrily, "You won't have to tie a handkerchief over our eyes; and you'll know for certain that we won't cheat by taking a peep on the sly."

From these experiences we learned that happiness is from within; that the real light shines in the heart, not in the eyes, and that everybody who *will* be glad, may be.

At one time Prof. C. B. Woodruff and his wife had charge of the "Blind Institute," as it was oddly called, and the mathematical miracles wrought by the pupils under his care, disheartened at least one of mother's three children about ever "cutting any figure" in that line, and perhaps made me the more determined to excel in some other direction since I was so outdone in this by my well-beloved companions. For life grew less lonely as the years went by and neighbors were more numerous. A handsome German gentleman called one day and proposed to buy a slice off the most distant part of the old farm. He was Prof. Gustave Knoepfel, of New York, since well known as an accomplished organist. He wished to bring his old father and mother with his many brothers and sisters, from Germany and locate them in peace and quiet in the "far West," which Wisconsin then was. His father was a Lutheran minister and a "Herr Professor," besides, having a title that he said meant "head covered with moss." Father thought these would be good neighbors and sold them the land. The young professor gave music lessons to us that summer, while he superintended the building of a house for the family that was to come. They were a new window into the great world, these cultured Germans with their neat, frugal ways, pleasant manners and many accomplishments.

But I noticed that the learned Doctor did not seem to think so much of his girls as of his boys, and that his wife had no such place in her home as my mother had in hers. Nor did the boys treat their sisters as their equals, as Oliver did his, and the Hodge boys theirs. They seemed to be more like convenient drudges—good to have about, but not companions. All this touched my free spirit with a sense of pain and I "pondered much why these things were."

The last teacher I had at Forest Home was mother's youngest sister, Miss Sarah B. Hill. She had gone with us in 1841, in the large carry-all, from Churchville, to Oberlin, Ohio. After study at Oberlin College she had been Preceptress of Riga Academy, New York, and Columbia Female College, Tennessee. Her fame as a teacher had gone out far and wide, and we thought nothing could ever give us so much pleasure as to see "Aunt Sarah." Our own dear mother had taught "eleven summers and seven winters," as we had often heard her say; but here was a woman who had been a teacher all her life long, who was a mathematician, an historian, a mental philosopher, and what-not, besides! She was to come from Buffalo to Milwaukee, "around the Lakes," and then by cars to Janesville, for we had the cars at last, and the screech of the locomotive sounded as we thought the voice of a horrid dragon might have done.

Father, who was fond of a secret, had tried to keep this great event as a surprise, but in hunting his pockets for the latest newspapers I had come upon my aunt's letter and shown it to mother, who knew all about the matter, but counseled silence on the children's part. So when he went to town one night,—a thing he almost never did at such an hour—advising us to sit up until his return, which was exactly opposite to his general counsel, we knew very well what it meant. The usual style of children, whose lives are so brimful of happenings that they have learned to take almost everything as a matter of course, can hardly imagine what it really *did* mean to us to have Aunt Sarah come! Here we had lived alone, year after year, in a place where most people would have thought that nothing ever happened; hardly a person of our own blood had we seen since the white-covered wagons started from Oberlin so long ago; letters were now and then exchanged, to be sure, but each letter cost twenty-five cents, hence was an infrequent luxury; and here, at last, was coming the wonderful woman who had studied many books and knew the world! Loren declared that he should stay at the barn—he did n't dare to see her. Bridget said "she knew enough of great people to lay in a good stock o' provisions when they was comin' 'round"; the Hodge children and Louise said there would be no more fun and they wished she would n't come, and meanwhile father rejoiced in the wonderful surprise he had in store for all of us! At the unheard-of late hour of ten, whose clear stroke on the old brass clock we young people had almost never listened to before, the rumble of wheels along that unfrequented road told of Aunt Sarah's coming. Loren rushed out to take care of the team and Oliver to help bring in the trunk. Mother's calm face was wonderfully lighted up ; how lonely she had been and how much hard work she had done since she saw her sister last ! Candle in hand she stepped out on the piazza ; a tall lady in a handsome blue traveling dress threw her arms about her and both women cried. I relieved mother of the light, father and Oliver brought in the trunk, my aunt gave me a hug and took sweet Mary on her knee.

'Well ! for country folks you don't surprise worth a cent, that's certain,'' said my father, but he never knew how much *we* knew, meek-eyed deceivers that we were !

It took but a short time to get acquainted. Mary said, ''Aunt Sarah is so much like mother that I'm not afraid of her.'' Oliver agreed to this, and so did I, but as I was the shy one of them all, I was on my good behavior longest. But Aunt Sarah was such a brave and sunny spirit, that I very soon ''thawed out,'' as Oliver laughingly called it, and became a walking interrogation point, giving my aunt no rest in my desire to learn all about the people, customs, etc., which the ''learned lady'' had found out in her wide experience. Teaching was such a passion with her, that in a few days she had me studying mathematics, derivation of English words, and history, while Mary listened to these recitations and took another set better suited to her years. Aunt Sarah was a devout Christian, and all her lessons led toward God. The Bible was one of her text-books in astronomy, and she delighted to explain its references to the Pleiades, Arcturus, and Orion. She was very clear in everything she taught. Standing up in all her ample proportions, she said one day, ''Now I will represent the sun ; Frank shall turn round and round, and so turning shall also go in a circle around me, and while she does this, Mary must move slowly around her ; thus Frank will represent the daily and yearly motions of the earth, and Mary of its satellite.'' So she made our work seem play. She illustrated as clearly, the tides, the zodiac, precession of the equinoxes and many other points usually ''skimmed over,'' rather than learned. Meanwhile, I read Dr. Dick's ''Christian Philosopher'' and ''Future State,'' and was so wrought upon that when I had to help get dinner one Sunday, I fairly cried. ''To come down to frying onions when I've been away among the rings of Saturn, is a little too much!" I said, impatiently. Poor ignorant child! I had not yet learned that

"To sweep a room as for God's laws,
Makes that and the action fine."

At the end of a delightful winter's training under our aunt, with whom we afterward spent (before leaving Forest Home) a term at the Milwaukee Female College, where she was Professor of History, we girls had the sorrow of seeing her go away to her home at the East.* After twenty years devoted to teaching, almost wholly in the college grades, this dear aunt married Mr. Ward Hall in 1862 and lives near the old home in Churchville, N. Y.

In the spring of 1857, when I was seventeen, our parents sent us to Milwaukee because Aunt Sarah was then one of the leading teachers there, and they had entire confidence in our well-being when we were with her. We boarded in the home of Dr. M. P. Hanson, for so many years the Dr. Dio Lewis of Milwaukee, and found its Christian atmosphere was like that of our own father's house. Miss Mary Mortimer, the Principal, was absent from the college on leave, and I have always regretted missing the contact of a pupil with that great, philosophic soul. The Misses Mary and Carrie Chapin, and Miss H. Huntington, all accomplished New England teachers, had us in hand.

The college was Congregational in leadership, though really unsectarian. We went with our aunt to Plymouth Church where I greatly enjoyed the preaching of Rev. Dr. Z. M. Humphrey, and the Bible class conducted by his accomplished wife.

I was never in an institution where the moral atmosphere was so clear and invigorating as that of the Milwaukee Female College. We used to sit in the great study hall without a teacher present, and any girl who would have misbehaved or laughed or whispered would have been looked upon as beneath contempt. We were all "upon honor,"—the teachers trusted us. I remember on the first day, I went to my class in geology, and, not knowing that it was against the rule, I spoke to a classmate about the lesson as we were climbing the stairs toward our teacher, and entirely

*Two of Miss Hill's visits are here included in one.

away from supervision; my school-mate looked at me brightly and kindly, evidently perceiving that I intended no harm, and laid her taper finger on her sweet, shy lips. I could not forget in a thousand years the majesty of the occasion, as it impressed my mind, the sacred sense of truth it gave me and the determination that it deepened in my spirit to be just as trusty and conscientious as was she.

My admiration for Marion Wolcott, daughter of Dr. E. B. Wolcott, the city's chief physician, was beyond words. Immaculate in character, conduct and scholarship, I set her up as my standard at once, and never rested until, like her, I heard "Ten, Ten," meaning "perfect in punctuality, behavior and lessons," read out each week after my name.

My diligence in study was so great that Aunt Sarah feared for my health. Each evening I rehearsed to her the lessons of the coming day or wrote on my forthcoming "composition." As an intellectual guide, she was my greatest inspiration; and other pupils felt no less enthusiastic over this "born teacher" and devoted Christian.

Our history class was memorable. This was her favorite branch—in teaching it she was thoroughly individual, making the lesson vivid, even to the dullest mind. Often she was very humorous, at other times pathetic even to tears, as she depicted great characters and achievements vital to the progress of humanity.

The "examination day," just previous to Commencement was the climax of all that I had known. Our "middle class," was seated on the high platform of the great study hall. My aunt went to the opposite end, and in her clear voice called out the topics by number. We had to speak loud enough to be heard throughout the room, or she would not allow us to proceed. Mother was present and this was a day of joy to her, for she could see how hard her girls had worked. I had an essay on "Originality of Thought and Action," also a little poem, "Lighting the Lamps," written on a sweet evening as I watched from my window that city sight to me so novel. This was read by my friend, Anna Barnes, one of the leading pupils.

Sitting by my window,
  On a summer eve,
List'ning to the billow,
  List'ning to the breeze;
Dark the shadows falling,
  Bright the stars and clear,
Men have ceased their toiling,
  To their homes draw near;
Hear the drowsy beating
  Of the city's heart,
As the hours are fleeting,
  And 'tis growing dark.

See! a light is gleaming
  Down the fading street!
Ah! 'tis brighter beaming,
  Guiding weary feet.
Wake from out thy dreaming!
  Wander not away!
Soul of mine, what seeming
  For this night of May.
Let the light now shining,
  Glist'ning through the gloom,
'Round thee gently twining,
  Cause thee not to roam.

But notwithstanding all that is honestly avowed in the foregoing lines, my heart ached when I left Milwaukee, and I was downright sorry to go home.

My journal of the last days reads thus:

Milwaukee, July 16, 1857.—Terrible times preparing for examination. I have studied hard, and ought to do well. How will it be? I pause for a reply. Practiced reading my composition on the rostrum, reviewed my history, geology and botany for examination; meltingly warm; all the seats are taken out of the school-room. Father and mother came and stayed a few moments and then went out to Mr. Gifford's. Later.—Nice times thus far; have recited botany, geology and history. Father only heard me in history; mother, in everything.

July 23.—Left the city at half-past ten. Felt fully as bad as when I left home, even worse.

It seemed as if I had here found "where to stand," and among noble mates. Marion Wolcott, Belle Flanders, Lizzie

OLD SCHOOL HOUSE NEAR FOREST HOME.

MILWAUKEE FEMALE COLLEGE

NORTHWESTERN FEMALE COLLEGE

Wiley, Susie Bonnell, Abby Walton, Dora Smith—to these and other leading spirits I was utterly devoted, and most of all to Marion. It was the greatest grief my life had known up to that time, when I learned that my father had determined not to send us back again, because he was a Methodist and preferred a school of that denomination. This being settled, we importuned the good man of the house until he told us he thought more favorably of Evanston, a new town a few miles north of Chicago, than of any other place. We had read in our church paper, *The Northwestern Christian Advocate*, that this was to be the Methodist Athens of the West. Dr. Clark Hinman, newly-elected president of the University, had spoken before the Conference in our own church, Bishop Morris presiding—the first "real, live Bishop" we had ever seen, and reverenced more in those years than he would be in these, when pew and pulpit almost meet.

Our cousin Morilla Hill came to see us at the holidays, 1857–58, and spoke so enthusiastically of Evanston, its present educational advantages and its assuredly metropolitan future, that we gave up our dream of Oberlin and our devotion to Milwaukee, and one day in early spring father was packed off, by the combined energies of wife and daughters, to "spy out the land" at Evanston. He attended the closing exercises of the term, was pleasantly impressed by Prof. and Mrs. Wm. P. Jones, the united head of the school family; Miss Luella Clark, the poet, who had the literature department; Miss Lydia Hayes, teacher of mathematics; Miss Baldwin, Miss Dickinson, and various other leading lights of the Ladies' College. So he brought home a good report, and we girls sang and shouted in glee; the spell was broken, the great world-voices charmed our youthful ears, so long contented with the song of zephyrs among the tasseled corn, or winds in the tall tree-tops that sheltered our sacred altar fires; our country life was ended, and forever ended, except that on our return from four months at Evanston, I taught a summer term in the "old school-house," in which Mary did the "art department," and our old playmates gathered in "for fun," while six delightful weeks proved that we could have our good times all the same, and yet be doing good to somebody.

The first sorrows that came into our girlish lives were caused by the departure from this world of our gifted, fine-souled cousin,

Charlotte Gilman, and our thoughtful, gentle playmate, "Reverend Jamie." "Heaven's climate must be more like home to them than ours," said lovely Mary, herself so soon to follow. Life took a serious color from the loss of these sweet souls, and Nature's voices had thenceforth a minor key amid their joyfulness.

Evanston, twelve miles north of Chicago, on Lake Michigan, was founded in 1854, by Dr. (afterward Governor) John Evans, Orrington Lunt, and other leading laymen of the M. E. Church. Here they located the Northwestern University and secured a large tract of land for its endowment. The Garrett Biblical Institute, a theological school, was founded here also by Mrs. Eliza Garrett, of Chicago. But the school which most interested this father of young women, bent on their higher education, was the Northwestern Female College, owned and managed by Prof. William P. Jones, a graduate of Alleghany College, and his wife, a graduate of Mt. Holyoke Seminary. This was the only woman's college of high grade at this time known. Its course of study was almost identical with that of its neighbor, the University, and its advantages were of a high order. It was soon arranged that we should enter the College which was to become the Alma Mater of us both.

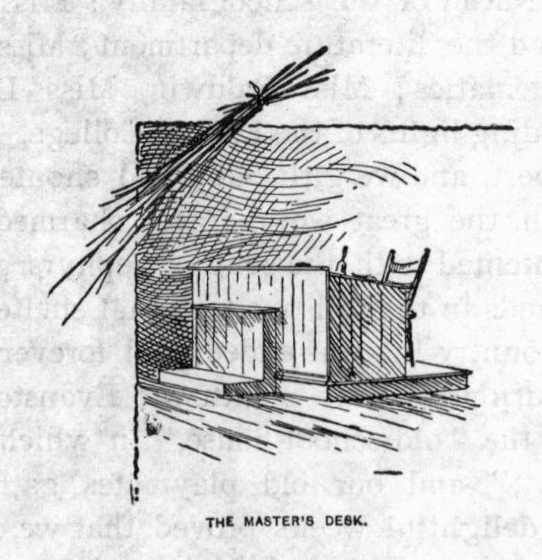

THE MASTER'S DESK.

CHAPTER II.

COLLEGE DAYS.

Here comes in a sketch prepared by request of "the powers that be" by my schoolmate, my sister Mary's classmate, and our beloved sister-in-law, Mary Bannister Willard. Her father was Dr. Bannister, long Principal of Cazenovia Seminary, N. Y., and for nearly thirty years Professor of Hebrew in our Theological Seminary at Evanston. With her two daughters, Katharine and Mary, Mrs. Willard has been for some years in Berlin, Germany, where she has a fine Home School for American girls:

None of the pupils who attended in the spring term of 1858 will fail to recall the impressions made by two young girls from Wisconsin on their entrance upon this new school-life. Mary, with her sweet, delicate face, winning, almost confidential manner, and earnest, honest purpose, conquered the hearts of teachers and pupils at once. School girls are a conservative body, reserving favorable judgment till beauty, kindliness, or fine scholarship compels their admiration. Frances was at first thought proud, haughty, independent—all cardinal sins, in school-girl codes. The shyness or timidity which she concealed only too successfully under a mask of indifference, gave the impression that she really wished to stand aloof from her mates. When it came to recitations, however, all shyness and apparent indifference melted away. The enthusiasm for knowledge and excellence shone from the young girl's face on all these occasions. After "class" her schoolmates gathered in groups in corridor and chapel, and discussed her *perforce* favorably. "My! can't she recite? Look out for *your* laurels now, Kate!" "The new girl beats us all,"—these were the ejaculations that testified of honest school-girl opinion, and prophesied her speedy and sure success.

It was but a few weeks till she was editor of the College paper, and leader of all the intellectual forces among the students. She was in no sense, however, an intellectual "prig." None of us was more given over to a safe kind of fun and frolic; she was an inventor of sport, and her ingenuity devised many an amusement which was not all amusement, but which involved considerable exercise of wit and intelligence — and our beloved "Professor" soon found that he could always rely upon her influence in the school to counteract the tendency to silly escapades and moonlight walks with the "University boys." A young man would have been temerity itself who would have suggested such a thing to her. In fact she came to be something of a "beau" herself—a certain dashing recklessness about her having as much fascination for the average school-girl as if she had been a senior in the University, instead of the carefully dressed, neatly gloved young lady who took the highest credit marks in recitation, but was known in the privacy of one or two of the girls' rooms to assume the "airs" of a bandit, flourish an imaginary sword, and converse in a daring, slashing way supposed to be known only among pirates with their fellows. If one of those school-mates had been called upon to sum up in a sentence a rough estimate of her friend she would probably at this period have given as her opinion, "She's wild with the girls and does n't care a snap for the boys."

At some "grammar party," or sociable, she was heard to begin a conversation with one of these "rejected and despised" individuals with the very *nonchalant* remark, "We all seem to be in good health, the company is pleasant and the evening a fine one. These subjects being duly disposed of, what shall we talk about?" Rumor had it ever thereafter, that the young man was so bewildered that he surrendered his heart upon the spot.

Her teachers at this time were, first of all, "Professor,"* than whom it would seem from the speech of those days and the girls of that time, no other ever existed. He was the moving spirit within all the wheels; the indomitable, unconquerable man whose energy and perseverance had twice built the college, the

---

* Prof. W. P. Jones, already mentioned as the president of the Northwestern Female College, died in the summer of 1886, at Fremont, Neb., where he was president of a flourishing normal school founded by himself.

last time after a disastrous fire, and whose faithful devotion to woman's higher education long before it became the popular, fashionable thing it is to-day, holds all his former pupils in reverent, loving admiration.

Next came his good, true wife, greatly beloved by the students and a most conscientious teacher. One of the deepest impressions of her school life, Frances often says, was made by the tender appeal of this teacher-friend urging her pupil to give heart and soul to God, and coming to her room and kneeling by her side to pray that she might be brought to the point of yielding herself in "reasonable service" to Him who died for her.

Miss Mary Dickinson, of Massachusetts, a women of queenly grace and dignity, and fine abilities as an instructor, occupied the Chair of Natural Sciences during the first year, and Miss Louise Baldwin the same position during the last year of the college course. Miss Luella Clark, loved and prized no less for her friendly heart and beautiful character, than for her poetic soul, was Professor of Literature and Philosophy, and general confidential adviser of each one who made any specialty of composition. Both Professor Jones and Miss Clark had rare ability to inspire the literary ambition in the minds of their pupils. They possessed high ideals themselves, and knew how to place these so attractively before the young beginner, that, without discouragement, there was endless dissatisfaction with crude effort, and endless trying for better things.

In the vacation summer of 1858, on returning from Evanston Frank (as everybody called her) took possession of the little school-house near Forest Home, and for six weeks carried on the school herself, with great comfort and pleasure. Early in the autumn the Willard family removed to Evanston, Tenants were placed in charge of their beloved "Forest Home," and "Swampscott" became their residence—a pleasant place near the lake, the large grounds of which became Mr. Willard's pride and pleasure, as he saw them, under his skillful management, growing constantly more beautiful. Nearly every tree and vine was set with his own hands, often assisted by Frank, and all were imported from Forest Home.

The last year at school was one of great strain for Frank, for she carried six or seven studies, and twice before graduation suffered severe illnesses, interrupting her progress, but not permanently interfering with her health. One of these occurred at the time of the marriage of one of her favorite teachers, Miss Lillie Hayes, to the Rev. J. W. Waugh, who was under appointment as a missionary of the Methodist Church to India. This was a sore grief, as Frances was one of her chosen brides-maids. The long journey before her friend seemed never so weary and unending as viewed from a sick-bed, and the parting never so final and appalling.

Some small glimpses of her busy student life are given in the following extracts from her journal kept in the spring of 1859.

May.—I am now in the midst of the cares, duties and troubles of my last term at school, and you must expect less frequent visits for a few weeks, my silent confidant.

Here's a pretty thought, from what source I know not. "Twilight flung her curtain down and pinned it with a star." "Duties are ours; events are God's." (*The Methodist.*) Definition of History: "Philosophy teaching by example."

Dr. Foster closed the Bible, after his discourse at the University chapel yesterday, with these words: "Brothers, with most men life is a failure." The words impressed me deeply; there is sorrow in the thought, tears and agony are wrapped up in it. O Thou who rulest above, help me that my life may be valuable, that some human being shall yet thank Thee that I have lived and toiled!

Have written my "piece" for the "Grammar party paper;" subject, "Living and Existing."

> "Boasts will not pillow thee where great men sit,
> Would'st thou have greatness? Greatly strive for it."

I am reading in *The Methodist* a new novel (religious) by Miriam Fletcher, alias Mrs. Cruikshank, of Cincinnati. Will write what I think of it, afterwards.

Miss G., a new pupil from Beloit, is an honest, generous, good girl (it is refreshing to see one such), and I like her. Mr. Emery has sent me a package of rare flower seeds and Breck's "Flower Garden." I have planted the seeds—have a garden of my own.

Professor detained me after devotions this morning and with his most "engaging" smile made this announcement: "By the vote of your teachers, you are appointed valedictorian." I was glad, of course; 'tis like human nature. To others it will seem a small thing; it is not so to me.

Mr. Gifford came last night, left this morning. I like him. He is a much endowed man, he is a good man. He lent me a little Swedenborgian book, "Rays of Light," which I am to read and to write him my views upon. I am glad he asked me, it will be a source of advancement. Have just commenced to read "The Memoirs of Margaret Fuller Ossoli." Thus far I am enchanted. I think her views are so essentially correct; they appeal so directly to my consciousness of right and fitness. Oh, to have known such a person! Oh, to possess such a mind! We of the lower stratum are improved, refined, by such communication. I think Margaret Fuller Ossoli would have been, could have been, was, so far as she went, the greatest of reviewers.

Humboldt is dead! He who has for a life-time ranged over the countries of the earth, is admitted to new realms of action. He has been promoted. He has passed an honorable probationship in the academy of the earth, and has entered the college of the universe. As says my friend, M. H. B., so say I, "'Tis well when a great, good man dies." Not well for us, but glorious for him.

Have finished reading story in *The Methodist*. It is good. Its influence must be good. It is not so very strong. "Buckeye" hazarded much in saying it was equal to "Uncle Tom's Cabin"; it is not, *nearly*. Harry Bradford is a noble character, almost equal to John Halifax, but he weeps too much, and so does Willie Hunter. Let a man *be a man*. I don't like Harry's ideas about a wife's obeying her husband. That I scout wherever I see it. I do not think I am unreasonable; I think I have good ground for my belief. If I truly believed that the fifth chapter of Ephesians (twenty-second to twenty-fourth verses) was to be understood literally and applied to *me*, if ever I'm any man's wife, I should think the evidence sufficient that God was unjust, unreasonable, a tyrant. But as it is I do not. This is my opinion now; will it change? It may seem wrong to others. It is *my* way of thinking, and I have a right to it. That right I will maintain.

Study did not end with the abandonment of the class-room, but, as she had planned, went on in new forms, and with the intent and intensity of original research. Her school-mates when they visited her in her quiet little room, with its bright south and east windows brimming the cozy nook with warm sunshine, found her always at her desk with books, paper and pen, for with her independent mind, the thoughts and investigations of others were not properly her own until she had fixed them in the mould of personal judgment, and phrased them in the forceful language of her own opinions.

While society, or the superficial intercourse known by this name, had little charm for this studious young woman, whose keen spirit soon pierced its disguises and rated it at its real value, to her journal she philosophized about it in this wise:

As I gain in experience, I see more and more distinctly that a young lady must have accomplishments to be of value in society. That august tyrant asks every candidate for preferment in its ranks: "What can you do for me? Can you tell me a story, make me a joke or sing me a song? I am to be amused!" Society is not for scholarly discipline. Study is for private life. Benefactions, loves, hates, emoluments, business—all these go on behind the scenes. Men grow learned, and good, and great otherwhere than in society. They ponder, and delve, and discover in secret places. Women suffer and grow uncomplaining in toil and sacrifice and learn that life's grandest lesson is summed up in four simple words—"Let us be patient"—in the nooks and corners of the earth. Into society they may bring not their labors but the fruit of their labors. Public opinion, which is the mouthpiece of society, asks not of any man: "When did you do this, where did you accomplish it?" but, "What have you done? we do not care for the process, give us the results."

Society is to every-day life what recess is to the school-boy. If it has been crowded from this, its right relation, then it is for every right-thinking member to aid in the restoration to its true position. Let no cynical philosopher inveigh against society. Let none say its fruits are simply heartlessness and hypocrisy. Man is a creature of habits; when among his fellows, he does his best studiously at first, unthinkingly afterward. I will venture to assert that the man who was greater than any other who walked the earth was the kindest, the best bred, the most polite. Society is not an incidental, unimportant affair; it is the outward sign of an inward grace. Let us, then, if we can, be graceful; cultivate conversational ability, musical talent; improve our manners—and our beauty, if we are blessed with it. Harmonious sounds cheer the heart. Fitness is admirable. All these are means of happiness to us who have sorrow enough at best. It is no light thing to perform the duties we owe to society, and it is better to approximate than to ignore them.

Scattered all along through this year the journal shows many an ardent longing for the best and most symmetrical of all lives—that of the Christian. The sacred song, the faithful sermon and many an earnest conversation calls out this deep desire and its expression.

The life of the home was a very bright and merry one at this time, for the three children were all together, all earnestly at work, but all as uniquely bent on enjoyment as ever they had been in the old delightful days of Forest Home. Oliver having finished his college studies, was preparing for the ministry; Mary was joyfully nearing her own graduation day—full of enthusiasm for knowledge, for happiness, for all the real values of life. Frances alone at home, deep in a young girl's philosophy of existence, was nevertheless as fond of a romp, a joke, and a good time, as any girl to-day of the particular fun and frolic that young people nowadays engage in.

Deeply envious of the brothers and friends who were so fond of their college fraternity, and so tantalizing with their half-displayed secrets, the girls of 1859 and 1860, an exceptionally bright and clever company, organized a secret society of their own, in which Frances and Mary were among the deepest plotters. Since Greek letters were in order, ours was the Iota Omega fraternity, or sorority; dark and dreadful were its ceremonies, grave and momentous its secrets. It was not allowed to degenerate, however, into anything worse than autograph hunting, and even in these early days of that nuisance, we received some sharp reprimands for our importunity. Horace Greeley, particularly, berated us in a long letter, which, fortunately, we could not entirely decipher, and which was so wretchedly illegible that we could exhibit it to envious Sigma Chi brothers without fear of taunt or ridicule. Abraham Lincoln gave his friendly "sign manual," Longfellow wrote out a verse of "Excelsior" for the collection, but Queen Victoria, alas! to whom we had applied in a letter addressed:

Victoria,
Buckingham Palace,
London,
England, The World,

never deigned us a reply.

We had a department of Notes and Queries, also, that was given to Frank's especial charge, and she was never more herself than when setting all of us at work with slender clues upon the hunt for some valuable bits of information, more than she or we knew at the time. She was our instructor and leader.

To the foregoing generous statement of my case as a student I hold myself in duty bound to add sundry particulars. On March 2, 1858, Mary and I left Forest Home, and that afternoon we saw Evanston for the first time. I was nearly eighteen and a half years old, and three days later my sister was sixteen.

Mary thus wrote of our new life:

March 2, 1858.—Up in the morning at three o'clock, ate breakfast, said good-by to Forest Home with many inward sighs, and were off to Janesville by four; took the cars and went, and went, and went, until we arrived at Chicago about one; took dinner at the Matteson House, started for Evanston, only twelve miles away. The college is really a beautiful building. We are in our own room now, tacking down the carpet, unpacking trunks, etc.

Evening.—We have our room quite in order. Hope, and guess, we shall like to live here, for our room is quite pleasantly situated, overlooking the railroad track, where the cars pass often, on the very road that connects us with our home. Good-night.

March 3.—Got up in the morning, made toilet and bed, took our new and beautiful silver forks and napkin rings, and went down to breakfast, came back and arranged our room. Father gone to Chicago to get us some necessary things. We are doing very well ; have been into the chapel, heard the rules and regulations of the school, a good many, to be sure, but I guess we shall be able to keep them. Have not decided what to study yet. Professor Jones, the president, is a noble looking man and his wife is just as nice as he is.

March 4.—Commenced operations to-day. Study natural philosophy, algebra, elocution and penmanship. Begin to get acquainted ; like Miss Dickinson, our division teacher, very much. Went down to prayers. Father expects to return home to-morrow morning. I felt very lonely this afternoon.

March 10.—Went to the store and got weighed, result ninety-four pounds.

March 11.—Miss Kidder came to our room and invited us to her house Saturday. She is a very pleasant, pretty girl. This morning, in company with teachers and scholars, went to the lake ; it was beautiful to see the great waves come riding along, then break and doff their white caps to the lookers-on.

Sunday, March 28.—Pleasant day, went to church in the morning and evening. Journal, I don't know whether I am a Christian or not. Hope I am. I spoke in class to-day, the first time I ever did such a thing in my life.

March 31.—Frank is busy with her paper, she is editress ; my composition is about the mosquito.

April 1.—Had a great time fooling people, fooled Professor ! A man rode up and down by here dressed in woman's clothes, and right in the midst of church to-night there was a great cry of fire, all being April-fool.

April 9.—In the afternoon we read our debates, and listened to the paper. When we came up from chapel, what did we hear but that father and mother had come—and were n't we glad ? We put on our "best bib and tucker" and went to the hotel as quick as we could go. They brought us cake and oranges, nice head-dresses, and all. Oh, what pleasure it is to see home friends !

April 12.—Had a good mind to be lonely but thought I would n't. Father thinks he shall be here in two or three weeks again ; good !

May 18.—The grammar party is the all-absorbing theme ; the boys are going to get the evergreens ; we have collected part of the money for the cake.

May 20.—I went around to help notify the company ; such getting ready of cake and candies, such sweeping of parlors, such arranging and hanging up festoons of evergreens was never seen.

May 21.—The people, too, came, and kept coming until the parlors were jammed full. We promenaded, and played, and waited on the table until twelve o'clock.

May 22.—Went up to the Biblical Institute and saw some idols that look like devils.

May 26.—Have been appointed to read at Commencement, so has F. and several of the other girls.

May 28.—Up in the teacher's room, playing all sorts of games, wringing water out of the handle of a knife, and so on.

Dear little heart! She liked the railroad because it was a palpable link binding us to Forest Home!

At the college in Evanston, I at once fell in with a very bright, attractive, but reckless young school-mate for whom I conceived a romantic attachment, although she was "the wildest girl in school." She was from Chicago, from an irreligious family, and while I think she had a noble nature, her training had led her away from the ideals that mine had always nurtured. It soon fell out that, while my gentle sister consorted only with the "Do-weels," I was ranked with the "Ne'er-do-weels," that is, those who did not go to prayer-meeting on Sunday evening, when all the good students assembled in the library; and did not give devout attention to the seventy rules of the institution, though I certainly started out to do so, having copied them and hung them up on the door of my room the very first day, that I might learn them by heart. But this bright girl, to whom I took a fancy, poked fun at the rules, and at me for keeping them, telling me that I was to be a law to myself, and that if I did not disturb the order of the institution, that was all anybody could expect and all that the spirit of the rules required. So I used to perch myself up in the steeple of the college building, alongside of her, during the study hours, unbeknown to the authorities; and once went into a girl's room and took possession of the prayer-meeting with my ill-doing band; whereupon, I was promptly asked to lead the meeting, and did so in all seriousness, for I would as soon have thought of insulting my own mother as making light of religion, at least inside a prayer-meeting. I can see now that group of sweet, true-hearted girls, with the look of surprise that came over their pleasant faces when half a dozen of us who belonged to the contrary part came in. They handed me a Bible, perhaps thinking it the best way of making us behave. It was a shrewd expedient, to say the least. I read a chapter, commented upon it as wisely as I could, and then said, "Let us pray." They all knelt down but one, a harum-scarum girl, who was among my special associates. There she sat bolt upright, with the rest all kneeling, and before I began my prayer, which was most seriously offered, I said, "Lineburger"—for we were so demoralized that we called each other after this fashion,—"why don't you kneel down, and behave? If you don't, you are a disgrace to yourself and the whole Lineburger tribe." At this nobody smiled, though when I think of it now, it seems so whimsical that I can not help doing so. Suffice it that "Lineburger" knelt, and the devotions proceeded with the utmost decorum.

One of the original features of the college was the grammar party given toward the close of every term. For each mistake in grammar we were fined one cent, and the pupils were constantly on the watch for each other, memorandum-book in hand or pocket. We were also allowed to call attention to mistakes by the teachers, even including the professor himself, and they were charged five cents apiece. A goodly sum was thus accumulated, to which we added by special assessment, and the grammar party was thus made of every creature's—worst! But in spite of this it was the great day of the year, almost rivaling the Commencement exercises in the church. Four large parlors were arranged in delightful juxtaposition for promenading, and we festooned them with evergreens brought in great loads from the lake shore. The dining-room usually bore some motto like the following, "All hail to the Queen's English!" The "cake of errors" was of great size and beauty, and was metaphorically supposed to have been purchased with our forfeited pennies. As the crowd gathered around, Professor Jones would brandish a formidable-looking knife above this wonderful creation, and in a witty speech descant on the importance of language, and of good language, at that. This feature furnished themes for conversation, so that a piece of good fortune in the way of a topic came to the guests with every piece of cake. I remember once being escorted by a most accomplished gentleman, who, as he critically tasted a slice from our cake of errors, made a familiar and witty extract from Goldsmith's famous poem in the words,

> "And e'en their errors leaned to virtue's side."

Turning to my journal I find these entries of school days:

The grammar party is over. There were one hundred and fifty guests, and all passed off pleasantly. Misses Gordon, Bragdon, Atkins, Stewart, Hattie and Julia Wood, Maggie McKee, Lizzie Wilson and myself were waiters. My dress was nearly ruined. Mary and I were considered worthy to "hold a candle" to Miss Stowe and Miss Shackelford, editress and assistant editress of the paper, while they read. My dress was tight and I was very faint once, in the heated rooms, but I quickly recovered. I never enjoy "mixed society." I was not made, I am not fitted, for it. I am, in this one respect, like Charles Lamb. He enjoyed the society of a few persons, his equals, and companions, with whom he was well acquainted and in whom he had entire confidence. In such society he was interesting; by those few friends he was much beloved. Beyond that circle he was not himself; appeared grave and confused and was considered uninteresting. This is my position now, as nearly as I know how to state it. I am sorry. It is unfortunate, it will cause me much unhappiness, but I can not help it. Somehow, I have an unconquerable aversion to intercourse with my superiors in position, age, or education. This is unpleasant, too. I shall lose many opportunities for improvement by this means. I have had the opportunity of becoming acquainted with Mrs. P., Mrs. N., and several others, but the dread I have of such relations I can not overcome. When speaking with such individuals I can never divest their characters, their intellects, of the accidents of wealth, age and position, and hence I can never be at ease. This is one reason why I like books so well. They do not chill me, they are content that I should absorb the knowledge-nectar they contain, without reminding me of my inferiority to them. They are great, yet most familiar; they say to every reader, "I am for you, my greatest pleasure is in having your attention." They are great without arrogance, wise without *hauteur*, familiar without degradation. They are full of power and pathos, yet not conscious of it; "they make no sign." And this is natural, for each man gives us his *best self* in his books, and our *best* selves are above and beyond our fortunate accidents. To books, then, let me flee. They never frighten me. They "never molest me, nor make me afraid."

I conversed a short time with Mrs. Hayes, Lillie's mother. She is rather aged, and is a fine, intelligent lady. She spoke of Lillie on the ocean to-night, and while the feelings of the mother were prominent, I could also discern the fortitude of the Christian.

I am more interested in the "Memoirs of Margaret Fuller Ossoli," than in any other book I have read for years. Here we see what a woman achieved for herself. Not so much fame or honor, these are of minor importance, but a whole character, a cultivated intellect, right judgment, self-knowledge, self-happiness. If she, why not we, by steady toil?

I have my Butler's Analogy lessons satisfactorily, I think; my astronomy lessons, (whenever mathematics present themselves), *awfully*. I was exceedingly mortified to-day by my stupidity.

Memorandum.—To have, always, some fixed rule of action in my mind.

To have two objects: A life-object and a daily, hourly object. To study systematically. To inform myself first on the subjects of importance of which I feel most ignorant.

Annie Foster called and invited Mary and me to a party at Doctor Foster's to-night, to which the senior and junior classes of the University are also invited. At the appointed time we went, at twelve o'clock we returned. Much as I dislike "mixed companies" in general, I enjoyed this occasion. I made two grand discoveries. The first was this: Dr. Foster so far understands what he is, what his position is, and how impossible it would be to compromise his dignity by any honorable act; in fact, he takes such extended and (I think) correct views of facts and relations, that he thinks it no sacrifice of dignity to talk with a school-girl, to walk with her, to honor her with his company to supper, and to forget for awhile the D. D., the genius, the position, the scholar and the orator, in acting the part of a true host and a most genial gentleman. When I see his beautiful home life and home character, when I see him leaving his guests to relieve his wife from the care of a fretful child, when I see him rocking back and forth and murmuring a song to soothe the child to slumber, when I see his nice appreciation of the characters and abilities of those whom he is entertaining, when I see him adjusting his conversation to their capacities, how vastly is my reverence, my appreciation of his merit, increased. At present I have a more exalted opinion of Dr. Foster than of any other living man.

The other revelation is that Annie Foster is, in all the respects mentioned, like her father, and worthy of him.

Everything humbles me, but two things in the highest degree. One is to stand in a large library, the other to study astronomy. In both cases I not only see how much there is to be known, how insignificant my knowledge is, but I see how atomic I am, compared with other human beings. Astronomers "think God's thoughts after him." Alas, I can hardly think *their* thoughts after them, when all is clearly represented!

After school, yesterday, I went to C. G.'s room and stayed till dark. It was pleasant, and reminded me of the joyful old times when I, too, was a boarder. I believe that to be connected in some capacity with a school is what I am intended for.

Memorandum.—Margaret Fuller's "Conversation Classes." I believe, though not fluent in conversation, I can benefit school-girls by a similar arrangement when I'm a teacher. C. G. is a good, sound writer and in this respect, as in others, will be an acquisition to our school.

I have been looking over the first few days of this installment of my journal and find that I complain bitterly of school duties and cares. From this, hereafter, when I have forgotten, I may infer that I was so narrow-minded as to hate study. I will defend myself. The case is this: I truly love knowledge. I thank God most that He has made us so that we may make ourselves great and wise and good, that we may change ourselves in mind from helpless babes to strong, steadfast characters. At school we acquire discipline. We learn how to use the implements with which we are provided for "working" the mine of truth. Along with this, rules are, perhaps necessarily (I'm not certain), imposed upon us. Rules are unpleasant; and the reason why I'm glad to leave school is this: I can learn, I truly think, as well alone, now. I shall be free from a restraint that is irksome to me. But then, I love my teachers, the institution which has been truly to me an "Alma Mater," the fellow-students who have been uniformly kind and loving. I hope I take a correct view of the case. O the glory of *knowing* always when you are in the right! I shall arrive at it.

Nowadays and until Commencement, *I am, and am to be* in a perpetual furor. I have no time to think steadily or do anything carefully and well. Consequently, I don't think. Oh, I'm tired and fretted and I long for the rest that is to follow.

Am reading the second volume of Margaret Fuller Ossoli's "Memoirs." Like it, even at the first; here's an extract: "Among this band was the young girl who, early taking a solemn view of the duties of life, found it difficult to serve an apprenticeship to its follies. She could not turn her sweetness into 'manner,' nor cultivate love of approbation at the expense of virginity of heart. In so-called society she found no sustenance for her truest, fairest self, and so preferred to live with external Nature, a few friends, her pencil and books. She, they say, is 'mad!'"

Now, in some respects, I'm like that. I've no "sweetness" to lose, 'tis true, but I have some character, some individuality, instead. The last part of the quotation is like me as I would be. Books I have, Nature I have. I have no melodeon or organ—my favorite instrument; I will learn drawing. Then I shall have pleasure enough, except—oh, I want a young friend of my own age, nearly, who shall love me, understand me, bear with me! Often I have thought that I had such an one, but have found to my bitter regret that I was mistaken.

Received letter from Oliver. He has the second "Honor" of his class, viz., Latin oration. He is the President of the Archæan Society; I'm glad, of course.

"The girls" say I am fickle; I have always had that reputation, I believe. And yet it is not my fault. In Emerson's essay on "Circles" I find the solution of the problem. Listen: "Men cease to interest us, when we find their limitations. The only sin is imitation. As soon as you once come up with a man's boundaries, it is all over with him. Has he talents? Has he enterprise? Has he knowledge? It boots not. Infinitely alluring and attractive was he to you yesterday, a great hope, a sea to swim in? Now you have found his shores, found it a pond, and you care not if you never see it again." This is hard philosophy, but, with some abatement, it is true.

June 22.—Beautiful day. We should be very grateful to Him that ruleth. Last night Mary and I went to hear Rev. W. McKaig lecture before the literary societies of the Garrett Biblical Institute, whose anniversary exercises are now progressing. His subject, as nearly as I can remember the wording of it, was: "The Study of Philosophy as Necessary to Liberal Culture, and in its Application to Theology." I have heard that some of the *élite* of the town think little of the production. In most cases the opinions of those to whom I allude would have great weight with me, for they are learned men, and have had experience, but in this instance my own convictions decide so strongly, so involuntarily, that I do not regard their decisions as material in the least. For me the lecture was, without exception, the best I have ever listened to. The thoughts were original, the language forcible Anglo-Saxon, the metaphors beautiful, and most of the conclusions just. The word "postulate" occurred too frequently, "mind" was pronounced "mine." Two words were incorrectly accented, I forget what they were; one word was used, which, I think, the dictionary does not contain, "parageum," and one word "dis ——" something, was coined. One of the conclusions I thought incorrect, viz.: That the Bible is to stand even in opposition to known facts; i.e., out of two cases, in one of which, the Bible says so and so, in the other of which science plainly declares the contrary, the lecturer said we were to believe the Bible and disbelieve science. This seems unreasonable; Bishop Butler declares the contrary, and he is good authority. Once Mr. McKaig said that men should confine themselves to specialties, or he made a statement very much like that; soon after, he accused Hugh Miller of wrong judging because he had so closely confined himself to his specialty, geology. I have bluntly mentioned all the errors I noticed. Deductions must be made for misapprehension on my part, for the narrowness of the views which I of necessity take, for my slight knowledge of the mighty subject considered, of the writers referred to, etc., etc. But, letting the errors stand as I have placed them, abating nothing, the lecture was yet a fine one. It was as refreshing to the mind to look from the pure heights to which we were led, as to the lungs is the bland evening breeze of the country after a dusty city day. It would be presumption and mockery in me to attempt a synopsis, so, out of respect to the lecturer, I forbear. God speed him always, say I. The vulgar mind will not appreciate him. He will have few friends (Emersonian) because few equals among his companions. Yet he is enough for himself. With his head among the stars it will be nothing to him whether dogs fawn or nibble at his shoeties. "Little he'll reck!" I have spoken enthusiastically, as I feel.

Memorandum.—I must study mental philosophy by myself after I leave school. It was rather deep, and I had to keep up a terrible thinking to get any benefit, but think I succeeded partially.

About this time, my dear friend and gifted preceptor, Prof. William P. Jones, president of the college, stated my case in prayer-meeting over at the church and asked prayers on my behalf. When this came to my ears I felt considerably wrought upon, for he had said I was an infidel, and I considered myself an inquirer. However, he had done it in good part and I took it the same way. Revival meetings were soon begun, and one Sunday evening Professor Jones urged some of us "wild girls," as we were called, to go to the altar. I was very loth to do this, but, to please him, consented. Going home after the meeting I wrote the following letter, returned to me after an interval of thirty years by Mrs. Jones:

PROFESSOR—I thank you very much for the interest you manifest in me and at the same time I feel very guilty.

I do not think you know how hard my heart is, how far I am from feeling anything. I see I have no excuse to offer for my conduct. Three facts stand out before me as facts, nothing more. I view them calmly, coldly. They are these. I am a great sinner; it is a sin greater than I can comprehend to doubt God, or to refuse submission to him, for a moment. I have no excuse for delaying to become a Christian. The third fact is, I am as cold as an iceberg, as unconcerned as a stone. I am not proud of it, I am not ashamed of it. I view it simply as a truth. I disconnect it from myself. I seem to think that all these things concern others, but do not concern me. You will say that I shall feel in hell (a hard word); I shall see that these things did concern me, when I come to die. I acknowledge it. If there is a God, a heaven, a hell, a devil, then I am undone. I have been taught to think that all these exist, yet from childhood I have doubted.

I have been told that man feels a lack, a longing for something not possessed, when away from God. Candidly, honestly, I feel no lack, no want. I would not ask for more happiness than I have always had, if by asking I might obtain it. You will say I ought to be thankful for this to God. I am thankful to something, thankful to whatever has thus blessed me, and I wish I was as sure that a good Spirit ruling the universe had done this, as Christians are.

If I were to pray, I should say, if I were *candid*, "Oh God, if there be a God, save my soul, if I have a soul!"

It is humiliating for me, the child of pious parents, for whom a thousand prayers have been offered up, to confess thus. I had thought no human heart should be permitted to look so deeply into mine. But I think it just that you should know.

And now, in view of all these facts, I ask, respectfully, yet earnestly, ought I to go to the altar, to kneel before the Christian's God, to hear the Christian's prayer, careless and unconcerned? Soon it will be expected that I speak in church. Congratulations will be numerous, that I have "returned to the fold," and my dark, wicked heart alone shall know how far I have wandered, how hypocritical I am.

I am willing to attend church, though it interferes very much with my progress in science. I am willing to go, if you think it will do any good, but until I feel differently, I *dare not* go to the altar again. When I do I will go unasked. I am,

Gratefully and respectfully yours,

FRANCES E. WILLARD.

During my last year, the follies of my early days at Evanston (mentioned in the sketch of Companionships), were not renewed. My *inamorata* was in New England, and though the reception of her letters marked the red-letter days of each week, I had promised my mother better fashions, and consorted almost wholly with the "good girls" among whom my nickname was "the favorite," and the only escapade of which I was guilty was having my hair neatly shingled, a rare delight, the continuance of which until this hour would have added incalculably to the charms of existence for me.

That last year at school, of which my sister-in-law has spoken in her sketch, was one of unceasing application. I often rose at four o'clock, and more than once have been found on the sitting-room floor asleep, with my face in my "Butler's Analogy," or some other of those difficult studies that crowded my senior year too full for satisfaction.

My only classmate was Miss Margaret McKee, of Batavia, Ill., a tall, handsome brunette. She was a young lady of the highest character, a devoted student and an earnest Christian. We were warm friends always, her great reticence of nature, and my frankness proving mutually attractive. We had no quarrel over class honors, she taking the salutatory, and I the valedictory.

Up to that time, my life had known no greater disappointment than the decision of my mother that I could not study Latin and Greek. One year longer devoted wholly to these studies, with my habits of application, would have given me at least a rudimentary knowledge of them both, but mother has always strenuously objected to the study of the classics, believing that the time might be far better expended in a well selected course of English literature, which she said I should have at home, free from the trammel of rules and the unescapable bondage of the school-bell. I think she was in error here, and that the mental gymnastics furnished by such studies would have been incalculably valuable to one of my tastes and temperament. I remember playing for hours, a piece of classical music that seemed to me to express the pathos of the situation, and, at its close, the jubilant triumph even over this deprivation and sorrow.

July 23.—Since I last wrote in my journal, under date of June 22, I have suffered much, physically and mentally. I have borne great disappointments (for me) but, as I have suffered, I have thought, and I am the wiser and the better for my trial. I have had typhoid fever; am just re-

covering. Very much of interest has occurred during these unchronicled days. I have seen Oliver's diploma and my own. We are *graduates!* How very little does the word mean, and yet how much! It means years of patient, silent brain work, discipline, obedience to the will of others. It means that we have started on the beautiful search after truth and right and peace. Only started—only opened the door. Thank God! we may go on forever alone. I was unable to be present or to receive my diploma and Mary took it for me. * * * * * *
I am very sorry I was vexed. There was no valedictory. The examinations and Commencement exercises passed off creditably to the institution, I have been told. Oliver has gone with several classmates and friends on a trip to Lake Superior. Of course we are anxious about him. C. G. left school just as I was taken sick. Her mother is dead. Poor girl! She is having a hard trial, and a weary life, but if she bears it well, it will be better for her. Dr. Ludlam, our honored and beloved physician, has gone to the beautiful Land o' the Leal. What we used to see walking the streets, and smiling pleasantly, the chrysalis he inhabited, sleeps in Rose Hill cemetery. The spirit is happy to day with God and Christ. *It is very well.* If I had had his preparation, joyfully would I have exchanged places with him. But I have come back to life to suffer, and toil, and earn,—in some degree,—the rest of the hereafter.

It was the disappointment of my life, that I was unable to bear my examinations, read my essay and graduate regularly. I have borne it stoically; I have shed no tear, and said little about it, but I have thought. *His* hand has crushed me, and not without reason, not, I hope, in vain.

I shall be twenty years old in September, and I have as yet been of no use in the world. When I recover, when I possess once more a "sound mind in a sound body," I will earn my own living; "pay my own way," and try to be of use in the world. It will—it shall—be better that I did not die. My acquaintances have been kind during my illness; especially I name with gratitude Mary Bannister and Rowena Kidder. Mrs. Noyes has shown an interest in me, and has done me a kindness which I can not forget, and for which, I think, I am as thankful as I am capable of being. This verse from one of Longfellow's poems has comforted and quieted me:

> And thou, too, whosoe'er thou art
> That readest this brief psalm,
> As one by one thy hopes depart,
> Be resolute and calm.

Take them all in all, my school days were a blessed time, full of happiness and aspiration, having in them the charm of success and the witchery of friendship, deepening in my heart the love of humanity and exalting my spirit to the worship of God.

Perhaps the most unfortunate outgrowth of the harum-scarum period of about four months on which I entered, as a student at Evanston, was the peculiar construction of the rules by the "Ne'er-do-weels," and after a few weeks adopted, I grieve to say, by me. That is, they said the rules were so numerous that nobody could remember them all, and that if we were quiet and orderly we should, in effect, keep the rules, because the end they sought would be attained, even though we did not technically observe each specification. Every night at prayers, those who had violated the rules were to rise and report. We simply did not rise. I think I never in my life had such a sense of ill-desert as when at the close of the term, our beloved Professor Jones called the names of all who had violated the rules, asking them to rise, whereupon they reluctantly stood up, among them my sister Mary, who was the saint of the school. He then called the names of all who had not violated the rules, that is, who had not reported having done so, and we stood up, none of us knowing to what all this was preliminary. Now came the keenest moment of self-contempt I ever knew, for the Professor made a beautiful speech, in which he gently labored with those who had broken the rules, and then, with enthusiasm, thanked those who had not, in the name of himself and the other members of the faculty, and held them up as an example! The fact that we were not suspected, proves that we did not do anything particularly out of the way, and that our general reputation was good; but I was so disgusted with myself at this false standing, that but for a miserable sense of what they call "honor," subsisting among school-mates and thieves, I should have risen then and there, in obedience to my strong impulse, and stated the facts in the case. These circumstances had much to do with my radical action when I became president of the same institution twelve years later, and almost altogether put rules aside, having instead a Roll of Honor, and a system of Self-government.

I wish I had not had those months as a "law unto myself," though nothing worse occurred in them than I have told, except that one night Maggie and I dressed up as two pirates. I had been reading that greatest of pirate stories, "Jack Sheppard," the only one of its kind that I had ever seen, and we were planning for the adventures that were before us as highwaymen of the sea, and were using, I am sorry to say, as much of the language that such men would have used as we knew, which was not much, and, horrible to relate, were armed and equipped, not only with wooden pistols and bowie-knives, but with a cigar apiece, and I am afraid that on the table between us stood a bottle of ginger-pop, which was as far as we dared to go in the direction of inebriation. We were not accustomed to estimate the permeating power of cigar smoke, whereby we were very soon given away; for there came a gentle little rap at the door, and without waiting for any response, a tall, elegant woman came in, Miss Mary Dickinson, my division teacher. She it was who, entering my room each day, would run her finger along the window-frame to see if there had been careful dusting. She was an exquisite woman in look and manner, as fresh and dainty as a rose. It must, indeed, have been a spectacle to her to see a girl who never failed in her recitation room sitting, in the character I had assumed, beside another who was known as "the wildest girl in school." But Miss Dickinson had remarkable clearness of mental vision. She made no ado whatever, but said, "Well, if this is not fortunate! The mosquitoes have almost driven me out of my room this hot summer night, and if you girls will just come in and smoke them out, it will be a great favor to me." So we had to follow after her, in our high-top boots, and there we sat, as imperturbable as we knew how to be, but with very heightened color, I am sure, and she insisted on our smoking, while she threw up the windows and drove before her the fluttering mosquitoes. She never alluded to the subject afterward, neither reported nor reproved us, for she wisely reasoned that the charm in all we were doing was the dare-devil character of the performance, and that if it was treated as a very commonplace affair, this charm would soon be gone.

My Bible class teacher at this time was Mrs. Governor Beveridge, who had a very happy way of presenting the truths of Christianity, for she did not speak in a canting tone or use certain prescribed forms. She was so fortunate as to be able to talk of sacred things in a pleasant, companionable way that used to be quite rare in Christian people.

Our Minerva Society was the literary pet of the college, and the debates, essays and literary papers to which its "Publics" gave rise, are still familiar in my memory as household words. For these occasions I was wont to prepare the poetic effusions, which, fortunately, were chiefly confined to that early period of my development.

Following the fashion of my home, I asked Professor for ground enough to make a little flower garden. The idea was popular and soon each girl in my set had her own little garden spot, where we worked each day like beavers, vying with each other as to whose flowers should be the best kept and most attractive.

I do not remember often losing my temper during my stay at the college, and never so far as the teachers were concerned, save when in an examination in Silliman's chemistry, after I had borne, as I knew, a successful part in the recitation, nearly every other member of the class was sent to the front to perform an experiment, writing the formula thereof on the board. Knowing that I was "well up" in the entire list, I went to my room unspeakably angry with what I considered the favoritism of the oversight, and expressed myself with so much freedom that my sister Mary, as usual, called me to order. Another display occurred when my diploma came home, my sister having received it in my stead, as I was confined to my room at the time in the convalescence that followed an attack of typhoid fever. Finding that the diploma was totally blank when I had been expecting to see it filled out in due form, and counting so much on the pleasure of it all, I tossed it out of the window with an exclamation of utter disgust.

Commencement Day in the old church was a great day indeed. We exhausted ourselves on decoration, a profuse growth of evergreens in the then primitive Evanston favoring our plans. An immense stage was built out and over the pews, and under a beautiful arch stood the performers. I shall never forget the day in June of 1858 when, although I was not a Senior, I was put down on the program for an essay that I duly wrote and delivered, nor the inward tumult of delight as the bouquets from all parts of the house fell at my feet, the gifts, no doubt, of my loyal set of "Ne'er-do-weels."

An amusing letter from my father to his daughters when they were at school in Evanston, gives a glimpse behind the scenes:

Mary, my dear, you will find inclosed my scribblings in response to your request, but you must not copy, but take any thought, or suggestion, or illustration, which seems to correspond with the genius of your piece. Frances must help you to select and arrange. I think the whole thing of "doubtful tendency."

Frances, your letter of eighteen dollars' notoriety nearly upset my equanimity, and I was on the point of sending for you to come home, but upon second thought concluded to forward six dollars to Miss Dickinson to buy the material for your dresses, which will be amply sufficient, and more too. As for the sashes, I shall buy them here, if necessary. I am somewhat at a loss whether or not to ask Professor Jones whether he prefers to have your tuition and board bills paid, or to have twenty or thirty dollars paid to fix you up in white for the Commencement! I am quite sure what his choice would be. The fact is, I have no money. I have sold some wheat for fifty cents per bushel to get money for actual necessaries. "You can't have more of a cat than her skin." Candy! Candy! Candy! Mary looks ominous. What shall I say? Wheat at fifty cents per bushel to buy candy for farmers' daughters!!! Eighteen dollars! My horrors! That is a pretty serious prelude to the perpetuation of college honors. I am done and say no more. Mary's letter is all right, Frances says, except that "it lacks force." Mary, you had better write all the letters if the force comes to me in this shape! All in tolerable health. Bridget "sings praises" and Mike says "Oh," and John looks amazed as they hear of all your goings on.

YOUR AFFECTIONATE FATHER.

The various teachers that I had before I was converted, were all excellent men and women and all Christians. I saw nothing in their conduct to make me doubt this, but as far as I can recall not one of them ever spoke to me on spiritual things other than indirectly, except Mrs. W. P. Jones. She came to my room one night when I belonged to the class of "wild girls," talked to me in the gentlest and most tender way, not reprovingly, for I was by no means an outbreaking sinner, only had a happy-go-lucky, reckless spirit full of adventure, at least, as far as she knew, for we girls were apt to put the best foot foremost to the teachers always. Before leaving she asked if she might pray with me. I told her I would be very glad to have her, whereupon we knelt down beside my bed and with her arm around me she prayed earnestly that I might be led to see the light and do the right. I am sure that every school-girl if approached as wisely and sincerely as I was by that good and noble woman, would respond as gratefully as I did. Teachers lose very much when they fail to utilize the good-will they have enlisted for the good of the cause to which they are devoted.

A few years since, Professor Jones wrote out his recollections of me as a student in respect to the vital question of Christianity. He did this a quarter of a century after I was his pupil, and though he is mistaken as to some of the dates, the general historical statements of his letter have afforded me much consolation, and I reproduce them here, disclaiming all responsibility for his too generous and partial estimate of his old pupil. This was the last paper penned by him:

You have requested me to contribute a few reminiscences of Miss Frances E. Willard and her sister Mary when students at the Northwestern Female College. Those are memories very precious to me, and some of them I will gladly sketch, so far as I can do it in words. How certainly I know, however, that I must fail to give them to you with the freshness and inspiration of life!

In the first of these Willard memories, I recall only the father—a man of singularly original manner and expression. Always urbane and polite, while always observing, he was as full of inquiry on almost every topic as a novice, yet ready at any moment to express an opinion on nearly any subject in thought and language breathing the fragrance of originality. He came to inspect the institution for himself before placing his daughters in it. He had evidently caught the prophecy that they were to make the world better, and was determined to aid them all he could. He told with natural pride of the prize taken by Frances for the best essay read at the State Fair of Illinois—a truly meritorious production—and described her so fully that when she entered college I needed no interpreter of her state of mind and character. She had reached an age when every old belief was required to give a reason for being retained, or else was told to stand aside. Many of father's and mother's teachings, once accepted without question, were being quietly subjected to further inquiry. Fragments of sophomorean eloquence from a neighboring college, questioning nearly everything in morals taught by college professors or believed by the Christian world, had reached her ears and helped to excite her doubts. The parents had hitherto attended to her instruction in a model way under their own roof;—the mother being by heredity a teacher, and by education and experience unusually fitted to lay the foundations of her children's education deep and broad. But the time had come when Frances longed to go to college, and the parents were convinced that it was fully time to place her under other instructors than themselves, and to let her contend in all the higher branches of study with minds of her own age.

When the daughters entered college, what I had learned of the father, kept closely locked in my own breast, was of priceless service to me in giving direction to other members of the faculty, as well as in my own treatment of them.

It did not take long to discover the taste of Frances as regarded studies. She would take mathematics as a disagreeable mental tonic recommended by the learned of all ages. The sciences drew her strongly, and won close study, but her delight was, first the *Belles-lettres* studies, and then, as she advanced in her course, mental and moral science and the argumentative Butler's Analogy.

From the day she entered, she made friends rapidly. Among the students, she was an emotional and intellectual loadstone. They loved to cluster around her and hear her talk. She would set them to discoursing on subjects quite out of the ordinary range of college girls' conversations, interspersing her own wise, quaint and witty speeches, to the great delight of her listeners. Possessed of a worthy ambition to live for a purpose, she inspired the same feeling in many of her school-mates. Her lively imagination drew plans for the future, not only of herself but of those around her, into which they entered with a spirit that showed itself in all their work. If they built castles in Spain, they, nevertheless, laid foundations for character and future achievement in real life, which endured long after their airy visions passed away, as their lives since have well attested.

Though inclined to be reticent in presence of the older teachers, it was not long before her novel questions and original remarks in the recitation rooms, uttered in the agreeable spirit she always manifested, won the hearts of all the faculty. Very soon what proved to be a life-long attachment grew up between her and one of the junior teachers, Lydia M. Hayes, subsequently that devoted missionary to India, Mrs. Rev. Dr. Waugh. The influence of the sweet, consistent, Christian life of this excellent woman worked as a constant rebuke to any doubts Miss Willard might have of the truth of Christianity.

Imagine, if possible, with what joyful surprise these two congenial spirits met years afterwards in far-off Egypt, as Miss Willard was making her pilgrimage to Palestine and Mrs. Waugh was returning with her children from India. One moment the hotel register revealed to Miss Willard the fact that Mrs. Waugh was under the same roof; the next, they were in each other's arms. There, oblivious for the time being of the monuments of fifty centuries, eloquent with the marvelous history which fills that wondrous land, they thought only and talked only of life in the college and Evanston, and of the friends of college days.

From the first, I was concerned to learn whether in the gatherings of students in her room and elsewhere Miss Willard was disseminating skeptical notions. I soon ascertained that her skepticism was of a mild form. Most of all, she doubted all her doubts, and in regard to other students, was of her own good judgment pursuing very nearly the course I would have advised. Of course, it was impossible for one so frank as she to conceal her doubts altogether, although she did not try to foster them in others. One day, one of her dearest friends came to me exclaiming,

"What a queer girl Frank Willard is! She won't confess that she knows or believes anything. She says she does n't know whether there is a God, and she does n't know whether the Bible is true;—she is trying to find out."

"Don't be distressed, Mattie," I said, "if she will only keep on trying to find out, she will find out. All her friends have to do, is to pray that she may persevere."

There were students' prayer meetings, class meetings, and missionary meetings, revivals came and went, and few except Miss Willard failed to take lively interest in them. Still I was confident that she was not indifferent. She never scoffed at others' piety, never sought to deter any one, but always encouraged her friends to do what they believed was right. At the same time, it was evident that she was not one to be brought into the faith by the mere entreaties and importunities of her friends, and I discouraged attempts of that kind. And yet the incident so tenderly recalled by Miss Willard in one of her addresses when she spoke of Mrs. Jones as the only teacher who had ever gone to her room, and, putting an arm about her, asked her to let her pray for her, shows how deeply she appreciated any manifestations of interest in her spiritual welfare.

Miss Willard grew dearer to all, and every one, teachers and students, grew prouder of her as she moved on to what we knew would be a brilliant graduation. Her intellectual lineaments had grown stronger, and shone brighter, and, best of all, the unrest of doubt seemed to be disappearing. It began to be remarked by teachers that she took more interest in the college religious meetings, attending them without solicitation.

We were reviewing Wayland's Moral Science, preparatory to the final examinations. I entered the class without a book, and having occasion to ask for one, Miss Willard handed me hers. It opened of itself at the beginning of the chapter on "Virtue," and on the blank half page opposite, I read (as nearly as I can recall the words) the following memorandum: "When I began this study, I could not say whether there was a God or no—and if there was, whether He cared for me or not. Now, thanks to President Wayland and my faithful instructors, I can say from my heart I believe that there is a God, and that He is my Father."

I exchanged glances with Frances, and sat silent until the mist of joy cleared away from my eyes, and the swelling of my heart subsided enough to allow me to proceed with the recitation. The students began to look at each other in surprise; then I poured questions in upon them, and in the midst of question, answer and discussion, the unusual opening of the recitation was overlooked.

Of course, I seized the first opportunity to tell Miss Willard how overjoyed I was to learn that she had escaped from her doubts, and how much I hoped she would soon frankly acknowledge her Heavenly Father before the world, and zealously work for Him.

"She did not know that there was a God;" "she did not know that the Bible was true;" "she was trying to find out." The Divine Spirit had led her on in her search. The many influences of the college had aided her, and the child of God had felt her way back to His arms. Father's and mother's teachings were holy truths to her once more.

Weeks passed on—weeks full of the arduous labors preceding the college Commencement, absorbing the minds and hearts, and consuming the days of teachers and students. Miss Willard was as busy as the rest, yet, unknown to us, a subject of still greater importance commanded her chief concern.

It was Sunday evening. A large congregation in the Methodist church had listened to an ordinary sermon and seemed somewhat impatient for dismissal, when the pastor, to the surprise of every one, extended an invitation to those who wished to unite with the church on probation to meet him at the altar. The revival wave of the last winter had rolled by; there had been no special meetings; not a ripple of religious excitement was discoverable on the smooth current of the church. Under the circumstances, no one was expected to respond to the pastor's invitation. A moment's pause, and a single young woman moved out into the main aisle and with a firm step approached the altar. Instantly, all eyes converged on her. There was no mistaking that form and face; it was Miss Willard.* No sign or faintest token of doubt clouded that countenance now. There was that firm expression of the features which clinches faith, and says, "Here I stand. I can do no other." The effect on the congregation was electrical. For a few moments the solemnity of the occasion held all other feelings in check, but soon hundreds of faces turned to hundreds of others, filled with surprise and joy, and many an eye was moist with tears. Some one began the doxology, "Praise God, from whom all blessings flow," and it was sung as if the very stars were expected to join in the chorus.

Of Mary Willard I shall write but little. That charming memoir, prepared by her devoted sister, through which she still lives and works with saving power, "Nineteen Beautiful Years," reveals her pure, loving nature so transparently and faithfully that I can not do better than refer to the latter part of it, immediately preceding her final sickness, to point out Mary Willard as known to her college teachers. From the first, it was easy to read in her serene, open, intelligent face that she was less troubled about faith than works. She was a close student, punctual in her performance of all her duties as the coming of the days and hours. After the parents removed to Evanston, and she had to brave all kinds of weather between home and college, this punctuality seemed still more remarkable. But it was not merely her studies that engaged her mind; ways of making others happy—particularly her friends at home and college mates—occupied much of her thoughts and time. If spiritual doubts came to her, she was so busy struggling to perform what was her duty, that she had no time to pursue them. "If everybody would only do right," she exclaimed, "that would end all the trouble in the world, would n't it?" "Why don't people do more to make the world good?" She had an extremely sensitive conscience rendered quicker and stronger by her constant practice. I never knew a more endowed nature ethically, and her love of all high and beautiful things was a perpetual delight to her teachers and friends. It is a comfort to know that this bright intelligence lives on "in minds made better by her presence" the world around.

---

*This was one year later than Professor Jones supposed.

CHAPTER III.

THE FIRST YEAR OUT OF SCHOOL.

This period, often very dull and sometimes very gay, according to the nature of the graduate and the sense or nonsense of her family, is, perhaps, the most difficult in a young woman's life. She has not yet found her "vocation." Friends wait and watch. Materfamilias fears and paterfamilias hopes. It is a time full of unuttered pathos for a gentle, refined and modest girl. The truth is, she ought never to be put into a position so equivocal — one whose tendency is to tinge her soul with at least a temporary bitterness. Girls should be definitely set at work after their school days end, even as boys are, to learn some bread-winning employment that will give them an independent status in the world of work. Better still, this education of the hand should be carried on for both, side by side with that of head and heart.

But these high views had not dawned on the world in my day, so for two years after my graduation I stayed at home, with three brief intervals of school teaching. My journals show that the unfailing resource of books and pen kept me in pretty good heart, while our delightful home life, rounded into completeness by my brother's return from college, rose "like the swell of some sweet tune," then died away forever in the pitiful minor strains of my sister Mary's death.

September 28, 1860.—I remember that I used to think myself smart. I used to plan great things that I would do and be. I meant to become famous, never doubting that I had the power. But it is over. The mist has cleared away and I dream no longer, though I am only twenty-one years old. If it be true that we have need to say, "God help us when we think ourselves strong," I believe that the opposite is equally true; nay, that we need Him most when most distrusting our own capabilities. And I have come to this point; I think myself not good, not gifted in any way. I can not see why I should be loved, why I should hope for myself a beautiful and useful life or a glorious immortality at its close. Never before in all my life have I held myself at so cheap a rate as since I came home this last time. It is a query with me, however, whether really I amount to so little as I think. I can not quite content myself to belong to what Dr. Ludlam once called, much to my disgust, then, "the *happy* mediocrity." Is it, then, inevitable that I am to account myself one of the great "commonalty" during life? Let us see. Jump into the scales, F. E. W., in honesty as before God, and, I say it reverently, you shall be weighed. *What you believe of yourself is vital to you.* Let others think as they will, if you feel "the victory in you," as my father says, all things are possible. Then deal generously with yourself; let not overweening modesty (of which I think you never have been accused) cause you to pass lightly over any redeeming traits you may possess. Let us have just weights and measurements in all respects. Beginning at the lowest and yet the highest department (let the paradox go unexplained), you are not beautiful, pretty, or even good looking. There is the bald fact for you, make what you can of it. And yet (offset No. 1,) you are not disagreeable nor unpleasant, either in face or figure. You have no shocking defects in respect to personal appearance, and that is something. Your expression is perhaps rather resolute than otherwise, and naturally, perhaps artfully, you tell but little with your face. In manner you are reserved toward those to whom you feel indifferent. You are too much inclined to moods, and yet you are as a rule exceedingly careful not to wound the feelings of others and you intend to be deferential toward those you think superiors, kind to your inferiors and cordial with your equals. You are hardly natural enough when in society, and have a certain air of self-consciousness sometimes that ill becomes you. However, as you think much upon the subject, it is not unlikely that by and by your manner will assume the half cordial, half dignified character that accords best with your nature. You have a good mind, but one not evenly balanced or developed. Your perceptions are rather quick, your memory on the whole, unusual, imagination good, reasoning faculties very fair; your judgment in practical matters not extraordinary, but elsewhere excellent. Your nature is appreciative; you are not cross-grained. You feel with a surprising and almost painful quickness. An innuendo or *double entendre* smites you like a blow.

Your nature, though not of an emotional cast, is not unfeeling. You lack the all-embracing love for man as man that is so noble and admirable, yet the few friends that you count among your treasures, have more devotion from you than they dream of, doubtless, for your love for them approaches idolatry. And yet your affections are completely under your control, are never suffered to have "their own wild way," and they fix themselves only upon those objects among the many that might be chosen, where they are manifestly desired. As for your will, I can not find out whether it is strong or weak. I hardly think it particularly powerful, and yet there is something about you for which I hardly know how to account on any other supposition. There is a sort of independence and self-reliance that gives the idea of will and yet is not really such. However the facts may be on this point, I think you would not be accounted a negative character. For the religious qualities of your mind, you are not particularly conscientious, you are rather inclined to skepticism and sometimes haunted by thoughts of unbelief. The æsthetics of Christianity have rather a large measure in your creed, both theoretical and practical, and yet you have right wishes and great longings after a pure and holy life.

The conclusion. Dear me, I don't make you out half as bad as I feel you ought to be. Placed in the scale against your beautiful ideal character by which you fain would mould yourself, you would kick the beam quickly enough, but somehow my *consciousness* affirms that the picture I have drawn has not all the shades it merits. In a spasmodic way, you are generous, yet beneath this, *selfishness* is deeply rooted in your heart. You are not a bit natural; you are somewhat original but have not energy or persistency enough ever to excel, I fear. However, you have some facility as a writer; less, I candidly think, than you had a year or two ago (that is encouraging)! Well, on the whole, I do not seem to make you out so poor and commonplace as I thought you to be, and perhaps if you keep your eyes wide open to your faults, and God will help you, you may yet come to be rather good than bad. For this, thank God and take courage. But oh, forget what you will, Frances, my best friend in all the world, ask the mighty, infinite Helper to model you by His plans, *let them be what they will*, so that every year you may grow 'calmer and calmer,' richer in love and peacefulness, and forgetting the poor dreams of less thoughtful years, have this and this only for your ambition; to be gentle, kindly and forgiving, full of *charity* which suffereth long, and patience, which is pleasing in the sight of God and man.

On the next page my sister Mary, as was her custom, skipped into my journal without leave or license and wrote the following paragraph:

I hope Miss Willard, though she be not conscious of it, does not hold herself at such a low rate as some of the foregoing remarks would incline one to think she did. When she calls herself neither beautiful, pretty nor good-looking I think she errs, as I am of the opinion she does come under one of these heads; of course I shall not say which one, however. I think she is right when she affirms that she has a good mind, but she contradicts this in the next breath, at least this might readily be inferred. I must say that in her dissertation on her affections, I notice nothing that would convey to the average mind the overpowering affection she cherishes for her sister! It may have been modesty that prevented her from mentioning this. I can not tell. I have a great interest in both these young ladies, Miss W. and her younger sister, and though my heart "yearns" more for the younger of the two, I can not say but that my affection for both is unbounded. Hoping that Miss W. will take no offense at my remark, I remain, hers very truly.

January 19.—I have united (on probation) with the Methodist church because I like its views of the doctrines taught in the Bible better than those of any other branch of God's church militant; because I have been reared in it, and for me to attach myself to any other would cause great sorrow and dissatisfaction in quarters where I should most desire to avoid such consequences, other things being equal. I honestly believe that I regard all the churches, the branches rather of the one Church, with feelings of equal kindness and fellowship. For myself, under existing circumstances, I prefer the one to which I belong, but that a person belonged to that church and was a true Christian, would be to me no more of a recommendation than that he was a true Christian and belonged to any other. The churches are all fighting nobly and zealously to make the world better and happier. Oh, I earnestly pray that as I grow older, the kindly, all-loving, catholic spirit may more deeply ground itself in my heart! I intend to observe all the customs and usages of the church. I have resolved never to be absent from Sabbath services, communion, Sunday-school, prayer-meeting and class-meeting, save when it is unavoidable. I will talk with any person upon the one great subject in the world whenever my prayer-guided judgment teaches me that it will be appropriate. That is, when it will not be so ill-timed as to jar upon the individual's prejudices and modes of thinking, so as to be the means of ill to him rather than good.

January 30.—Mary and I have been busy from morning until three o'clock renovating, changing and improving our room, and now I will describe it. In the southeast corner between the windows, stands my desk, with its friendly, familiar look. Once it was father's, but I have owned it many years and it has seen hard service. On my desk lying one above another are Butterworth's "Concordance," Niebuhr's "Life and Letters," Watts "On the Mind," Carlyle's "Schiller," Mercein's "Natural Goodness," Kames' "Elements of Criticism," Boswell's "Life of Johnson," Tennyson's "Poems" and my Bible. Below them a copy of *The Home*, for which I write, cousin Lottie's portfolio that she gave me and which I use for my unanswered letters, Webster's Dictionary and *Blackwood's Magazine* for May, 1838, which contains an article relating to insects, that I wish to read; my sand-box, microscope, inkstand, memorandum paper, pen-wiper and a cork bristling with beetles, "Cicindella," "Belostoma Americana," and many other varieties, though by the way, the last is a bug and not a beetle. Over my desk hangs an engraving of Schiller, and close beside, pasted to the wall, is my "program of daily occupations," which, I am sorry to say, is an illustration of the form without the power. Above it is a bit of excellent advice by Dr. Todd, whose Student's Manual I have very much enjoyed "and over all, softening, mellowing," a very pretty picture of a flower-girl. Suspended from the upper part of the casement of the east window, by a straw-colored ribbon, is Gypsey's cage, and its occupant is exhausting himself in a vain endeavor to collapse the tympani of Mary and me. On the north side of the window Mary sits, inflicting a letter on our mutual cousin, Sarah Gilman. She calls the affair at which she is writing, "Her book-case and desk." In point of fact, it is a pine-board arrangement, more valuable for its convenience than for its beauty. In it are her books, on it her portfolio, dictionary, etc.; over it a photograph of the Madison State Fair grounds when father was president; a Grecian painting representing a girl feeding a canary, my own handiwork, and a curious piece of whittling by Eben Marcy, a boy we knew when we were children. In the northeast corner of the room, Oliver's college cane maintains an unshared supremacy. Then follow the closet door, and one of the parlor chairs, over which hangs a beautiful engraving of grapes in clusters; and then there is the bureau, with Mary's portfolio, books of my borrowing, daguerreotypes, a painting, "Sunset," by myself, Mary's cute little basket, Oliver's hunting knife and Sac Gilman's drawing of the house in which her mother and ours lived when they were children. Over all this is the mirror, grandly looming, surmounted by a battered and shattered statuette in plaster of Paris, supposed to represent Devotion. This record is made in view of the pleasure it will give me to read of these passing days, when more sorrowful years shall draw nigh.

February 16.—Attended last evening a temperance lecture by Parker Earle, Chicago agent of the Illinois Temperance League, I believe. It was the best lecture of the kind I have ever heard, almost the only one. Forbearing to refer to orphans' groans and bloodshed, the usual material on such occasions, he reasoned the case, dealt chiefly in logic, presented interesting statistics, all in good, even elegant language. His subject was the relation of government to society and temperance. There are in Chicago at this time fifteen hundred shops for the sale of intoxicating liquors, exclusive of those which sell it for medicinal and mechanical purposes. Outside of Chicago, in the state of Illinois there are five hundred such shops. Twenty million dollars are annually expended in Illinois for intoxicating drinks, more than the cost of all the schools from universities to district schools. In one shop, on a certain day in Chicago, $2,000 were paid in for rum in its various forms. All this was astonishing to me. Thus we go on, one half of the world knowing not how the other lives.

February 25.—Received a letter from Lillie Hayes Waugh, describing her home in India. She gave me the Hindu definition of woman: "That afterthought of God which was sent to bring woe to man!" That single sentence gives the key to India's awful degradation.

Have resolved that neither public opinion, nor narrow-minded pride, nor any other creature, shall prevent me from showing, whenever I can, kindness as delicate, and respect as genuine, as I know how, to those whom the community as a rule treats slightingly or with positive meanness. If I do this I shall be of value to the world whether the world knows it or not. I shall, I think, bring some happiness into troubled and wounded hearts, and, oh, will it not be sweet to remember in the hour when I shall most need comfort, the hour in which I am to die!

THE OFFICE — REST COTTAGE

Below stairs Dr. Bannister and father are talking of secession, the cabinet and the prospect of civil war, topics of startling interest to every patriotic heart. The opinion generally expressed is that a collision is inevitable, and will occur within a very few days. God pity us and forgive the accumulations of crime and folly that have brought so near us a result so terrible as this would be.

March 5, 1860.—What am I doing? Whose cares do I relieve? Who is wiser, better or happier because I live? Nothing would go on differently without me, unless, as I remarked to-day to Mary with bitter playfulness, the front stairs might not be swept so often! Now these are awful thoughts. But come, let us reason together. What more could I do if I would? Mother does not work, she says, more than is healthful for her, keeping the front room in order and giving instructions to "Belinda" (father's invariable name for "a lady in a subordinate capacity"). There are no younger brothers and sisters to be cared for as is the case in many homes. Evanston has no poor people. Nobody seems to need me. In my present position there is actually nothing I might do that I do not, except to sew a little and make cake! Now that is the fact. I may acknowledge a feeling of humiliation as I see so plainly how well the world can spare me. But perhaps I may be needed some day and am only waiting for the crisis. Who can tell? We are told that God in his wisdom makes nothing in vain. Thus having moralized I lean back in my easy-chair and resume the reading of Poe's ghostly tales, which, with a little twinge of conscience at the thought of my uselessness, I laid aside a moment since.

March 15.—Let us see, mother and Mary have been sick but are getting well again. Xantippe of the kitchen has left; I have been doing the work as well as I could for a few days, and now a gentler spirit rules over the culinary department.

April 20.—How many unwritten romances careful observers might find in the lives of the so-called "commonplace people" whom one meets every day! A story as powerful as Rebecca Harding's "Life in the Iron Mills" might be woven from materials I wot of, the characters being men and women who live and labor within a circle of a mile from where I sit this minute, men and women whom I pass on the street now and then, or see at church.

A hungry soul and a bruised heart are objects more pitiful, I think, than a maimed limb or abject penury. I wish my mission might be to those who make no sign, yet suffer most intensely under their cold, impassive faces. The pain of a sensitive nature feeling that it does not adequately represent itself, that it is misapprehended and placed below its deserts, that its efforts to rise are viewed with carelessness by the most generous in the community, that it is denied companionship with those whose society it craves or feels that it deserves—no words can measure this. These people whose souls sit on the ends of their nerves, and to whom a cold look or a slighting word is like frost to the flower—God pity them! This world is a hard place for natures so fine as theirs. They are like the rare porcelain out of which beautiful vases are made. The coarser natures whose nerves, after coming to the surface, bend back again, can no more comprehend their finely constituted brethren than I can conceive of a sixth sense. This non-recognition of claims she was too sensitive to push before the public, pinched the face of Mrs. S. and killed her at last, I steadfastly believe. This carelessness and coldness makes B., splendid fellow as he is, reserved and untrusting; why, practically, no one cares for him more than if he were a dog, and his burrowing place is a matter of as much indifference as a gopher's might be. Mr. A., a man of fine intellect and large cultivation, lies year in and year out on his bed upon the "Ridge," helpless and alone. Who goes to see him? Who tries to make his life happier or more endurable? Who tries to lead him into the beautiful life of the heaven we talk about and stupidly expect, somehow, to gain? What wonder that he is cynical and misanthropic, wasting the years of middle life when other men's pulses thrill with strength; shut out from active duty when his need for work is sorest; laid aside in the darkness of his curtained chamber and left alone while the busy hum of life goes on as ever, and he sees he is not counted, needed nor regarded in any way. He hears the whistle of the engine and the cars go thundering by; the college bell rings every hour and its tones fall on his listless ear. Teams rumble past. He hears men's voices talking with each other. All this comes to him heavy with reproach and taunting him with the unfulfilled promise of his youth. In summer in the fields he hears the click of the reaper and knows that they are using his invention; knows how the wonderful automatic hand stretches out and grasps the heads of wheat that the sunshine and rain have ripened, the hand so human in its motion that he contrived by much of thought and study. He hears quick steps on the walk under the window, but he is a deformed man and will never walk again; thrown from a carriage in Chicago, years ago, he was taken up as dead, and since then he has done nothing of the work of the world. He looks into the fireplace where the coal is kept blazing winter and summer—his only company. Does anybody think God takes no notice of all this?

The B.'s who are kept out of the literary society by the unkindness of some of its members and the stupidity of the rest; Miss A., who is not asked into the reading circle, where it is her right to be by virtue of the exertion she has made to cultivate and enrich her intellect and character; Mrs. J., at whom a shallow school-girl could laugh if she attempted to recall the music she learned years ago when better fortunes were upon her; Mrs. M., who is disregarded utterly, though refined and educated; even "Ruth Ann," at whom we laugh unblushingly—all the cases of these people cry to heaven for justice and will have it, too, at last. These look like little matters, yet nothing is trivial, as Mrs. Stowe has said, "since the human soul with its awful shadow makes all things sacred." Nothing is a light matter that makes my heart ache or the hearts of any of my human kin. God accounts nothing slight that brings a tear to any eye, a stinging flush to any cheek, or a chill to the heart of any creature he has thought fit to make and to endow with body, brain and soul.

I hate the spirit in any one that seeks to gain the notice of the influential in society by fawning, or undue attention of any sort. I love a brave, strong character that walks the earth with the step of a king, and an eye that does not quail before anything except its own dishonor. All can not do this, but there are some who can. The man, woman or child that makes me uncomfortable, that stabs me with an undeserved reproach or rebuke, that dwells upon my faults like a fly upon an ulcer, that slights me or needlessly wounds me in any way—that man, woman or child I may forgive, but only through God's spirit striving with my wrath. I will shun them, and in my heart I must despise them and this, not because I am weak or clinging, according to the views of some people, but because, be I weak or strong, I will stand up for justice so long as I have power, and I hereby declare that I will speak more kindly and considerately to those whose claims are unrecognized by the society in which I live, than I will to any others. I will bow more cordially to those to whom persons of position do not bow at all, and I will try in a thousand pleasant, nameless ways to make them happier. God help me to keep my promise good!

Another branch of this same subject relates to those who live among us and do our work, perform the menial services for us that we think ourselves too good to do; who are cared for as we would care for the dogs and horses, well fed and warmed and promptly paid, but spoken to with harshness often, treated with unreasonable severity as if they had not brains and souls, but were animals conveniently gifted, somehow, with the power of speech. Who says kind words to the man that blacks his boots, to the maid that makes his bed and sweeps his hearth? Who employs the graceful "Thank you," and "Won't you please," that softens down the sharp tone of a command? O we forget these things! We are just mean enough to disregard decency and kindness in the cases where we dare to do it. I have called at houses where in the room a girl sat sewing, more beautiful, graceful and well-bred than my hostess ever dared to be, yet she has taken no more notice of this girl than if she were a brute, nor attracted my attention to her by an introduction or the faintest indication of one, though descanting eloquently on the virtues of the sleek skye-terrier at her side. The poor and the unlovely fare hardly in this world of ours. Climb the ladder yourself to enviable distinction, or reach a comfortable mediocrity by your own exertions, and you will be treated with all-sufficient consideration; but while you are *climbing*, look only for cold indifference, at best, and if you begin to stagger or fall, then kicks and cuffs will shower upon you with an energy surprising to contemplate. Oh, that I were a Don Quixote in a better cause than his, or even Sancho Panza to some mightier spirit, who I trust will come upon the earth some day!

April 21, 1861.—On this beautiful Sabbath day the unusual sound of the whistle and the thundering cars, has been heard for the first time, and our thoughts have been more of war, I fear, than of the God of battles whom we tried to worship. It is twilight and soon I shall go peacefully to sleep, but while I am asleep a thousand soldiers will pass through our quiet village on their way to "the war," that terrible Something which hangs over us black and portentous. Somewhere in Wisconsin, and on the broad, bright plains of Minnesota, mothers and sisters, daughters and wives will be weeping and praying to-night for these soldiers. God pity them and give them peace.

April 27, 1861.—I want to tell how with all their beauty sadness has been interwoven with these bright days, for Oliver has signed the pledge that he would go to the war if called upon. The students of the Theological Institute have organized a company and are drilling every day, preparing to go if it becomes their duty. I can not tell how my heart sickened and was rebellious for awhile as I thought of what might be. Went with mother and the other ladies to the Theological school to attend the exercises in honor of the banner presented to the students by Mrs. Bishop Simpson. We enjoyed it greatly.

May 5, 1861.—An eventful day to me. Mary and I publicly declared our determination and endeavor, with God's help, to live as Christians. We were baptized and received into the church and partook of the sacrament. Those were solemn vows we took ; I almost trembled as our voices mingled in the responses to the questions asked us. I felt how solemn a thing it was, how awful the responsibility that would henceforth rest upon us, and yet the ceremony seemed very beautiful to me. We knelt there at the altar, we whose lives and hearts and thoughts had been one ; it was most fitting that we should in this, as in everything, be together.

IV.

EVANSTON COLLEGE FOR LADIES, AND LATER, WOMAN'S COLLEGE OF THE NORTHWESTERN UNIVERSITY.

"Talent is nurtured best in solitude, but character, on life's tempestuous sea."

CHAPTER I.

DISTRICT SCHOOL NO. 1.

Not to be at all, or else to be a teacher, was the alternative presented to aspiring young women of intellectual proclivities when I was young.

Graduating in 1859, convalescing slowly at Forest Home that summer and autumn, studying, reading and writing all winter, I grew restive, and solemnly determined that *I would teach.*

Between 1858, when I began, and 1874, when I forever ceased to be a pedagogue, I had thirteen separate seasons of teaching, in eleven separate institutions, and six separate towns; my pupils in all numbering about two thousand. In my summer vacation at Forest Home, 1858, I taught our district school; in my own home-town of Evanston, I taught the public school one term; in Harlem, two terms; in Kankakee Academy, one term; in my Alma Mater, the Northwestern Female College, two; in Pittsburgh Female College, three; in the Grove School, Evanston, one year; in Genesee Wesleyan Seminary, at Lima, N. Y., three terms; the Evanston College for Ladies, two years; the "Woman's College," one year, and I was a professor in the Northwestern University, one. Nor did I ever relinquish any of these situations save of my own free will, and in every case but one, I had from the authorities a warm invitation to return. This I say very gratefully and gladly.

A desire to learn the methods of different institutions and to see more of the world were the chief motives that led me into an experience so varied.

It is also but fair to confess that routine has always been immensely irksome to me, and to be "tied to a bell rope," an asphyxiating process from which I vainly sought escape, changing the spot only to keep the pain.

I was determined to "teach school" because I wished to be independent, so I wrote a letter to John F. Eberhart, who was then superintendent of Public Schools for Cook County, of which Chicago is the county-seat, but it was a little late in the season, and he replied, advising me not to begin until fall, saying he had but one school left and it was the least desirable of all upon his list, away on the prairie beyond Oak Park, in a little red school-house and attended almost exclusively by the children of foreigners. I wrote him, as soon as a letter could return, that I would take the school. What the wages were I do not at all remember, but they were small. He gave me a certificate based on the fact that I had the diploma of the Northwestern Female College, asking no questions and charging no fee. This was somewhat irregular, perhaps, but at that date these questions were not as carefully adjudicated as they are now. Professor Eberhart, as we called him, had for years been editor of a family journal, for which I had often contributed, and he knew that I was abundantly qualified from a literary point of view, for the position aspired to by me and deprecated by himself. When all was settled I informed my father, who naturally felt humiliated. He was a business man in the city, having joined S. A. Kean, now a well known banker, in founding a brokers' office on Clark street, nearly opposite the Sherman House; he strongly objected, as has been said, but I parried an argument which, while it has very little force in these days, had a great deal in 1860, and pleaded with him to let me carry out my purpose of bearing my own weight in the world.

So the arrangement was made, and my father accompanied me to Harlem, for with his ideas of the protection that should be accorded to women, he could not conceive of my going there alone, although I was in my twenty-first year. When we alighted at a little wayside shed which served the purpose of a station, for there was no town there then, a kind-faced, but rather rough-looking man, with long, black hair, a slouched hat, a red shirt rolled up to the elbows, and blue overalls, appeared at the car and said, "Is this the schoolmarm? I am school director and came to take her over to her seminary," pointing with his finger across the prairie at the little red "nubbin'" of a school-house. My father looked volumes and whispered sardonically, "You see what you have got yourself into." A return train for the city passed soon after ; he took it, and I was left alone with my new fortunes. Arriving at the school-house I found the boys had not been idle. Among other things they had broken several windows and engaged in sundry forms of controversy, emphasized with fisticuffs. One or two American families were represented, the rest were of different foreign nationalities. I knew nothing about teaching, had been a "probationer" in the church only a few weeks, but I took my little pocket Testament and went into the school-house. The school came to order tolerably well ; I read a few verses, led them in singing some familiar Sunday-school hymn, which they seemed to know quite well,—I think it was, "I want to be an angel!" Its incongruity struck me so forcibly that I could easily have laughed, but in a moment later I could easily have cried, when I bent my head to try to pray. But to their credit be it said, the children stood by me far better than I had feared. The school was not large, having some fifteen or twenty scholars, only one of whom was so insubordinate as to require a whipping. He was a boy almost as tall as myself and I had no small ado to hold him by the collar while he did his utmost to show he was more of a force than his young teacher, but without success. Fathers would come to the door with a bit of a stick, asking me to beat their children with that particular one, which was the only form of aristocracy recognized in my institution. However, there was small need of discipline. In a few days the children would sit quietly at their lessons while I solaced myself by reading Plato and other philosophical books with which I had taken care to provide myself. I went through several of Bohn's translations from the classics, besides a variety of lighter reading. In every way I could devise I tried to interest the scholars, and I think they enjoyed the school, which I certainly did, although often feeling forlorn as I opened my little dinner-pail at luncheon time when they were all playing and hurrahing outside. It was not what I would have chosen in life ; indeed, I hardly know what it would be freely to choose what one would like, but the next best thing is to like what one must choose, and I think I have learned that art quite thoroughly. Next to the New Testament, Epictetus has helped me beyond all others to do this ; I mean all others except my mother, who, when nearly eighty-four years of age, said to me one day, "Did you ever see me forlorn?" and stoutly claimed I never had; which is true, except in the crises of our family bereavements.

I boarded that summer in the family of David Thatcher, a returned Californian, who was the richest man in those parts. He was an American, his wife was English. I have seldom seen a finer head than his; he was not, however, a man of education, though he had remarkable native force of intellect, and under happier fortunes might have been a senator. His wife was one of the kindest, most cheery women I have ever known. Two of his sons, George and David, were in my school and were staunch friends of mine; George, then sixteen years of age, being as true and loyal as if he were my younger brother. I think his good behavior set the key-note for the school. He was a very bright scholar and is now a lawyer in Chicago. Mr. Thatcher's only daughter, Clara, was at this time a student in the Chicago High School, a girl of unusual powers of mind, and a genial, kindly heart. When she came home on the first afternoon and saw a demure young stranger at the supper-table, she did not know whether she liked it or not; on the whole, she thought she did not, and though she said nothing, her atmosphere was somewhat chilly on that bright night of June. It is my nature to withdraw within myself when the environment is not propitious, so I said nothing and went to my lonely room as soon as possible. I had brought my writing-desk, a very pretty one that had belonged to father, and which was my most cherished earthly possession, except a little Bible given me by a favorite aunt who had recently died. This blessed book I read, and opening the desk, I placed upon the shelf, near by, the pictures of my nearest and best, and looked at them with a tugging at the heart such as can be appreciated only by those who remember the pang it brings when endured for the first time. Then I tried to read, and tried to write, but the time hung heavily. I did not cry, for I had made up my mind that I would not. It was clearly a case of "mind-cure," for the occasion certainly warranted a demonstration. Pretty soon there was a rap on the door and Miss Clara came smiling in, grasped the situation at a glance, spoke to me with great gentleness, and said, "You are lonesome, are n't you? It is too bad. I wonder if you would not rather come into my room?" From that hour to this we have been warm and trusty friends. I was glad to leave my bare little room for hers, so much more tasteful and attractive, but here was a new dilemma. I knew it was my duty to kneel in prayer before retiring, as had been my custom all my life, except the few weeks of my first term in Evanston, but I knew from various indications that Clara had not been trained to do this. She was a gay, laughing girl, and I dreaded her criticism, but when the time came I lifted up my heart to God and fell on my knees beside the bed, feeling myself to be a spectacle and with a sense of sacrifice which, absurd as it was, cost me more than anything had done in many a year. But in a moment this generous-hearted girl had knelt beside me with her arm around my neck, and from that hour she became thoughtful concerning spiritual things. She helped me found a Sunday-school in the little red school-house, which we conducted all summer long, and out of it grew the prosperous, well-ordered Methodist church at River Forest, once Harlem, of which my friend and her husband, Solomon Thatcher, well known in Methodist circles, have been pillars for many a year.

This incident may give to some young heart the courage that is needed in a more difficult emergency than mine.

When I went home toward the close of the term I took Clara along and we had a delightful visit, she being henceforth endeared to every friend of mine.

It pains me even now to remember how grieved my sister Mary was that she could not teach school. She graduated the same summer that I began my work as a teacher, and in the autumn she had an invitation to be an assistant in a private school, but she was the pet and darling of the house, and it was not strange they were unwilling to have her go from home. But I have seen her pretty face all stained with tears as she said to me, "Oh, to have earned a little money of my own, my very own!" and I have seen her on her knees praying to be helped and guided out into a larger life. So she was, in one more year, but in a way how different from anything she dreamed! She was guided out into the largest life of all, which is an heavenly.

The voluminous journals of my earliest period as teacher have this entry:

April 27, 1860.—Professor Jones informed mother in my absence last evening, that he knew of a school which he thought I could get, and with the items of information he furnished, I sallied forth bright and early this morning to learn more about the matter. The result of my investigations was a letter duly composed, copied and mailed, inclosing a kind recommendation from Professor. I hope to obtain the situation, for I have not yet been out in the world, to "do and dare" for myself. Single-handed and alone I should like to try my powers, for I've remained here in the nest, a full-grown bird, long enough, and too long. It is an anomaly in natural history!

This school was at Elk Grove, a country place not far from Chicago. The next entry says:

April 30.—On coming home from Dr. Foster's examination of his University class in moral science—which, by the way, Bishop Simpson quizzed unmercifully—I found a letter, stating that if I'd been a very little earlier I might have secured the situation. This was a disappointment, and one so hard to bear that I said several harsh, un-Christian words, for which I'm very sorry. I then wrote another school-seeking letter to Prof. J. F. Eberhart, who is Professor Jones's friend, and superintendent of the public schools in this county.

May 1.—Received a letter from Professor Eberhart, which amounted to but little.

May 22.—Another letter from Professor Eberhart saying that he thought he had secured me a school. It is very kind of him, for I ought to be earning money for myself and doing something useful, as every one else is. *Of course*, it will be very hard for me, for I am not "used" to care or trouble. Evanston is a beautiful place to live in, and those I love best are here, but I would rather go, notwithstanding, and I think God helps me to say with truth, "I would rather go because it is right that I should, and because of this alone."

It will be hard to leave mother, who cares for me as no other human being ever can, and to go where everybody is indifferent to me.

The first school is a greater epoch to the young teacher than any that can follow. I have been thus minute in its description, hoping to cheer some "new beginner," to furnish some suggestion, and to preserve the picture of a school within ten miles of Chicago, yet primitive as any upon Western prairies. Twenty-five years later I went back, stood upon its doorstep like one in a dream, and had a photograph taken of "the old place" as a new gem in my collection of "antiques." As my brother had taught in the new school-house during one winter vacation (1861) of his theological course, and I had followed him in the spring of that year, I went there also with my kind friends, Mr. and Mrs. Solomon Thatcher, and we formed another group, in which the young lady then teaching there, my dear friend Clara and her husband, and Anna Gordon, standing beside me, illustrated somewhat the developments of history.

Here follow journal extracts written just before I went to Harlem, and while there:

May 19.—Yesterday the Republican convention at Chicago nominated Abraham Lincoln for president of the United States. I wish I had been in the Wigwam when this was done. The accounts that father and Oliver give us of the excitement, the hand-shaking, handkerchief wavings, etc., have made us very enthusiastic. They say men's hats were knocked about like foot-balls, and one man took off his coat and waved it. They say we must have laughed or cried if we had been there. I would like to test myself, to try my self-control in some such way.

May 27.—Father asked our Heavenly Father this morning to "make us feel the responsibility that these peaceful, painless hours impose, and to help us to prepare for the storms that will come, we can not say how soon." I have thought much of this. But now, when there is not a grief at my heart or a shadow on my path, I find it almost impossible to lead a Christian life. Just what I need is discipline. Sorrow alone can melt my heart and make God more to me than all the universe besides. I want to be right, at whatever cost, and so I feel sure that if I am ever made perfect it will be through suffering. I am twenty years old and I have neither dignity nor womanliness, I am giddy and thoughtless as much as I ever was, I verily believe. There is something I can hardly define, but the word character seems to me to express what I lack and what I must acquire. I am neither self-reliant nor self-contained. There is not that about me which those of my age ought always to possess and which causes people to keep their distance, a certain well defined self-respect that is not haughtiness. Belle Stewart had it and she was only twenty; Annie Foster, and she was barely eighteen when I used to see her last summer; Lillie Hayes was a grand exemplification of this element that I find missing in my nature; I name these young ladies to you, "myself," for your favorable consideration. Now, while it is a shame that I am not as they are, it is yet but little wonder, for I have not been brought on as they have been. They have seen much of society, have attended school all their lives, and been trained, possibly, to dignity of manner, while I knew no more of society than a baby or a goose until I came to Evanston, and I know almost nothing now. In all these twenty years, although I have graduated after a fashion, I never spent four years in school, and I was trained to live outdoors as much as possible, ride, and walk, and garden, and go fishing, if, peradventure, my life might be spared to me, for I was always "slender," as my mother calls it. I have never been out in the world, have had no care or trouble, no grief worth mentioning, no "lovyer" as "Bub" says, nor any love affair to sober me. And so, since I am not naturally a person of character,—why should I be one at all when the artificial method has never been employed in my case! I am determined to be just, if not generous, with myself; indeed, who has a better right? Now, I am sorry that I am not more like my ideal young lady, and I am anxious to be more like her if I can. But I must get my discipline in a rougher school than most young ladies do. I see clearly that I shall never be the grown-up person that I ought to be until I have borne sorrows and had cares.

If I become a teacher in some school that I do not like, if I go away alone and try what I myself can do and suffer, and am tired and lonesome; if I am in a position where I must have all the responsibility myself and must be alternately the hammer that strikes and the anvil that bears, but always one of them, I think I may grow to be strong and earnest in practice, as I have always tried to be in theory. So here goes for a fine character. If I were not intent upon it, I could live contented here at Swampscott all my days.

It is quite curious that just as I wrote the last word, our hired man came in with the mail, and on opening a letter addressed to myself, post-marked "Noyesville, Harlem Postoffice," I found the words, "You may consider yourself engaged to teach our school." So I am to go this very next Saturday and to begin my hard battle for myself alone.

May 29.—I trained the vines this morning; it is all the pleasanter working around home since I am to leave it so soon. Professor Eberhart, school commissioner for Cook county, called, and I went with him to visit Minnie Holcomb's school. In the afternoon I went, under the same auspices, to visit Miss Automaton's school. I learned very much from what I heard and saw. The two teachers were as different as light is from darkness. Minnie was patient, kind and slightly diffident. Miss Automaton was perfectly cool, metallic in voice and manner, and calmly despotic in government.

May 30.—I have been arranging my dear old desk and getting ready for my departure. Will copy here what I have learned in the way of "rules for conducting a country school successfully":

1. Never let your pupils feel that they understand you or know what to expect from you. Be a mystery to them. Invent punishments. Resort to expedients they least expect.

2. Demand implicit obedience in small as well as great matters and never yield a point.

3. Introduce general exercises when practicable. This concentrates every mind on one idea, and when they all think alike by your command, you can do with them what you will.

Memorandum.—Introduce gymnastic exercises—Miss Beecher's, as we practiced them in Milwaukee. Ever so much singing, those chipper "rounds," and dear old-fashioned songs I used to sing in school. Have them sing the multiplication table. Have them sing the capitals and bound the states so as to make it a sort of game and less distasteful, while they point out the places on the map, à la Mrs. Hovey. Give them all sorts of extra lessons, viz.: have them bring flowers and name the parts; teach them the bones of the human body; the rulers of all countries, and as many other things as I can think up; all this in concert. Say to them all of a sudden, "You see now I am talking, clap your hands together. Now I am silent. See how quickly you can fold your arms; look me in the eye and be perfectly silent for one minute;" I click the bell and note your watch. This trains them to promptness.

4. Accustom them to take their seats for recitation at the right moment, as indicated by the clock. This cultivates attention.

5. Give them a good deal of outside information on all sorts of topics, to liven them up all you can. Have them spell on slates.

Miscellaneous.—Offer no prizes. Read the record of the deportment and lessons on the afternoon of literary exercises once a week. Have the head and foot in spelling classes, besides slate spelling, have them toe the line and put their hands behind them. Have No. 1 take the floor and call No. 2 to come, etc. Have them number as they take their seats. Give a perfect mark for each good lesson. Make a specialty of map-drawing. Practice reading classes in the sounds of the letters. Have them learn abbreviations, Roman numerals, words pronounced alike, but spelled differently, etc. Draw figures on the blackboard and let the little children copy them on their slates, to keep them quiet. Let the little ones go out and play a good deal during study hours. Call the roll at the close of school and have them report "Correct," if they have not been absent or tardy, then let the boy nearest the door go out when you call his name, and so on, having them leave one at a time, that there may be no confusion. Post up an order of exercises in a conspicuous place. Have everything systematized to the last degree. Make only four rules, namely: "Don't be tardy; don't leave seats without permission; don't be absent; don't whisper;" but wink at the latter unless it becomes too palpable. Have the whole school as far as possible read in concert, from time to time. Have the more mischievous ones sit alone and at a distance from each other. Make out a list of general questions for the whole school to answer, propound them to two divisions, if the house has four, and when they fail have the others respond, alternating in this way to stir their emulation and enthusiasm.

All my friends are very kind; they bring me flowers, write me notes, invite me out to tea and seem to be sorry that I am going hence. Am full of errands and last things to be done. Mary and I had just retired on Saturday night, when Mary Bannister and Kate, Han, and Mollie, and Charlie Smith, and Mr. Wood, and Watson with his melodeon formed in line under our window and they sang beautifully for my sake, because I am going away, "Auld Lang Syne," "Sweet Home," "Good-by" and two or three other pieces. And I lay there very quietly, I who have not shed a tear since last September, and cried like a child while they sang.

Harlem, Cook County, Ill., June 5.—I could not write last night, I felt too desolate. After leaving home, walking from the Harlem station to my ugly, dismal, red school-house, through a marsh; riding through the flying mud, with some kind-hearted ladies, to my boarding-place to leave my trunk; walking more than half a mile back to my den—for it is nothing else, it is the most comfortless house I ever saw; going through the tiresome routine of teaching the A B C's, spelling, and the like; helping sweep out the school-house—which is dirty beyond description, with broken windows, baked floor, and cobwebs mingled; walking home again, unpacking and arranging my effects, writing out my order of exercises, I sat down very tired and full of heartache. It is doubly hard for me because I have been sick and have done very little for a year, because home is so pleasant and everybody so kind to me. My head aches as badly as my heart to-night. Somehow I am afraid I can not bear it. Father came out from the city—it is only ten miles, though it seems a hundred—to bring me a bundle. I took it and turned away, saying in answer to his half cheerful, half sad words, "Keep up a brave heart and don't let it discourage you," "Good-by, father, I am not afraid," but the tears blinded me so I could hardly see to go back to my teacher's-desk again, and yet the people here don't know. These rough school directors don't dream that I am not exactly in ecstasy although I am teaching in "their deestrict," and they will not know either, never fear. I turned to God, the Heavenly Father, who presides over our destiny, with new eagerness. I prayed last night as I have not for many days, and went to sleep in the cold and dark and lonesomeness with a feeling that somehow the Arms that reach around the world enfolded me. If I can learn to look to Him and try always to obey Him, this bitter life will not have been in vain. Just now I took my Bible and it opened at the passage, "Like as a father pitieth his children, so the Lord pitieth them that fear him," and I could hardly see the words, the page became so blurred as I tried to look at it. Those who know my nature would understand that I am indeed getting my discipline, for I almost never cry, not once in a year, often not so frequently, and no one shall know save God, and you, book, that the inside and the outside life are vastly different, that while one is quiet, unaspiring and firm, the other is full of longing and heartache and misery. All this last I shall not write even in my letters home, for it will do me no good and will worry mother.

June 6.—Last evening had a pleasant talk with Clara Thatcher, the daughter of the house in which I board. Congenial outside surroundings are a great deal to me as yet. Looking at the case as hopefully as possible, I think Clara will make my boarding-place a pleasant one, for she is attractive and seems kind-hearted, but my school life is almost unendurable. I have twenty-seven scholars, five A B C-darians, the rest all under twelve years old, except two girls and one boy. The children are more than half German, the rest mostly Irish, except a few Americans, including Clara's two bright brothers. I have classes in botany, United States history, algebra, arithmetic and grammar. It is very cold to-day, and I have no material for making a fire. "It rains and the wind is never weary." The house leaks, my desk is wet and I am completely chilled. I can hardly hold the pen to write this about the life which I knew was coming to me. I must stay three hours longer and then walk home through mud that will come over my shoetops.

Evening, ten o'clock.—Am half ashamed of the dolorous tone in which the above is written, and yet I need not be, for it is all true, and in stating it *here* I made nobody unhappy with the consciousness that I was miserable. I only wrote it down for the future. After all, I have much to be thankful for. Billy Thatcher carried me to school and brought me back, and Clara and I have had a very pleasant evening together. We have been talking science, art and books as well as we were able, and I find her highly intelligent. Her ideas in general seem just and broad. The part of my summer that I spend in her home will be pleasant and profitable. We have already planned to pursue together the following studies: entomology, conchology, aquarium-making, botany and herbarium-making, study of the constellations, drawing from copies, and the manual alphabet. Clara is quite skillful with her pencil, sketching from nature. I think there is something else, but here is enough for once. Clara is a senior in the Chicago High School classical course and we have in tastes and education many things in common. She is the last person I thought to find in this rude neighborhood, and I thank God for it humbly and sincerely, and will try to exert a good influence over this new friend of mine. I think she has not been reared religiously, and so I pray here in her room even as I try to in my morning devotions at school, and then go to sleep more peacefully and happily than I dreamed I could two days ago, or than I shall deserve to ever.

June 7.—In the school-house, half-past eight. Am quite content this morning and disposed to look with some complacence on my lot in life. My school will be thoroughly organized before the end of the week, and I shall not find it hard to teach, only wearisome. They are very kind at my boarding-place, and I am altogether comfortable there. Wrote a cheerful letter home last night. I asked two of my pupils in the Second Reader class why we have such a day as Christmas, when it occurs and what it commemorates. They said, "It comes sometime in cold weather, and we have it so we can hang up our stockings and get something nice." Beyond this they had not the faintest idea of the day.

Evening, ten o'clock.—Clara and I have been having a royal time ever since she came from the city on the six o'clock train. After supper we went walking to the Desplaines river where Clara wished to show me some of the scenes we are to sketch, then we walked up the railroad track and talked, and I had a beautiful time. We gathered bouquets of roses, and rosebuds which are better than blossoms, and after a walk of nearly two miles we returned and found the three directors waiting to examine my certificate. After they had dissected it, we came up to my room, traced constellations, I learned the manual alphabet, and now I am going to bed tired, but happy and thankful. But before I go I shall tell my troubles and joys to God, and pray Him to take care of all of us, especially the Four, until death us do part; nay, until after death.

June 4.—One thing particularly troubles me. I am afraid I do not try enough to influence Clara in the right direction. I am naturally thoughtless, and a playful remark with a hidden meaning which is irreverent does not meet in all cases a negative response, or silence even, but I see that I am inclined to laugh myself if the wit of the words is sufficiently apparent. But I have told her how I am trying, and am praying earnestly and have sincere wishes after righteousness in my heart. There is no church here, nor are there any Christian people, but the Infinite One is everywhere, and "His greatness flows around my incompleteness."

Afternoon.—The scholars are more vexatious than usual and I find it rather difficult to keep my temper, though I have succeeded thus far. The children overwhelm me with flowers, the desk is piled with them; they enliven this doleful place wonderfully. And alas! for me the time even now is when I must make comfort to myself out of roses and lilies instead of friends and home. One of my scholars had a fit in school and we all were frightened, but I was "schoolma'am" to the best of my ability.

Evening.—I have not laughed so heartily in months as over a scientific result obtained by Clara and me this evening, and have been just as wild and thoughtless as I ever was at home. Clara is eighteen and her enthusiasm on the subjects we are to investigate together, awakens mine. Perhaps my life is not going to be so very hard, but I can not tell. One moment I am in the sunshine and the next I am in the shade; so delicate is my spiritual thermometer that from zero to summer day a pleasant breath of the sweet south wind will raise the mercury.

June 10.—Sabbath morning. Rose at nine o'clock, breakfasted, arranged my room, and am wondering at the strange day that I shall spend, so different from Evanston with all its Christian privileges. This family is not religious. There is no church that I can attend, no outward form of worship in which I can show the gratitude and love that fill my heart this beautiful day. I can see father and mother, sister and brother, in the old pew. I know they all have prayed that I might be shielded, strengthened and comforted by our God who is over all, blessed forever. Mother has wondered what I was doing to-day and has hoped in her heart that I might be happy and serene and that I might live and act like a Christian under whatever circumstances I may be placed. The younger members of this family have taken their pony and ridden off to the strawberry patch to spend the day. The proprietor sits in the library below with six or seven friends who have ridden out from the city; they are smoking their cigars and talking of horse-races, sporting, and the like. The mistress of the establishment is busy superintending the preparation of the Sunday dinner, for Mr. T. is a rich man and fares sumptuously every day. It is a queer Sabbath, I never spent one like it. God, help me to remember Thee and heaven and holiness while all around is of the earth, earthy. I have stayed in my room with Clara, read a little, talked with her the rest of the time. I do not know what I should do without her. She is a petted child, the only daughter, not used to thinking much of others' comfort, but she is very kind to me and marvelously thoughtful of my happiness. Clara and I did not go down to dinner, which was a comfort. Have read my favorite 119th Psalm with solid satisfaction.

Evening, June 11.—School has been positively zestful, my pupils enthusiastic and easily governed. The sun has shone and the sky has been as blue as a violet, and, best of all, I have had four letters from home.

June 12.—My pupils have not been as studious or as easily governed as usual, to-day, and have troubled me greatly. Have been obliged to box the ears of two reprobates, ferule the brown palms of four, and lay violent hands on another to coerce him into measures that did not meet his views. All this I have done; I am sorry it became necessary, for I feel kindly toward them all and never speak a harsh word only as they force me to do so by the total depravity they manifest in their conduct, and yet the little creatures bring me flowers and evince in many little actions a kind of regard for me that is most pleasant.

I have given these extracts showing what a young teacher once endured, because I know ten thousand others have had a similar experience, and I have hoped to bring somewhat of good cheer and courage to those as faint-hearted in their new endeavor as I was in mine so many years ago.

CHAPTER II.

KANKAKEE ACADEMY.

(1860).

After a few months at home I engaged to go to Kankakee, an Illinois county-seat about sixty miles from Chicago, as assistant teacher in an academy started by Prof. Charles B. Woodruff (the former principal of the "Blind Institute" at Janesville, Wis., and my father's friend). Here I remained one term, but owing to the urgent wishes of my parents did not return after the Christmas holidays. My cousin, Miss Sarah F. Gilman, of Churchville, N. Y., took my place and made a decided success of the venture, in more ways than one, as she here made the acquaintance of Harry Dusinbury, whom she married within the year. The story of this second effort as a pedagogue is best given in journal language:

September 26, 1860.—Very busy getting ready to go. Letter from Professor Woodruff in answer to my telegraphic dispatch, giving me further particulars and saying that he will secure my boarding-place and meet me at the night train. As nearly as I can find out, I am to teach philosophy, history, drawing, grammar, and all the reading classes, how many soever there may be. I received from Clara Thatcher one of her warm-hearted, impetuous epistles. What a heroine that girl has proved herself to be! Right on through summer's heat she has carried, all alone, the Sunday-school we founded in the little red school-house so forlorn. She says Oliver is to have their school, and he is glad and so are we, for the wages are excellent. What an unromantic consideration! But he will not have half so hard a time as I had, for he will be in the nice, large, brick building instead of my wretched little wooden house. Yet when I think of spending all the winter there, I can but murmur, "Poor fellow," to myself, for Evanston is a town that makes almost any other seem half barbarous. The fact that the University charter forever forbids saloons tells a whole dictionary full about our moral status.

And so I am to go from home before our dear relatives come from the East, and I have not seen them in many years, not since I was a young girl.

They are all very dear to me and I was especially anxious to see my Aunt Elizabeth who is loved with more than the love of near relationship by me, and for whom I am named. In the lonely days that will follow my going I shall think of those whom I have left behind and the other loved ones who are coming, as they enjoy themselves together in our home, while I am lonesome, tired and heart-sick. In the evening Mary and I sang for hours to father, who is not particular about the quality and cultivation of our voices, it being sufficient for him that, as in the olden days, his daughters sing together "Bonnie Doon," "Come this way, my father," "Star-spangled Banner," and the rest; when we closed with Longfellow's "Rainy Day," mother sat with her hand shading her eyes and a sad expression on the dearest face in all the world to me. I knew she was thinking about my birthday so near at hand, about my going off again, about her birds that are making longer flights at every trial and need no more to have her bear them up upon her wings. I knew that she was being sorry for me as only one can be, that one my mother. Oliver and Beth Vincent were upstairs making the library catalogue for the Sunday-school. Aunt Sarah sat with us, listening quietly to everything. Father threw in a remark now and then, sometimes lively, sometimes sad, but always quaint and curious. And thus endeth the last home-picture I shall draw for many a day. I have been trying to think why I go away to this new work so soon. I can not tell. I only know that I have some dim sense that it is right and best. Certainly it is not the happiest. But I have come to believe that it is well for us, well for our characters, those beautiful fabrics we are weaving every day, to do those things that do not make us happy, but only make us strong.

I have never felt reluctant to tell my age. It early came to me that nothing was less dignified than to make a secret of one's personal chronology. Marketable values in many instances depend on freshness, and if a girl has no broader view of her relations to the world than the relation she may hold to some man who will prize her more if she is younger, then she does well to hide her age. But if she is a dignified human being, who has started out, "heart within and God o'erhead," upon an endless voyage wherein she sails by the stars rather than by the clock, she will never hesitate either to know or to announce just where she is on that long voyage; how many days out from childhood-land. The first mention I find in my journal of this way of looking at the subject is the following:

September 27, 1860.—I have often wondered why it is that people generally, and ladies especially, are so unwilling to have their ages known. We are immortal, and, for aught we know, eternal. We never regard Gabriel as old, though the prophet Daniel first introduced him to us. Our baby brothers and sisters who have died are babies still to us, lambs in the flock that the gentle Shepherd leads. If we do not think of age when we think about eternity, why should we in time, which is only eternity cut off at both ends? And yet we do regard it very much. This was accounted for to me recently, in the case of ladies, on the ground that their attractions diminish as their years increase, after a certain point, and that consequently the number of years is made a mystery. Ah, I have it! If "one" is beautiful, there is some reason in one's keeping one's age a secret, but if one is not, one has little or nothing to lose by the flight of years in this respect, while one is constantly adding to one's attractions in other ways, that is, in knowledge of the world, intelligence, culture, conversational ability, etc.; therefore, if one is not beautiful, it is foolish to make a secret of one's age. Corollary: My course is plain, because I myself am plain! It shall always be in order for any one to propound to me the usually much-dreaded question, "How old are you—if I may be so bold?"

Why should men universally tell their ages? Because a man is an individual and not dependent upon others for his support. I early resolved that I would not be dependent, either, and later that I would try to help all other women to the same vantage-ground of self-help and self-respect. I determined, also, that I would set them a good example by always freely speaking of my age, which I have not shunned to declare, my mother facetiously contending that I keep it, and hers, too, for that matter, just one year ahead of the current calendar.

I have not done much in these years, yet God knows I will try to make up if He will spare me, and somehow I believe He will.

September 29.—Going away to Kankakee to-morrow to begin my work. Packed my trunk so as to have it out of the way. Oliver kindly lent me Nolte's "Fifty Years in Both Hemispheres," D'Aubigné's "History of the Reformation," Scott's "Bride of Lammermoor," and the first volume of Bohn's edition of "Plato," to take with me.

Kankakee, Ill., October 2, 1860.—Another book to begin and a new, strange life to tell of. What a world this is, to be sure, and how we struggle about in it, straying off from those whom we love and those who love us, to strange, unfriendly regions, resolutely turning away from books and quiet to take in their stead pain, weariness and toil; yet in it all there is the comforting reflection that we are right, that in our nature there still exists, notwithstanding all our sins and ignorance, a spark of Godhood, a shimmering ray from the stars that shine serenely in the zenith of the angels, a breath of divinity which stirs within every human soul. Father left me yesterday evening, and I prayed quite trustfully and went to sleep with a broad grin on my face, put on through sheer strength of will. Well, this morning, I went to the Kankakee Academy, where I am second teacher, and on the whole have had a tolerable day. I am going to try not to cry once while I am here, for I am twenty-one, I would have you understand. It is not so very bad, and I won't care. I wish I were a better *woman*. I shall always call myself that now.

I now feel competent to work, and work I will. I can accomplish a great deal between now and the holidays, so good-by to home and friends until then. You can well do without me, and I have proved that I can live without you, as well. Each of us is sent into the world by himself, to fight and conquer for himself, and when all is said an infinite remoteness from every being, save God, encompasses each one of us from the cradle to the grave.

A little poem in Harper's for this month struck me unusually. I will copy from it as a text to a short sermon. It closes thus :

> " In this poor life we may not cross
> Our virtuous instinct without loss,
> And the soul grows not to its height
> Unless it love with utmost might."

I believe the doctrine of this poem divested of its imagery. I believe no woman ever knows the depth and richness of her nature until she has loved a man, some man good and noble, better than her own life. I believe that unless she does this, much of pain and want must be endured by her, and with all that I have admitted, my journal bears me witness that I say little or nothing upon the subject. Once only I will give the reason here, and then I shall not revert to it again. In truth, it is not one of which I often think. I have never been in love, I have never shed a tear or dreamed a dream, or sighed, or had a sleepless hour for love. I never treasured any man in my heart until he became sacred to me, until his words were as oracles, his smiles as sunshine, his voice like music. I never hung upon any man's words or took any man's name into my prayer because I loved him, but I might have done all this had I so willed it. I was too cautious, loved my own peace too well, valued myself too highly, remembered too frequently that I was made for something far more worthy than to spend a disconsolate life, wasting my heart, the richest gift I could bestow, upon a man who did not care for it, and who never thought of me save in friendly, common fashion. I was too proud for that, I had too keen a sense of right and justice ; too strong a desire to work out from the seclusion in which I live, and try to become wiser and better and more helpful to the world each day. I have known several men for whom I might have cared. I have seen enough nobility in their natures, enough culture of intellect, enough purity of mind and heart and life, to inspire the choice emotion. I have looked after them as they passed me on the street, as I saw them in church or met them in society, and have tranquilly thought to myself, " You might care for him, but remember you must not do so," and I have gone on my way calmly and in great peace. It is not that I am hard-hearted or insensible, but because I know perfectly well these men think nothing about me except as an acquaintance, and therefore I am determined to be even with them and have shut the door upon them and said, "Get hence," and that is the end of it. I am sure it is right for me to do so. I have not known as yet what it is to lean on any being except God. In all my friendships I am the one relied on, the one who fights the battles, or would if there were any to fight. Yet every night I say to God in prayer, "Sometime, if it pleases Thee, give me the love of a manly heart, of one that I can trust and care for next to Thee. But if this can not be, make it up to me in some other way. Thou knowest what is right. And in it all may I be very quiet and restful, remembering that the fashion of this world perisheth and ere very long I shall be gone beyond the light of sun or stars, beyond the need of this blessing for which I have asked." I am quiet. The present situation does not trouble, nor turn the song of my life into the minor key, and for this I thank God fervently. Burke says that the traits most admired in women are dependence, softness, trust, timidity, and I am quite deficient in them all.

October 11.—As an indication of the literary standard of the family in which I am to stay for the next ten weeks, I might mention that the *Mercury*, the *Ledger* and *Godey's Ladies' Book* adorn (?) the parlor table, and I find twenty or thirty copies of *Littell's Living Age* stuffed away in a closet under an old chair.

October 13.—"To know, to esteem, to love and then to part,
Make up life's tale to many a feeling heart."

In the afternoon I went to Sunday-school; they have given me a class of boys to teach; then went to class-meeting. My class-leader I like very much. He looks to me like a Christian, he is rather old, has silvery hair, dark eyes, sweet, calm mouth, finely-cut features. I told them that Christ, their friend, was also mine. After all this I am going home peaceful and content, if not happy. What a thing it is to be a Christian minister! How glad and proud I am that Oliver is one! My landlady gave me those *Living Ages* to which I referred a few pages back. Took Plato to school and finished "Phædo." It requires close thought to follow the arguments, particularly the last one. The reasoning is like Butler's in the "Analogy" as to one or two of the points, and I think reason could not more clearly prove the immortality of the soul. I do not like to affect such contempt for the body as Socrates seems to have felt. It looks to me to have a certain dignity of its own besides that reflected upon it by its kindly occupant, and it is so fearfully and wonderfully made. The following words partake of a universal spirit in man that looks and longs for a divine revelation: "For we ought with respect to these things" (concerning the immortality of the soul), "either to learn from others how they stand, or to discover them for one's self, or if both these are impossible, then taking the best of human reasoning and that which is the most difficult to be confuted, and embarking on this, as one who risks himself on a raft, so to sail through life *unless one could be carried more safely and with less risk on a surer conveyance, or some divine reason.*" The tears came into my eyes when I wrote the lines I underscore, they seem so mournful, have such longing in them for the revelation of which Socrates lived and died in ignorance. One of the speculations in these dialogues pleased me particularly, that is the one where the philosopher inquires what will become of the souls of those who have not loved wisdom, after this life. He thinks that some may be changed into wolves, or hawks, or kites, while those of a milder type may become wasps, or ants, or even change again into the human species. I can never rid myself of the idea that a spirit alien to them, looks out of the eyes of dogs, cows, and horses I have seen. The expression is so wistful, as of those that long for something forever unattainable. It is a curious thought, of which I can not clear my mind; in its practical workings it is a good one, too, for I try always to be kind to animals, particularly those of the large, hungry eyes.

It is so cold that I am obliged to spend my evenings in the parlor downstairs with the rest, and therefore I can not write as I would, but I will do my best.

Evening.—There, I did not intend to cry during all my sojourn at Kankakee, but sitting here alone, writing to my sister Mary, I have cried like a child, no, like a strong man, rather, until I quivered with trying to suppress the sobs that would make themselves audible. I am going to copy the few sentences that had power to make a woman forget her self-reliance on such short notice, for I sat down almost gayly to write, talked on with Mary in business style until this last: "I am sorry I have nothing to tell you, and have written so much about my own little affairs, but I could hardly help it just this once. Remember I shall never live with you all at home again. In all your careless, pleasant times, think now and then of your sister that loves you, and who feels as she writes these words with tears in her eyes, that she is to have a sterner life than you will know about. I am afraid you will forget me there at home, now that I am always to be gone; and I wish you would not quite, father, mother, brother, sister, for I shall not have many to love me while I live. I know your pleasant life and how you are used to be without me, and how I was often impatient and indolent, too, perhaps. I wish I had been better. There, I did not mean to write all this, but here it is, and though it will sound strange to you coming from me, I will let it go. Oliver need not say, in his droll fashion, that this last part of my letter is all 'hypocrisy,' for I have written what I mean, though you do not know me in this character."

Sunday.—Went to church with my little pupil, Fanny. While the first hymn was being sung, my mind came into tune with the calmness and Christian quiet of the place. I believe I have a soul more susceptible to the influence of music than any one who knows me dreams of, or than I fully understand myself, for a few words played *con expressione* will thrill me strangely, and sacred music most of all. There is something so spiritual about music, so unearthly, it stirs me like a voice from purer, better regions than these of ours. It was Coleridge who said a painting was something between a thought and a thing. This definition seems to me as truly to apply to music, and when I use this word I mean music; not twanging of strings and swelling of bellows merely, but the waking up of sweet and solemn sound. No one, I think, can be truly a player who has not a fine, cultivated mind, a delicate, sensitive nature. I have friends who, when they are in loftier moods than usual, play so that the music seems simply to drop from their finger-tips upon the keys. Miss Kellogg plays Beethoven's "Spirit Waltz" that way. Five minutes of beautiful singing or playing will change my entire mental attitude, and like Philip, as George Eliot pictures him under its influence, I think "I might be capable of heroisms." Well, so it was this very morning, as the solemn bass, the mournful alto, the ringing tenor and exultant soprano united in singing:

"The whole creation joins in one
To praise the glorious name
Of Him who sits upon the throne
And to adore the Lamb."

I quite forgot my doubts and fears, my troubles and temptations, and turned a reverent, wistful face unto the Lord. A strange thing is this soul, this wonderful presence within my breast.

I told Professor Woodruff, speaking of my propensity to give away my books, that I was spasmodically generous, which he laughingly remarked was a species entirely unknown to him. I must be very dignified-appearing, for this evening a pair of young gentlemen called to see Professor Woodruff about attending the Academy. The other ladies present and I talked and laughed together about some trivial matter, after which one of the boys asked me a few questions concerning the school, which I answered promptly enough. Whereupon he inquired if I was attending school, and I answered that I was one of the teachers. The boy put his hand to his mouth and indulged in an ill-bred snicker at this. Upon relating the incident to Professor Woodruff he inquired, with well-feigned petulance, "Why don't you look older? How dare you masquerade in this false character?"

As I sat here writing the above, a neighbor came in; he is a smart sort of man, of middle age. I was not thinking about him or his talk until the following sentence was thrust in upon my reverie, "Well, this old orthodoxy is running down, running down in my opinion. I suppose everybody would not say so, but that is my way of thinking." I never heard such scandalous language before from the lips of a decent person. The poor, blind fool! I am so indignant at him that I can hardly sit here and let him go on with his ignorant, blasphemous nonsense, but I will bear it quietly unless he says something on the subject to me, and then I will declare myself instanter. I am decidedly of the church militant, I see, but I can not help it, I am so thoroughly disgusted with this man.

Subjects on which I am to write: "Mental Projectiles," "Religion," "According to Law." But what is the use of putting down these themes when I have no privacy or chance to write? When I thought up these subjects I thought up fine ideas to match them—fine ones and valuable, too, as I steadfastly believe, but I was foolish enough to imagine if the subjects were kept and remembered, the thoughts would come back to me, and the pity of it is they don't, so I look regretfully over the words full of suggestion when I wrote them first, but comparatively empty now. Have been reading of Hypatia, about whom I always think with admiration and a sort of reverential love.

October 23.—Such a kind letter from father! I am going to make an extract: "My Dear Daughter: I take up my pen a third time to write without provocation on your part, but feeling symptoms of loneliness which I presume are imparted to me through the affinities of father and child, knowing that my little 'news' will not be unacceptable." Then the dear man went on and gave me every item that would be of interest; among them, that Mr. Thatcher told him this morning that if Oliver did as well as Frank had done when she taught at Harlem, they would be perfectly satisfied. I am glad to hear that he said so, though the praise is late in the day.

October 25.—Here comes a letter from mother and here is an extract: "It gives me pleasure to learn that you are not lonely nor unhappy. Though you have not the exuberant gleefulness of the little girls whom you saw from the window that day with such a thoughtful face, I am thankful you have calmness, and quiet endurance, and something that you can almost call peace. Your excitement you must now seek in the vitalizing influences of the Holy Spirit. An infinite soul may not find contentment in the gifts of a finite world. Some writer said, 'For suffering and enduring there is no remedy but striving and doing.' This remedy you have early adopted." I thank God for my mother as for no other gift of His bestowing. My nature is so woven into hers that I almost think it would be death for me to have the bond severed and one so much myself gone over the river. She does not know, they do not any of them, the Four, how much my mother is to me, for, as I verily believe, I cling to her more than ever did any other of her children. Perhaps because I am to need her more. I am very proud of her, and few women that I have ever seen have satisfied me as she does. She has a fine intellect, and as she said to me once, in the regretful tone of one who felt the world did not know her full capacities, "I might have been a singer with the heart under more kindly circumstances."

Mary and I were talking together once and I said I could not imagine what it would be to love any one better than mother, to cling to any one more than I did to father, brother and her. The tears were almost in my eyes, I spoke so earnestly; but Mary answered lightly yet decidedly, that she believed she could love the man she should marry more than all others, and then I knew that in a few years longer my sister will love some one alien to us better than her mother who has been bone of her bone and flesh of her flesh, better than her brother and sister whom that mother has carried under her own heart; better than her father who has watched over her ever since she was born into the world, and had many an anxious thought about her even before that time. She is to love the stranger better than these who are so dear to her, and who have been faithful to her always, and who will be to the end of the world, when he may grow careless and indifferent. And it is right that she should do so, it is an instinct of God's own appointing, but my heart ached to hear her speak the words.

October 26.—Father is the cleverest of men. Just listen to him: "Dear Frances, this day I forward by American Express, care Professor Woodruff, a package directed to you, containing a book, a watch and belt fixings such as all the girls are wearing now. The watch I took out of my pocket as I would an eye out of my head, for I do not know what I am to do without it. And I hesitated some time as to what was my duty in the case without coming to any determination on that point."

The great event of this evening was Professor Woodruff's attempt to mesmerize me. He tried eighteen minutes, looking me straight in the eye, but never a bit of dazedness did he put upon me "at all at all," although I will admit he has a very peculiar eye, and two or three evenings ago when he tried it I felt a curious dizziness, everything seemed going away except his eyes and they glared at me like a serpent. My landlady's daughter came down to be mesmerized, if he could do it, and within two minutes she was unconscious. I knew her to be perfectly honest and she was greatly chagrined that he had conquered her, particularly after his laughing boasts. I have been heretofore wholly skeptical on the subject, but I am now a convert to this much: I believe it to be a species of animal magnetism, manifested under certain conditions and dependent for force upon the will of the operator. That is all Professor Woodruff claims. The symptoms all go to prove this theory. The young lady said she felt prickings in the ends of her fingers like those attending a shock from a battery.

We have most amusing times singing; Miss C. takes the soprano, Professor W. the basso, and I attempt the alto; when Sam is here he helps and we have quite a concert. "Oft in the Stilly Night," as rendered by us is really quite heart searching.

October 27.—This is Oliver's birthday. I wonder if he remembers it. I dare say not, the careless fellow! I am vexed with him for not writing, but I suppose he can hardly find time, as he is preparing for examination. Went down town with my landlady and she kindly helped me to select a dress, which I have earned with my own money, as I shall joyfully think when I wear it in school.

Later. My two boys who laughed at the idea of my being a teacher, are in one of my classes and I take great delight in magnifying my office for their illumination. Had a letter from Oliver after all; I am very proud of my brother and very thankful for him. I like him, he suits my ideas better than any other young man I have ever seen. He has delicacy, quickness of perception, cultivation of mind, and physically the look that I particularly admire. I let my hostess read the letter and as she laid it down she said, "He is a good brother, I know." I admire her sagacity and sense. I believe I will copy some of his words: "Evanston, October 20, 1860. My Dear Sister Frank: I ought to have answered your letter at once, and should have done so but for poor health, a great deal to do, and a very foolish aversion to letter writing, becoming, from long indulgence, almost insurmountable. I am disposed to make amends and hope you will accept my apology coupled with a promise to do better hereafter. I was very sorry for the incident attending our parting, for I was unconscious of an intention to injure your feelings in any respect, though part of what I said would have been better unsaid. I am glad you gave me credit for innocence of intention. As to the construction given my words, I was surely guiltless, for I never thought there was any foundation for remarks based upon the assumption that you were in any particular inferior to the rest of us, because I feel, and have always felt, the opposite. 'To err is human'—in this respect I acknowledge myself related to humanity; 'to forgive, divine,'—in this respect I am glad to believe you are affiliated with spiritual existences."

For little Fannie's amusement I have this evening become almost a child again, having an interest that surprises me in the old games of the dead years. I have ransacked my memory for stories of witches, robbers, fairies, told her about Jack and his bean-stalk, Blue Beard and Cinderella, with variations ; played all imaginable games, from the tick-tack to the labyrinth ; showed the wonderful pictures of the wolf and sand-hill crane, and closed the exhibition by achieving the Spanish student in the highest style of the art, which the bright-eyed little girl is now imitating with astonishing success.

November 4.—Anniversary of the Kankakee County Bible Association. When they took up a collection and I wrote, "F. E. W., $1, " I felt a new thanksgiving that I could earn and use money according to my own judgment. I hereby promise myself that I will give as much as I can from all my earnings to promote the doing of good in the world.

Received a letter from Amelia I., one of my former pupils at H. I smiled as I observed how careful she was to place all her capitals and punctuation marks. She is doing well and trying to learn and satisfy the hunger that is given by the gods to their favorites among men. The closing words of her letter are enough to reward me for the little I have done and shall do for her : "I thank you for your kind offer to lend me some books, and trust I shall learn much from them. Do write soon, Miss W., for it does me good to hear from my old teacher. I feel resolved to take your advice and to learn all I can and try to remember all that I learn."

November 7.—Lincoln is elected President of the United States. Hurrah ! Under the present system I was not allowed to vote for him, but I am as glad on account of this Republican triumph as any man who has exercised the elective franchise can be. It is amusing to observe the interest children take in politics. This morning Professor W. read the returns aloud, and all my little girls, some of them but six years old, crowded around and listened attentively, clapping their hands at the announcement of an unusual majority in any state. It was a curious and suggestive side-picture ; a tall gentleman reading in triumphant tones ; twenty young men around him listening eagerly ; a group of smaller boys in the rear ; several young ladies paying careful attention, and "the other teacher" looking with expectant eyes toward the newspaper, and surrounded by a dozen little girls, holding by the hand the rosebud who dances up and down exclaiming, "Are n't you glad, Miss Willard, that Lincoln is elected ?" A picture representing this scene would not inaptly indicate the genius of a Republican government, an organization in which every member, male and female, large or small, feels a keen, personal interest.

Our reading lesson to-day was about God and his goodness to us. I wished to impress it upon my pupils, and after going over the ground at some length, said by way of application, "Now, Sarah, what ought we to do when God is so kind to us ?" She looked up with a fresh sparkle in her eyes and exclaimed, "Why, pay Him for it !" Oh, we all have that idea, heaven pity us ! We can not take the gift of Christ humbly and thankfully. In all the ages men have been trying to climb up some other way to God, trying after all His love and mercy, to pay Him for it.

I gave my pupils these three questions: How do we know right from wrong? What is the difference between morality and religion? How do we know the Bible is true? My recollections of moral philosophy and "Leslie's Method with the Deists" were of great use to me in making these things intelligible. Florence listened with attentive face and flush on cheek and brow that delighted me. Nothing is so refreshing as these evidences of a thinking, reasoning mind in a child. Nothing seems so hopeful for future usefulness and growth.

My landlady has been telling me about Bunker Hill and the dedication of the monument by Daniel Webster when Lafayette was present, and the wonderful address delivered by the greatest orator of his time. I wish I had seen something of the world, and I think I shall some day.

In the evening Mr. N. called; he is a pleasant, good-hearted fellow and very entertaining. He almost terrified me by his familiarity with Beaumont and Fletcher, the poets Rogers, Pope, Addison, Dryden, etc. Talked with him in friendly fashion and rather enjoyed the evening. He is going to teach me to play chess. I lent him Plato's "Dialogues"; wonder what he will make of them.

November 13.—Was weighed to-night; result, one hundred and nineteen pounds. That is gaining more than a pound a week ever since I came here.

Evening.—Here Mr. H. sits, ridiculing the vicarious atonement and the divinity of Christ. It almost makes me shudder to hear him. I know it injures me and I know it vexes me beyond expression. What a terrible creed is this of the spiritualist! I believe it is from the bottomless pit.

My little Flora looked up discontentedly into my face to-day, and said, "Miss Willard, I want to draw, *I am suffering to draw!*" I burst out laughing, nobody could help it. Between you and me, I am not the most staid, decorous "school-marm" in the world.

November 18.—After dinner I went to Sunday-school. One of my boys came in early and said, "Were you sick that you did n't come for these two weeks?" I felt reproached and ashamed. Then he said, "I have remembered the answers to those questions all this time." The other boys came up and whispered the answers, "Paternoster," and "Apocrypha." I was sorry I had stayed away. It was on account of a headache once, and the next time some frivolous excuse, unworthy of my profession, but really they behaved terribly the last time. They said to-day they would behave like gentlemen hereafter and seriously began by being very quiet and attentive. I will try not to stay away again. I spoke in class-meeting to the following purpose: I wish I were a better woman. My conscience reproaches me for my thoughtless words and actions during the last few weeks. My life is very different now from what it was at home where every morning my father prayed that we might be guided aright. I seem to stand alone, almost, and have many new temptations.

Then the class-leader said he had thought of me often and prayed for me, had been sorry that I was away from my father and my friends. His gentle words brought the tears to my eyes. I resolved again and again to live better than I have done, and in Christ's strength to be "a good girl" as my father has so often and so kindly counseled me.

November 19.—Father says that Mary has been ill, something resembling typhoid fever. That is why she did not write. I am worried about it, poor child. I love my sister almost as I love myself, I think she is even nearer to me, though not dearer, than my mother. She seems a part of my heart. We have been together all our lives; I have no secrets from her, none in the world. I admire her for her frank, ingenuous manner, her pleasant, pretty face and fine figure. I love her for her true, good heart, her intellect and her strong good sense, but most of all for her unyielding conscientiousness, her firm religious character, her entire devotion to truth and righteousness. "Absence makes my heart grow fonder" toward her and toward them all. God pity me if any evil should befall her! If she should be cut down in her youth and her prime, while the bloom is on her cheek, the light in her eye and the luster on her brown hair! I can not conceive of anything so terrible. God will not curse me so. He will not send such a blight over my life and mother's. She is mother's youngest child. I can not bear to think of it, it makes me shudder.

Father fears I am wandering off and forgetting my allegiance to God and Christ, but he need not, I *am* trying to be good. I wrote him so to-day. If he did not love me very much he would not write me as he does.

November 21.—Letter from mother and a note from father. Mother insists that I shall spend the winter at home and not return here again. I can not tell, it will be just as I think best, but as I go through the cold and frost and bear many unpleasant things and hear unjust words sometimes, I often wonder that I do not stay at home where they love me and where I am warm and comfortable.

November 22.—Letter from father containing this comforting sentence at the conclusion: "Keep up good courage, pray in faith, and remember you have my poor prayers, as well as your mother's, every day."

We have pleasant times in our drawing-class. Besides the regular matters, we talk physiognomy. My recollections of Lavater are invaluable here. We analyze faces, hands, figures and feet, classic noses, eyes and eyebrows, disagree about the curve of the nostril, or the aristocratic elevation of an instep, define the Roman nose, studying the school generally in respect of all these and their finger-nails and hair besides. I talk Rubens, Landseer and Rosa Bonheur as well as I am able, and I think my pupils like the hour in which we do these things as well as any in the six. I have each one of them bring in a drawing from nature and reproduce the day's lesson from memory every day.

November 23.—To-day came a letter from my sister, the first she has written since her illness. She speaks more seriously than usual, proposes that we be baptized on Christmas Day. She has done a good deal of reading since I left home, and sums it up with pardonable importance. She is a smart girl and I am glad of her. Here is an extract from her letter: "My dear Frank, you did not know when you wrote your last letter that I should read it on my sick-bed. Yes, I have been quite ill, a sluggish sleep for thirty-six hours, with fever and headache, only waking up long enough to take a little medicine. I don't know as I ever was worse. I had the doctor this time and I was put in a pack, like Oliver, you know, and all the ugly doctoring things done, and so it was and so I might have died. Just think of it! And then—no, I am not ready for that. There are matters of form to be gone through with, saying nothing of the lack of polish that the jewel in its case is suffering for."

In the evening Frank N. came and gave Professor W. and me a lesson in chess playing. He says we are apt pupils and shall do well. I like the game exceedingly. It is quite intellectual, does not admit of cheating, and is the king of games. Went to the "Reading Circle" of this town and enjoyed it very much. We read "Washington's Life," by Irving. These young ladies seem well educated and quite appreciative; they are critical about pronunciation, etc., and I learned several things.

November 25.—Went to Sabbath-school and my boys seemed really unusually interested in the class. It amused me to hear them whisper among themselves, "You must be polite, *she* told us to act like gentlemen."

Monday.—We play chess all our spare time. I do not read a bit and am ashamed of myself generally. From Goethe: "Every day one ought to hear a song, to read a little poetry, to see a good picture, and, if it is possible, to say a few reasonable words." Thus we are better for everything refined and beautiful that meets us in our lives, for every flower, dewdrop and rainbow. In my working life I see these glorious things not often, but receive, with hearty, loyal gratitude, the little that falls to my share. I wish I could hear Beethoven's "Spirit Waltz" to-night. I wonder what he thought of as he played it for himself. I wonder what it said to him. I shall know some day when, on the peaceful shore, I talk with the good and great ones who have lived on earth. This faith of mine renders me patient and hopeful. There is another life than this of ours.

November 28.—Mary Hickok and her brother spent the evening with us. She beat me at chess, after which we sang the song-book through, and Frank N. came and we enjoyed ourselves in a general way till twelve o'clock. I received my first invitation to a ball, which I respectfully declined.

November 29.—Thanksgiving Day. Much to my regret, our school was not adjourned. I thought many things this morning while I heard my geography class and they were singing upstairs (the academy rooms being in the basement of the M. E. Church). Then came the prayer. I heard the minister's gentle, earnest tones thanking the Divine Father for the mercy and goodness that have followed us all the days of our lives, mingling with the words I heard from Professor W. explaining the value of x and y in an equation of three unknown quantities. I stopped my class, and we all listened with bowed heads to the prayer; my little girls were strangely silent and attentive. Though I teach to-day as usual, instead of praising God in the great congregation, yet in my heart I keep Thanksgiving, and God, who seeth not as men see and judgeth not by the outward appearance but by the intention of the heart, knows this.

Evening.—Finished Nolte's "Fifty Years in Both Hemispheres." He is a keen, quick-witted, garrulous man, with no idea of humor or decency. Much of the book concerning individual speculations and like subjects is uninteresting to me, yet I have learned a good deal from it. The letters to painters were especially attractive. It has been much fresh entertainment to read sketches of great men with whom the writer is personally acquainted, as in the present instance. Chantrey, Delaroche, Charlet, and a dozen other writers, were the author's friends. Of the latter he says that he was so strongly impressed with the face and figure of Napoleon, that he could draw him with his eyes closed. "He frequently did this for me," says Mr. N. "Once asking where he should begin, 'At the heel of the right boot,' I said. He did so, and drew the whole figure perfectly well."

December 3.—That grand student of men, Chamfort, who far surpasses the philosopher, De la Rochefoucault, remarks: "In great matters men show themselves as they wish to be seen; in small matters, as they are." I heartily indorse this sentiment, my experience with myself approves it.

December 6.—I must own that all my talk about self-abnegation is becoming every day more like poetry and less like reality. I do not try to control my temper as I did at Harlem, I do not try to grow good and noble as I really did when I first came here. True, I have very little cause for the exhibition of temper, and I do nothing really bad, as the world views it, but the glorious Christian life I know little about. Finding that loftiness and Spartan-like severity and dignity can not well be attained with my disposition in my present surroundings, I accept my lower destiny and grasp the straws, content since I can not have the roses. I am not noble-natured, I own it humbly, and with infinite regret. I descend to puny thoughts, I sing songs instead of quiet and lofty psalms, talk localisms and nonsense instead of morality and religion; play chess instead of reading history and the Bible; use amusing, quaint expressions instead of well-selected, elegant English; laugh instead of think; make efforts at satire instead of trying to control my temper; think more of doing up my hair nicely than of exerting a pure, refining influence. And thus my life goes on, my poor make-shift sort of a life. I am more sick of it than my best friends can tell. I must not be unjust with myself, I am not wicked, only thoughtless and rather degenerating even from the place to which I had attained, and yet the case has lights as well as shadows.

I have more charity for the world, more faith in it, than I ever had before. I see these people "without God and without hope in the world," exhibiting a nice sense of honor, much tenderness of conscience, and an emphatic love for justice and for truth. I see a thousand signs of nobleness and right-heartedness that I would not before have dreamed of seeing in a community of "non-professors." It enlarges my charity, my faith in mankind as such, my catholicity, my cosmopolitan spirit. Certainly this is a gain. I shall not cry, "Surely we are the people" with half the emphasis that I once put upon the words, and it is better that I should not. I see men making no profession of Christianity and yet contributing liberally to the support of the church and all its enterprises, manifesting the deepest respect for its rights and ordinances, professing the greatest reverence and regard for its institutions. I hear young ladies not bred to orthodoxy, nor affecting an experimental knowledge of its worth, murmuring their prayers each day with sincerity and faith. I see the children of careless, worldly women reverently kneel to say "Our Father," taught by their mothers. I see lying and dishonesty frowned upon and noble deeds applauded. All this in Kankakee, the most irreligious community in which I was ever placed. I walk their streets quietly and they think me a humdrum person, doubtless, but in my poor, wavering, silent heart there are, perhaps, more longings and more purposes "than they have ever dreamed in their philosophy."

Some one has said: "My conceptions were grander when they were inarticulate, in my youth, than when, in after years, they found a voice. The wave, crestless in the deep sea, swelled like a mountain; it broke in shallower water, and rippled ineffectually on the shore of utterance."

After a foolish evening I go to sleep and dreams—of dearer, holier things than I had talked about, for every heart knoweth its own sacred possessions; every heart hath its faces

"That it muses on, apart."

I am reading now Plato's "Lysis," on friendship, and the "Gorgias," on rhetoric. From the former I take this paragraph, which has in it wholesome counsel: "If then you become wise, my boy, all men will be your friends, and all friends will be attached to you, for you will be useful and good; but if you do not, neither will any one else, nor your father be a friend to you, nor your mother, nor any of your kindred."

By the noon mail a missive arrived from my school-mate X., coolly begging her "very dear friend Frank," with the "very dear" underscored, to give her some ideas of a composition to be read on a special occasion in two weeks. Oh, Finley Johnson, thou who advertisest to concoct speeches for senators, poems for freshmen, odes on "My own little boy," à la Tom Hood, for "doting parents," come to the relief of a dazed school-teacher, who amid all her other cares and troubles must take the additional one of writing a composition for a *very dear* friend. Well, I must arm myself with paper and pencil and bring to light a few scattered thoughts on the curious and flowery theme, "The living strive, the dead alone are glorious."

Never be afraid to question your author, and to stop him in his loftiest thoughts and profoundest depths with the question, "Is it so?"

That is a beautiful idea contained in the writings of Schiller, I believe, that "deprived of earth's gifts by want of alacrity in suing for them, the poet received from Jove the key of heaven." Happy poet! In having this he has all things, and can well afford to miss the joys of common folks.

December 16.—Taught my school with a joyful heart, I am going home so soon. Went to the book store for prizes for my Sunday-school class. Professor W. wrote a commendatory letter to father about me. Now, evening, having regaled myself upon the Chicago daily *Tribune*, I will devote the remainder of the time to the study of Agnew's "Book of Chess," and to

mental congratulations of this character: "Well, you are going home, going home in two or three days; your hard times will all be over. You will see your mother and father, your sister and brother, and all the kind well-wishers that you count among the inhabitants of dear, delightful Evanston. You will see the old, familiar rooms, and the lake, and the college, and the church. You will sleep in your own little room with your sister by your side, and your cousin not far off—your bright cousin Sarah, *Lottie's* sister. So thank God, and be sorry that you have not better deserved the blessings He is showering on your head." This is the melody of my life, all else is but seeming, and variations upon this beautiful reverie.

December 18.—Attended my classes and walked to and from school through rain and mud unutterable. I sent to Chicago yesterday for prizes for my Sunday-school boys, to-day went to the depot and wrote their names in their books. They met me there, and as fast as this was done, the graceless little scamps snatched their "winnings" and scampered off without as much as "By your leave," much less, "Thank you." Such an instance of unkindness and ingratitude I have not seen in a long time.

Quotation from our reading lesson at school: "That which each man can do best, no one but his Maker can teach him. Insist on yourself, never imitate. Every great man is a unique." (Emerson's "Essay on Self-reliance.")

Packed my trunk to-night, and so it is almost all over, and I am going home.

December 21.—An awful snow-storm has commenced. I walked through the drifts to school. The elements seem determined to wreak their vengeance upon me to the last. Well, let them, they have but a little longer.

Here are some lines written by Stillingfleet that contain "my doctrine," as father says:

"Would you both please and be instructed, too,
Watch well the rage of shining to subdue.
Hear every man upon his favorite theme,
And ever *be* more knowing than you seem."

Evanston, December 26.—I doubt if there is a person living who has greater cause for thankfulness than I have. I am in my little room once more; the fire burns brightly; the old, familiar furniture is about me; the pictures look down benignly from the walls; my sister Mary sits at my feet, writing in her funny, off-hand journal; my cousin "Sac" sits opposite; my brother in his room across the hall is writing a sermon; down-stairs father and mother gather cozily around the home hearth, and with heart brimming full of thankfulness, I come to Thee, Father of every good and perfect gift.

CHAPTER III.

THE PUBLIC SCHOOLS IN HARLEM AND IN EVANSTON.

(1861-1862.)

In the spring of 1861 I once more taught Harlem school for a few weeks. Here at the Thatcher homestead, "Shady Dell," came in June the climax that I then thought would close my independent career. But in the following February that spell was broken and I resumed the spelling-book in April of the same year.

The first I knew about the war was when my father came home from Chicago, April 13, 1861, in an agony of mind, saying, "Fort Sumter has been fired upon and our flag is there no longer." This produced great consternation in our household. When I think of the love that fills my heart toward the Southern people in general and my own great circle of friends there in particular, I can hardly believe that I exhausted language in anathemas upon them when this news came. Soon after, the Bull Run defeat showed us what we did not till then believe, that we had foemen worthy of our steel! Up to that time we looked with disdain upon "the lily-handed Southrons" and thought that General Scott would soon teach them the difference between "a lot of idlers" and the horny-handed and lion-hearted soldiers of the North. After that terrible defeat the students in the University immediately formed a company commanded by Alphonso C. Linn, one of the truest of men and a favorite teacher there, who left us with a thousand blessings on his noble head and returned to us no more. A company was also formed among the theological students in which my brother enlisted for one hundred days, but they were not called out. All the relatives I had were too old to go as soldiers except my brother and two cousins; the latter had dependent families, my brother was never physically vigorous, and I am compelled to admit that we were well content that the company to which he belonged was not called away from home. I used to be sorry at the time that none of my kindred, so far as I knew, was in the army, but I can not say at this distance that I am now, and while I know that if my understanding of the Southern people had then been what it now is, I should have felt altogether different toward them, I have the poor satisfaction of knowing that they anathematized us as bitterly as we did them! It grated strangely on my ear when the first Sunday trains I ever knew rumbled by loaded with soldiers from my own Wisconsin. The day is fresh in memory when Gen. Julius White, on Sunday morning after church, stood up in his pew near the altar and made an impassioned speech calling upon all patriots to convene in the church the next night and declare what they were going to do to save the country. They came; the old "meeting-house" was filled to overflowing and our hearts beat fast when students whom we knew and thought much of, went up the aisle and placed their names upon the muster-roll. Governor Evans presided, and he with other rich men and many not so rich, pledged large sums to the families of those who agreed to go to the front. I was a young school-teacher, but according to my narrow income, perhaps I gave as generously as any. I would have given myself to care for the wounded, indeed, was earnestly desirous of so doing, but my father would not for a moment listen to such an idea, and I must say mother was not particularly heroic in that connection. But we scraped lint and prepared bandages; went to all the flag-raisings, Professor Jones's College flinging the first one to the breeze, and we prayed the God of battles to send freedom to the slave.

In 1862, the Public School of Evanston was my theater of action. Dr. Bannister, professor of Hebrew in our Theological Seminary, was a director. Meeting him on the sidewalk near his own door, I asked him for the place. He thumped meditatively with his cane, then said, abruptly, "Are you sure that you can do it, Frank?" All my forces rallied on the instant in the words, "Try me and see!" His daughter was my associate, and ours was a difficult portion; two young women essaying to teach their neighbors' children in the town where they themselves were lately students.

My journal says:

April 20, 1862.—This is the hardest work I have yet done. There are two rooms, eighty pupils, thirty-two classes, of which we teachers have six apiece that are "high." I study on my mathematics all the time I can possibly get out of school hours. I have algebra, and arithmetic away over in the back part of the book. It is almost impossible to keep order, but we do our best and have *hope*, though every night we *ache*.

We had two big overgrown pupils, "the O. boys," who had been a terror to all preceding pedagogues. Their open insubordination one day obliged me to go toward them with a stick, whereupon both vaulted out of an open window and we never saw them more! The school was a thoroughly American type. There sat the sons and daughters of men cultured, distinguished, rich, beside the barefoot boy and girl from humble cabins, and melodiously their voices mingled as they sang Coates Kinney's lovely song:

"When the humid shadows gather
Over all the starry spheres,
And the melancholy darkness
Gently weeps in rainy tears,
O 'tis sweet to press the pillow
Of a humble cottage bed,
And to listen to the patter of the raindrops overhead,
To the patter, patter, patter of the raindrops overhead."

Their fingers drumming gently on the desks, in imitation of the falling rain, helped to make the sweetest music that my teaching years recall.

April 25.—We try to teach well and to do good. Dear knows I "give my whole mind to it," to say the least. Aunt Sarah has been with us all winter, and is my main-stay in mathematics. She thinks it would be beautiful for me if I could go East to teach next fall, and will do her best for me. She has considerable influence with Mrs. Stanton, principal at Leroy, and some leading ladies in Rochester. It looks pleasant to me to think of carrying out this plan.

May 11.—School goes well, is very hard, but can be compassed. Some of the pupils I love. I play ball with them at recess and "spell them down" myself, or take one "side" and put them all in competition with me on the other, to enliven the proceedings.

At devotions in the morning, when I read and pray before them I feel their weight a little, and a thrilling desire to help them toward eternal life.

It is hard for me to conduct devotions, yet I prize this possibility of doing good.

Among other things I teach natural philosophy, botany and physiology.

If I were not often beclouded by physical weariness I should always thank God, every moment, that I am *of use.* I think I have a rather healthful nature and I get on comfortably with life. To-night Freddy Huse brought me a little bouquet arranged after his own fashion. He did not know how grateful it was nor how it stirred my heart to hear him say, "We've missed you very much in Sabbath-school." It was a simple, boyish sentence, but I have felt better ever since, and I think hardly so tired.

I had not been able to take my class as usual because my sister Mary was not well and my Sunday afternoons were passed with her.

Mary getting better very slowly—it is a painfully familiar sight—her thin face on the pillow, when I come in from school.

We talked a little, she and I, about old times at home, before any of us had other loves than those of the dear ones there. She said, "I have never been so happy as when we used to 'keep store' under the trees, and go walking with father and mother in the orchard and pasture. Just think, Frank, of the vine all over the house, of the splendid well, the evergreens, the animals of all sorts, and the dear old barn!" She is so anxious to go back—says she shall never get well unless we take her home. Just as soon as she can bear it, mother will go with her.

I have "inspirations" about the old home. Some day I shall write a pleasant book about it. I have believed I should, for years.

May 30.—Every day school grows pleasanter, and I think a little easier. I have such a liking for Emma, Minnie, Ella, Eda and her sisters; Darwin, Harry, Verner and many more. And my pupils like me, too, I think.

Nine days after this, June 8, 1862, I lost out of this life my sister Mary. The record of her life is fully given in "Nineteen Beautiful Years."

June 8, 1862.—*Mary is dead.* I write the sentence—stop and look at it—do not know what it means. For God is merciful and the awful truth of my desolation does not shut down close around me all the time; it comes in paroxysms and goes again.

At the request of Dr. Bannister, who will preach the funeral sermon, I shall write out many of the things that she has said during her illness—and at her death. Sweetness, purity and childlikeness were remarkable features throughout her trial. She expected to recover almost down to the last hour, and her most ardent wish was to get well enough to go to Forest Home, where she had spent her childhood. The very night she died she told us to talk about returning there. She used to say, "I never have had such pleasant times as when Frank and I were children and used to play among the trees and in the garden." The physician considered her hopefulness her best symptom, so we did not talk to her of dying, though of Christ and of religion a great deal. She used to wander in her sleep, and often thought she was a child again. One night when I slept with her, she put her hot hand against my face and said, "You're with me in the trundle-bed, Frank, as you used to be, are n't you?" And that night she thought she was talking with Emma White (one of her Sunday-school scholars), and she said, "Emma, I hope you remember your promises made in Sabbath-school, and read the Bible, and pray, and try to set a good example, and don't think too much about this poor world, but about that wonderful, wonderful, infinite world where God is. And remember that where your treasure is, there will your heart be also—so you can easily tell whether you are right or not. And don't worry about joining the church, but ask that kind man, Mr. Goodrich, to put your name on some of the class-books and then be proud to be a Christian, and to have it known that you are, and not be like people who say, 'I'm not *ashamed* to own my Lord' when they ought to feel *so* honored."

She seemed anxious to do good and worried for fear she had not. Once she said to mother, "I would like to be well if only for one day, so that I could do some good to some one. I've never done any, unless a little in my Sabbath-school class, and I am not quite sure about that. I've tried to learn, and to improve, and to prepare myself to be useful, and now I'd like to live and do something in the world."

She thought much about the kindnesses shown by her friends. Bouquets, notes, messages, were received so joyfully. She was thinking about these things one day and said to me, "How good people are to me; how thoughtful and kind! Oh, Frank, humanity, humanity, what a wonderful thing!"

On the last day of her life she was lying with her head in father's lap and she asked to have the Bible read. He said, "Where shall I read?" She told him, "Oh, where it makes Christ seem beautiful!" He read a psalm. She said, "Please read where it says Christ was sorry for sick folks."

Father read about the healing of the daughter of Jairus. She liked it, but when he had finished her plaintive voice cried out, "Please read where it says He is sorry now." After awhile she added, "We believe that God loves us better than our mothers; yet mother would have liked me to get well, and God does n't seem to care—He does n't seem to see fit to make me well—yet He knows what is right." In the night she was worse. She wanted everything still; kept moving her hands in a soothing, caressing way, and murmuring, "So quiet, so quiet, no noise, so quiet!" At four o'clock on the morning of the eighth of June, Sabbath morning, we became greatly alarmed and for the first time father and I decided that she could not get well. I went at his suggestion for Mrs. Bannister and Mary. Father said to our Mary, for the first time coming directly to the subject of her danger, "My child, if God should think it best to take you to Himself should you be afraid to go?" She looked quickly at him with a rather pitiful face, she seemed to consider a moment, and then said in her low, mournful voice,

"I thought I should like to get well for I am young; but if God wants me to go I should n't be much afraid, but should say, 'Take me, God.'" We asked if there was anything that we could do for her. "Pray," she said, "pray thankful prayers." Mother asked her if she saw Christ, if He was near her. "Yes, I see Him" she said, "but He is not very near, I wish He would come nearer."

I asked her if we should pray, she said "Yes," and I prayed aloud that Christ would come close to her, that she might see and feel Him plainly, that since she had tried to love and obey Him, He would come right to her now in her great need. She clasped her hands together and said so joyfully, "He's come, He's come! He holds me by the hand, He died for me, He died for all this family, father, mother, Oliver, Frank" (and Mary Bannister says she added, "my dear sister").

"I'll have Him all to myself," she said and then seemed to remember and added, "I'll have Him and everybody may have Him, too—there is enough for everybody. He is talking to me, He says 'She tried to be good, but she wandered, but I will save her,'" and added, "I see Him on the cross, He died for the thief; He did n't die for good people, but for bad people; He died for me." I said, "I want to ask you to forgive me for all my unkind actions to you, for everything bad that I ever did to you." She answered very earnestly, "Oh! I do, but you never did anything bad, you were always good." Mother asked her if she did not wish to leave a message for Oliver. "Don't you think he will be with us in heaven?" she said; "Of course, he is working for God. Tell him to be good, and to make people good," and when I asked for a message for her Sunday-school class she said, "Tell them to be good," and then added with great earnestness, "*Tell everybody to be good.*"

She said to us, looking so sweet and loving, "I wish I was strong enough—I'd like to talk good to you."

Almost at the last she said, with a bright smile on her face, "Oh! I'm getting more faith!" Mother questioned, "My darling, you will meet us, won't you, at the Beautiful Gate?" "Oh, yes! and you will all come, and father. Christ wants you right off!"

She moved her hands convulsively and said, "I've got Christ—He's right here!" Then she said to me, "Oh, I'm in great misery," and then, "Dear God, take me quick!" She held out her hands and said, "Take me quick, God—take me on this side," turning toward the right. She lay still, bolstered up by pillows; I asked if she knew me, and she repeated my name. Father asked her often if Christ was still near her, she would nod, but did not speak. She seemed troubled, after a few moments father bent over her and slowly and with difficulty she told him of her dread of being buried alive and he promised her over and over again that she should not be. Then she gave some little directions about preparing her bed, as she said, "For those who lay me out," showing her perfect consciousness. She never spoke again, but opened her eyes and looked at us with such intentness, the pupils so wide, the iris so blue. I never saw such soul in human eyes before. She groaned a little, then, and for some time she did not move, her eyes closed slowly, her face grew white. Father said, "Lord Jesus, receive her spirit; Lord, we give her back to Thee. She was a precious treasure, we give her back to Thee." Mrs. Bannister closed Mary's eyes. Father and mother went into the sitting-room and cried aloud. I leaned on the railing at the foot of the bed and looked at my sister—my sister Mary—and knew that she was dead, knew that she was alive! Everything was far off; I was benumbed and am but waking to the tingling agony.

August 21.—O dear! I don't know what it is that I would like to say. I am crowded with feeling, and it was never before so plain to me that I am without power of expression. "*Mary did' nt get well,*" that is the key-note to all my thoughts. I was so sure she would; I refused to think it possible that she could die. And now under the experiences that crowd upon me faster than ever before, like a wave, the consciousness of what has happened us flows back and forward in my heart, and put in words it all amounts to this: "She is dead. Mary is dead. Her hands are on her breast so cold and still; she takes no note of us, or any thing; and she used to be so merry, so full of motion; she was always with us, she never went away."

Oh! this has crushed out all other feelings, except a vague sense of incompleteness, of wanting some one, some thing—of reaching out toward the future life almost with yearning. Sometimes I don't look upon her as dead—I ought not to have said so. And oh! last Sabbath evening when we walked up to church, all that is left of us, father, mother and I, so clear and beautiful I saw her in her unconditioned life—somehow, somewhere, so radiant, so painless, so secure—very near to Christ, the glorious, satisfying Christ, and perfectly complete in heart and life, thinking of us, knowing that it will not be long till we shall come. And I was quite content to go to church, to pray and trust and work awhile longer and then I believed I should go, too. It is His will, He is as well pleased with us who pray as with those who praise; with us who try as with those who triumph. This is one stage, it is all arranged by Him. The time will be brief, the eternity will pay all, will give us what we missed here, will round everything to symmetry. All this if we love and trust the Father of our souls, and do as well as we can what He has given us to do. And Mary is the favored one, not sleeping in the grave, but conscious as we are, only so well off, so glorified, so restful. It may be only a fancy, yet I think I shall be with her before many of our little years are past. O Father of my spirit, take it to Thyself, any time, any where, only love it, take care of it. Let it see Christ and Mary.

Sept. 1.—I have been to the old home, Forest Home, since I wrote last. Mary was to have gone there, Mary wished to go more intensely than any of us—spoke of it not more than two hours before she died. The place is sold now. Mary did not live to see it go out of our hands, she never mourned a friend lost by estrangement or by death, and no reverses ever came to her.

CHAPTER IV.

"PRECEPTRESS OF THE NATURAL SCIENCES."

We were so heart-broken after my sister left us, that a few weeks later the old home was given up and by the kindness of Professor Jones I went to the Northwestern Female College, whence I had graduated three years earlier, as teacher of the natural sciences.

My brother was married July 3, 1862, about four weeks after my sister's death, to her class-mate and my friend, Mary Bannister, and their home was in Denver, Col., for several years, where he founded the M. E. Church and Seminary, and was a Presiding Elder when but twenty-seven years old. Thus unbefriended and alone, for the first time in my life homeless and for the first bereft, I returned to the scene of my girlish escapades a thoughtful, chastened woman—at least I thought so, but my pupils of those days declare, to my astonishment, that I was "full of fun." Surely, they did not know my heart as here revealed:

August 29, 1862.—On Monday I move over to my Alma Mater, the Northwestern Female College. I am elected "Preceptress of Natural Sciences." Very humbly and sincerely I pray to God that I may be good over there and do good. I was wild and wicked as a pupil; in the same building may I be consistent and a Christian as a teacher. The last days are passing in this broken home. Life changes so, Thy heart must ache for us, O God, but that Thou knowest we are soon to enter the unchanging home. I have been at camp-meeting four days. It is a glorious place, I love it dearly. God has brought me nearer to Himself. My Sunday-school girl, Jennie, is trying to be good, and her noble sister Hattie, and ever so many more. What names I could write here of those for whom I pray and hope, who have not yet come to the light. Help me to act aright in these my new relations! I want to live a good life and get ready to go to my sister in heaven. I am afraid that Mary's death will kill my mother.

August 31.—

"Man may trouble and distress me,
'Twill but drive me to Thy breast.
Life with trials hard may press me,
Heaven will bring the sweeter rest."

September 2.—Sitting in my room at the "Female College," a teacher regularly installed in a ladies' school. The sensation is agreeable. I have a natural love of girls, and to have them around me as pupils and friends will be delightful. To think that I am sitting here in the room that was Luella Clark's, my poet friend, as much a teacher as herself; my dear old books around me, my pictures and familiar things; and then such admirable girls to teach, Emma, Hattie, and the rest. Went for the last time to the class-meeting of which I am so fond, at Dr. Bannister's, since I must as a teacher attend here at the college. George Strobridge led it. Kate Kidder and Josephine Evans came home with me here to the steps below.

September 7.—Sabbath evening. My first Sabbath in the college. All the teachers are at church except myself. It is sweet and full, busy and fatiguing, at once, the life I lead. In the parlor to-night, how beautiful was the grouping after tea: the graceful figures of the girls, Miss Fisk at the piano, Captain Jones with his wife, Dr. Charlie, and spiritual-faced Professor with his wife, and the children, all of them soon to start for China, where Professor has been appointed consul; the kind old father and mother looking on contentedly at their three handsome sons; the folding-doors affording glimpses of the piazzas; music in the air. I liked it. The bell rang for church, the picture dissolved. Professor did not die, as we all thought he would last winter. He is well and going on a voyage half around the world. Mary, my sister Mary, who went with me to see him in his illness, took that longest of all voyages in his stead!

Am reading Peter Bayne's "Christian Life." It will help me to prepare to go to Mary. I wish everything might.

September 8.—After school hours I ached—there are so many flights of stairs, forty in a day or more. Went home at dinner time. Father and mother are soon to go away. Oh, mother, with your sad, sad face, and your black dress! Heaven has much to restore to you for all your weary years! I pray God to show me how I can be most comforting to you, how I can justly fill an only daughter's place. Life reaches out many hands for me, with manifold voices. I am intensely alive. I, who am to lie so still and cold beside my sister Mary.

Sabbath morning, September 14.—Sitting in my room dressed in a pretty black silk wrapper that mother and Miss Burroughs made. The autumn sunlight is pouring in. I am here, but Mary, who was always with me, where is she? The question mocks me with its own echo. Where is she who was so merry, who knew the people that I know, who studied the books that I study, who liked "Bleak House," who laughed at Micawber and Traddles and read the daily *Tribune*. Where is she who picked up pebbles with me by the lake and ran races with me in the garden; who sang Juniata and Star-spangled Banner? She was so much alive, I can not think of her as disembodied and living still. Then there is that horrible doctrine held by many who are wise and good, that the soul is unconscious until the resurrection. That idea worries me not a little. Then, too, I am coming right straight on to the same doom: I, who sit here this bright morning, with carefully made toilet, attentive eyes, ears open to every sound I, with my thousand thoughts, my steady-beating heart, shall lie there so still, so cold and for so long. It is coming toward me every moment, such a fate as that! But my religion tells me that my life shall be unending. One interpretation of my creed says that consciousness shall be uninterrupted both here and there, that fruition awaits us in the years where every minute shall be full of overflowing and nothing shall have power to disappoint. How much a human heart can bear, and how it can adjust itself! Four months ago to-day I thought if Mary died I should be crazed; it made me shiver just to take the thought on my brain's edge, and yet to-day I think of Mary dead just as naturally as I used to think of her alive. Yet God knows how well I loved my sister and how deeply she is mourned. Here on a piece of blotting paper I keep in my book is her name written over and over again in her careless round hand. She used to borrow this same piece of paper to dry the fresh pages of her own journal not many weeks ago. Oh, dainty little hand, I should not like to touch you now!

September 17.—This young person, F. E. W., reports herself tired and proceeds to show cause therefor. Rose a little after six, made my toilet for the day and helped to arrange the room; went to breakfast, looked over the lessons of the day, although I had already done that yesterday; conducted devotions in the chapel; heard advanced class in arithmetic, one in geometry, one in elementary algebra, one in Wilson's "Universal History"; talked with Miss Clark at noon; dined, rose from the table to take charge of an elocution class, next zoölogy, next geology, next physiology, next mineralogy, then came upstairs and sat down in my rocking-chair as one who would prefer to rise no more! Now I have to-morrow's lessons to go over.

September 18.—I have the sorrow to write here that Forest Home is sold. The time has been when I could not for a moment have contemplated the probability of its passing into other hands than ours who created and who loved it. Alas for the changes of the great year of my history, 1862. I am to lose sight of the old, familiar landmarks, old things are passing from me whose love is for old things. I am pushing out all by myself into the wide, wide sea.

"The shadow of a great rock in a weary land."

October 3.—My twenty-third birthday has come and gone without even a passing remark. On Monday my brother Oliver started for Denver Col., after having been ordained a Methodist minister, at Joliet, by Bishop Baker. Mother is going East to see our relatives; she greatly needs the change. Father will board in Chicago this winter, probably, and for the first time in my life I shall have no home. There is a grave in Rose Hill cemetery; most of these changes may be traced to it as their cause.

"The same fond mother bent at night
O'er each fair sleeper's brow;
She had each folded flower in sight,
Where are those dreamers now?"

October 11.—Have been ill a week since I wrote last. Dear, unforgetful mother has nursed me up again. It almost paid to be sick to have people so sweet and mindful. My girls were marvels of loving kindness. Well, I conclude that I can not stand very much, not so much as I supposed. I am just a trifle discouraged to-night about the prospect before me. I thought this last week as I lay in the bed, that perhaps God, seeing how I wonder about that other life, would let me out into it, and it would seem so natural to my sister Mary to have me with her once again. I refresh myself little with reading nowadays. Miss Clark and I corrected the compositions all the evening. I stipulated for Ada's in my lot. Ada, dear, refined girl, fit to be Charles Gifford's sister. I like the ideal, Heaven is that! We get hints of it here though, some of us. Luella Clark does and it is her chief charm for me. Things are not so endlessly commonplace to her as they are to most folks. A red leaf out of the woods, a bouquet, a cluster of grapes, these are a great deal to her. She puts her ear close down to nature, listens and hears. I wish I might do this more, but then I shall when mortality drops off, and I have those acute, tense senses of my spiritual self that Swedenborg tells us of, and I believe him. Ella Simpson, dear unfailing friend, for all these years, has had my classes while I have been ill. Dr. Tiffany is our minister and I am more thankful than I can express for the prospect of hearing good preaching once more.

October 12.—Up here in my room, while the people go to church, I watch the long procession of young ladies file out along the walks and through the trees. The gate under the pretty arch bangs together as the last one passes through. One of my pupils, Josie, is sitting with me, and I have made her talk, trying to draw her out a little, in a friendly way, asking her if she likes her studies, if she likes to learn new things, if she likes to read refined books, if she loves people, if she tries to make them love her, if she tries to do them good, if she has ambitions and what she expects from life. She answers with frankness and enthusiasm. There is rare delicacy in the girl. Then we sit by the window in her room. This was Mattie Hill's once, and in it I have played many a school-girl prank. I tell Josie so as we sit here. She lets me into the history of her life, which has been sorrowful, and we make a few wondering remarks over God's providences. Then we talk a little of being good, and I speak somewhat of my sister Mary, and how she lived and died, while I get a little nearer in heart to pretty, sad-faced Josie. As I turn to leave her room, she kisses me, and says, "You are the first one that has talked to me about being good since I have been in this school. I wish you would do so often." I go back to my room, praying that God may make me well again, and that I may love all these girls and they me, and that I may do them only good. Then I sit down cozy and contented to read Harbaugh's "Sainted Dead," looking out often at the window on the bright trees and sunshine of this pleasant, pleasant world, thinking my thoughts between the author's sentences, and feeling very full of wonder about my sister Mary. I learn that this author thinks heaven is a place somewhere far away, and that the soul never sleeps, not even for a single moment, and I find this sweet quotation: "*Selig sind die das Himmelreich haben, denn sie sollen nach Hause kommen.*" (Blessed are they who have heaven within them, for they shall come home.)

I think the book has not a page worth that. I read a chapter in my German Testament, "Come unto me, all ye that labor and are heavy laden." Then the folks come back from church, and my queer little pupil, Lizzie B. comes to my room. I ask Miss Fisk, my room-mate, about the sermon, she comments briefly, the bell rings, and they all go down to dinner. My room-mate brings me mine in her quiet, kindly way, and Misses Harvey, Sewall and Bunnell sit around me while I eat. I like the toast, and have some zest for the delicate, amber-colored jelly. Miss Sewall tells me of her home between the two Miami rivers. Miss Holmes comes in to get excused from "Biblical Antiquities." My dear Luella Clark enters with the last *Repository*, and Dr. Johnson's book of sermons labeled "Consolation." She tells me she went "way up to Professor Noyes' for the book on purpose to read from it to me." How very kind she has been to me always, when I was a pupil and now when we are both "faculty folks"! The girls go off to Sunday-school, Miss Clark sits with me and we talk. She gets me to wrap up, and we go to walk in the garden, for she thinks a sun bath is what I need. Swedenborg's book is in her hand, brought at my suggestion, and she reads here and there as we sit on the stile, while we talk of the Swedish seer and his professed revelations. I incline to look with favor on it all, and say, "Why should not God in some way supplement that mysterious apocalypse of John; for we are all longing to know more about the other life—at least I am, in these days." She says Swedenborg's belief is too materialistic, but his ideas of special providences she likes exceedingly. A little gray cat comes and sits by us. We wonder at the graceful little creature, and fall into a dozen queries over it, for we are in a querying mood. Miss Clark takes it up in her arms, smooths its fur, and says, "Poor creature! You noticed us and followed us with your big, curious eyes. You make the very best of life you can; you like to jump and play about, and it grieves me to think how your life will all flicker out after a little, not to revive again." Then I tell her how fond I am of the kind old "Country Parson" ("A. K. H. B."), and repeat what he said to his horse, "Old Boy," out in the stable, in that genial, generous passage with this sentence in it: "For you, my poor fellow-creature, I think with sorrow, as I write upon your head, there remains no such immortality as remains for me." Then Miss Clark tells me anecdotes about her pets when she was a little child, away off in New England, where I have never been. I fall to wondering about this strange Being who made the little cat and gave to her feet their active motion, who pushed out of the ground the little flower that Miss Clark plucked for me from the borders as she walked, who made my favorite heliotrope. I hold two leaves of it on the palm of my hand, one green with sap, one black with frost, and wonder at the difference between the two. I see the leaves dying on the beautiful trees of the college grove, and I wonder what God thinks as He sees this world that He has made, and we poor, blind creatures groping along through it. Then I remember that "God is love," and that thought quiets me. We go into the house, up to my room again, and Miss Clark begins to read to me from the book she brought. Soon comes a low rap at the door, and my friend Emma enters, a very welcome visitor to me, with her refined face and large gray eyes. Pretty soon my pupil Lizzie comes in, for a chance to read her Bible in peace, I guess, and then the smart Bishop girls bring me news that Dr. Tiffany heard my "Biblical Antiquities" class at church, telling me who had their lessons and who had not. Then my friend Ella Simpson, tried and true, with Mollie Ludlam appear upon the scene; soon after, Mary, my kind sister-in-law. Now I will lay aside this writing and try to go to sleep. I pray God to make me well again, to take away my uncertain, ghostly feelings, and to restore to me something of the zest and enthusiasm that have always been my portion. And oh, above all other things, may I rest in the belief that Thou art love!

Northwestern Female College, January 1, 1863.—"Abraham Lincoln has fulfilled the pledge, the slaves are free," so said Father Jones to-night, coming down late to tea, and on the instant all the girls clapped their hands so heartily that it was fine to see and hear them, and far down in my heart something stirred, some chord was struck that gave out music. How much there was to think about just then! Our girls sitting there so well kept as they are, so good looking, so happy and contented, with the thought in their heads that four million of wretched beings became this day constitutionally free, and the feeling in their hearts of what a gift this freedom is to a human soul. It was a thing that thrilled me beyond my power to tell, one that I am thankful has transpired in my experience, and that I shall think over with frequent pleasure.

The future rises before me misty, dark, moist, like an advancing wave. Steadily I march toward it, there is no help, and God is in it, God who manages affairs. My soliloquy was: "F. E. W., why do you plan to go on teaching ad infinitum, now here, now there, and then some other where? Why do you content yourself with such a hedged-up life, with acquiring money so slowly, with an allotment so obscure? There is no need of it. You have abilities for something beyond this. Don't cheat yourself out of your rights. Do you know that sometimes as you help arrange the room, or make your toilet, or take your solitary walks, you think of splendid paragraphs that you never write out—idle creature that you are? Do you know that you have a great many kind, fresh, beautiful thoughts that you never tell? Do you know that new and striking comparisons come to you, and pleasant, queer ideas, and you let them pass in and out, leaving not even a sedimentary deposit there. Stir yourself; be determined to write books if you please. Why not? Be intent upon it. Your flight of usefulness might be very much extended. God thinks it right to have ambitions; you are on the earth, now deal with the earthy, 'feel the victory in you,' that is your father's quaint, expressive phrase. And now, to be pointed and make the application, write next year, write. It is nonsense to think you can not do it while you are teaching. You expect to visit Boston in the summer. Take to that city an essay on the writings of William Mountfort, an essay on a tolerant spirit, a novelette entitled 'Philip,' and a chastely written memoir of your sister Mary. Now, do this without fail. You can.

CHAPTER V.

PITTSBURGH FEMALE COLLEGE.

(1863-1864.)

Several persons have stood at the parting of the roads for me, and almost all of them have been animated finger-posts pointing towards a better and an upward path. Mrs. Bishop Simpson was the first whose presence brought to me a greatly widened circle. The Bishop had lived for several years only one street from us, and the young people of the two families had been quite intimate. The Bishop, though at home only during brief intervals was the central figure and beloved hero of the town, where during his three or four years' residence he preached and lectured not less than thirty times. His eldest daughter, Ella, more like himself than any other of his children, was a school friend and companion in many a pleasant, confidential ramble through the woods and down by the lake shore. Now when my sister's mystical departure had changed all, and my parents were so heart-broken that they went away and boarded in Janesville, and afterwards in Chicago, while I was teaching, in this small, rudimentary way, I found what friends I had in this now historic family. Heartsick and homesick I had taken to my bed, and from very listlessness seemed disinclined to leave it. Hearing of this, Mrs. Simpson came down to see me, and in her emphatic tones said to me, "Frank, it is absurd for you to stay here in one village all your days. My husband is President of the Board of Trustees of Pittsburgh College; it is a fine, large institution in the heart of a leading city noted for the remarkably good health of the inhabitants. Now, you just have your trunk packed and be ready to start within a week, for I am sure we can arrange it so that you can have classes to hear, enough, at least, to pay all your expenses and doubtless something more." Her words did me a world of good. I consulted with the faculty, of which I was a junior member, and they agreed to let me go, so that a new world opened before me as widely different from anything heretofore known as is conservative Pennsylvania, with its mountains, mines and valleys, from the broad prairies and progressive spirit of the West.

The new life will best be told in its own vernacular, as my journal sets it down:

PITTSBURGH FEMALE COLLEGE, January 26, 1863.

"Give battle to the leagued world;
If thou art truly brave
Thou shalt make the hardest circumstance
A helper or a slave."

Very aimlessly I have scrawled the above heading. Very aimlessly now I am racing my new "Gillott" across the first page of Journal Book No. 17. Sitting here in Doctor Pershing's office, in his easy-chair with the writing-table attachment, coal glowing in the grate, teams passing through the muddy street outside, the tinkling of the school pianos in my ears mingling with the voices of the girls in the halls, sitting here thus surrounded I thank God for life,—for life continued on the earth. My last winter day, may be gliding away from me now just as our Mary's were one year ago, when we laughed and studied together. Next January my grave may be curved under the snow as now her's is, oh, Mary! But now I live, I am surrounded with matter, or, to put it more truly, I am a spirit enshrined in matter, and for this I am thankful, I hardly know why. Perhaps simply because it is so natural. I am glad I came here, I am to like it, I know. By-and-by I, who am a stranger here, may find sweet friends and be called by beautiful, endearing names, and I am to learn much that is new and good; indeed, I have already. I mean to do my best to be as good a teacher as my abilities will permit, and to win the love and respect of these strangers to myself, if it be possible. I wish to made it a happy thing for some of them that I came here among them, and not a thing unpleasant for any one. This first Monday of my new experience, my classes have gone off creditably and I am not dissatisfied with the result of the day's effort. Before it was light, nice Fanny Fish, my room-mate, and I, rose, dressed and went to devotions in the chapel before breakfast. Professor Johnson, a refined, sweet little man—whom, with his wife I greatly like, indeed, I like him rather better—read and prayed. After breakfast we returned to our room and did our work. Then I went to smart Miss Scull's room and together we called on Miss Teel; the first is the head teacher among the ladies, the second is teacher of drawing and painting. By much maneuvering we arranged to have Miss Scull take the arithmetic, for which I have no "call," and I am to take her class in elocution. What a weight went off my shoulders then! I looked over my geometry, history, etc. Being the youngest teacher I have no school-room to superintend.

Genesee
Wesleyan Seminary
My
First School House
Harlem - 1860.
New School
Harlem.
Pittsburgh Female College.

"The Open Secret" fascinates me; sometimes it looms up misty and awful for a moment, but when I fairly look, it has disappeared unread. Habitude is its safe mask. And that is one reason why habits seem half hateful to me, but I know this is not right. Oh, if I could but see! Two afternoons ago I was upon the street. A child was coming toward me with a basket on his arm; opposite, a servant cleared the sidewalk with her broom; just as I passed a forge where blackened men were working, a lady crossed the street ahead of me. The instant that I looked at her, a hint at the open secret of the universe flashed through me, taking away my breath. It went again an instant afterward. I can not tell you what it was, but oh the vastness of it weighed me down. Are we to read it in this life, I wonder, even when the Ripest Age has come? I almost think that no man shall look it in the face and live. We may talk of it, long for it, learn its alphabet, but with our last breath only shall it stand before us clear and—perhaps terrible! Schiller's final words, "Many things grow plain to me," gives a hint of this. But oh, of late it is almost always in my thoughts, it winds itself in every reverie of Mary. I have thought of God to-day, of "that wonderful, wonderful world," as Mary called it in her incoherent sentences the last night that we ever slept together, when the misty depths beyond us seemed to have been penetrated a little way by her sweet spirit so soon to depart. Social life in this world blinds us and stupefies us as too much confectionery makes a child ill. The kind God of many a well-bred family on their knees around their glowing grate, with warm and sense-pleasing things about them, is little better than the Lares and Penates of Æneas and his people. He is a domestic God, or at least, He is the one we worship "in our church." This is said without bigotry by them, too, and only in memory of their luxuriously-cushioned pews, beautiful stained-glass windows and melodious organ, and with the thought of their well-dressed, gentlemanly pastor, besides. I write this not in bitterness. I have seen that it is true. Oh, for a glimpse at Him who is without beginning and without limitation! We use these words, the wonder is that we have got so far, but a little bird raising its head in grateful acknowledgment to heaven as the water-drops pass down its throat, knows what the words mean as well as we do. *Ecce Homo!* Let us take that in as best we may.

I thought to-day of another church where often and often I have sat contentedly listening to what was given me to hear. Father and mother were no doubt in opposite corners of the old pew, to-day, and they have dreamed sadly of those who used to sit between, of me, of Oliver, away by the Rocky Mountains, of Mary, away by the River of Life. I have the feeling of one who walks blindfold among scenes too awful for his nerves to bear, in the midst of which we eat and drink, wash our faces and complain that the fire won't burn in the grate, or that the tea-bell does n't ring in season. We are like a spider's web in some remote angle of St. Peter's Cathedral. I suppose the cunning insects flurry greatly if a gnat flies past without being entrapped! All that appertains to the building from floor to dome is accidental in their sight.

A letter from Emma has made Pittsburgh with its smoke and forges to be quite forgotten for awhile, and put me into a Utopia all my own.

May 2.—It is a queer place that I am in. I would give a good deal for a painting of the scene around me. Professor G.'s botany class, with a few invited friends, is spending the day among the hills. About thirty of us took the street-cars this morning and came out into a beautiful valley, took a long walk on the bank of the Ohio, amid charming scenery; climbed the highest hills, that I, a prairie girl, have ever seen, and are now encamped on Jack's Run, a murmuring little stream. The scene is picturesque. I am painfully conscious that my pen can do no justice to it, can hardly give a hint, a sign, to stand for its calm beauty. Perched nearly on the top of a queer mound of limestone, I am sitting, monarch of nothing that my eye surveys, and yet in my poverty content. I wish Emma could see me just now, or Luella Clark; they would know the costume, all black, with a little hat Emma has seen rising out of a hollow many times as I took my evening horseback ride and always went to her. The eye-glasses and veil drooping to one side would be less familiar, for I never wore eye-glasses until submerged in this Pittsburgh darkness in the midst of which I can not see my pupils in the chapel except by artificial aid. I think of Shirley, which I finished reading this morning and of Louis Moore. No female character in any book suits me, like Shirley. Such fire and freedom, such uncalculating devotion to a master, command my hearty admiration. Oh, so much better to wait for years and years, if we may hope to find at last the one who can be all things to the heart! I am glad, heartily glad, that I did not perjure myself in 1862. But I digress. The highest kind of hills inclose us; the water drips, drips, drips, over the uneven stones, and I listen while the music and the murmur sink into my heart and make me richer-natured for evermore. At my right a ledge of rocks rises perpendicularly, and on its top grow trees. At the foot of it a group of girls recline in various graceful attitudes, a botany among them, and a rare flower, a yellow trillium, going through the ordeal of analysis. Across the little stream is a small, white house, the home of some quiet farmer and those who love and look to him. A peach tree in full bloom is in his yard; his son, as I choose to think, sits in a chair by the open door, while he himself is plowing near by. The furrows are not those shining black ones that we used to like to walk on as they fell off from the plowshare, Mary and I. Two of the smaller girls run about gathering flowers; sweet, gleeful faces they have, their childish enthusiasm I look upon with smiles, partly in memory of my own sunny years of early life. It is a kind, sweet scene about me. Its beauty makes me glad. Thank God for this pleasant day of spring. All these things talk to me, though I can not translate every message which the wonderful, mysterious Power sends to me by way of bud and blossom, sky and tree. If only some one dear to me would take my hand and look into my eyes with wise, kind words to-day! If I might speak as I can not write what fills my heart, I should be as complete as we can be on earth. A rain-drop falls on the page as I am writing. A sudden shower, while the sun shines; the group of girls below me scramble after hat and shawl. The day outside of town is passed. I too, must go; so, fair, gentle scene, good-by.

May 5.—Evening. Sitting in my room. What is it, I wonder, that I keep wanting to say? It never comes to my lips nor to the point of my pen. I am almost sure that God does not mean that I shall say this while I live on the earth, and yet it stirs in every pulse, it lies back of every true thought, but it has never yet been told. Some of my best essays are studies for it; sentences that I have hurriedly, earnestly, spoken to a friend's soul with which for the hour I was *en rapport*, have been guesses about it; the kindling eye and flushing cheek have told a little of it, but it will never be uttered right out loud except in deeds of happiness and valor; it lives on in my heart unsaid, and even in my prayers unsaid. It comes so strangely near me, how or why I can not tell. I have seen in the eyes of animals, so wistful, so hopeless in their liquid depths, some hint at what I mean. That mournful flower, the gentian, with its fringed corolla, is to me like the sweeping eyelash that directs a loving, revealing glance, and gives a new hint at that which I can feel, but can not tell. The dripping of water tries to spell out some simple words of it, and the blackbird's note or the robin's song, these help me wonderfully. The royal colored clouds of sunset make it clearer and a long gaze upward through the depths of the night,

> "When the welkin above is all white,
> All throbbing and panting with stars,"

makes the secret clearest of all. The thought of this, which I can only speak about, has been with me all day, like an ethereal perfume; has wrapped itself around me as a cloud of incense, and yet I have been through with the usual number of classes, absorbed the plain, substantial fare of breakfast, dinner and tea eagerly, and read the daily papers. Hooker's triumphant march thus far toward Richmond has made my heart beat faster than love or pride has done since the Garden City was left behind.

Two letters have been received from two poet-souled women in obscure life, and for the time they have transfigured me. Full of insight they were, for these women love much and read the significance of destiny by clear burning tapers lighted at the altar of consecration to their homes. I have read of the French Revolution, and Charlotte Corday, and the Unknown and Invisible has risen before me misty and dark as I wonder what vision burst on the freed soul of that marvelous girl as she lay on the plank of the scaffold and "the beam dropped, the blade glided, the head fell." I have listened to the Bible reading at our quiet chapel prayers, and pondered much over Job's words, "Why should a man contend against God?" and as I thought, my soul went out after Him, this awful, overwhelming Power that holds all things in equilibrium, and has come back again with some dim, shuddering consciousness that He is, and some sweet faith that "He is a rewarder of all such as diligently seek him." I have looked at my pliant, active fingers, and wondered over this strange, imparted force that is o.dained to live a while in me, that joins itself in some weird way to muscle, sinew, tissue and bone; that filters through my nerves and make all things alive, among them the organic shape that is called me. I wish I could talk to-night with some one who would say, with quick, emphatic gesture, "Yes, I understand, I have felt so, too." "Be Cæsar to thyself." The words are brave, but to-night I am too tired to say them truly, and so I will pray to God and go to sleep.

May 15.—Mary Willard is my one thought, even more truly now, I think, than when I was in Evanston. But the stunning weight is not always upon me. Like an object held too near the eyes to be distinctly seen, so has her memory often been; but to-night I held the awful Providence at arms-length and looked at it fairly. Oh, if I could keep my face and form for-ever young, if I could save myself from such a fate as Mary's! But there is no release. In all nature there is no law so inexorable as this: "Dust thou art, and unto dust shalt thou return." Oh, Frances Willard, aspiring mortal! Hungry for love and fame, and thirsty for the nectar of life, grasping after the beautiful and bright, but crying out so often at the thorns that prick when you would feebly reach out for the good—God pity you! And so He will. "He doth not willingly afflict." He who loves us best is at the helm. If He has ordained that we shall die, it is but that He may take us nearer to Himself. Mary knows that.

May 17.—I have been reading the *Presbyterian* account of the first anniversary of the United States Christian Commission, also a sketch of the orator, Anna E. Dickinson. My heart thrills with the hope of a long life on earth and of seeing these persons that I read about; walking up and down the cities, feeling the salt sea-breeze in my face, being at one with the great, pulsating heart of my race. I will try for it. I am bound to try. And yet, on such a morning as this Mary went into the Silent Land, with her hopes on earth all blighted, with unsatisfied ambitions, and unawakened love. The earth side of that Providence is pitiful and touches me even to tears. The heaven side, doubtless, is aglow with brightness, such as I could not see and live. Oh, the untold wonder of my soul!

May 27.—For two nights I have been up till twelve or one. Night before last we had a faculty meeting—the girls have been "acting up," as they call it here, in a ridiculous manner. Their "pahs" and "mahs" will be ashamed of them. "You'uns," they will say, "stop your scrouging." (Specimens in neat mosaic of Pennsylvania idioms.) N. C. sat before the assembled awfulness of the faculty so gracefully, answered so readily, interpolated her "no, indeed," with such pretty emphasis, and cried so charmingly that I was duly charmed. I wanted to go up and kiss her. Even A., naughtiest of pretty-faced girls, I felt sorry for. Mollie quite won me with her introductory sentence, pronounced in that tired, childish voice, which corresponds with her invalid state, "I mean to tell you just what I have done, the best I know how." The bell has rung, and I have to go to another faculty meeting. This makes the third night that I have been up at all hours.

May 29.—Two little incidents have stirred my heart and taught me that I am not fossilizing. Yesterday on the street-car, coming from the House of Refuge, several negroes sitting opposite us, a man in the blue uniform signaled the car. He came limping up and eagerly the driver helped him on the platform. One of the negroes, a very black and noble-looking young fellow, sprang forward and motioned him to his seat, but before he could reach it a place was given him nearer the door. A thrill came to my heart as the poor negro turned toward the soldier. They were types, the two men,—one so dark and one so fair, the lower one looking to the higher, grateful for his aid, turning to him for help. The negroes know quite well for what this war is waging.

The other scene. Virginia Hart is a sweet girl among my pupils. We read for our lesson this morning Alice Cary's story of her little sister Dillie, to whom she was unkind, and who died from the effect of a fall on the very day she used her ill. The story is very pitiful, and touchingly told. Virginia turned toward me when we had finished, as I dismissed the class, and with tears in her honest gray eyes, said, "Miss Willard, I was never unkind to my little sister that died." "That must be a comforting thought, my child. How old was she? When did she die?" I asked. "Oh, a good many years ago," she said. "She was only nine years old." "Have you no other sister?" I inquired. "No; only a brother," she replied. Poor child! I wanted to tell her that I had no sister, either, and that was why I was wearing this black dress, but there were so many in the room I could not mention it. Through my heart went the sad question, "Was I ever unkind to Mary?" And very mournful came the reply, "Many a time I was thoughtless and gave pain to the gentle, gentle girl. I can make no wrong right now,—not one." Oh, how sweet and strange was the voice in which, one year ago, she said to me, "You never were unkind, you were always good to me," and she spoke to me no more.

Extract from my poor father's last letter: "Yesterday, for the first time this spring, we caught up Jack and drove him to Rose Hill. We put some flowers on Mary's grave, but oh, how tame, when I would see her face and clasp her to my heart, that I must be satisfied with merely putting a few flowers on her grave. Oh, vacant and pitiful substitute! Well, we must control ourselves."

Sabbath Day, May 31.—One year ago to-day Mary spent her last Sabbath on earth. I stayed from church; we talked pleasantly together of old, familiar scenes. I read the Bible to her; she was better than she had been for weeks. She was really merry toward night, and made many a humorous speech. She did not seem to think of death. I felt sure she would get well. Ah, on that calm, momentous Sabbath I did not see the grave so soon to be added to the number in Rose Hill. I did not see my brother severed from us, my home in the hands of strangers, father and mother left childless, myself far off from all, at Liberty Street Church in Pittsburgh, and in the afternoon at the mission school on Prospect Hill. To-day the superintendent brought flowers for every one. It was a pretty sight to see the boys holding out their caps for the blossoms, to see all the poor children going gayly down the street, each with a handful of flowers. And then, with Mrs. Holmes and Fannie, I went into a cellar where, for four years an old man, who can not hear or speak, has lived upon the charities of the benevolent. It was something new to me, and impressed me painfully. I gave the man some tea that I had brought at Mrs. Holmes' suggestion. He looked at me gratefully, and put it into his pocket, he could not speak.

June 1.—Saddest, sweetest of months! I am sorry to spend it in a place so dirty, so dusty and so dull.

June 8.—On this same side of the page in my red journal one year ago to-morrow I wrote the words, "Mary is dead." And I have n't the heart to write now that this, the first return of that awful day, has come. "Speech is silver, silence golden." In silence I will think my thoughts. A letter written to father and mother, the lonely, heart-aching pair, shall be my record of this day.

June 12.—Two weeks from to-day I start for home. I am very eager for it, more so than I can tell. Indeed, I think about it all my spare time. Father and mother, the house and garden,—Mary's grave. "Thoughts that do lie too deep for tears" go through me as I think of my changed home, and the pleasant face shut out of sight. It is idle to write about it. Death is unspeakably mysterious and awful. The feeling of this grows stronger in my soul. The terrible sentence rings in my ears, "I am to die! I am to die!" No matter to what it conducts, the earth side of it—and that is what we see—is fearful enough to strike one dumb. Mary always viewed it so herself, and yet it has passed upon her!

June 16.—Pittsburgh is in a ferment, two thousand men are working on fortifications, Gen. Lee's army is said to be approaching, and martial law is to be declared. Trains from the South are forbidden to come to the city. Miss Dole, our New England teacher, is very much alarmed. The girls are distressed, especially those living to the southward, but I am not troubled a bit, nor any of the teachers except Miss Dole. It is quite exciting, though. The President has ordered out 100,000 men, 50,000 of them from Pennsylvania, but there are so many false alarms that it does not do to receive all we hear as gospel on any subject.

Last night came a long letter from Oliver, the first since he went to Denver last fall. It was interesting and characteristic. Though our roads lie so far apart, and our interests are so unlike, yet I always think fondly of my brother and proudly of his success. It is nice for him and Mary B. to love each other and to be together.

June 25.—Doctor P. just now called me into the music-room and complimented me so much that I must write it down, for this book is my safety-valve. Ahem! He said my success in the essay before the Alumnæ was something wonderful. He said it made a marked impression, that he wanted me to come back, would make it pleasant for me, and that if he had only thought of it in time, he would have had *me* make the address to the graduating class upon the occasion of receiving their diplomas, instead of Dr. Herrick Johnson, pastor of one of the first Presbyterian churches in this city and one of the oldest, and furthermore that he wanted me to write an account of the Commencement for "Tom Eddy's paper," and insisted on my taking a five dollar bill for the same. So now, in great haste and honest joy, I have written this and will proceed to prepare the article. Praise, when it is meant, is life to me, "in a sense." I am afraid I think too much about it. Anyhow, I know that I am glad of all this and would like those who love me to know of it.

Evanston, July 7.—Thank God for my safe return.

July 9.—Sabbath morning before church. Sitting alone in my little newly furnished room that father and mother have had fitted up for me, the one where Mary and I once sat together when I was merry-hearted. Mother has just been in and read to me some beautiful thoughts of Hannah More's, on prayer. Mother is wonderfully spiritual since Mary is among the spirits, and her thoughts are only incidentally of earth, habitually in heaven. Father and she are in the front room now. He is reading the *Northwestern Christian Advocate*, she lying on the lounge, perhaps thinking of Mary in heaven. Down-stairs the pleasant housekeepers, Mr. and Mrs. Hanchett, otherwise Alfred and Cynth, with active little Tillie, the small maid of all work, are walking about or reading in the rooms where we used to lounge on Sabbath morning; and under this room where I sit, that one where Mary died is darkened and left solitary. Oh, life is strange and full of change! If these things did not come to us slowly, they would craze us, I am sure; but as it is, we adjust ourselves to them and manage to get on. Though the fresh air and sunshine are taken away, we live in darkness and from long habit breathe on, struggling to inhale the heavy, unreviving air.

July 15.—I am writing with enthusiasm the book about Mary and think it will be interesting. Her journals are delightful. I did not know she had such talent as they evince. Evanston is different, though I say little about it. I have been to the city to visit dear, true Clara Thatcher, one of the best friends I have on earth. Life is rather queer, but it pays, for all that. I want to be good and get ready for something better in the way of animated existence. I do not expect to live to be old. If I were sure about the Future, I would like to go there right away.

July 24.—Not because I have the least thing to write, but just from habit, sitting at my table, I take the pen and scratch away. If it were not for "Mary's book," at which I work almost constantly of late, I could hardly get on. I go out very little, which is foolish, I presume. My book is so well commenced now, that I mean to write only forenoons and visit more; read, study German, and play a little. I am really happy over books, they are the true magicians. They take me back across the chasm of years and make me as fresh-hearted as when the leaves sent their shadows dancing to and fro on the pages which I read in the garden or on the piazza at home, with the tinkle of the distant cow-bell in my ears, and the fragrant breath of flowers cooling my cheek.

Sitting here alone, so often, I think about my future life out there in the mystic country, and glimpses come to me of an atmosphere golden as sunbeams and inspiring as ether, of crystal towers and snowy cushions of cloud, of streams that sing songs as they flow, of perfume delicate as the color of rose-lined shells, of infinite repose and that unspeakable feeling never to be won on earth by prayer or penance—that we are *satisfied*. Christ has in

His nature the elements that will make all this true when we behold Him face to face. We do not know what we are seeking here when we strive so hard and fret so much. Human love no doubt comes nearest, but it is only the melody of an anthem, the study for a picture, the twilight of a morning that shall dawn, and oh, to think! "the fret and jar gone from our souls forever," how we shall erelong awake to life and be restless and hungry and thirsty no more!

This may be as good a place as any in which to state that when we wrote in our journals or elsewhere, as children, mother was wont to help us with points, and sometimes with sentences. In extreme cases, father would do the same. It never occurred to me that this was at all out of the way, any more than to have them help me with my mathematical problems. When I went away to school, it soon became known to my fellow-students that I kept a somewhat voluminous journal, and was very fond of writing. Naturally enough, they flocked around me for aid and comfort in their composition work, which I was by no means slow to render, for I think no school-mate ever asked my help without receiving it. Indeed, I am afraid that I had an undeveloped conscience on this subject, for one of my most lively remembrances is a "change of works," by which my clothes were mended, and my room set in order, while I plied my pencil in the interest of some girl whose harp was on the willows in view of the fact that next Friday afternoon she must bring in a composition.

When I was a teacher, while disposed to be helpful to all my pupils, I did not write their essays, though given to "interlarding," as my father used to call the help furnished us children at home. In a single instance I remember writing an important paper for a pretty young lady, who received a class honor on the basis of her good looks rather than upon her facility with her pen. This was a deadly secret between us two, and one never before divulged. It is mentioned now only by way of warning, for in the confession of sin that I deem it right to make, as a true witness in this autobiography, I am obliged to include not only sins of omission but of commission in the particular treated of in this paragraph.

In the autumn of 1863, I returned to Pittsburgh and taught in the Female College two thirds of that school year.

CHAPTER VI.

THE GROVE SCHOOL AND THE BUILDING OF HECK HALL.

(1865–1866.)

Mr. Edward Haskin, of Evanston, having six children of his own and plenty of money, determined to found a select school near his own home where they could have the best advantages. He enlisted several leading gentlemen to coöperate with him as trustees. Their children also attended the school, which was in two departments, primary and intermediate, with a tendency toward academic, in exceptional cases. My talented cousin, Mrs. Minerva Brace Norton, was the first teacher. She was a woman of intellect so penetrating and experience so large, that to follow her was not a holiday undertaking, but it fell to my lot to make this attempt in the winter of 1865. Associated with me were the "two Kates," as we were wont to call them, Miss Kate Kidder, the accomplished daughter of our Professor in Homiletics, and Kate Jackson, for so many years my friend and comrade. The building where we exercised our gifts is still standing on Hinman avenue, near the corner of Davis street, and I never pass it without seeing those two rooms full of the best-born and best-mannered children in Evanston, kindly, quick-witted and studious. If there were any naughty children I do not recall them. One or two who were dull formed the background for the rest. Our school had many unique features, but perhaps none more so than the custom of the pupils to write questions on the blackboard for their teachers to answer. This turn about was but fair play, stimulated the minds of all concerned, and added to the good will and confidence between teacher and pupil. As we had all grades, from the toddler of four years old to the elegant young lady of sixteen, the problem of government was not so simple as it might appear. After trying several experiments, I introduced the Bank of Character, opening an account with each student in my room, and putting down certain balances in his favor. Then by a system of cards of different values, which were interchangeable as are our bank notes of different denominations, that is, one of a higher value being equivalent to several of a lower denomination, the plan was carried out. Every absence, tardiness, failure in recitation, case of whispering, was subtracted from the bank account, and so emulous were those children that my tallest boys were as much on the *qui vive* to know their standing, as were their youngest brothers. Aside from the lessons, into which we introduced as much as possible of natural history, object-lessons, drawing and gymnastics, we gave out questions at each session, keeping an account of the answers and putting at a premium those who brought in the largest number of correct replies. I remember my honored friend, Dr. Raymond, told me that his boy, Fred, one of the brightest and most exceptional pupils I ever had, when not in school was lying on the sitting-room floor with his face in a book, hunting up the answers to some of this continuous game of twenty questions. It was certainly delightful to see the enthusiasm of my young folks in that Grove school.

We had our exhibition duly at the end of each term, on which occasion the University chapel would be packed with the appreciative throng of fathers and mothers to hear the exercises, in which their children had been most carefully drilled, and to see who got the prizes, for, thanks to the generosity of L. L. Greenleaf, at that time one of our wealthiest citizens, we always had several attractive rewards of merit, usually in the form of books, which seem to me the most unexceptionable prize that can be given. As I grow older, however, I doubt more and more the propriety of offering prizes. Competition is so fierce in this country and age, and the "set" of children's brains is so strong toward it from the first, that I have become an ardent believer in coöperation as a principle destined some day to overthrow the selfishness of competition, and with my present views, would hardly re-enact the scenes that made the "last day" so exciting in that school.

Oddly enough, the prosperity of this pleasant enterprise gnawed at the root of its life. The trustees were urged to make common cause in building up the public school system whose success was greatly hindered by this more select institution, and we all saw that the best interests of the town required such action.

The spring of 1866 witnessed our closing exercises, and made the pleasant school in the grove a memory. I have always thought that some of my most satisfactory teaching was done here and have cherished a warm regard for the bright and winsome pupils who helped me to succeed.

One of my hobbies as a teacher was to interest the children in the history, poetry and morals that are bound up in single words. Dean Trench was among my favorite authors, read early and often, and I collated from his sparkling pages many a picture for the children, drawn out from a single word written by me on the board and copied by them as they sat behind their desks. Every geographical word was thus analyzed, so far as our knowledge permitted, and the chief words in reading and spelling lessons. All except the dullest, were delighted with this variation in the order of the day. In teaching composition, I tried to make the lessons vivid, concrete ; giving few rules, but taking a subject with which the children were familiar, and drawing them out, or, if their little minds were empty concerning some character or event, pumping in ideas by a familiar talk, and then asking them to write out what had been said. In the formative period of my mental habits, writing out recollection of books, characters, addresses, etc., has been the most valuable discipline that ever came to me.

I had list of tabooed subjects in my composition class, among which were Home, Hope, The Seasons, Spring, especially Beauty, Youth, Old Age, The Weather I did not allow them to use 'twas, 'tis, 'neath, th', e'en, though they much inclined to drop into poetry to this extent.

I find a list of words for studies of literal meaning in my memorandum book for composition classes :

Poltroon, supercilious, astonished, sarcasm, imbecile, affront, halcyon, fortnight, scape-goat, daguerreotype, mythology, disaster, asunder, apparent, sandwich, volcano, horse-radish, didoes, telegraph, surname, bayonet, vermin, currents, windfall, caprice, desultory, silhouette, miser, trivial, happiness, heaven, Holy Ghost, consciousness, sincere, Paternoster, enthusiasm.

I found that children ten years old could be well-nigh fascinated by the study of words like these.

An interlude in my work as a teacher brought me my first introduction to a really public career. I was made corresponding secretary of the American Methodist Ladies' Centenary Association, that helped to build Heck Hall, at Evanston, in 1866. This was an addition greatly needed by the Garrett Biblical Institute, our theological school, and our appeal was made to Methodist women throughout the country for contributions to ministerial education. But this new idea of organizing women in a large way for Christian work was seized upon by other institutions, and so many "good objects" were soon before the public that ours did not attain the prominence we hoped. About $25,000 was raised, however, and the certificate for framing sent out by us, and representing Mrs. Garrett presenting a Gospel commission to a very nice, spiritual-looking young man, had more of prophecy within it than met the eye. These certificates hung up in many a Methodist family of the nation, and bearing the honored name of Mrs. Bishop Hamline as president, and mine as corresponding secretary, first gave me a public larger than that implied in any school constituency. I have often thought of this first associated work of the most progressive Church women in America — for Methodist women are confessedly that — and wondered if the sense of power they then acquired did not pave the way for their great missionary movement started about two years later, and of which Mrs. Jennie Fowler Willing was so long the moving spirit in the West.

My father had now become pecuniarily embarrassed, through no fault or failure of his own, and it was necessary that I should earn enough to float myself financially.

I was very grateful to the kind friends who secured the situation for me, and I found in Rev. Dr. James S. Smart, whose keen brain thought out the "Ladies' Centennial" idea, a brother indeed. He helped me in every possible way, and so did my dear father, for I was not good at accounts, and these had to be carefully kept. Father built "Rest Cottage" three blocks from our first home in Evanston, on some new lots reclaimed from the swamp and embellished by him with as much enthusiasm as he had felt in the creation of Forest Home. My parents moved into this house, December, 1865. While it was building, my home was with the families of Dr. Raymond and Simeon Farwell, whose kindness in those days of difficulty I shall not forget.

In the autumn of 1866, I went to Lima, N. Y., Miss Kate Kidder taking my place in Evanston as corresponding secretary.

CHAPTER VII.

GENESEE WESLEYAN SEMINARY.

(1866–1867.)

For many years I had heard of this oldest seminary of the Methodist church, located at Lima, Livingston Co., N. Y., not more than thirty miles from my birthplace. Rev. Dr. B. F. Tefft, whose story of "The Shoulder Knot," published in *The Ladies' Repository*, had fascinated me many years before, was in early times principal of this famous institution. Associated with it as teachers or students were such names as U. S. Senator Angus Cameron, Henry J. Raymond, founder of the *New York Times;* Orange Judd, the greatest among agricultural editors; Prof. William Wells, of Union College; Prof. Alverson, and many others of whom I had heard with great interest. It had a history, and to a Westerner this was a fascinating fact. It was a co-education school and Oberlin life had proved to our folks that this was the natural, hence the wise, way.

With such history and traditions the school could but be attractive to me, and when, one fine winter day, in Evanston, in 1866, a letter reached me from Prof. Charles W. Bennett, who was then at its head, inviting me to become "preceptress," I was delighted, and, with the approval of my parents, wrote him at once that I would gladly go in the following September. I was greatly disappointed to learn later on that Professor Bennett, about whom Dr. Bannister's family had told me many pleasant things, had gone abroad, and that a new principal, Professor Fuller, unknown to fame, and certainly unknown to me, was to be my chief associate.

It was a beautiful autumn day when I reached this historic village nestling among the hills of Genesee. Its pastoral peace was welcome to my spirit as dew on the mown grass. An entertainment was given to the faculty that evening at the home of Rev. Dr. Lindsay, president of Genesee College, which was located on the same campus. Here I met the leading members of both faculties, with all of whom I was remarkably well pleased. The seminary building, large, rambling, old, had special fascination for one who came from a country where everything was new. I thought of the historic characters to whom this place was familiar and by whom it was beloved. My own pleasant suite of rooms had been occupied for two generations by women of the highest character and exceptional abilities. My friend, Kate Jackson, came with me, for I had secured her the promise of French classes. Her object in going was to be with me, as she had no occasion to make money for her own use, and there we spent a year with very much of brightness in it, and somewhat of shadow.

I can not more correctly depict the year at Lima, than by giving in conclusion the following extracts from the journal of the period:

Lima, Livingston Co., N. Y., September 15, 1866.—Father went with me to Lima. From Avon I had my first stage ride, seven miles across, the driver blowing his horn as we entered a town, in the good old-fashioned style. Stopped at the pleasant home of Rev. A. D. Wilbor, agent and treasurer of the Seminary. We were warmly welcomed, had a nice dinner, and walked over to the Seminary with bright E., a sophomore in the gentlemen's college (Genesee), were introduced to Mrs. Hale, wife of the steward, conducted to our rooms, sitting-room, bedroom, and closet, up one flight of stairs on the front side of the building; nicely furnished, Brussels carpet, pretty bedroom set, a fire ready in the stove, house plants in the windows; they had evidently done all they could to make it pleasant for us. We went to work and put up the pictures, etc., and in a couple of hours, I was nicely established in my new home. Then Professor Lattimore and daughter, Professor Steele and wife, and several others, called.

September 18.—After father had helped me put up the pictures and got me nicely settled, he went away yesterday just after breakfast; he stood on the steps before the great front door, held out his hand with his face turned half away, and said, "Well, good-by; take care of yourself, and don't get sick." I shall not comment upon my many thoughts and emotions as he walked off with carpet-bag in hand, looking so gentlemanly, so tall and slight and fragile—too much so for my peace.

Am getting acquainted with all these excellent people; the bugbear, Lima, is nothing so dreadful after all. Have had my first duty as preceptress to welcome a lot of new-comers. Two are Indians from the Seneca reservation; another is a peculiarly thoughtful, religious, book-loving girl of seventeen. I brought her into my room and she looked with much interest at my pictures, and we fell into talk. I happened to mention that I had a sister who graduated young, and that I was nineteen when I left school. Soon after, I handed her the new circular where my full name is printed. She glanced over it, looked up with flushed face, and said, "May I ask a question? Did you write 'Nineteen Beautiful Years'?" I answered, "Yes, of course," and showed her Mary's photograph while tears fell from her eyes. New students are coming all the while, new teachers, and I am not a bit blue. We had a long, tedious faculty meeting in the ladies' parlor. They gave me rhetoric and composition, and I am perfectly delighted.

September 20.—To-day began my onerous task. At nine A.M., prayers in the chapel, conducted by the principal. Afterward I went to my recitation room and spent the forenoon registering young ladies who brought slips of admission from the treasurer. I then took the names and addresses of guardians, studies for the term, and number of rooms in the Seminary, or, if an out-boarder, the place of residence. They are most of them interesting, attractive girls. Then came to my room and had a call from one of my Seneca Indians and also from polite Miss Waite, the assistant preceptress; Mrs. Hale, the stewardess, gave me a cup of tea in her room and consoled me, the dear, motherly woman. Have had several homesick girls to look after. Poor things, I like them, and pray that I may do them good, in all true and pleasant senses. Have been registering all day, have received numerous calls on business from my strange-faced and pleasant-mannered young ladies, a few anxious fathers, and some of the professors. Gave them this afternoon a chapel talk and took the postoffice addresses of them all. Think I shall greatly like Lima when I get seasoned.

September 24.—Mrs. H. is a woman of mother wit; witness her inveighing against people who parade their bookishness; she brought me a private cup of tea and a cooky, kissed my cheek and said, "You dear little kitten, you, if anybody hurts you, I'll bite 'em, that's all."

October 6.—Girls, girls, girls! Questions upon questions! Dear me, it is no small undertaking to be elder sister to the whole one hundred and eighty of them, but it is pleasant, truly so. Tried to write on a talk to them but can get no time nor much inspiration. This term, I will extemporize, I guess. Went up to the room of the "Ladies' Literary," was introduced, the whole society rising. They treat me beautifully, and I think I reciprocate. Never saw such a thing as Lima sociability.

October 13.—We have changed works; I hear Kate's physiology class and she "does up" our room.

October 15.—Have had a letter from Nina Lunt, dated Geneva, Switzerland. What would I not give to have her opportunity in life, for my pet desire is to travel. If I had been a man I would have liked Bayard Taylor's portion under the sun.

October 24.—Prepared talks to my girls about room-keeping. This is my hobby. I believe, whatever I can not do, I *can* make a home attractive. My own room I delight to have a pleasant place to dwell in. For this I care more than to dress. Heard my rhetoric scholars, of whom I have thirty-four.

October 29.—I went down to a political mass meeting addressed by Horace Greeley. Here was American politics as manifested in a crowd of yeomanry with bands and such mottoes as "Down with the One Man Power!" "Congress Must and Shall Be Sustained!" "Andy Johnson Swinging Around the Circle!" This motley throng surged to and fro, nearly taking us off our feet. It was somewhat to study, to be sure, but we did n't stay long, the place was so breathless and full in spite of the rain. I like Horace's quiet, unwritten face. Life has n't hurt him much—the noble old philosopher. I liked to watch him standing there in his nice black suit, with velvet vest, wide collar and queer ruffle of whiskers gray; with his bald head, ring on third left hand finger and red bandana in his hand. He is a historic figure and embodies well the idea of our government—freedom in all right things, to all. Give everybody a fair chance and let the out-come come! Honor to H. G., the self-made chief editor in the United States for the last score of years.

November 2.—Kate and I have great fellowship with Mrs. Fuller, the principal's wife, she is so straightforward, and common-sensical, that one likes her of right.

November 5.—In the evening, went to the twenty-two rooms of my girls. I like them all. I really think I shall do these girls good in composition lines. The seniors improve and I give them unsparing criticism. Regents' examination is going forward, to the great disgust of the students. Kate and I went into the chapel to see the poor victims undergoing their ordeal. It is the perfection of a system.

Sabbath, November 11.—Stayed at home all day and read "Ecce Homo." It has mind in it, it has body, it *is* something. I have enjoyed it and concluded it certain, from internal evidence, that the author believes in Christ's divinity. If our faith could but be separated from cant and hackneyism it would touch the world more nearly.

November 16.—Professor Fuller laid down the law to the lawless young men in a way that did my heart good. In the boarding-hall there is ever so much that goes amiss, and some people that precisely answer to the "Country Parson's" description of a "cantankerous fool."

November 26.—Girls are ten times as quick as boys. In Rhetoric the last do wretchedly. I should think they would take hold and study for very shame.

The term grows dreary and monotonous. I am an inveterate lover of variety and should have made a traveler if I had been a man—as I sometimes wish I had been. My life is a free and happy one—surfacely so. How strangely accommodating are our natures! With nothing just as I wish it; with chasms and voids in my life too numerous to name, I yet have a good time and no complaint to make!

November 28.—Went down town in the rain to see about my new dress, bonnet, etc. These evils of a lady's life are very irksome to me, yet quite inevitable. For to express in toilet, manners, and the room (some day I hope the house) I live in, that I am civilized of soul, I expect and intend.

November 29.—The first national Thanksgiving Day appointed by the Chief Executive is here. Thirty-six millions of people at once offering their thanks to the Source of life and of all that comes through living! Alas that "my policy" Johnson instead of our beloved Lincoln, the emancipator, should have written the proclamation setting this day apart to its delightful uses! Rain falling, windows open, no fire, dandelions golden in the grass. Spent the day reading Carlyle on the religious life of Dr. Johnson. Life is "sort o' rich," but might readily be more so.

One of the cross-currents came to the surface when I declined to hold myself responsible for the locking and unlocking of the outside door, a little distance from my room, at ten o'clock at night and half-past five in the morning. They said, "The preceptresses have always done this." I replied, "More's the pity, it is the janitor's business." Good Professor Fuller stood by me and we carried the day, though it made no small jangle in the faculty for a brief period. But we were in the main harmonious, and I heartily liked all my associates.

It soon occurred to me that we might improve the name of "The Young Ladies' Literary," which was the immemorial designation of one of the societies. This caused no small amount of contention and criticism, but finally we christened it "The Ingelow," and when I went to New York, at Christmas, I expended $100 that the young women had accumulated for the purpose, in plaster of Paris busts of the great lights of literature, one or two handsome chromos, and I know not what besides, to brighten up their large, old-fashioned assembly room, with its low ceiling and solemnities of president's chair and critic's desk.

At Lima for the first time I gave a church-roll talk each week, having the young ladies all to myself in the huge, old chapel, and after calling the church-roll to know if they had been in attendance punctually upon the Sabbath day, I talked to them in a familiar, sisterly fashion about all sorts of things interesting to them and to me. It was an hour of genuine pleasure on my part, and they professed to like it, too.

Squire Hale and his wife were characters, indeed, known and read of all men and women who were at Lima during the forty years of their stewardship. To them I was indebted for many kindnesses; their accomplished daughter Dora and her genial husband, Rev. C. C. Wilbor, were my next-door neighbors on the same hall. Dr. Lindsay was greatly looked up to by us, and always seemed to me one of the noblest of men. Dr. Daniel Steele was a special friend of ours, a man of independent mind and sterling character. He had not then come to the vision of "Love enthroned." Professor Coddington, the eloquent preacher of Syracuse University, gave high promise in those early years; Professor French, honest and skilled; Professor Lattimore, the son-in-law of the lamented Professor Larrabee of Dickinson College, was the exquisite man of the faculty; the afterglow of Professor Alverson's great name still lingered on the hills; Dr. Cummings was spoken of reverently, Dr. Reid pleasantly, and an important chapter in the history of Methodism was here studied by me at first hand.

In our own seminary faculty we had in Professor Fuller a man of excellent ability, who had succeeded in the pastorate, but was hardly at his best in this new calling, a fact for which, because I thought so highly of him, I was often sorry. His wife was a true friend, whom I have not seen since, but whom I have remembered always with unchanged affection. Miss Bannister, now Mrs. Ayers, of Penn Yan, the teacher of Fine Arts, had a nature delicate as a porcelain vase, and a spirit tremulous with aspirations toward God. With her I took sweet counsel, and oftentimes we walked to the house of the Lord in company. Professor Hudson, the Latin teacher, was phenomenal in memory, and has since become one of the leading stenographers at Chautauqua. I remember he took my White Cross address with marvelous celerity and accuracy when I spoke there in 1886. Professor Locke was chief of the Conservatory, a young man of harmonious character, great activity, and zeal that his pupils should improve, and that all the students should be religious. For many years now he has held the same position in the Northwestern University, at Evanston, loved and trusted by all who know him. Prof. Delevan C. Scoville was probably the most unique man of either faculty; born among the hills of Oneida, devoted to the Adirondacks and to books, worshipful toward his mother and sister—two rare women, worthy of his devotion,—working his way to high culture, and phenomenally successful as a teacher, with a certain magnetism in look, voice and manner that made him a universal favorite among the students, he should, to my mind, have been a minister, and I think he had this purpose, but in some way was deflected from it, went to New York City, and has become a first-class lawyer there.

I remember that Professor Scoville, who was very liberal-minded on the woman question, urged me to consent to speak before the United Societies at Commencement in the College chapel, saying that if I would only agree to do this, it was the easiest thing in the world for him to secure the invitation. But I stoutly declined, saying that while I would rejoice to speak were I a man, such a beatitude was not for women, and I would not face the grim visage of public prejudice. This was at the Commencement exercises of 1867. Something less than four years later, I was glad to accept Mr. A. E. Bishop's generous championship, and under his auspices to speak an hour and a quarter in Centenary Church, Chicago, without manuscript. So goes the world. It is always broader and better farther on.

I left Lima at the close of the school year of 1867, with the pleasantest of memories and prospects, as shown by the following correspondence:

July 8, 1867.

To the Board of Trustees of Genesee Wesleyan Seminary:

GENTLEMEN—Opportunity to visit Europe under circumstances most advantageous having presented itself since I entered upon my duties here, I have decided to avail myself of it, and therefore tender my resignation of the position of Preceptress. Wishing continued prosperity to the institution in which I have spent a year so pleasantly, I am,

Yours very respectfully,

FRANCES E. WILLARD.

This was their courteous and brotherly reply:

GENESEE WESLEYAN SEMINARY,
LIMA, N. Y., July 9, 1867.

MISS FRANCES E. WILLARD, *Madam*—I am directed by the Board of Trustees of Genesee Wesleyan Seminary to transmit to you the following resolution, unanimously passed by the Board as an expression of their regard for you personally, and approval of your conduct as the Preceptress of the Seminary.

Trusting that the good Lord will preserve you during your travels, I am,

Yours truly,

D. A. OGDEN, Secretary.

Resolved, That in accepting the resignation of Miss Frances E. Willard as Preceptress in Genesee Wesleyan Seminary, we feel great pleasure in expressing our high appreciation and grateful acknowledgments for her valuable services during her connection with this institution.

Hoping for a pleasant tour and safe return from her journeyings abroad, we will pray for her safety, her continued success, prosperity and happiness in any sphere of labor and usefulness she may be called to fill in the future.

[Unanimously adopted.]

D. A. OGDEN, Secretary.

My generous Senior girls gave me a beautiful ring like their own, with my favorite motto from Goethe, which they had adopted, *Ohne hast, ohne rast;* the under-graduates gave me nearly one hundred dollars with which to buy a dressing-case.

CHAPTER VIII.

PRESIDENT OF EVANSTON COLLEGE FOR LADIES.

The circumstances that led to my being elected president of a new college, and the first woman to whom that honorable title was accorded, though so many others have deserved it better, are thus narrated by my mother to the stenographer:

In 1868 Frank went to Europe. Her good friend, Kate Jackson, paid all the expenses of their trip, which cost about $12,000 in gold, at the time when gold was at a premium. We rented Rest Cottage to Rev. Mr. Safford and family, friends of ours from Oberlin, and I boarded with them for a year. The next year my son and his family moved into our house, and I boarded with them a year. Then we closed the house, and I went to Churchville to visit our relatives and await my daughter's coming. Frank and Kate returned in September of 1870, and we three reopened Rest Cottage, where I have lived ever since.

That winter we did all of our own work, not because we could not have a girl, for Kate had no lack of money, but after such a tremendous outing as those two had been through, they seemed to enjoy hugely the idea of hiding away out of sight and hearing, and keeping house for themselves. Frank occupied herself chiefly with the outdoor part, chopping kindling, bringing in wood and coal, and doing the rougher work, while Kate and I attended to the culinary and ornamental departments. One day when Frank was busy nailing down the stair-carpet, Mrs. Dr. Kidder, whose husband was then leading professor in the Theological Seminary, came from her home across the street, and taking a seat on the stairs, said, "Frank, I am amazed at you. Let some one else tack down carpets, and do you take charge of the new college." "Very well," answered Frank; "I shall be glad to do so. I was only waiting to be asked."

Comparing the opportunities for womanhood then and now, the old Persian proverb comes instinctively to mind, "More kingdoms wait thy diadem than are known to thee by name." Coincident with the advance of woman into an unknown realm, began another epoch in my life, as I was made President of the Evanston College for Ladies.

On St. Valentine's day, 1871, I was elected to this position, and at once entered on my duties.

Our college was, indeed, something new under the sun. Its beginning was on this wise: Mrs. Mary F. Haskin, wife of the kind friend who gave me my first financial send-off, was a woman of decidedly progressive thought. She believed that women should be a felt force in the higher education, not only as students, but as professors and trustees. She believed that to have men only in these positions, was to shut up one of humanity's eyes, and that in the effort to see all around the mighty subject of education with the other, a squint had been contracted that was doing irreparable damage to the physiognomy of the body politic. Therefore, Mrs. Haskin ordered her handsome carriage and notable white horses one fine day, and calling on half a score of the most thoughtful women in Evanston, proposed to them to found a woman's college, in which women should constitute the board of trustees, a woman should be president and confer diplomas, and women should be, for the first time, recognized and proved as the peers of men in administrative power. She pointed out that even at Vassar College the president and all the trustees were masculine, while at Mt. Holyoke, where one would think the spirit of Mary Lyon would have left more liberal traditions, men only were trustees, and a man always conferred the diplomas that young women's study and older women's teaching had combined to earn. Evanston is the paradise of women, and Mrs. Haskin found abundant preparation of heart and answer of tongue among the earnest Christian matrons to whom she addressed herself. A meeting of ladies was appointed in her own home, at which measures were instituted to secure a charter and empower Mrs. Bishop Hamline with fourteen other ladies, and their successors, as trustees.

Our genial townsman, Hon. Edward S. Taylor, was in the Legislature that winter [1869–70], and through his influence the Charter was secured. Meanwhile, my own beloved Alma Mater, the "Northwestern Female College," was in full career, for although its founder, Prof. Wm. P. Jones, had been consul in China for several years, he had placed the institution in 1862–63 under care of Mrs. Lizzie Mace McFarland, and, later, that admirable College president, Rev. Dr. Lucius H. Bugbee, had been at its head. Professor Jones himself had now returned and for a year resumed the leadership. But by wise diplomacy Mrs. Haskin, president of the new board of trustees, and those associated with her, secured the transfer of the Charter of the old college into their own hands, with a choice list of alumnæ, the formalities of the change taking place in the old Evanston church at the final "Commencement" of the old College in 1871. Meanwhile, in 1869, Rev. Dr. (afterward Bishop) E. O. Haven had resigned the presidency of Michigan University to accept that of the Northwestern University at Evanston, none of whose advantages had been open to women until this man, who stood second to no college president in the nation, made it a condition of his coming to us, that every door should be flung wide to the gentler half of humanity. How many times have I thought, with regrets unutterable, of what it would have meant to my own education had all those doors been open in 1858! But this was not at all in the plans of the good men who founded and controlled the University, and had not Dr. Haven been born with the diplomatic skill of a Talleyrand he never could have fitted the conflicting elements of the three educational interests—old College, new College, and University—into one, of which the University was from the first, not only helm, but wheel and rudder. It was he who held high counsel with Professor Jones when the latter, strenuous—and justly so—for the dignity and historic perpetuation of an enterprise into which he had poured heroic years of toil, was loth to see his pet College merged in ours. It was Dr. Haven who arranged for the Evanston College for Ladies to be so correlated with the University, that, under his presidency, the two moved on in perfect unison; and had he remained until the new order of things became fully established it is my confident belief that ours would have been to-day the greatest, because the most thoroughly American University extant.

I see him now, medium-sized, alert-moving, most modest and unostentatious of men, with his fine brow, mild, but keen-flashing eyes, dominant nose of Roman mould, and his "smile as sweet as summer." His voice was musical, his manner winsome, but behind all, his purpose was unconquerable as Cæsar's. Unlike almost every other person I have known, he had the piercing mental gaze that could divide the accidental from the necessary in this purpose; the latter he followed with the rapidity and lightness of a greyhound. Most men carry luggage in following their purpose; he laid aside every weight; they load with small shot and their fire is scattering; his was always Sharpe's rifle—one ball, and hit the game; they tithe mint and cummin, he tithed nothing, but made all gleaners welcome to his harvest-field. More than once I heard him say, "I think a man who has the ability and who manifests the spirit of Professor Jones, should have a good position in our University. He gives up the hope of a lifetime in order that the educational interests of Evanston may become unified, and this action should be recognized not in words only but in deeds."*

He wanted only what came to him naturally as the result of his own reaction on the forces about him, and rejoiced to see the dignity and prerogatives of others fully acknowledged, not fearing for his own. How much of life's present friction will be avoided when the average mind discovers that the central aim of any life is best conserved by choosing for one's motto "*In non-essentials, liberty*"! But the trouble is, only a great mind can so take in the scope of life to perceive that most things are relatively, and all things are absolutely, non-essential except "*truth in the inward parts*"; and that to apply that truth more perfectly to heart and home, to state and world affairs, is more than all burnt-offerings and sacrifices. Dr. Haven saw the truth of family government—the fatherly plus the motherly eye applied to the problem of educating young people; and he followed it more grandly than any other educator of his time.

With such a master spirit among us, so intuitive in thought, magnanimous in heart, and harmonious in action, we launched the fearless ship that flew the pennon "Evanston College for Ladies."

But we suffered from plethora of plans coupled with such a dearth of dimes that something had to be done, and that right speedily.

Now came to the front, with her unmatched gift of imparting enthusiasm, Mrs. A. H. Hoge, the new president of our "Women's Educational Association," and the distinguished

*Both these true men have passed onward now: Bishop Haven in 1881; Professor Jones in 1886.

yoke-fellow of Mrs. Mary A. Livermore in the days when a sanitary fair meant victory. I shall never forget the morning when this woman, one of the few truly great whom I have ever known, stood up in a meeting of ladies in the Evanston Presbyterian Church, of which she was a leader, and told us to preempt at once the coming fourth of July, the University campus and the Chicago press, in the interest of "our girls." Forthwith, we said we would, and verily we kept our vow. But Mrs. Hoge had never recovered from the rigors of her army work, and she had many cares besides, hence could only give us the splendid impetus of her magnetic words and presence. It remained for the new "college president," minus a college, to show what she could do, and to carry out the plan. Two years of foreign study and travel were hardly the best preparation for a work so practical, but it was a case of "sink or swim," and I took my lessons in the middle of the stream as many another has been forced to do. For three months I slept and woke FOURTH OF JULY. It haunted me like a ghost, nay, it inspired me like a good fairy. Men and women rallied to my help as if I were their very own.

Although ours was a Methodist college, Episcopal ladies were on the Committee, Presbyterians bore the battle's brunt, Congregationalists cheered on the battalions and did not a little of the fighting, while Baptists were outdone by nobody, and Methodists headed by Mrs. Mary F. Haskin, president of our Board of Trustees were "at it and all at it," intent upon making "*The Women's Fourth of July*" celebration what it was, the most complete ever known in the Northwest and the most unique ever held upon the continent.

As a key-note I prepared a circular, of which the following is a synopsis. It went out by cartloads, indeed Uncle Sam's special express was our chief base of operations, next to the newspapers:

CIRCULAR LETTER.

Addressed to all who are interested in the girls of the Northwest:

It is a very easy matter to sneer at the "Girl of the Period," to discourse upon her frivolity, lack of perseverance, and general "shiftlessness."

It is a less easy, but not at all an impossible matter to cure her of these faults.

Is not this last the more excellent, as it is the more generous, way?

How can we better begin this cure than by proving to the period's much-berated girl that we set no higher value upon any member of our complex American society than upon herself; that we believe her worthy of the best we have to offer; that we regard her faults, not as inherent, but, rather, as the result of a defective training, for which, not to put too fine a point upon it, she is to be pitied, and we are to be blamed?

We believe the common sense of the American people has arrived at this conclusion, and that a higher education for women is demanded by the spirit of the age.

Perhaps this sentiment has nowhere found a more correct exponent than E. O. Haven, LL.D., to whose efforts women owe their admission to the foremost University in the United States, that of Michigan, and, more recently, to the Northwestern University at Evanston, near Chicago, of which Dr. Haven is now president.

And perhaps no attempt to utilize this new and noble public sentiment has been so commensurate with its progressive character as the establishment of the

EVANSTON COLLEGE FOR WOMEN,

under the control of a Woman's Board of Trustees, and intended to supplement the advantages of the

NORTHWESTERN UNIVERSITY.

To foster the interests of this new institution, an

EDUCATIONAL ASSOCIATION

has been formed, of which Mrs. A. H. Hoge (whose name is endeared to all hearts by her devotion to the "Boys in Blue" throughout the great Rebellion), is the President, and of which prominent ladies, connected with the various denominations, are officers.

Under the auspices of this association, it is proposed to hold at

EVANSTON,

NEXT FOURTH OF JULY,

A GRAND CELEBRATION,

at which time the corner-stone of the new building will be laid; orations will be pronounced by some of our most celebrated countrymen, and

A BANQUET

worthy of the occasion will be served.

Notice is hereby given of the PRE-EMPTION OF THE FOURTH OF JULY in the interest of

THE GIRLS OF THE NORTHWEST.

Then followed an appeal to editors, pastors, etc., to help in the new movement; also a call for "supplies" for the tables, fancy articles, flowers, "and any curious or useful objects which will add to the interest and profit of the occasion." The call was signed by the "Committee on behalf of the Evanston Woman's Educational Association," consisting of Emily Huntington Miller, corresponding secretary Ladies' Board of Trustees; Mrs. Mary B. Willard, recording secretary of the same; Mrs. General Beveridge, Mrs. Sarah B. Bradley, and myself, as president of the college.

We went to the village authorities and modestly asked for one of its parks as the building site of our college, and, to their everlasting credit be it said, they gave it. We had the foundation laid for the elegant Woman's College Building and arranged that the corner-stone should be set in place at the great celebration. We induced the famous Ellsworth Zouaves to come and drill inside an inclosure on the campus, for an admission fee; we got a generous jeweler to give a silver ball for which the College base-ball-ists of the country were invited to compete. On the lake we arranged (that is, Gen. A. C. Ducat did) for a regatta with a winner's prize; in the University chapel we had an amateur play, in which our young "society people," led by my friend, Kate Jackson, performed three separate times that day to crowded audiences, at so much a head. A general of the army (afterward Gov. John L. Beveridge) was persuaded to act as marshal; a United States Senator, Hon. J. R. Doolittle, of Wisconsin, pronounced the oration; a distinguished public reader, Prof. R. L. Cumnock, gave the Declaration of Independence; Gov. John Evans, of Colorado, for whom our town is named, headed a subscription list that aggregated thirty thousand dollars, and the ladies served three thousand dollars' worth of dinners, notwithstanding all the picnickers that filled our groves. The Chicago press had during three months given us ten thousand dollars' worth of free advertising; special trains and steamboat excursions bore the people to our feast with waving flags and bands of music, but there was no clang of war; no cannon, fire-cracker or torpedo was tolerated at the *Women's* Fourth of July. The climax of the day was the laying of the corner-stone, a woman, Mrs. Haskin, assisting in the ceremony, at which a beautiful dedication song by Emily Huntington Miller, one of our trustees, was sung. On this occasion we all walked over from the campus to the park in long procession, and my place was beside my brotherly and prescient friend, Rev. Dr. E. O. Haven, who told me, as we went, how deeply he rejoiced in all the on-going movements by which women were coming to their kingdom. "When they are fully come," he said, with that beautiful smile not to be forgotten by any who have seen it, "there will be peace, even as here to-day they have preserved the peace for us; never before was there a Fourth of July without noise or accident."

It now became my duty to present the plan of the new college to good people wherever I could get a hearing. The Congregational Church in Evanston was the scene of my first appearance, and the ordeal was difficult, but Dr. Haven also spoke, and that made my trial less. Rock River Conference welcomed me most courteously, and in many towns of the Northwest I sang the praises of the great "Northwestern" and its sturdy little sister, the Evanston College for Ladies. All that summer we planned the course of study, and my pen was busy in pursuit of pupils, who, on the opening day, filled the old college where I had graduated twelve years before, and which we had leased until our new building should be completed.

Our pupils of the Evanston College for Ladies were to have all the school privileges of the University at the regular tuition rates; they were to take music, art, and several other studies at our own college building, and were to be under our care exclusively as to morals and manners. For those who did not wish to pursue any of the University courses, one having a larger proportion of English and modern languages was carefully prepared. As planned by Dr. Haven and ourselves, we had, in fact, five departments; Modern Languages, Fine Arts, Music, Health, Home and Home Industries.

CHAPTER IX.

SELF-GOVERNMENT FOR GIRLS.

As I follow, in these later years, the thorny path of a reformer, I sometimes think how good and pleasant would have been the quiet life, so universally approved, of a teacher of girls. But one confident belief gives me grace and courage to go on, and it is this:

> "My bark is wafted to the strand
> By breath divine,
> And on the helm there rests a Hand
> Other than mine."

In Evanston College for Ladies, for the first and only time in my history as a teacher, I was for one year free to work my will as an elder sister of girls—for this was then my idea of my relation to them; now, I would say, "a mother to girls."

Dr. J. B. Chess, of Chicago, yearly gave a gold medal for good manners, which keyed the whole school to a higher ideal, and Miss Kate Jackson, who had the French classes, joined me in offering prizes for neatness and tastefulness in rooms.

Every Friday afternoon a lecture was given in the College chapel at which the "Church Roll-Call" was had, to which all lady students were expected to respond. History, biography, books and reading, art, travel, manners, health, and many other kindred subjects were brought forward. Mrs. Kate Doggett, President of the *Fortnightly* (Chicago), gave several illustrated lectures on art; Rev. Dr. L. H. Chamberlain, spoke on his favorite "Philip Van Artevelde," and a lawyer of Evanston, Mr. L. H. Boutell, gave his reminiscences of Margeret Fuller Ossoli. My own talks were frequent, and related chiefly to what I am fond of calling "Moral Horticulture." Every day each pupil had twenty minutes alone in her room. We did not at all prescribe what should be done, but what we hoped was perfectly well known—it was a breathing place for heavenly thoughts. I valued this time more than any other except evening prayers.

I constantly visited the young ladies in their rooms, never once being met with coldness, and almost always we knelt together to ask God's blessing on those at home, and those here, who were often lonely because home was far away.

On the first Sunday after the college opened, one of my pupils came to my room saying: "Miss Willard, we can't bear to go in a procession over to the church. They say it has always been the custom, but if you would trust us to go independently, I feel sure you would never have occasion to regret it; for we would all be loyal to you and to the school."

My heart responded, "Amen and amen. We will find a more excellent way." Very soon a request came that the young women might be members of the (open) literary societies of the University, of which there were four, the Hinman and Adelphic in College, the Philomathean and Euphronian in the Preparatory School. But these societies all met in the evening, the distance from our college was six or seven squares, the young ladies had always been strictly kept to many rules, and when they left the college grounds to go to public audiences were to be accompanied by teachers. The idea of their participating in debates with young men, and making orations, was unheard of, and "besides," quoth some objectors, "some one of them might prevent a young man from having as frequent opportunity to speak as he otherwise would have had, or might possibly be elected president of a society—such an improper position for a young lady to hold!" But Dr. Haven thought the objections were all mole-hills, and the advantages were mountain high. "Here they can measure swords," he said; "here, even more than in the recitation room, young men will learn that young women are their peers. It will break down the prejudice against woman's public speech and work; it will refine the young men and develop intellectual power in the girls—precisely what each class most needs."

But he warned me more than once that the success of the venturesome experiment was in my hands. Teachers could not well attend the societies; their presence would be irksome. The girls must go and come at night, and they must do this always and strictly *by themselves*.

I remembered the clandestine visits of "University boys" to our college grounds in former days, the secret sleigh-rides and moonlight walks, from which my sister and I had always kept aloof, but of which we dared not tell, and I knew that in our alma mater there had been no more, if as much, of this as in the average girls' boarding school. Could I brave public opinion and take the risks on a method never before applied to a co-education school? Was it right thus to hazard our sacred cause? Much I mused and often prayed.

One evening soon after these requests for larger liberty, I asked my pupils to remain after prayers. I can see the bright double parlors planted out to my beautiful garden of girls. I told them all that has been stated here, all my scruples, aspirations, hopes. I told them how I came to Evanston as a school-girl about thirteen years before, and of my "ne'er-do-weel" term in this very college, of my conversion, and, finally, of my heart-break when my sister Mary died. Then I laid before them my plan of school government, which was to put it almost wholly into their own hands, to have no rules except those that they and their teachers felt to be of vital importance, and closed with some such statement as the following: "Here is an enterprise the like of which was never seen, a college with women trustees and faculty, a woman president and women students. Up yonder in the grove is a first-class men's college, and to every one of its advantages we are invited, on one condition—all of us must at all times be Christian ladies. Now, girls, I place your destiny in your own hands; I confide mine to you, also, for this is my own home town, and my good name is more to me than life. Besides all this, and greater, the destiny of this woman's college, and, to some degree, that of the co-education experiment, rests with you young creatures, fair and sweet. God help you to be good!" We knelt in prayer for grace and guidance, and then, with my faithful faculty, I passed from the room, leaving the girls to organize, according to the written plans I had previously explained to the leading pupils, their "*Roll of Honor*" and "*Self-governed Societies.*"

How nobly they fulfilled their trust! I used oftentimes to wish that I behaved as well. On Sunday, when they entered church after their own sweet will, with what pride, even such as might thrill a mother's breast, I noted their unexceptionable manners. No whispering, no tittering; and woe to the youth

BENSON AV. School.
GROVE SCHOOL
NORTHWESTERN UNIVERSITY.
NORTHWESTERN FEMALE COLLEGE
EVANSTON COLLEGE FOR LADIES.

who tried to slip sly *billets-doux* into the hands of "my girls" as they entered or left the sacred edifice. How many a Friday night at ten o'clock, lying in my bed at Rest Cottage, four blocks from the Woman's College and on the same street, I have heard the light steps of that long procession going home from the University building, where they, separating into four groups as they entered the campus, had attended their respective societies, and I have wept to think how true and self-respecting a college full of girls could be! The town pronounced my method "a success"; Dr. Haven was satisfied — which meant everything to me—and a teacher not now in the University, one who thought my "government" was "hair-brained," said, "The trouble is, these girls are quite too loyal; they make a hobby of it."

Here are my first letter as president to the Roll of Honor girls, and their "general principles," together with the pledge of the higher grade:

DEAR AND TRUSTED FRIENDS—In your novel and important position, you have need of all the guidance Divine and human that you can possibly obtain; the reputation of the college is largely in your hands, hence as you already possess the unreserved confidence of your teachers, you have been intrusted by them with intricate and delicate responsibilities. Your conduct, your conversation, your scholarship, your manners, will be henceforth carefully observed by all your fellow-students. Impressed as I am most deeply with these thoughts, I shall implore for you the guidance of the Supreme Power in your new undertaking, and I especially urge you to do this in your private devotions and in each one of your committee meetings. When we begin with prayer, we may be sure we are on the right track to a genuine success.

Now, as to the practical workings of this new venture, the faculty suggests:

1. That you appoint a regular time and place of meeting.

2. That you send in each week a written report to the faculty meeting on Monday evening.

3. That to this end you appoint a secretary.

4. That you have a committee for each literary society at the University and the Preparatory department, and also a church committee.

5. That you get a list of all the lady boarders in the college who propose to join, and ascertain which society is preferred. Then assign to each sub-committee those going to its society.

6. That you all go together and return together, and in all cases unaccompanied by gentlemen, and that you never go in companies of fewer than four.

7. That you leave at the close of the literary exercises at ten o'clock.

8. That if experience proves it to be impracticable for the University and Preparatory detachments to meet after the exercises, that the two return separately, but those from both the Preparatory societies together, and those from both University societies together.

9. That the young ladies sit together and choose certain seats, which they can retain henceforth.

10. That in regard to quiet deportment on the street, attention during the exercises, faithfulness in performing duties of the society, the committee report to the faculty as a committee, thus relieving every one from personal embarrassment.

11. Any member of the Roll of Honor who regards this as too much to undertake must speak now or ever after hold her peace.

On behalf of Faculty,
FRANCES E. WILLARD.

GENERAL PRINCIPLES OF THE ROLL OF HONOR.

Roll of Honor girls must be examples to the flock. They will not, of course, disregard the smallest of our few regulations. They will not ignore study hours, enter rooms in study hours, keep lights burning after bell, be late at meals or recitations, be noisy or uproarious either in or out of school hours. They will be low-voiced and gentle-mannered, kind and considerate toward all, and just as much above reproach as any of their teachers.

They will not be regarded as Roll of Honor young ladies after they have transgressed a single regulation, and their places will be supplied by others, and the number enlarged by those whose lives among us are above reproach.

[By order of the Faculty.]

PLEDGE OF THE SELF-GOVERNED GIRLS.

I promise so to conduct myself that if every other pupil followed my example our school would need no rules whatever, but each young lady would be trusted to be a law unto herself.

I promise that I will always try to do the things that make for peace.

I wish to have in my book the list of the original members of this society who are among the choicest of my friends.

ELECTED BY THE FACULTY.

Sarah Heston, Belle Webb,
Emma Warner, Susan D. Mitchell.

ELECTED BY THE PUPILS.

Mary Pattison, Jennie Pattison,
Ella Wheeler, Belle Miller.
Alice Yaple.

The first list was limited to nine, because we wished to make it a high dignity to belong, and because we could rally around this nucleus, when its character was established, more successfully than if we had placed a larger number on the list at the beginning.

The constitution of the Roll of Honor Club contained the following:

> The general principles of this club shall be to coöperate with the Faculty in securing good order and lady-like behavior among the boarding pupils, both in study and recreation hours, in inspiring a high sense of honor, personal responsibility and self-respect, and especially conducting in this spirit the attendance of the young ladies at the literary societies and church.

As this method developed, it was my custom to say at the beginning of a term, "We will have no rules whatever, just so long as everything is quiet, your time diligently occupied and your punctuality without flaw. We have no need of rules. Let us see how long we can go without them. I will post a time-table in the hall, and let us live by it. Regard the teachers as you would your mother and elder sisters at home. You advise with them as to what is best for you in every way, feel free to do the same with us; that is what we are here for."

The girls were so delighted to have no rules that the older ones gave little comfort to the younger when they began misbehaving, which they did, not from bad intention, but on account of thoughtlessness. After awhile, however, we would see the necessity of some one rule, then it would be announced. Every girl in school was a candidate for the Roll of Honor, which distinction could only be reached by one month of faultless deportment and punctuality. So it fell out that for the first month we had no rules, on the principle that "A new broom sweeps clean." In the second month, we had almost no need of rules, for every one was on the keen stretch to reach the Roll of Honor, and the third month all being anxious to remain at that high grade, there was an *esprit de corps* in the school that held the pupils to the mark. So that the bondage of school discipline, of which I had had so much always as a teacher and member of faculties, was reduced to a minimum, indeed, became almost inappreciable. This was especially true when we had graduated from the Roll of Honor grade enough of our older and more prominent girls into the Self-governed class, so that their noble behavior was indeed "an example to the flock," an incentive to every one below them, because the self-governed grade was open to the youngest. I remember that my little cousin, Rilla Norton, when only twelve years of age, not only attained this honor but ever afterward maintained it.

I sent this letter to my pupils when the second term began:

EVANSTON, ILL., January 11, 1873.

MY DEAR "SELF-GOVERNED" AND "ROLL OF HONOR" GIRLS—There are two things of which I wished to speak at your meeting to-day, but I shall not be able to attend, hence, I send you this "encyclical":

1. In relation to the standing of the old pupils whom we welcome back to the college this term. Having great confidence in your judgment, I ask you to take their cases into careful consideration and report to the faculty what, in your judgment, will be the best way to arrange the matter. Remember that you thus establish a "precedent" and that "precedents" are often inconvenient unless very general in their application.

2. The subduing and controlling of the vexing spirit called "noise" is one of the most difficult problems to a household that aspires to be harmonious and peaceful. Last term I spent more breath upon this theme than I intend to spare from nobler occupations for the future. During vacation this revelation has come to me:

That Roll of Honor club can do whatsoever it will. Thanks to the high-minded integrity and good common sense of its members, the problem of membership in the literary societies is solved to the satisfaction of all concerned. Thanks to them, also, the uproar that once disgraced our chapel on Friday afternoon is quelled. What can they not achieve? I will submit to them this subject of quietness in the college building, ask them to secure it for us by such means as they see fit, and to be examples of it in the future as in the past. Let us see what their inventive faculties can do about it. They have proved themselves, thus far, equal to any emergency; they will again.

So I leave the subject with you. The good order and quiet of your temporary home ought surely to be as important to you as it can be to your teachers.

One thing more. Please elect ushers for next Friday P. M. Don't let your meetings stagnate. Get up new things. Have wide-awake critics to tell you your faults, appoint at least two, one for our end of the street and one for the opposite.

Always affectionately yours,

FRANCES E. WILLARD.

They replied by sending me the following:

We, the undersigned, do pledge ourselves, in order to subdue the noise and disturbance which has been of late and is now a growing evil in our school, to faithfully observe the following resolutions:

Resolved: 1. That we will not congregate in the halls or on the stairs.

2. That we will avoid loud talking in passing through the halls.

3. That in going to and from the dining-room we will be quiet, also while at the table.

4. That in passing to the chapel and before the exercises commence, we do each take it upon ourselves by our example and otherwise to do all we can to maintain the best of order.

5. That, during the meditation hours, those of us who remain in the parlor will try so to conduct ourselves as not to disturb the teachers, or those who desire to study.

6. That we, as members of the Roll of Honor, do pledge ourselves to remember and live up to the vows which we made when placed on the roll, that we may retain the confidence of our teachers, the respect and esteem of all, and that the injunction, "Study to be quiet," shall not be forgotten by us.

After one year's successful trial, the plan was officially outlined for the public in the following language :

GOVERNMENT.

The phrases made and provided for literature of the catalogue style will not be employed under this head. "Mild but firm," "of the parental type," have been the usual changes rung when this fruitful topic was under consideration.

The general basis of government in this institution is, that *merit shall be distinguished by privilege.* Any young lady who establishes for herself a trustworthy character will be trusted accordingly. After a probation of one month, any one who, during this time, has been loyal to the regulations of the school, and has not once required reproof, will have her name inscribed upon the Roll of Honor, and will be invested with certain powers and responsibilities usually restricted to the faculty. The Roll of Honor has its constitution, officers and regular meetings, and sends written reports to the teachers relative to the trusts of which it is made the depository. A single reproof conditions, and two reproofs remove any of its members, who can regain their places by the same process through which they were at first attained. Those who during one entire term have not been conditioned (by a single reproof) upon the Roll of Honor, are promoted to the Self-governed List, and give this pledge : "I will try so to act that, if all others followed my example, our school would need no rules whatever. In manners and in punctuality I will try to be a model, and in all my intercourse with my teachers and school-mates, I will seek, above all else, *the things that make for peace.*"

Thenceforward, these young ladies do as they please *so long as they please to do right.* Every pupil in school is eligible, first to the Roll of Honor ; next to a place among the Self-governed, hence there is no ground for jealousy. Scholarship does not enter into the requirements of admission—*character* is placed above all competition here.

A year's trial of this plan has proved that it is practicable, and that school discipline may vitally contribute to the growth of noble, self-reliant character. The ideal set before each pupil, the sum of all "regulations," the proverb of the school, is this : "*Just be a Christian Lady.*"

N. B.—At the close of the year, twelve young ladies were on the Self-governed List, and *all the rest* were on the Roll of Honor.

Successful candidates were promoted to the Roll of Honor, or the Self-governed grade, at evening prayers, pledging themselves before the school and receiving the right hand of fellowship.

I think our girls felt as did the young knights of old, and held their vows as sacredly. To show the care they exercised, I copy a note from the Roll of Honor girls at College Cottage:

MISS WILLARD AND MEMBERS OF FACULTY—The Roll of Honor have decided that Miss —— and Miss —— remain on the Junior Grade, and Miss —— should be on the same grade *if at all* on the Roll of Honor.

Also by unanimous vote that *none* be promoted to the Self-governed List until next term.

We pasted in the parlor the list of the Roll of Honor, and Self-governed girls, and printed in the catalogue, next to the faculty, the names of their leaders. I will copy them here, for I like to link those noble names and memories with the story of my life:

Chairmen of the Roll of Honor, Belle B. Webb, first term; Julia D. McArthur, second term; Jemmy E. Pattison, third term. Chairmen of Roll of Honor, at College Cottage, Sarah E. Cathcart, first; Mary E. Wood, second; R. Frank Remington, third.

Without noble coadjutors in the faculty, this system could not have succeeded, but we were a unit in purpose, plans and personal affection. Our faculty meetings were a refreshment to jaded nerves. Never as a white ribbon leader have I been supported more ably or more warmly than by those devoted and gifted women whose names I wish to string on a rosary of perpetual and endeared remembrance: Minerva B. Norton, Kate A. Jackson, Evelyn C. Crosby, Harriet E. Reed, H. Maria Pettengill, Ada F. Brigham, Fanny D. Smith.

Among our teachers not boarding at the college were Oscar A. Mayo, Anna S. Lewis, Mary L. McClure, Ida M. Kessler, William Arnold. As lecturers on physiology and hygiene, we had at different times the following physicians: Mary A. Thompson, Sarah Hackett Stevenson, Mary J. Safford.

My friend, Professor Charles C. Bragdon, reared in Evanston, a graduate of our University, and with his mother and her family our nearest neighbors during his college life, sends me the following reply to the question, "How long have you governed by my method, and how does it work?" He says, "Used this method fourteen years," and adds this letter:

LASELL SEMINARY, AUBURNDALE, MASS., January 24, 1889.

DEAR FRIEND—After a residence of three months, a committee of twelve pupils, chosen indiscriminately by the pupils, nominates candidates for the Self-governed List and Roll of Honor. Each one of the twelve, without consultation with any one, and without knowledge as to how any other one of the committee votes, writes her list of candidates. Those who receive a majority of the twelve votes for the Self-governed rank are made into a list, and those receiving a majority for the Roll of Honor, into a second list. The teachers review these lists in assembly, talking over each name and discussing such facts as to each pupil's conduct and spirit as may be brought out, more weight being given to spirit than conduct. Where the teachers' votes agree with the pupils' list, the candidates are confirmed. Where the teachers differ, the pupils' judgment is usually taken, though not always. If grave reason for differing appears, the teachers change a name from one list to the other, or remove from both lists. The lists thus settled are read before the school with such comments as seem fitting. We try to emphasize trustworthiness as against petty details.

At the end of the next term (three months) the same is repeated, some elevated, some, though not often any, demoted.

Our Self-governed do as they please, have all the privileges of teachers, subject only to the general order of exercises, such as to go to bed at 9:30, to rise at 6:45, etc.

The Roll of Honor have certain privileges, inferior to those of the Self-governed. Those not on either list are not reckoned as degraded, but as "not having yet attained." If at any time special reason arise, members are removed from either list, rarely some are promoted "between times." I believe in the method. I believe all our teachers come to believe in it although new ones may not at first.

The pupils of both grades are put upon their honor and helped to live for the general good, to be good because they are trusted to do well. There are cases always of incomplete comprehension of the spirit of the thing, owing to incomplete moral development. The effort is to develop the honor sense in such, and to hold up to disrepute the "being good" for the loaves and fishes, i. e., the privileges. The danger in the plan is the discouraging of those who do not attain so soon as they think they ought, and in the development of self-conceit among those elevated. These dangers are constantly striven against by personal interviews as symptoms develop, and the attempt is to deepen a sense of both obligation and privilege to do right because it is right and because they are responsible, first and last, to themselves.

Yours sincerely,

CHARLES C. BRAGDON.

The Woman's Educational Society gradually merged into the Educational Aid Association, to which Rev. O. Huse, Isaac Hitt and Dr. D. K. Pearson were the earliest contributors; Mrs. Hannah Pearson is the present chairman of the committee. It owns a large building called College Cottage and many women of exceptional gifts and earnestness have been helped to help themselves to an education under its auspices.

Concerning physical education, we made the following declaration :

The young ladies walk over a mile a day in going to and returning from their various recitations. Lectures on the care of health are given by Dr. Mary J. Safford, the well-known Chicago physician. *Common sense applied to dress* is one of the problems in the solution of which we earnestly solicit the co-operation of our patrons.

Another of our inventions was "The Good Behavior Club," which proved to be a favorite feature of the school. Teachers and pupils were all members and shared the offices. Representations were given of all social observances, from the White House reception to the morning call ; personations of distinguished characters, adding the dramatic charm so attractive to both young and old ; the fact that gentlemen participated in these, by no means detracted from the interest manifested.

"The Good Behavior Club" had its "Question Box" into which were dropped anonymous queries and criticisms of all sorts relating to care of the toilet, the etiquette of occasions, and the small, sweet courtesies of daily life. While many of these were based upon observations involving the deficiencies of individuals, the strictly impersonal character of the comments shielded the sensibilities of each and all. I found this club a barrier against the "self-activity" that in my own student days had led me to plan escapades just for the novelty of doing so, and that to have the amusements of my girls going forward under their teachers' eyes, contributed greatly to that *esprit de corps* which is the first requisite of success in all organized effort from the family circle to the great circle of nationality.

I believe there is a hint here for our "Y" societies of the white ribbon, and so will copy an article of mine from *The Tripod*, in my day our college paper at Evanston, hoping that its hints may help them to a new line of work :

Why it is not just as sensible to teach good manners as a theory and art as it is to teach singing, I can not understand. In a democracy like ours good manners ought to be a branch specially attended to in all the schools. Especially would I have it introduced into the public schools and continued throughout the course of study.

Suppose the perpetrators of the "pudding-stick fun," to which we were treated in Philomathean Hall the other evening, had been trained from the pinafore-age to "habits of good society"—should we have had to blush that they and we belonged to the same race?

Americans are angular, uncouth, unkempt. Nothing is more palpably true than this. A French gentleman recently exclaimed after an interview with a high official in our state who, on leaving the room, turned his back to the company: "I will not say that American men have bad manners, but I will say that they have no manners at all." The proofs of an uncultivated origin that meet us on every street corner of our own classic town are beyond enumeration. The "student's slang" (not to mention other varieties!) salutes our ears at every turn. And yet, when it is proposed to teach good manners as one would any other art, to give line upon line, and precept upon precept, and to illustrate and enforce the teaching given by practice and example, many people have only weak sarcasms to offer by way of commentary.

The need of some such teaching, to supplement the random and often nugatory instructions of home, finds another salient illustration in the excuse of Christian parents for sending their children to dancing-schools. "They say our young people must learn ease and grace of deportment, and become familiar with the etiquette of occasions, so that no social entertainment will find them ill at ease." True; and it must be confessed that the drill of the dancing-school renders them more graceful and self-possessed. We have nothing special to say in this connection of the harm that grows out of dancing (not, mark you, out of dancing "*in itself*," any more than out of swallowing brandy "*in itself*," but in its associations and results). Read Dr. Bushnell's admirable sermon on "Free to Have Amusements: But Too Free to Want Them," if you would see our position defined at length. Our creed is clear in its declarations on this subject. The people who help the world, and whose names are praised and blessed—whose memories yield perennial fragrance and form the examples of our times—are not the people who have excelled in polka or in waltz. But aside from the merits of the case, there are large numbers of Christian people who send their children to dancing-school for the same object which a class in etiquette would subserve equally well, thus removing the temptation to that concerning which the thoughtful *mater familias* can not fail to have misgivings.

The foregoing are "after-thoughts" connected with the pleasant entertainment given at the Ladies' College, on a recent evening by the "Good Behavior Club." This organization, numbering nearly forty members, has been for the past term under the care of Miss Smith, of Chicago, teacher of etiquette. Miss Smith has also had classes in the Normal University, the Wesleyan University, at Bloomington, and other institutions. President M. speaks in the highest terms of her success in the institution over which he presides, where a large class of young gentlemen and ladies has been formed.

As for the entertainment at our Ladies' College, it was tasteful, and well conducted, the young ladies having entire charge of the arrangements.

Whatever others may think, the experiment is a success here; and we congratulate the accomplished young lady who is quietly opening to women a new and attractive employment, and to students an added opportunity to learn and to illustrate "the habits of good society."

In an address on "School Government," before the Woman's Congress, New York City, 1872, I said:

And this brings me to look carefully in upon that model home once more, to find the system of government that shall most conduce to the formation of genuine character in our young people at school. I find there very few fixed rules, and that the continued observance of these by the children as they grow older depends almost wholly upon the disposition they display as they advance in years. I find that the noble, trustworthy boy and girl are trusted, the deceitful and ignoble, governed. So in the school I simply "go and do likewise," applying rules to the unruly, regulations to the irregular. All are placed under a system of restrictions at the first, the simplest that experience pronounces safe, and many find it impossible to work their way up through these to the bracing heights of self-control. I open a "character bank," of which the faculty act as "directors," in which the "deposit" is reputation, of which each student may accumulate as much as he will, and on which he may freely draw, his paper being honored at sight and discounted only when his debit exceeds his balance on the books. Self-government is then the noble possibility of each, the eagerly sought goal of every student, and the exemplars of the school are the "tried and true" of whom it is openly declared that "unto such there is no law" or, to put the point with more decision, "they are not under the law, but under grace." I know these are advanced positions, but I beg you to believe they are not the result of dreamy theorizing, nor the mirage of an unvisited Utopia.

Between the first and second evening study hours, we had a prayer-meeting of fifteen minutes in a teacher's room. This was perfectly voluntary, but overwhelmingly attended. I can hear yet those clear young voices, singing

'Rock of ages, cleft for me,
Let me hide myself in Thee.

* * * * *

In my hand no price I bring,
Simply to Thy cross I cling."

How little did I dream that erelong I, who loved it now so well, should gain new love for it, and that the "Crusade," undreamed of then, would bring the "arrest of thought" to these dear girls and to me. Of temperance I never spoke, taking it for granted that all was well. Now and then, when especially "worn out," I would take a little of mother's currant wine; on the last winter of my teaching, Dr. Jewell, one of the leaders in our Sunday-school, ordered a keg of beer into my cellar, of which I drank a nauseating glass at dinner, rebelling at every dose, experiencing no benefit, and abjuring it forever when the blessed Crusade wrought its miracle upon our hearts. I then introduced temperance themes to my classes, one and all, as mentioned in the temperance chapters of this chronicle. A missionary society was organized in the college, coöperating with the local auxiliary of the Methodist church at Evanston.

I had all the young ladies (numbering several hundred) in my English composition classes. One feature that was attractive to them was reporting for the Chicago and Evanston papers, for which I arranged, so far as practicable, and with good results.

In teaching my art class at the college, I availed myself of my friend Kate's remarkably fine selection of photographs and stereoscopic views, numbering about eight hundred, including all the leading places that we saw in our long trip abroad. Many of these I had produced on glass so that they could be thrown on the screen of the stereopticon, and described to the entire class at once. It was my earnest hope that, after I had taught the theory and history of the fine arts for a few years, I might be able to prepare a text-book that would be used generally in schools and would furnish the introduction, of which I so much felt the need, to a study of the European galleries and of art in our own land.

It was my wont to open or close my recitations with a few words of prayer, and I could feel the lofty spirit thus imparted to teacher and to pupils.

Good Mrs. Van Cott came to Evanston this first year of the new college (1871–72) and no one present will ever forget the scene in the college parlors when, with illuminated countenance, she talked of God and sang with us her favorite hymn:

> "Come, Holy Spirit, heavenly Dove,
> With all Thy quickening powers,
> Kindle a flame of sacred love
> In these cold hearts of ours."

Then she placed her kind hands on every head as going

around that large circle she asked a blessing upon each and all. The revival that followed was the most memorable ever known in Evanston, and all my girls but two — one of whom was a Catholic, and a very good Christian, by the way — became members of the church. Among all the noble girls whom I had the happiness to see kneeling at the altar, none rejoiced me quite so much as my brilliant Belle Webb, who had fancied herself an infidel, but who from that time steadily developed Christian character throughout her six years' classical course, and is now with her gifted husband, Rev. Dr. Edward Parks, connected with the Methodist University, in Atlanta, Ga.

The Senior class bequeathed us by Professor Jones was the only one, up to the date of its graduation (1872), whose diplomas were conferred by women. I think at Wellesley, during the administration of President Alice Freeman, this was done, as also at Rockford (Ill.) Seminary by Miss Hillard — now Mrs. McLeish — a Vassar graduate and teacher.

It was a noteworthy circumstance that at our first Commencement a woman gave the baccalaureate sermon, Mrs. J. F. Willing, the same who, two years later, presided over the first convention of the National W. C. T. U. At my suggestion our women trustees voted her the title of A. M. I shall never forget the beautiful appearance of our new church at Evanston, bedecked for this "Woman's Commencement"—words significant in many ways. Only the basement was finished, but it was endeared to us by the services of Mrs. Van Cott, and as I stood there under the beautiful arch of evergreen, conferring the diplomas on my six charming seniors, the scene recalled, by contrast, the laying of Heck Hall's corner-stone only six years before, when my gallant friend, Rev. Dr. J. S. Smart, read in sonorous tones the address I had composed, but lacked courage to pronounce.

This was my first presiding on a momentous public occasion, and in looking over the data for the present history I came upon the handsome printed program of that Commencement ceremony. For the benefit of other on-coming presidents among women, I will divulge the fact that what I was to say was all written out inside that program, and the memorandum read as follows:

(Preliminary.) There is a time-honored request "made and provided" for occasions like the present, which must be reiterated, I suppose, at this time, or "Commencement" will be shorn of a cherished prerogative.

It is my duty, then, to remind our intelligent and thoughtful friends that we are in a *church*, and that, however much the eloquence of our graduating class may unfit you to carry out the terms of the treaty, it is, nevertheless, expressly stipulated between us that no ruder method of applause shall strike our ears than the mild concussion of manly palms or the fragrant breath of the ever-welcome bouquet.

* * * * * * * * * *

(On giving the medal for good manners.) A word in explanation of the intention of this award. It does not imply loyalty to school regulations (though the young lady who receives it has not been once reproved for word or act during the entire year); it refers, rather, to the minor moralities, the "small, sweet courtesies" of life; to habitudes of gentle speech and graceful, kindly action; to that nameless charm of manner which springs not alone from a *kind*, but from a *cultured* heart and brain. While it affords me profound pleasure thus to decorate Miss Patterson, I beg you to believe that a vast amount of embodied good manners still remains undecorated among "our girls."

* * * * * * * * * *

Immediately after these exercises there will be a reception at the Ladies' College, to which the Board of Trustees and officers of the College cordially invite all our patrons and friends from abroad, as well as those residing here, also the faculties, alumni and students of all the institutions here.

Please consider the invitation *general*, *cordial* and *emphatic*.

* * * * * * * * * *

Miss Annie Webster, by the authority of the Board of Trustees of Evanston College for Ladies, I confer upon you the degree of Laureate of Liberal Arts, and in testimony thereof I present you this diploma. By the same authority, I confer upon you (five) each the Degree of Laureate of Science, and in testimony thereof, I present you these diplomas.

My dear young ladies, you have now received from your young Alma Mater the first honors she has given. May He who is the strength of all who trust in Him, help you to fulfill the bright promise of this hour. *Farewell!*

In the midst of this first school year occurred that terrible calamity, the Chicago fire. We were sitting at breakfast in Rest Cottage, on Monday morning, October 8, 1871, when a neighbor came in and said, "Did you know that Chicago is burned up?" We thought the lady joking, but her grave face belied the supposition.

"Yes, burned up," she continued, "Court-house and all." We rose with one impulse and went into the beautiful, quiet street. It was more quiet than ever—business seemed suspended, no man was to be seen. A dull, dun-colored atmosphere settled over us as the day wore on ; its odor was peculiar, composite, and stifling, a total contrast to the pleasant, earthy smell of the prairie fires to which my childhood was accustomed. At ten o'clock the young ladies composing my class in moral philosophy came to recite. They brought me tidings of stone houses crumbling like cardboard in the fierce heat ; of the entire business heart of the city taken out ; of the homeless, famished ones, many of them now on their way to Evanston, whither they fled, with the flames on their track. The awful situation engrossed us altogether ; lessons were not to be thought of, and we all knelt in prayer to God for the friendless and forsaken.

Later, the rumor came that the fire had gained such headway it was possible that it might come on through twelve miles of woods and fields to Evanston. Absurd as such a supposition seemed, the panic was sufficient to set men plowing furrows of defense, while a corps of students was fitted out with buckets of water and told to stand on guard between our peaceful village and the fiery foe ! A committee of safety was organized and we were told to be ready to entertain any refugees that might be sent us. Kate Jackson was keeping our house then, and in her busy, Martha-like fashion she hurried to grocery store, market and coal-dealer that we might be fitted out in a manner suitable to the hard fortunes we would alleviate. We went to the evening train at six o'clock and such a sight I never saw. Our well-favored, tailor-dressed business men crawled off the cars, ragged as cinders and black as chimney-sweeps. Their eyes were red with involuntary tears called out by smoke, not by their gigantic losses, for the Chicago man never bates a jot of heart or hope. Now and then there was one who had not lost, and the rest would pound him on the back in boisterous play, shouting, "String him up to a telegraph pole !—what right has he not to be ruined with the rest ?" Men and women were loaded down with baskets of silver, boxes of valuable papers, household relics, and the like.

We had no guests, after all ; the distance was too great for those who walked, and most of those who came by cars went to their friends. Several persons brought baskets of precious things, however, asking us to keep until called for.

Thousands camped on the prairie near the city that night,

and little babies were born, and the sick moaned helplessly under the wide, calm heavens. At midnight the fire was burning so brilliantly that standing on our piazza I could distinctly read my fine-print Testament.

The fire began at 9:30 on the evening of Sunday, October 8, and ended about ten o'clock Tuesday morning, lasting through thirty-six horrible hours. It covered an area of three miles in length by one and a half miles in breadth, or two thousand one hundred acres. The number of buildings destroyed was about seventeen thousand; of people rendered homeless, ninety-eight thousand. Of these, about thirty thousand left the city and about fifty-five thousand were fed by charity. It is estimated that about two hundred persons lost their lives, and over two hundred million dollars' worth of property was destroyed. The cow-barn on DeKoven street, where a frightened bovine kicked over a kerosene lamp, started this greatest conflagration of all history.

I have hardly heard a more heroic story of this unmatched calamity than that of Ina Coolidge, one of my pupils. On the day before the fire I had gone with her to the city Eye Infirmary, Dr. Annie Reid being with us, and a skilled hand had operated on one of Miss Coolidge's eyes for strabismus. The quiet way in which she laid her little form down on the operating table, crossed her hands in prayer and submitted to the anæsthetic; the sweet, bright look when she said, "Oh, Miss Willard, we are all in heaven and you are the center of our band!" have always remained with me, since they brought the tears to my eyes as I stood by her side. The flowing blood and bandaged eyes—both bandaged, so that she was helpless—were pitiful to see. We sent her to the Sherman House with her trusty room-mate. There they were to stay for a few days, but that night came the awful conflagration, and the hotel was just in its path. My pupil said the scene was terrible, with screaming women and cursing men, nobody willing to help another; people and trunks bumping their way along the stairs, while din of bells and puff of fire-engines made up a horrid orchestra. In all this the blindfolded girl never once lost her equipoise of mind. She would not take the bandage from her eyes, but waited till the scampering crowd was well-nigh gone, took her room-mate by the hand, and the two girls started out alone. She noted the quarter from which came the wind and roar of flames, and away they sped through the livid inferno, not knowing, in that strange city, what direction they had taken until, hours afterward, they found themselves at the Milwaukee depot, on the West Side, and the next day, while we were in breathless anxiety about them, they appeared climbing the college stairs at Evanston!

All the newspaper offices were burned, but I remember the *Evening Mail*, with which my brother was soon after connected, and all the other dailies, soon came out as usual, looking primitive as the frontier. We found Oliver and his friend Hobart in a downright "piney-wood shanty," a few days afterward, working away at a drygoods-box table with all the importance of Chicago editors who had survived. I took my mother and several wagon loads of my pupils to see the ruins,—that being for some time the chief occupation of suburbaners. Tolerably familiar though I was with "the wreck of time" in Egypt, Palestine and at Baalbec, these were the most colossal ruins I had ever seen. The towering fragments, smouldering embers, charred trees and half lifted smoke-cloud; the groups of men and women, roaming about as if bewildered, or delving into the heaps of débris that covered their pulverized homes and melted hearthstones; and, in awful contrast, the sparkling waters of the great lake stretching before us in mocking uselessness and selfish security—the only thing unchanged—made up a picture the most frightful that my eyes have mirrored.

But with a wish to see some smile of hope across the blackness, I asked my girls to take The Greatest Conflagration as a subject of debate, one side advocating the view that good was to come out of it. I think we were first in the field for the optimistic view now generally accepted, and so far realized that when I welcomed the National W. C. T. U. to Farwell Hall, just six years afterward, I was able to say to them, with all the pride of a Chicago suburbaner:

> You will see for yourselves our parks and boulevards, the palaces in which we transact our business, and lodge our travelers; the costly churches where we worship, and the costly mansions in which our money-kings are wont to eat and sleep. As you drive along our streets, a vacant lot here and there, a heap of shattered stones, a bit of charred pavement will be

shown you as the only remaining traces of that city of stone that in a night became a city of ashes, and six years later gleamed forth a city of marble.

That fire touched humanity's heart, and endeared our smitten city to the whole world. Sailors have told me that at the farthest point of the Aleutian Islands, they found that most of the natives knew three English words—Victoria, a dollar, and Chicago.

CHAPTER X.

WHY I LEFT THE UNIVERSITY.

That fire changed the outlook of our college. Its hot breath shriveled our generous Fourth of July subscription list, impoverishing some of our most trusty friends and obliging us to cover up the newly-laid foundations of our great building. We furled our sails and went scudding as best we could before the blast. The year 1872 witnessed the election of Rev. Dr. Haven as Secretary of the Board of Education of the M. E. Church, and his change of residence to New York City. And there rose up as his successor one who "knew not Joseph."

Rev. Dr. C. H. Fowler (now Bishop), a man of brilliant gifts, came to us from the pastorate, never having taught at all, unless very briefly in district school when a student in college. His concept of the situation was totally different from that of Dr. Haven with his long experience in the work of higher education.

To go into the details of this most painful period of my whole life is not my purpose. Suffice it that the bone of contention was the relations of the Evanston College for Ladies to the Northwestern University. Dr. Haven's plan, indorsed by the University trustees, was as follows:

> We would recommend that all young women receiving instruction in the University, be requested to enroll themselves as members of the Evanston College for Ladies * * * * and that the young women be under the moral oversight of the faculty of the Ladies' College.

But the new president held that the University faculty of men was the final authority in everything pertaining to those who received instruction there. Hence, when a young woman preferred not to take lessons in penmanship (required of all under our care); when she fell from the Roll of Honor list, or for any reason desired to go outside our college building and thus be free from all restrictions except such as related to her recitations at the University, or its Preparatory department, the new president said she might go, and still be in good standing so far as those classes were concerned, when the old president would have said she must do as the women's faculty thought best. This was the "rift in the lute"; it was a readjustment that removed the center of gravity outside the base so far as the Evanston College for Ladies was concerned, and introduced so much friction into our educational machinery that, perceiving the impossibility of going on another year under the same disadvantages, I strongly advocated what the new president favored, viz., such a union of the two institutions as would make their interests identical.

A principle which I always tried to inculcate in the minds of my girls was this—a sentiment of true honor and dignity favors the school not the delinquent. How is it in society? Every noble man brings rogues to justice. He never dreams of shielding them, yet pupils think it honorable to shield each other. And I had myself the same absurd idea during a part of my years at school, but it is a sediment of barbarous ages wherein espionage took the place of free government. What I urged most in the basis between the College and the University was that the University trustees should reaffirm the action which made all young women members of the Woman's College, and that the University faculty should do this with such minutiæ of legislation as would relieve the Woman's College from all embarrassment, making our faculty responsible for the young women in all cases save when they were in the recitation room.

In my annual report to its board of trustees, as president of the Evanston College for Ladies, I said (June, 1873):

> The general policy during the first year of the college was frequently expressed by Doctor Haven in terms like these:
>
> "I wish the Ladies' College to be responsible for all the lady students in everything; but their recitations, so far as advantageous to them, will be with us, and when they pursue our courses of study they will receive our diploma."
>
> But the practical workings of the school this year indicate a different view of the subject, and it is necessary to the harmony we all desire to maintain that the question be settled.
>
> Will you, therefore, please detail, with as much minuteness as possible, the duties of the president of your college toward the young ladies whose

names are placed upon its register, stating wherein they are amenable to her authority, and wherein they are not?

For my own part, unless I am thoroughly self-deceived, I desire "the greatest numbers' greatest good"; and I earnestly seek such a solution of the problem, which I now present to you, as shall most directly tend to fulfill the hopes and expectations of those who have stood by our enterprise from the beginning. But I frankly acknowledge that I can not, with self-respect, longer sustain relations so undignified as the last few months have witnessed.

I have no aspersions to make against any one. We have simply arrived by a rather circuitous route, but a no less certain one, at the logical sequence of relationships too dimly outlined at the beginning.

To your combined wisdom, energy and prudence, I submit questions with which I have been loth to burden you, but with which I can no longer contend alone.

I have great confidence in the power of a free and kindly interchange of sentiment between the authorities of the two institutions to set these questions at rest, and to develop a policy which shall render their harmonious interworking practicable.

Let me add a single sentence from an article written by Dr. E. O. Haven, in *The Methodist,* in which he gave an outline of our plans. He says:

"It is our intention to show that 'opening a university to women' and 'giving ladies an equal chance with gentlemen,' means something more than to control a university wholly by men, select courses of study fitted only to men, give instruction mostly by men, and then, forsooth, 'open the doors *alike to both sexes.*'"

Let me, finally, put myself upon the record, as not at all unfriendly to a closer union between the two schools, providing always that the advance positions we have gained for woman be not sacrificed.

We represent the most progressive educational movement of the world's most progressive age, and timorous as well as weak should we prove ourselves, did we surrender the trusts of which Providence has made us the depositories.

EVANSTON COLLEGE FOR LADIES UNITES WITH NORTHWESTERN UNIVERSITY.

An agreement was now made to this effect:

In consideration of having turned over to it all the property of the Evanston College for Ladies, the Northwestern University agreed to assume all financial obligations of said college, to complete its building and maintain the institution on a basis of which the principal features were the following:

The party of the first part (University Trustees) further covenants to maintain in all future time a representation of women in the Board of Trustees of the Northwestern University of not less, at any time, than five; and in the Executive Committee of the Board of Trustees of the party of the first part there shall always be, at least, one woman, if the women of the Board shall so require; and provision shall also be made, by the party of the first part, for an Advisory Committee of women, to be appointed by the Board of Trustees of the party of the second part, to confer with the Executive Committee on all matters of interest to the party of the second part hereafter, and the chairman of this committee shall always be received at the sessions of the Executive Committee of the Northwestern University; and the party of the first part shall also elect a woman to the presiding office of the Woman's College as annexed to or affiliated with the party of the first part, with the title of "Dean," who shall be a member of the Faculty of the University. And the party of the first part shall elect at least one woman to a Professorship in the University, and this perpetually; and shall also confer degrees and diplomas on the students of the said Woman's College entitled thereto, and this in the name of the Trustees and the Faculty of the University; and shall also maintain the same friendly relations now existing between the Woman's Educational Association and the party of the second part (Evanston College for Ladies), and keep up the same as between the said Woman's College and the said party of the first part, so far as is consistent with the charter of the University.

And in consideration of each and all of the matters aforesaid, the said party of the second part has this day assigned, granted and conveyed to the party of the first part, all its property, real and personal, together with all its choses in action, moneys and subscriptions set forth and enumerated in a schedule hereto attached, and hath agreed and covenanted and doth hereby agree and covenant to change its present corporate name to that of "Woman's College of the Northwestern University," etc., etc.

A method was also provided by which, should the University trustees fail to carry out the contract, the trustees of the Evanston College for Ladies could obtain redress.

One year more was invested in an unavailing effort to make the Woman's College and the University keep time together. Charles V. had not more trouble in his famous effort to make two watches do the same!

Having been elected Professor of Æsthetics in the University, I heard my recitations in the president's room of the University building. It was entirely a new thing to the students to recite to ladies, my friend, Kate Jackson, having all the French classes in the University, while I had part of the English composition. They tested us in various ways. One day on entering, I saw written on the blackboard, "Miss Willard runs the Freshman like a pack of girls." Without admitting by word or look that I had seen the flattering sentence, I went to the blackboard behind my desk, and while with one hand I erased it, with the other I was looking into my note-book for illustrations of different rhetorical styles, and sending the young men to the black-boards around the room each to write out a specimen sentence.

Another time they entombed a howling cat in the large drawer of my desk, and its orchestral accompaniment did not intermit one moment during the hour of my recitation, but if ever any one had the appearance of being stone-deaf I think I may claim to have been the person and this the occasion.

Their last attempt was on this wise: The recitation room door began to creak vigorously, the weather being damp. A young man would enter the class a minute late, open the door the whole arc of its liberty, and close it carefully while the squeaky creak went on, disturbing us not a little. The moment he had taken his seat, another young man just a minute later would open the door, enter, and close it in the same percussive manner, and so on until a dozen, perhaps, came in — there were no more mischievous ones in my large class of seventy. I made no comment, went on with the class as best I could, but that night a trusty student who was working for his board at Rest Cottage, was armed with a lantern, a piece of soap and the key to that recitation room, and he so limbered up those hinges that there was quite a surprised look on the faces of the boys when next day the door swung to and fro as if on velvet instead of iron.

I was reminded of these occurrences in the anteroom of Moody's great tabernacle in Boston,.where I spoke one Sunday afternoon in 1877 to five thousand people or more. Some excel-lent ladies who accompanied me said in anxiety when I was about to go before the audience, "Are n't you frightened? Does n't it make your heart beat faster to step out, one lone woman in sight of that great amphitheater?" And it came instantly to my mind to reply, "You never taught the Freshman class in Northwestern University or you would not expect one who has done that to be frightened at anything." To me an audience is like a well-bred person, quiet, attentive, sympathetic, and, best of all, not in a position to answer back! In all of these particu-lars it is the diametrical opposite of a lot of roystering youths who never before recited to a lady teacher and who are trying her mettle and their own. I ought to say, however, that the large majority were gentlemen and brothers, whom I recall with the kindest remembrance and in many cases with sisterly affection because of their manly considerateness toward me in those difficult days.

In the meanwhile, however, my system of self-government had fallen into "desuetude" that did not seem to me to be "innocuous." The new executive did not consider it compatible with the dignity of the great institution wherein our Woman's College was but a minor fraction. Some attempts to revive it in a modified form failed to meet the exigency that now came upon us, for the lease of Professor Jones's school building having expired, our girls boarded in the village during two thirds of my last year. A "self-report" was then devised to be filled out by them in writing. But it caused great dissatisfaction, the young men students, who were not under rules, being particularly hostile to this device which was only intended to tide us over the complex difficulties of a woman's college that was "all about town." When the spring term of 1874 opened, the new college being ready for occupancy, we moved into its spacious rooms and I believed, and do believe to-day, that if the internal management had been left with the ladies' faculty there, we could have restored the good order and good feeling that were the chief features of that single, bright, untrammeled year—1871–72. But, our chief now took the ground that the young women would get on very well with very little supervision, and I, who had thought myself an emancipator of college girls, saw myself designated "a female Bluebeard" by the press. On the test question, I voted all alone in one of the last faculty meetings of my history—my good friends being either absent or not voting. They knew the utter uselessness of making an issue with the president. I knew it, too, but my resolve was taken, the world was wide, and I would not waste my life in friction when it could be turned into momentum.

With but two exceptions, my generous girls stood with me and declared that they would gladly submit to any rules I might think best. There may be other instances on record, but I have not found them, of a college full of girls crying for rules like housekeepers for sapolio! But the fiat had gone forth: Practically equal freedom for all students and the method of self-government disfavored. This being settled, I determined to resign. My mother, brother and dear friends protested with might and main.

If I would state the case to the trustees, they felt sure that I would be sustained; Evanstonians were all my friends, they thought, and with a clearly defined issue like this, the local pressure in my favor would be strong. I had been elected to a most honorable life-position at a salary of $2,400 per year, had no money laid up, and no other means of support; it was consummate folly to resign a position so congenial as "Dean of the Woman's College, and Professor of Æsthetics in the Northwestern University." How could I think of leaving such a post? Thus they reasoned long and loud. But to my trusted few I stated my decision as unalterable, and then as always they stood by me, loyal, loving and true. To no trustee did I give the slightest intimation of my purpose, but went quietly on with my work; saw the steward of the Woman's College, who had been authorized to do so, conducting evening prayers while I sat by on the platform and my girls looked whole encyclopedias of rebellion and wrath; conducted my art classes at the new building to which from Rest Cottage I removed my residence; went to the University Hall to hear my college classes in English composition, and to the Preparatory for similar classes there; and all the time this refrain was in my heart:

"I am to go, I am to go! This college has been dearer to me than anything save Forest Home. Three years of my life's hardest work and best are here enshrined; brick by brick I've watched these handsome walls as they climbed high above the trees, and thought, "This is Professor Jones's college of which he was so fond, and it is my sister Mary's that died and it is mine." With a faculty of women gathered around me that are like a band of sisters, with pupils loving and beloved, with a life-position as professor of the branches I like best and know most about, and an adequate income assured, with mother and Rest Cottage only two blocks away, I felt too tranquil and secure. But as the eagle stirreth her nest and leadeth forth her young, so the Lord alone shall lead me; I must go; the world is wide and full of elbow room; this atmosphere is stifling—I must leave it."

On June 16, 1874, I went to my last faculty meeting. How I dreaded it! The beautiful stone building, the blue lake seen through the trees, the pleasant sky—I took last pictures of them all. In the president's room they were assembled—those men of culture and conservatism of whom I knew that none were my enemies, and several were my friends. Kate Jackson was with me, as usual, having the position of acting professor of French. I asked and received permission to read my report which was as follows:

TO THE FACULTY—Authorized by a resolution of some weeks since, I will indicate briefly, the principal points developed during the past term in the working of the "Rules for the Woman's College."

1. The demand of a certain class of patrons and of students for equality between young men and women in their relations to the government seems to have been met in a manner generally satisfactory, by making no special requirement of young women boarding outside the college building; thus placing them, in all regards, on the same basis as young men.

Those parents who desire to entrust their daughters with the responsibilities and prerogatives of self-government, can certainly make no complaint that this is not practicable in the Northwestern University.

2. On the other hand, allow me to call your attention to the fact that a large and estimable class of patrons do not find their wants met by the system of regulations at present prevailing *within* the college building. From the first, I have been impressed with this, but particularly so within the last fortnight, on being questioned by those who contemplate intrusting their daughters to the care of this faculty and who are not entirely disabused of old time prejudices against "mixed schools." One of the first inquiries of such parents is: "To what extent will the acquaintances formed by my daughter, and the social attentions she receives, be regulated by those under whose care I place her?"

A gentleman from Kansas applying on behalf of his motherless daughter of fifteen, asked me this question with much anxiety. In view of the fact that young ladies in the building receive calls from whom and when their judgment dictates (out of study hours), that they can be attended by gentlemen to nearly all the public exercises of the institution, and to all the regular religious meetings, without any special permission; in view, also, of the fact that they leave the grounds at all times freely out of study hours, (and thus, on Saturday and Sabbath can be absent for hours at a time without a teacher's cognizance), I have found it impracticable to answer truthfully such questions as I have referred to, and at the same time to secure the patronage of the inquirer.

3. The principle having been recognized, that, within the college building, the social relations of young ladies are, in the main, left to be determined by the girls themselves, I have found it extremely difficult, indeed impossible, to impress them with the dignity and importance of such exceptions to the general rule, as the faculty has seen fit to make.*

*The young ladies were, under these rules, free to go with young men to all meetings pertaining to the church and school, and only asked my permission when invited to concerts, lectures, etc., outside these "regular exercises."

When by the authority of this faculty, a young lady can receive a call daily, if she chooses, from Mr. A. (even if the teacher in charge deems his acquaintance an undesirable one for her), when, if she chooses, she can attend Monday evening prayer-meeting, Tuesday class-meeting and Wednesday prayer-meeting, and on Friday evening can accompany him to a literary society, is it to be wondered at if she regards it as unimportant that she obtain permission before going with him on Thursday evening to hear the Hampton singers?

Once admit that a lady student is competent to decide upon four fifths of the "social privileges" of a given week and she will soon learn to speak as flippantly as she thinks lightly of the restriction placed upon the remaining fraction of her liberty.

4. As an inference from what has been stated already, let me record the opinion that one and the same system of self-government for all lady students within the building as well as without, is more logical and will prove more successful than the present partial measures, which suit neither the radicals nor the conservatives and are, as experience and their own testimony conbine to prove, unsuited to the girls themselves. Indeed, I think girls boarding out have, under the present system, moral advantages over those in the building; for, being few in number in any one family, they are not likely to go to such extremes as when assembled in one building they are sure to reach, when left so largely to their own immature judgment. My own conviction that a more responsible "*home* government,"—one more worthy of a name involving an interest so deep, and a duty so high—is the truer solution of the problem, need hardly be repeated here!

5. It has been my task to administer, during the past few weeks, laws to which neither rewards nor penalties had been attached. Mild as is the code, and few as are its requisitions, I have greatly felt the need of some incentive to its observance on the part of the young ladies; and though no instance of violation of rule, which has come to my knowledge, has passed unrebuked, I have found a growing unconcern on the part of our well-meaning girls, and a hardly-concealed carelessness on that of others. Let me suggest that the hope of advancement to a higher grade, the certainty of a report sent home to parents, or some other expedient, will greatly aid in the administration of the rules.

6. The effect on the young ladies, of being left to the guidance of their own judgment, has not, in my opinion, been fortunate. Aside from the slight esteem in which they have come to hold the rules, there has been a stronger tendency toward sociability than toward study on the part of many, and a lightness of bearing, a pertness of speech and manner, and a tendency to disorder, such as my long experience in a school family has never witnessed hitherto.

7. I do not deem it inappropriate to express, in this connection, the decided opinion that, as at present conducted, the experiment of receiving young men into the Woman's College building as day-boarders has not warranted the expectations of its friends. I am confident that this opinion is

shared by all who have thoughtfully considered its developments. The young men should, in my opinion, be more carefully chosen ; should have certain restrictions or should be discontinued altogether, the latter being, as it seems to me, much the better course to be pursued. Though a few have been gentlemen, the majority have, by their rude behavior, much increased the unpleasantness of the family life, while their influence over the young ladies, uniformly directed against order and discipline, has rendered the problem of government much more complicated than it would otherwise have been.

8. In conclusion, let me ask your attention to the *duty* of a plain understanding with the public on the question of the government of young ladies in this institution.

The supposition is as natural as it is universal, that a school having a ladies' department, undertakes special supervision of this class of pupils, particularly in regard to their social relations. The public mind is fully persuaded that this is the policy of the Woman's College, not only from the nature of the case, but from the newspaper controversy of last winter, at which time the supposition was correct.

Repeatedly have mothers who intended sending their daughters to this institution, asked me within the last month "If this were not a strict school?" and it has proved an ungracious task to correct this quite erroneous opinion.

But consider expressions like the following from the new catalogue : "A home for young women, where their morals, health and manners can be constantly under the special care of women ;" "special advantages of watch-care," and others, of the like import, and see if there is not a discrepancy, of which you have not been aware, between these statements and the system now in force.

My own relation to the Woman's College has brought out the difficulty above referred to in a light more vivid than agreeable. With the parents on one side asking, "What safeguards can you offer to my daughter in her youth and inexperience ?" and the financial interests on the other urging the utmost possible conciliation of patronage (in view of an impaired exchequer), I have newly illustrated the peril of being between the upper and the nether millstones.

Clearly there are but two courses open to the University : First, no special requirements for young women, either in the building or in private families, and a frank avowal of such policy to patrons and inquirers ; or, second (the idea of general supervision having been abandoned by the faculty), a systematic oversight of the daily life and associations of those boarding within the college walls. I do not mean the old-fashioned boarding school system, which I never advocated, but I do mean such care and oversight, as will replace, so far as it can be done, *the influence of home.*

All this I can say to you, gentlemen, with the more directness, because of its being my last utterance in my present relations to you.

I have long thought there was but one fitting sequel to my experiences of the past school-year, experiences of which but little has come to the surface in the meetings of the faculty. Yet, from time to time, I have hoped for an improvement in the outlook of the Woman's College. I finally determined, some weeks since, upon a careful reconsideration of the whole question of my relations to the University, and, as a result, I wrote my resignation several days ago, which I shall present to the trustees on Tuesday next.

As my last word concerning the vexed question of government (one which, in my opinion, involves that of the success of the co-education experiment to which I have, in Evanston, given some of my best years), let me ask that the faculty carefully review the whole question, not only on its merits, but in the light of this term's experience; that you allow some weight to the womanly judgment of her who shall succeed me as Dean; that the daily devotional exercise at the Woman's College be placed under her care; and that, upon whatever course you may determine, the policy be clearly stated to the public, especially to parents who contemplate sending their daughters to this institution.

Respectfully submitted,

FRANCES E. WILLARD,

Dean of the Woman's College of Northwestern University.

June 13, 1874.

The reading over, I asked if Miss Jackson and I might be excused. The president nodded, and I went forth, not knowing whither I went, but glad, though grieved, to go. I pass over the trying ordeal of a "trustee meeting," in which it seemed to me that those opposed would fain have put me in the attitude of a culprit, while those who were my friends said, very properly, "We'd fight for you if you would stay, but you are bound to go and we must work for peace." I remember walking into the University chapel, where this trustee meeting was held; and what a stay and solace it was to grasp the arm of my beloved friend and sister, Mrs. Hannah Pearsons, who has reminded me always of the blessed Hannah of old. I can see my brother at the reporter's table,—though an editor-in-chief, he chose to hear for himself that day,—erect, alert, and deeply angered; my loyal knight always. I can see the sad faces of those faithful women, the trustees of the old college, and the thoughtful looks of the officers of our educational association, and my dear pupils with their sympathetic eyes. My resignation was read and referred, without debate, to a "Special Committee on the Woman's College." It read as follows:

EVANSTON, June 13, 1874.

Gentlemen and Ladies of the Board of Trustees of the Northwestern University:

It has slowly, but surely become evident that I can never carry into execution my deepest convictions concerning the interests of the Woman's College under the existing policy of government.

I therefore resign the office of Dean of the Woman's College, and Professor of Æsthetics in the University to which you elected me one year ago.

There are other reasons for this action, which justice to myself would require me to name in the hearing of the trustees, but I refrain from doing this out of regard to interests which must take precedence of any personal consideration. Respectfully submitted,

FRANCES E. WILLARD.

Relative to the foregoing documents by me presented, the following reports were made by the special committee and unanimously adopted by the trustees:

Your committee to whom has been referred the consideration of the interests of the Woman's College and in connection therewith the resignation presented to the board of trustees by Miss Frances E. Willard of her position as Dean of said College and Professor of Æsthetics in the Northwestern University, would respectfully report that, while they profoundly regret that any reasons should be supposed to exist sufficient to induce such resignation, they would recommend the acceptance of the same by the board of trustees. They further report that in view of the intimation contained in the letter of resignation of Miss Willard that the existing system of government in the Woman's College is in her conviction defective, the committee ask leave for further time to inquire into the grounds upon which the objections are founded, and to mature and indicate the proper remedy for any such defects they may find to exist.

This report was accepted and adopted, the substance of the latter part being laid over for further action. The final report was as follows, and was also unanimously adopted;

The committee to whom was referred subjects of interest pertaining to the Woman's College would respectfully report upon the question of rules for the Woman's College and for women attending different departments of the University, which question is suggested for present consideration by the resignation of the Dean of the Woman's College; that the system of co-education is new to the trustees of the University, and new, as well, in its University form to the faculty of the University and the Dean of the Woman's College, and it is not surprising that there should have been a difference of views with the members of the faculty as to the proper rules required under the circumstances. That the existing rules were not the exact views of any particular member of the faculty, and not precisely what any single one would have suggested, that they were in the nature of a compromise of different views, seems true. There is no doubt that the Dean of the Woman's College supposed in the formal union of the Woman's College with the University, all authority to make rules and regulations for the Woman's College was reserved to itself, and was not to be exercised by the faculty of the University; that subsequently she cordially united with the president in framing rules that after much public and private discussion were regarded as defective, and in this view she was understood by a majority of the faculty to concur; that, at a later period, when public discussion had ceased with reference to the rules, the faculty of the University took up and fully considered the question; that in this discussion the Dean of the Woman's College was not in full accord on the general principles of government for young women with the faculty, or a majority of them; but it was understood that in the main, all parties assented to the rules as adopted, though in some points they were not entirely satisfactory to the Dean of the Woman's College. Distinct provisions were made by the faculty that the Dean of the Woman's College shall, from time to time, report to this faculty upon the success of the rules adopted by the faculty. That the Dean of the Woman's College was greatly solicitous for the welfare and successful administration of the Woman's College, the committee fully believe; that she believed herself without adequate authority for a satisfactory administration of the Woman's College is also manifest.

The committee on the other hand fully believe the faculty of the University were equally anxious for the successful administration of the Woman's College, and were ready and willing to render any aid that they believed would contribute to that end, and that they regarded the rules adopted as an experiment. That the Dean of the Woman's College made no request to the faculty of the University for additional rules seems to be conceded. That she did not, may be explained by the fact that she did not wish, with too great haste, to pronounce the existing rules insufficient, or by the consideration that she would delay such suggestion until by her announced resignation all personal considerations should be eliminated from this subject.

The committee believe that the Executive Committee of the University made arrangements without consulting the Dean of the Woman's College, or the faculty of the University, with reference to day boarders in the Woman's College, that proved not wise, and which have been discontinued.

The committee would recommend to the faculty of the University that at an early day they reconsider and re-examine the rules of the Woman's College, and that in any respect in which they shall be found inadequate by administration to a complete and thorough safeguard of the students, that they be amended or added to.

The committee are persuaded that the trustees and faculty of the University have a united purpose to make the Woman's College, in its departments of instruction and government, worthy the fullest public confidence.

This "Special Committee" was, as I then believed, mortgaged from the first to the side of the stronger, and before it, when arraigned as not having carried out the rules efficiently, I burst out crying, and left the room. Finding my brother with a carriage at the gate, I soon reached friendly shelter.

So it was over, the greatest sacrifice my life had known or ever can know. For, lying there alone in our beautiful college, so thankful to be out of sight in my own quiet suite of rooms, planned for me by the loving care of the good women whom I had worked with so happily, there came to me the sense of an injustice so overwhelming that no other experience of mine compares with it in poignancy. "I tried so hard and meant so well!" Over and over again, I said those words and with agony of tears I pitied myself then and there, so that they heard me all through the hall, and were frightened by my anguish. Evening wore on, and at his handsome residence near by, the president's levee went forward. I could see its flashing lights and flitting forms as I lay there alone, and music by the band smote my tired ears.

At last everything grew still and sweet and holy, while far into the night the deep June sky bent over me with a beauty that was akin to tenderness. The storm in my soul ebbed away slowly, the sobs ceased, the long sighs were less frequent. As dies the wave along the shore, so died away for evermore my sorrow to lose the beautiful college that my heart had loved as other women's hearts love their sweet and sacred homes. In the long hours that followed, the peace that passeth understanding settled down upon my soul. God was revealed to me as a great, brooding Motherly Spirit, and all of us who tried to carry on the University, while He carried on the Universe, seemed like little boys and girls, who meant well, but who did n't always understand each other. The figure was of children playing in a nursery, and one little boy had more vigor than the rest of us, and, naturally, wanted us to play his way, while a little girl, whom I thought I could identify, said, "No; my way is best!" Then a deep voice declared, "This is the interpretation—good to forgive, best to forget." And then the happiness that mocketh speech, flowed, like the blessed, tranquil river of dear old Forest Home, all through my soul, and overflowed its banks with quiet, happy tears.

My cousins, Rev. S. and Mrs. M. B. Norton, who were associated with me from the first in all this college enterprise, and my friend Kate, were sent for at this point by my room-mate, Miss Harriet Reed. The record as my cousins have written it out, is this:

Well do I remember (writes Mr. N.) the rap upon our door in the then new Woman's College building at Evanston, one morning in June, 1874. It was an early hour, while it was yet dark. To the question, "Who is there?" a friendly voice responded, adding, "Mrs. N., I wish you would come to Miss Willard's room. She has not slept during the night. Something is the matter with her, I don't know what."

The call was instantly heeded, and we found Miss Willard, though surprised, yet glad to see us.

She seemed very anxious to have everything right between herself and those from whom she had so widely differed. And so intent was she upon this purpose that she urged us to send out at once to call in those who had been so eagerly engaged in opposition to her, that she might ask pardon of them all. But we who were then present were slow to believe that this was any part of her duty. Yet we could not fail to see *how easy it now was with her* to obey the best impulses of her heart in putting away everything that seemed un-Christian; sins of omission and sins of commission, of "word, thought or deed," for since the heavenly vision was present, nothing must be kept back. The joy of forgiveness was with her. Of this I have never known a brighter example.

It was now fully morning and Miss Willard's mother was sent for, who came with a carriage, saying that "her own home and her own folks were what Frank needed," so she was carried away from her well-beloved college forever. Mrs. N. and myself took an early train for Wisconsin. As we passed from this scene of "heavenly vision," in which, as Miss Willard had said, "God seemed so great, so loving, and human plans so small," I remarked to my wife, "Our cousin is either soon to go to her heavenly home or *from this time her life is to be enlarged!* This wonderful manifestation of Divine grace means something unusual."

FIFTEEN YEARS LATER.

In the foregoing pages I have tried to set forth the facts as they seemed to me at the time, and to do this with all possible considerateness and charity. But seen through the long telescope of fifteen years, and from a totally different angle of vision, the whole affair takes on a different aspect. I now perceive that our Woman's College building, its traditions, plans and purposes, all suited admirably to an independent institution, were not adapted to our relations as a department. The cost of this building greatly embarrassed the trustees, upon whom the failure of our subscription list, after the Chicago fire, threw burdens greater than they felt able to bear, and probably prejudiced them somewhat against our movement. The steward, who was authorized by the president to conduct prayers in my stead, was a Methodist minister and a gentleman of fine attainments, for whose dignity his brother minister showed a consideration that was perhaps no more than due.

But the clashing of my theory of a woman's college against our president's theory of a man's university was the storm center of the difficulty. An executive chief, the law of whose mind made general supervision his policy in the departments, was suddenly exchanged for one, the law of whose mind made special supervision the necessary policy and I, at least, as a departmental leader, did not take kindly to the change! Young men students helped on the revolt against the restrictions that seemed to me essential after my plan of self-government was set aside, and their watchword, "Equal rights for us all," was certainly chivalric, and in a deep sense, just. So far as the difficult question of government in such an institution is concerned, I would now say, with what seems to me to be the clearer sight of these more impartial years: put all on the same plane, but lift the plane on which young manhood stands to the higher level of young womanhood. Have a college senate of students made up of representatives from all departments, and let them conduct the government. This would break down the false ideas of "honor" that are among the student's greatest temptations; banish the hatefulness of espionage and give the noblest incentives to truthfulness in word and deed. With present light, I would organize a school as the national Government is organized — the college president and faculty being analogous to the Supreme Court—and would make the discipline of our young people's formative years a direct preparation and rehearsal for their participation in the government of their country, later on. This would leave the minds of teachers free to develop their specialties of instruction, and to lay deep and broad foundations for the ripe scholarship that is the glory of a great seat of learning. Moral horticulture at home and at school must always be the basis of success in developing Christian character among students, but participation in the government would place them in organic contact with the wisest and most parental minds among their teachers, and thus head and heart culture would go on side by side. So much for my present outlook and theory of school government, which, if I were to begin my district school in Harlem at fifty, as I shall not, instead of at twenty as I did, should be at once instituted in place of a set of rules with a rattan back of them. And were I now at Evanston, I would urge this view with what I fear might be regarded as "pernicious activity" upon the grave and revered leaders who very likely know a hundred times better than I do how to conduct a university.

It grieves me that I can not truthfully say I left the Deanship of a college and a professor's chair in one of America's best universities on purpose to take up temperance work, but the unvarnished tale here told must forever dispel that rare illusion. It is however true, that having left, I determined upon temperance work in face of tempting offers to teach in New York City and several other centers, and held to temperance work though delightful positions outside its circle have been open to me all along the years. Nor is there any merit in this constancy; I had, at last, found my vocation, that is all, and learned the secret of a happy life.

A few months after I left Evanston and while I was president of Chicago W. C. T. U., Mr. Robert Pearsall Smith, a wealthy Philadelphia manufacturer, and at that time a leading evangelist, came to Chicago and gave Bible readings of wonderful power, in Lower Farwell Hall. I remember he was staying at the Sherman House, where he invited several ladies and gentlemen to dine with him, and afterward I had an earnest conversation with him about the Christian life. I told him of the circumstances under which I left the University, and that I had unkind feelings toward several who were then connected with it, that it was the first time in my life that I had for any length of time felt other than cordial good will toward every human being, and though I was now greatly ameliorated in mind toward all, I still felt and wished to do something farther in the direction of a more friendly understanding with some of those whose associate I had so recently been. "There is but one thing to do, my friend," he said; "take the morning train for Evanston, see each and all between whom and yourself there is the faintest cloud, and without asking them to make any acknowledgment whatever to you, freely pour out in their ears your own acknowledgment, with the assurance of your affectionate good will." And this I did next day. The recital of my experience in going back on such an errand to "my ain familiar town," would be both pathetic and humorous. At first some of my dearest friends declared I should do nothing of the kind, that the bad behavior had been wholly on one side, and it would be an undignified and hypocritical admission of ill-conduct if I should go and make apology. My brother was specially strenuous on this point, but I said to him, "I am going to see the president of the University; you are my only near male relative, and I think it behooves you to act as my escort." When the matter was put before him in this light he could not refuse to accompany me. There was a revival meeting that night in the University chapel that we attended and in which I was called upon to participate, which I did. When it was over and nearly all had left the chapel, my brother went forward to the president and said I wished to speak to him and he would please tarry for a moment. How plainly I can see at this moment the tall, slight figure of my brother as he strolled up and down the aisle, at a distance, while in a recess of the chapel I went to the president, saying as I extended my hand, "I beg your pardon for everything I have ever done and said that was not right," with other friendly words, assuring him that I desired to be at peace with God and every human soul. He received me with the utmost kindness and responded in about these words: "To one who comes to me as magnanimously as you have done, I surely can not say less than that I beg your pardon," and from that hour we have been the best of friends. He and my brother shook hands, too, which was no small victory. Others whom I saw received me with tenderness even, and we knelt in prayer with many tears, so that when I left the dear home village and came whizzing back to my duties in the city, the buoyancy of my spirit was greater than if I had been made that day the heir to some rich inheritance. Nor do I know, nor ever mean to know in this or any world, a reason why any human being should hesitate to speak to me with cordiality and kindness, or why any middle wall of partition should exist between my spirit and any other human spirit that God has made.

The vexed question of government received special attention after I left, and I have every reason to believe that the Woman's College has been under the accomplished Deans, Ellen Soulé and Jane M. Bancroft, and is under the present gifted Dean, Prof. Rena A. Michaels, doing for young women all that their parents could expect from a first-class institution, while the University as a whole, with its two millions invested, its eleven elegant buildings, twelve departments, one hundred professors, and nearly fifteen hundred students, greatly outranks any other west of Lake Michigan, and richly deserves its name of the "NORTHWESTERN" in the modern sense of that great and comprehensive designation. Steadily may its star climb toward the zenith, growing clearer and more bright with each succeeding year!

COLLEGE COTTAGE, EVANSTON.

V.

A Tireless Traveler.

"SLEEP SAFE, O WAVE-WORN MARINER!
FEAR NOT, TO-NIGHT, OR STORM OR SEA.
THE EAR OF HEAVEN BENDS LOW TO HER:
HE COMES TO SHORE WHO SAILS WITH ME."
—*N. P. Willis.*

THE TIRELESS TRAVELER.

EARLY JOURNEYINGS.

One lonesome day in early spring, gray with fog and moist with rain, a Sunday at that, and a Puritan Sunday in the bargain, I stood in the doorway of our old barn at Forest Home. There was no church to go to, and the time stretched out before me long and desolate. I cried out in querulous tones to the two who shared my every thought, "I wonder if we shall ever know anything, see anybody, or go anywhere!" for I felt as if the close curtains of the fog hedged us in, somehow, from all the world besides. Out spoke my cheery brother, saying, "Oh, I guess I would n't give up quite yet, Frank!" and sweet little Mary clasped my thin hand with her warm, chubby one, looked into my face and smiled that reassuring smile, as sweet as summer and as fresh and fair as violets. "Why do you wish to go away?" she asked.

"Oh, we must learn—must grow and must achieve! It's such a big world that if we don't begin at it we shall never catch up with the rest," was my unquiet answer.

Always in later years when the world has widened for me, as it has kept on doing, I have gone back in thought to that gray, "misty, moisty morning, when cloudy was the weather," and been ashamed and sorry for the cross child I was, who had so little faith in all that the Heavenly Father had in store.

My mother says I never crept, but, being one of those cosseted children brought up by hand, started at once, by reason of the constant attention given me by herself, when I was less than two years old, to walk, having declined up to that time to do anything except sit in her arms. The first independent traveling of which I am cognizant was running away, with that primitive instinct of exploration that seems well-nigh universal.

Our overland trip to Wisconsin in my seventh year, two visits to Milwaukee, the fair, lakeside city, and one to my birthplace, comprised all the traveling done by me until we came to Evanston to attend college.

I well remember the profound impression made upon me, at nineteen years of age, by the first hotel I ever entered — the Matteson House, Chicago. I can not pass the building that now bears this name without shuddering recollections of the impressive spectacle when we all sat down to dinner at what was then one of the chief hotels; the waiters (all white men) standing in solemn line, then at a signal, with consummate skill and as by "one fell swoop," inverting the covers on all those huge, steaming dishes, without letting a drop fall on the snowy table, and marching out like a detachment of drilled soldiers! And never did a sense of my own small size and smaller knowledge settle down upon me quite so solidly as when one of those faultlessly attired gentlemen in claw-hammer coat and white cravat asked me "what I would have." I glanced helplessly at my good father; his keen eyes twinkled, he knew the man oppressed me by his likeness to a clergyman; he summoned him for a conference, and chose my dinner for me. But I was distressed for fear I should do something awkward under these strange circumstances, ate almost nothing, and had a wretched, all-overish sense of being unequal to the situation. Helplessly I envied the fair girl of sixteen who sat beside me, and was full of merry quips with father, and not at all concerned about her conduct or herself--my beautiful sister Mary.

When we came home from my year as "preceptress" in Lima, in the spring of 1867, we found my dear father in what proved to be the last stages of consumption. Hoping that a return to his early home and the society of his near relatives would be beneficial, Kate Jackson and I induced him to go with us to Churchville, in September, where he remained with his only brother, Zophar Willard, and his youngest sister, Mrs. Caroline Town, until the 24th of January, 1868, when his worn body succumbed to its inexorable fate, and his triumphant spirit wafted its way to heaven

Inasmuch as my father was with his family and had mother to care for him, I sought employment as a teacher once more, the impaired fortunes of our house seeming to make this requisite. I had secured a situation as teacher of English Composition in Lasell Female Seminary, Auburndale, Mass. My trunks were packed to go there from Kate's home in Paterson, when a letter from mother made me feel that my destiny did not lie in that direction. I therefore telegraphed to father, "I wish to come to you; shall I not do so?" Receiving his reply, "Come at once," Kate and I set out for Churchville, where for two months or more my only thought was to help as best I might in the care of my father, who was confined to his bed, and with whom mother and I took turns in watching for sixty nights, she having already, with my uncle and aunt, had the care for nearly two months. This season of solemn vigils was the most reflective of my life. In the silence of the night, how many times I sang to my father the old hymns dear to us at home, and read or wrote while he slept. The devotion of my mother and of my father's relatives can not be described—it was complete. Our loyal friend Kate settled herself in a quiet home across the street and was with us daily. When the sad home-going came, she was one of the company. A committee sent for the purpose met us on the train some hours before we reached Chicago, and when we arrived in Evanston at midnight with our precious burden, lights in the homes of our friends all along the streets we traversed, spoke eloquently of the sympathy and thoughtfulness they felt for us in our sorrow, and our home was bright with their presence and the manifold tokens of their loving care.

All that winter, mother, Kate and I kept house together. In the spring we went to visit my brother Oliver and his family in Appleton, Wis., where mother remained, and whence going to New York, Kate and I sailed on our long, adventurous journey.

And now, to show how it came about that I had the great advantage of living, studying, and traveling abroad from May 1868 to September 1870, I will give a sketch of my dear friend,

KATE JACKSON.

On my return from Pittsburgh in the summer vacation of 1864, I went according to my custom to the regular prayer-meeting in our old church in Evanston, and participated according to my custom in the exercises. At the close of the meeting when I greeted my true and tried friends, Dr. D. P. Kidder and family, I found with them a young lady who had been for some months their guest. Many years before, her father had been a member of Dr. Kidder's church, in Paterson, N. J., and the two families were special friends. The young lady's name was Katharine A. Jackson, and her father was James Jackson, founder, and at that time proprietor, of the New Jersey Locomotive Works. He was a self-made man, of great force of character and the sterling uprightness and energy of a North-of-Ireland Protestant. He had built up a fortune for himself and family, and his daughter Kate had received a careful education at the Ladies' Seminary in Wilmington, Del., where she was foremost as a scholar, having a very exceptional gift for the languages, especially Latin and French. She had been the salutatorian of her class, and since graduation had gone on with her studies until she was remarkably accomplished in her specialties. This young lady, not then a Christian, nor, as it would seem, even "seriously disposed," always declared that she took a liking to me on sight, or rather on sound, for I think it was my simple and fearless testimony as one who wished to lead a Christian life that first attracted her, a fact that has always made me thankful.

Being of a very enterprising disposition, Kate went a year or two after her graduation away down to Brenham on the Brazos River, Texas, where she taught French in Chapel Hill Seminary, only coming home when the war broke out. She had lost her mother early in life, and for that reason did not live at home.

We were much together that summer, and when I assumed the principalship of the Grove School in Evanston, she, just for the novelty of it, assisted me, and gave much additional popularity to the school by teaching French. When I was chosen corresponding secretary of the American Methodist Ladies' Centenary Association, in 1866, Miss Jackson did much writing for me, and helped me on in every way she could; and when I went as preceptress to Lima, N. Y., she accompanied me, having the French classes there.

One pleasant day at Lima, she said, "Go home with me at Christmas, for I am bound to coax my father to agree that you and I shall make the tour of Europe." I looked into her face with large-eyed wonder and delight. To see the countries of which I had read so much, and the homes and shrines of the great and good, had been one of my cherished dreams. I thought that its fulfillment would sometime come to me, but supposed it would be late in life.

When the holidays came, Kate and I went to Paterson, N. J. A handsome carriage with a high-stepping span and coachman in livery was at the train. A gentleman of about sixty years of age, with iron-gray hair, shrewd face as keen as it was generous, and the slightest suspicion of Scotch-Irish brogue, beamed upon us as we approached, and welcomed us to his beautiful home. It was James Jackson, a man whom my long acquaintance with his daughter had prepared me to admire and respect, and through whose liberality I was soon to have one of the crowning blessings of my life. He readily fell in with the project of his daughter Kate and told me not to feel in the least under obligations to himself or to her, for he had long desired that she should go abroad, but had never until now found any one with whom he felt inclined to send her. This gracious speech of the generous gentleman dispelled my scruples, which, indeed, were not strong, as Kate and I had been for years devoted friends. And so it came about that good James Jackson and his daughter are among the foremost of the beautiful procession of helpful souls that have so many times stood for me at the parting of the ways and pointed onward.

When we started on the long journey, May 23, 1868, I saw that honest, brotherly face with the sweet countenance of his youngest daughter, Carrie, close beside it, as the two stood under one umbrella in the soft May shower and watched us as our steamer parted from the wharf, we gazing on them with loving eyes until in the distance they grew dim and faded out of sight. That manly face we never saw again. In less than two years Kate's father had gone home to heaven.

PRELIMINARY.

Previous to going abroad I had visited my birthplace and Milwaukee, as already stated, been once to Pittsburgh, and twice to New England; the ocean, Niagara and the White Mountains being all that I had seen of Nature's loftiest mood. To visit the Capital of our own country, the only Eastern city that we had not yet seen, struck us as eminently fitting, and we went there just before sailing. Its glories fired our patriotism tremendously, and nothing that we beheld beyond the sea was ever admitted to be so grand as the great dome "where Fame's proud temple shines afar." We shook hands with President Johnson at the White House and were present, thanks to cards from Hon. Norman B. Judd, at one session of the Impeachment Court. My former friend of the Northwestern Female College, Evanston, Mrs. Jane Eddy Somers, now principal of Mt. Vernon Seminary, was our hostess and cicerone.

While abroad, we visited almost every European capital, large city, and specially interesting haunt of history, learning and art, besides going north as far as Helsingfors, Finland, east as far as the Volga banks in Russia, and Damascus in Syria; making the tour of Palestine, and going south far enough to look over into Nubia on earth, and up to the Southern Cross in the heavens. In all these journeyings, so varied, difficult and distant, we did not lose a day through illness save by my brief attack in Denmark, and our comrades paid us the compliment of saying that we were "as good travelers as men." We traveled with four hundred different persons during our different trips and had the comfort of believing that we were seldom, if ever, an incumbrance. Dr. Bannister, through whose influence we were admitted to the rare advantages of going through Palestine in the company of a party of distinguished Christian scholars, was especially proud of their verdict that we had not hindered them nor made any complaint throughout the trip, though it involved hardships to us unheard of and unknown until we braved the terrors of "camping out." My friend, Anna Gordon, has estimated the distance traveled, abroad, and since then in the temperance work of fifteen years, with the little flutterings that preceded, as making a total of two hundred and fifty thousand miles for the poor little girl that stood in the barn doorway and thought she should never see anybody nor go anywhere! But the story will best be told from records made when the impressions of all we saw were fresh upon the brain of one to whom the world was new. From twenty volumes scribbled on the spot, besides articles and letters, I make the wholly inadequate extracts that follow:

So the long dream was coming true, and yet, somehow, "it was not like"—how could it be? The Ideal world can never stoop to shore or sea, but we are slow and sad to find this true. Kate and I looked into each other's faces; "I could cry this minute, but I won't," she said. And then we talked of the kind, shrewd, grave face of her generous father and my noble benefactor; of his anxious, pathetic look after us as we started off all alone for strange, unfriendly shores, and faces of other friends unknown as yet.

All this while the nice looking little waiter, No. 2, left-hand side, at two o'clock dinner—was putting on the dishes, and dinner would be ready soon. We sat there silently, full of unusual thoughts. Looking over the passengers we were disappointed in them. They were for the most part quite mediocre in every sense—and probably they said the same of us! After a tolerable dinner we went below (the steamer now lying still waiting the tide), and set our house in order for the voyage, changed our dresses, and were innocently and unapprehensively putting the last touches upon our ship-toilets, when, lo! a pain that was not all a pain, but part a prophecy of dreadful things to come, seized each of us. Five minutes thereafter I had tumbled tumultuously into berth No. 1, at the top, and was "reaching" as our stewardess calls it, and groaning with all the more vehemence because so suddenly and totally surprised, for I had calculated with certainty upon the very opposite of this result. Kate lay in her berth below me moaning dutifully, but then, she had expected it. Well, for the next two or three days I thought and did unutterable things. Sunday is a perfect blank. In it I had just this one thought: "Let me lie still · let me keep this saucy diaphragm in equipoise."

Our lively and unique companion, Miss C., of Columbus, Ohio, between her "bad spells" and her tears, regaled us with exclamations of this character: "Why did n't they tell me it was *this way* and I would not have left my country! Oh! why did n't somebody tell me it was *this way?*" emphasizing the words with sounds more expressive than all human language could interpret, while listening to her I laughed like one who lived for laughter's sake alone. It is idle to attempt recounting the horrors of this voyage. All these notes I am scrawling on Sunday, May 31, leaning my head against the berth's side, and dipping my pen from a wine glass, furnished by our stewardess, whom at first we voted a virago, but have now "learned to love," have blessed with a sovereign, and voted a power in the earth.

June 1.—This bright Monday morning we were a hilarious ship's company, for to-day we should tread solid ground once more. We dressed "for shore," packed our portmanteau, and went on deck, where blue and distant loomed the longed-for land. Keen indeed was our pleasure in the sight of it. The scene was charming. All about us gently rippled the quiet sea; sails shone against the far-off, slate-hued horizon; birds, white and graceful of motion, careered around us; clouds lay anchored here and there; lines of dim coast stretched out alongside to the left; bunting flew merrily aloft; everybody was on deck in better dress than usual and with sunnier faces; the sailors furled the hanging canvas and made all trim for entrance to the harbor. And so the first bright day passed with talk and laughter, and toward evening a tug shot out from Queenstown harbor and we stepped gingerly upon its slippery deck, endured its wretched accommodations cheerfully, though rain began to fall and wind to blow, until they moored us alongside the steamer "City of Cork," and the inevitable custom-house officers took us in charge. They went rapidly through the form of unlocking our trunks, while we stood by unconcerned, looking over the magnificent Cove of Cork, and wondering that it did n't feel queer to be in sight of Queenstown shores. Soon we sped across the steamer's deck, went on shore, walked up strange streets, striking jubilant feet firmly upon beloved terra firma; peeped into curious looking shops, talking and laughing, half beside ourselves with pleasure, dangerously amused at the little donkeys, almost delirious over that intrinsically ludicrous, extravagantly rollicking contrivance, an Irish jaunting car. And so we reached the depot at nine o'clock, P. M., broad daylight at that, and took the cars for Cork, fourteen miles away. We tried to notice everything, even to the shape of the chairs and pattern of the paper at the Queenstown station; asked questions *à la* Yankee, and learned a great deal; drove to the Imperial Hotel, Pembroke street, Cork, had supper at eleven o'clock in an elegant coffee room, and went to bed. In the morning we chartered a jaunting car for Blarney Castle; rode enchanted through hedge-bordered roads to the famous castle, kissed both the Blarney stones (a gentleman giving us pieces of the real one, that we might carry the spell away with us); climbed to the topmost peak of the castle, and went down into its dungeons; got shamrock from inside the castle, went through Blarney groves, and what not. We then went laughing back to Cork, in the dear, ridiculous, old jaunting car; were invited by friends to go with them to Killarney, overland, one hundred miles by private coach. So at ten o'clock we all departed amid smiles and bows of waiters and chambermaids (thinking of "gratuities"), for the classic lake scenery of County Kerry.

"SHALL WE EVER GO ANYWHERE?"

ITINERARY OF FOREIGN TRAVEL.

May 23, 1868.—Sailed from New York in steamship City of Paris, Inman Line.

June 3.—Landed at Cork, Ireland.

June 3 to June 13.—Ireland.

June 13 to 30.—Scotland.

July 1 to 25.—England.

July 25 to 29.—Paris, France; Geneva, Switzerland.

July 29 to September 12.—Geneva to Nijni Novgorod via Denmark, Sweden, Finland, Russia, returning via Poland to Germany.

September 12 to December 20.—Berlin, Dresden, Leipsic.

December 20, 1868 to June 26, 1869.—Paris.

June 26 to July 28.—Belgium, Holland and the Rhine.

July 28 to September 2.—Switzerland.

September 2 to January 24, 1870.—Italy.

January 24.—Sailed from Brindisi for Alexandria, Egypt.

February 1 to 21.—Cairo, to the first cataract of the Nile (Island Philæ) and return.

February 23.—Climbed the Pyramid of Cheops.

March 6.—Sailed from Port Said to Joppa.

March 7 to 18.—Jerusalem.

March 18 to April 9.—Camped out in Palestine and made a trip to Damascus and Baalbec.

April 9.—Sailed from Beyrout to Cypress, Smyrna, Ephesus, Athens and Constantinople.

April 29.—Sailed from Constantinople via Bosphorus, and up the Danube to Vienna via Hungary.

May 4 to 16.—Vienna to Paris.

June 15.—Paris to London, Southampton, Isle of Wight, etc.

July 15.—Returned to Paris.

August 23.—Left Paris for Liverpool.

August 27.—Sailed from Liverpool in steamship City of Russia, Cunard Line.

September 5, 1870.—Arrived in New York.

THE GIANT'S CAUSEWAY.

A morning's ride through broad and prosperous fields brought us to the pretty village of Port Rush, with its fine outlook over the sea and far away. The Antrim Arms hotel received us hospitably and an appetizing dinner fortified us for the afternoon's performance.

Chartering a huge and jolly jaunting-car for our party of six explorers, we dashed off in pursuit of Nature's freakiest freak. Our road lay along the shore but lifted high above it. We looked down to see fantastic carvings of the waves upon the yielding rocks. "Tell us everything you know," was our moderate injunction to the middle-aged Hibernian who held the reins, and to do this he spared no pains.

"There's the Pope's nose!" he called out, soberly pointing with his long whip to this striking feature of the Holy Father's face, wave-sculptured, glistening in the sunshine and outlined on the blue-black ground of the sea. Our bright little friend, Willie, excelled us all in his appreciation of this piece of chiseling, and voted it, afterward, worth the whole Causeway.

"His lordship's residence" was pointed out, a fine country-seat, at a distance, almost concealed by the trees (as is "exclusively" done in these aristocratic regions), and a question brought out this brief "charcoal sketch" of the high-born gentleman who owns the "Giant's Causeway."

"Sir Edward's not a bad landlord, only he sweeps everything away. Just runs down here for money when he's out, and then off again to London, to spend it on his pleasures. But, ah! his steward is the man we're all in dread of. If one of the tenants would give him an offense in the least thing, then you'd see the beauties of a free government! Out goes the tenant into the street after getting a notice served on him to quit. Some of us try to improve our little farms, but what good is it? Down comes the man they call a "val-u-*a*-tor," and because we've made them worth so much the more, on goes more rent to keep us always sweating away just the very same as our fathers did before us, for if we don't pay the rent we have nothing to do but just tramp off as fast as we please. But Sir Edward, he spends nothing at all on the soil, and we've no ambition in consequence of it."

"You must come to our country across the water," said we, much interested in the man's straightforward words.

"Then, ah! I knew you was from America, Miss," said he; "that's the country where they'll give a well-doing man a chance, we all know that, and we'd go there on our hands and knees only for the water being in the way!"

Palaces, museums, picture-galleries are fine things in their places; sometimes as we wander over these rich lands we contrast their splendid treasures with our emptiness at home, and feel a moment's discontent. But we think of these words, and are too grateful for complaint, too proud for boasting, "America's a country where *they'll give a well-doing man a chance*—we all know that."

About a mile from the Causeway, two guides came trotting along the road, anxious to enlighten us as to the merits of the case in hand, and we engaged one as a refuge against the other and any who might subsequently present themselves.

"Will you please look over my book of recommends?" said John McLaughlin, the chosen of our judgment, hanging on precariously to our rapid car, and we examined sundry soiled autographs of tourists, noble and otherwise, all of whom concurrently attested the varied virtues of the said John in his capacity of guide.

"Indeed, I'm the man that Harper says ye ought to have, in his fine leather-covered book," quoth he, winking triumphantly at his disappointed rival, who whined out, "It's my turn, anyhow, and I'll be even with ye yet."

We dismounted in front of John's cottage, the tonguey owner thus introducing it: "Ye must know, ladies and gentlemen, that I have the honor to live in the house fartherest north of any in old Ireland. Here I have lived for twenty years, and a snug place it is, as ye all see."

Not altogether unattractive looked the man's home, with white-washed walls, and grass and trees about it. Not far off, around the curving crags, we came, by diligent and dangerous scrambling in a down-hill direction, upon a cove, where tossing upon the restless waves was a small boat in which we embarked for a general in-look on the Causeway. Four oarsmen had the boat in charge, and with tossings and dippings not conducive to content on the part of the timid, nor to interior tranquility in those of dizzy head and squeamish stomach, we put to sea, while John McLaughlin, oblivious to fears or qualms uttered or unexpressed, proceeded with great fluency to give the following "true history of Giant's Causeway." "Ye must know, ladies and gentlemen, that long and long ago it was, we had here in Ireland a giant, the like of which was never before seen nor will be seen again. His name was Fin McCaul, and what he could n't do nobody else need try. It so happened that at the same time they had in Scotland another giant, a tremendous fellow and jealous of our Fin, as a matter of course. Well, this Scotch fellow sent word to Fin that the only reason he did n't come and fight him was, there was no bridge across. So what does Fin do but falls to work right immediately and all his servants with him, and they make the genteelest road (or 'causeway' as they used to say in old times) from here to the other side. Then they had their matched fight, and you may be sure Fin did n't leave a whole shred of the other fellow, but pounded him up fine, and that was the last of him. So then when there was no use of it any more, in the course of time the Causeway sank into the sea, and there's nothing left of it now but some remains on the far side, called Fingal's Cave, and this here that you can see for yourselves. This is just the very same as it was in his day, and when the sea is still you can notice it going out into the water as far as you can see at all."

Highly instructed and entertained by this historical account, we viewed with increased interest the outlines of this astonishing piece of engineering, though its general appearance, at this distance, hardly met our expectations. Indeed, some of us vociferously informed the imperturbable exhibitor that it did n't pay to be tossed about in this fashion, and risk one's life in the bargain, just to see some sloping, irregular rocks, stretching for some distance along the shore. "Gentlemen and ladies have many times observed the same to me, madam," he replied, touching his old blue cap, "but I just get them to wait a bit, and afterwards they look upon it quite different to that."

The name-worthy heights and depths before us were now duly indicated and described, a geography lesson "with illustrations" worth talking about. We declined to row into Portcoon Cave, the waves being so high that our heads must inevitably be bumped against its roof, a tribute we would not pay even for a new sensation. "The Steckan," or chimney-tops, a couple of tall, conspicuous rocks, were pointed out with the story that when the Spanish Armada passed this coast they fired upon these rocks through some misapprehension, and that right here, some of its ships going to pieces, the organ upon which King Philip said his *Te Deum* should be played in Westminster Abbey (after the victory that he did n't win) came ashore and was conveyed to Trinity College, Dublin, where we had seen it within a day or two. We now returned to land, having as yet but a dim notion of the great sight we had taken so much pains to see. Of our disappointment our guide was made repeatedly aware, but he bided his time with an air of superior wisdom inspiring to behold, and profound faith in the ultimate triumph of the great show over whose wonders he had so long presided. Marshaling us in line, he led us up steep rocks and along devious ways, to inspect narrowly the Giant's Road. From that time forth, our progress partook of the character of an ovation. How very thoughtful everybody seemed! Here came a young Hibernian of impecunious aspect, who urged on our acceptance his collection of stereoscopic views illustrative of scenery hereabouts. Each one of the four boatmen presented a little box of pebbles, crystals, shells, "Picked up right here at the Causeway, sir." Half a dozen ragged urchins, none of them over half a dozen years old, clamored for us to accept their herbariums of sea-weed, their curious bits of stone, their printed "guides," their gathered flowers.

"Ye'll do as ye like," whispered the crafty McLaughlin with an air of great disinterestedness, "I don't say but what all these poor things have is very good, but, to tell the truth, I think ye'll do better to look over me own assortment at the house when we've done here."

Now we began to see that what we came to see was surely worth the seeing. We stepped upon the Causeway, its surface at the edge being, save for irregularities, quite like an incipient Nicholson pavement; traversed its whole extent (made up, some careful counter says, of four thousand columns set side by side), and every moment the wonder grew upon us that purest nature could so mimic purest art. A monstrous puzzle it must all be,

17

which some well-instructed giant hand might take apart; or else a honey-comb of the Olympian gods, gone gray with age and hardened into stone.

On we went, over the ends of those most curious columns, which extended, nobody knew how far below us, now stepping up, now down, as the arrangement of the surface varied, for the appearance everywhere is startlingly like that of intention, as if the great artificer had turned aside to rest a little while, leaving his carefully wrought plan to be completed on his return.

I have no wish to attempt a description in the abstract, but to relate in the concrete what we saw, and how we saw it, hence it becomes essential to confess that for thought deeply interesting to the observer and inspired by the peculiarities of his surroundings, we had little peace. Our retinue of pests increased in geometric ratio as we proceeded; we reached "The Well," a several-sided indentation, whence an old man with a ready cup dipped water for us, drinking which we were to "wish a wish," which in a year was surely to "come true." A crowd of witnesses surrounded us as we went through this ceremony and silently chose our choicest wish, with as much sincerity as if we had believed the story of its prospective fulfillment; and while it was in our thoughts, the dear, sacred, mystical desire, a ruthless, wrinkled hand thrust before us a bunch of dripping sea-weed and the old woman owner of both exhorted us to buy, with this clinching argument, "The nobility and gentry, they always buys of me!"

At the same time, bright little Jessie P. was assailed by an itinerant shell dealer with his flattering unction, "Indade, darlint, yer have the most illegant foot that ever came upon the Causeway in my time, and I've been here since ever I can remember anything at all." And she was a Chicago girl!

On we labored, perseveringly, until we reached the "Wishing Chair," a depression formed by the removal of a section or two of these carefully-fitted stones, and a most unluxurious seat. We were now introduced to what the guide called "The Particular Stones," those of shapes less frequent than the four, five and six-sided, which make up the body of the Causeway. There are septagons and octagons, two nonagons and a single triangle among all the one thousand stony illustrations of geometry that make up the vast structure. Specimens of every style having been examined and a tiny piece of the triangle hammered off (strictly "by permission"), we next analyzed in cursory sort the background of the picture, the tall basaltic columns that rear themselves farther from the sea, behind the shelving floor that we had thus far trodden. One of these is sixty-three feet high above the surface of the ground. How far it may extend beneath, the wisest can not estimate. In one of the columns, of which we got a long profile view instead of the mere surface one seen in the foreground of the Causeway, there are thirty-eight different pieces, all fitted with the nicest accuracy, but each so separate from that above and below itself, that an arm strong enough could unjoint the whole column as children do toy steeples made of spools.

"The Giant's Loom Post," is a splendid tower made up this way, standing out in strong relief, but not facing the sea, and hence invisible in general views. Here the old Road Builder was wont to spin, including that effeminate accomplishment among numerous more weighty ones. His organ, splendid but tuneless in its basaltic pipes, stands opposite. The jack-stones with which he was fond of playing in intervals of labor, the prints of his huge knees made while enjoying this game; the fan mosaicked by him in his road for a lady admired and admiring, and, incongruously, perhaps, the pulpit whence he sometimes preached, all were pointed out and served the guide as reminders of anecdotes, sometimes witty, often dull, always related with an air of deep conviction, and listened to in a similar spirit, by me, at least. Our expressions of appreciation satisfied him fully at last, and he begged permission to pack and send to Liverpool for shipment to the land of lands, at least one specimen joint apiece for us, from those unclassified fossil remains. Pentagons were dear, octagons at a premium, but hexagons could be had, I think, of ordinary size (say a foot or two in length and four to six inches in diameter) for the paltry sum of eight or ten golden dollars. We began to wonder whether Lord Antrim, or Sir Edward (whose income is set down as two hundred and fifty thousand dollars annually), had farmed out the eighth wonder of the world, but we remain ignorant on that score.

We returned from the "Grand" across the "Honey-Comb" and "Well" causeway (the three divisions which are yet undivided, being designated thus). "A belemnite and two ammonites and all for one half crown!" screamed a little ne'er-do-weel who might have offered herself as a specimen Bedlamite with some propriety, as she outskipped her comrades and presented herself prominently beside us. Terms so geological from a young nondescript like that, seemed whimsical enough.

Along the crag-bordered road we walked as evening fell, breathing the vivid ocean air, a straggling procession at our heels, through whose clutches we had passed unscathed.

We gathered for ourselves sweet flowers with faces strange and new, and then rode homeward in the shadow of the limestone cliffs, with outlook on the far, mysterious sea.

MY TRIP TO THE GARDEN OF EDEN.

"The gentle reader" will surely be decoyed by such a heading into a perusal of my first sentence. But my conscience drives me to the avowal that I have in mind only some notes of an excursion to the Isle of Wight. I realize the duplicity of trying to sail into the uncertain harbor of "the public ear" on false pretenses. England calls its pet island "Eden's Garden," but the mother-land is so fair that I should hesitate to give the palm to a daughter even so lovely as this. We landed at Cowes,—the paradise of yachtsmen,—rumbled through its narrow streets on top of an omnibus, overgrown and overcrowded, to Newport.

Leaving Newport, we jogged on to the pretty little town of Carisbrooke, whence we walked up to the castle, the more active of our party making its circuit, and finding every lonesome room haunted by thoughts of Good Queen Bess and stubborn, unfortunate King Charles I. A young woman of quite literary aspect, with a wise looking book under her arm, opened the wicket for us, and we thought her an obliging tourist till she took the proffered coin, so seldom refused in Her Majesty's dominions, and told us how to "do" the fine old ruin. But, somehow, after Netley Abbey, Carisbrooke seemed tame and too far gone for much enthusiasm. What I shall remember longest is its fortress well—excavated in forgotten centuries to a depth of three hundred feet or more—from whose black abyss the most forlorn, demented-looking donkey I ever saw drew a full bucket for us by toddling along a great wheel in tread-mill fashion.

Going to Carisbrooke village, near by, we had a homely, but most toothsome English dinner at the Bugle Hotel. The mistress of the house waited on us herself, cutting the "half-gallon loaf," and telling us she once saw Tennyson : "that is, an ordinary looking man passed by, and afterward somebody said 'he'd wrote a book about a sailor that went off and got ship-wrecked, and when he came back, his wife was married again.'" She always thought the person that pointed this man out to her called his name Venison! Over the midday meal our party decided upon a separation. Four of them openly declared their indifference to the "Dairyman's Daughter" and all the haunts pertaining to her, and expressed their fixed determination "to see the inside of Osborne" if money would purchase that beatific vision. But Kate and I decided on the daughter of the dairy-man, so, complying with the suggestion of our landlady, we chartered "our vicar's chaise, and the nice, stiddy young man that drives it," and off we bowled through the shadiest and loveliest of lanes. Of all the hamlets that English authors set before us, or pensive fancy conjures when we read about the mother-land, this of Arreton, at which we soon arrived, seems to me the most perfect fulfillment of one's ideal. What a good and ignorant life one might here lead ! How distant from the pleasures, sins, and numberless amenities of this our wide, wide world; "so near and yet so far" from all that pains and pleases on the turbulent, but buoyant sea of art, business and politics, that we call life ! What a host of intricate relationships to the world we touch at points so many and so varied, are brushed aside like cobwebs, as one enters the still graveyard where simple Elizabeth Walbridge has slept so sweetly and so long !

In the cool shade of the gray and friendly church—the very quaintest in the kingdom—how many a fitful fever has been quenched ; and looking far above its dim old spire into the quiet heavens, what downlike peace has fallen into tumultuous hearts ! If one should ask me the place of all that I have seen in my restless wanderings over the earth which lent itself most readily to sober second thought—the place where one could be most truly "in but not of" this world ; did any seek the sanctuary of a silence sacred, but not terrible ; of a serenity profound as that which glorifies the brows undreaded death has touched, yet sweet and human as the smile upon a sleeping baby's face—I would point him to this tree-embosomed hamlet. Here the invisible spirit's breath alone seems to stir the quiet leaves, and the very sunshine is toned and tempered as one sees it not elsewhere. The clustered homes look as if they had grown here, like the trees which hide them; one's fancy can not make itself believe that ever sound of hammer or of saw was heard in a retreat so still. The solemn church has a look so venerable, one well might believe it a feature of the scene as natural as the bowlders on the highway.

Around it the silent graveyard stretched its quiet shadows on that still summer noon. A little child, not six years old, was playing near the roadside as we alighted from the carriage, and at a sign from the "stiddy young man," she conducted us to the church-yard, walking demurely down the narrow lane before us, finger in mouth, and looking a strange, elfish little guide, as she threaded her way among the thickly strewn graves, guided us to the rear of the church, quite under the shadow of its solemn walls, crossed a small bit of sunlit sward, and stood beside a plain white headstone much larger than herself. Resting her hand upon it, she pointed to the name we sought and sententiously observed, "That's it." Beside the grave were two others—that of the parents and sister of good Leigh Richmond's heroine—the parents without tombstones, those of the two sisters having been secured by public subscription. Nothing could be simpler than these little monuments; and Leigh Richmond's epitaph written for that of the "Dairyman's Daughter" is very touching and appropriate.

I brought away with me a dandelion that was growing on the grave I came to see, for I thought it a fit emblem, with its modest stem and globe of gold, of the lowly life which yet was glorified by some of the loveliest beams that make bright the Sun of Righteousness.

The gray-haired sexton came across the little meadow to show us the old church, in whose plain and unadorned interior he seemed to take fully as much pride as the elegant beadle of unmatched York Minster evinces in his own especial charge. "There his some very hold brass in the chancel, ladies, you really hought n't to miss of seein' hit," he said, touching his old straw hat. But we anticipated seeing so much "brass," ancient and modern, in that museum of antiquities called "Europe," that we declined, to the evident disgust of the exhibitor.

Reluctantly we turned away from Arreton hamlet—the ideal home of a Rip Van Winkle sleep—and told our "stiddy young man who drives the vicar's carriage" to take us next to the cottage of the dairyman. But that worthy felt called upon to reason with us in this wise: "Hit's a long ways off—three good miles there and back; and I'm persuaded you'd miss the six o'clock boat for Southampton that I've given you my word you should be in time for. Then again hit's nothing to see, I assure you, ladies—being as common a cottage as there is on the whole island. I can show you many a one like it. And, besides, you could n't get in if you went; for the present proprietor don't like troubling himself for visitors, and it was recently a question of pulling the hold thing down altogether." We ranged ourselves as usual on different sides of the argument—Kate the conservative, I the radical; she cautious, I adventurous; she saying, "We must n't miss the boat," and I, "But we must see the cottage." However, with two against one, it is manifest who gained the day; we drove off regretfully to join our friends at Osborne—the "stiddy young man," true to his word, pointing out a cottage now and then with his long whip and turning toward me with his squint eyes, saying, "Hit's very like the dairyman's, I do assure you, Miss, only far prettier, and better worth your while." Alas, for those to whom a primrose is a primrose only!

We looked down the cool vista of Osborne from "without the gate," and were glad that within a home so sheltered and so noble the lonesome queen can shut herself from the obtrusive world, and hide her wound as does the stricken deer in the deep wilderness; and as we went our restless way we mused upon the lesson to be gleaned from the reflection that the saddest woman in England's realm wears England's crown upon her head, and lives, sometimes, at least, in its "Garden of Eden."

It was a great transition to find myself next day swinging in the globe at the top of St. Paul's Cathedral spire in London—impelled to a gymnastic feat so senseless by the declaration of a young Boston snob, that "No woman had done this, or could, or should."

THE MONKS AND DOGS OF ST. BERNARD.

It was the twenty-seventh day of August, 1869. The Doctor "did n't think 'twould pay to climb such a tall hill just to see a few dogs and some monks," and his wife was not physically able, so we three insatiables, Kate, Sophie and I, gladly accepted the invitation of Messrs. Smith and Jones to take the long-desired excursion in their company. We did our best to get up and off early, but it was half-past seven before ourselves, our bags, guide-books and umbrellas were all fairly stowed away in a carriage meant for four. We drove six hours along a well-built road, through scenery much finer than we had looked for on this pass which the books feel called upon to characterize as inferior to most other Alpine heights. We did not at all agree to this, particularly Mr. Jones, who was in a sort of fine frenzy all the way—only Mr. Jones is dry in manner, and, like a glacier river, apt to burst forth "on a sudden." The villages we traversed far surpassed in age, dirt, narrowness, and direct antagonism to their natural surroundings, all that had preceded them in our two months' observation of Switzerland. At Orsieres we spent a spare half hour in the curious old church, which has a crucifixion quite too sanguinary and awful to be long looked upon, and a contribution-box with a jingling bell attached, which Mr. Smith shook in our faces, with his great laugh, frightening us lest priest or sexton should appear. Nobody was present, though, except two sober-faced little girls, who said that they had come to pray, and who responded in pretty, serious fashion, to Kate's shower of French interrogations.

There were quaint and curious explanations written in a hand like our grandfathers', on paper yellow as theirs, of the dim, but tawdry pictures on the wall, stating that certain purgatorial exemptions might be reasonably hoped for by the faithful who should repeat in front of them a certain number of *Aves* and *Paternosters*. There was also a huge eye painted in water-colors, likewise an ear, and a hand holding a pen, under which, respectively, were written, "The Eye that sees all!" "The Ear that hears all!" "The Hand that writes all!" This, perhaps, is good—for peasants. I was indignant at the contrast between the bedizened wall and the high, stiff, narrow seats for the humble congregation. It seemed curious, in such squalid villages, to come upon Latin inscriptions over the houses, but these were numerous, also saintly symbols and monograms. Great crosses spread their sheltering arms along the roadside, almost always with inscriptions, of which the most impressive was, "*Cruci fidelis inter omnes.*"

Erelong we struck the trail of the great Napoleon—that is, its palpable remains. Mr. Jones kept a bright lookout, for he thinks there never was but one man, and his initials were N. B. The old, broken-down bridge by which the "greatest captain of his own or any other age" crossed this deep gorge, is near the ancient village of St. Pierre, and a tavern hard by is called the "Hotel of Napoleon's Breakfast."

I went back in thought to my old "McGuffey's Third Reader" and the rough Wisconsin school-house, where I first studied out its account of the great warrior's passage here, and gazed upon its rude wood-cut of David's splendid equestrian picture, which I saw last year in the palace of Frederick the Great. I linked the present and the past by a strong effort of imagination, and repeopled the silent cliffs and valleys with the invincible army of thirty thousand men, and the dauntless leader who said, "Is the route practicable?" and being answered, "It is not, perhaps, impassable," cried, "Move forward the legions!" and a few days later won Marengo and lost Desaix. To my unskilled eyes the route did not appear so difficult as I had fancied, but it was August, that was May, and snow blocked up the passage and benumbed the troops. Yet even Mr. Jones, the hero-worshiper, who would have followed to the bitter end the leader whom Madame de Rémusat does not love, admitted that it "did n't really look so dreadful as he had hoped it would."

At a lonely wayside inn we left the carriage, and Kate and Sophie took mules while I went on foot with the two gentlemen. Kate's muleteer was a handsome fellow with a mouth gleaming in ivory, and a tongue which proved that perpetual motion is no impossibility. As a peasant woman with fantastic head-piece, passed on her way to church, he remarked in French, "Men are not good at prayer, no more have they the time; they leave it to their wives. Women's eyes are always fixed on the sky, but men's eyes are rooted to the ground." As he said this, he saluted the woman and exclaimed, "Pray for us husbands."

The way was enlivened by interesting talk, and I forgot to change with Sophie at the place agreed upon, but climbed upward on foot in the sudden twilight toward the famous home of animals of whose noble deeds men might be proud, and of men whose saintly lives recall that of the Master who pleased not Himself. The way grew very dreary, the chill in the air seemed to penetrate our bones; bare, gray and pitiless rose the cliffs on every hand, and the eternal snows seemed not a stone's throw distant. Travelers of all nations passed us on this strange road where nature was so pallid and so cold; quick-footed young pedestrians from England, leisurely gray-mustached French gentlemen on horseback, fat German ladies in chairs borne by two stout-armed peasants, delicate-featured Americans, the women riding, the men lightly walking at their sides. On we climbed, while Mr. Smith impelled our flagging steps by an explosive recitation of Longfellow's "Excelsior," the scene of which is here. Around a sharp, rocky bend, up an ascent as steep as a house roof, past an overhanging precipice, I went, leaving the gentlemen behind me, in the enthusiasm of the approach, and then the gray, solemn, friendly walls of the great Hospice, which had seemed to me as dim and distant as the moon's caverns, rose before me outlined upon the placid evening sky. I stopped and listened eagerly as I approached its open door, no sound but the gurgle of a distant brook; no living object but two great St. Bernard dogs seated upon the broad, dark steps of stone.

A gentleman may be defined as a being always wisely and benignantly equal to the occasion. Such a character appeared upon the scene in the person of "Reverend Besse," the "Hospitable Father" and chief of the establishment. Our party in committee of the whole (and no "minority report"), voted him the most delightful man we ever saw. All that is French in manner, united to all that is English in sturdiness of character, all that is winning in Italian tones, united to a German's ideality, a Yankee's keenness of perception, a Scotchman's heartiness, and an Irishman's wit—these qualities seemed blended in our "nonesuch" of a host, and fused into harmony by the fire of a brother's love toward man and a saint's fidelity to God. Young, fair, blue-eyed, he stood among our chattering group like one who, from a region of perpetual calm, dispenses radiant smiles and overflowing bounty. So quick was his discernment and so sagacious was his decision, that almost without a question he assigned us, in detachments correctly arranged, to fitting domiciles ; made each one feel that he or she had been especially expected and prepared for, and within five minutes had so won his way into the innermost recess of everybody's heart, that Mr. Jones expressed in his own idiomatic way the sense of fifty guests when he declared, "To such a man as that even the Little Corporal might well have doffed his old chapeau." Who shall do justice to the dinner at that L-shaped table, where the Father sat at the head and said grace, beaming upon his great cosmopolitan family with that young face, so honest, gentle and brave? Who but the jestful climbers to whom rice soup, omelet, codfish and potatoes, stewed pears, rice pudding, figs, filberts, cake and tea, seemed dulcet as ambrosia on these inspiring heights? Then came the long evening around the huge and glowing hearth-fire. How soon we felt "acquaint"; how fast we talked in frisky French or wheezy German, minding little how the moods and tenses went askew, so that we got and gave ideas. The Father turned from side to side answering with solicitous attention every question that we asked, so that a mosaic of his chief replies would read something like this:

"Mademoiselle asks the indications of the thermometer this August evening? I learn the mercury stands already at forty-five degrees Fahrenheit, and the boundary line of Italy is but five minutes distant. Here, Brother Jean, please provide the beds of all our guests with warming-pans.

"Yes, lady, our Hospice was founded nine hundred years ago, by Count Bernard, of Savoy, who devoted forty years of his life to entertaining and protecting, as we still try to do, the many travelers who annually pass through these mountains between Switzerland and Italy. About twenty thousand were cared for each year in olden times, without the smallest charge being made of rich or poor. Now, we have not so many, the facilities for travel having so greatly improved. But a great number come over the Pass who are out looking for work, and there are also many beggars. These we limit to three days' entertainment. We would gladly keep them longer, but can not. Our dogs are a cross between Newfoundland and Pyrenean, and after seven or eight years become rheumatic, and we are forced to kill them. In winter travelers are obliged to wait at a place of refuge we have provided, at some distance from these buildings, which are on the very top of the Pass, until we send out a man and dog, with refreshments fastened to the neck of the dog, who never once loses his way, though the distance is long, the snow is often thirty feet deep, and the only guide the man has is the great banner-like tail of the dog waving through the storm. Last winter we lost one of our noblest animals. A strange dog bit him and severed an artery. The monks always go out in the most dangerous weather. I lead them at such times. They are not obliged to go—we make it perfectly voluntary."

Here Kate broke in with an important question: "How do you occupy your time in summer?" "Oh, Mademoiselle, we study and teach—we had fifty students last season." "What do you teach?" "All that a priest ought to know—theology, philosophy, the laws of the church. We know contemporaneous events, except politics (!) which we do not read." "What is your age?" here chimed in the practical Jones. "Monsieur, I am thirty-one." ("But he does not look a day older than twenty-three," whispered poetical Sophie, and we all nodded our energetic acquiescence in her figures.) "How long have you been here?" "Eleven years, and I remain in perfect health. My predecessors in the office could not endure this high latitude—three of them left in a period of four years." "Why are you here?" persisted Jones. The scene was worthy of a painter—that shrewd Yankee, whose very figure was a walking interrogation point, and that graceful, urbane monk, in his long cassock, as leaning in his easy-chair and looking forward and a little upward, he answered with slow, melodious emphasis, "Brother, *it is my calling*, that is all." So simple was his nature, that to have heard "a call" from God and not obeyed it, would have seemed to him only less monstrous than not to have heard any call at all! At early dawn we were wakened by men's voices in a solemn chant, led by the Hospitable Father—and never did religion seem more sacred and attractive than while we listened as through the chapel door came the words of the *Te Deum*, consecrated by centuries of Christian song, "We praise Thee, O God, we acknowledge Thee to be the Lord."

PARIS.

January 3, 1869.—In the evening we were all assembled in the *salon*, and Madame P., our teacher, telling us not to be scandalized, brought in the cushion cover she is embroidering and her sister's sewing, and they both proceeded to put in a solid evening at work. Her son, with two friends, sat at the card table throughout the evening, and this was my first Sunday with a French family in Paris.

Memorandum.—A man of all work is cleaning out Madame's *salle à manger* floor with a brush on his foot, and his foot plying actively from side to side. A more excellent way this than to see Antoinette, the maid of all work, on her knees with a scrub broom!

January 6.—Rejuvenated, recreated, by eight hours' continuous repose, I have a mind to indicate here what has much occupied me of late, but what I am not brave enough to execute, perhaps, though, if I were, I believe my usefulness would exceed the measure it will reach in any other line of life. Briefly, it is to study so far as possible, by reading, learning the languages and personal observation, the aspects of the woman question in France, Germany and England, and when I return to America, after two or three years' absence, and have studied the same subject carefully in relation to my own land, to *talk in public* of the matter and cast myself with what weight or weakness I possess against the only foe of what I conceive to be the justice of the subject, and that is unenlightened public opinion. Sometimes I feel "the victory to be in me," often I do not. Always, I have dimly felt it to be my vocation, but a constitutional dread of criticism and too strong love of approbation have held me back. With encouragement, I believe myself capable of rendering services of some value in the word-and-idea-battle that will only deepen with years, and must at last have a result that will delight all who have helped to hasten it.

Antoinette, the *bonne*, from whom we are also striving to learn, as everybody is fish for our net at present, told us that Monsieur M., husband of Madame P., was the architect of the thirteenth ward of Paris; that no one could make the least alteration in his house, either to put in a window or a pane of glass, without his permission. We told her how in free America every man chose the material and style that suited him, and no one dared to interfere. She thought it evidently a liberty not to be envied, and said we must have all sorts of odd looking streets as the result. Paris is to be beautiful, that is decreed, and no private tastes or ignorances are permitted to interfere with the plan.

This evening Madame talked frankly with us of her affairs. She said that to-day the reader of the Empress brought her a message from Eugénie, in answer to a request made on Madame's behalf by the Duchess de Sesto. It seems that Madame applied for the rent of a tobacconist's shop to increase her income, a curious thing on its face, and a request lodged in a curious quarter. But harkee! All the tobacco that comes to France is the property of the government. There is no permission given to private individuals for its importation or manufacture. The only manufactory in France is at Paris.

The shops in which it is offered for sale buy their license of the government at a fixed yearly sum. To the wives and daughters of military men who have distinguished themselves, these license moneys are given as a support by the government. Vacancies only occur on the death of some lady to whom a license has been given. The Empress sent word to Madame that it would be as easy to bite the moon with one's teeth as to get her a tobacconist's shop within six years, but that anything in her power she would do, and she offered the Bourse to her for Henri, her son, that is, the right of gratuitous education in the Napoleon Lyceum, one of the chief schools of Paris; but through the city, on account of her husband's services as an architect, Madame already has that privilege. The Empress also offered to put the little girls in a school of high grade, but Madame wisely says she will never be separated from them. She expects, however, to obtain something desirable through the kindness of the Empress.

Later, came in Captain Rollé, a soldier of the regular army, full of conversation and of contradiction. He told us a marvelous story of an American born in France who has just inherited a million by the decease of a miserly uncle, and from his fruit-stand on the streets of New York he has been transported to the elegant establishment in this city of delights. The Captain brought in his various crosses of the Legion of Honor, one for evening, one for the parade, and a ribbon for daily use, with the various official papers relating to his promotion, in all of which we were much interested. I think a Legion of Honor would be a decidedly good novelty to introduce into America.

"This is a funeral of the fifth class," said Madame, scrutinizing a passing procession with her lorgnette from our lofty balcony. It seems there is one grand establishment in Paris which takes charge of all the funerals. There are seven grades, one orders whichever he can best afford for a friend, and has no further concern about any of the details. At the church, whither everybody is carried after death, whether he ever went before or not, one orders a dozen or a half-dozen choir boys and many or few prayers, according to the style of purse he carries.

January 24.—Just one year ago to-day my father died. How changed is life since then for mother and for me! In the twilight Kate and I have just been singing the hymns he liked the best, and which I often sang in the midnight hours to him, in those last times, so sad, so brightened in their clouds by his victorious faith. No other hymns will ever be to me like those on which his fainting spirit, sorely tried, was often borne aloft toward the calm regions where he has now enjoyed our Saviour's presence for one whole year, has learned so much, and delighted in the company of those he loved most dearly when in this world.

In the evening came Mr. U., an accomplished French gentleman, with whom we have fine opportunities for improving our grammar and accent. We fell into a spirited discussion of the late war, our own at home. He favors the South, thinks the liberation of the slaves without compensation to the master is theft; thinks the proclamation of emancipation was but a vigorous stroke of policy to enfeeble the enemy and to curry favor with

Europe; thinks the North has crushed the South, which sentiment he illustrated by raising his boot with force and bringing it down upon the well-waxed floor of the *salon* with ringng emphasis; thinks the South was not bound to stay in the Union, on the principle that what our ancestors agree is nothing to ourselves, and prophesies another assassination of the nation's chief officer, and a second effusion of blood. Nevertheless, he says the South was not wise in going to war, and slavery is wrong, and ought to end, but by fair means. He says that France and England should have helped the South, for America is growing so powerful that, joined with Russia, she will "meddle herself" in European politics one of these days. It is very interesting to listen to the absurdity of these foreigners. I have not yet seen one who did not at heart lean a little toward the South.

January 26.—The lecture over, we went to Madame Farjon's for the evening and to tea, and had hours of what we most delight in—solid French. It was pleasant to me to be able to understand a whole conversation in another language, with the help of an occasional word from Kate, who is always ready and willing to come to my aid. It is odd, but when she is a moment absent, I do not altogether understand sentences that would give me no trouble if she were within earshot.

January 31.—We go almost daily to the Collége de France, where ladies are allowed to listen to the lectures of the ablest men in Paris. I have already acquired enough French to understand quite well.

I like my peeps at the domestic life of the intelligent, but undistinguished, in this wonderful city. In only one *salon* have I seen a carpet over the entire extent—and the fire, or the want of fire! Talk was had about the fine coal and the cheerful flame, when we made our bargain to come, but to-night we sat in the great barn of a room with a foot-stove apiece filled with warm ashes, and shivered with the cold, although such a day as this in an American January would be thought spring-like. Finally, Kate and I, in desperation, sat down before the chilly grate and absorbed what heat it had, since we paid so much a week therefor. While the others, with wraps about them, took their sewing and gathered around the great lamp on the center-table, resigned to their habitual fate, and possibly gained some heat from that luminary, I quietly mended the scattered fragments of the fire, at which one of the children said, "*Oh, malheureuse!*" (unhappy one) for to touch a thing so sacred is presumption. If father were here he would say, "The French know no more about comfort than my goose."

I have been noting the industry of Madame's little girls, one nine, the other seven years old. They rise at six o'clock, breakfast on a bowl of tea and bread, stay at their work-table and are employed with their governess until noon, three days in the week, at grammar, reading, English (such English!) lessons. Twice a week their aunt gives them lessons on the piano; two or three times they go for a walk with Antoinette; in the evenings, directly after tea, they bring forth their light work from their neat and orderly workboxes and sew an hour, read a little quietly by themselves in books taken from the Sunday-school library, and retire at eight or nine o'clock after "embracing" all present in the most dutiful and affectionate manner. The other evening Madame made a little sketch for them to copy by way of variation. She keeps them to their tasks with gentle firmness, calling them all endearing names from "my angel" to "my little one," and admirably directs their young activities.

February 8.—I remember reading in the traveler books that in Paris one rarely saw a drunken man on the streets. This morning four reeled past us as we went to church. I repeated what I had read to Madame P. She said no error could be greater, that such sights were common, but gentlemen never became intoxicated here either at home or on the streets. She claimed that it was the blouse, not the broadcloth, that covered the back of the inebriate, but said that other pleasures no less fatal attract "the better class" of Frenchmen! What standards have the Parisians and what wonder that their language has no word for home!

In the evening, Madame's brother and sister were here. He has lived in South America, believes in slavery, and says in the funniest pronunciation that he is a copper-head. He laughed at the "pretty President" we have in General Grant, and when Kate, acting as mouthpiece for us both, because she speaks French more readily than I do, pushed him to the wall in argument, he asked if she would marry a colored man. She replied with spirit, "No, nor would I marry a Frenchman, either!" at which remark general horror was expressed and the argument was ended.

February 10.—We have been to see the process of making both tapestries and carpets at the Imperial manufactory. In the former, the artist stands behind his work, because every thread must be tied on the wrong side of it, to leave a perfectly smooth surface upon the other. The picture he is to copy is behind him. From time to time he puts a little mirror between the threads and in it sees the progress of his work. The busy bobbin flies in and out in the expert hand of the invisible worker. Then the mirror is pushed through for an instant's scrutiny, and again the bobbin resumes its motion. I do not believe that a quarter of an inch is wrought in a single day. Watching a long time, I could see no growth in the delicate flower petal that was under the fingers of the artist of whose work I took special notice. The men who make carpets, on the contrary, have their work in front of them, and the picture they are to copy hangs above their heads. They loop upon a little iron instrument many loose stitches, then turn a sharp edge that is on one side of this tool against the loop, cutting it in two and leaving the severed ends exposed. These they clip down, smooth off and their work is finished. But this work, too, is very slow, being on a much larger scale than the tapestries. Some carpets take ten years, and none are ever sold. The manufactory belongs to the government and its products go to palaces at home or are the princely gifts of France to foreign potentates. The largest carpet ever made here or elsewhere, probably, was for the picture gallery of the Louvre. It was in seventy-two pieces, was more than thirteen hundred feet long, and cost $30,000. It seems curious that women are not at all employed here, where the delicacy of the work would seem so well suited to their fingers. Large, heavy, unwieldy looking men were clipping at the carpets, seated comfortably on their benches, some of them with a scissors' end picking out the ends of the woven threads, but not a woman was to be seen, except the one who laid hold of our umbrella and confiscated it at a cost of two sous. The men who work here are poorly paid. There are about one hundred and twenty of them, and they receive prices ranging from three to six hundred dollars annually in gold, and when disabled by age or illness a life pension ranging from one hundred dollars to two hundred dollars annually. We did not see the establishment for dyeing, but in one room was a dazzling collection of the colors used in making the tapestries, the loveliest blues, greens, reds, and other shades, that I ever saw.

At our evening lesson and talk Madame P. fell upon the subject of the strictness of the marriage laws of France, saying that the ceremony at church had no authority apart from that at the Mayor's office, whither goes every pair from the Emperor and Empress down. She told us about her own trousseau, and disapproved the action of her cousin, who at her marriage had a dozen dozen of each linen garment; she thought four dozen enough. She said the proper way for the parents of the bride was to put a sum of money at interest at her marriage, sufficient to keep her in linen for the rest of the time, instead of getting such a senseless quantity on hand to grow old and fall to pieces. She told us that she was married at the mayor's one day and at the church the next, but that the common people usually went direct from one place to the other. The church gave the benediction of heaven upon the union, that was all, it had no validity apart from the legal forms. She mentioned a curious custom that every child must be dispatched within three days after the tenth birthday to the mayor's office to be registered and examined as to its sex to prevent deception on the part of parents, who would avoid the conscription of their children. If a boy, he was not examined, but if a girl was announced, an examination must be had in presence of witnesses. That single law would bring about a war within twenty hours if passed in America. The idea is, "If you have sons, I, the Government, will know it, and they shall fight to uphold my throne. I will examine for myself, and you have no way to escape from the conscription which I ordain."

Kate recounted several instances about American customs to Madame P., giving among them the incident of a young lady who broke off a "desirable" engagement, because she did not love her lover. Madame replied with spirit, "There is but one thing in the world that a woman has to give and that is her hand. I like now and then to hear of her having refused it, just as a token of her independence." I was much amused at an out-cropping of the national sentiment which followed my remark that, if I ever married, I hoped a minister might be my lot, as I needed the influence of such surroundings and companionships. Madame replied: "Why, I know a young man, well educated, very religious, a fine fellow, every way. I will write to him, I owe him a letter, and will show you his reply. You can judge from that what sort of a person he is." She imagines that like all Americans who have gone before me, I should be desirable by reason of my dowry!

18

ITALY.

I never dreamed in those lethargic years at home, what a wide world it is, and how full of misery. Indeed, in a thousand ways, it was Rome's office to teach me this. Walking along her streets with grief tugging at my heart for all the wretchedness that they disclosed, how many times have I repeated to myself those words of St. Augustine, "Let my soul calm itself, O God, in thee!"

Hollow-eyed beggars asking charity, at almost every step; troops of tonsured monks, barefooted and steaming in their moist, dirty, old garments; skinny hags, warming their knotted hands over the smouldering coals in their little "scaldino" pots; dirty little children, whose tears make the only clean spots upon their pitiful faces, old before their time; soldiers standing as sentries in wind and rain, for no real purpose save to subserve the pride of Prince and Cardinal; horses, whose bones but just refrain from protruding through their rusty skins, driven rapidly over the sharp stones, and falling, only to struggle and throw out their wounded legs in the effort to rise and continue their journey under the pitiless lash. All these sights smote my eyes every time I walked the classic streets of Rome. Whoever can fail to feel the fires of a quenchless philanthropy kindling in his breast as he contemplates such scenes is either too frivolous for thought, or too hardened for emotion. For myself, whatever I did not learn there, Rome taught me an intense love and tender pity for my race.

OPENING OF THE "ECUMENICAL COUNCIL."

I doubt if Rome, old as she is and varied as her experience has been, was ever earlier astir than on the morning of this day. Lights glimmered in the Roman garrets, the cavernous depths of Roman basements, and the lordly middle heights of Roman palaces, at a most unseemly hour, looking like jack-o'-lanterns through the cottony mist of the most unpropitious morning that ever dawned, at least considered from a meteorologic point of view. Crowds had already assembled at St. Peter's before the bells struck off the cheerless hour of five, and when our comfortable carriage load, invigorated by the breakfast that awaited our appearance at seven o'clock, set out for the scene of action, the tide of emigration in the same direction was frightful to behold.

We rolled on through the chief thoroughfares in the long double line of carriages, while on each side the army of umbrella-carrying pedestrians could be compared to nothing but a forest of mammoth mushrooms. They poured in from all directions; processions of school-boys, colleges of theological students, their symbolic "leading string" hanging limp and spiritless behind them; white-bonneted sisters of charity, solitary priests, adventurous women; "don't-care" urchins of the street, and gaunt-faced beggar women, with ragged petticoats gathered around their heads; a monstrous, motley throng, all candidates upon exactly equal footing as the wealthiest or most lowly occupant of the hurrying carriages, who joked about them as they passed, for the "Holy Father" had ordained that perfect fairness should prevail at the day's ceremony, and prince and peasant would jostle each other this morning in their efforts to get a good look at the procession. In the street, however, slight distinctions still prevailed; mounted soldiers, wrapped in dripping cloaks and wearing draggled plumes, guarded the approach to the bridge of St. Angelo, and he must be at least a Bishop who would pass unchallenged, while all lesser lights of church or state must make the grand détour, pass the Tiber's classic muddiness by a distant bridge, and pay roundly for the privilege of doing so.

Alas for human foresight! Had we not planned to be among the earliest to take possession of the great Basilica, and behold! the streets many squares distant from St. Peter's were lined on either side by empty carriages which had already deposited their too-enterprising burdens, though it was but seven, and the ceremony would not take place till nine. Arrived at the great square we became fully convinced, perhaps for the first time, that early birds alone can hope for toothsome morsels. The place was red with Cardinal's carriages and black with commonplace humanity, all of whom were engaged in a break-neck race for the wide, inviting, blocked-up doors of the cathedral. We filed in between gigantic guards with old-fashioned muffs upon their heads, carrying the burden of our wilted hopes. What a sea of human faces; what a deep ground-swell of human voices; what waves of human forms! Along the dim, damp, lofty nave was stretched a double line of soldiers, keeping an aveune from the great central door, now open for the first time that we had ever seen it, to the council hall. Against this moveless wall beat the eager, hopeless crowd. Thousands were between them and us so the pleasant fiction of "seeing the procession" was exploded at a glance. Still we made desperate efforts to get nearer the soldiers and soon found ourselves crushed between three peasants, two monks and a fishwoman, the mingled odor from whose wet garments was more invincible than bayonets, and we worked our way to a breathing place without loss of time. Then we tried for the high altar opposite which is the open door of the council hall, but Leonidas and his Spartans were not more steadfast than the multifarious monster that held position there. Then desperately we forced our way into the entrance portico of the church, but this was packed and had he passed at the moment, we could not have seen the topmost feather of the Pope's peacock fans. At last becoming weary and dispirited, we retired to the chapel of the Presentation of the Virgin, *vis-a-vis* with the splendid chapel of the Holy Sacrament, and our escort, Signor Paolo Caveri, a Genoese lawyer, devout Catholic that he was, insisted on our taking sitting positions on the marble railing that surrounded the altar, turning our backs upon the sacred symbol. We had our scruples, but a glance revealed the startling fact that several sanctimonious priests had been guilty of a like irreverence, and so we mounted the rich balustrade, and thence "assisted" at the pageant of the day. Time wore on and the human stream still gurgled through the open doors. The beautiful marble floor was deluged with water dripping from cloaks, shoes and umbrellas; the air was dark with incense from the "unseen censer" of ten thousand pairs of panting lungs; the Babel of voices grew louder, the crush more formidable, but along the endless nave the lines of troops stood firm. Side scenes were not wanting to make the hours less long. At every altar in the church, mass was being celebrated, and to us irreverent heretics the struggle in the Catholic breast between curiosity and devotion was a curious study. One solemn-faced gentleman in holiday attire elbowed his way through the crowd and knelt to take the sacrament, but being closely pressed on either side, he inadvertently knocked from the altar one of its tall candles which dripped upon his fine new coat in swift revenge. The priest pretended not to see, and went on decorously with his genuflexions; the communicant affected not to feel, but assumed an apoplectic hue, and the people hid their laughing faces in their prayer-books while they muttered the responses in broken tones. We saw our good friend and escort, the Italian lawyer, and his daughter on their knees, but with faces that would have become them far better at the comic opera than before the sacred altar. A worthy priest intent on seeing all that passed and yet on escaping the pressure of the crowd, had abused his prerogative so far as to climb the projecting ornaments of a column beside the altar, and was making most industrious use of his eyes, when, lo! another priest in glittering vestments and with attendant choir boy came to say mass within arm's-reach of him. The struggle between duty and inclination was ludicrous enough; the poor priest wriggled himself into a position of compromise and nodded and mumbled toward the altar while he kept one eye sharply opened on the passage way for the procession. Opposite him, standing up on the altar railing, was a portly dame who courtesied and responded from her statuesque position and ran a dreadful risk of becoming cross-eyed for life by trying to look two ways at once — toward God and Mammon. From time to time ladies were carried out in fainting fits, with faces ghastly white and chignons trailing on their shoulders, or purple-cheeked children were lifted over the heads of the crowd to purer air. Now a gentleman's hat or his umbrella would be swept from his hand and lost irrevocably, or a lady's shawl drop from her shoulders to be seen no more. And in all the tumult the automaton boy who kneels beside the priest would ring his little bell, and as the wind bends the prairie grass, so the warning sound would bring the faithful to their knees. The liveried servants of cardinals and bishops, in their cocked hats and knee-breeches, went down upon their "prayer-bones" like men who feel that their position demands a certain decorum at any sacrifice, while, mindful of their white stockings, they tucked a handkerchief under their knees. Now and then a purple-gowned bishop, preceded by his secretary and servants, forced his way through the crowd which always made room for a personage so distinguished. But at last the boom of minute-guns announced the long-looked-for moment; the peal of bells joined its rich alto to this solemn bass, and the clear, seraphic voices of the Pope's choir completed the chorus. Every soldier stood with lifted bayonet; the crowd existed but for the sake of its eyes, and dizzily poised on tiptoe on my marble balustrade, I—one of this august army's fifty thousand fractions—beheld the passage of the august procession. Beheld it, yes, but at a distance of one of the aisles and half the nave of the hugest existing church; over the heads of the greatest crowd ever gathered within doors and on the darkest morning that ever rained down shadows. As a veritable chronicler I can pretend to nothing more than having literally looked upon the heads of the Catholic church, which I would respectfully report as for the most part gray, when not bald, tonsured, or concealed by skull-caps. The procession was half an hour in passing, and Monsieur l'Abbé, who also went with us, but was more fortunate in his place of observation, reports it as having numbered eight hundred or more. The venerable priests moved very slowly, as became their dignity and the majesty of the duties to which they were going, and last of all came the Pope who left his official chair at the door and walked to the council hall with his brethren, to the scandalization of the commonalty, who had comforted one another with these words, "At least we shall get a good view of his Holiness borne in his chair of state."

What was done at the high altar and in the council hall, deponent saith not. We all crowded as close as possible to the great open door of the latter when the members had taken their seats, and were rewarded by a glimpse of white-robed Bishops, sitting in wide semicircles as the saints are represented in the heavenly visions of Fra Angelico, and above them royal personages, the Empress of Austria and the Queen of Hungary, looking very black and unseemly in such a shining company. Four times we charged upon the phalanx that had crowded around the open door aforesaid, but were driven back in confusion and disgust.

We drove home fatigued beyond measure and thankful beyond words that Ecumenical Councils happen not more frequently than once in three hundred years.

UP THE NILE.

Steamer "Behera," borrowed of the Pasha for a three weeks' trip by "Cook's tourists" and "us Americans." February 11, 1870.

One week of my restless, ranging life has now been passed upon the quiet river that was once the god, and is ever the good genius of the Egyptians.

Let me try to give a true sketch of an experience entirely unique. We thought to make the trip by "*dahabeah*" (boat) would take too long; we found that to charter a small steamer would be difficult. Cook and his tourists came along; they wished us Americans, sixteen in number, to join them in engaging a large steamer; in an evil hour we yielded, and behold us "in for it" and afloat upon the Nile, a most uncongenial crowd of forty-seven persons, in a big, bloated, blustering steamer, all to be dined and wined, walked on shore and mounted on donkey-back, by wholesale; marshaled by a dragoman in green clothes, an interpreter who speaks nine languages, and an important "tourist-manager," whenever an Arab village, a venerable temple, or a tomb old when Joseph was governor of Egypt, is to be "done."

Well, a sorry day it was in which Warburton, in his "Voyage up the Nile," taught me what the East might be to a pale-faced traveler from chilly shores and stormy skies.

The Real is a dragon under whose scaly feet the airy form of the Ideal is almost always trampled in my life's cheerful history.

We came to feel the subtle spirit of the East; instead, we feel Egyptian fleas. We came to float musingly along the mystic waters of the world's most curious river; instead, we go snuffing, snorting, shaking, over its tolerant breast—eyes full of smoke, ears full of discord, noses full of smells from kitchen and from coal-bin. And yet, in spite of all, I shall never forget one evening's ride; it was the culmination of what the East can yield me, and very grateful I am for its golden memory. Above me were new heavens; in the frame of a violet sky hung constellations I had never seen before, their palpitating golden globes like the fruit waving in the trees of Hesperides. And dear, familiar stars were there, only in places very different from those they occupy in the "infinite meadows of heaven" that bend above my home. The Dipper lay on the horizon's edge, tipped up most curiously;

the Pleiades had nearly reached the zenith and the changeless face of the North Star I could hardly distinguish in his new surroundings. Around me was a new earth, and the sandy plain stretched away into the purple darkness full of attractive mystery. Far off gleamed the fire-fly lamps of an Arab village, and on the cool, invigorating breeze which had succeeded to the day's stifling heat came the lonesome bark of dogs and jackals so characteristic of the East. I rode under magnificent palm trees of a symmetry unequaled by any hitherto seen, and casting shadows in which the moonlight mingled so that they looked like an emblazoned shield. The white walls and graceful dome of a sheik's tomb gleamed through the trees.

My thoughts flew across the sea—dear mother, for whom all things lovely and noble have such significance, never looked upon a palm tree's feathery crest, nor saw it mirrored by an oriental moon upon the desert's yellow sand! Dear mother! did she think of me that night and pray for her far-away child? The landscape was dim for a moment as my heart stirred at thought of home.

I rode along the avenue of sphinxes that once extended over the mile that separates the temple of Luxor from that of Karnak. How still it was, and how significant that stillness in the highway through which for more than two thousand years had passed what was choicest and most royal in the wide earth—processions of kings and priests and captives, compared with which those of Rome were but the sport of children; and this, ere Romulus laid the first stone of his famous wall or Æneas fretted the blue waves of the Ægean with his adventurous prow. The pride and glory of a world had had its center here ere Cadmus brought letters into Greece, or Jacob had his vision on the Judean plains.

But of what value is the "dramatic justice" which pleases us in romance, compared to the visible hand of vengeance with which a merciful God, who loves the creatures he has made, has smitten this stronghold of cruelty, wrenched from their lofty places the statues of bloodthirsty tyrants, and sent the balm of moonlight drifting through the shattered walls, and mellowing the fallen columns?

We sat upon a broken pedestal in the great court of the Temple, Kate and I, and let the wondrous beauty of the place fall on our hearts. One isolated column, the last remaining fragment of a stately colonnade, outlined itself against the liquid sky—its white shaft brilliant in the moonshine and its broad, corolla-shaped capital gleaming far above us, while beyond, the shattered propylon once gay with the banners of Isis and Osiris frowned like the bastion of a fortress, and nearer by, an avalanche of fallen rocks of huge dimensions marked where ruin had struck the Temple of Jupiter Ammon with its relentless hand. Farther on was the forest of columns, which in its kind is unequaled by anything ever wrought by man—one hundred and thirty-four pillars, each seventy feet in height and thirty-five feet in circumference—covered from base to abacus with carefully wrought sculptures, brilliantly painted in their day. One of them was broken and leaned heavily against its giant neighbor, one of the most pathetic, indeed the most mournfully significant fragment that human hands have ever carved from stone, and time and ruin consecrated. Still beyond, in the white moonlight, climbed the tapering finger of the largest obelisk in Egypt, as fresh and clear-cut in its outline as on the day the chisel left it—the chisel held by that unknown artisan who was a mummy before Phidias wrought in Greece, or Zeuxis and Apelles had their rivalries. Against the obelisk leaned an old Arab in graceful turban, and around were seated several others, all by their costume and their bearing as perfectly in harmony with the scene as human accessories could be, and lending it a strange yet human charm.

In what far-off realm of our endless life shall we some day meet those mighty builders whose works we contemplated under the moonlit heavens? What a thought is this, that in the changeful round of being we shall doubtless encounter, somewhere, the awful king, Sesostris, the witching Cleopatra, the Pharaoh who was overwhelmed in the revengeful sea!

I firmly believe that they are all upon some stellar world, seen by us, probably a thousand times, when we looked up into the great, gleaming, kindly heavens. And I can not help an earnest heart-welcome for every student of pyschic laws; spiritualism and all the occult phenomena that shall doubtless build up new sciences some day—just as alchemy became chemistry and astrology changed into astronomy. Only these new investigators must be disinterested students, not money-seeking jugglers.

THE PYRAMIDS.

A wise man once wrote in my autograph album, as follows: "There is an *Up* in life." (I remember he commenced the word "Up" with a capital "U.")

Always after that, I dimly believed in his idea, but on February 23, in 1870, I found out its truth for certain. To the airy hypothesis that there is actually, *Up*, I then applied the substantial test of "that experience which one experiences when one experiences one's own experience." Briefly, I climbed to the tip-top stone of the biggest of the pyramids.

Our party drove from Cairo to the pyramids in a barouche worthy of the Champs Elysées at Paris, along twelve miles of splendid road, built through the sands by the Viceroy in anticipation of a visit from the French Empress, and lined with shady sycamores and delicate mimosa trees. Quite a different way of getting there from the one reported by earlier tourists, who toiled on donkey-back through burning sands, accompanied by an escort of vociferous Arabs.

The barbarous scenes of which our Bible speaks, lived and moved again before our saddened eyes. A part of the embankment of the regal highway where we rode was broken down, and a hundred ragged laborers with baskets on their heads were bringing mud for its repair, while scattered at small intervals among them were swarthy overseers, each with his whip, which he plied almost unceasingly about the heads and shoulders of those bearded workmen, of those women who were mothers, while they all crouched like dogs, beneath the lash.

We drove on through fields of lentils, like those for which hungry Esau sold his birthright to long-headed Jacob; we saw men in ample gowns of blue and turbans of red, scratching the earth with one-handled wooden plows, leisurely dragged by stolid buffaloes; the whole scene having apparently walked out of the "Pictorial Family Bible" that we left behind us. We saw at frequent intervals, stalking along the road with listless tread, a tall, solemn woman of the Egyptians, with a little child sitting astride her shoulders, as Ishmael may have sat when Hagar was turned away from Abraham's inhospitable tent, over which the palm tree bent its feathery head as that one did beneath which the woman leaned to rest.

We talked of the theories concerning the use of pyramids, which have been held at different times by learned men. We knew that the stately group toward which we moved was not the only one in Egypt. There are several others scattered in groups for a distance of about seventy miles, along the Nile's west bank, averaging one to each mile. They, like those of Gizeh, are on the western or sunset bank of the mysterious river, the point of compass which receives the declining sun, being supposed to indicate the region of the dead. These pyramids are by no means rivals of Cheops and its mates, either in size or history, but are a conspicuous feature of the Nile's west bank for seventy miles or more south of the capital.

Why this laborious effort to preserve from decay the bodies whence life and spirit have departed? The doctrine of metempsychosis, or the transmigration of souls, offers the only answer to this interrogation. According to this belief, every spirit not thoroughly purified on its departure from the body, must pass through a long exile, entering, successively, into the bodies of different animals, and returning after cycles of these transformations, to its own corporeal form again. The importance of finding its own still in existence and in a tolerable state of repair will readily occur to thoughtful minds! But besides the horrid possibility of failure here, the disembodied spirit had a thousand other things to dread. Whenever the body it had last left became subject to corruption, the course of its migrations was suspended, and its ardently desired return to a human body—its own—delayed. Hence, every form of animal life became precious, as the possible shrine of a departed friend. The greatest care was employed in preserving all, so far as possible, from becoming decomposed. This was effected by the intricate and mysterious process of embalming, in which certain orders of the priesthood were almost constantly employed.

After migrations of three thousand years through inferior animal forms, the spirit was permitted, as has been said, to return to its own human body, and to try its chances once again.

Now, if we could, by a prodigious effort of imagination, put ourselves for a moment in the place of an Egyptian of the olden time, and if we could conceive of the anxiety with which we should guard against the possibility of a "failure to connect" in the endless whirligig I have described, we might appreciate why their tombs are finer than their palaces; why the dead were in their thoughts more than the living, and why, when this grotesque belief had passed into the life and heart of the nation, the king, who had all resources at his command, should, on his coronation day, put his whole empire under contribution to begin for him a tomb which should rival the mountains in its stability and guard his paltry dust from every chance of harm.

With constant notes and queries about the uses and abuses of the pyramids, we passed along. We crossed the limits of the belt of green, which is old Father Nile's perpetual gift to Egypt; the desert's golden edge came nearer, and at last, our white-robed Arab checked his steeds at the foot of Cheops' pyramid, where—shade of great Pharaoh, forgive us prosaic Yankees!—the Cheops restaurant treated us to Smyrna dates and Turkish coffee. A banditti of Bedouins, fierce-eyed and unsavory, surrounded us as we emerged from our retreat, and clamored for the privilege of pulling and pushing, hoisting and hallooing us up the saw-tooth side of the monster pyramid. We got speedily to windward, assured them that, as for us, we'd "not the least idea of going up" (at least, not now) and turned aside to visit the tomb-pits at the left, hoping to shake off the odious crew. But you might just as well try to dismiss the plague by a dancing-room bow; the old lady Fates, by raising your hat; or the neighborhood bore by a glance at your chronometer. They careered before us, a tatterdemalion throng; they lagged behind us; they helped us over the stray stones the pyramid has shed, with officious hands under our nervous elbows, and when, at last, Dr. Park cleared a breathing space for us by whirling his cane, they danced about us, beyond the circle thus marked out; they grinned, they groaned, they laid their hands upon their hearts and pointed with melodramatic finger to the serene heights they would so gladly help us climb, while the one refrain from which, for two consecutive breaths they were utterly incapable of refraining, was: "Goin' up, mister—madam?" "Yankee Doodle goin' up? Ver' good, thankee. Yankee Doodle go up ebery time!" But we passed on regardless, and they were left lamenting. We walked upon sealed tombs; the whole ground for miles about this group of pyramids is honey-combed with them. This is a grave-yard in which they are but chief monuments.

Some distance from old Cheops, we saw a sandstone rock much worn and rounded. While we were wisely theorizing as to how it came to be here on this almost level plateau, we walked around to the other side of this queer, rounded rock protruded from the clasping sands, when, lo! the oldest, wisest and most baffling face the world has seen, looked grandly into ours; and our ephemeral forms passed from the unhistoric sunshine into the shadow which the Sphinx has cast for forty centuries! The worn and rounded rock which had deceived us, was only its "back hair," which I am obliged to report as very much spread out, and hence, not "stylish" in the least. It is an unique moment in which a flitting creature, such as we are, pauses in his changeful haste, folds his weak arms and confronts the steadiest gaze that has ever met his own! That this calm and not unfeeling face has looked out thus, over the level sands and emerald meadows and toward the steadfast Nile since history's glimmering dawn, we know. That Abraham stood where we are standing, and mirrored (in the eyes that witnessed the deliverance of Isaac!) these flowing outlines, this low brow, these rounded lips, we deem altogether probable. That Moses, grandest figure of antiquity, has gazed upon this stern, but not unpitying face, is certain. That Eastern emperors have turned aside from their pompous march to see it; that Herodotus asked of it many an unheeded question; that thoughtful Plato measured glances with it; that fierce Cambyses may have struck its nose off with iconoclastic hammer—all this is true as history. And stranger than it all—throughout the three decades of the world's one matchless Life, with Bethlehem at their beginning and Calvary at their close, this gaze neither brightened at the first nor faltered at the last. Thinking about it all—sending bewildered fancy onward into the wondrous future, upon whose happier myriads and milder destinies this changeless face shall gaze, one sinks beneath the contrast this mystic creature's history affords to one's own trivial joys and petty griefs so like to those of gossamer-winged insects which the evening taper blots from being. But, afterward, one has a thought more worthy of a soul for whom the Mightiest died; it is a thought which brightened Plato's eyes when he stood here more than two thousand years ago, though he knew not the wondrous truth which dims my own with happy tears, and that thought is: I am immortal! The centuries flow onward at thy feet, O weird and mystic Sphinx! yet from their fertile waves thou dost not gather aught that enriches thee. But for me each breath yields blessings that shall last forever, and all climes and ages are my gleaning fields. Not like an ignoble worm do I crawl beneath thee, but like a tireless bird I soar above! For a moment I have paused to muse on thy strange, unproductive history, but now I spread my wings and fly away to other scenes, and by and by, weary of one small world, I shall journey to another, and so on and on through the beneficent universe of God whom I love, and who loves me, and whose boundless heart is my eternal home! Gaze on over the desert and the still meadows, solemn Sphinx! One landscape can not satisfy eyes so insatiable as mine, and so, farewell!

Cheops lifted his dimensions toward the sky in a style so thoroughly uncompromising that we felt quite in haste to set our feet on his bald crown. But our hurry did not at all compare with that of the wild Arabs gathered at his base and eager for their prey. They knew it had been only a question of time when we threw them off, with such indomitable purpose, an hour ago; alas! we knew it now. For the first time in all our journeyings, my friend Kate, who side by side with me had climbed half the cathedral spires of Europe, executed marvels of mountaineering in Switzerland and scrambled to the summit of Vesuvius, confessed herself vanquished, without striking a blow, and retreated to the carriage to watch the attack gallantly conducted by the rest of us. Taught by all the guide-books, warned by all the tourists, I took my purse—although it was not dangerously plethoric—from my pocket, placed it in the hands of my friend who stayed below, and told the three men who, *nolens volens*, had taken my destiny in hand, that if I did not hear "backsheesh," until I regained *terra firma*, I would parody, for their benefit, the famous lines of Uhland:

> "Take, O boatman, thrice thy fee,
> Take, I give it willingly."

I then resigned myself to fate.

Just here I will confess something not usually divulged, viz.:

I cherished a secret determination to reach the top before any of my comrades. The undertaking was by no means trivial. I had a dim suspicion of this before I started, which became, as I set out (or set up, rather), the most vivid "realizing sense" of all my history. Three feet and a half at a step is a "departure" hardly excelled by Weston of pedestrian fame, and when the inclined plane one is trying to walk is set on edge, as in the present instance, you can imagine such "a getting upstairs" as it would be hard to beat! Just try, some day, in the solitude of your apartment, to step "genteelly" from floor to mantel-piece, or on top of the bureau; do this one hundred times in fourteen minutes, and see if the achievement is n't a *feat*, though it may not prove a "success."

It is to be remembered that the huge slabs of granite and porphyry which once smoothly covered the pyramid, were scaled off in the time of the caliphs and taken, with about twenty feet from its apex, to be used as building material at Cairo. Climbing the side of Cheops, then, is nothing more nor less than going up the most outrageous "pair of stairs" on earth, under circumstances the most harrowing. But I got on bravely, in spite of all. Climbing rapidly, I did not once sit down to rest, and stopped but briefly, thrice, to breathe, or rather to puff, like an asthmatic locomotive; my Bedouins, meanwhile, tranquilly watching the spectacle, and cool as if they had but just emerged from a refrigerator. Below, I could hear the advancing steps of my rivals in the race, and this lending ardor to my flagging zeal, I clambered on.

Ever above me, with extended hands, were two solemn, but never silent Bedouins; ever beneath my shoulders were the strong hands of a burly Egyptian, while for me, the only possible thing to do was to fix my foot firmly against the upper edge of the stone step before me, and to grasp with desperate grip the steady hands of those above, they going up backward with an agility which put to shame my own backwardness about coming forward in this business!

Well, when one measures off dimensions in this straightforward fashion, one soon learns that they amount to something. I had no more narrow "flings" about the Pyramids of Cheops. It was huge. I said this with starting eyes; I felt it with panting breath and purpling cheeks. There was no more spirit in me.

The wind blew almost fiercely, as I neared the summit. The voices of my friends grew silent, a long way below. High up in the crystal air I saw a great bird sailing with strong and steady wing. How I envied his calm flight!

At last, I lost all consciousness of everything save the frightful, sledge-hammer beating of my heart.

"Yankee Doodle 'most got up!" shouted a kindly Arab, and in a moment more I was standing, tremblingly, on the broad summit of the pyramid. Though more dead than alive, I insisted (in deference to the heroic name of "Yankee") in crawling to the loose rocks piled on the center of the platform, and seating myself triumphantly upon the topmost stone. Taking from my pocket a Jaffa orange (brought with this same intent) I tore it open and buried my parched lips in its juicy pulp. If I were called upon to name the most delectable sensation that ever human palate knew I should refer to the foregoing incident.

You've no idea how quiet and composed I was, though, as the rest came wheezing into view, three minutes afterward; opera-glass in hand, I was counting the minarets of Cairo, as the fainting trio struggled to the top, and were met by my Arabs grinning from ear to ear at our achievements!

And here we were, as the purple twilight fell, a thoughtful, and, strange to say, a silent company. There were eighteen of us, Arabs and all, and yet we were not crowded.

It had required no ordinary eloquence to still the clamor of our dozen swarthy escorts. To put the much-desired quietus upon the noisiest of them, I had agreed that if he would but hold his tongue for fifteen minutes, I would do what in no instance I had done in famous places hitherto (save on the white forehead of a skull in the Paris Catacombs), inscribe my name. The Arab carefully scraped out the autograph of some member of the Smith family to make room for me, the whole summit being as thickly planted out to names as a Dutch garden to cabbages. While he erased the autograph of this luckless candidate for immortality, my Bedouin assured me (in most startling English) that he kept his big knife for no other purpose than to cut the names of the heroic few who reached this goal, and that

Kate A. Jackson.

when I came again I should just see how he had cared for mine and kept its sprawling capitals in good repair (more particularly if I paid him a shilling for such service). In this last statement, however, my faith was irremediably weakened by the scratching-out process through which poor Smith's autograph had just now passed!

But all this time we had been sitting dangerously near the western edge of Cheops' pyramid, with the most significant of panoramas spread out before us. The charm of evening's earliest hour, the zest of novelty, the spice of danger, the chastening thought of pathos — all these united to make the time forever memorable.

That was a break-neck scramble down the side of Cheops as the darkness fell! The Arabs said to me (as they doubtless say to each ambitious tourist), "Yankee Doodle ver' good fust rate." As they conducted me — and a long way I found it — from the point where I alighted, back to the carriage, two of them put a hand apiece under my elbows and I fairly flew over the ground, they delighting in the sport and telling me that I had "Arab feet," which (if I had) they lent me.

With facts, fancies, and "guesses at truth" in mind, we walked on in the gathering twilight toward the entrance of the King's tomb. This entrance, carefully concealed during thousands of years, but discovered by the indefatigable Belzoni, now yawned black and ominous in the uncertain light. Above its solemn doorway, in letters several feet long, done in black paint, we had the mortification of seeing this inscription:

"PAUL TUCKER, OF NEW YORK."

All the way up the Nile, even to Philæ, we had found this same epitaph of American refinement; carved in the Temple of Jupiter Ammon at Thebes; scrawled upon Memnon's pedestal; and cut beside the mystic sculptures of Abydos. But on a tablet so tempting as the front angle of the "big pyramid," the confiding Paul had vouchsafed a bit of personal history eleswhere withheld. Beneath his name he had printed in straggling capitals, this time not more than a foot apiece in altitude:

"AGED 18 1-2."

It was a pleasant and consoling thing to know how tender were his years. There's always hope—more than we churlish old folks may be inclined to think, "concerning veal"—as the country parson said.

The entrance to the tomb, for the sake of which the pyramid was reared, had been carefully concealed in former ages. We can but admire the ingenuity which located this opening twenty-three feet to the right, rather than in the center, where one would naturally look for it. Another precaution hardly less surprising, was to seal up the passage-way, narrow and intricate as it is, when the royal builder had been laid in his tomb, with blocks of granite, so much more difficult to break through than the ordinary, calcareous stones of the pyramid, that a passage has been forced around them. In these, as in every feature of the pyramid, it will be seen that *the security of the body one day to be called for by the soul* was the controlling purpose of its design. Through a passage three feet eleven inches high, and over three hundred feet in length, along a downward and then upward angle of about 26°, we wended our weary way to the king's tomb. Clinging now to slippery, now to cobwebbed walls, anon to the sleeve of some officious Arab; blinded by dust from the wings of countless bats, and finally measuring off the distance on our hands and knees, we made a dolorous procession to the center of the pyramid with its empty sepulcher. We found as the reward of our pains a rectangular-shaped chamber, lined with red granite. In its center stands a sarcophagus of red granite, too large to have been introduced through the entrance passage, and therefore necessarily placed here before the pyramid was built around it.

Notwithstanding all the precautions mentioned, this sarcophagus has been empty and without a lid since the time of the Caliphs, when, in the expectation of finding treasure, an entrance was forced and the king's body was thrown out and treated with the grossest indignities by the rabble in the streets of Cairo. *Sic transit gloria mundi!* Vandal tourists have hammered the corners of the sarcophagus till they look as though a grindstone had been scooped from each one of them, and straightway our Arabs began to pound off "specimens" for us at five piastres each.

Waving them solemnly aside, Dr. Park marshaled our entire party of five into this coffin of the elder world, where we stood in a strange looking row, with the flickering torch-light on our faces, while at the bidding of our leader, we sang that curious old hymn:

"Hark, from the tombs a doleful sound!"

Our voices woke some most lugubrious echoes; our Arabs listened, looking more than "dumb-founded," at our performance. Dr. Park smiled audibly. But his mood quickly passed from gay to grave. "Sing 'Rock of Ages, cleft for me!'" were his next words. With swelling hearts we joined in the dear old hymn we learned so long ago, so far away. At its close, solemn and deep sounded the good man's voice; I shall not soon forget the words:

"The pyramids may crumble, but the Rock of Ages stands firm and secure. The old idolatry that reared this awful tomb has had its long, its little day. The kingdom of our Lord and of His Christ is ushered in, and we, His ransomed sons and daughters sing of Him who hath so loved us, standing in the empty coffin of the idolatrous and cruel Pharaoh."

After all, this was the lesson we shall cherish longest, the truest lesson of Cheops, old and gray.

Let Egypt boast her mystic monuments, which, in the race with time, have come off grimly victorious; a Christian's eye pierces the boundless blue above their heads, and gets a glimpse of more enduring habitations, while, as he turns away from their pitiless masses of stone, his humble, happy faith sings of the "Rock of Ages, cleft for me!"

SYRIA—THE HOME OF OUR SAVIOUR.

"Over whose acres walked those blessed feet
Which eighteen hundred years ago were nailed
For our advantage to the bitter Cross."

On the night of March 6, 1870, I closed my eyes upon Egypt, and in a comfortable cabin of the Russian steamship, "Grand Duke Constantine," after a tranquil passage, opened them at six o'clock upon a low sandy coast and hill-top crowned by a white-walled town, while sunlight from behind the clouds spread broad blades of light over the distant lands—light lovelier to me even than that of home. Between me and the shore shimmered the sea, even in the unwonted calm, sustaining by its motion the unsatisfactory reputation of the port, or want of port, at Jaffa. Yonder the Great Apostle had his vision, which gave even to me, a Gentile maiden, a right to look upon the country of God's chosen people with a sense of home stirring my heart, and such thoughts of Him with whom "there is neither Jew, nor Greek, bond nor free," as filled my eyes brimful of tears, and silenced my voice which, in earlier, less tender years, nothing ever could unsteady or place beyond my own control.

March 8.—*En route* for Jerusalem. The day has dawned on which my eyes shall mirror the city of our Lord. From yonder valley to the right, Joshua made the sun stand still. On this side is the supposed site of Emmaus. Here we first strike the trail of the Divine Pilgrim; in that village yonder John the Baptist was born; in this brook David got the stones to slay Goliath; here the Philistines were encamped; there across the valley were the Israelites. Boy-peddlers would have slings to sell here, if they had any "gumption"! I ride on alone, ahead and out of sight of our procession, pass wretched women, fierce-looking men, files of camels, flocks of sheep, processions of donkeys with bells on. At last I am alone—in sight of Jerusalem!

March 9. — First promenade in Jerusalem through the Via Dolorosa. Saw a fallen pillar where Christ is said to have reposed—covered with pilgrims' kisses; another pillar where the cock stood to crow; a stone in the wall with the impress of the cross—a boy comes up, puts his fingers in the hole of this stone and goes off kissing them; wretched pavements, no carriages, no realization whatever of the glorious city of our God.

Jerusalem is the most disagreeable, dismal, ugly city I have anywhere seen. There is so little that attracts, and so much that repels; everything is so shut up, streets not only narrow, but with heavy stone arches running sometimes their whole length. I can heartily echo the sentiment of some author I have recently read, that he congratulated himself upon the fact that the Jerusalem of David's song and Solomon's wisdom and magnificence, and, above all, of Christ's divine love, is half a hundred feet below where we are walking.

Reading up Murray half an hour is worth a whole morning of "barn-door flights of knowledge" from the regulation guide, even when he is as nice a man as ——, who, however, pointed out the Angel of the Annunciation in one of the absurd daubs of the Armenian Convent, as "the devil"; and when, not liking to hurt the poor fellow's feelings, we mildly hinted that it was curious the devil should have wings, and carry his hands filled with white lilies, he said, anxiously, "But they dress the old gentleman very oddly sometimes, you know, that is, these rascals do." But at the Holy Sepulcher this afternoon, when he stoutly maintained that the Mater Dolorosa and John the Beloved, on either side the crucified Saviour, were the two thieves, I could hardly contain my amusement, and his "stock" as "*un homme savant*" took a mighty fall!

THE TOMB OF CHRIST.

I would approach that spot with reverent feet for its name's sake, and because of the reverence of ages which has been here so freely spent. I always thought it would be to me a solemn and a tender hour in which I stood beside the place where men have even said that mystic body lay in which He bore our burdens, in which He tasted for us the bitterness of death. But after seeing Moses' rod, and Adam's tomb, and "the stone that cried out," my mood was spoiled; grief at the wounding of my Saviour in the house of his friends, at the example given to infidels in the very temple of his sepulcher, displaced all other thoughts. I bent at the low entrance door, made with a view to exacting this homage, and stood beside the marble slab on which, "they say," the angel sat whom the gentle Mary saw. Some pilgrims from Armenia were just folding and putting in cases an altar-cloth of the dimensions of the tomb which they had consecrated by contact with this slab. A frightful daub representing Christ hung over it; bouquets of weed-like flowers, tinsel and tawdry adornings unworthy of a child's doll-house surrounded the most august of tombs. A frowzy monk stood beside it on guard. Kate sat down upon the tomb, being quite weary, and forgetting what it was; luckily his head was turned at the moment, and before he observed the sacrilege I gave her a push that spoke volumes. The pilgrims knelt and kissed the ground before entering the sepulcher and went forth from it backward. I thought I would have given something just then for a little of this faith, but, dear me! fervor and filth, sanctity and smells seem to go hand in hand. Here at Jerusalem, processions of the different creeds are marching about constantly. In the Greek chapel there is continual hopping up and down; prostrations of forehead to floor, and all the ardor we had observed so often at St. Izak's and the Kazan in Russia. The Catholics seemed very business-like, keeping excellent time, stepping about briskly, and going through their genuflexions in a most workman-like manner; while the Armenians droned out sonorous prayers, and their long black garments trailed not ungracefully behind them as they paced off to their appointed altars. The quarrels amid these brethren are such that a key to the holy sepulcher is kept by the Mohammedans who act as peace-makers!

Most pitiful of all the places shown. is the summit of Calvary. In the great open court before the church, squat venders of beads, ivory crosses, *cigarholders*, Jericho roses, and other souvenirs of the so-called sacred place.

March 10.—A day of unrivaled execution. Mr. Floyd brought us permission for the Mosque of Omar, which a few years since could not at any price be entered, and later, often required a hundred dollars for the privilege; but thanks to the efforts of the American Consul it is now open to our countrymen at five francs each. We are obliged to take off our shoes and put on slippers, that are furnished, and our party scuffs along through the world-famed Mosque, looking with watchful eyes for traces of the temple, dear to Jew and Christian, whose undoubted site was here. It is comforting to come at last upon something true, and to find it even in Jerusalem! Through courts and archways, carven pulpits and places of prayer, we reach the Mosque itself. In its external appearance from any point yet seen, I have been gravely disappointed in it. The interior is still more unsatisfying; dark, gloomy, and heterogeneous, made up of little bits and big bits of Oriental marble and other choice stones, all said to be fragments from the temple. Many columns stand in double rows around a great bare rock; the peak of Mount Moriah, projecting from the floor, surrounded by a railing and overhung by an old silk quilt, is the central point of attraction to infidel and Christian eyes alike. This looks so genuine and is so palpable, that the prints of Gabriel's fingers, made in holding the rock down in its place, instead of permitting it to follow its impulse and Mahomet to heaven, when that worthy took his flight, did not destroy our belief in its authenticity. Under this rock is a grotto where are shown the "praying places" of Solomon and David. The latter is very curious. The top is a trefoil, and at each side there are two little capitals and two little columns, each divided into two strands, and each pair braided together in a very curious, graceful style, the whole in design entirely different from anything hitherto seen. This we all examined with great interest, believing it may really once have been a part of the Temple of Jehovah. Another fragment in similar design also interested us, as did old bits of marble in the walls and on the floors. The real Jerusalem is so far beneath our feet that we shall never press a stone where our Saviour's feet have passed, if it be not here and now. This thought gave an inexpressible sweetness and pathos to the dark, old Mosque of the Moslem. I reached my hand through the jealous bars, and laid it on the naked rock which once supported the altar of the Most High, whereon the offering was typical of Christ. I felt as if that contact placed me in sympathetic union with the long line of prophets and the sad elder race who waited and hoped for a Redeemer, who foretold the rising of the Star which should shed the only light of love and hope our world has ever known. But jealous eyes were on me, for Moslems hate the Christian intruders from the noble lands they fear, and harsh voices called me to "come along," using the only English word they had acquired, and I left the gloomy Mosque, sad that in the City of Christ, hate and intolerance had undisputed sway.

Later we went to the Garden of Gethsemane, all planted out to flowers, and sat under one of the great olive trees, while an old Italian monk, twenty years an exile from his country, clipped flowers for us with the long scissors at his girdle. We cut for ourselves twigs from the solemn old trees; accepted the olives given us by the old monk; made the acquaintance of his comfortable cat; mounted to his pleasant rooms in one corner of the garden for a drink of water, and raised our eyebrows contemptuously as the opposition "garden" of the Greek Church was pointed out near by. But not at Gethsemane as in some other places, did I realize that One had been here to whom the wide world offers no rival—One who was mystical—Divine! To close the day's investigation we went under the city into the great cave made by the quarriers of the temple, whose tool-marks are fresh upon the lofty walls.

March 13.—Upon the Mount of Olives in the afternoon. We went out on our donkeys, followed the path by which David went with ashes on his head when Absalom rebelled against him, and climbed to the summit of the middle division of the mountain—for, as all the world knows, Olivet has three. Here we contemplated Jerusalem from the top of a Moslem minaret; studying its topography and getting into our minds more thoroughly than we could elsewhere, the relation of the so-called mountains on which it stands to the desolate, stony valleys that surround it on every side. Here we had our first real view of the Dead Sea, which in this crystal air seemed but a little distance off, though we shall sadly learn the contrary, I suppose, when we measure it inch by inch over the worst paths ever tried by human enterprise and patient horses' hoofs. Here the blue mountains of Moab spread themselves dimly "as a dream when one awaketh," and the Judean hills touched our hearts with manifold suggestions of the blessed Presence that vanished from them to the mount of God many a sad century ago. Away beyond the stony promontories that overhang the stonier valleys, was Bethlehem. Yonder was the path where Jesus walked so often seeking the home of his friends, Mary, Martha and Lazarus; by the winding road nearer us he made his triumphal entry into the city; from some blessed height beneath our eyes—what matters it that we can not tell which one!—he floated into the airy regions suited to his resurrected body, and thence away to the mystic heavens we love to think about in our exalted hours. What a matchless landscape this, impossible to rival on the wide face of the beautiful earth; more significant to the Christian heart than all the classic plains or poetic mountain heights of Europe, the grand peaks and vales of Switzerland, or the tender beauty of the home scenes his longing heart recalls.

But around us were clamoring Arabs intent upon showing us the very spot whence the Ascension took place, the very prints left by the upward tending feet of the Redeemer. We go to see them duly, and escape down the hill-side, gathering flowers for dear ones at home who will never have this landscape under their wistful eyes, and picking up bits of agate and onyx which have lain here for unnumbered ages, been turned a thousand times by the rude plowshare of the husbandman, and we please ourselves by fancying that possibly our Saviour's footsteps may have touched them as he passed along the hill-side.

A Sabbath in Jerusalem! An afternoon upon the Mount of Olives! To a devout soul this were worth a pilgrimage longer than any other that the earth's wide belt makes possible. And yet—and yet—we were so cold; the wind blew so searchingly; curious Arabs pursued us so relentlessly; the intellectual part of studying the landscape, and the practical part of keeping on the backs of slippery donkeys distracted our attention so that the spiritual part, those shy, sweet feelings of the heart—those tender, child-like aspirations—those deep and solemn contemplations more suited to the spot than to any other in all the earth, had little chance to hold us. But I had some quiet moments of priceless worth. Gleams and glimpses of what all this may mean flashed through my soul. The gentle, helpless face of Mary—my sister Mary—shrined forever in the center of my heart, looked out upon me from her dying pillow, and that failing voice uttered again the words: "Oh, Christ has come to me! He holds me by the hand; He says, 'She tried to be good, but she wandered; but I'll forgive and save her'!"

That same Christ to whom we trusted Mary walked upon this mountain; here spent the night of His infinite agony, and purchased her sweet soul's redemption on the bitter cross, within sight of where I stand!

Pale and wasted and framed in hair made gray by suffering, more than age, another face looked on me, and my honored father's voice rang in my ears: "Christ lived, and died, and rose again! Upon this faith I walk right out over the awful gulf of death—and I am not afraid!" Ah, how these tender memories, so sad, so sacred, so inspiring, bring home to me the reality of that religion which was born in yonder gray and mournful city, and hence has swept its way to the remotest corner of our world! The poet's song brings relief to my heart, which is surcharged with trembling love and timid hope, and prayerfully I sing,

> "Rock of Ages, cleft for *me!*
> Let me hide myself in thee;
> Let the water and the blood,
> From thy wounded side that flowed,
> Be of sin the double cure;
> Save from wrath and make me pure."

Oh, I must go again and yet again to Olivet; no experience of all my life has seemed so sweet and so significant as this!

It is a mournful thing to see the white-robed women of Jerusalem, their beauty or hideousness concealed by colored handkerchiefs wrapped about their faces, congregating around the graves that fleck the valleys and the hill-sides of Jerusalem beyond the walls. I wonder why they go there, poor things! and whether it is to be merry or sad. Sometimes I have seen flowers upon a little stony grave and children playing around, while the women, patient and still, sat beside the lonesome mound. As we toddled in at the Damascus gate (my odd word describes, not inaptly, the motion of our droll little donkeys), a cannon was fired, and another and another still, signals for closing the gates at evening. The Spanish Consul here, a pleasant gentleman who sits opposite us at *table d'hote*, says that at Ramadan, the fasting time of the Mohammedans, the firing of a cannon informs the people when they can eat, when they must commence their rigorous abstinence, which lasts from sunrise to sunset and in which no good Mohammedan eats, drinks, or even smokes; also, in the night, it arouses the faithful to prayer. This is the first religious use to which I have heard gunpowder put in all my travels!

I can never tell what force and added pathos I found in all the wonderful Bible words after the experience of this marvelous week, and this chief Sabbath of my life. Why, the Bible is going to be a new book to me after this! God grant it may be "new" in a deep, *spiritual* sense; that it may take hold upon my careless life, may make me what all teaching and the most golden opportunities must fail unless they accomplish, a better human creature, nearer to what God meant when He created me; more as Christ taught us we must be to serve Him on earth and live with Him in heaven.

Bishop Kingsley, Dr. Bannister, Dr. March and company reported themselves as comfortably encamped beyond the Jaffa gate, and we lost no time in getting our luggage into the prescribed compass, and walking behind the same as piled upon the broad back of El Hani's servants it traversed the dark and winding streets. With the least possible ceremony we introduced ourselves in camp, where three large tents, besides the "kitchen," were in order, the star-spangled banner floating from that occupied by the wide-awake Presbyterian quartet, Drs. March, Goodwin and Hayden, and Brother Ezra Coan. We found our quarters quite comfortable, one large tent adorned within after the manner of a patch-work quilt of the "basket pattern," red, white, blue and green calico in circles and triangles, and at the top branching out into a flaming star; pieces of carpet cover the ground, four iron bedsteads stand thickly around (Mr. and Mrs. Paine, of Boston, are our companions), a table occupies the center with a decent red "spread" thereon; there are two tin wash-basins and pitchers, and one brass candlestick suitably equipped for evening. We hunt up the gimlets we have provided (at our friend Warburton's suggestion), bore into the tent pole, regardless of any sensitiveness on El Hani's part, and hereon hang curtains to divide the tent, riding-whips, waterproofs, carriage-top hats, and so on. Things begin to "look like living." I get out our books, and finding in my Bible the description of the temple built by Solomon, read it, placing myself in fancy where I stood last evening, imagining its glories replacing the swelling dome of the Caliph's Mosque and listening with ear intent to that stately prayer of the wise king with its impressive iteration of "Hear us, O Lord, in heaven thy dwelling place, and when thou shalt hear, forgive!" Ah, but it is a new book altogether, this Bible I have read so long and left so long unread; what would I not give now to have it all "at my tongue's end"! I also read "Esther," being interested particularly in the account of the pilgrims to the Holy Land; and make out from the various guide-books a list of such places as I yet must see or must revisit in this city, which has a charm for me—although it is the darkest, dreariest and most comfortless I ever saw—that no other can ever attain. Jerusalem and Paris! What contrast greater does our various earth afford! They are at the two opposite poles of human life and history. The one gratifies every sense, pleases every taste, is the bright, consummate flower of modern civilization, the long result of time in its most winning sense, the admired of all admirers; the other girt about with gray and barren hills, hedged by stern and solemn walls, with no beauty, no attraction, hardly even the ordinary comforts of life to offer to the weary pilgrim; and yet drawing him to her withered bosom with a spell to which he gladly yields, and melting his heart with a love, pity and hope that take fast hold upon the dearest ties, that reach backward through all ages and forward to the consummation of creation's mystery.

But the wiry little luncheon bell disturbs my reverie. We repair to the tent of the banner, in which Dr. March & Co. have lodgings, and find cold beef, cold chicken, bread, nuts, dates and oranges awaiting us, from which, thanks to our keen appetites, we make a hearty repast. Thus far we like tent-life, seeing nothing to dread, save the mosquitoes which have set their crimson seal on the foreheads of our hardy comrades, and against whose attacks we have been trying to provide by rigging out a net apiece, made of our veils with our Garden-of-Gethsemane whips bent across them.

In the afternoon we went to Bethany. Here lived Jesus' friends and here his nature showed its most human side; here affection won from him the tears that torture could not force; here he performed his crowning miracle; somewhere hereabouts from the side of Olivet he passed through the pure air that fans my cheek into the blue above us. All that our hearts most dearly cherish in the crisis hours of life centers in this ascent of Jesus from some spot beneath our gaze, as it wanders over the low and lonesome hill that stands out in the history of our race, more lofty in its meanings, more heavenly in its hopes than all the summits of the earth. For "if Christ be not risen, then is our preaching vain, and your faith is also vain."

They showed us Lazarus' tomb: a deep, disagreeable excavation by the roadside, suspiciously convenient to "the house of Mary and Martha," and not a stone's throw from that of "Simon the leper." We crawled dutifully into the cave and mounted a housetop to look down upon the ruins, but should have been puzzled to reply had anybody asked why we did so, why we paid the tribute of a thought to these barefaced impostures, when around us were the faithful face of nature, the changeless outlines of the hills, the unvarying rocks, all of which Jesus had seen, and these alone. Doubtless, our unanalyzed impulse to look at these impostures, was a certain kindly sympathy with the army of pilgrims from every land, who have honestly venerated these shrines. Well, I am glad that since "I am human, whatever touches humanity touches me." We lingered long upon the housetop, while the village sheik stood near us, watching curiously our movements and listening attentively to our reading of the chapter about how Jesus came from beyond Jordan, up yonder rugged path before us, and Martha went to meet him, and his potent voice called her brother from the grave—perhaps one of the very holes in the rock before us.

TO THE DEAD SEA AND JERICHO.

March 18.—We rise at about six o'clock and breakfast out-of-doors at seven. This morning it rained upon our omelette, toast and coffee. The wind was chilly, the sky a leaden gray, and matters looked a little dubious for starting on the grand route, "doing" the Dead Sea and the Jordan, and reaching Jericho to-night. Mr. Wilson, Kate and I made it our first business to ride up to Jerusalem in the rain and buy ourselves rubber coats, a precaution we had stupidly neglected up to this time. Not until nine o'clock did our long line get in motion, led off by a couple of formidable-looking Arabs who, for a consideration, acted as our escort.

It really takes a good deal of "impedimenta" to start a baker's dozen of tourists over these break-neck hills, paradoxical though it may seem. In and out, up and down, around and over we wind by the worst road that ever outraged that respectable name. And what has set us all to wriggling thus among these barren hills? Why, one called Jesus walked here often, in olden times, and with him went twelve others, whose humble names have gained a luster brighter than those of kings and have gone into all the world. After the fall from my horse I thought perhaps the feet of Christ might have pressed the very stones that bruised me; could I but know it, how I should prize the wound! We lunched beside an old wall inclosing the summit of the "Pisgah" of the Mohammedans, the only trouble with which is, that it ought to be the other side of Jordan; but one must not be exigent.

To pass rapidly through this wilderness is nothing, but to live here would be simply impossible, for no green thing is seen for miles, unless sometimes in the valleys the gray, weird-looking shrub made for the camel's nourishment and found in the great deserts. But the hills have such variety of form, are so harmoniously rounded, circle around each other in dance so intricate, display such curious lines of stratification, and abound in such tempting pebbles, that, flecked by the bright sunshine that the newly swept and garnished skies have yielded, their white and yellow colors light up cheerfully, and the scene is far more pleasant than travelers teach us to expect. And as for the desolation of the Dead Sea, I surely was unable to discover it. A more beautiful sheet of water I have rarely seen, blue as a mountain lake, its distant promontories standing out grandly and mellowed with a light that Claude need not have disdained, while to-day the effects of cloud and the hue of the sky were magnificent enough to be memorable. I certainly never saw a more splendid display in the heavens, and even as we bent over the smooth and glassy water a rainbow in the east gave the last touch to a picture that we all thought marvelous. Neither is the approach to the Dead Sea desolate; there was far more vegetation than we had looked for—tall, rank cane, juniper, tamarisk, and a few flowers. Some apples of Sodom, at least our knowing ones pronounce them such, were gathered here (also at the Jordan and Jericho), but they are a pretty, yellow fruit, and on the same twig with them grows a purple flower which is in appearance, compared to that of the potato, what a race horse is to a mule. (I become, naturally enough, equestrian in my comparisons!) But the water of the

Dead Sea is worthy of its reputation. I tasted it slightly when filling the little can we are going to take home. It is unbearable to the tongue, but the feeling of it is smooth, almost slippery, and the gentlemen who took the bath, self-prescribed here to all tourists, report it as buoyant even beyond their expectations and almost blistering to lips and eyelids. Master El Hani (up the Nile we had an English, here an Arab commander-in-chief), told us we had "just ten minutes" to spend at the Dead Sea. What with scolding and display of temper I managed to get twenty, and the gentlemen, some of them, a little longer; but the train departed, leaving many loiterers, long before half an hour was passed. Pleasant, is n't it, to come seven or eight thousand miles to a renowned spot and be told by a wild ignoramus that he allots you ten minutes in which to make observations? Well, well, some people don't even have ten.

March 21.—Far off, Gerizim and Ebal loom, and here is Jacob's well. There the pleasant fields on which Christ looked, when He said, Behold the fields are white and ready for the harvest! I have hardly seen a landscape more suggestive of sweet and hopeful thoughts, and certainly, go where we may, we can never be so certain as here that we have found our Saviour's footsteps, that we are actually in the same place where he once was. Only those who have been fortunate enough to prove it can know what life, what vividness, must ever invest that beautiful fourth chapter of John when it has been read beside this well, with Gerizim on the right hand, Ebal on the left, Joseph's tomb a little distance off and the fields stretching away on every side. Horseback-riding is fatiguing work sometimes, living in tents is not the method of existence one would choose, but a single experience like that I have described repays a thoughtful traveler for more of hardship than he would have believed himself capable of enduring, until the spell of such a land as this was laid upon him.

That night we sat at *table d' hote* as usual an hour and a half, there being time for a nap between each of the courses, only the opportunities were small as we were perched on camp stools all on a slant and leaned our elbows on the table to maintain our equilibrium. And in the night how the rain poured, the lightning flashed, the thunder roared with short explosions among these sacred hills; yet so weary were we all that we slept very soundly, rising a little after five, in hopes to get off to Mt. Gerizim after an early breakfast. Not so however was it written in the almanac. The rain poured, the wind blew, and thick clouds shut down over our heads. But we bravely prepared for a day's ride; "the ladies" each fastening her big hat on her back and drawing over it her rubber coat, fastening the hood tightly under her chin until she looked like an Esquimaux, buttoning on her riding-gloves with whip attached to one of them; taking her bag of books intended to swing from the pommel and containing the Bible, Murray, and a book for flowers, and a pincushion in case of anything "giving out." The tents were knocked down over our heads and we stood out in as "big a drip" as ever poured its wet sheets upon defenseless travelers. It was very amusing to look around and see thirteen drenched, but cheerful mortals looking out from under their umbrellas and longing for a better time. I was especially struck by the mild, smiling countenance of Bishop Kingsley, shining like a full moon from under his wet and shapeless sombrero. But the dragoman decreed that the weather was too bad, we could not move to-day, so we mounted our horses and rode slipping along over the mud and through a roaring torrent to the town where, at the present writing, we are toasting our feet around a brasier of charcoal in a great, dirty, nondescript room of an Arab hotel; some reading their Bibles, others their Murray, others asking hard questions in history and chronology pertaining to our whereabouts, others still cracking dry jokes, and some curious scribblers sketching this room where we have taken refuge.

April 6, 1870.—So I am in Damascus—city of so many vague and pleasant fancies—even I!

We clatter along the muddy, wretchedly paved streets, where walk the same parti-colored processions of barbarians that trail their soiled, but brilliant garments through all the highways and byways of the East. We pass under the gigantic palm tree, down in all guide-books as one of the marvels of Damascus. Grand and brave it looks, the sunshine sifting through its million leaves and the mild breeze singing a hymn away up in its branches. What a lesson it has preached here, quite unheeded, during all the centuries of its noble growth; rising from these dirty streets and dingy dwellings into purer air and sunny skies, without a spot upon its emerald garments or a distortion among its vigorous branches. In a sense this palm tree pleases me better than anything else in all Damascus.

We clatter on at the discretion of our guide.

A slave market, the first and only one we ever saw, is among the "sights" he sees fit to place before us. Through several courts, up shaking stairs and into miserable little dens we are conducted with much discomfort and outrage upon our olfactories. Here are several miserable negro women, tattered boys, and one pretty Circassian girl waiting to be sold. They hold out their hands for alms. Some are in bed, sick in body or in heart. It is a sad sight to behold, in some regards the saddest upon which I ever gazed.

The great Mosque is of interest from its history, though I see little there except its vastness, which attracts me. This Mohammedan religion is by no means the harmonious affair one ignorantly supposes, but has its divisions and its rancors, all the more fierce from the fanatical stupidity of its adherents. We climb one of the minarets—that of "The Son of Mary," and get the ripest fruit of a journey to Damascus—namely, a view of the city itself. There it is, the emerald in its setting of gold, which poets have sung of, artists painted, and tourists spent pages of verbiage upon; one of the strangest, choicest sights of our beautiful earth, one to drink in with the eyes, one to cherish in the memory, one that Moore might have described in Lalla Rookh, or Warburton in his best mood might have presumed to touch, but which should have the tribute of silence from such pens as mine. The hill whence Mahomet first beheld it is thickly covered with snow, so we can not climb it as we have so much desired to do, as I have a thousand times dreamed of doing, even in Wisconsin groves and upon Illinois prairies.

Through dark, crowded streets we go to the "goldsmiths' hall" of Damascus, where hundreds of workmen, seated tailor fashion on their tables, are hammering away at all imaginable kinds of jewelry, and where from rude cases gleam pearls, rubies and diamonds of incalculable price, from earliest ages the heritage of the splendid Orient. But we hasten through this golden bedlam and emerging upon its roof come upon what we are seeking—the old, walled-up door that led to the Mosque we have just visited, when it was a Christian church, and where we read, or might if we knew Greek, an inscription placed here twelve hundred years ago, "Thy kingdom, O Christ, is an everlasting kingdom, and Thy word endureth to all generations!" There is almost the inspiration of prophecy in these words, and no one whose early and most innocent hopes Christianity has cherished, can look upon it without emotion. I stoop to gather a leaf that is growing from a crevice of this sculptured doorway.

The uninviting exterior of Oriental houses is proverbial, but those of Damascus are so much uglier than any other city of the East can show, that it would seem as if the fashion started here and its imitators had fallen as far behind their model, as is the fate of imitators generally. Our donkeys pick their way along a street outrageous in its filth, and so dark and narrow that it reminds us of the entrance to the pyramids, and stop before a small door let into a wall twenty feet high. A vigorous application of our whips to the same, unearths a withered-up old servant who flings wide the bird-cage portal, and bending nearly double we stumble into the finest of Damascus houses; into the place which brings us nearest to the dear, impossible, story-book world, and banishes in the twinkling of an eye that matter-of-fact old world, where we have lived so long, to the greatest distance to which it has ever yet been banished from our eyes. The transformations of the stage are nothing to it; the charm of Lalla Rookh's enticing pages can not go beyond; nay, rather, can not approach this scene. Look! As we pass from the entrance court to a second in the middle of the house, where fountains sparkle and the native Damascus roses bloom, a lady from an upper window salutes us with graceful courtesy, regards us for several minutes, no gentleman being of our party, and retires. She looks worthy of her surroundings, indeed, is just the human creature to lend a harmonious charm to all the beauty lavished here, where every sense is pleased. The very sight of her makes us commonplace Europeans ill at ease; our thoughtful faces and travel-worn garments have no rightful place in this exotic dream. We feel relieved when that fair face withdraws from sight and yet our foolish thoughts go with it wondering, and envious for one impulsive moment of the strange, glowing life one here might lead amid so much embodied poesy. We wander through the cool and shady rooms that open on the central court where orange trees in marble basins sift the sunshine that the sweet-voiced fountains cool. We enter by windows wide open as doors and on a level with the court-yard's marble floor. An ample space, also marble-covered and with a fountain in its midst, marks the limit beyond which shodden feet can not be allowed to trespass. Before stepping to the higher level where Turkish carpets indicate the sanctum sanctorum of the apartment, slippers must be put on or shoes put off. Velvet furniture of graceful, airy shape adorns the principal *salon.* Bright colors greet the eye wherever it may rest, from silver lamps to tapestried doorway, and large mirrors of surprising frequency repeat the rich hues that fall through windows of stained glass. In an alcove of the parlor are the delicate coffee, and wine cups with curious holders, peculiar to the East. In one great room are thirty or more windows, but all high above the loftiest head; no sound or suggestion of the outer world can penetrate this beautiful retreat. It is a place apart, a paradise unforfeited. The only thing I saw there which reminded me of the world from which I came and to which I must so soon and so inevitably return, was a plate of visitors' cards from all parts of Europe, showing that the charm of this strange spot has seized upon a thousand tranquil imaginations from the cooler zones. I am quite sure that when in my dear, quiet home in Evanston I shut my eyes to summon the most glowing picture that my fancy can afford, the least like what is around me there, the least, indeed, like what my notions of our old world would lead me to expect it could contain, I shall see a sunny bit of sky above an odorous garden walled in by the brightly colored interior walls and made musical by the clear fountains of a Damascus home.

Athens, April 18, 1870.—It is very much of a moment in one's life, I hold, when he looks first upon the birthplace of the arts, the capital of earth's most heroic land—even though its glory is departed and its children are enslaved.

And so it happened that when those stout-armed, swarthy-faced Greek boatmen took us in charge, tumbled us like so much merchandise into their little boats and rushed us off to the shore, I saw, instead of them, a blue-eyed, fair-haired race, the same to whom were given those visions of Minerva and of Venus which a colder age crystallized into religion; and before me on those azure waves loomed the fleet of Xerxes driven by Themistocles and his helmeted warriors away from the paradise they had menaced.

A pleasant carriage ride along the line of wall built by the prudent Athenians to afford a sheltered passage from their city to their port, and we enter the city which has succeeded to that of ancient times. It is a fresh, cheerful looking place, altogether European, even American in seeming, to our Asiatic eyes! The streets are clean, shops large, windows bright and clear, pavements and sidewalks smooth and well arranged. Our hotel seems like a palace, and I don't wonder that a dozen different travelers have extolled its merits in the guide-book, if all came hither from the East as we do. What rooms we have, covered with rich carpets, and planted out to huge easy-chairs and pretty escritoires, with clean beds covered by a scarlet blanket apiece. Engravings of Kings George and Otho are on the walls, and out of the windows views of the Acropolis! What a dining saloon is this, and what a breakfast they give us—crisp cutlets, fresh eggs, fresh rolls and coffee, and honey from Mt. Hymettus!

The creature comforts duly attended to—and who forgets them? even long-haired artists, and starry-eyed poets confessing their indolent sway—we engage "Philosopher" as our guide, a plump man of middle age, dull as his own eyes and good natured as he is well fed. By his exertions a nice carriage, and driver in short white petticoats, à la Greek, are speedily in readiness, and obedient to the order, "To the Acropolis"; we drive off in high spirits to the goal of our long voyage. We wind around the base of this famous hill, which has several much higher and fully as steep in its vicinity, and passing through three comparatively modern gates enter the Propylæum, pass its beautiful, though ruined portal, climb the bare rock, where the brilliant processions of the Golden Age were wont to pass, and take up our position before the Parthenon. Gray and broken as is this ruin it is yet among the most impressive I have had the good fortune to behold. So simple, almost austere, in its beauty; so satisfying in its proportions; so nobly dignified in its *tout ensemble*—one feels a reverence for the Parthenon, not exceeded by that inspired by any other fane that reverent hands have reared to any deity. Three or four hours of scrutiny, as honest and as earnest as we could bestow, gave us somewhat of a home feeling in this temple.

We studied the Propylæum, the Temple of Victory, the Parthenon and Erechtheum and found where the old altars had stood, the glittering statues on their sculptured pedestals, and followed the road by which the splendid processions used to wind up the steep rock in the Age of Pericles.

PARIS AND THE FRANCO-PRUSSIAN WAR.

We returned to Paris after another visit in England and remained until the investiture of the French capital by Germany became imminent. Our sympathies were with King William and "Unser Fritz," Bismarck, Von Moltke and the "Red Prince," but to say this would have been treason, and we maintained that "guarded silence" in which diplomatists rejoice and honest people grow impatient. The results of the struggle form a part of history's record to-day. But we who watched its beginnings from within were not surprised at the sequence.

August 12, 1870.—Even so soon, the outmost ripple of the widening war-wave has reached me in my quiet life and quietest of Paris homes. This morning the cream cheese which helps out my slender breakfast failed, because the man who was wont to bring it was conscripted and has gone to the frontier. The garrulous old custodian who conducted us this afternoon to the Arc de Triomphe, said that most of the trees in the park were to be cut down in the progress of the home defenses. We saw hundreds of men working on the fortifications which are soon to shut off communication with the outer world.

Thiers spoke in the Corps Législatif to-day, for the first time since three weeks ago, when he was hissed and howled at and silenced, and his house stoned a while later by the populace, because his voice was not for war. To-day he was applauded. To-day Marshal Lebœuf, then Minister of War, head of the army, the nation's hope, the most eager of them all in his shrieks for combat, has handed in his resignation. What a people is this, and how short-lived the glory so dear to all who love the name of France!

News on the bulletin posted up at the mayor's: "The Prussians have surrounded Strasbourg. The French are retreating in good order. But her soldiers performed prodigies of valor in the recent engagement."

As Thiers said, "All the failure is due to the incapacity of their chiefs." To which Picard replies, "An incapacity that has lasted twenty years." Many think, and all who have not loaves and fishes to lose by it, hope that the second Empire is in its dying hour. It looks ominous—the number of men working on the fortifications and the number of places where the grass has been cut away to make space for the cannon, of which six hundred will very soon be mounted.

Père Hyacinthe publishes his determination to work on the fortifications, since he thinks a priest should only fight in extreme cases. He will take his spade to-morrow after mass.

All other considerations are evidently overshadowed when the gay Parisians reflect that the whole French army is in retreat, closely followed by "the German brutes," as polite France does not hesitate to call the challenged invaders of her soil. Great, but quiet crowds stand waiting upon the boulevards and in the street of the newspaper offices. The varying aspects of Paris are like those of a handsome woman's face swayed by contending passions.

News of two indecisive French victories are reported by Marshal Bazaine, with the words, "Our losses have been great." The people seem as disconsolate as ever, for who does not know that if real success should crown the French armies, the streets would bloom with flags and the air be rent with the noise of minute-guns? This state of things can not endure much longer.

A lengthy placard posted on the columns of the Rue de Rivoli, and on all available spots along the boulevards, announces that "General Trochu is governor of Paris in the peril of the nation, and that his motto is, 'I am for the country, with the help of God.'" Everybody feels relieved, because he is a very able man and much beloved.

We have another batch of London papers, and the news we gather is altogether different from what the Paris papers give us.

Let me here set down one corollary on my European study of the Sabbath problem. Even if the observance of one day in seven by cessation from ordinary pursuits, particular observance of divine worship, and thoughts of destiny and duty, be not required of us by our Creator, it is at least proved to be for our highest good and best development, first, by comparing nations where such observances are habitual with those where they are not; and second, in individual experience, by instituting a similar parallel between the periods when we have and when we have not regarded the injunctions of the fourth commandment. I look hopefully toward the better country of America and the better life that it is easy there to lead. For me and for my work in life it is a happy thing that I am going home. I would that I had the ambition of goodness even as strongly as I have the ambition of knowledge!

Three things I did, once in awhile, during my two years and four months of foreign travel, that I never did and never do at home. I went to see sights on Sunday, went to the theater, and took wine at dinner. I reflect upon these facts with undisguised regret, but will frankly mention how this apostasy occurred. Never having been inside of a theater but once in America, and that on my first visit to New York City, in 1863, I went a few times in London, Paris, Berlin, and once in Moscow—perhaps half a dozen times in all. The universal judgment of tourists is that one's impression of the class that has best opportunity of culture is best gained by one's observations at the play, and their native language is spoken with greater purity by actors, perhaps, than by any other class.

There are some important sights in Paris never to be seen except on Sunday, so we went a few times, probably not half a dozen, in the nine months of our residence there.

Having been reared a total abstainer, the thought never occurred to me to take wine until my violent illness in Copenhagen, when a kind-faced physician bent over me and told me in French that if I ever expected to see my home again, I must avoid drinking water as we journeyed from one country to another, that being the most fruitful source of disease among travelers. The subject had not then been studied as it has been since, and I was more reverent towards physicians than I am now, so these words came to me as law and gospel. From that time on I thought it right to mix a little wine with the water at dinner, taking tea and coffee at the other meals. Kate also carried a bottle of wine with which to moisten our box of Albert biscuit, which was a requisite on our long car rides. Coming home, the custom was at once abandoned by us both and not renewed by her in her many years of foreign travel since, nor by me save as herein confessed.

At the International breakfast in Philadelphia, which was a part of the Centennial celebration by temperance people in 1876, I heard testimonies from travelers who had circumnavigated the globe many times, to the effect that they never drank wine. I know it is the testimony of all of our Methodist Bishops, and their duties take them to every clime, and my honored friends, Mr. and Mrs. Joseph Cook, of Boston, tell me that they found a bottle of thoroughly boiled water to be a perfectly safe and satisfactory substitute for wine in all their world-wide travels, so that were I now to set out for a voyage around the world, as I suspect I shall some day, I should have no anxiety in my character of total abstainer. I firmly believe that had I never tasted wine while on the other side of the water, and had I scrupulously followed the American customs in my Sabbath observances, it would have been much better for me every way.

August 14.—I went to the Louvre to see my favorite among Venuses, that of Milo, for a leave-taking. In the long, dim perspective, she gleamed like a divinity. She has a soul, a brain, a heart, which one can not say of the Medici and hardly of the Capitoline, or of the Diana of Versailles and her antiquarian companions. The gallery of modern sculpture, including Canova's Cupids and Psyches, and many other chefs d'œuvre were our last sights in the Louvre, most artistic of all galleries and the one that more than any other contributes to the culture of the public taste. It is the noblest thing in France, worthy of what is highest and most generous in the great Latin race. How it has pleased and taught me by its lessons manifold as the panorama of evening clouds, and free as the air from Swiss mountains. To-day, as always, when I have been there, many poor workmen in their blouses were passing through this gallery, looking delightedly from side to side, holding their caps in their hands, not awkwardly, but with a certain timid grace, until they observed that gentlemen wore theirs, when they replaced them suddenly and commenced staring more diligently than ever at the pictured walls.

August 23.—Our adieus to our dear French hostess and her children were indeed hard to be said. We felt that we should probably never see again this gracious and accomplished woman and her lovely little children, who, with their invariable happy heedlessness, went smiling to the carriage door, throwing kisses and repeating their good-bys without cessation. Dear Madame, from her I hastened away, so as not to cry outright. She has a firm and loyal friend in me, and I am sure that while she lives I shall not lack one on this side the water, nor shall I lack, while she has a roof over her, a home, where I am as welcome as anywhere on earth save in the little Gothic cottage on the sunset shore of Lake Michigan.

September 5.—With respect to sea-sickness, I would offer a recipe of my own, inasmuch as every one has at his tongue's end a deliverance of this sort—I mean if he has never been sea-sick. My recipe is, however, an exception to the rule, for I am never anything but sea-sick while on the sea! Crossing the Mediterranean is perhaps as much worse than crossing the Atlantic as the latter is worse than navigating a mill-pond. But on both these watery highways,* I got relief by just one method, namely, rolling the pillow into a cylinder and rolling back my neck over that, while I held my arm above my head and with eyes well up in their sockets and fixed with

*Also on the Pacific Ocean where I eked out a miserable existence during the voyage from San Francisco to Astoria at the mouth of the Columbia river.

desperate clinch upon the pages of an interesting book, I performed my cure and defrauded Old Neptune to the, at least intermittent, quietude of my diaphragm. I thus read the Life of Robertson, and his sermons, many of the best novels of Bulwer, and choice excerpts from Tauchnitz's Edition of Great Authors.

September 6.—New York almost in sight, silver sails all out in the west, silver moon in the clear sky, breakfast in the American fashion; port-holes all open for American air. We fill out our custom-house affidavits, pass Sandy Hook, the Narrows, the forts, the shipping, with the Star-spangled Banner at the mast-head, feel choky over it, vote unanimously that there is no nobler harbor; see the German flag everywhere, and learn amid tremendous excitement that Napoleon is a prisoner, McMahon's army has capitulated and France is a Republic. We are so delighted we know not what to do or say. Our friends, the German Doctor and his wife, hop up and down!

Wait three hours for our baggage to be taken off, enthusiasm ebbs to a low point; get our eight trunks and packing boxes together with infinite pains. A gentleman of the police fraternity takes our effects in hand, asks me solemnly, "In which trunk are all those handsome new dresses from Paris?" to which I innocently reply, "In this big black one, sir." Asks me if we have any piece goods, to which I replied, "Oh, yes, enough to make our dresses over when they get out of style!" He smiles wisely. "Have you worn all your clothing?" "Well, yes, that is, we tried it all on at our dressmakers', but we have worn it very little." He sees that we are so tremendously honest that he does n't look into a single trunk, merely cuts the rope, saying, "You understand these have all been examined. I do this for you as a personal favor, I peril my position by so doing, but you say you are in haste to take a train, and I wish to annoy you as little as possible." Poor fellow! It were more than human charity to say that he did not look for a fee, but at least he did not get any from two such upright and patriotic women as Kate and I, for, in the first place, we were "principled against it," and in the second place, our finances were at such a point of exhaustion, that only my ten-dollar gold piece, that I had when we left America, bought for fifteen dollars in greenbacks and sold at a premium of one dollar at the New York railway station, saved us from bankruptcy. We talked of taking a carriage from the wharf, and asked the price. "Five dollars," said the hackman, which frightful words we repeated after him in holy horror and wrath and toddled off to take the street cars, meditating on the nice Paris cabs that would have carried us for thirty cents, and agreeing that America was not perfect, but then it was America, and that was enough.

And now, in conclusion, follow my rough notes made like Captain Cuttle's, "when found"; for my native land, which seemed a little strange at first, was now as closely scrutinized as those lands had been whence I was newly come, and no home-fondness was allowed to dim my glistening spectacles as I drew forth pencil and paper and took up my task.

First. Wooden wharfs, general look of temporariness, as one approached the shore; no imposing buildings; droll ferry houses, and steamers that look as "skating bugs" did on Rock River of old; cars going like wild-fire; unpaved streets full of weeds, as we passed through the villages going out to the home of Kate's genial Aunt Jane in New Jersey; cow-catcher on the engine; the screaming whistle instead of the mild, cultured whistle of the continent; an ear-splitting ding-donging of the engine bell; "Lookout For the Locomotive," at every turn. In Europe no railroad or path, or passenger, is ever, under any circumstances, allowed to cross a track. "Coal, brick, lime, cement, mortar," these are signs frequently met with and of proportions that indicate a thriving business and a new country. We have stood upon Mt. Calvary, and here we are at the Morris and Essex depot; we have eaten pomegranates at Damascus, and behold us with mouths watering for prairie melons. "Fust regular stop's Milburn, don't pay no 'tention, it's only to let off a passenger." Spruce conductor, ring on finger, gold chain, well-kept mustache, not a man adapted to climbing along outside of car from one door to another after the manner of conductors on the other side. Raw, stubby fields, smell like a prairie on fire, as we cross the Jersey marshes. Polite gentleman changes seats with us because ours is a back one; anticipates our raising of the car window; an employé conducts us to the car, carries our baggage, opens door and seats us *without charge!* "Pop-corn for sale." The cars are like a meeting-house, where people decorously and comfortably face one way instead of glaring at each other from benches opposite all the weary day long. Every man, well-dressed and ill-dressed, has a newspaper. Cost of a carriage, five dollars! Truckman with trunks, five dollars! In France, all that for five francs (one dollar) or less. Railroad salutation between two men of business; rough shake of the hand, "Good-by, give my respects to your folks;" "Thankee, I will;" wooden houses everywhere, glaring white; whole forests manufactured into fences glaring white. Amazing gentility of custom-house officers and street conductor; first advertisement that we saw plastered on a bowlder by the roadside, "Watt's Nervous Antidote." We have got home to a nervous nation. Tremendous play bills, with huge portraits, caricatures, etc.; circuses predominating; newsboys allowed to hop on the street and other cars with papers, without being taken by the collar and jerked off by a policeman. You would know that the street-car conductor did not always expect to be one, by the very style of his making change for your tickets. He has the air of a man holding on to one round of the ladder while he reaches up to grasp the next. Street barber's poles instead of little brass basins, concave on one edge. Street-car conductor to Kate, "Excuse me, but have n't you just come from England? you said station."

All this was twenty years ago or more, when we were less "English, you know," than Henry Irving, daily cable dispatches, and plenty of money have made us since. But we are true Americans at heart, and we know beyond all doubt or contradiction, ours is GOD'S COUNTRY.

CAR-WINDOW JOTTINGS.

NEW MEXICO.

Albuquerque, nearly as ancient in its origin as Santa Fé, is the "Wide-awake" of this mercurial continent. We were there on Good Friday, and wagons of nondescript appearance thronged the streets, while teams were in the corral, and men lounged about the street corners and saloons. "That's the way the men go to church here," dryly remarked a friend. "They think they've done their whole duty when they fetch the women to mass." Sure enough, the dingy old church was full of devout women, prostrate in acknowledgment of sin, while their liege lords were drinking *ardente* at the next corner. It needed no prophet to declare the doom of such an unequal civilization. Whatever makes the beliefs, tastes, habits and education of men and women more congenial, providing always that we must level up and not down, will most rapidly hasten the sway of happy homes and regenerated hearts.

The Pueblo Indians have a very simple form of election, one that might, with propriety, be recommended to the politicians of Gotham. It is this: The mayor of the city is chosen once a year. He can not have a second term. On the morning of election day, the outgoing mayor nominates two candidates for the succession. One of these goes to one end of the field, the other takes his station opposite. Every man (why not every woman, pray tell?) goes to the candidate of his choice and literally "stands up for him." Rapidly the lines lengthen on either side. The old men of the tribe count the number in each, and thus the election is absolutely without fraud, and, best of all, they can dispense with caucuses. The Navajoes a tribe of 16,000, trace their line of descent wholly along the mother's side, and the inheritance of property is from mother to daughter, so that a man when married goes to his wife's house. This is in accord with the philosophy of that most brilliant French thinker, Emile de Girardin, who descants at length on the intrinsic advantages of this plan as being founded in nature, ancestry being far more easily and surely traced on the mother's than on the father's side.

SOUTHERN CALIFORNIA.

We are at last in the land of enchantment, where heliotrope climbs all over the fronts of the houses; where corn grows seventeen feet high, and one can have a bouquet of fresh roses and a strawberry short-cake on the table all the year round. We are with a people as genial as the climate and breathe an air that makes wine seem more than ever an unnecessary and absurd exhilaration. Mrs. Dr. Gray, the dignified president, and Mrs. M. E. Congdon, the keen-brained secretary of California W. C. T. U., came five hundred miles to welcome us. Capt. A. D. Wood, our noble friend, of *The Rescue*, with Mr. and Mrs. Will D. Gould, of Los Angeles, the former a gifted lawyer, and the latter a grand woman, met us at the depot after our long overland trip. But I must not tell all our delightful impressions and haps with no mishaps, until I bring up the log by noting down some items of our stay in Tucson, for ten years the capital of Arizona, and still its chief city.

Outsiders say that Arizona means "arid zone," but insiders insist that its real significance is "beautiful zone." The latter we will not dispute, only its beauty is below ground, for its deserts are wide and its mines the most famous of the period. Roads leading nowhere, desert plains, strange, useless vegetation; no fences, general appearances not unlike Arabia Petræa, according to the books; one dollar charged for an aged canned meal; now and then an emigrant wagon, with wild-faced, bearded men driving oxen or mules; lone mountains, tranquil, treeless and distant, like vast, heaped-up shapes of sand or stone; a saw-tooth sky-line; needle-pointed shrubs; seven-branched candlestick cactus trees, forty feet high, these items include some of my impressions of Arizona. The only living things indigenous to the plains that cheered our eyes, were six graceful antelopes, discerned at early dawn, coming no whence, going no whither. What a strange juxtaposition, this wilderness outside, and the race-horse of the East, puffing his undaunted way; the elegant "silver car," with its artistic decorations, its tapestry cushions and curtains, and way-wise men and women reading the Chicago dailies, the last *Century*, of New York, *Atlantic*, of Boston, or *Spectator*, of London, and looking out through costly glass (adjusted from "opera" to "field") over this waste of primeval lonesomeness!

SAN FRANCISCO.

Of all places on the globe, go to the California metropolis if you would feel the strong pulse of internationalism. Few have caught its rhythm, as yet, but we must do so if we would be strong enough to keep step with that matchless, electric twentieth century soon to go swinging past. You can almost hear his resonant tread on San Francisco pavements; his voice whispers in the lengthening telephone, saying, "Yesterday was good, to-day is better, but to-morrow shall be the red-letter day of all life's magic calendar." I have always been impatient of our planet's name—"the earth." What other, among the shining orbs, has a designation so insignificant? That we have put up with it so long is a proof of the awful inertia of the aggregate mind, almost as surprising as our endurance of the traffic in alcoholic poison. With Jupiter and Venus, Orion and the Pleiades smiling down upon us in their patronizing fashion, we have been contented to inscribe on our visiting cards, "At Home: *The Earth!*" Out upon such paucity of language. "The dust o' the ground" forsooth! That answered well enough perhaps for a dark-minded people who never even dreamed they were living on a star. Even now an army of good folks afraid of the next thing, just because it is the next, and not the last, will doubtless raise holy hands of horror against the proposition I shall proceed to launch forth for the first time, though it is harmless as the Pope's bull against the comet. They will probably oppose me, too, on theologic grounds, for, as Coleridge hath it,

> "Time consecrates, and what is gray with age becomes religion."

Nevertheless, since we do inhabit a star, I solemnly propose we cease to call it a dirt heap, and being determined to "live up to my light," I hereby bring forward and clap a patent upon the name

CONCORDIA.

By the same token, I met half a dozen selectest growths of people in San Francisco who, in the broadest international way are doing more to make this name Concordia descriptive, rather than prophetic in its application to our oldest home, than any other people I can name. They work among the Chinese, Japanese, and "wild Arabs of the Barbary coast," they go with faces that are an epitomized gospel, and preach to the stranger within the Golden Gate that he is a stranger no more; they bring glad tidings of good which shall be to all people, for to them, as to their Master, "there is neither Jew nor Greek, bond nor free, male nor female in Christ Jesus."

Among the many such, I can here mention only two: "See Otis Gibson, or you have missed the moral hero of Gold-opolis"—this was concurrent testimony coming from every side. Garfield left no truer saying than that the time wants men "who have the courage to look the devil squarely in the face and tell him that he is the devil." Precisely this fearless sort of character is Rev. Otis Gibson. He has been the uncompromising friend of "the heathen Chinee" through all that pitiful Celestial's grievous fortunes on our Western shore. When others cursed he blessed; while others pondered he prayed; what was lacking in schools, church, counsel and kindness he supplied. It cost something thus to stand by a hated and traduced race in spite of hoodlum and Pharisee combined. But Otis Gibson could not see why the people to whom we owe the compass and the art of printing, the civil service examination, the choicest porcelain, might not Christianize as readily on our shores as on their own! In this faith he and his noble wife have worked on until they have built up a veritable city of refuge for the defenseless and despairing, in the young and half barbarous metropolis of the Pacific slope.

We afterward visited the "Chinese Quarter," so often described, under escort of Rev. Dr. Gibson. We saw the theaters where men sit on the back and put their feet on the board part of the seat; where actors don their costumes in full sight of the audience, and frightful pictured dragons compete with worse discord, for supremacy. We saw the joss-house, with swinging censer and burning incense, tapers and tawdriness, a travesty of the Catholic ceremonial, taking from the latter its one poor merit of originality. We saw a mother and child kneeling before a hideous idol, burning tapers, tossing dice, and thus "consulting the oracle," with many a sidelong glance of inattention on the part of the six-year-old boy, but with sighs and groans that proved how tragically earnest was the mother's faith. Dr. Gibson said the numbers on the dice corresponded to wise sayings and advices on strips of paper sold by a mysterious Chinese whose "pious shop" was in the temple vestibule, whither the poor woman resorted to learn the result of her "throw," and then returned to try again, until she got some response that quieted her. Could human incredulity and ignorance go farther? We saw the restaurants, markets and bazaars, as thoroughly Chinese as Pekin itself can furnish; the haunts of vice, all open to the day; the opium dens, with their comatose victims; and then, to comfort our hearts and take away the painful vividness of woman's degradation, Dr. Gibson took us to see a Christian Chinese home, made by two of his pupils, for years trained under his eye. How can I make the contrast plain enough? A square or two away, the horrid orgies of opium and other dens still worse, but here a well-kept dry-goods store, where the husband was proprietor, and in the rear a quiet, pleasant, sacred home. The cleanly, kind-faced wife busy with household cares, her rooms the picture of neatness, her pretty baby sleeping in his crib, and over all the peace that comes from praise and prayer. Never in my life did I approach so near to that perception, too great for mortal to attain, of what the Gospel has achieved for woman, as when this gentle, honored wife and mother said, seeing me point to an engraving of "The Good Shepherd" on her nursery wall: "*Oh, yes! He gave this home to us.*"

How firm and fine the etching that should accurately show the features of Mrs. Sarah B. Cooper! whose strong, sweet individuality I have not seen excelled—no, not even among women. From the time when our Eastern press teemed with notices of the Presbyterian lady who had been tried for heresy and acquitted, who had the largest Bible class in San Francisco and was founder of that city's Kindergartens for the poor, I made a mental memorandum that, no matter whom I missed, this lady I would see.

So at half-past twelve on a mild May Sabbath noon, I sought the elegant Plymouth Church, built by Rev. Dr. A. L. Stone, formerly of Boston, and found a veritable congregation in its noble auditorium. Men and women of high character and rare thoughtfulness were gathered, Bibles in hand, to hear the exposition of the acquitted heretic, whom a Pharisaical deacon had begun to assail contemporaneously with her outstripping him in popularity as an expounder of the gospel of love. She entered quietly by a side door, seated herself at a table level with the pews, laid aside her fur-lined cloak and revealed a fragile, but symmetric figure, somewhat above the medium height, simply attired in black, with pose and movement altogether graceful, and while perfectly self-possessed, at the farthest remove from being self-assertive. Then I noted a sweet, untroubled brow, soft brown hair chastened with tinge of silver (frost that fell before its time, doubtless at the doughty deacon's bidding); blue eyes, large, bright and loving; nose of the noblest Roman, dominant yet sensitive, chiseled by generations of culture, the unmistakable expression of highest force and mettlesomeness in character, held in check by all the gentlest sentiments; a mouth firm, yet delicate, full of the smiles that follow tears.

When the delightful hour was over, among the loving group that gathered around her, attracted by the healing virtue of her spiritual atmosphere, came a temperance sojourner from the East. As my name was mentioned, the face so full of spirituality lighted even more than was its wont, and the soft, strong voice said, "Sometimes an introduction is a *recognition*—and so I feel it to be now." I consider that enough of a compliment to last me for a term of years. I feel that it helped mortgage me to a pure life; I shall be better for it "right along." For if I have ever clasped hands with a truth-seeker, a disciple of Christ and lover of humanity, Sarah B. Cooper held out to me that loving, loyal hand. A more hospitable intellect I have not known, nor a glance more wide and tolerant; "Christ, and him crucified," is to that loyal heart "the Chief among ten thousand and altogether lovely."

Among the best types of representative women America may justly count Sarah B. Cooper, the student, the Christian exegete and philosopher, and the tender friend of every untaught little child.

If I have not yet written up my California trip it is not for lack of material, but rather because I have such a bundle of notes that I dread to begin. California! "She is made up of every creature's best."

THE YOSEMITE.

Who can fitly tell of the condensed impressions about God made by a valley only six miles long, one mile wide and half a mile high, wherein all forms of solemn, majestic and pastoral beauty are combined?

When, after a mountain ride of half a day, surrounded by inclined planes of evergreens, each of which would have been a world's wonder at the East, with superb curves in the road evermore opening fresh vistas of illimitable height, verdure and beauty, we rounded Inspiration Point, "there was no more spirit in us." Word-pauperism oppresses one upon this height as nowhere else on earth. There is in Europe a single revelation of art that has power to silence the chatter even of fashion's devotees, and that is Raphael's Sistine Madonna. I have been in its seraphic presence for hours at a time, but never heard a vocal comment. The foamiest natures are not silenced by Niagara, by Mount Blanc, by the Jungfrau's awful purity, or the terrors of Vesuvius, for their flippant tones have smitten me in all these sacred places. But from the little child in our midst—a bright-faced boy of four—to the rough, kind-hearted driver, not one word was spoken by our party as the heavenly vision of Yosemite, framed in fleecy, flying clouds, greeted our thoughtful eyes, and spoke of God to our hushed souls. Except beside the dying bed of my beloved I have never felt the veil so thin between me and the world ineffable—supernal. What was it like? Let no pen less lofty than that of Milton, less atune with Nature's purest mood than that of Wordsworth, hope to "express unblamed" the awful and ethereal beauty of what we saw. "Earth with her thousand voices praises God," sang the great heart of Coleridge of the vale of Chamouni, but here, the divine chorus includes both earth and heaven, for El Capitan rears his head into the sky, while Sentinel and Cathedral Rocks and sky-climbing Cloud's Rest round out the full diapason of earthly and of celestial praise. A holy awe rested upon us, and tears were in all eyes. At last the sacred silence was broken by a rich voice, beloved by me for many a year, as Mrs. Dr. Bently led the "Gloria in Excelsis," in which the jubilant soprano harmonized with the melodious bass of humanity's united utterance of praise. "O come, let us worship and bow down, let us kneel before the Lord, our Maker," these inspired words leaped to our lips, and we found that in this supreme moment of our experience, beyond all poets, was the fitness of grand old words our mothers taught us from the Book of God. "The Lord is in his holy temple, let all the earth keep silence before him," "What is man that thou art mindful of him?" "Stand in awe and sin not," these were the words that came first to us, and I believe we shall be better men and women always for that vision of eternity from which the curtain of mystery was for a moment drawn aside. We learned afterward that as our two coaches rolled on into the valley a third rounded "Inspiration Point," and Judge ——, of Sydney, Ohio, a dear old gentleman, rose to his feet, clasped his hands as if in prayer, and exclaimed "Mercy, mercy, mercy! Have I lived seventy-six years that I might see this glory! God made it all!" and he lifted up his voice and wept. Such a scene as that is once for a life-time.

We saw the valley from an hundred points of view afterward; we waved our good-by to it a week later from this very spot, but the first remains the unmatched view—its like will never greet our eyes again—not in this world.

As we sped onward into the valley I thought of the sightless children with whom I used to play at Forest Home and said: "I never before felt such pity for the blind."

PUGET SOUND.

Beautiful for situation is Puget Sound. A generation hence it will be the joy of this noble Republic. Oregon with its matchless mountains and river, Washington and its wonderful forests, are both included in this name. Here is the Pacific cowed and conquered, purring like a tamed tiger at the feet of marvelous young cities. No one can appreciate the transformation save those who, like ourselves, have experienced the untold miseries of the voyage between San Francisco and Astoria, Oregon. For fifty-four hours I lay motionless in the upper berth suitably assigned to one who, during that interval when "deep calleth unto deep," had no part in this world's hurry or delight.

Welcome Puget Sound with its fathomless harbors of land-locked blue, and the imperial pressure of such snow-clad mountains as are found nowhere else, no, not in Switzerland!

Twice Anna Gordon and myself visited Victoria, the capital of British Columbia, receiving a royal welcome. The second time, we went to organize a Provincial W. C. T. U. The climate of the Sound is perhaps its greatest surprise. It is so mild that the English ivy grows out-of-doors all the year round. The ladies told me they could gather flowers always up to March, when slight frosts generally appear, but of snow or ice there is nothing to signify. It has the summer of Denmark and the winter of Italy. It is a rare climate for clear thinking and quiet, rational living, a soil in which the temperance reform has readily taken root. The forests, chiefly of fir and cedar, are of unequaled magnificence. Frequently more wood is cut from an acre of ground than can be corded thereon. "Go West, young woman, and grow up with the country," would be our advice to aspiring girls.

MONTANA.

Bishop Hargrove of the M. E. Church, South, had it about right when he said, "Montana has barely enough valleys to slip in between its hills." Never was a territory more aptly named. For beauty of railway scenery I should like to know what country furnishes anything superior to the panorama between Spokane Falls, W. T., and Missoula, Montana. Spokane Falls itself is an almost ideal town in situation, and the cataract is better worth a day's journey to visit than several on both sides of the water that I have made a pilgrimage on purpose to behold.

"Clark's Fork" of the Columbia is the absurd name of a river quite comparable in dash and beauty of color with the "arrowy Rhone," only this is of the most delicate emerald, and that, as all the world knows, is the most cerulean blue. But the towers, spires and bastions of the American river are unique beyond those of any other save the glorious river toward which it runs—the Columbia, Oregon's pride and, erelong, the tourist's favorite rendezvous.

We left Missoula July 26 in a covered conveyance for Helena and Deer Lodge—a distance of one hundred and eighty-two miles—Rev Mr. Shannon, his wife and little girl accompanying us. The two horses and entire outfit had been loaned Mr. S. in-token of good will. He had sent it ahead the night before eighteen miles beyond Missoula, as the railroad authorities had kindly permitted us to ride on the construction train to that point, which was the western terminus of this great iron track. Here we clambered into our wagon behind the unmated steeds loaned us from two separate establishments, packed away "big box, little box, bandbox and bundle" almost to the overflowing point, and set out overland. Anna dubbed our horses "Thunder and Lightning"; for what purpose did not appear, unless, as cheery young Mr. Riggin, superintendent of Methodist missions in Montana, said, "One of them looked as if he had swallowed an avalanche of thunder, and it had n't agreed with him, and the other seemed to have been struck by lightning." We perambulated along through wooded valleys, the sun's light obscured by forest fires and great pines in process of ignition on either side our path. We camped at noon beside a gurgling brook, spread our table-cloth, boiled our eggs and tea over a fire made of pine cones, washed our dishes in the little mountain stream, got some nice milk for the baby from a way-side farm, and took up our "jog trot" over the hills and far away. Our dark horse "Thunder" stood from under the heavy load upon hill-sides dangerously sloping, and it was droll indeed to see Mr. S. balance on the hind wheel to strengthen the "brake" while his wife drove, and we ran with stones to block the hind wheels. Thus we worked our passage the first day and wished for lands with railroads. It came to pass, however, that when we stopped at night, having made fifty-six miles, cars and all, we found that it was "all along of" the misfitting collar that poor Thunder had led us such a hard life, whereupon he became the pet of the party. I could but think whether it be not true that a galling, ill-adjusted yoke, may explain much, in many cases, of the criss-cross and contradiction of this our mortal life.

Our second day's ride was much ameliorated by the experience of the past and the increased adequacy of our thunderous steed. We had leisure to take in the changeful beauty of Montana, a territory with an individuality all its own. It is the fourth in size among the grand divisions of Uncle Sam's estate, the order of extent being as follows: Texas, California, Dakota,

Montana. It is emphatically the pasture land of the Republic, and its cattle kings are justly famed.

Montana sometimes exhibits a thermometer marking fifty-seven degrees below zero, but so light and clear is the atmosphere that the people declare they "do not feel the cold as they used to back East." The territory is thinly settled as yet, but railroading is simply rampant there and in Idaho, and we shall soon regard both as next door neighbors.

On our third day's ride, we passed the place where robbers sacked a stage and killed a horse a few days previous. Though unarmed and mostly of the timid class, I don't think we felt a qualm. Somehow, though distance lends enchantment, proximity brings grit to bear, and we went on our way rejoicing. On our fourth day's riding we passed the logs beside the road from behind which, not twenty-four hours earlier, three masked men had pointed guns at the stage load, and afterward at a private conveyance, making them stand and deliver. Perhaps it was on the principle, they that know nothing fear nothing ; anyhow, we did n't mind, but jogged on over endless reaches of hill country, till we reached a stage station where we slept the sleep of the weary, if not of the just.

We were glad to learn that the robbers were captured in a few days after their crime. Brother Garvin told me that Plummer, the greatest "road agent" of the far West (for by that euphemism do they absurdly soften down the atrocious occupation of these men) could in two and a half seconds take his pistol from his pocket, and fire three bullets, hitting a little percussion-cap box at ten paces. Woe is me, to think of such quickness of mind and dexterity of hand turned to an unmixed curse.

A couple of droll speeches were reported to me on this trip. One was by an emigrant woman in Washington Territory, who was seated in a rude wagon behind a weary-looking ox team, while the lordly owner was refreshing himself in a saloon. A tourist accosted her with the words, "How do you like it out here ?" and she answered, "Well, stranger, it may do well enough for men, but I tell you what, it's drefful poor country *for women and oxen !*" Another passing traveler asked a Montana girl if she had ever seen the cars and received this philosophic answer which might be appropriately headed "sweet satisfaction": 'No sir, I can't say that I ever saw the cars, but I don't care, I'd *just* as lief see the stage."

UTAH.

After leaving Montana, we boxed the compass of Utah, home of the strangest civilization of modern times, the "Church of the Latter Day Saints."

First of all our train entered Cache Valley north of Ogden, and we watched out sharply for signs of the new departure. Early in the day, we passed numerous farms and little villages, utterly treeless and forlorn, whereupon we ejaculated: "There! we've struck Mormondom, no doubt of it; plain to be seen as a pikestaff." When, behold, we were informed by the conductor of our mistake, for these dreary burghs were "Gentile" beyond a peradventure. Later on, they grew more winsome, with trim little homes, trees and vines, yellow harvests and solid comfort everywhere. *Mirabile dictu!* These were the Mormon settlements! We soon learned that their most salient features were the presence of willow fences around the fields, woven somewhat like a basket—an Old World notion, imported by the Mormon emigrants, which, combined with the churchless aspect of the villages themselves (for the Mormon "Tabernacle" has an architecture peculiar to itself, not unlike our notion of what the temple might have been) gave a novel aspect to the scene. Noon came, and we stopped for dinner at the notable Mormon town of Logan, where we first saw one of these stately buildings. Our breakfast in a Gentile village had been simply execrable. Here, it was the most toothsome we had tasted in a year. It was homelike, wholesome and appetizing; "Mother's cooking!" was my immediate exclamation. The butter, with flavor and fragrance of sweet pastures and new-mown hay, reminded me of the cool cellar and delightsome dairy of my old Wisconsin home. What a contrast to the frouzy abomination usually taken as medicine in railroad waiting-rooms in that sultry month of August! The bread was worthy of its companionship, with cheese that was the ambrosial essence of sweet cream, the vegetables simply delightful, the meat could be prepared for deglutition without the ten minutes of assiduous grinding we so often laboriously give, and the table-cloth, dishes, etc., were absolutely whole, fresh and clean! A neat, modest, rosy-cheeked girl was our attendant—the first real, live Mormon I had ever seen "for certain." This was her sorry classification as the following brief dialogue disclosed:

Gentile Temperance Traveler.—Is this a Mormon town?

Modest Waitress.—I suppose it would be called so, though some Gentiles live here.

Traveler.—Is this Gentile or Mormon cooking? that's what I want to know.

Waitress.—Well, since you ask, I can assure you it is Mormon like myself.

Traveler.—Well, it is an unspeakable credit to the Mormons, that's all I have to say, and I'm a judge, having learned by the things I have suffered. The Indian chief asked, "Who is there to mourn for Logan?" and I promise you here is one weary wayfarer, of microscopic appetite, who will hereafter "mourn for Logan" every time the brakeman pipes his dreary warning, "Train stops for dinner at this place."

We reached Ogden toward night. Sabbath morning we went to the Mormon Tabernacle with our host and Mr. Cannon, son of the famous George Q. Cannon of Washington memory. Forgetting for a moment this significant fact, I asked the accomplished young man if he had brothers and sisters, whereupon he meekly answered, "*About twenty.*"

We entered the tabernacle, which seats three thousand persons. It was almost surrounded by horses and wagons from the country, and was tolerably well filled with a motley throng of what would be called the common people. There were no windows save very large ones just beneath the oval roof at each end of the building. The seats sloped toward the wide platform where, behind a choir of nice-looking women and a few men, sat the speakers of the hour. Nobody knows who will speak, there are no paid ministers, but every man is free to exercise his gift of exhortation and of prophecy, the younger brethren being put forward with a kindly tolerance on the part of the fathers in Zion, which our churches might wisely emulate.

It was the annual meeting of the "Mutual Improvement Societies" of this county; or as it is curiously called, "This Stake of Zion."

Reports were given by half a dozen honest-looking young men, evidently accustomed to public speaking, for their voices reached without effort the seat far back, where, in the middle tier, we sat with the rest of the women, the men forming a sort of guard on either side. There was not an instance of whispering, even the children, though evidently not under repressive training, keeping remarkably quiet. All the men spoke in the same style—as if following a certain model.

There were no figures of speech, no anecdotes, only a certain equipoise, deliberateness and dreary level of mediocrity. They talked about the meetings in which they study the history and doctrines of their church. One said: "We have purchased a book-case that cost us somewhere in the neighborhood of sixty dollars, and we hope, after awhile, to have a reading-room to put it in." Another told about the "benefits to be deriven" from this mutual improvement society. All who spoke, and there were half a dozen at least, conspicuously murdered the Queen's English. Nearly all closed with a perfunctory "This is my prayer, in the name of Jesus, Amen," pronounced with eyes wide open.

A son of Apostle Rich ("one of the twelve") preached a brief discourse. He has just returned from England, and is one of the two hundred and fifty missionaries who go out minus purse or scrip to win converts in distant lands. He had more culture than his brethren, and proceeded on this fashion, using the Bible as a sort of fulcrum. His text was, "Blessed art thou, Simon Bar-jona: for flesh and blood hath not revealed it unto thee, but my Father which is in heaven." Matt. 16:17. "My brethren and sisters, I ask the prayers of the Latter Day Saints who are here, and also of those who are not. I ask the good wishes of all. Our religion is different from all others. Christ is the head of His church, even as the husband is the head of his wife, but a wife would be of very little use to her husband, if she had no head of her own, would n't she? [Smiles and nodding of the women's heads in approbation!] Even so Christ has never left His church without a head. Some say there is no need of a farther revelation, but I declare that the first proof that any revelation is real must be that it goes right on. We believe that there is no people on this earth who really follow Christ, except those who receive the revelation of His latest prophet, Joseph Smith, who stood up at fourteen years old and went into the woods and declared that there he received a revelation. The world says: 'We don't care how much you believe in your revelation, if you will let alone the principle of plural marriage which we are bound to stamp out.'

"But it is not for this principle that our fathers and mothers were driven into the wilderness. In the early days of the church my mother had muzzles of pistols at her head to make her tell where my father was. She has seen him fired at when carrying a flag of truce. Was this because of his belief in polygamy? No, it was because he held to the Bible, its form of government, its teachings and examples *all through*. I believe the Bible prophets have had successors, and that Joseph Smith, Brigham Young and John Taylor, are true prophets of God. If the Gentiles could bring up as many proofs that our doctrine is false as a sixteen-year-old Mormon boy can that it is true, they could stamp it out quick enough. But here are we according to prophecy. Don't the Bible say, 'Let us go up to the temple of the Lord, that is in the tops of the mountains?' Well, here we are, and 'seeing is believing.' The people who drove us here had little idea that they were fulfilling prophecy! Our elders carried to the wilderness the promise and prophecy of Joseph Smith, that in baptism they should receive the testimony that ours is the true religion. They have taken the medicine and know it does what it agrees to. If you who are here this morning will take it also you will rejoice in the same result. Let us not have theory, let us have experience. I can take my Bible under my arm and go to the ends of the earth and testify for the religion of the Latter Day Saints. I know it will yet fill the earth as the waters do the great deep. It can be so deeply stamped upon the youthful mind that all hell can not prevail against it."

The young man spoke earnestly and with evident conviction.

As a temperance worker I was glad of the testimony of Anson Call, one of the leaders, who said, "Young men who attend our Mutual Improvement Society can readily be known by the greater purity of their habits. As a class they do not drink, use tobacco, nor swear."

The last speech was by H. Anderson, a pure-faced young man, who publishes the Mormon paper. Our keen-witted lawyer host (the scalpel of whose criticism does n't spare the Mormon leaders), said to me as he came forward, "There is a native product, a thorough gentleman, one whose life illustrates every Christian virtue, though he is a Mormon through and through." He said:

"When we have young men who can expound the principles of our church as has been done this morning, it is indeed a comfort and refreshment. We are willing to be judged by our fruits. Take the Mormons of Cache Valley and Ogden, and our own county as a class, and compare them with others as to truth, kindness and uprightness. We have learned to be good—for I went to Sabbath-school when a boy, and learned to honor God and my parents, and those by whom I was surrounded. We are becoming better, nobler, more upright. Why, then, do the Gentiles object to our polygamy? But then God's people are always persecuted—this is one of the surest marks of God's favor. The time is short. The Gospel is to be preached to all nations, and then shall the end come."

The services were closed with a beautiful anthem, that Anna Gordon says they sing in her own home church near Boston.

One of the men lifted his hand, whereupon all rose and he pronounced the benedictory prayer.

I walked up the street with young Mr. Cannon, who little guessed the turbulent subjectivity beside him. He was too polite to ask an opinion and I was too considerate to offer one. But never in my life have I been more profoundly disturbed. The service was such an awful travesty of "the faith once delivered to the saints." For the moment I thought I never wanted to hear those words again. It was as if Christianity had died and they were galvanizing its corpse into hideous contortions imitative of life. "Wounded in the house of his friends" has our Christ always been and far more grievously than any free-thinker can ever wound Him! For whatever may be true of Brigham Young and his hierarchy, these were honest, simple, kindly souls, and believed what they had said about Joe Smith as a prophet and polygamy as a sacred tie. But for the self-control which years and discipline have brought me since my impetuous girlhood days, I would have lifted up my voice and wept.

Partly was I grieved for them in their awful delusion; for human reason brought so low, for deadly fanaticism that blights every fairest flower of the beautiful soul, so rampant in its credulity, when in our own sublimated land and sunlit century it ought to be so balanced and serene. But as a woman, my sense of outrage and humiliation was beyond language. The highest ideals of noble souls in all ages were here trampled under foot by those who verily thought they did God service. The lofty companionship of "*Two heads in council, two beside the hearth,*" on which Home's sacred citadel is founded, how it is blotted out in the "Church of the Latter Day Saints"! Woman becomes the servitor of man, having no promise of heaven save through her relations to him, and he, whose relations to her are intended to exalt and purify every faculty of his nature, loses his loftiest and sweetest hopes of manly character. Childhood, too, is defrauded of its most precious inheritance, the tender guardianship of faithful parentage, and fond tie of brother and sisterhood. "*About* twenty brothers and sisters," said young Cannon. What can he know of the close love of our fireside groups in Christian families? A young lady of Salt Lake City said with a twinge of pain upon her face, "My father has at least forty children; I do not think he would know me should he meet me on the street."

Three Mormon ladies called upon me at Salt Lake; one was the editor of *The Woman's Exponent*, another was an accomplished lady physician, educated in Philadelphia and Boston, the third had been a wife of Brigham Young. All were bright women, leaders of their church. At first I did not know that they were Mormons, and when, in speaking of that as voting day, two of them said, "The government of the United States has disfranchised us because we are polygamists," I simply replied, "On that question I have my own opinion, but the temperance work is the only reform about which I care to express myself in Utah." They had avowed their interest in our society, and I was glad of this. Said Mrs. Young, "A wise general will not on the eve of battle, ask the religious opinions of his soldiers, but rather this question, 'Are you ready to do battle against our common foe.'" As years have passed, our society has, however, taken higher ground than this and come out squarely against such Mormons as persist in the practice of polygamy.

We went to Brigham's grave as a wonder of its kind, being to an American woman the most obnoxious on the whole circle of the planet. Three tons of granite in one block were hardly needed to hold him from aerial heights, his own specific gravity settled that matter! But he is thus hedged in to keep his bones from desecration, probably, and his only dead wife (poetic justice that, with this exception, the whole outfit should survive him!) has no stone nor flower to mark her grave. What an oversight on the part of the loving sisterhood, who, with her, shared his affections.

By the way, we saw a most inferior woman hurrying from a Mormon house, when one of us commented upon her stolid appearance and the other remarked, "Eternal fitness! only the fifth part of a woman would ever take up with the fifth part of a man." The prettiest place we saw was "Rose Bud Cottage," a Mormon, but not a polygamous home, completely embowered in trees and vines, the latter being trained over strings, so that they lay as a roof of greenery overhead, along the garden paths. Nothing more sylvan, cool and restful could greet one's eye.

Salt Lake with its Mormon and "Gentile" population has every convenience and luxury of any city; has "Gentile" society of the forcible type that dares consecrate life to setting up the American civilization among a people essentially alien in purpose and life. Altogether we never had a more curious, pleasant, pathetic trio of days than in far-famed "Deseret."

Ogden, Utah, is a far lovelier town than we are taught. Doubtless it has improved since becoming a railroad center of five different roads. Its summer climate is delightfully tempered by "the canyon breeze," which blows nearly one half of the twenty-four hours, and the near neighborhood of this same delightful valley affords to the home people such facilities for camping out as must go far to conserve their health, rejuvenate their spirits and drive dull care away. If asked in my own life, and that of our fevered Americans, the greatest mistake and deprivation, I would say: "Great Nature has n't half a chance to soothe, enrich and nurture us; we 'go touring,' but we do not let the calm old mother take us to her heart and sing the lullaby that we sigh for without knowing what we miss." Only blurred and misty revelations of God can come to souls so worn and travel-stained. When we temperance workers go to the sea or to the mountains, it is still to wring from our tired brains a few more thoughts for public utilization or a little "stored up energy" of magnetism for a "summer audience." May the valleys, trees and skies forgive us this profanation of their sanctuaries and this profane substitution of our restless glances and babbling tongues for their sacred liturgy.

SOUTHWARD HO! *

My first trip of three months (1881) spent in blessed work for the homes and loved ones of a most genial, intelligent and heartily responsive people, made me quite in love with the South. To think they should have received me as a sister beloved, yet with full knowledge that I was that novel and unpalatable combination (as a Richmond gentleman said) "a *woman*; a *Northern* woman, a *temperance* woman!" I had been told that to speak in public in the South was "not to be thought of, that all would be lost if I attempted anything beyond parlor meetings. But instead of this, their liberality of sentiment was abundantly equal to the strain; their largest churches were filled with the best, most influential and thoughtful people; their ministers were more united and earnest in the temperance cause than ours at the North; their editors, without the slightest subsidizing, were as kind and helpful as my own brother could have been. Nay, the only grief I had was in being spoken of so much better in every way than my own consciousness bore me witness that I merited.

From the first the Southern ladies took up our quiet, systematic lines of work with an intelligence and zeal that I have never seen exceeded and seldom equaled. There was an "our-folks" air in audiences, cars, and on the streets that was quite refreshing. The native population is so regnant, colored popula-

---

* In my book entitled "Woman and Temperance" I have given an extended account of my Southern trips, now numbering six, hence these brief notes.

tion is of such home-like nature, and the foreign element so insignificant in influence and numbers, that temperance has an immense advantage at the South. Beer has no such grip on the habits or the politics of the people as at the North. Almost without exception the gulf and seabound states have taken advance ground. The time is ripe; "the sound in the mulberry trees" is plainly audible. I have now made five trips thither, and always with the same warm welcome.

On a later journey I spent a week in New Orleans at the time of the famous Exposition.

Here our natural point of rendezvous was the booth of the National W. C. T. U.; *en route* thither we passed through an immense park with an avenue of live-oaks that would be a glory in itself were it in Central Park or the Bois de Boulogne. We climbed the slow, graded stairs of the great government building, and turning to the right came upon a home-like oasis in the desert of strangeness, for from a hundred costly banners, white and golden, blue and emerald, representing every state and territory of the great Republic, gleamed on every side the magic legend that we love, "For God and Home and Native Land." Here at last were the flags, and pennon fair, and brilliant *gonfalon* of the Ohio Crusade and the Continental white ribboners!

At three o'clock of that day, I was expected to preside and speak on behalf of the National W. C. T. U. The auditorium seated over eleven thousand persons, and the only blunder of the Exposition was that the music of the Corliss engine drowned all competing voices. The engine did not stop until four o'clock and we were to begin at three. Fancy a vibrant soprano unable to hear itself in all the whiz and roar of a cataract of sound where the most capacious lungs could not reach over a thousand persons even when the machinery was motionless! But the advantage of speaking there was that a stenographic reporter sat just beside me, and the audience that hears with its eye, got my ideas next morning in the *Times-Democrat* and *Picayune.* We went through the pantomime of a meeting. Bro. Mead pitched the tune "Coronation," but to the rumbling orchestra of that remorseless "Corliss," our singing was like the chirping of a sparrow when an avalanche is falling. I went through the motions of calling off the parts, and bravely that sweet-voiced gentlewoman,

Mrs. Judge Merrick, went to the front and articulated the Crusade Psalm, after which Mary T. Lathrap offered prayer. Then gallantly came to our rescue broad-shouldered Governor St. John, and talked against time until the horrible mouthing of that pitiless engine ceased. The great audience was in good humor, and deserting the chairs, stood closely around him, eager to catch every word, while he spoke in frank, soldierly fashion to the men who once had worn the gray, even as he had the blue, and predicted the good time coming. That Governor St. John is a man who can "tire out" almost any other on the platform is well known, but as a *tour de force* I have never seen equalled the speech of this afternoon when, as he declared should be the case, he "wore out" the Corliss engine. At four o'clock Mrs. Lathrap and I made brief addresses, and Mrs. Wells read the song salutation dedicated to Louisiana W. C. T. U. by Indiana's white ribbon poet, Mrs. Leavitt, of Vernon. Wearier women have slept the sleep of the just, perhaps, but more willing dreamers never were, than the twain—Matilda B. Carse and I—who retired from view at seven P. M. that night.

As a temperance worker, I was devoted to my "stint," as I called it, which consisted of presenting the white-ribbon cause, not only in every capital, but in every other town and city in our country that by the census of 1870 had 10,000 inhabitants. This was completed in 1883.

"EN ROUTE" IN MONTANA.

VI.

A Temperance Advocate and Organizer.

HOME PROTECTION PETITION. 200,000 NAMES.

"THE WOMAN'S CHRISTIAN TEMPERANCE UNION IS ORGANIZED MOTHER-LOVE."

—*Hannah Whitall Smith.*

CHAPTER I.

ON THE THRESHOLD.

From my earliest recollection there hung on the dining-room wall at our house, a pretty steel engraving. It was my father's certificate of membership in the Washingtonian Society, and was dated about 1835. He had never been a drinking man, was a reputable young husband, father, business man and church member, but when the movement reached Churchville, near Rochester, N. Y., he joined it. The little picture represented a bright, happy temperance home with a sweet woman at the center, and over against it a dismal, squalid house with a drunken man staggering in, bottle in hand. Unconsciously and ineffaceably I learned from that one object-lesson what the precepts and practice of my parents steadily enforced, that we were to let strong drink alone.

In 1855 I cut from my favorite *Youth's Cabinet*, the chief juvenile paper of that day, the following pledge, and pasting it in our family Bible, insisted on its being signed by every member of the family—parents, brother, sister and self.

> "A pledge we make no wine to take,
> Nor brandy red that turns the head,
> Nor fiery rum that ruins home,
> Nor brewers' beer, for that we fear,
> And cider, too, will never do.
> To quench our thirst, we'll always bring
> Cold water from the well or spring;
> So here we pledge perpetual hate
> To all that can intoxicate."

It is still there, thus signed, and represents the first bit of temperance work I ever did. Its object was simply to enshrine in the most sacred place our home afforded a pledge that I considered uniquely sacred. Nobody asked me to sign it, nor was there a demand because of exterior temptation, for we were living in much isolation on a farm three miles from Janesville, Wis., where my childhood was invested—not "spent."

Coming to Evanston, Ill., in 1858, we found a prohibition village, the charter of the University forbidding the sale of any intoxicating liquor as a beverage.

Temperance was a matter of course in this "Methodist heaven" where we have lived from that day to this, from the time it had but a few hundred, until now when it claims seven thousand inhabitants.

About 1863-'65 a "Temperance Alliance" was organized here by L. L. Greenleaf, then our leading citizen, the Chicago representative of the Fairbanks' firm, who have made St. Johnsbury, Vt., a model temperance town. Before that Alliance I read one temperance essay when I was a quiet school teacher amid these shady groves, and one evening at the "Alliance sociable" I offered the pledge for the first time and was rebuffed by a now distinguished literary man, then a pastor and editor in our village. This was my first attempt and his brusque and almost angry negative hurt me to the heart. We are excellent friends all the same, and I do not believe he dreams how much he pained me, so little do we know what touches us, and what we touch, as we wend our way along life's crowded street.

In all my teaching, in Sunday-school, public school and seminary, I never mentioned total abstinence until the winter of the Crusade, taking it always as a matter of course that my pupils did n't drink, nor did they as a rule.

I never in my life saw wine offered in my own country but once, when Mrs. Will Knox, of Pittsburgh, a former Sunday-school scholar of my sister Mary, brought cake and wine to a young lady of high family in our church, and to me, when we went to call on her after her wedding. "Not to be singular" we touched it to our lips—but that was twenty-five years ago, before the great examples burnt into the Nation's memory and conscience by Lucy Webb Hayes, Rose Cleveland and Frances Folsom Cleveland.

That was truly a prophetic innovation at the White House when our gracious Mrs. Hayes replaced the dinner with its wine-glasses by the stately and elegant reception. Perhaps while men rule the state in their government "of the minority, by the minority, for the minority," its highest expression will still be the dinner-table with its clinking glasses and plenty of tobacco-smoke afterward, but when men and women both come into the kingdom for the glad new times that hasten to be here, the gustatory nerve will be dethroned once and for evermore. For there are so many more worthy and delightful ways of investing (not "spending") one's time; there are so many better things to do. The blossoming of women into deeds of philanthropy gives us a hint of the truer forms of society that are to come. Emerson said, "We descend to meet," because he claims that we are on a higher plane when alone with God and nature. But this need not be so. Doubtless in the outworn and stereotyped forms of society where material pleasures still hold sway, we do "descend to meet," but when a philanthropic purpose determines our companionships, and leads to our convenings, then we climb together into purer and more vital air. The "coming women," nay, the women who have come, have learned the loveliest meanings ot the word "society." Indeed, some of us like to call it "comradeship," instead, this interchange of highest thought and tenderest aspiration, in which the sense of selfhood is diminished and the sense of otherhood increased. We make no "formal calls," but the informal ones are a hundred-fold more pleasant. If a new woman's face appear in church we wonder if she won't "come with us" in the W. H. M. S., the W. F. M. S., the W. C. T. U., or some other dear "ring-around-a-rosy" circle, formed "for others' sake." If new children sit beside her in the church pew, we plan to win them for our Band of Hope or other philanthropic guild where they will learn to find "society" in nobler forms than this poor old world has ever known before. The emptiness of conventional forms of speech and action is never so patent as when contrasted with the "fullness of life" that crowns those hearts banded together to bring the day when all men's weal shall be each man's care. Wordsworth wrote wearily of

"The greetings where no kindness is."

From 1868 to 1870 I studied and traveled abroad, not tasting wine until in Denmark, after three months' absence, I was taken suddenly and violently ill with something resembling cholera, and the kind-faced physician in Copenhagen bending above my weakness said in broken French: "Mademoiselle, you must put wine in the water you drink or you will never live to see your home." This prescription I then faithfully followed for two years with a gradual tendency so to amend as to make it read, "You may put water in your wine," and a leaning toward the "pure article," especially when some rich friend sent for a costly bottle of "Rudesheimer," or treated me to such a luxury as "Grand Chartreuse." At a London dinner where I was the guest of English friends, and seven wine-glasses stood around my plate, I did not protest or abstain—so easily does poor human nature fall away, especially when backed up by a medical prescription. But beyond a flushing of the cheek, an unwonted readiness at repartee and an anticipation of the dinner hour, unknown to me before or since, I came under no thralldom, and returning to this blessed "land of the wineless dinner table," my natural environments were such that I do not recall the use of intoxicants by me, "as a beverage," from that day to this.

Thus much do I owe to a Methodist training and the social usages of my grand old mother church. Five years in Oberlin, Ohio, in my childhood, also did much to ground me in the faith of total abstinence and the general laws of hygiene.

In 1873 came that wonderful Christmas gift to the world—the woman's temperance crusade, beginning in Hillsboro, Ohio, December 23, and led by that loyal Methodist woman, Mrs. Judge Thompson, daughter of Gov. Trimble and sister of Dr. Trimble, the oldest member of the last M. E. General Conference. All through that famous battle winter of Home *versus* Saloon, I read every word that I could get about the movement, and my brother, Oliver A. Willard, then editor of the *Chicago Evening Mail*, gave favorable and full reports, saying privately to me, "I shall speak just as well of the women as I dare to"—a most characteristic editorial remark, I have since thought, though more frequently acted out than uttered! Meanwhile it occurred to me, strange to say, for the *first time*, that I ought to work for the good cause *just where I was*—that everybody ought. Thus I first received "the arrest of thought" concerning which in a thousand different towns I have since then tried to speak, and I believe that in this simple change of personal attitude from passive to aggressive lies the only force that can free this land from the drink habit and the liquor traffic. It would be like dynamite under the saloon if, *just where he is*, the minister would begin active work against it; if, just where he is, the teacher would instruct his pupils; if, just where he is, the voter would dedicate his ballot to this movement, and so on through the shining ranks of the great powers that make for righteousness from father and mother to Kindergarten toddler, if each were this day doing what each could, *just where he is*.

I was teaching rhetoric and composition to several hundred students of the Northwestern University and my eyes were opened to perceive that in their essays they would be as well pleased and would gain more good if such themes were assigned as "John B. Gough" and "Neal Dow" rather than "Alexander the Great" and "Plato the Philosopher," and that in their debates they would be at least as much enlisted by the question "Is Prohibition a Success?" as by the question, "Was Napoleon a blessing or a curse?" So I quietly sandwiched in these practical themes to the great edification of my pupils and with a notable increase in their enthusiasm and punctuality. Never in my fifteen years as a teacher did I have exercises so interesting as in the Crusade winter—1874.

Meanwhile in Chicago the women of the Churches were mightily aroused. They gathered up in ten days fourteen thousand signatures to a petition asking that the Sunday closing ordinance might be no longer a dead letter, and while some remained in old Clark Street Church to pray, a procession of them led by Mrs. Rev. Moses Smith, moved across the street to the Court House and going in before the Common Council (the first and last time that women have ever ventured into that uncanny presence), they offered their petition and made their plea. Their petition was promptly tabled and the ordinance for whose enforcement they had pleaded, was abrogated then and there at the dictate of the liquor power while a frightful mob collected threatening them violence; the police disappeared and only by the prompt action of such men as Rev. Dr. Arthur Edwards in finding a side exit for them, was Chicago saved the indelible disgrace of seeing some of its chief Christian women mobbed on the streets by the minions of saloon, gambling den and haunt of infamy. All these things we read at Evanston next morning and "while we were musing the fire burned."

Events moved rapidly. Meetings were held in Chicago to protest against the great indignity and to organize for further work. There were fewer writers and speakers among women then than now. Some missionary and educational addresses of mine made within the two years past caused certain Methodist friends to name me as a possible speaker; and so to my quiet home eleven miles up the lake-shore came Mrs. Charles H. Case, a leading Congregational lady of the city, asking me to go and try.

It is my nature to give myself utterly to whatever work I have in hand, hence nothing less than my new-born enthusiasm for the Crusade and its heroines would have extorted from me a promise to enter on this untried field, but I agreed to attend a noon meeting in Clark Street Church a few days later and when the time came went from the recitation room to the rostrum, finding the place so packed with people that Mrs. Dr. Jutkins who was waiting for me at the door had much ado to get a passage made for us. Ministers were on the platform in greater numbers than I had ever seen before or have seen since in that or any other city. They spoke, they sang, they prayed with the fervor of a Methodist camp. Philip Bliss was at the organ and sang one of his sweetest songs. For myself, I was frightened by the crowd and overwhelmed by a sense of my own emptiness and inadequacy. What I said I do not know except that I was with the women heart, hand and soul, in this wonderful new "Everybody's War."

Soon after, I spoke in Robert Collyer's Church with Mrs. Mary H. B. Hitt, now president of the Northwestern Branch of the Woman's Foreign Missionary Society. Here, for the first and last time, I read my speech. I believe it was Rev. Dr. L. T. Chamberlain, who called it a "school-girl essay"—and served it right. Robert Collyer took up the collection himself, I remember, rattling the box and cracking jokes along the aisle as he moved among his aristocratic "Northsiders." I went home blue enough and registered a vow as yet well nigh unbroken, that I would never again appear before a popular audience manuscript in hand.

My next attempt was in Union Park Congregational Church a few weeks later. Here I had my "heads" on paper, but from that time forward I "swung clear" of the manuscript crutch and the "outline" walking-stick. In June I resigned my position as Dean in the Woman's College and Professor of Æsthetics in the Northwestern University. It has been often said in my praise that I did this for the explicit purpose of enlisting in the temperance army, but it is my painful duty in this plain, unvarnished tale to admit that the reasons upon which I based that act, so revolutionary of all my most cherished plans and purposes, related wholly to the local situation in the University itself. However, having resigned, my strongest impulses were toward the Crusade movement as is sufficiently proved by the fact that, going East immediately, I sought the leaders of the newly formed societies of temperance women, Dr. and Mrs. W. H. Boole, Mrs. Helen E. Brown, Mrs. Rebecca Collins, Mrs. M. F. Hascall and others of New York, Mrs. Mary C. Johnson, Mrs. Mary E. Hartt, H. W. Adams, and others of Brooklyn, and these were the first persons who befriended and advised me in the unknown field of "Gospel temperance." With them I went to Jerry Mc Auley's Mission, and to "Kit Burns's Rat-Pit," and saw the great unwashed, unkempt, ungospeled and sin-scarred multitude for the first time in my life as they gathered in a dingy down-town square to hear Dr. Boole preach on Sabbath afternoon.

With several of these new friends I went to Old Orchard Beach, Me., where Francis Murphy, a drinking man and saloon-keeper recently reformed, had called the first "Gospel Temperance Camp Meeting" known to our annals. Here I met Neal Dow and heard the story of Prohibitory Law. Here I saw that strong, sweet woman, Mrs. L. M. N. Stevens, our white ribbon leader in Maine, almost from then till now; and here in a Portland hotel, where I stayed with Mary Hartt, of Brooklyn, and wondered "where the money was to come from" as I had none, and had mother's expenses and my own to meet, I opened the Bible lying on the hotel bureau and lighted on this memorable verse: Psalm 37:3, "*Trust in the Lord, and do good; so shalt thou dwell in the land, and verily thou shalt be fed.*"

That was a turning-point in life with me. Great spiritual illumination, unequaled in all my history before, had been vouchsafed me in the sorrowful last days at Evanston, but here came clinching faith for what was to me a most difficult emergency.

Going to Boston I now sought Dr. Dio Lewis, for, naturally enough, I wished to see and counsel with the man whose words had been the match that fired the powder mine. He was a considerate and kind old gentleman who could only tell me o'er and o'er that "if the women would go to the saloons they could soon close them up forever." But we had already passed beyond that stage,so I went on to broader counsels. Convinced that I must make my own experience and determine my own destiny, I now bent all my forces to find what Archimedes wanted, "where to stand" within the charmed circle of the temperance reform. Chicago must be my field, for home was there and the sacred past with its graves of the living and dead. But nobody had asked me to work there and I was specially in mood to wait and watch for providential intimations. Meanwhile many and varied offers came from the educational field, tempting in respect of their wide outlook and large promise of financial relief. In this dilemma I consulted my friends as to their sense of my duty, every one of them, including my dear mother and my revered counselor, Bishop Simpson, uniting in the decision that he thus expressed: "If you were not dependent on your own exertions for the supply of current needs, I would say, be a philanthropist, but of all work, the temperance work pays least and you cannot afford to take it up. I therefore counsel you to remain in your chosen and successful field of the higher education."

No one stood by me in the preference I freely expressed to join the Crusade women except Mrs. Mary A. Livermore, who sent me a letter full of enthusiasm for the new line of work and predicted success for me therein. It is said that Napoleon was wont to consult his marshals and then do as he pleased, but I have found this method equally characteristic of ordinary mortals, and certainly it was the one I followed in the greatest decision of my life. While visiting in Cambridge, Mass., at the home of Mr. and Mrs. John S. Paine, with whom I had traveled in Egypt and Palestine, I received two letters on the same day. The first was from Rev. Dr. Van Norman, of New York, inviting me to become "Lady Principal" of his elegant school for young women, adjoining Central Park, where I was to have just what and just as few classes as I chose, and a salary of twenty-four hundred dollars per year. The other was from Mrs. Louise S. Rounds of Centenary M. E. Church, Chicago, one of the women who had gone to the City Council on that memorable night of March, 1874, and she wrote in substance as follows:

"I was sitting at my sewing work to-day, pondering the future of our young temperance association. Mrs. O. B. Wilson, our president, does all she can and has shown a really heroic spirit, coming to Lower Farwell Hall for a prayer-meeting every day in the week, though she lives a long distance from there and is old and feeble, and the heat has been intense. She can not go on much longer and it has come to me, as I believe from the Lord, that you ought to be our President. We are a little band without money or experience, but with strong faith. I went right out to see some of our leading women and they all say that if you will agree to come, there will be no trouble about your election. Please let me hear at once."

I can not express the delight with which I greeted this announcement. Here was my "open door" all unknown and unsought—a place prepared for me in one true temperance woman's heart and a chance to work for the cause that had in so short a time become so dear to me. I at once declined the New York offer and very soon after started for the West.

The first saloon I ever entered was Sheffner's, on Market street, Pittsburgh, on my way home. In fact, that was the only glimpse I ever personally had of the Crusade. It had lingered in this dun-colored city well nigh a year and when I visited my old friends at the Pittsburgh Female College I spoke with enthusiasm of the Crusade, and of the women who were, as I judged from a morning paper, still engaged in it here. They looked upon me with astonishment when I proposed to seek out those women and go with them to the saloons, for in the two years that I had taught in Pittsburgh these friends associated me with the recitation room, the Shakspeare Club, the lecture course, the opera, indeed, all the haunts open to me that a literary-minded woman would care to enter. However, they were too polite to desire to disappoint me, and so they had me piloted by some of the factotums of the place to the headquarters of the Crusade, where I was warmly welcomed, and soon found myself walking down street arm in arm with a young teacher from the public school, who said she had a habit of coming in to add one to the procession when her day's duties were over. We paused in front of the saloon that I have mentioned. The ladies ranged themselves along the curbstone, for they had been forbidden in anywise to incommode the passers-by, being dealt with much more strictly than a drunken man or a heap of dry-goods boxes would be. At a signal from our gray-haired leader, a sweet-voiced woman began to sing, "Jesus the water of life will give," all our voices soon blending in that sweet song. I think it was the most novel spectacle that I recall. There stood women of undoubted religious devotion and the highest character, most of them crowned with the glory of gray hairs. Along the stony pavement of that stoniest of cities rumbled the heavy wagons, many of them carriers of beer; between us and the saloon in front of which we were drawn up in line, passed the motley throng, almost every man lifting his hat and even the little newsboys doing the same. It was American manhood's tribute to Christianity and to womanhood, and it was significant and full of pathos. The leader had already asked the saloon-keeper if we might enter, and he had declined, else the prayer-meeting would have occurred inside his door. A sorrowful old lady whose only son had gone to ruin through that very death-trap, knelt on the cold, moist pavement and offered a broken-hearted prayer, while all our heads were bowed. At a signal we moved on and the next saloon-keeper permitted us to enter. I had no more idea of the inward appearance of a saloon than if there had been no such place on earth. I knew nothing of its high, heavily-corniced bar, its barrels with the ends all pointed towards the looker-on, each barrel being furnished with a faucet; its shelves glittering with decanters and cut glass, its floors thickly strewn with saw-dust, and here and there a round table with chairs — nor of its abundant fumes, sickening to healthful nostrils. The tall, stately lady who led us, placed her Bible on the bar and read a psalm, whether hortatory or imprecatory, I do not remember, but the spirit of these crusaders was so gentle, I think it must have been the former. Then we sang "Rock of Ages" as I thought I had never heard it sung before, with a tender confidence to the height of which one does not rise in the easy-going, regulation prayer-meeting, and then one of the older women whispered to me softly that the leader wished to know if I would pray. It was strange, perhaps, but I felt not the least reluctance, and kneeling on that saw-dust floor, with a group of earnest hearts around me, and behind them, filling every corner and extending out into the street, a crowd of unwashed, unkempt, hard-looking drinking men, I was conscious that perhaps never in my life, save beside my sister Mary's dying bed, had I prayed as truly as I did then. This was my Crusade baptism. The next day I went on to the West and within a week had been made president of the Chicago W. C. T. U.

CHAPTER II.

THE OPENING WAY.

No words can adequately characterize the change wrought in my life by the decision I have chronicled. Instead of peace I was to participate in war; instead of the sweetness of home, never more dearly loved than I had loved it, I was to become a wanderer on the face of the earth; instead of libraries I was to frequent public halls and railway cars; instead of scholarly and cultured men I was to see the dregs of saloon and gambling house and haunt of shame. But women who were among the fittest gospel survivals were to be my comrades; little children were to be gathered from near and from far in the Loyal Temperance Legion, and whoever keeps such company should sing a psalm of joy, solemn as it is sweet. Hence I have felt that great promotion came to me when I was counted worthy to be a worker in the organized Crusade for "God and Home and Native Land." Temporary differences may seem to separate some of us for awhile, but I believe with all my heart, that farther on we shall be found walking once more side by side. In this spirit let me try to tell a little of our story.

One day in September, 1874, a few ladies assembled in one of the Young Men's Christian Association prayer rooms adjoining Farwell Hall, and elected me their president. One of them came to me at the close of the meeting and said, "We have no money, but we will try to get some if you will tell us your expectations as to salary." "Ah," thought I, "here is my coveted opportunity for the exercise of faith," and I quietly replied, "Oh, that will be all right!" and the dear innocent went her way thinking that some rich friend had supplied the necessary help. It was known that my generous comrade, Miss Kate A. Jackson, had taken me abroad for a stay of over two years, so the ladies naturally concluded that she was once more the good fairy behind the scenes. But this was not true. She had not approved my entrance upon temperance work. She was a thousand miles away and knew nothing of my needs.

Having always been my faithful friend I knew she would help me in this crisis, but I chose not to tell her, for I had a theory and now was the time to put it to the test. To my mind there was a missing link in the faith of George Müller, Dorothea Trubel and other saintly men and women who "spoke and let their wants be known" by means of annual announcements, reports, etc., so I said to myself, "I am just simply going to pray, to work and to trust God." So, with no financial backing whatever, I set about my work, opened the first "Headquarters" known to Woman's Christian Temperance Union annals—the Young Men's Christian Association giving me a room rent free; organized committees for the few lines of work then thought of by us; started a daily three o'clock prayer-meeting at which signing the pledge and seeking the Lord behind the pledge were constant factors; sent articles and paragraphs to the local press, having called upon every editor in the city and asked his help or at least his tolerance; addressed Sunday-schools, ministers and mass-meetings and once in awhile made a dash into some town or village, where I spoke, receiving a collection which represented financially "my little all." I remember that the first of these collections was at Princeton in October of 1874 and amounted to seven dollars, for I had small reputation and audiences in proportion. Meanwhile my mother, who owned her little home free from incumbrance, held the fort at "Rest Cottage," Evanston, dismissed her "help" and lived in strict seclusion and economy. I was entertained by different ladies in the city or was boarded at a nominal figure by my kind friend Mrs. William Wheeler, one of the truest of my coadjutors. Many a time I went without my noonday lunch down town because I had no money with which to buy, and many a mile did I walk because I had not the prerequisite nickel for street-car riding. But I would not mention money or allow it named to me. My witty brother Oliver, then editor of the *Chicago Mail*, who with all his cares, was helping mother from his slender purse, and who had learned my secret from her, said, "Frank, your faith-method is simply a challenge to the Almighty. You've put a chip on your shoulder and dared Omnipotence to knock it off." But for several months I went on in this way and my life never had a happier season. For the first time I knew the gnawings of hunger whereat I used to smile and say to myself, as I elbowed my way among the wretched people to whom I was sent, "I'm a better friend than you dream; I know more about you than you think, for, bless God, I'm hungry too!"

When in Italy I had been greatly moved by the study of St. Francis d' Assisi, whose city I had visited for this purpose, a nobleman who gave his life to the poor and who was so beloved of Christ that legends say he was permitted to receive the stigmata.

Thinking of him, my small privations seemed so ridiculously trivial that I was eager to suffer something really worthy of a disciple for humanity's sweet sake. I had some pretty rings, given me in other days by friends and pupils, these I put off and never have resumed them, also my watch-chain, for I would have no striking contrast between these poor people and myself. To share my last dime with some famished looking man or woman was a pure delight. Indeed, my whole life has not known a more lovely period. I communed with God; I dwelt in the spirit; this world had nothing to give me, nothing to take away. My friend Kate came back from the East and I told her all about it. "Why, you are poor as poverty," she said with pitying amazement. "True," I replied, "I have n't a cent in the world, but all the same I own Chicago," and it was a literal fact; the sense of universal ownership was never so strong upon my spirit before or since that blessed time. "I'm the Child of a King" was the inmost song of my soul.

I find this record in a little pocket note-book of the time:

Came back to the city from my evening temperance meeting at ——; almost froze getting from Lake Shore depot to my office—did freeze indeed. No women in the streets, everything stark and dead. Found lovely Mrs. F. J. Barnes and faithful sister Wirt trying to help three poor fellows who had come in, learning their stories and trying to do them good. We have more "cases," histories, crises, calamitous distress revealed to us than could be told in an octavo or helped out by a millionaire. Verily, we are in the "real work." How good it is to watch the men grow clean and shaved and brightened; the outward sign of an inward grace. This work is by far the most blessed of my life. My "Gospel talks" are in demand to an extent that surprises me. Dr. —— wishes me to conduct meetings right along in his church, Dr. —— invites me to —— church and so does ——. If I were fit for it how this work would enthrall my heart, as no other ever could—as I used secretly to wish, with hopeless pain, it might, but thought it never must since I "was but a woman." Engagements crowd upon me for Temperance, but

(FROM A PHOTOGRAPH OF A BAS RELIEF.)

(FROM A PHOTOGRAPH OF A BAS RELIEF.)

still more for "Evangelical" talks, and persuasions come to me from friends to abandon the first and devote myself to church work. But I can not perceive, I can not feel as yet—and hope I never may—that a cause so forlorn as that of temperance should be deserted by a single adherent. I'm strong in the faith and believe that I am in the path of duty.

Our Daily Gospel Meeting in airless, sunless Lower Farwell Hall grows constantly in interest; the place is two thirds full of men who never go to church and who are deep in sin. Christian men come in to help us and a few ladies, perhaps one to every eight or ten men. This last is the saddening feature, but only temporary I feel sure. Daily, many ask for prayers and ever so many sign the pledge. My strongest intellectual thirst is to know more of the WORD. Who is sufficient for these things—these hours when destiny hangs trembling in the uncertain balance of the human will?

Did n't go to the Conversazione on Oriental and Greek Thought, though General B—— urged me. I can not serve my intellect at the expense of my Master, and our church prayer-meeting comes at the same hour. Went out to Evanston to see my dear seventy-year-old mother, finding her blithe as a lass and active as a cricket.

I called on O. C. Gibbs of the City Relief Committee and asked him to post notice of our prayer-meetings and talked to him of my grief over the homeless, dinnerless condition of men whom I met daily and proposed a Workhouse where they could render an equivalent for food and lodging. He looked at me in his sad, thoughtful way and said: "Ten years ago I believed that I could solve the problem of the unemployed, that it was a sin and shame for them to suffer. I investigated and studied the whole question carefully. It will seem strange to you, but now I have no remedy to offer. Their own volitions have brought them where they are, others surrounded just as they were, have pushed on to good conditions; these have not, what can we do?"

Found the manager of the Museum waiting to see me and to invite our Union to free seats at the "new and highly moral drama, 'Three Days in a Man Trap,' a strictly temperance play!" He seemed to think it so desirable for us, so "just the thing," and was apparently so much in earnest that I had much ado to make my voice sound friendly, out of a world of thoughts so different from his own. But I did the best I could, thanked him for his courtesy and said we had opinions widely at variance, that my own experience was that my life was far less helpful when I used to go to places of the sort, that I needed all my time for higher things and I believed our ladies felt the same.

—— is converted and, sure and swift "fruit of the Spirit," has made up with his wife to whom he had not spoken in a fortnight, and has asked me to forgive him for his inconsiderate language. O "heart of flesh!" how gentle and easy to be entreated; but the "heart of stone," how hard and cold and self-absorbed! What is the matter with me is that I'd like to go out by myself, looking only to God, and preach the unsearchable riches of Christ!

When Bro. —— wrote me that offer to be editor of a New York temperance paper, it did n't stir my soul a bit, but this little Gospel meeting, where wicked men have wept and prayed and said they would see Jesus—it thrills me through and through.

Went to hear Nathan Sheppard on George Eliot. Don't believe I'll ever attend another literary lecture. It was keen, brilliant, flinty as flint, cold as an icicle. Poor, grand George Eliot, who sees no light beyond the sepulcher, who thinks we are snuffed out like candles! Dear me, it is n't even æsthetic, that! As a cute critic said, purely from an artistic point of view our poor old Religion has some notions that ought to commend it to the attention of cultivated personages.

Dr. —— discourages me what she can in my work and says "a cheaper woman would do it just as well." Ah my dear friend, is it then "cheap" work to be God's instrument in delivering men from voluntary insanity?—to bring them back to themselves? to help *enthrone the conscience* in a human breast? A letter read just after Dr. ——'s, from a mother in Fishkill, N. Y., thanking us for helping her wayward son, was antidote enough, if I had needed one.

Heard Rev. George Coan, newly returned from Persia. If I were younger I believe I'd be a missionary.

Went home to mother, read to-day's mail aloud to her, in which she was greatly interested. Found her well up in the events of the day—President's message to Congress on Louisiana, Collyer's sermon on Gerrit Smith, etc. Told her of Dr. ——'s invitation to me to "preach" for him and how glad I was the way was opening so for me to speak of the glad tidings, and she, too, rejoiced.

I wonder what the "Women's Congress" will think about my plan of Literary Clubs for women.

In P. M. studied my Bible and thought about "my sermon." In evening went to Rail Road Chapel and heard Captain Black, a Christian lawyer, preach a simple Gospel sermon. We are to have temperance meetings here if the South Side ladies will rally. It is an intemperate neighborhood, the red light "danger signal" gleams from scores of saloons.

January 18, 1875.—A hurried P. M.—large prayer-meeting, twenty drinking men present, only four ladies! Dear Mrs. Barnes, of New York, my little Quakeress, is my main-stay. I don't know what I could do without her. I should often be here alone with the office full of men. This would n't worry me, to be sure, save that it is better to have a *little* help. I've given up expecting the ladies of Chicago to come to the rescue at present. They will sometime—in the Lord's own good time. For me, my hands are overrunning full of Christian work, and that's enough. Large meeting—one poor fellow, gray-headed, washed-out looking, hands shaking with effects of drink, came in for the first time. He was once a church-member and promising business man of the city, but is now at ebb-tide.

January 19.—Well, last night I preached—the word grates somewhat, but has no business to—at Ada Street M. E. Church (Dr. McKeown's). Text, "Lord, what wilt thou have me to do?" Had a few "heads" on a slip of paper. Took my little Bible that father gave me, and just talked. I greatly regretted to go to my first most sacred service from the lightness and repartee of the pleasant parlor at Mrs. N——'s and felt ill-attuned at first. But perhaps that was forgiven; anyhow I was in earnest and greatly enjoyed the evening, and my large audience was thoughtful. O God! can I live near enough to Thee to *dare* tell the good news to Humanity?

January 25.—Have spoken again at Ada Street, with more efficiency and spirit. Subject: "Thou requirest not sacrifice, else would I give it." My friend, Kate Jackson, says I'm better as a gospel talker than anything else. O I wish I might be one; that I enough communed with God!

After several months invested in this fashion, I went to speak one night at Freeport, a few hours' ride from the city; became ill from overwork, addressed my audience while in a burning fever, came home to mother, and went to bed with inflammatory rheumatism. I asked her to send for our family physician, then Dr. Jewell, of sainted memory, the man who had prayed at my bedside six months before, when I was sick with heartache at leaving my dear college. "No," said that Spartan matron, "You are going by faith—you do not need a doctor."

The truth was she always believed that she best knew what her children needed, whether they were well or ill. "Now I want you to listen to your mother," she quietly continued, "I believe in faith as much as you do, but you have, with pure intention, yet ignorantly, flown in the face of Providence. Those good women spoke to you about a maintenance on the very day they chose you president. That was your Heavenly Father's kind provision, and you turned away from it and dictated to Him the method of His care. The laborer is worthy of his hire; they that preach the gospel shall live by the gospel; this is the law and the prophets from St. Paul down to you. God is n't going to start loaves of bread flying down chimney nor set the fire going in my stove without fuel. I shall soon see the bottom of my flour barrel and coal bin. You are out at the elbows, down at the heel, and down sick, too. Now write to those temperance ladies a plain statement of facts, and tell them that you have made the discovery that God works by means and they may help you if they like."

My mother's words were a needed revelation. I wrote a

letter to my dear women. Later on I learned that they cried over it in Executive Committee. That night a tender note came from them with a $100 check inclosed, and my "faith test" was met upon the Heavenly Father's basis, not upon the one I had prescribed for Him. But I enjoyed that episode and shall be the better and the richer for it evermore.

One of my best and brightest coadjutors from the first has been Mrs. Matilda B. Carse, of Chicago, the chief financial woman of our white ribbon host. Her first money-raising venture consisted in getting a hundred men to give ten dollars apiece to keep me going when my blissful episode of impecuniosity was over. Rev. Dr. J. O. Peck, "of ours," was the first name she secured. From that day to this she has been on the war-path, financially, raising hundreds of thousands for the Foundlings' Home, the Woman's Christian Temperance Union with its huge cheap Lodging House for men, its "Anchorage Mission" for women, its Gospel Meeting, Kindergarten, Temperance Restaurant and other philanthropic enterprises, until now she has set herself with perfect equanimity to collect eight hundred thousand dollars for the building of a Woman's Temperance Temple in Chicago, to serve as the Headquarters for our National Woman's Christian Temperance Union, also for the great "Woman's Temperance Publication Association" founded by her, and which printed in 1888 over sixty million pages of temperance literature. From this Temple she expects to derive, beyond all expenses, over a hundred thousand dollars a year rental, with which our work will be still more widely carried on.

But to return. A few weeks after my election as President of the Chicago Woman's Christian Temperance Union (October 8, 1874), the "Woman's Congress" met in Farwell Hall, Chicago, Mrs. Livermore presiding. It was her wish to have me speak upon the temperance question. For years I had been vice-president of the organization for Illinois and had prepared a paper read at the New York "Congress" on the "Higher Education of Women." But in my new character I was less welcome and only by taking a brave stand did Mrs. Livermore succeed in having me recognized. I wish here to record my sincere appreciation of her loyalty to the great cause and to one of its "new beginners" at a time when her championship before the most intellectual body of women then existing, was particularly valuable to both.

That same autumn of 1874 the Woman's Christian Temperance Union of Chicago sent me as a delegate to the Illinois Woman's Christian Temperance Union Convention, called by Mrs. J. F. Willing, at Bloomington, where she was then professor in the college. As a hundred of us marched, two by two, along the street, under cover of the stars, I felt that we were marching to victory. My life had hardly known a more exalted moment. I seemed to see the end from the beginning ; and when one has done that, nothing has power to discourage or to daunt. Of this meeting I was made secretary (my first appearance in the state arena), Mrs. Willing being elected president. A few weeks later, (November 18, 19, 20, 1874), the great National Woman's Temperance Convention, which had been called by a committee formed at Chautauqua, of which Mrs. Willing, Mrs. Emily Huntington Miller and Mrs. Mattie McClellan Brown were leaders, convened in Cleveland, Ohio. Its object was to preserve the fruits of Crusade victory—indeed, it may be justly called the sober second thought of that unparalleled uprising. Women from eighteen states were gathered.

> "Hear the call, O gird your armor on ;
> Grasp the Spirit's mighty sword,"

was their stirring battle-cry. Something divine was in the air—a breath of the new dispensation. Introductions were at a discount—we shook hands all round and have been comrades ever since. Here I first met Mrs. Annie Wittenmeyer, Mrs. Mary T. Lathrap, Mrs. J. Ellen Foster, Mrs. Governor Wallace, Mother Stewart and Mrs. Judge Thompson, leader of the first praying band and the "mother of us all."

Very few could make a speech at that early period—we gave speechlets instead, off-hand talks of from five to fifteen minutes. The daily prayer-meetings were times of refreshing from the presence of the Lord. There was no waiting, everything was fresh, tender and spontaneous. Such singing I never heard ; the Bible exposition was bread to the soul. Everybody said it "was n't a bit like men's conventions." "And it's all the better for that," was the universal verdict.

As I sat quiet, but observant, in my delegation, Mary T. Lathrap sent me a note to this purport: "We Michigan women are going to nominate you for corresponding secretary of this national society."

Now it is my nature to accept every offer that means a wider outlook from a higher point of observation, and my heart sprang up to meet this kindly call. But the heavenly forces had me pretty well in hand just then. I had already been nominated for President by Mrs. M. B. Reese, of Ohio, and had promptly declined, with the statement that I was but a raw recruit, and preferred to serve in the ranks; when they had proved me, I would be at command for anything they wished; but, though I met this overture from my new-found friend, Mrs. Lathrap, with a similar refusal, her eloquence prevailed, and I became first mate on our newly launched life-boat of reform, under the captaincy of Sister Wittenmeyer.

The only resolution written by me, so far as I can now recall, was this:

"*Resolved*, That, recognizing that our cause is, and will be, combated by mighty, determined and relentless forces, we will, trusting in Him who is the Prince of Peace, meet argument with argument, misjudgment with patience, denunciation with kindness, and all our difficulties and dangers with prayer."

There was some debate about inserting the word "Christian" in the name of our society, the point being made that to leave it out would broaden and thus benefit the platform, but then, as always since, the Convention said by its deeds, "We are not here to seek a large following, but to do what we think right."

Returning to Chicago with the duties of national secretary upon me, I found my generous comrades saying, "Go right ahead as our local president, and we will pay you a hundred dollars a month and give you time to work for the National in the bargain." So I struggled on, blessed with good health, blithe heart and warm co-operation. The summer of 1875 I spent with Mrs. Wittenmeyer at Ocean Grove, where our pens flew from early morn till dewy eve in the interest of the National Woman's Christian Temperance Union. Here she wrote her valuable "History of the Woman's Crusade." By Dr. Vincent's invitation, I spoke at Chautauqua, and with Mrs. Wittenmeyer visited several summer camps in New England and the Middle States. After a second winter's work in Chicago, during which I prepared "Hints and Helps for the Woman's Christian Temperance Union," I made a trip through Ohio, and while in Columbus for a Sunday engagement, remained at home in the morning for Bible study and prayer. Upon my knees alone, in the room of my hostess, who was a veteran Crusader, there was borne in upon my mind, as I believe, from loftier regions, the declaration, "You are to speak for woman's ballot as a weapon of protection to her home and tempted loved ones from the tyranny of drink," and then for the first and only time in my life, there flashed through my brain a complete line of argument and illustration—the same that I used a few months later before the Woman's Congress, in St. George's Hall, Philadelphia, when I first publicly avowed my faith in the enfranchisement of women. I at once wrote Mrs. Wittenmeyer, with whom I had always been in perfect accord, telling her I wished to speak on "The Home Protection Ballot" at the International Temperance Convention of Women, then being planned by us as a Centennial feature of the movement. She replied mildly, but firmly, declining to permit the subject to be brought forward. We had our convention in the Academy of Music, Philadelphia, and an International Woman's Christian Temperance Union was organized, with Mrs. Margaret Parker, of England, as its president, and Mrs. J. Ellen Foster, of Iowa, secretary, but the time was not ripe for such a movement and it advanced but a short distance beyond the name and letter-head. I spoke, but not upon the theme I would have chosen, and Mrs. Mary A. Livermore who was present and to whom I offered to give my time, so greatly have I always honored and admired her, was not allowed to speak, because of her progressive views upon the woman question.

At the Newark National Woman's Christian Temperance Union Convention, held that Autumn (1876), disregarding the earnest, almost tearful pleading of my friends, I repeated my "suffrage speech" with added emphasis. The great church was packed to the doors; Mrs. Wittenmeyer was on the platform, Mrs. Allen Butler, a Presbyterian lady of Syracuse, then president of New York Woman's Christian Temperance Union, presided. I remember her quoting at the outset an anecdote of Mrs.

Lathrap's about a colored man in the war who saw a Confederate boat approaching an island where several Union soldiers of whom he was one were just landing, whereupon they all lay flat in their canoe, colored man and all, until he jumped up, saying, "Somebody's got to be shot at and it might as well be me," pushed the boat from shore, and fell pierced by bullets, but saved the day for his comrades. I then gave the people my argument, and though I could but feel the strong conservatism of an audience of Christian women, in New Jersey in 1876, I felt far more strongly the undergirdings of the Spirit. At the close I was applauded beyond my hopes. The dignified chairman came forward saying, "I wish it clearly understood that the speaker represents herself and not the Woman's Christian Temperance Union, for we do not propose to trail our skirts through the mire of politics." These words were received in silence, and I knew then that the hearts of the women were with the forward movement. As we left the hall my honored chief whispered regretfully, "You might have been a leader, but now you'll be only a scout."

It is true that at the Cincinnati convention, held in St. Paul's M. E. Church just one year previous, Mrs. Governor Wallace of Indiana (the original of that famous mother in Gen. Lew Wallace's "Ben Hur"), had secured the adoption of a resolution favorable to submitting the question of prohibiting the dramshops to a vote of men and women. But it is equally true that this was done by her great personal influence in privately securing from leaders strongly opposed, an agreement to let her make the test, whereupon the resolution went through without debate. Thus it is an historical fact that the first time the subject of prohibition came before the temperance women of America was upon the proposition that the united home forces should vote out the saloon. We knew that we could not at Newark get such a resoution passed, therefore we tried another plan, asking that in the territories and the District of Columbia the sale of alcoholic drinks should be legalized only "when a majority of men by their votes and women by their signatures should ask for the legalizing of such sale." A petition to Congress embodying this request led to our first work at the capital.

It was at this Newark convention that the national motto, "For God and Home and Native Land," was first indorsed. It had come to my thought early in the work and been accepted as the motto of our Chicago Woman's Christian Temperance Union, then of the State of Illinois and lastly of the nation. It was at the Newark convention that a majority of the members pledged themselves to pass the cup untasted at the sacramental table, if they knew that it held alcoholic wine. It was at Cincinnati the year previous, though on recommendation of the New Jersey convention, that we pledged ourselves to observe the "noon hour" for prayer that God would help the temperance work and workers, overthrow the liquor traffic and bring in the universal reign of Christ.

At the Newark convention our national organ was found to be so heavily in debt that its committee of publication resigned, and Mrs. Jane M. Geddes, of Michigan, Mrs. Mary T. Burt, of New York, Mrs. C. B. Buell, of Connecticut, and myself volunteered to save the day for this new journalistic venture and literary outgrowth of the Crusade. We put in what money we had as a free-will offering, gathered up gifts from our friends, gave several months' gratuitous work, during which I was entertained in Brooklyn by my good friends, Mr. and Mrs. J. F. Stout, and we were so happy as to see the enterprise placed upon a paying basis. It was removed to Chicago in 1882, by action of the Louisville convention, merged with *The Signal*, organ of the Illinois Woman's Christian Temperance Union, founded by Mrs. T. B. Carse in 1880, and under the name of *The Union Signal*, was at first edited by Mrs. Mary Bannister Willard, and is now by Mary Allen West, issuing a weekly edition of from fifty-five to sixty thousand. It is one of half a score of periodicals brought out by our Woman's Temperance Publication Association, a joint stock company of women only, which declared in 1886 a dividend of four per cent, in '87 one of five and in '88 one of six per cent, besides owning its machinery, handling in 1888 a hundred and thirty thousand dollars and sending out over sixty million pages of literature.

In the winter of 1877 I went to Washington and spoke before the House Committee on Judiciary, Hon. Proctor Knott of Kentucky, chairman, urging the claims of the Home Protection Petition adopted at Newark as aforesaid. I remember the presence of Gen. Ben Butler with a red, red rose in his button-hole. I remember the blandly non-committal Garfield, the friendly Frye, the earnest Blair, the polite Samuel J. Randall who invited us to a seat in the speaker's gallery during the presentation of our huge petition, which was so large that the pages required help to bring it in. I remember being most hospitably entertained for ten days in the home of Rev. Dr. and Mrs. John P. Newman, where I said nothing about my intention to speak before the Committee on Judiciary, supposing that my kind friends were opposed to a movement so progressive, and I remember, too, how glad I was when they told me afterward of their hearty sympathy and took me to task for not inviting them to be present. From Washington I came home to Chicago and was somewhat identified with the Moody meetings then being held in the huge Tabernacle there. I shall never forget a stormy Sabbath day when, through blinding snow, nine thousand women gathered to hear a sermon specially for them, from that most successful evangelist of the Christian era. We then met for the first time and he asked me to lead in prayer. The mighty significance of such an army of wives and mothers, sisters and daughters gathered to pray for their beloved absent ones, surged in upon my heart like the sea at high tide. I never beheld a more impressive scene. A few weeks later I introduced John B. Gough in this Tabernacle to the largest temperance audience I have ever seen assembled within four walls. How magnificently he spoke! his good wife, Mary Gough, sitting near by with knitting-work in hand. As he retired from the audience and the tremendous evening's task, a little boy's autograph album was thrust into his face and as he wrote his name the page was wet with perspiration. Alas for kind but thoughtless hearts!

> "Strange we never heed the singer
> Till the sweet voiced bird has flown,"

would be the truthful epitaph of a thousand Greathearts of pen and voice killed by kindness and appreciation no less than by the stress of their prodigious industry and boundless versatility in the sacred causes upon whose altars they are laid and by whose steep stair-ways they climb to fame and death. We "heed" them in eulogies, in resolutions of condolence, in marble-cut epitaphs; would that we might heed them earlier by lifting off the wholly needless cares we heap upon their shoulders in token of our love!

I remember being in the Tabernacle when it was draped in

black for Mr. and Mrs. Philip Bliss, whose death by the frightful railroad accident at Ashtabula Bridge, shocked the whole world. They were to have been present on Christmas day, the announcements were out and the public expectant. Mr. Moody stood before the multitude and cried. We all cried with him, and he said between his sobs, "O that lovely, lovely man!" I could but say of Mr. Moody then, and often since, "Thy gentleness hath made thee great."

CHAPTER III.

MOODY'S BOSTON MEETINGS—OLIVER'S DEATH.

Toward the close of his meeting, sometime in January, Brother Moody—that is the only name for him—asked me to call at the Brevoort House. He stood on the rug in front of a blazing grate in his private parlor, and abruptly said to me, "Good-morning—what was that trouble you and Dr. Fowler had in the University at Evanston?"

I was not a little "set back," as the phrase is, but replied, "Dr. Fowler has the will of a Napoleon, I have the will of a Queen Elizabeth; when an immovable meets an indestructible object, something has to give way."

He said "Humph," and changed the theme. "Will you go with me to Boston and help in the women's meetings?" he asked. "I think I should be glad to do so, but would like to talk with mother," was my answer. "What are your means of support?" was his next question. "I have none except as the Chicago Woman's Christian Temperance Union pays my current expenses, and in leaving its work for yours, I should have none at all," I said. "Let's pray about it!" concluded Brother Moody, falling upon his knees. We did pray and he shook hands, dismissing me to admit some other individual of the endless comers-in. My mother liked the plan. "Enter every open door," she said, and every friend I had, seemed glad. At a farewell meeting in Farwell Hall, Mrs. Carse presented me a Bagster Bible, and John Collier, a reformed man whom we all liked and believed in, gave me on behalf of himself and others who had signed the pledge, a copy of Cruden's Concordance, saying, "We did n't know about the Bible, let alone this big, learned Concordance, till the women fished us up out of the mud and set us walking on the heavenly highway."

I had studied the Bible a few weeks with Rev. W. J. Erdman, a scholar of beautiful spirit and great knowledge of the

Scriptures. But I went to Boston with no material on hand save a few temperance lectures. On a fly leaf of my new "Bagster" I find this entry, my only record of that fruitful three months of work and study, for I kept no journal and have not since my return from Europe in 1870:

"My first *whole day* of real, spiritual, joyful, loving study of the kernel of God's word, simply desirous to learn my Father's will, is this 17th of February, 1877, with the Boston work just begun. And on this sweet, eventful day, in which, with every hour of study, the Bible has grown dearer, I take as my life-motto henceforth, humbly asking God's grace that I may measure up to it, this wonderful passage from Paul: "*And whatsoever ye do, in word or deed, do all in the name of the Lord Jesus, giving thanks to God and the Father by him.*"—Col. 3:17."

I had lacked specific Bible teaching, having almost never attended Sunday-school, because of being brought up in the country. Mrs. Governor Beveridge is the only teacher who had me in charge whom I clearly recall, and she for a brief period. I had taught in Sunday-school, somewhat, but with the pressure of academic and college cares, my temerity in undertaking a Bible reading daily before the most cultured audience of women on the footstool surprises me as I reflect upon it. Entertained in the beautiful home of Mrs. Fenno Tudor, an Episcopalian lady of broad views, on Beacon Hill, I went to my room at eight o'clock each morning, studied until noon, then met my audience, spoke twenty minutes without manuscript, conducted the inquiry meeting afterward, attended to correspondence for the National Woman's Christian Temperance Union all the afternoon, save when I had an extra meeting, which was not infrequently, and made a temperance address, usually in the suburbs, at night.

I never studied by lamp-light and I had my requisite eight hours of sleep. Sometimes I had four or six hundred, often a thousand, and occasionally twelve or fourteen hundred women in my meetings at Berkeley Street and Park Street Congregational Churches. Usually I spoke on Sabbath evening in Clarendon Street Baptist Church, and when Mr. Moody called a "Temperance Conference," in the Tabernacle, at which Gough, Tyng, Wanamaker and others spoke, he placed my name upon his program, also had me literally preach—though I did not call it that—one Sunday afternoon. I said to him, "Brother Moody, you need not think because I am a Western woman and not afraid to go, you must put me in the forefront of the battle after this fashion. Perhaps you will hinder the work among these conservatives." But at this he laughed in his cheery way, and declared that "it was just what they needed and I need n't be scared for he was n't."

The Christian womanhood of Boston rallied around me like sisters indeed. I never had more cordial help, even from my own white ribboners.

Mrs. Myra Pierce, the leading Methodist woman of the city, was made chairman of the Committee to arrange for my meetings, and, with Mrs. Rev. Dr. A. J. Gordon, stood by me steadily. I tried my best to make the temperance work a prominent feature, and had the satisfaction of seeing some grand new workers develop, among whom were Miss Elisabeth S. Tobey, and Miss Bessie Gordon, now president and corresponding secretary of Massachusetts Woman's Christian Temperance Union, and Miss Anna Gordon, a gifted girl, born in Boston, christened by Rev. Dr. Nehemiah Adams, to whose church her parents belonged, and now for twelve years my devoted friend, faithful secretary and constant traveling companion.

One day as I was about to open my noon meeting in Berkeley Street Church, Mr. Moody came running up the pulpit steps, for his own meeting was waiting, and said, "I see by the papers that you're talking temperance all around the suburbs. Why do you do that? I want all there is of you for the Boston meetings."

"It is because I have n't any money and must go out and earn some," I replied.

"You don't mean that I've given you nothing?" he said striking his forehead.

"Of course you've given me nothing," I replied with mildness.

"Who paid your way from Chicago?"

"I did."

"Did n't those fellows"—naming some of his immediate friends—"send you money for traveling expenses as I told them to?"

"I guess they forgot it," I replied.

"Well, I never heard the like!" and he was off like a shot.

That evening, as I was going into my meeting, he thrust a generous check into my hand, saying, "Don't you go beating about in the suburbs any more."

Everything went on smoothly until a Woman's Christian Temperance Union Convention was announced at Malden, and I was asked to speak there with Mrs. Livermore, then president of Massachusetts Woman's Christian Temperance Union. I agreed to go, and was again taken to task by Brother Moody, but this time on another ground. He held with earnestness that I ought not to appear on the same platform with one who denied the divinity of Christ. In this he was so earnest and so cogent, by reason of his deep convictions and his unrivaled knowledge of proof-passages, that I deferred to his judgment, partly from conviction and partly from a desire to keep the peace and go on with my good friend in his work; for I deem it one of the choicest seals of my calling that Dwight L. Moody should have invited me to cast in my little lot with his great one as an evangelist. But on returning West, I went over the whole subject of an "orthodox" Christian's duty, for myself, and as a result, sent the following letter to my honored brother, through my gracious friend, his wife:

EVANSTON, September 5, 1877.

DEAR MRS. MOODY—In view of the fact that when I last saw Mr. Moody, I agreed to go with him in his work, I think a simple statement of the ground of my changed purpose, due to myself, though I dislike to take his time to listen to it; you will consult your own judgment about presenting my reasons to him.

For myself, the more I study the subject, the more I fail to see that it is for us to decide who shall work in this cause side by side with us, and who shall not. I cannot judge how the hearts of earnest, pure, prayerful women may appear in God's clear sight, nor just when their loyalty to Christ has reached the necessary degree. If to the communion table we bid those welcome who feel themselves fit subjects to come, then surely in the sacred communion of work for poor humanity, I dare not say, "You may come," and "You must not." "With you I will speak on the same platform,—with you, I will not." Rather let the burden of this solemn choice rest on those who come, and whosoever will may work with me, if only she brings earnest purpose, devout soul, and irreproachable moral character. This has been my course always, and it would be denying my deepest and most sacred convictions to turn aside from it. In denominational lines, we certainly have safeguards enough for the defense of the faith, and I am sadly aware that within these lines there are myriads less true, less Christ-like than many whom I must disfellowship if I take the dilemma by the other horn.

All my life I have been devoted to the advancement of women in education and opportunity. I firmly believe God has a work for them to do as evangelists, as bearers of Christ's message to the ungospeled, to the prayer-meeting, to the church generally and the world at large, such as most people have not dreamed. It is therefore my dearest wish to help break down the barriers of prejudice that keep them silent. I cannot think that meetings in which "the brethren" only are called upon, are one half as effective as those where all are freely invited, and I can but believe that "women's meetings," as such, are a relic of an outworn *régime.* Never did I hold one of these meetings without a protest in my soul against it. As in the day of Pentecost, so now, let men and women in perfectly impartial fashion participate in all services conducted in His name in whom there is neither bond nor free, male nor female, but all are one. Nobody is more than half himself who does not work in accordance with his highest convictions; and I feel that whenever I surrender the views herein stated, I have the lever by the short arm when I might just as well grasp the long one, nay, when I am in duty bound to do this. No one knows better than Mr. Moody, that to work at our best, we must work out our own ideas. To represent the views of another, no matter how much we may love, honor, or revere him, is like pulling with the left hand when we might use the right.

Mr. Moody views the temperance work from the standpoint of a revivalist, and so emphasizes the regeneration of men. But to me as a woman, there are other phases of it almost equally important to its success, viz., saving the *children*, teaching them never to drink; showing to their mothers the duty of total abstinence; rousing a dead church and a torpid Sunday-school to its duty; spreading the facts concerning the iniquitous traffic far and wide; influencing legislation so that what is physically wrong and morally wrong shall not, on the statute books of a Christian land, be set down as legally right;—and to this end putting the ballot in woman's hand for the protection of her little ones and of her home. All these ways of working seem to me eminently religious—thoroughly in harmony with the spirit of the most devoted Christian man or woman.

So I cannot believe myself called upon to discontinue these lines of work, nor to cease hearty co-operation with those thus working; and yet it remains true, that best of all I love to declare the blessed tidings of salvation, and would gladly do so still, if I might act in my own character, under the auspices of the greatest Christian leader of our day.

It costs me much to turn away from such a future and from such a guide—but I believe it to be right, and this is a decision resulting from a whole summer of thought and earnest prayer for wisdom.

Pardon me for going so much into detail, and yet I think your kindly nature will appreciate my wish to be understood by those for whom I have so great regard, and with whom my relations have always been so pleasant.

With sincere Christian affection, I am, as I shall always be,

Your friend, FRANCES E. WILLARD.

In the wider fields that would have opened to me as a coadjutor of the great evangelist, no doubt the widest that could by any possibility be open to a Christian worker, whether man or woman, in our day, my work for the Woman's Christian Temperance Union and the World's Woman's Christian Temperance Union would have been immeasurably greater than it is now, for Mr. Moody made no objection to my being president of the first society, and I doubt not he would have welcomed my becoming president of the larger one. I should have gone to England with him and been able, both there and here, to acclimate the white ribbon movement in conservative circles never yet penetrated by its broad and genial influence. It was my dream to do this—to rally under Mr. Moody's indirect influence, all the leaders, men and women, of our growing host. But for this one objection, so unlooked for, how different might have been my future and that of the white ribbon cause! My friends were grieved again, and many told me what many more told others, that I had once more made "the mistake of a life-time." For myself I only knew that, liberal as he was toward me in all other things, tolerant of my ways and manners, generous in his views upon the woman question, devotedly conscientious and true, Brother Moody's Scripture interpretations concerning religious toleration were too literal for me; the jacket was too straight—I could not wear it.

In the autumn of this year, 1877, our annual convention was held in Chicago, where, after a lively discussion over the report of the committee on badge (they having recommended royal purple as the color), we adopted a simple bit of white ribbon, emblematic of purity and peace, on the principle of "first pure, then peaceable." Miss Margaret Winslow, of Brooklyn, then our editor, made a telling speech upon this subject, which I wish might have gone upon the records. After debate, a resolution known in our annals as "the famous Thirteenth" was adopted, declaring that "woman ought to have the power to close the dram-shop door over against her home."

At this convention I resigned the corresponding secretaryship of the National Woman's Christian Temperance Union and again declined the use of my name as a candidate for president, because I felt, after much prayer, unwilling to appear as an opposing candidate.

Throughout the next year, 1878, I was a free lance for the Woman's Christian Temperance Union, during which period I proceeded to "go on a bureau." My friends had long urged me to quit the guerilla warfare of hap-hazard engagements, so to speak, and to put my invitations into the hands of a Lyceum Lecture Bureau. In an evil hour I listened to the siren's voice, went to Mr. Slayton, the gentlemanly manager of such an institution, he having repeatedly invited me to do so, handed him some of my letters and lists of invitation, of which I had enough to cover more time and territory than I could ever exhaust; submitted to the indignity of placards, small bills and a big lithograph; was duly set forth upon glossy tinted paper in an imposing "Annual"—in common with one hundred others—as a light of the age, no newspaper to the contrary being quoted; contracted to pay my per cent, and was started out. I remained on that bureau, to which I had climbed at the expense of a hundred-dollar lithograph and all the rest of it, just three weeks. It was what is called "a damper" to one of my temperament and habitudes. To go from the genial, breezy, out-doorsy temperance meeting, the warm, tender, exalted gospel meeting, the home-like, sisterly, inspiring Woman's Christian Temperance Union Convention, into a human snow-bank of folks who have "paid to get in" and are reckoning quietly, as one proceeds, whether or not they are really going "to get their money's worth," is an experience not to be endured with equanimity by anybody who can slip his head out of its noose. To have a solemn "Lyceum Committee" of men meet you at the train, take you to a hotel of funereal dreariness and cooked-over cuisine; to march upon a realistic stage that no woman's hand has beautified or brightened; to have no heartsome music or winsome prayer preceding you and tuning your weary spirit to the high ministry for which you came; to face the glare of footlights; and after you have "gone through" your speech and are feeling particularly "gone," to hear the jeremiad of the treasurer that "they had n't sold so many tickets as they hoped," or "the weather was against them," or "counter attractions had proved too powerful;" all this is "nerve-wear" to no purpose. Then to be exploited over the country with as little regard for comfort as if you were a case of cod-fish or a keg of nails, the heart of the night being all the symptom of a heart that your time-table reveals, the wee small hours being made consciously present with you in order that you may "make" the next engagement, the unconscionable "wait" at side stations and uncanny junction depots, all these are reasons of my hope never again to see a "Bureau,"—indeed, I can hardly tolerate one in my room since an end was put to that abyssmal epoch of three weeks. I think my manager was as glad to have me go as I was to say Good-by, for I would n't raise my price ($25), even when double and three times that amount was offered for an "option." "No," I replied with reproving tone, "a philanthropist can't afford to make money. It shall never be said that I charged more as I became more popular. I've set my price once for all and I'll never raise it and I'll never lay up money and I'll never be rich,—nobody shall ever bring that reproach upon me no matter how else I may fail." Whereat my handsome manager was wont to look upon me as mildly lunatic, changing the subject lest I might become violent.

Returning to Anna Gordon's tender mercies, a young woman who has repeatedly convinced ticket-agents that they make mistakes concerning train-time; who has a face so honest that (before that wretched Interstate law!) she has often got passes for me from entire strangers on her simple say so; who understands traveling as well as Robert Bonner does Maud S. and who has n't her superior as a business woman on this continent, I have gone my way in peace since 1878, visiting with her every state and territory and all but two capitals, those of Arizona and Idaho, in a single year (1883, our temperance "round-up," ten years after the Crusade), and reaching, since my work began, a thousand towns, including all that by the census of 1870 had ten thousand inhabitants, and most of those having five thousand. Mother says that for about ten years she thinks I averaged but three weeks in a year at home, and Anna Gordon says she thinks I averaged one meeting daily throughout that period.

In 1878 the white ribbon regiment of Illinois placed me at its head and we entered on our home protection campaign, collecting in nine weeks nearly two hundred thousand names to the following petition:

To the Senate and House of Representatives of the State of Illinois:

WHEREAS, In these years of temperance work the argument of defeat in our contest with the saloons has taught us that our efforts are merely palliative of a disease in the body politic, which can never be cured until law and moral suasion go hand in hand in our beloved state ; and

WHEREAS, The instincts of self-protection and of apprehension for the safety of her children, her tempted loved ones, and her home, render woman the natural enemy of the saloon ;

Therefore, Your petitioners, men and women of the state of Illinois, having at heart the protection of our homes from their worst enemy, the legalized traffic in strong drink, do hereby most earnestly pray your honorable body that, by suitable legislation, it may be provided that in the state of Illinois, the question of licensing at any time, in any locality, the sale of any and all intoxicating drinks, shall be submitted to and determined by ballot, in which women of lawful age shall be privileged to take part, in the same manner as men, when voting on the question of license.

We had great hearings at the State House, which we decorated with the Petition,* all the names being pasted upon a strip of cloth nearly a quarter of a mile long, bound with blue to represent the Murphy, and red to indicate the Reynolds reform movement ; we sang "Home Sweet Home" in the Senate chamber ; held prayer-meetings in the committee rooms and on top of Lincoln's monument, and convened mass-meetings throughout the state to the tune of:

"Rally then, rally then,
Ye men of Illinois ;
Give woman home protection vote,
To save the tempted boy."

That we did not get an iota from the Illinois legislature goes without saying. It is chosen by the saloon and legislates for it almost exclusively. The beer and whisky interests of the world are nowhere centered as in our state, with Chicago and Peoria as the foci of an ellipse in which our politicians move as in an orbit. But all the same we roused the people so that, under our local option law, six hundred and twenty-five towns went for prohibition out of eight hundred and thirty-two voting that spring, and nothing so encouraging was ever known before nor has been since.

Rest Cottage was like a rag-bag by reasons of the petitions stacked everywhere. My dear old mother, president of the local

*This petition was sealed and placed in the rooms of the Chicago Historical Society, not to reappear until the day of Jubilee when women *vote* in Illinois.

union when she was seventy, took turns with Anna Gordon, ironing the "Big Petition" smooth as a shirt bosom. I used to take my little tin dinner-pail as of old in district school days, and go over to the Illinois State House every morning, some kind ladies being there with their sewing to stay with me, and we thus kept house for weeks. The state geologist let us fix up his room with flowers and birds and pretty home devices. A good temperance man was in attendance to take our cards in to the legislators when they were not busy, and we interviewed them man by man, setting down their names as plus or minus, according to their promises. One day all the grangers came in a body and pledged us their votes. Another, a party leader agreed to make the speech of presentation when our petition should come up, but a week later he came in and said the caucus (Republican) had threatened him ; he had also, "heard from home and did n't dare to go back on the men that had voted him in." "If you women had votes, and could reward them that stood by you and punish them as would n't, your bill would be all right," he said commiseratingly as he slunk out of the room. Another leader with whom we had a private interview, said: "Ladies, I'm ashamed to admit that I'm bound hand and foot, and can't do as I would. My wife put her hand on my shoulder when I left home and said, 'Won't you please stand by the temperance ladies?' and she looked straight in my eyes so earnestly I could have cried. But I said, 'No, my dear, I can't; my law practice is nearly all from the saloons, my hopes of promotion are from them, I have no sons to help me earn money, and I'm bound to support you and the girls in good style, so don't say another word,' and then I left her. Now, ladies, if I denied the plea, of the woman I love better than any other being on earth, you'll not urge me, I know." As we still pressed our plea this man of kind nature had tears in his eyes ; his lips quivered, and he left us saying : "I want to help you, ladies, more than you know, *but I just can't.*"

I have not named the most significant experience of my life in 1878.

My only brother, Oliver, of whose great gifts and genial nature I can never say enough, after his graduation from Beloit College in 1859, took a diploma from Garrett Biblical Institute in 1861 and became a Methodist minister, founding that church in Colorado, and being chosen presiding elder when he was twenty-seven years old.

Afterward he was for years editor of the *Chicago Mail*, then the *Chicago Post*, and on March 17, 1878, he died quite suddenly at the Palmer House, Chicago. One of the last efforts of his life was to help work up for me my first Evanston audience since I had left the University four years earlier. Temperance was a threadbare theme and he feared I might not be greeted by the attendance that is the most grateful of all to a speaker when it consists of his or her own towns-folk.

But I had a fine audience in our own church. My mother, my brother's wife and their four children were all present, but where was he who had cared so much about this meeting?

At the close we were informed that he had been taken suddenly, but not at all dangerously ill, and had remained in the city, but would come home next day. His faithful wife drove in at once, reaching the Palmer House at midnight. He rallied her on her needless anxiety and asked "how Frank had got along?" When she told him of the meeting's success, he smiled and used a favorite phrase of his (borrowed from a song about "Brave Wolfe," at Quebec), "I die with pleasure."

How little he dreamed of leaving us was shown in his bright greeting to me when I went to see him in the morning and our good Dr. Jewell assured me he would be able to go home by the next day, and advised me not to miss the appointments I had, in company with Mrs. S. M. I. Henry, at Saginaw, Mich., for the next day but one, which was Sunday. So I left my dear, kind brother, life-long comrade and friend, without any thought of the sorrow that was so near.

Mrs. Henry and I had what ministers call, "a good time" in our meetings on the Sabbath day.

Monday at family prayers in the Christian home where we were sheltered, Mrs. Henry breathed this petition:

"Grant, Heavenly Father, that each one of us may this morning so find our balance in Thee that no sin or sorrow may be able to surprise us."

Going upstairs to my writing, five minutes later, I heard the door bell ring and a telegram was put into my hand. This has long been an experience so frequent as to cause no surprise, but

I have never yet opened a telegram without first lifting up my heart to God in prayer. What need I had to do so now! The message was dated Sunday and read as follows:

"Your brother Oliver died this morning—Funeral Tuesday."

I read it aloud, friends being in the hall, and crouched upon the stairs without a cry, like one who had been struck. They led me to my room, and my saintly Sister Henry took me in her arms, as I repeated the words of her prayer, and we knelt once more together. I shall never forget the tenderness of her voice as for my consolation she read that blessed psalm, "Lord, thou hast been our dwelling-place in all generations."

I had been announced to conduct a temperance prayer-meeting that afternoon. The Chicago train would go at an hour that left me time to fulfill the engagement. I said, "He would have wished me to do this; he was punctual to his religious duties all this blessed year, no matter what might come." And so I went and told the people all about it while we cried together, praying and talking of a better life which is an heavenly. They went with me to the train and we had a sort of meeting in the depot while we waited, and as I departed alone, they stood there with their sorrowful but kindly faces, those dear new friends in Christ Jesus, and sang:

"Rescue the perishing, care for the dying." *

When I reached my sweet Rest Cottage home, there stood my mother, seventy-four years old, upon the steps. He was the pride and darling of her life, and I had almost feared to see her sorrow. But no, her dear old face was radiant and she said, "Praise Heaven with me — I've grown gray praying for my son— and now to think your brother Oliver is safe with God!"

I went up the street to his pleasant home beside the College campus—

"Dead he lay among his books,
The peace of God was in his looks,"

but the dear face was tired and worn. His last words to his wife had been, "All your prayers for me are answered; I have a present, perfect, personal Savior."

---

*Afterward, I had the comfort of learning that a young and gifted man that day decided in the meeting to be a missionary.

CHAPTER IV.

CONSERVATIVES AND LIBERALS.

I was much taken to task because I would not allow my name used as a candidate for President of the W. C. T. U. at the Chicago convention in 1877, and the papers tried to make out that I said, "Nothing but a unanimous choice would induce me to accept the position." The facts were that we then had an unpleasant method of nominating our candidates; namely, by means of a very complimentary speech made by some leading orator. Mrs. Foster generously made such a speech in my behalf, although I had said all I could to the women against their taking such action. A friend of Mrs. Wittenmeyer then rose and made a very complimentary speech about her, and put her in nomination. Then I rose and said I would not allow myself to come forward as an opposing candidate when the President of the society, a much older woman than I and one who had borne the burden for some years, was in the field, and I withdrew my name.

If no other name had been brought up I would not have done this, and the next year but one, when by a change in the constitution we had done away with the *viva voce* nominations and the flowery, complimentary speeches, I did not object, when elected by a large majority, to taking the position.

In 1879, at Indianapolis, I was elected president of the National Woman's Christian Temperance Union.

Two policies had in the five years' evolution of the Crusade movement become distinctly outlined under the names, "Conservative" and "Liberal." Our honored president, Mrs. Wittenmeyer, believed in holding the states and local unions to strict account, expecting uniformity of organization and method — in short, maintaining strongly the central power of the *National* Woman's Christian Temperance Union. She also vigorously opposed the ballot for women. In opposition to this, we "Liberals" interpreted the constitution of our society on the *laissez-faire* principle. We believed in making very few requirements of the state and local unions; if they paid their small dues and signed the total abstinence pledge, we asked no more, believing that the less we asked the more we should get, and that any amount of elbow room was good for folks, developed their peculiar genius and kept them hard at work and cheerful. So we declared for state rights and intruded not at all upon our thrifty auxiliaries, save that we were ready to go to them, work for them and build them up all that we could. In respect to woman's ballot we believed it was part and parcel of the temperance movement, one way out of the wilderness of whisky domination, and that any individual, any state or local union ought to have the right to say so and to act accordingly.

At our previous convention (Baltimore, 1878) we had debated one whole day over this question, taking it up in two parts as follows:

1. Shall we indorse the ballot for women as a temperance measure?
2. Shall our official organ publish accounts of work within our societies along this line?

The debate was a marvel of mingled courtesy and cogency, at the close of which the first question was decided in the negative, but the second affirmatively, which opened the columns of our paper, and henceforth the process of educating our women in favor of the ballot went forward rapidly.

At Indianapolis the principles of the liberal wing of our society became dominant, not so much by specific declaration as by the choice of leaders who incarnated those principles.

The number of delegates at this convention was one hundred and forty-eight from twenty states, no Southern state save Maryland being represented. Total receipts in national treasury for the year, $1,213.00.

At Boston the next year, there were one hundred and seventy-seven delegates from twenty-five states, and the receipts were $2,048.00. The debate begun the year before on a change in our mode of representation was earnestly continued. As the constitution had stood from the begining, each state was entitled to as many delegates in the national convention as it had representatives in Congress, but this operated unjustly because several states having the largest number of local unions had fewer congressional districts than others having but few unions; it also put a premium upon unorganized states which were represented on the same basis.

The liberal party held that representation ought to be on a basis of paid memberships, but the conservatives claimed that "praying not paying" was the only true foundation of the movement, while their antagonists declared that we must both *pray and pay*. No change was made at Boston and as a consequence the work was greatly hampered financially. But at Boston the cumbrous system of "standing committees" was abolished and that of individual superintendence substituted on the principle that "if Noah had appointed a committee the ark would still be on the stocks." The departments were divided into Preventive, Educational, Evangelistic, Social, Legal and Department of Organization.

Under the first head we had a superintendent of Heredity and Hygiene; under the second, a superintendent of efforts to secure Scientific Temperance Instruction in the public schools (Mrs. Mary A. Hunt); under the fifth a superintendent of Legislation and Petition (then Mrs. J. Ellen Foster, now Mrs. Ada Bittenbender), etc., making one woman responsible for one work, and giving her one associate in each state and one in each local union. The plan of putting a portrait of Mrs. Lucy Webb Hayes in the White House as a Temperance Memorial was here adopted by request of Rev. Frederick Merrick, of Ohio, its originator.

From my annual address at Boston—my first as President of the National W. C. T. U.—I make this extract:

> Two-thirds of Christ's church are women, whose persuasive voices will be a re-inforcement quite indispensable to the evangelizing agencies of the more hopeful future.
>
> A horde of ignorant voters, committed to the rum-power, fastens the dram-shop like a leech on our communities; but let the Republic take notice that our unions are training an army to offset this horde, one which will be the only army of voters specifically educated to their duty which has ever yet come up to the help of the Lord against the mighty. For slowly

but surely the reflex influence of this mighty reform, born in the church and nurtured at the Crusade altars, is educating women to the level of two most solemn and ominous ideas: *1st. That they ought to vote. 2nd. That they ought to vote against grog-shops.* The present generation will not pass away until in many of the states this shall all be fulfilled, and then America, beloved Mother of thrice grateful daughters, thou shalt find rallying to thy defense and routing the grimy hosts that reel about thee now, an army of voters which absenteeism will not decimate and money cannot buy. Under the influence of our societies may be safely tried the great experiment that agitates the age, and which upon the world's arena most of us have feared. When we desire this "home protection" weapon, American manhood will place it in our hands. Though we have not taken sides as yet, in politics, we cannot be insensible to the consideration shown us in the platform of the Prohibition party—a prophecy of that chivalry of justice which shall yet afford us a still wider recognition. These benign changes will not come suddenly, but as the result of a profound change in the convictions of the thoughtful and conscientious, followed by such a remoulding of public sentiment as this class always brings about when once aroused.

At Boston the ballot for woman as a weapon for the protection of her home was indorsed, and the action of the president in opening official headquarters in New York City was confirmed. Mrs. Caroline B. Buell was elected corresponding secretary, an office which she still retains.

In the spring of 1881, following this convention, I went to Washington to be present at the inauguration of General Garfield and to meet the commission of the Mrs. Hayes' Temperance Memorial of which I was president. The Woman's Christian Temperance Union of the North—it was then practically non-existent at the South—had stood solidly for the Republican candidate whom we then believed to be a friend of total abstinence and prohibition. His name was cheered whenever mentioned in the Boston convention, and being personally acquainted with him, I had written him at Mentor, immediately after his nomination, that if he would hold to total abstinence during the campaign, he might count on our support—although Neal Dow was in the field, and I had been invited, but declined, to go to the Prohibition convention at Cleveland. For I had not then beheld, therefore was not disobedient to, the heavenly vision of political as well as legal suasion for the liquor traffic. The disappointment of our temperance women was great over the reply of President Garfield, when, on March 8, we went to the White House and I presented the picture of Mrs. Hayes. His manner seemed to us constrained. He was not the brotherly Disciple preacher of old, but the adroit politician "in the hands of his friends" and perfectly aware that the liquor camp held the balance of power.

Surprised and pained by his language, we at once adjourned to the Temple Hotel (conducted by Mrs. S. D. La Fetra, one of our members) and such a prayer-meeting I have seldom attended. The women poured out their souls to God in prayer that total abstinence might be enthroned at the White House, that a chief magistrate might come unto the kingdom who would respond to the plea of the nation's home-people seeking protection for their tempted loved ones.

From Washington I started for the South, accompanied by Mrs. Georgia Hulse McLeod of Baltimore, a native of Tallahassee, Fla., a gifted writer and corresponding secretary of our society in Maryland. I had also with me my faithful Anna Gordon and her sister Bessie. In the three months that followed we visited nearly one hundred towns and cities of the South, and I have made four trips since then, attending, in different years, a state temperance convention in almost every one of the fourteen Southern states. By this means I have become acquainted with the men and women who lead the movement there, and so know them to be, in the old New England phrase, "just our sort of folks." The Methodist church is in the van, and here I found my firmest friends. Good Bishop Wightman, when not able to sit up, wrote me letters of introduction as hearty as our own Northern bishops would have penned, and they proved the "open sesame" to many an influential home in the Gulf states; brought many a pastor out from the quiet of his study to "work me up a meeting"; conciliated the immense influence of church journalism and paved the way for the recognition of the white ribbon movement throughout the Southern states. I would gladly name the noble leaders who thus stood by me both in Methodist and other churches, but the roll would be too long. It is written on my heart, where it will never grow dim.

I have always believed that I had an unexpected element of power in my name. The first night at Charleston and in each Southern audience from then till now, lovely women came forward to take my hand and said, "Are you Madam Emma Willard, of

Troy?" or else, "Are you her daughter?" Often and again have I been told, "We came to hear you because our mothers were educated in Mrs. Willard's school, and we wanted to see if you were kin to her." Once I have been introduced as "Emma Willard," and more than once, gentlemen old enough to be my ancestors have shaken my hand with vigor, saying, "We studied your United States History when we were little boys." Many a time in the passing crowd I was unable to contradict these declarations and often I smiled internally and thought, "My people love to have it so," but whenever the opportunity presented itself, I frankly discounted my standing and crushed their hopes by the mild announcement that "Madam Emma Willard was the second cousin by marriage of my great-grandfather!" I have that elegant lady's historic picture, the "Temple of Time," on my study walls, her life on my shelves, and have dutifully visited her relatives in Troy; but I did not thank them so warmly for the good she had done me as I would now, for that was before the events occurred which, at the South, showed me how truly "a good name is rather to be chosen than great riches, and loving favor than silver and gold."

That trip was the most unique of all my history. It "reconstructed" me. Everywhere the Southern white people desired me to speak to the colored. In Charleston I had an immense audience of them in the M. E. Church, North; in New Orleans, Mrs. Judge Merrick, a native of Louisiana, whose husband was Chief Justice in that state under the Confederacy, invited the Northern teachers to her home, and wrote me with joy that the Woman's Christian Temperance Union would yet solve the problem of good understanding between sections. I was present repeatedly in the gallery when legislatures of the Gulf States voted money for negro education, and for schools founded by Northerners. "We were suspicious of the Northern school-teachers at first," said Southern friends to me, "we thought they had come down here, as the carpet-baggers did, to serve their pockets and their ambitions by our means, but we don't think so now."

I found the era of good feeling had indeed set in, and that nothing helped it forward faster than the work of temperance, that nothing would liberate the suppressed colored vote so soon as to divide the white vote on the issues, "wet" and "dry"; that the

South "Solid" for prohibition of the liquor traffic might be exchanged for the South Solid against the North, by such a re-alignment of those moving armies of civilization popularly called "parties," as would put the temperance men of North and South in the same camp. Therefore it was borne in upon my spirit that I must declare in my next annual address, as President of the National Woman's Christian Temperance Union, the new faith that was within me.*

---

* To avoid repetition, descriptions of the constitutional amendment campaigns, and many other phases of the work, besides personal sketches of the workers, are omitted in this volume, having been given at length in "Woman and Temperance."

VII

A Woman in Politics.

"As once He sat over against the treasury, so now Christ sits over against the ballot box to see what His disciples cast therein."

—*Mary Allen West.*

CHAPTER I.

THE HOME PROTECTION PARTY.

My purpose to adopt the new faith gained power at the Saratoga Convention in the summer of 1881. Called by the National Temperance Society, of which Hon. William E. Dodge was president, this great meeting was "non-partisan" in action, but not in utterance. There I first met James Black, of Lancaster, Pa., the James G. Birney of the new abolition war, in which Northern and Southern bayonets point the same way; John B. Gough was present, at his best, and Rev. J. O. Peck, of Brooklyn, outdid himself in eloquence; Rev. Dr. A. J. Gordon, of Boston, was chairman, and three hundred and thirty-seven delegates were present, representing many states. A noticeable feature was the presence of accredited delegates from the General Assembly of the United Presbyterian Church, the Reformed Presbyterian Synod, the Lutheran Synod, etc. Two ladies were designated to escort Doctor Gordon to the chair, and for the first time in history, a lady, who had been chosen as vice-president, presided over the deliberations of a convention made up chiefly of men. The keen, clear logic of those who declared in the convention their conviction that the temperance question must follow the liquor question into politics, the earnest talks I had with leaders, the fervent religious spirit of the convention, confirmed me unchangeably in my new political departure. To me, the central figure of the scene was James Black, the Presbyterian, with his noble gray head, his pure, true face, his sturdy figure, as he stood before us all on the first morning with the Bible in his hand, and read God's decree of downfall for despoilers of the people, and triumph for the truth. I shall never forget the night before the close of the convention, when I, who am one of the "seven sleepers," could not sleep; but, while dear Mrs. Carse, who was with me, peacefully reposed, I thought through to the conclusion of my personal duty and delight to take sides for the Prohibition party. It was a solemn and exalted hour in which my brain teemed with the sweet reasonableness of such a course, and my conscience rejoiced in its triumph over considerations of expediency. Nothing has ever disturbed the tranquil assurance that I was then helped to make a logical and wise decision inspired from Heaven.

Two months later, at Lake Bluff, Ill., thirty miles north of Chicago, we held our usual Temperance Convocation. This beautiful spot, on the sunset shore of Lake Michigan, has long been famous as the chief rallying place of Temperance leaders on this continent, and has borne a part unequaled in influence by that of any other rendezvous of the Prohibition army.

Coming here with a heart full of new love for the South and enkindled perceptions touching what might be done, I heard a reformed man of Illinois, Captain Lothrop, of Champaign, make a most touching plea for better protection from the legalized drink curse. As he left the grounds he shook hands with me and said, "Don't let this convocation end in talk—we want to hear that you folks who stand at the front have done something; taken a forward step against the liquor power."

His worn face and intense earnestness made a deep impression on my conscience.

"By the help of God we will do something," I said in my heart and immediately sought Dr. Jutkins, Colonel Bain and John B. Finch, who that year came for the first time to Lake Bluff and captured everybody by his great gifts as an orator.

I told them what I had heard from the reformed man; of the thoughts and purposes that came to me at Saratoga; of the stirring in my spirit when my brave cousin, Willard Robinson, also a reformed man, who signed the pledge at one of my meetings in Spencerport, N. Y., had said this very year, "Cousin Frank, you people ought to go into politics; you'll never succeed until you do. I've got where I write my own ticket and put it in all alone for men who, if they were but voted into power, would outlaw the saloon."

My temperance brothers listened and gave heed. What had been tutoring them for this same hour, I do not know; the living can speak for themselves. I do not profess to give all the links in the chain that led us, then and there, to found the "Home Protection Party," but only those that are most clearly impressed on my own mind. As a result of our deliberations at this summer camp, an address was issued to the temperance people of the country. R. W. Nelson, of *The Liberator*, Chicago—a bright young man, whose paper was devoted to political prohibition, was prominent in all this movement and his journal gave us at once what we needed most, a medium of direct communication issuing from a metropolitan city.

A committee on organization was subsequently appointed, a form of constitution for Home Protection clubs prepared and the co-operation of all Prohibition leaders sought.

On the 13th of March, 1882, a Call for a national convention on the 23d of the following August, to be held in Chicago, was issued by Gideon T. Stewart, chairman of the Prohibition Reform party of the United States.

In the autumn following the Lake Bluff Convocation, our National Woman's Christian Temperance Union met in Washington, D. C. When I prepared my annual address, this thought came to me: "For you to favor the Prohibition party as an individual is one thing, and to ask the Woman's Christian Temperance Union in your official address to indorse that party, is quite another; are you going to do it? Such action will cost you much good-will and many votes." But a voice from loftier regions said: "*You ought to declare for the party officially as well as individually.*" I knelt to pray, and rose to write as follows, without one misgiving:

BELOVED SISTERS AND CO-WORKERS—When the National Prohibition party held its convention in Cleveland in 1880, women were invited to attend as delegates; but while I admired the progressive spirit thus indicated, it seemed to me clearly my duty not to go. Always profoundly interested in politics, as the mightiest force on earth except Christianity, and trained to be a staunch Republican, both my education and sympathies were arrayed on Garfield's side; moreover, I labored under the hallucination that the South secretly waited its opportunity to reopen the issues of the war. During all that stormy summer of the presidential campaign, I did not hear Neal Dow's candidacy spoken of with interest by the workers of the Woman's Christian Temperance Union, and yet we all honored and gloried in that brave father of the Maine Law. In contrast to the apathy with which we regarded the "Third Party" movement, you will remember the profound enthusiasm that greeted General Garfield's name at our annual meeting in Boston, and that, later on, we hailed his election as an answered prayer. Dear sisters, since then, by your commission, I have visited the

Southern States, and met in every one of them representatives and leaders of opinion. I have seen their acceptance in good faith of the issues of the war—a good faith sufficiently attested by the great loyalty they invariably manifested toward President Garfield, in spite of his army record, his radical utterances in Congress, and the uncompromising tone of his clear-cut inaugural. I have seen Northern capital pouring into those once disaffected states in untold millions, and I know there is no stronger bridge across the "bloody chasm" than this one woven out of national coin, and supported by the iron-jointed cables of self-interest; I have seen their legislatures making state appropriations for the education of the freedmen, and helping to sustain those "colored schools" whose New England teachers they once despised; I have learned how ex-masters cheered to the echo the utterances of their ex-slaves in the great Prohibition convention of North Carolina, and my heart has glowed with the hope of a real "home government" for the South, and a "color line" broken, not by bayonets nor repudiationists, but by ballots from white hands and black, for prohibitory law. Seeing is believing, and on that sure basis I believe the South is ready for a party along the lines of longitude,—a party that shall wipe Mason and Dixon's line out of the heart as well as off the map, weld the Anglo-Saxons of the New World into one royal family, and give us a really re-United States. With what deep significance is this belief confirmed by the South's tender sympathy in the last pathetic summer, and the unbroken group of states that so lately knelt around our fallen hero's grave! But this new party cannot bear the name of Republican or Democrat. Neither victor nor vanquished would accept the old war-cry of a section; besides, "the party of moral ideas" has ceased to have a distinctive policy. Was its early motto, "Free Territory"? We have realized it. Later did it declare the Union must be preserved and slavery abolished? Both have been done. Did it demand negro enfranchisement and the passage of a bill of Civil Rights? Both are accomplished facts, so far as they can be until education completes the desired work. Was the redemption of our financial pledges essential to good faith? That noble record of the Republican party cannot be erased. If we contemplate questions still unsettled, as Civil Service Reform, both parties claim to desire it; or a National Fund for Southern Education—each deems it necessary. But when we name the greatest issue now pending on this, or any, continent—the prohibition of the manufacture and sale of intoxicating liquors as a drink—behold, the Republicans of Maine, New Hampshire and Vermont vote for, and the Republicans of North Carolina, Ohio and Illinois against it, while the Democrats of Kansas oppose, and of South Carolina favor it! Now, I blame neither party for this inconsistency; it is simply the hand-writing on the wall, which tells that both are weighed in the balance and found wanting. For they are formed of men who, while they thought alike and fought alike on many great questions, on this greatest of all questions are hopelessly divided, and a "house divided against itself cannot stand." This is saying nothing whatever against the house; it is recognizing the law of gravitation, that is all.

Believing that the hour had come for us, the Woman's Christian Temperance Union of Illinois, at its annual meeting, nearly two months ago, indorsed the action of the Lake Bluff Convocation, held a few days earlier, and composed of representative temperance men and women from twelve different states.

In many a meeting of our temperance women I have seen the power of the Highest manifest, but in none has the glow of Crusade fire been so bright as when these daughters of heroic sires who, in the early days of the great party whose defection we deplore, endured reproach without the camp, solemnly declared their loyalty to the Home Protection party, wherein dwelleth righteousness. Let me read you the statement of doctrine to which we women of Illinois subscribed:

"We recommend that, looking to the composition of the next legislature, we request and aid the Home Protection party to put in nomination in each district a Home Protection candidate, committed not more by his specific promise than by his well-known character, to vote for the submission of a constitutional amendment, giving the full ballot to the women of Illinois as a means of protection to their homes.

"Finally, to these advance positions we have been slowly and surely brought by the logic of events and the argument of defeat in our seven years' march since the Crusade. We have patiently appealed to existing parties, only to find our appeals disregarded. We now appeal to the manhood of our state to go forward in the name of 'God and Home and Native Land.'"

Ten days later the Liquor League of Illinois held its convention, the day being universally observed by our unions in that state in fervent prayer that God would send confusion and defeat as the sequel of their machinations. Let me read you their declaration:

"*Resolved*, That the district executive committee be instructed to make a vigorous fight against all such candidates for the General Assembly, no matter what political party they may belong to, who cannot be fully relied upon to vote in favor of personal liberty and an equal protection of ours, with all other legitimate business interests."

They want protection, too! and they know the legislature alone can give it. But we know, as the result of our local Home Protection ordinance, under which women have voted in nearly a dozen widely separated localities of Illinois, and have voted overwhelmingly against license, that our enfranchisement means confusion and defeat to the liquor sellers. Therefore, since for this we have prayed, we must take our places at the front and say, with the greatest reformer of the sixteenth century:

"Here I stand. I can do no other. God help me. Amen!"

Here, then, at the nation's capital, let us declare our allegiance; here let us turn our faces toward the beckoning future; here, where the liquor traffic pours in each year its revenue of gold, stained with the blood of our dearest and best, let us set up our Home Protection standard in the name of the Lord!

But the convention took no action; the sentiment of the society was not yet ripe for the declaration I so earnestly desired.

Of this convention, held in Foundry M. E. Church, the most notable feature was the large attendance from the Southern states, a delegation of thirty or more from a majority of these states, being present, headed by Mrs. Sallie F. Chapin.

At this convention the following resolution was adopted :

"*Resolved*, That wisdom dictates the Do-everything policy ; Constitutional Amendment, where the way is open for it ; 'Home Protection' [i. e., the vote for women on the temperance question only], where Home Protection is the strongest rallying cry ; Equal Franchise, where the votes of women joined to those of men can alone give stability to temperance legislation."

The Plan of Work Committee also recommended :

"A Committee on Franchise whose duty it shall be to furnish advice, instruction and assistance to states that so desire, in inaugurating measures for securing and using woman's ballot in the interest of temperance."

The Southern delegation requested permission not to vote upon these measures, but showed a degree of tolerance not to have been expected of them at their first convention. Besides, Susan B. Anthony was present as a visitor, was introduced on motion of a delegate and publicly kissed by an enthusiastic Quaker lady from the West. All this had alarmed the conservatives, and a few of them withdrew, stating that they could no longer keep us company.

The *New York Tribune*, which had never reported our work, nor shown the least interest in our proceedings except as an antagonist, now came out with displayed headlines announcing that our society had "split in two." The facts were that out of a total of two hundred and eighteen delegates, only twelve to fifteen delegates left us. They made immediate overtures to the Southern women to join them, stating that "then there would be a conservative movement divested of the radicalism that was destroying this one" ; but the Southern ladies said, "they had seceded once, and found it did n't work." Not one of them joined the malcontents, but the latter formed themselves into the "National Woman's Evangelical Temperance Union," which had, perhaps, a dozen auxiliaries, but soon died for lack of members.

At this convention the constitution was so changed that actual membership became the basis of representation instead of, as heretofore, allowing so many delegates to each congressional district, no matter how few its white ribbon women.

New women came to us continually with bright ideas about the work. Personal initiative was at a premium and a new department usually developed from the advent of a woman with a mission, to whom, after a study of her character and reputation, we gave a *com*-mission. We thus conserved enthusiasm and attached experts to our society.

CHAPTER II.

NATIONAL CONVENTIONS.

In August of 1882, a "Home Protection Convention" met in Chicago, to which rallied the "old liners" as well as the new converts. There were present three hundred and forty-one delegates from twenty-two states. A substantial reorganization of the party followed, the name becoming "Prohibition Home Protection Party." Gideon T. Stewart, of Ohio, was made chairman of the national committee, and Rev. Dr. Jutkins, secretary. I there became officially related to a political party as a member of its central committee and have been thus related almost ever since. A new force was added to the Prohibitionists by means of this convention, chiefly drawn from the Crusade movement and consisting of men and women who had dearly loved the Republican party and who retired from it with unaffected sorrow.

In the autumn of this year I renewed the political attack, closing my annual address before our National Woman's Christian Temperance Union Convention in Louisville, Ky., with these words:

Protection must be administered through a mighty executive force and we call that force a party. Happily for us, what was our earnest expectation last year, is our realization to-day. The Prohibition Home Protection Party stands forth as woman's answered prayer. In the great convention of last August at Chicago, where three hundred and forty-one delegates represented twenty-two states, where North and South clasped hands in a union never to be broken, we felt that the brave men who there combined their energy and faith were indeed come unto the kingdom for such a time as this.

"The right is always expedient," and the note of warning which this non-partisan convention may sound in the ears of partisans will serve the cause of constitutional amendment far better than the timid policy of silence. It will help, not hinder, our onward march ; for we must each year fall backward if we do not advance. God's law of growth does not exempt the Woman's Christian Temperance Union. Therefore I call to you once more, sisters beloved, "*Let Us Go Forward!*" As we now proceed with the duties in whose sacred name we are met, let it be said of us as of a gifted Southern statesman, whose biography I have read in the *Courier-Journal*, since coming here: "He never questions the motives of men. He always argues the merits of the case." As the great general said to the boatman, so the temperance cause is saying here to us, "Remember, you carry Cæsar and his fortunes." God grant that we may be so wise and gentle that the cause we love shall not be wounded in the house of its friends.

"We have no time to waste
In critic's sneer or cynic's bark,
Quarrel or reprimand;
'Twill soon be dark;
Then choose thine aim
And may God speed the mark."

But I saw that the convention was reluctant to make this new departure. Profoundly convinced that it ought to do so, I sought my friend, Mrs. L. D. Carhart, then president of Iowa Woman's Christian Temperance Union, and asked her to write a resolution bearing on the subject. She told me afterward that she went alone into an undisturbed corner of the church, lifted up her heart to God in prayer, and wrote the following, which was adopted with practical unanimity:

"*Resolved*, That we rejoice in the day that gives recognition to our prohibition principles by political partisans and we will endeavor to influence the best men in all communities to commit themselves to that party, by whatever name called, that shall give to them the best embodiment of prohibition principles, and will most surely protect our homes."

Nothing is truer than that most people are more afraid of words than of ideas, and as this resolution avoided naming any party, while really pointing one out by its description, the convention passed it with very little difficulty.

At this convention, *Our Union* was consolidated with *The Signal* and removed to Chicago. The Flower Mission, Kitchen Garden and other departments of work were added, and prejudices against the public work of women were broken down as never before among the Southern people. The number of delegates present was one hundred and forty-six, from twenty-seven states. Receipts from state auxiliaries, $4,046. The next year we called

"OUR TEMPERANCE ROUND-UP,"

borrowing the expressive phrase of the Western plains. I was determined that the completion of the first Gospel Temperance Decade should see every state and territory in the nation visited by me and organized if possible. Helped by the railroad men to passes, replenished financially by an appropriation of $300 from the Good Templars of California, and personal gifts from Dr. McDonald of San Francisco, Captain Charles Goodall, of the Oregon Steamship Company, and other wealthy friends (for I had no salary until 1886), I went the rounds accompanied by Anna Gordon. The Pacific Coast friends gave us royal greeting everywhere. We visited thirty-three towns in California, went to Oregon by steamer, and worked in that state and along the wonderful Puget Sound Coast, visiting British Columbia and going by the Snake River to Lewiston, the former capital of Idaho, the only town ever quarantined against us, so far as I remember. The "municipal authorities," learning of our intended visit, declared that on account of the danger resulting from diphtheritic contagion, no public meeting could be held. But we had traveled thirty-six hours by river steamer for the express purpose of meeting the good women at this head of navigation on the Snake River and did not propose to be defeated. Mrs. Judge Buck, our hostess, went out and arranged for a parlor meeting at a friend's house, we adopted a constitution and appointed officers for Idaho, finished up our convention and had an ice-cream reception in the omnibus as we went back to the steamer, and instead of shaking the dust off our feet we waved our handkerchiefs in loving adieu to the band of devoted women who had thus stood by us, as the river bank receded and the swift wheel bore us back from this nook and corner to the broad highways of civilization and philanthropy. Some account of that long trip—covering from twenty-five to thirty thousand miles—is given in the car-window jottings of the "Traveler's" department of this volume.

OUR FIRST DECADE.

At Detroit, in October of 1883, we celebrated our First Decade with rejoicings, every state and territory having that year been visited, and the Woman's Christian Temperance Union set in motion not only as a local, but also as a state and territorial society duly constituted, and with regularly elected officers, not chosen by the National Woman's Christian Temper-

My "Little Organist."

Boston. 1877.

ANNA A. GORDON.

ance Union, but by conventions held for that purpose in each one of the forty-eight subdivisions of the United States—Alaska not included.

In this Detroit convention we had an able and spirited debate on the resolution favoring equal suffrage, which was almost unanimously adopted. The following on political prohibition were also adopted practically without debate:

"*Resolved*, That we lend our influence to that party, by whatever name called, which shall furnish the best embodiment of prohibition principles and will most surely protect our homes.

"*Resolved*, That effort be made to secure in each state and territory, non-partisan prohibition conventions of men and women before the party nominating conventions of 1884 are held. At such conventions, efforts shall be made to unite electors in declaration that they will vote with no party that has not prohibition in its platform. These conventions shall adjourn to meet after the last nominating convention has been held."

This was intended to educate and urge men to the duty of forcing the prohibition issue upon the old parties if possible, and if unsuccessful in that, to put upon the same men such compulsion of reason and conscience as would drive them into the party that did make prohibition its issue—primary and supreme.

A memorial to the presidential nominating conventions was adopted, asking for a plank in their platforms in favor of submitting the question of national prohibition to the people, and it was made my duty to present the same. Another memorial asking the ballot for women was ordered to be presented to the National Congress.

The "World's Woman's Christian Temperance Union" was projected and the general officers of the National Woman's Christian Temperance Union were made a standing committee of correspondence and organization for that movement. Five fraternal delegates were present from Canada, headed by Mrs. Letitia Youmans, president of Dominion Woman's Christian Temperance Union. Total delegates present, two hundred and forty-two, from twenty-eight states and territories. Total receipts $5,045, balance in treasury, $919. No salaries were paid up to this date, save $1,000 a year to our corresponding secretary.

The following extracts from my annual address at Detroit, show the thought and purpose of that time:

"We are wiser than we were; our intellects ought to be all aflame with clear and penetrating thought. We are more loving-hearted than we were; our sympathies ought to move with more compassionate enthusiasm to the rescue where the onslaught is most fierce and the crisis most inevitable. We have a steadiness of purpose that comes of faith in God, and our wills ought to fly with resistless sweep to the execution of both thought and sympathy in glowing deeds.

Revolutions never move backward. Pillar of cloud, pillar of fire, where dost thou lead? This question has burned in my heart as I read the news of our defeat in Illinois and Michigan; our victory in the states that having eyes, have also seen—the Buckeye and the Hawkeye! Sisters, we must send the plea of "Home, Sweet Home," into the national conventions of the Republican and Democratic parties, when, six months hence, they meet to select candidates for the Presidency of these United States. Thank God, the nation has one senator who declares his purpose to insist on a prohibitory constitutional amendment plank in the platform of his party. You know his name: Henry W. Blair, of the Old Granite State. Let us give emphasis to his demand by rolling in such petitions in its support as never before bombarded a political assembly! Let us redeem the pledge made to the senator when he addressed our Washington convention, by intrenching him behind such towers and bastions of petition as will give decisive courage to the good, and bring confusion to the counsels of the base. All honor to the gallant Republicans of Iowa! Every true woman's heart blesses them with their rallying cry of "Home, Sweet Home." But there is not an organ of their party outside that state which has not pierced them like a javelin, nor a leader in its counsels who has not jeered them as the Don Quixote of the party camp. In Ohio the Republican candidate for Governor planted himself squarely on a license platform; the leading organs exhausted contempt and sarcasm upon our cause before the election, and bitterest curses since, while it seems not unlikely that their carelessness or complicity, or both, have combined with Democratic treachery to render doubtful or futile the most sacred "counts" known to the annals of this country, of votes "for God and Home and Native Land." But if the party that in 1872 at the dictation of the Germans passed the "Herman Raster Resolution," intended as a stab at prohibitory legislation; if the party that now champions license and deludes the unwary with the prefix "high," turns a deaf ear to our prayer; and if the party of Judge Hoadley remains true to its alliance with the rum-power, as undoubtedly it will, and our petitions are once more trampled under foot of men, I ask what then would be the duty of the hour? O friends, God hath not left Himself without a witness. There is still a party in the land to be helped onward to success by women. There is one now despised for the single reason that it lacks majorities and commands no high positions as the rewards of skillful leadership or wily caucusing, but which declares as its cardinal doctrine, that a government is impotent indeed which cannot protect the lowliest home within its borders from the aggressions of the vilest saloon that would destroy that home. It declares all other issues trifling when compared with this, and insists that the "home guards" shall be armed with the ballot as a Home Protection weapon. Here, then, let us invest our loyalty, our faith and works, our songs and prayers. To-day that party is Endymion, the unknown youth, but the friendship of Diana, the clear-eyed queen of heaven, shall make for it friends, everywhere, until it becomes regnant, and the two reign side by side. The Woman's Christian Temperance Union was never weak, but it is a giant now. The Pacific Coast, the New Northwest, the South are all with us to-day. But yesterday, Mary A. Livermore, of Massachusetts, sent to Sallie F. Chapin, of South Carolina, our forces being in convention assembled in both states, this telegraphic message: "If your heart is as our heart, give us thy hand." Back came this message from our gifted Southern leader: "For God and Home and Native Land, we'll give you both our heart and hand." The Woman's Christian Temperance Union, headed by a Woodbridge, an Aldrich, a Lathrap, West and Stevens, with the flush and prestige of success, can not go forth in vain. Auxiliaries are in every important town of all the nation, sometimes ambushed, it is true, little thought of by the great public, but ready to execute with promptness all military orders wisely planned and gently given. Our work grows most rapidly where the need is most imminent. Witness Ohio, with five hundred unions this year, out-leaping by half, its previous record, and forcing the issue of prohibition with a persistence like that of gravitation, and a faith high as the hope of a saint, and deep as the depth of a drunkard's despair. Look at Iowa, where Judith Ellen Foster started five years ago with a petition of which few took note, but which, like the genii of Arabian story, "expanded its pinions in nebulous bars" until the Woman's Christian Temperance Union has "Moulded a mighty state's decree, and shaped the whisper of the throne" from which a sovereign people declares its sovereign will. Look at Georgia and Florida, where the petitions of our women last winter resulted in the advance step of local option; and Arkansas, where their efforts secured the banishment of saloons from seventy-five counties by the united signatures of men and women. Look at Vermont, New Hampshire and Michigan, where we have already won the battle for compulsory scientific instruction in the principles of temperance, and tell us, has not God chosen the Crusade Army to be His warriors, indeed? Let no man say, "But you have not the ballot yet, and must not expect recognition from a party." Be it well understood, we do not come as empty-handed suppliants, but as victorious allies. Our soldiers are not raw recruits, but veterans, wearing well-won laurels. We have no more to gain than God has given us to bestow. Let not the lessons of history be disregarded. Of old the world had its Semiramis and Dido, its Zenobia and Boadicea, nay, better still, its Miriam and Deborah. Later on, Russia had her Catherine, and England her Elizabeth. But in my thoughts I always liken the Woman's Christian Temperance Union to the Joan of Arc, whom God raised up for France, and who, in spite of their muscle and their military prowess, beat the English and crowned her king! But evermore she heard and heeded heavenly voices, and God grant that we may hear and heed them evermore! To the martyrdom of public rebuke and criticism they will surely lead us, a sacrifice not easy for gentle hearts to bear; doubtless, also, with some of us, to the actual martyrdom by which a national history becomes heroic, but following where those voices lead, we shall steadily pass onward from the depths of this world's pain to the heights of eternity's peace, and, best of all, we shall help to lift Humanity, so weak and so bewildered, nearer to the law, the life, the freedom of God in Christ our Lord."

A strong controversy arose about the form of our Memorial to the national political conventions. The word used was "Memorial" and I supposed the description of my plan as given in the foregoing address was unmistakable. I had said that we would intrench Senator Blair in the Republican convention, behind "towers and bastions of petition" sufficient to "give decisive courage to the good and bring confusion to the counsels of the base;" that we would roll in such petitions as had never before bombarded a political assembly, in support of a Prohibition plank, and would "redeem the pledge made to the Senator when he addressed our Washington convention in 1881." A reference to the record of that convention shows that we then and there promised one million names for an amendment to the Constitution of the United States, prohibiting the manufacture and sale of all alcoholic liquors, fermented and distilled.

Because the passages in my address where I argued this petition were more earnestly applauded than any others: because in tabulating my recommendations I had called it a "Memorial," the terms "Petition" and "Memorial" being interchangeable; because nothing to the contrary was said when the exact wording of my recommendation was adopted by the convention, I claimed that a general circulation of the Memorial should be had in every hamlet and city of the nation, hoping thus to bring upon the Republican Convention such a pressure that the Prohibition plank would be adopted.

And now arose Mrs. J. Ellen Foster, of Iowa, until this time my warm and earnest coadjutor in every measure that had come before our conventions, in so much that we two were called "the wheel-horses of the W. C. T. U. wagon," but who (the Convention being adjourned and Executive Committee scattered) insisted that this was to be a Memorial in the sense of a document signed only by the officers of the National Woman's Christian Temperance Union. In this greatest surprise and disappointment of my life as a temperance worker, I turned to the women of Illinois, meeting with them in Bloomington at their mid-year Executive Committee. They had invited Mrs. Foster to be present and, weary as they were of the petition work in which they had largely lost faith, influenced by the urgent entreaties of Mrs. Elizabeth G. Hibben, then a devoted Republican, and impressed by Mrs. Foster's eloquent presentation of her views, they begged me not to insist upon a popular petition, but to be content with a simple memorial in the sense of that word upon which Mrs. Foster insisted, viz., a request officially signed by the state and national officers.

Twice in my life I have been moved to bitter tears, by the contradictions of my public environment. Once, when I left the Woman's College at Evanston, and now in the Illinois Executive Committee. I had believed with my inmost heart in that great popularly-signed Memorial, as an object-lesson that should condense and crystallize the thought and purpose of American manhood for the protection of the home by Prohibition ballots. I solemnly believed that the heart of the convention was with me in this understanding, and that faithful hands were ready to carry out the work on a scale commensurate with the greatness of the crisis and the sacredness of the interests involved. But after strong crying and tears on the part of many of us who bowed together in prayer, seeking for guidance, I promised that I would commend to the general officers (all of whom understood the convention to mean what I did), an official rather than a popular Memorial. But they did not agree to this and the Executive Committee was convened at Indianapolis — for the first and only time in our history, thus far—to decide the weighty question. Only seven out of forty-eight members answered the call, distance and expense being the chief explanation of their failure to appear. These declared their belief that my understanding was the correct one, but we all desired the opinion of the entire committee, and so sent out the question by letter, to which, almost without dissent, the answer came that a petition numerously signed was what they understood the convention to mean in its use of the word, "Memorial."

But the time was now far spent for securing a million names or anything approaching that number and only an official Memorial could be prepared. I have always thought that this decision hindered the growth of our party, believing that a national canvass with the petition as an educating force, would have enlisted an army of men in the old parties whose decision, when these parties denied their prayer, would have been like that of Governor St. John, to "come out from among them and be separate."

While the Woman's Christian Temperance Union had this unprofitable difficulty on hand, during the winter of 1884, the Prohibition Home Protection party had another. Our honored friends, the "old liners," who had stood sponsors for the party at its birth, had three points of disagreement with the new-comers: Our favorite name of "Home Protection" was distasteful to them because an innovation, and the purpose we had to hold the national convention in Chicago was distasteful also; they wanted it held in the East; besides all this, they thought we should not wait for the old parties, but hold our convention earliest of all. Hon. Gideon T. Stewart, of Norwalk, Ohio, chairman of the Central Committee, was strenuous on all these points, and was, perhaps, the most influential man in the party at that time. Although the "new-comers" were confident of a majority and clearly had one in the Central Committee, we felt the vital importance of unity in these decisions as to time and place. A commission was now given me by my associates on the committee, of which I have always felt proud; they sent me to Norwalk to see Mr. Stewart. He received Miss Gordon and me with the utmost cordiality, coming with his daughter to meet us at the early morning train, and introducing us to his pleasant home where his wife had prepared for us. A man of college education and a lawyer of prominence, Mr. Stewart had felt the "slings and arrows of outrageous fortune" because of his political Prohibition sentiments and deeds. His fellow townsmen had even condescended so far as to change the name of a street named in his honor, and to make him unmistakably aware of their social as well as their political hostility. After a friendly talk we agreed to disagree in this way; Mr. Stewart conceded the time and I the place. Pittsburgh was the choice of the "old liners," and this Chicago granted, while, in deference to our cal-low wish to "give the Republicans one more chance," the convention was to follow theirs. It now became my duty to wend my solitary way, after the manner of G. P. R. James's strategic horseman, to the four national conventions. Never having seen a political convention of any sort, I was quite shy and sat in a box at the Indianapolis Opera House with Mrs. Zerelda Wallace beside me, while Rev. Dr. Gilbert Delamater presented to the Greenback Convention our White Ribbon Memorial in a fine speech, received with hand-clappings by the good men and women delegates there gathered. But when it came back from the committee to which, without debate, it was referred, it had suffered a sea-change into nothing rich, nor, alas, strange. The temperance plank was suspiciously succinct, and stated that a constitutional amendment relative to the liquor traffic ought to be submitted; but how near a relative — whether a third cousin or a mother-in-law, was not indicated. This was not specially encouraging, and like poor Joe in Dickens' story, I heard a voice saying to me, "Move on!" In the great Exposition Building of Chicago the "Party of Moral Ideas" had gathered up its leaders. Although I had been working with the Prohibition party, my final farewell was not yet said to the Republican. I had yet fond and foolish hopes that it might take advanced ground, though the difficulties seemed insuperable and I believed that it and every other party should be obliged to go on record for or against the grandest living issue: Home or Saloon Protection, which shall it be?

Having been often urged to do so I will here write out some account of my visit to the Committee on Resolutions of the Republican National Convention in 1884. Commissioned by the National Woman's Christian Temperance Union, I took the memorial of our society to the Exposition Building and placed it in the hands of Hon. Mr. Donan, chairman of the Iowa delegation, who presented it in due form and it was referred without debate to the Committee on Resolutions. Senator Blair of New Hampshire then set at work to secure the opportunity for a brief hearing before that committee. Similar demands from other societies, reformers, etc., were many and urgent; I think it was not until the day before the resolutions were presented that we obtained an audience.

My impression is that this took place during the noon recess.

Word was sent me at Woman's Christian Temperance Union Headquarters that the Senator had been successful, and I asked Mrs. Mary B. Willard, editor of our organ, *The Union Signal*, and Miss Helen L. Hood, corresponding secretary of Illinois Woman's Christian Temperance Union, to go with me. We were escorted to the committee room at the appointed time and found but few of the members present—they being in an adjoining room, the door of which was, I think, open. I know that tobacco smoke was most uncomfortably noticeable throughout our stay, though I do not think that any member smoked in our presence, but the room was thoroughly distasteful, almost sickening to us, by reason of the sight of the many much-used spittoons and the sight and smell of the blue cloud of smoke.

We three women sat in one corner on a sofa, feeling very much like mariners stranded on a lee shore. There was no greeting for us or notice taken of our presence by any one so far as I remember. We were not asked what votes we could deliver or questioned in any way whatever. Senator Blair gathered in as many as he could of the committee and asked for a hearing. He then began to speak of our mission and after a few minutes was called to order and a motion made that the length of time to be granted be now fixed. The Senator asked that we might have half an hour but was greeted by a vigorous "no" from several throats. Some one, I never knew who, then moved that fifteen minutes be the limit, and this carried, though there were several sharp negatives. I then rose, took out my watch, made my speech in thirteen minutes and we at once withdrew. As we did so, several, perhaps half a dozen, members of the committee came forward and shook hands with us, some expressing their sympathy and hope that favorable action might be taken.

My speech read thus:

GENTLEMEN—The temperance women of America have never before asked for one moment of your time. Thousands of them have worked and prayed for your success in the heroic days gone by, but up to this hour they have laid no tax on the attention of the people's representatives in presidential convention assembled. Though the position is a new one, I can not count myself other than at home in your presence, gentlemen, as you represent that great party which, on the prairies of Wisconsin, my honored father helped to build, and whose early motto roused my girlish enthusiasm, "Free soil, free speech, free labor, and free men." But I rejoice to-day in the sisterhood of the women's party—the Woman's Christian Temperance

Union—where I may march side by side with that brilliant Southern leader, Sallie F. Chapin, of South Carolina, who, in our new anti-slavery war, the fight for a free brain, is my beloved coadjutor.

I am here in no individual character, but as a delegated representative of the Woman's Christian Temperance Union of forty-eight states and territories, including the District of Columbia, to present to you the memorial of the American home against the American saloon. You will notice that we make no note of foreign drinking customs, but speak and work directly against an institution which derives its authority directly from our own government. Our society is the lineal descendant of that whirlwind of the Lord known as the "Woman's Temperance Crusade," of 1874, and stands not only for total abstinence and prohibition, but for no sectarianism in religion, no sectionalism in politics, no sex in citizenship. We recognize state rights as to the adoption of these principles, but move forward in one grand, solid phalanx—a society as well known in Florida as it is in Oregon, by the results of the last ten years' work; a society that has an open hand for Catholic and Protestant, for the foreign as well as the native born.

We know that in America the great clanging mill of government, kept in motion at enormous cost, turns out just one product, and that is protection for life and limb and property. But it seems to us women that the citadel of purity, the palladium of liberty, the home, our brothers have forgotten adequately to protect. Therefore I am here to-day to speak on behalf of millions of women, good and true, but grieved and sorrowful; to ask that the guarantees and safeguards of law shall be stripped from the saloons of my country; that their tarnished gold shall no more pollute our treasury, and that the land we love may at once and forever go out of partnership with the liquor traffic.

Gentlemen, some political party will respond to this plea from the hearts of women asking for protection from a stimulant which nerves with dangerous strength the manly arm that God meant to be woman's shelter and protection, so that man's cruelty becomes greatest toward those he loves the best. Some party will declare that when our best beloved go forth into life's battle they shall not have to take chances so unequal in the fight for a clear brain, nor run the gauntlet of saloons legalized and set along our streets. Some party will lay to heart this object-lesson of the "Nation's Annual Drink Bill," shown in the chart I have had placed before your eyes to-day, with its nine hundred millions for intoxicating liquors, to five millions and a half for the spread of Christ's gospel.

The Greenback convention has already received with favor this memorial. Senator Donan, our gallant Iowa champion, has secured its reading in your own great convention and its reference to your committee. To-morrow you will act upon it. On July 8 it will be presented to the Democratic convention in this city, and on July 23 to that of the Prohibition Home Protection party, in Pittsburgh, Pa.

A great chief of your party, who was with us as the hero of your last convention, said that not in the turmoil of politics, but at the sacred fireside hearth, does God prepare the verdict of a great, free people. Let me say, gentlemen, that the party that declares for national prohibition in 1884 will be the one for which the temperance women of this land will pray and work, circulate literature, convene assemblies, and do all in our power to secure its success. Nor is the influence of these women to be forgotten or lightly esteemed, as the past has sufficiently proved. While I have tried to speak, my spirit has been sustained and soothed by the presence of that devoted army which I am here to represent. As womanly, as considerate, as gentle as the women of the Woman's Christian Temperance Union, from Alabama to Wyoming, would wish me to be in this presence, I have tried to be—that I might justly represent them—good-natured as sunshine, steadfast as gravitation, persistent as a Christian's faith. I have no harsh word to speak of any. The liquor traffic is the awful heritage of a less wise, less kind, and less enlightened past. For its existence in this gentler age we are all more or less responsible.

Let us combine to put it away, "with malice toward none, with charity for all." Daughters of heroes and sisters of patriots are those for whose dear sake I have dared to speak to-day. De Tocqueville said: "Life is neither a pleasure nor a pain; it is a serious business, to be entered on with courage, and in a spirit of self-sacrifice." Gentlemen, in that spirit I have tried to speak,—not because I wished to be heard, but to represent, as best I could, the homes of America in their sacred warfare against the American saloon. May God lead and guide us all into lives and deeds of tenderest charity and divinest toil for the sorrowful and weak.

Some of us have sung the Miriam song of this great party in other days, and whether or not we shall, erelong, chant its requiem, depends upon whether or not the party shall be as true to living issues of the present as it was true to living issues in the past. For

"New occasions teach new duties,
Time makes ancient good uncouth;
They must upward still, and onward,
Who would keep abreast of truth."

We ask you to declare in favor of submitting to the people a national constitutional amendment for the prohibition of the liquor traffic.

Gentlemen, on behalf of the National Woman's Christian Temperance Union, I thank you for this courteous hearing.

I ought to say that while I spoke, those present listened respectfully, so far as I observed. Indeed, I took no special exceptions to their conduct, which was, no doubt, from their point of view, altogether courteous. They were nearly through with their report, the convention was impatiently waiting, they had not the remotest intention of doing anything for the temperance people, and, weary and annoyed as they were, I think they did all in the way of politeness that we could expect from them. A different standard would most assuredly be applied by us to the Prohibition party, as to its manner of receiving ladies, for ladies themselves are members of and leaders in that party. This being so, there is, of course, no smoking in the committee rooms of Prohibitionists. The gentlemen of the Republican committee belonged to the old régime—they were, as Mrs. Hannah Whitall Smith so often and so charitably says of people, "in their conditions," and, being in them, they did the best they could. Whether or not they received the Brewers' Committee, and what length of time was accorded its members, if received, I do not authentically know. It is said that those men had an hour—I cannot say, and do not wish to do any one injustice, least of all my political opponents. Going upon the platform of the convention, thanks to a ticket from Senator Blair, I listened earnestly while Chairman McKinley, in his grand voice, read the resolutions. As he went on I said to myself, "Of course, ours will be near the close, if there at all," but when he had finished and there was not a word for temperance, I said to myself:

"'Tis sweet to be remembered,
'Tis sad to be forgot."

When the report was accepted without debate and without a single negative (although the Iowa delegates, the Maine and Kansas delegates, were out in full force), I said to myself, "Streams cannot rise higher than their fountains; men in the states cannot rise superior to their party nationally, and this Republican party, once so dear to me, I must now leave because here is the proof that even good men dare not stand by prohibition when they meet upon a national platform."

So then and there I bade the "Grand Old Party" an everlasting farewell and took up my line of march toward the Grand Army of Reform. By this I mean, that while I had already acted with the Prohibition party for a brief period, I had never until now utterly given up the hope that the Republican party might so retrieve itself that we could stand together for God and Home and Native Land.

The document that I presented to the four conventions read as follows:

THE MEMORIAL OF THE AMERICAN HOME FOR PROTECTION FROM THE AMERICAN SALOON.

To the National Convention of the...... Party:

We, members of the Woman's Christian Temperance Union of the United States (and of its forty-eight state and territorial Woman's Christian

Temperance Unions, with that of the District of Columbia), herein represented by the signatures of our officers, believe that, while the poison habits of the nation can be largely restrained by an appeal to the intellect through argument, to the heart through sympathy, and to the conscience through the motives of religion, the traffic in those poisons will be best controlled by prohibitory law.

We believe the teachings of science, experience and the Golden Rule, combine to testify against the traffic in alcoholic liquors as a drink, and that the homes of America, which are the citadels of patriotism, purity and happiness, have no enemy so relentless as the American saloon.

Therefore, as citizens of the United States, irrespective of sect or section, but having deeply at heart the protection of our homes, we do hereby respectfully and earnestly petition you to advocate and to adopt such measures as are requisite to the end that prohibition of the importation, exportation, manufacture and sale of alcoholic beverages may become an integral part of the national Constitution, and that your party candidate shall be by character and public pledge committed to a national constitutional prohibitory amendment.

After two such failures I had little heart to approach the Democrats, but in loyalty to my appointment I had this to do. The great Exposition Building was packed once more with delegates whose drink bill at the Palmer House was no larger than that of the Republicans had been—in both cases it was immense. Major Burke, of the New Orleans *Times-Democrat*, presented the Memorial which was referred without debate to the Committee on Platform; they reported against "sumptuary laws that vex the citizen." Meanwhile one more national party remained unvisited, and to that I went with the rejected Memorial, purposing in my heart henceforth to cast in my lot just there.

THE PITTSBURGH CONVENTION.

It was a gathering never to be forgotten! In old "Lafayette Hall," cradle of the Republican party, where in 1852 John P. Hale and George W. Julian were nominated for president and vice-president, were gathered on the morning of July 23, 1884, over six hundred delegates representing twenty-eight states. Women were there in goodly numbers, almost wholly from the Woman's Christian Temperance Union, which, in common with other temperance societies, had been invited to send delegates. It was a crowd not only of "real folks" but of "our folks"—the non-drinking, non-tobacco-using home-people, almost without exception members of the church. Careful hands had bedecked the old hall with mottoes and flags, pictures and banners, all symbolic of "Down with the saloon and up with the home." Mary A. Woodbridge, of Ohio, was chosen one of the secretaries, and women were on every committee. After an admirable address by Chairman Stewart I asked for three minutes in which to present the Memorial of the National Woman's Christian Temperance Union, which was adopted with cheers, and a general uprising.

The following droll resolution, offered by John Lloyd Thomas, of Maryland, shows the paternal interest manifested in us by leaders of the party which in its heroic days had waked the echoes of this same hall:

"*Resolved*, That the convention of the Prohibition party recognizes with due humility the anxious care for the welfare of our party displayed by the representatives of the national government, who in the persons of W. W. Dudley, Commissioner of Pensions, and Hon. Hiram Price, Commissioner of Indian Affairs, have violated civil service rules and used public time to come to Pittsburgh and to urge advice upon members of the convention, but,

"*Resolved*, that we timidly advance the claim that the intelligence of this assembly is ample to provide for its own security."

Here I met for the first time Prof. Samuel Dickie, now chairman of the Prohibition National Committee. Mrs. Mary T. Lathrap came to me, saying: "We have a man in our state who cannot be excelled as a presiding officer, Professor Dickie, the astronomer of Albion college." I knew he was what "the common people" call "a square man," square head and shoulders, strong Scotch face, and good Scotch blood. We women worked for him—he was elected chairman. I do not say we did it, for I do not know.

A pleasant surprise came to me when the Kansas delegation asked me to represent its members in seconding the nomination of Governor St. John for the Presidency. The stenographer thus reports my words:

Mr. Chairman, Brothers and Sisters in America's Great Battle for a clear brain:

The thing that has been shall be. History repeats itself. Thirty-three years ago, only eight years before the nomination of Abraham Lincoln under the increased impetus of the same movement, John P. Hale and Geo. W. Julian were chosen in this hall.

During their campaign a little girl, a farmer's daughter on the prairies of Wisconsin, sat up until unprecedentedly late at night to "hear the news from the Free-soil meeting" which her mother and brother had gone miles to attend because Hale and Julian were to speak, and she will never forget the eagerness with which she listened to that recital. But how little did she dream that in the interval between those days and these the world would grow so tolerant; old prejudices would roll away like clouds below the horizon, and women come forth into public work like singing birds after a thunder-storm! Least of all could she have imagined that a royal, free state like Kansas, by unanimous invitation of its delegation in the second great "Free-soil" gathering of Lafayette Hall, would accord to her the honor of seconding the nomination of Kansas' greatest leader. But so it was to be!

The heroes of America have been from the first, and will be to the last, men of the people. The name of John P. St. John, of Kansas, has already passed into history. His is the rare and radiant fame that comes of being enshrined, while yet alive, in that most majestic of Pantheons, the people's heart. Our action here to-day will neither lift nor lower his position, for he is "Fortune's now and Fame's; one of the few, the immortal names that were not born to die." His history, half heroic, half pathetic, has always deeply touched my heart, and I rejoice to rehearse it briefly here to-day.

Brother and sister delegates, picture to yourselves a lonesome little fellow in the wilderness of Indiana fifty years ago, trying, single-handed, to make his way in the world.

"Blessings on thee, little man,
Barefoot boy, with cheek of tan."

Picture an adventurous youth as, with but a dollar in his pocket, he crossed the "Big Muddy," bound for Pike's Peak, and, driving an ox-team over the Rockies, "footed it" to California. See him next delving in the mines by day and studying law by the camp-fire at evening. For

"The heights by great men reached and kept,
Were not attained by sudden flight,
But they, while their companions slept,
Were toiling upward in the night."

See him at the outbreak of the Civil war, waiting for no draft, hiring no substitute, but baring his own breast to foemen who, thank God, to-day are friends! See him next in the senate of Kansas, then twice elected governor, keeping always near the people and trusting them in spite of a thousand warnings from political leaders. I saw him first at Bismarck Grove, Kansas, in presence of a great concourse, when the campaign for constitutional amendment was at its height. As he came forward, every man's hat and every woman's handkerchief waved high in air, and while the loud hurrahs resounded, I saw tears on many a gentle face of mother, sister, wife, because they knew he was defender of their endangered homes.

They told me in Topeka, where he had lived for years, that he was always in his place at church and prayer-meeting, no matter how official duties pressed upon him. They told me how he went to Leavenworth when letters threatening his life warned him to stay away, and being met *en route* by a temperance delegation whose anxiety was so great they had come to protect him, he showed them the letters of which, until that moment, no one had been aware, saying: "Our cause must have its martyrs as well as heroes, and I might as well be ready."

It seems to me the world must have in every age the object-lesson of new lives dedicated to all that most exalts humanity, and here we have this one which God has set up high where all may read.

I never heard John P. St. John traduced, save by the myrmidons of the saloon. The party that now reviles would have adored him had he been even a little less loyal to our cause. The Senate's open door would have been just before him if indeed he had not entered it already. But now, forsooth, he is "an office seeker" when he holds on high the standard for us who can give him nothing but our gratitude; when he lays his lofty fame a sacrifice upon the altar of our holy cause!

I yield to none in admiration of these glorious veterans, John Russell, James Black, and Gideon T. Stewart. History will place their names beside those of Phillips and Garrison upon her roll of honor; they were the adventurous pioneers who struck out into a forest of prejudice and "blazed the trees." But to make our way across the Sierras of difficulty that still separate us from the Eldorado of success, we want a "Pathfinder," and we believe St. John to be the "Frémont" of our battles.

For Dr. R. H. McDonald I have the highest esteem, his lofty character and generous help command my admiration and my gratitude; but as between two noble men we must choose the one who, as a sun-glass, will focus the most votes, and I believe Governor St. John to be that man.

Dear women of the white ribbon, here assembled, you know that from all this land went up the voice of supplication when the call for prayer was made just before the first of these party conventions, in May last! We prayed that America might have a plank in some platform declaring for national prohibition for the sake of home protection, and a candidate whose character and personal habits mothers might safely commend to their sons. In Governor St. John we have an answer to that prayer. When I think of what he is to the temperance people of the nation, I know that in ten thousand homes these words of England's laureate will strike responsive chords:

"As some divinely gifted man,
Whose life in low estate began
And on a simple village green;

"Who breaks his birth's invidious bar,
And grasps the skirts of happy chance,
And breasts the blows of circumstance,
And grapples with his evil star;

"Who makes by force his merit known,
And lives to clutch the golden keys,
To mould a mighty state's decrees
And shape the whisper of the throne;

"And moving on from high to higher,
Becomes on Fortune's crowning slope
The pillar of a people's hope,
The center of a world's desire."

On behalf of the Kansas delegation, I second the nomination of John P. St. John, of Kansas.

When it was announced that all the votes of the convention had been cast for Governor St. John, the tumult was tremendous, and as we all stood up and sang,

"Mine eyes have seen the glory
Of the coming of the Lord,"

there were tears on many a cheek.

I was a member of the Committee on Resolutions, and especially interested in the one on equal suffrage. It read as follows, and was mainly written by James Black, of Pennsylvania, the Prohibition party's first candidate for president; my own part I will print in italics:

Resolved, That the activity and coöperation of the women of America for the promotion of temperance has, in all the history of the past, been a strength and encouragement which we gratefully acknowledge and record. In the later and present phase of the movement for the prohibition of the traffic, the purity of purpose and method, the earnestness, zeal, intelligence and devotion of the mothers and daughters of the Woman's Christian Temperance Union have been eminently blessed of God. Kansas and Iowa have been given them as "sheaves" of rejoicing, and the education and the arousing of the public mind, and the now prevailing demand for the Constitutional Amendment are largely the fruit of their prayers and labors. Sharing in the efforts that shall bring the question of the abolition of this traffic to the polls, they shall join in the grand "Praise God from whom all blessings flow," when by law victory shall be achieved.

Resolved, That believing in the civil and political equality of the sexes, and that the ballot in the hands of woman is her right for protection, *and would prove a powerful ally for the abolition of the liquor traffic, the execution of law, the promotion of reform in civil affairs, and the removal of corruption in public life, we enunciate the principle, and relegate the practical outworking of this reform to the discretion of the Prohibition party in the several states, according to the condition of public sentiment in those states.*

I had been so much in the South that its delegates confided to me their earnest hope that we would "draw it mild," but I felt that they would hardly disown their traditional doctrine of state rights as here expressed. They did not, nor do I believe that, as a class, they will antagonize those of us who are committed to the equal suffrage plank in the Prohibition platform.

There was some debate, lively and courteous, but the resolution was adopted with but little dissent. Not so the party name. Rev. Dr. Miner, of Boston, a chief among the old liners, moved that the old name "Prohibition" be restored. "Our side" amended with the proposition to retain the name given two years before at Chicago, viz., "Prohibition Home Protection Party,"—ten syllables! and on this rock we foundered. It was not in human nature to put up with a decahedron name, and one parted in the middle at that! If we had moved to substitute "Home Protection," we should have done much better. I remember uttering a few sentences in favor of retaining the long name, but the old liners were too strong for us, and almost without debate, the change was agreed to. This action scored another of those huge disappointments through which one learns "to endure hardness as a good soldier." Away back in 1876, I think it was, when our great and good Mrs. Yeomans, of Canada, spoke at Old Orchard Beach, my ear first caught the winsome and significant phrase "Home Protection." My impression is that she did not coin, but adapted it from the tariff vocabulary of the Dominion. Listening to her there in the great grove of pines, with blue sky overhead and flashing sea waves near, it flashed on me, "Why not call this gospel temperance work the 'Home Protection Movement,' for that's just what it is, and these words furnish the text for our best argument and go convincingly along with our motto: 'For God and Home and Native Land?'" The more I thought about all this, the more it grew on me, and in 1877, when invited by Henry C. Bowen, of the New York *Independent*, to speak at his famous "Fourth of July Celebration," I chose "Home Protection" for my theme and brought out from the *Independent* office my "Home Protection Manual," which I distributed among our white ribbon women throughout the nation. We called our petitions, "Home Protection," our great Illinois campaign in 1879 went by that name, and when I was converted, heart and soul, to the Prohibition party, I believed, as I do still, that its strength would be immeasurably increased by adopting Home Protection as its name. But the old name was endeared to those who had suffered for it, and

26

they were not disposed to give it up. In this I then, and always, believed them to be unwise.

Directly after the convention I went, by the earnest request of Mr. Daniels, vice-presidential nominee of the Prohibition party, to speak at a ratification meeting in Cumberland, Md. I dreaded the encounter, for, except at our temperance conventions, I had but once in my life, so far as I can recall, spoken on politics.* To meet the "world's people" in the opening of a fierce campaign was painful to me, and I did it only as a token of loyalty to our new candidate. This town among the hills is fore-ordained to be provincial, by reason of its physical geography. Its pretty little opera house was well filled that night; but the air felt cold as winter to my spirit, though July's heat was really there. Curiously enough did its well-dressed women look on me, standing forlorn before the footlights, on a bare stage, and sighing for the heart-warmth of a Woman's Christian Temperance Union meeting, where women would have crowded around me, flowers sent forth their perfume, and hymns and prayers made all of us at home. I spoke, no doubt, forlornly; anyhow, I felt forlorn. The gainsaying political papers said next day, that I was poor enough, and our candidate even poorer than I! Major Hilton, of Washington, D. C., was with us, and I think if there were honors that evening, he bore them away.

Meanwhile, we had heard that our noble martyr of the Prohibition army had accepted the sacrifice, not without intense reluctance and most bitter heartache, and our campaign began. I say "ours," because the white ribbon women were so thoroughly enlisted in it. By going as delegates to its convention, many of our leaders "lent their influence," and our five "general officers," Mesdames Buell, Woodbridge, Stevens, and Miss Pugh, with myself, issued a card expressing our hearty sympathy, and our belief that, since the Prohibition party, of all the four then in the field, had indorsed our memorial, we were bound to take its part. At the annual meetings of that battle autumn, nearly all our state unions did this in one form or another, Iowa and Pennsylvania being then, as now, on the opposing side.

*The single exception occurred in Canandaigua, N. Y., September, 1875, when, having spoken by invitation before the Conference Temperance Society of the M. E. Church, I also briefly addressed the first Prohibition party audience I had ever seen, by invitation of Rev. Mr. Bissell; but I did not speak as an adherent.

CHAPTER III.

THE ST. LOUIS CONVENTION.

When our National Woman's Christian Temperance Union Convention met in St. Louis, just before the swift arbitrament of the memorable election day that changed the national administration, the air was full of thunderbolts. For the first time, there was much ado to get a church. The Central Methodist agreed, and then disagreed to our assembling there. "Will you promise not to mention politics?" was the question. "Nay; but we will promise that the politics believed in by us shall most assuredly be mentioned," was the reply. "We can give up the high-toned churches, but not our high-toned ideas; we will meet in a tent in a public square, if need be, but we will never smother a single sentence that we wish to speak."

Our St. Louis women were brave and staunch, but not a little tried and tossed in the seething counter-currents of the time. Where to put either delegates or convention they hardly knew. But all their difficulties dispersed in due season. Good church-people of liberal spirit opened their houses; Rev. John A. Wilson, a generous-hearted pastor of the United Presbyterian denomination, secured for us the use of his church, saying, "I traveled with your national president some years ago in Egypt and the Holy Land, and I don't believe she will permit anything very bad"—albeit he was an ardent Blaine man and I fear he repented his bargain before we were through.

In my annual address I used as a theme Mrs. Lathrap's new and suggestive phrase, and spoke on

"GOSPEL POLITICS."

DEAR SISTERS—By the laws of spiritual dynamics this has been one of our best, perhaps because one of our most progressive, years. Stationary pools and people tend toward stagnation. The most senseless of proverbs is that about the rolling stone that gathers no moss. What does it want of moss when it can get momentum?

In the arena of National Prohibition we shall fight our hardest battles and win our most substantial victories. Nothing will alarm and anger our opponents like our effort in this field, because no effort less direct aims a blow so decisive at the very vitals of their trade.

Senator Blair, of New Hampshire, has made a more careful study of national prohibition, and with better opportunity to learn, than any other student of this subject in the nation, and he thus sums up his opinion: "For more than half a century, the working life of more than two generations, gigantic efforts have been put forth by noble men and women, by philanthropists, by statesmen, and by states, to restrain and destroy the alcoholic evil through the operations of moral suasion and by state law. Public sentiment has been aroused and public opinion created, and at times, in my belief, it might have been crystallized into national law had the labor been properly directed. But it has failed, as it will always fail, so long as we save at the spigot and waste at the bung, if I may borrow an expressive simile from the business of the enemy. The temperance question is in its nature a national question, just as much so as the tariff is and more than slavery was. It is waste of time to deal with it *only* by towns and counties and states. All possible local efforts should be put forth against the liquor-death everywhere. The yellow fever should be fought in the by-ways and hospitals, by the physician and the nurses as well as by the quarantine of our ports and the suspension of infected traffic by national law, but the enemy will forever come in like a flood, unless the nation, which is assailed as a nation, defends itself as a nation. *What the temperance reform most needs is unification of effort, nationalization. Samson was not more completely hampered by withes than is this giant reform by the geographical lines of states; and if its supporters would but use their strength, they would at once find their natural arena circumscribed only by the national domain.* How shall this be done? By concentration upon the enactment of a national constitutional law. The nation can act in no other way than by law; and now there is no national law for the removal of the alcoholic evil. On the contrary, we have seen how, by guaranteeing the importation and transportation and permitting the manufacture, the national Constitution is the very citadel of the rum-power."

Existing parties can not in the nature of the case, take up this question. Not to this end were they born; not for this cause did they come into the world. Upon this issue the voters who compose them are irrevocably divided. Twenty years ago Governor St. John and Senator John Sherman voted one way. Now the latter champions the brewer's cause, and the former is Prohibition's standard-bearer. Party inclosures must be broken down, that men who think and vote alike may clasp hands in a political fraternity where the issue of to-day outranks that of yesterday or of to-morrow. A friendly editor uttered his word of warning to us in terms like these: "There is any amount of political lightning in the air, and if you are not careful a bolt will strike the Woman's Christian Temperance Union." Whereupon our brave Mary T. Lathrap replied: "Women who have been fighting Jersey lightning for ten years are n't afraid of the political kind."

Dear sisters we must stand by each other in this struggle. Side by side, shoulder to shoulder, we must move forward, with no break in the ranks, no aspersions, no careless, harsh or cruel judgments, but the tenderest and most persistent endeavor to keep the unity of the spirit, if not of method, and, above all, the bond of peace. Let the criticising world see plainly that concord has the right of way in the Woman's Christian Temperance Union. In all the turmoil of these toilsome days, in which motives of which we never dreamed are foisted on us, words we never spoke attributed, and deeds we would spurn ascribed, may the law of kindness still dwell upon our lips and the spirit of a loving forbearance keep our hearts tender. Let me give you the sweet words my mother used to speak as the talismanic charm to still my turbulent spirit in girlhood days: "*Hath any wronged thee? Be bravely revenged. Slight it, and the work's begun. Forgive it, and 'tis finished.*" Permit me also to give you golden words, spoken by one of the clearest philosophic minds of our own or any age. They may cheer you in this battle-hour as they have strengthened me: "Whoever hesitates to utter that which he thinks the highest truth, lest it should be too much in advance of the time, * * * * must remember that while he is a descendant of the past, he is a parent of the future; and that his thoughts are as children born to him which he may not carelessly let die. He, like every other man, may properly consider himself as one of myriad agencies through which works the Great First Cause; and when that cause produces in him a certain belief he is thereby authorized to profess and act out that belief.' * * * * Not as adventitious, therefore, will the wise man regard the faith which is in him. The highest truth he sees he will fearlessly utter; knowing that, let what may come of it, he is thus playing his right part in the world."

We are slowly but surely attaining to the grandest mastership in all the world, mastership over our own spirits. The noblest figure of contemporary history is Gladstone, England's governmental chief, because with the people ready to mob him one day and to worship him the next, he holds right on his way quietly and patiently, but dauntlessly true to his convictions. God has set the Woman's Christian Temperance Union for a grander confession and defense of the faith than we have dreamed as yet; one which would blanch our cheeks, perhaps, and make our hearts heavy with fear, could we to-day know all that it involves. But if we are true and tender-hearted, holding fast the hand of Christ, we shall be equal to the emergencies as they arise, no matter how perilous or great. Let me give you De Tocqueville's words, for a motto in 1884: "*Life is neither a pleasure nor a pain. It is serious business, to be entered on with courage and in a spirit of self-sacrifice.*"

The general work of our conventions falls into the care of two committees, one on a statement of principles, called the "Committee on Resolutions;" the other on formulation of plans, called the "Plan of Work Committee," and the President's Annual Address is always referred to these. From the former committee the following resolution came, and led to the great

"St. Louis Debate" in which Mrs. Mary T. Lathrap so distinguished herself as a St. John, and Mrs. J. Ellen Foster as a Blaine, woman:

> We refer to the history of ten years of persistent moral-suasion work as fully establishing our claim to be called a non-political society, but one which steadfastly follows the white banner of prohibition wherever it may be displayed. We have, however, as individuals, always allied ourselves in local and state political contests with those voters whose efforts and ballots have been given to the removal of the dram-shop and its attendant evils, and at this time, while recognizing that our action as a national society is not binding upon states or individuals, we reaffirm the position taken by the society at Louisville in 1882, and at Detroit in 1883, pledging our influence to that party, by whatever name called, which shall furnish us the best embodiment of prohibition principles, and will most surely protect our homes. And as we now know which national party gives us the desired embodiment of the principles for which our ten years' labor has been expended, we will continue to lend our influence to the national political organization which declares in its platform for National Prohibition and Home Protection. In this, as in all progressive effort, we will endeavor to meet argument with argument, misjudgment with patience, denunciation with kindness, and all our difficulties and dangers with prayer.

This resolution was drawn up by Mrs. Mary B. Willard, but the last sentence was my own, being a resolution adopted by the first National Woman's Christian Temperance Union Convention as a basis of action immediately following the Crusade. Men who heard the long and brilliant argument, pro and con, on this political declaration—an argument that packed the church and crowded the aisles hour after hour with standing listeners—declared that it had not been equaled for courtesy, and not excelled in force, wit, pathos and earnestness by any they had known. At its close, the ayes and noes were called, for the first time in our annals, and here culminated the features that had made the debate itself so remarkable, for nearly every delegate gave, in a sentence, her reason for voting as she did. Mrs. Dr. Erwin, President of the Mississippi W. C. T. U., one of the saintliest and most motherly of women, standing with Bible open in her outstretched hand, lifted her eyes as one who prays, and said: "By God's grace, I vote this way for the sake of the poor, misguided colored people of the South."

Beloved as she was by them and a student of their needs and

wrongs, she felt that the new party would not only give them standing-room but would put away from them the curse that makes their votes a terror now to temperance homes.

That scene has passed into memory and will be recorded in history,—for then and there the fitting representatives of American womanhood, both North and South, "entered politics" for the sake of home protection, and when they came they came to stay.

The vote stood 195 (including seven who had to leave) in favor to 48 against the Resolution.

The situation "after election" is shadowed forth in the following call to prayer written by me and issued November 20, 1884:

BELOVED SISTERS OF THE LOCAL UNIONS—These are the times that try women's souls. To be tolerant toward the intolerant is a difficult grace, and yet its exercise is imperiously demanded of us.

A party long accustomed to success is in defeat. Thousands of leading men see their hopes blighted, ambitions overthrown, perhaps their occupations gone. Party journals denounce the Prohibitionists as having caused all this, and "fellows of the baser sort" hang ex-Governor St. John in effigy. The W. C. T. U. is termed "a political party," and subjected to the sharpest criticism by men who found no fault with our societies in Iowa, Kansas and other states where they "lent their influence" to the Republicans. Free speech and "a free ballot" have, within a fortnight, cost many a voter dear, in the good-will and business patronage of his neighbors, while obedience to the most profound convictions has called down bitter imprecations on many an earnest woman's head. Our own familiar friends in whom we trusted, have uttered these words in public print and private reprimand. Not from the ignorant or base, but from cultured scholars and Christian gentlemen have come these words and deeds. Not in a generation has such a cross-fire of denunciation whistled through the air as that now aimed at those who "lent their influence" to the Prohibition party.

All this you know from the things that you have suffered. But what is our duty in this strife of tongues?

Dear sisters, we stand before the people as followers of Him "who when He was reviled, reviled not again; when He suffered He threatened not, but committed Himself to Him that judgeth righteously." Let us, therefore, pray mightily to God that we may be replenished with heavenly grace according to our need, so that the law of kindness still shall dwell in our hearts and on our tongues, and charity (or love) which "vaunteth not itself, is not easily provoked, doth not behave itself unseemly," shall control our every action. Next to God's spirit dwelling in our own, nothing will so help us to be considerate and patient, as to pray for and speak gently of those who in our judgment, have done injustice to our motives, our record and our character. Let us be careful not to do them a parallel injustice, but by recalling their noble qualities and their kindness in the past, keep them hidden in the citadel of our generous regard and confidence until this storm be overpassed.

Let us try, also, to put ourselves in their places and to realize that they too, are sincere, even as we are, and acting, the great majority of them at least, from patriotic motives. We seek the same goal, but have chosen different roads, each one believing his way the best. In time we shall agree to disagree and go on without bitterness. "A soft answer turneth away wrath, but grievous words stir up anger." May God fill our mouths with soft answers in these wrathful days! If we women can not mitigate the asperities of politics, woeful will be the day of our influence therein, whether that influence be indirect, as now, or direct, as in some future time. But if God be with us we can save our country as surely as Joan of Arc crowned her king.

That the infinite Spirit of Christ may rule and reign in our hearts, making them tender, true and teachable, we ask you to observe, as a day of fasting and prayer, the fourth of December, reading on that day those passages of Scripture which relate to God's power in the affairs of government, and also such as illustrate the supreme fact that "he that is slow to anger is better than the mighty; and he that ruleth his spirit than he that taketh a city." Let us exhort you more earnestly than ever before to observe individually the noontide hour of prayer. Our prayer for you, beloved friends, shall also be that "your faith fail not," but that you "stand fast in the liberty wherewith Christ hath made you free," and "having done all, stand."

Yours, "with firmness in the right as God gives us to see the right,"

FRANCES E. WILLARD, *President.*

CAROLINE B. BUELL, *Corresponding Secretary.*

The next year, 1885, at Philadelphia, the same political resolution was again adopted by a vote of two hundred and forty-five to thirty, and Mrs. Foster presented a protest signed by herself with twenty-six others, to which, by order of the convention, a committee consisting of Mesdames Woodbridge, Lathrap and Hoffman made reply.

At Minneapolis, in 1886, the vote stood two hundred and forty-one for the Prohibition party to forty-two against, and at Nashville, in 1887, the protest had but fourteen names out of three hundred and forty-one delegates. Meanwhile, at Minneapolis, Mrs. Rastall, President Kansas W. C. T. U., offered the following, which was adopted:

Having for three years thoroughly discussed and established by a large majority vote our position in regard to the Prohibition party, I move the adoption of the following by-law:

"Any resolution referring to our attitude toward political parties is to be decided by vote without discussion."

GENERAL OFFICERS NATIONAL W. C. T. U.

CAROLINE B. BUELL, Cor. Sec. ESTHER PUGH, Treas.
FRANCES E. WILLARD, Pres.
MARY A. WOODBRIDGE, Rec. Sec. L. M. N. STEVENS, Ass't Rec. Sec'y.

This was in force at Nashville only, and was rescinded by an overwhelming majority at New York. At Nashville an amendment to our Constitution offered the previous year by Mrs. Foster, was voted down. It read as follows:

"This association shall be known as the National Woman's Christian Temperance Union, and shall be non-sectarian in religious, and non-partisan in political work."

The convention held that our non-sectarian character had been thoroughly established from the beginning, and as to being non-partisan, it was far from our intent. In St. Louis we had crossed the Rubicon forever, and with us it was a case of "sink or swim, live or die, survive or perish, I give my hand and my heart to this vote." We could not as a national society consent to remain in relations of equal friendship toward one national party that ignored, another that denounced, and a third that espoused, the cause of prohibition. But we did not appreciate the anger of a party in defeat—indeed, we had not supposed that defeat was in store for the Republicans.

PORTLAND (OR.) W. C. T. U. SHIELD.

CHAPTER IV.

WOMEN IN COUNCIL.

Patiently the "Old Guard" (for so we now called the National W. C. T. U.) held on its way. What it hoped and prayed for came true, the good men who were angry thought better of the situation after awhile. Ministerial brethren, even, who had declared that our pulpit notices should be read no longer, changed their minds and let us hold meetings in the dear old home churches as aforetime.

At our next National Convention in Philadelphia (autumn of 1885), forty churches were opened to our speakers on the Sabbath day, though we chose Association Hall in preference to the beautiful edifices that were offered us. Among the beautiful decorations of this Hall were the banners and other devices that had made our booth at the late Exposition in New Orleans a fitting symbol of our womanly work. That the woman-touch is thus to brighten every nook and corner of earth, has always been a cardinal doctrine of my creed, coming to me first as an intuition, later on as a deduction, but always as an emphatic affirmation.

Two hundred and eighty-two delegates were present from forty states and territories. Nearly eleven thousand dollars had been received by our treasurer and our convention was conceded to be by far the strongest and the best that we had ever held. Clearly, our branch of the temperance work had not "been set back twenty years." Forty-four district and national departments of work were provided for; a new constitution was adopted, requiring ten cents per capita to be paid into the national treasury, instead of five cents, as heretofore; our superintendents were organized into a committee to confer with the Executive Committee. Headquarters were removed from New York, where they had never flourished, to 161 La Salle Street, Chicago, Ill., where, in conjunction with our Woman's Temperance Publishing House, they have greatly gained in power, and the White Cross movement was adopted as a feature of our work.

I was made, *per force*, superintendent of this new department, also of our national department of publications, and had that of organization assigned me as an *ex officio* duty.

The Philadelphia Convention was remarkable for the large number of white ribbon women in attendance as visitors, for the number of distinguished persons outside our ranks who addressed it, also for the deference manifested by ministerial and other bodies in sending us fraternal delegates. Probably no convention ever assembled in America in an auditorium more beautifully decorated. The escutcheons of states, the banners of the forty departments, the gay pennons of state and local unions, of young women's societies, and of the children's Loyal Temperance Legion, recalled the pictures and pageants of the mediæval Crusaders and knights of olden chivalry. Mrs. Josephine R. Nichols, national superintendent of introducing temperance work at expositions, state and county fairs, and other great assemblies of the people, had set our women at work preparing these beautiful bits of color and emblems of sentiment and purpose, for the New Orleans Exposition, where we had a handsome booth. I fear, lest in setting forth the political attitude of our society and my relation thereto, I am doing injustice to its real, though less observed, activities. For example, at St. Louis nearly thirty distinct departments were passed in review by their chiefs, in reports printed and circulated throughout the convention, and methods for improving all of these departments were duly discussed and acted on; a strong corps of national organizers was selected, and all our publishing interests provided for.

Indeed, the versatility of our W. C. T. U. can hardly be better illustrated than by the fact that this same convention not only swung us into politics, but adopted the following petition to editors of fashion-plate magazines, reported to us from the Press Department, which sends out news, temperance literature and bulletins to thousands of papers, from Tampa Bay to Puget Sound, and of which Miss Mary Henry is our present Superintendent:

DEAR FRIEND—Knowing that the fashion in woman's dress which requires the constriction of the waist and the compression of the trunk is one which not only deforms the body in a manner contrary to good taste, but results in serious, sometimes irreparable, injury to important vital organs, and believing that the existence of the widespread perversion of natural instincts which renders this custom so prevalent may be fairly attributable, in part, at least, to erroneous education of the eye, and the establishment of a false and artificial standard of symmetry and beauty, which in our opinion, is largely the result of the influence of the popular fashion-plates of the day, we, the undersigned, most respectfully petition you that, in the name of science and humanity, you will lend your aid toward the elevation of woman to a more perfect physical estate, and consequently to the elevation of humanity, by making the figures upon your fashion-plates conform more nearly to the normal standard and the conditions requisite for the maintenance of health.

The Minneapolis Convention was held in an enormous rink which was packed to the doors whenever any speaker of special prominence appeared. During the great debate on one of the last evenings, the scene was full of a new significance, for women of the South as well as the North, with strong and ready utterance declared for prohibition in politics as well as in law. General Nettleton, a gentleman of local prominence and champion of the anti-saloon (Republican "non-partisan") movement, spoke to the convention, and fairly—or most unfairly—scolded us; the quiet self-restraint with which he was heard, and the immediate return of the convention to the order of the day, without making note or comment, as soon as he had finished, afford, as I believe, the most palpable proof on record that women are capable of constituting a really deliberative body.

Perhaps the most notable feature of that convention was the presence of Mrs. Margaret Bright Lucas, of London, England, the sister of John Bright, and the first president of the "World's Woman's Christian Temperance Union." This distinguished lady crossed the sea when nearly seventy years of age, in token of sisterly good-will toward American temperance women and their work. She came under escort of our own Mrs. Hannah Whitall Smith and accompanied by two other English ladies. Her reception was magnificent, the convention rising in separate groups, first the Crusaders in a body, second the women of New England, then of the Middle States, after these the Western, and the Pacific Coast, and last (by way of climax) the Southern representatives, while the English and American flags waved from the platform and all joined in singing, "God save the Queen."

One of the most important suggestions made by me to this convention was that of an address to the Labor Organizations. The following is a specimen of tens of thousands that were printed:

AN ADDRESS TO ALL KNIGHTS OF LABOR, TRADES UNIONS, AND OTHER LABOR ORGANIZATIONS.

FROM THE NATIONAL WOMAN'S CHRISTIAN TEMPERANCE UNION.

HEADQUARTERS OF THE NATIONAL W. C. T. U.,
161 La Salle Street, CHICAGO, ILL.,
November 11, 1886.

To all Working Men and Women—Brothers and Sisters of a Common Hope:

We come to you naturally as to our friends and allies. With such of your methods as involve coöperation, arbitration and the ballot-box, we are in hearty sympathy. Measures which involve compulsion of labor, the destruction of property or harm to life or limb, we profoundly deplore, and we believe the thoughtful and responsible among your ranks must equally deplore them, as not only base in themselves, but a great hindrance to your own welfare and success. We rejoice in your broad platform of mutual help, which recognizes neither sex, race, nor creed. Especially do we appreciate the tendency of your great movement to elevate women industrially to their rightful place, by claiming that they have equal pay for equal work; recognizing them as officers and members of your societies, and advocating the ballot in their hands as their rightful weapon of self-help in our representative government.

As temperance women, we have been especially glad to note your hostile attitude toward the saloon, the worst foe of woman, of the workingman, and of the home. We read with joy of the vow made by the newly elected officers of the Knights of Labor at the convention in Richmond, Va., when, with hands raised to heaven, they pledged themselves to total abstinence.

In addressing you at this time we wish to offer our sincere congratulations upon your achievements as practical helpers in that great temperance reform which engages our steadfast work and prayers, and which, as we believe, involves, beyond all other movements of this age, your happiness and elevation. Permit us to ask your careful consideration of this statement of our belief:

The central question of labor reform is not so much *how to get higher wages*, as *how to turn present wages to better account.* For waste harms most those who can least afford it. It is not over production so much as *under-consumption* that grinds the faces of the workingmen. Fourteen hundred millions annually drawn, chiefly from the pockets of working men, by saloon-keepers and cigar-dealers, means less flour in the barrel, less coal in the cellar, and less clothing for the laborers' families. We grieve to see them give their money for that which is not bread, and their labor for that which satisfieth not. We suggest that if, by your request, pay day were universally changed from Saturday to Monday, this would do much to increase the capital at home.

The life insurance statistics prove that while the average life of the moderate drinker is but thirty-five years and a half, that of the total abstainer is *sixty-four years.* The successful explorers and soldiers, the famous athletes, pedestrians, rowers and shots are men who do not cobweb their brains, or palsy their nerves with alcoholic drink.

We believe that the work of our societies, resulting in laws by which nearly one half the children of the United States are being taught in the public schools the evil effects of intoxicating liquors upon the tissues of the body and the temper of the mind, merits your earnest coöperation, and will prove one of your strongest re-inforcements in the effort to elevate your families to nobler levels of opportunity. We believe that the study of hygiene, including a knowledge of the most healthful foods and the discovery that these are of the cheaper and non-stimulating class, with a careful consideration of the scientific methods by which, in the preparation of food, a little can be made to go a long way in home economies, is well worthy of your attention. We ask you to aid us in our endeavors to have taught in all the departments of our public schools those beneficent laws of wealth which relate to wholesome living in respect to diet, dress, sleep, exercise and ventilation, so that this teaching shall be given to every child as one of the surest means to its truest happiness.

We ask your attention to our White Cross pledge of equal chastity for man and woman; of pure language and a pure life. We ask your help in our efforts to secure adequate protection by law for the daughters of the poor and rich alike, from the cruelty of base and brutal men. We ask your help in our endeavors to preserve the American Sabbath with its rest and quiet, redeeming it from being as now the harvest-time of the saloon-keeper, when he gathers in the hard earnings of the workingman, and we promise you our co-operation in your efforts to secure the Saturday half-holiday, which, we believe, will do so much to change the Sabbath from a day of recreation to one of rest at home and for the worship of God. We rejoice to note that the Central Labor Union of New York City petitioned the municipal officers to close saloons upon the Sabbath Day, and we earnestly hope that all such societies may soon petition for their closing every day, and order a perpetual boycott upon the dealers in alcoholic poison.

We call your attention to our departments of evangelistic temperance meetings; work for railroad employés, lumbermen, herdsmen, miners, soldiers and sailors; also to our efforts to organize free kitchen gardens and kindergartens, and Bands of Hope; to supply free libraries and reading rooms, temperance lodging-houses and restaurants, and to reach a helping hand to fallen women as well as fallen men. We have a publishing house at 161 La Salle Street, Chicago, which sent out thirty million pages of temperance literature in the last year, which is conducted by women, its types being set by women compositors. Our National organ, *The Union Signal*, has good words for all lawful efforts made by working men and women for their own best interests.

We ask you to do all in your power for the cause of prohibition, which is pre-eminently *your* cause. With the dram-shop and its fiendish temptations overthrown, what might you not attain of that self-mastery which is the first condition of success; and what might you not achieve of protection and happiness in those *homes* which are the heart's true resting places! Your ballots hold the balance of power in this land of the world's hope. We ask those of you who are voters to cast them only for such measures and such men as are solemnly committed to the prohibition of every brewery, distillery and dram-shop in the nation. And that women may come to the rescue in this great emergency, also as an act of justice toward those who have the most sacred claim on your protection, we hope that you may see your way clear to cast your ballots only for such measures and such men as are pledged to the enfranchisement of women.

In all this, we speak to you as those who fervently believe that the coming of Christ's kingdom in the earth means *Brotherhood.* We urge you with sisterly earnestness and affection to make the New Testament your text-book of political economy, and to join us in the daily study of His blessed words, who spake as never man spake. His piercèd hand is lifting up this sorrowful, benighted world into the light of God. In earnest sympathy let us go forward to work out His golden precepts into the world's life and law by making first of all His law and life our own.

Yours for God and Home and Every Land,

FRANCES E. WILLARD, *President.*

CAROLINE B. BUELL, *Corresponding Secretary.*

N. B.—Local unions please have this printed in all the papers practicable.

It was intended by the convention's action at Minneapolis to recommend each local union to take copies of the preceding address to the local labor organizations of its own town or city, and ask them to discuss and adopt a resolution concerning it; also to bring the address before district, state and national conferences of workingmen for their action. By this means, great good can be done, in an educational way, for the cause of temperance and of labor.

In 1887 we once more wended our way southward, Baltimore (in 1878), Louisville (in 1881) and St. Louis (in 1884), having been the three points farthest south, at which the National Convention had been held up to this date.

Ample preparations were made for us by Mrs. Judge East, Mrs. Judge Baxter, and other ladies of Nashville, the Athens of the nation as well as of the South—if the proportion of students to inhabitants and the number and variety of institutions of learning is considered.

On the opening morning a rare picture was presented in the elegantly adorned hall with three hundred and forty-one delegates present from thirty-seven states, five territories and the District of Columbia, and the platform crowded with notables of Vanderbilt University and the M. E. Church, South, with whom this great institution outranks all others as Harvard does with the people of New England. The Southern delegates were out in force and it was admitted by the press, which treated us most courteously, that there was no denying the fact that this convention was not made up of the kind of women dreaded in that conservative region, but that our delegates were well-dressed, sunny-faced, winsome, home women, but at the same time, women with minds of their own.

William Jones, the noted English Quaker, and Peace philanthropist, was our guest at this convention and a magnificent reception was given in his honor by Colonel and Mrs. Cole, at which the National W. C. T. U. officers and leading Southern ladies assisted in receiving.

Rev. Dr. Alfred A. Wright, of Cambridge, one of the best Greek scholars in the country, was our guest also, and then and there began his work as instructor in our Evangelistic Department, which has widened and deepened until now he has charge of the Course of Study for Evangelists and Deaconesses in that branch of the service.

Pundita Ramabai, in her white robes, was a central figure, and her plaintive appeal for the high-caste Hindu widows, a memorable event in the convention.

Mrs. J. Ellen Foster was not present this year, being on a health trip in Europe. The non-partisan Republican delegates were not, therefore, a strong force in the convention, though the usual protest was circulated and received fourteen signatures.

We adopted our customary resolutions on controverted points, the Southern press making certainly no more ado than the Northern had often made under like circumstances. The following resolutions would have been bomb-shells in the camp a few years earlier, but now the first couplet occasioned almost no debate, and the second was adopted with practical unanimity, excepting the dissent of Iowa and a few other delegates.

Resolved, That the success of municipal suffrage in Kansas convinces us that no stronger weapon has been hurled against the liquor power; we therefore urge upon our members the importance of trying to secure this power in any and all states and territories where there is a prospect of success in such an undertaking.

Resolved, That an amendment to the national Constitution is the final goal of all those efforts for the enfranchisement of women which shall deal the death blow to the liquor traffic, and for the first time provide adequate protection for the home.

Resolved, That we rejoice in the great successes that have been gained by the Prohibition party during the past year and we again pledge it our hearty co-operation, assuring it of our prayers and sympathy.

Resolved, That we ask the Prohibition party at its coming National Convention to re-affirm its former position in regard to woman's ballot.

We placed on record our protest against personalities in politics, sending the same to the leaders of all parties, and we rejoice that the campaign of 1888 largely fulfilled our hopes, except that the after-election abuse of the W. C. T. U. and its leaders, by old party organs, has been, in view of the beneficent work and record of the society, nothing less than unmanly, and we feel assured that history will so pronounce it. This is the Nashville resolution:

Resolved, That with a deep sense of the significance of such action we women, representatives of thirty-seven states and five territories, do most solemnly urge upon all political parties and partisan papers the duty of avoiding, in the pending Presidential campaign, the personal vilification and abuse that characterized the last, and we call upon them to consider the fact that the women of the North and the South have clasped hands in concord and co-operation, which is a most practical proof that war issues are dead, and that the land should have rest from reviving them for campaign purposes. We protest as women against this outrage upon the growing spirit of fraternity, and reiterate the cry of the great general, "*Let us have peace!*"

We lost that most brilliant of our leaders, John B. Finch, October 3, 1887. At once the thought came to many of us, "Samuel Dickie, Michigan's trusted leader in the Constitutional Amendment campaign, is his natural successor."

A meeting of the National Committee of the Prohibition party was held in Battery D, Chicago, at the close of 1887, to elect a new chairman. The attendance was general and enthusiasm at white heat. Professor Dickie was chosen; woman's ballot as a plank in the platform was warmly indorsed, Rev. Anna Shaw making a most telling argument in its favor, and plans for the campaign of 1888 were outlined. At this meeting a memorial service was held in honor of Mr. Finch and I was chosen to pronounce his eulogy.

CHAPTER V.

WHITE CROSS AND WHITE SHIELD.

The most pointed and practical standard of daily living of which I can think, is to permit in one's self no open habit in word or deed that others might not safely imitate, and no secret habit that one would be ashamed to have the best and purest know. Anything less than this is vastly beneath our privilege. Having thus made the only adequate preparation for a work so holy, we may send out our plans and purposes to the wide world of manhood and of womanhood, calling upon all to climb the heights whence alone we shall see God.

When the Crusade began, no one would have predicted that twelve years later we should be as earnestly at work for fallen women as we were then for fallen men.

That we are so doing, is because we have learned in this long interval, that intemperance and impurity are iniquity's Siamese Twins; that malt liquors and wines have special power to tarnish the sacred springs of being; that every house of ill-repute is a secret saloon and nearly every inmate an inebriate. Unnatural and unspeakable crimes against the physically weaker sex make the daily papers read like a modern edition of Fox's Martyrs. A madness not excelled, if indeed, equaled, in the worse days of Rome, seems to possess the inflamed natures of men, let loose from the two hundred and fifty thousand saloons of the nation upon the weak and unarmed women, whose bewildering danger it is to have attracted the savage glances of these men or to be bound to them by the sacred tie of wife or mother in a bondage worse than that which lashes the living to the dead.

But our Iowa sisters were in the field as early as 1879, and at the annual meeting of their State W. C. T. U., in response to the plea of Mrs. L. B. Benedict, they resolved to found a Home for penitent, erring women, and to that end established a department of work. Maine W. C. T. U. has set us a grand example with its Industrial Home, New York with its "Christian Home for Inebriate Women," Cleveland with its "Open Door," Chicago with its "Anchorage," and many cities East and West by the appointment of police matrons to care for women under arrest; all these things prove that temperance women have never been indifferent to this branch of work.

But, after all, it was the moral cyclone that attended the *Pall Mall Gazette* disclosures, which cleared the air and broke the spell, so that silence now seems criminal and we only wonder that we did not speak before.

Some sporadic efforts had been made in this direction from time to time, but the action of our Philadelphia Convention in 1885 launched the new life-boat nationally, and because no other woman could be found to stand at its helm I have tried to do so, though utterly unable to give to this great work an attention more than fragmentary. My faithful office secretary, Alice Briggs, has really been the main spoke in the wheel at my home office, and Dr. Kate Bushnell, in the field, for I have only spoken in large cities, and the heroic doctor is going everywhere and has made such a reconnoissance of the North Woods lumber centers as ought to place her name among the Grace Darlings of moral rescue work. Mrs. Dr. Kellogg has developed the Mothers' meetings into a potent factor of the department, and Hope Ledyard (Mrs. C. H. Harris) has taken up this specialty at our request.

My own "call" is hinted at in these words from my annual address, only a few weeks after the *Pall Mall Gazette* disclosures.

How hard men work for votes! They do not assemble the faithful by general bell-ringing and let that end it. Nay, verily! They obey the Gospel injunction: "Go out into the highways and hedges, and compel them to come in." Carriages are running all day between the voters and the polls, no matter how hard it is to bring the two together. Thus must we go out to seek and save the lost; as eager for our Master's triumph in the individual soul, as politicians are for the election of their candidates.

This work can not be done by proxy nor at arms-length. We ought to have always, in every local union, an active committee of visitation to the homes of those who drink. I beg you to do this, though you do nothing else. Go into homes and saloons, inviting lost men to come to Christ. We must *go*; we can not send. As an earnest-hearted minister recently said in my hearing: "Salvation by tongs is a failure." The grip of our own hands can alone convey the unbeliever's hand to the firm and tender clasp of the Hand once pierced for us and him.

The Bishop of Durham founded the White Cross League. Its pledge predicts the time when fatherhood shall take its place beside motherhood, its divine correlate, as equal sharer in the cares that have so ennobled women as to make some of them akin to angels. Its blessed pledge declares: "I will maintain the law of purity as equally binding upon men and women; I will endeavor to spread these principles among my companions, and try to help my younger brothers, and will use every means to fulfill the sacred command, '*Keep* thyself pure.'"

Those noble men, Anthony Comstock, of the New York Society for the Suppression of Vice, and Rev. Dr. De Costa, of the White Cross League, will address our convention. Their work relates to the overthrow of those Satanic means by which the theory and practice of abominable crimes against social purity are carried on in our great cities, and from thence spread their leprous taint to every town and village.

Our Department for Suppression of the Social Evil is as yet inoperative. It is greatly to be regretted that we do not yet succeed in winning the services, as superintendent of this most difficult work, of a lady who combines the rare qualities of a delicate perception of propriety with practical ability and leisure. The special aim of this new superintendency will be to trace the relation between the drink habit and the nameless practices, outrages and crimes which disgrace so-called modern "civilization"; especially the brutalizing influence of malt liquors upon the sexual nature. Besides this we should emulate the example set us by Mrs. Stevens, of Maine, and her clear-headed associates, in providing a temporary home for the women whom our police matrons rescue from the clutch of penalties whose usual accompaniments often render them still more familiar with sin. But the effect upon our minds of such unspeakable disclosures as those of the *Pall Mall Gazette*, and the horrible assurances given us by such authority as Dr. Elizabeth Blackwell, that we should uncap perdition in the same direction, were the hidden life of our own great cities known, has so stirred the heart of womanhood throughout this land, that we are, I trust, ready for an advance. Had we to-day the right woman in this place of unequaled need and opportunity, we could be instrumental in the passage of such laws as would punish the outrage of defenseless girls and women by making the repetition of such outrage an impossibility. Woman only can induce lawmakers to furnish this most availing of all possible methods of protection to the physically weak. Men alone will never gain the courage thus to legislate against other men. Crimes against women seem to be upon the increase everywhere. Three years ago the Chicago *Inter Ocean* gathered from the press in three weeks forty cases of the direst outrage, sixteen of the victims being girls. In a majority of cases, where the gentler sex is thus hunted to its ruin, or lured to the same pit in a more gradual way, strong drink is the devil's kindling-wood of passion, as everybody knows. Hence the relation of this most sacred work to that of the W. C. T. U. is so close that the press, through some of its noblest representatives has, in the last year, appealed to us to ignore the tempted and the fallen of our own sex no longer. It is not by the vain attempt to re-introduce the exploded harem method of secluding women that they are to be saved. It is rather by holding men to the same standard of morality which, happily for us, they long ago prescribed for the physically weaker, that society shall rise to higher levels, and by punishing with extreme penalties such men as inflict upon women atrocities compared with which death would be infinitely welcome. When we remember the unavenged murder of Jennie Cramer, of New Haven, and the acquittal of the ravishers of Emma Bond, a cultivated school teacher in Illinois; when we reflect that the *Pall Mall Gazette* declares "the law is framed to enable dissolute men to outrage girls of thirteen with impunity"; that in Massachusetts and Vermont it is a greater crime to steal a cow than to abduct and ruin a girl, and that in Illinois seduction is not recognized as a crime, it is a marvel not to be explained, that we go on the even tenor of our way, too delicate, too refined, too prudish to make any allusion to these awful facts, much less to take up arms against these awful crimes.

We have been the victims of conventional cowardice too long. Let us signalize the second century of temperance reform by a fearless avowal of our purpose to take up the work of promoting social purity by the inculcation of right principles and the serious demand for more equitable laws. The Society of the White Cross will warmly coöperate with our endeavors in this righteous cause. Oh, may some clear brain, true heart and winsome spirit in our great fraternity cry out under the baptism of the Heavenly Spirit, "*Here am I, Lord, send me!*"

These are the first words I ever publicly uttered on a subject that had been farther from my thoughts than I like to acknowledge, all my life long. When I was first a boarding-school pupil, at Evanston, in 1858, a young woman who was not chaste came to the college through some misrepresentation, but was speedily dismissed; not knowing her degraded status I was speaking to her, when a school-mate whispered a few words of explanation that crimsoned my face suddenly; and grasping my dress lest its hem should touch the garments of one so morally polluted, I fled from the room. It was, no doubt, a healthful instinct that led me to do this, but I am deeply grateful that the years have so instructed and mellowed my heart, that, could the scene recur, I would clasp that poor child's hand, plead with her tenderly and try to help instead of deserting her as I did in my more self-righteous youth.

The next time this subject was thrust upon me is described in my first address after becoming superintendent of the department. It was given to an audience of women at the twelfth annual meeting of the Chicago W. C. T. U., in 1886:

In the year 1869, while studying in Paris, I used often to see passing along the pleasant streets, great closed wagons, covered with black. Inquiring of my elegant landlady the explanation of these somber vehicles, she answered, sorrowfully, "It is the demi-monde, who go to be examined." I then learned for the first time that in Paris, fallen women have a legal "permit" to carry on what is a recognized business, but must remain secluded in their houses at certain hours, must avoid certain streets, and must go once a week, under escort of the police, to the dispensary for examination and certificate that they are exempt from contagious disease. Always, after that, those awful wagons seemed to me to form the most heart-breaking funeral procession that ever Christian woman watched with aching heart and tear-dimmed eyes. If I were asked why there has come about such a revolution in public thought that I have gained the courage to speak of things once unlawful to be told, and you may listen without fear of criticism from any save the base, my answer would be:

"Because law-makers tried to import the black wagon of Paris to England and America, and Anglo-Saxon women rose in swift rebellion."

Even a worm will turn at last, and when her degradation was thus deliberately planned and sanctioned by the state, on the basis of securing to the stronger partner in a dual sin the same protection from nature's penalty which society had granted him so long, and of heaping upon the weaker partner in that sin all the disgrace and shame, then womanhood's loyalty to woman was aroused; it overcame the silence and reserve of centuries, and Christendom rings with her protest to-day.

Thus do the powers of darkness outwit themselves, and evils evermore tend to their own cure. It is now solemnly avowed by thousands of the best and most capable women who speak the English tongue, not only that the contagious-diseases acts shall never be tolerated upon a single inch of British or American soil, but that houses of ill-fame shall be not only prohibited but banished altogether. The system of license must not come. The let-alone policy must go. The prohibitory method must be achieved.

Having determined on a great petition to Congress, asking for the better protection of women and girls through severer penalties for assaults upon them, and that the age of protection might be raised to eighteen years, I went in company with my dear friend, Mrs. Hannah Whitall Smith, of Philadelphia, whose guest I was at the time, to see Mr. Powderly, chief of the Knights of Labor, at their headquarters in the same city. A score of clerks were busy in the office below, and I was told that it was difficult to get access to Mr. Powderly, delegations often waiting for hours to take their turn. But Mrs. Bryant, editor of the journal of the Knights of Labor and a white ribbon woman, used her influence for us, and the detention was brief. Mr. Powderly came into her office from the inner room, where he sits from morning till night in counsel with six other men, I think, who, with himself, form the executive of this great organization. I saw a man of something more than medium height, broad-shouldered but of not specially robust physique, with a noble head, full, arching and slightly bald; the brow particularly handsome, also the clear-cut profile and magisterial nose; the eyes weary-looking but most intelligent and kindly, protected by light-bowed spectacles; the mouth, as I should judge, fine, but almost concealed by a military mustache. In the fewest possible words I told him my errand. He said, "Please show me your petition." Glancing at it a moment, he added, "Excuse me, I will consult my brothers"; he was gone perhaps three minutes, and returning, said, "If you will send me ninety-two thousand copies, they shall go out to every local assembly of the Knights of Labor without expense to you and with the recommendation that they be signed, circulated and returned to you at Evanston." I rose, reaching out my hand, and said, "Brother Powderly, you are a Catholic, and I am a Methodist sister, but I have sincere respect and high regard for you and I shall pray Heaven every day to bless you and your work." There was, perhaps, a little tremor in my voice as I said this, and the faintest token of the same in his as he replied, warmly grasping my hand, "I thank you, friend and sister. Good-by." I had asked him for his photograph, which he soon sent me, and it has stood on my desk ever since with those of Elizabeth Fry, Josephine Butler, Mrs. Cleveland and Pundita Ramabai. I know that Mr. Powderly is a thorough total abstainer, that he never uses tobacco and can not tolerate any symptom of it in his presence, that he is a man mighty in deeds as in words, having, as I believe, a single eye to the best interests of the working-classes, and the purpose to advance them only by the noblest methods, namely, education, coöperation, arbitration and the ballot-box. Repeatedly we have sent our delegates to the annual meeting of the Knights of Labor. Mrs. H. A. Hobart, president of the Minnesota W. C. T. U., spoke for us when the convention was held in Minneapolis; Mrs. Henrietta Monroe, president of the Ohio W. C. T. U., in Cincinnati, and in 1888, Mrs. Josephine R.

Nichols, president of the Indiana W. C. T. U., in Indianapolis. Our representatives have always been most cordially received, and as Mrs. Nichols was on the platform after her speech, Mr. Powderly came forward, taking her hand, and saying, "The Knights of Labor pledge themselves to stand by the W. C. T. U.," while applause, loud and hearty, rang out through the assembly.

When the petition for the protection of women came winging its way back to Rest Cottage from every quarter of the nation, no copies were quite so welcome as those soiled by the hardy hands of toil, largely signed in pencil, sometimes with the sign of the cross, and showing the devotion that binds lowly to lofty homes for the protection of those they hold most dear.

In the winter of 1888 our great petition was presented at the Capitol by Senator Blair, Mrs. Ada Bittenbender, our legal adviser, making all the arrangements, and the Senate giving respectful heed to the words of our illustrious champion as he read the petition and urged that action upon it be not delayed. A bill passed the Senate raising the age of protection to sixteen years, and it is pending in the House.

The petition, well known throughout the country, having been presented to almost every state and territorial legislature, reads as follows:

PETITION

OF THE

WOMAN'S CHRISTIAN TEMPERANCE UNION

FOR FURTHER PROVISION FOR THE

PROTECTION OF WOMEN AND CHILDREN.

To the Honorable, the Senate and House of Representatives of the State of—

The increasing and alarming frequency of assaults upon women, the frightful indignities to which even little girls are subject, and the corrupting of boys, have become the shame of our boasted civilization.

We believe that the statutes of——do not meet the demands of that newly awakened public sentiment which requires better legal protection for womanhood and childhood;

Therefore we, the undersigned citizens of——, County of——, and State of ——, pray you to enact further provision for the protection of women and children. And we call attention to the disgraceful fact that protection of the person is not placed by our laws upon so high a plane as protection of the purse.

The first time the thought ever came to me that a man could be untrue to a woman was when on entering my teens I read a story in the *Advocate of Moral Reform*, entitled, "The Betrayer and the Betrayed." It haunted me more than any story in all my youth, except "Uncle Tom's Cabin." It was brief but it was tragic, and the lovely young girl was left at the close in a madhouse, while of the man, I remember this sentence, "I see him often, passing to and fro in his elegant carriage. Beside him sits his wedded wife, around him are his happy children, and he is a candidate for the state legislature." As I used to think over the situation there came a deep, honest purpose in my inmost spirit always to stand by women in every circumstance. I was thirty years of age before I had the opportunity. I then found that a Swede girl, Bertha by name, who had served us several years, who seemed to be an earnest Christian, to whom we were all attached, was very sorrowful and strange. Erelong, she told us that a handsome young Swede who was then a student in our Theological Seminary and highly thought of, who had been her boyish lover and for whose sake she had come to this country, had betrayed her, and in my own house, too. Instead of driving her from our door, I sent for this young man, talked the whole matter over with him, and urged him to allow me that very evening to send for a justice of the peace and put a legal stamp upon what was already true. I told him he might then go his way, if he desired to do so, and we would keep Bertha. But he stoutly declined to do anything of the sort. Whereupon I walked over to the home of the President of Garrett Biblical Institute, my good friend, Dr. Bannister, and told him the situation. A faculty meeting was held the next morning, and by noon the young man had been ousted, under ban of professors and students, and went his lonely way to the depot, nothing having been heard of him since. We kept Bertha, and she was a few years later happily married to an honorable countryman of hers. "He is thrice armed who hath his quarrel just."

When the great International Council of Women was held in Washington, D. C., in 1888, at the women's meeting to discuss Social Purity work, it fell to my lot to speak as follows:

Now, in closing this magnificent meeting, a poor little Protestant nun comes before you, and feels that she hasn't much right to talk to you; feels that the high and solemn mysteries that have been spoken of in such varied tone and manner to-day, are those that she ought not to try to deal with; feels more than ever the inadequacy of one whose life has been set apart from the sacred tie of home, to utter her thought on themes like these. While the ladies have spoken so bravely or so tenderly, on this historic morning, my thoughts have been at work. I have seemed to see those two who went forth hand in hand from Eden on the saddest of all mornings, after the fall, and I have said to myself many times, "Oh, if those close clasped hands had never parted company, our poor world had been to-day the place God wants to see it, and the place Christ came to make it." I have said to myself many times, "Would that the other half the audience were here!" This is only half the circle; we ought to have had it builded out into completeness. So I have only to offer you the thought, that every objection brought forward here to-day, every philosophical statement made, is based upon the fact that out of the aggregation of men by themselves always comes harm; out of the coming of men and women both into true, and noble, and high conditions, side by side, always comes good. Where is it that you have this curse most deeply rooted and most apologized for by men? In the camps of the soldiery. What would woman's coming forward in government tend to bring about? The reign of peace. The mother heart that can not be legislated in and can not be legislated out would say: "I will not give my sons to be butchered in great battles," and we would have international arbitration.

My noble friend, Mrs. Hoffman, who spoke so bravely, said: "Until woman has complete industrial freedom, until woman has the purse jointly in her hand, marriage will never be the thing we want to see it." This blessed change is involved in all the magnificent enterprises represented by the women who stand on this platform, while doubtless you who are in the audience are true to this emancipation in your own circles. So that my heart is full of hope, and, out of the long savagery and darkness and crime, I see humanity coming up into the brightness and beauty of a new civilization. I see the noblest men of the world's foremost race, the Anglo-Saxons, who made this audience possibie, the men who have worked side by side with us, to bring about these great conditions, placing upon woman's brow above the wreath of Venus the helmet of Minerva and leading forward the fair divinities who preside over their homes to help them make a new and nobler government.

There is nothing on this earth that I tried more earnestly to instill into my girls' hearts, when I was teaching, than a genuine womanly self-respect. I doubt if we have this ourselves as the women of the future will. Why, I pass signs on the street, I pass pictures of women in the cigar-stores and saloons, that, if we were as self-respectful as we ought to be, could n't stay there over night; I see fair women in beautiful robes walking on the streets, or hear of them in fine social surroundings, with a man at their side puffing tobacco smoke into their faces and eyes, and I say that is a survival of past savagery and debasement and of the immolation of women. If there is anything on earth I covet that pertains to men it is their self-respect.

No man would be seen with a woman with the faintest taint or tinge of tobacco about her; no man would allow himself to enter into marriage with a woman of known habits of drinking or impurity; it is n't thinkable. When I see women coming out before men, or when I know they do—I do not see them, they are not women with whom I am socially acquainted—revealing the sacredness of the pure symbol and badge of their womanly nature, coming out dressed so improperly that the joke, the jest, and jibe, are uttered in the dressing-room where young men smoke cigars and hobnob together, I could weep my life out that a woman thus appears, borrowing that style from women the hem of whose garments she would be ashamed to touch. Let us have self-respect. Let us be clothed with the raiment of purity that ought to guard the virgin, the mother and the wife.

When we assemble socially and allow scenes to be put before us that are indecorous and shameful, we have passed away from the purity and self-respect that must and shall characterize the women of the future. Oh, friends, these things are deep in every thoughtful woman's heart! Girls come and ask me, "Would you dance round dances?" Dear little sister, no; don't dance a round dance. The women of the future will not do it. I walked the aisles of the picture galleries of Europe. I saw the men in those great historic paintings, with their ear-rings, and their fingers covered with rings, their necks bedecked with ruffles, their forms dressed in all the hues that the peacock and rainbow could supply. They were nothing but an exhibition of sycophants, a collection of courtiers. That was the time when King Louis XIV. said: "The state, it is I!"

Woman is courtier and man is king to-day, in the sacred realm of government. But when a woman shall be able to say to the state, "I am part of you, just as much as anything that breathes"; when she shall say, "I am part of society; I am part of industrial values, I am part of everything that a man values; everything that a man's brain loves to think about in philosophy, in philanthropy, in history, or science," then the calm equipoise of human forces shall come; and for that I would like to live; for that I would like to speak. Persons who know more about it than I, tell me that women who give their lives to shame, women who are on the street-corners with their invitations at night, are women who have, from the very look of the face and configuration of the head, the symbols and emblems of no self-respect. The superior, queenly woman is the one who has most self-respect, who sees its application to everything around her, and who makes every man feel that he would as soon die as offer her an insult.

The Arabs love to say of a pure man that he is "a brother of girls." The brotherly man will come forward to meet and respond to the sisterly woman. When we are not toys, when we are not dolls, when we stand before them royal, crowned with heart of love and brain of fire, then shall come the new day. I ignore nothing that has been said. I am in hearty sympathy with all. But, in my own thought, this is the key-note that must be struck. God grant that we may be so loving and so gentle in it all, that there shall be no vanity, no pride. Evermore the grandest natures are the humblest.

Let me speak a word of hope. I have heard this statement from a woman who has just come from Germany, a woman for years a student in the universities. She says the professors' wives tell her that the new science has developed this thought, and that professors are saying to their young men: "If you want a scintillating brain, if you want magnificent power of imagination, conserve every force, be as chaste as your sister is, and put your power into the brain that throbs on like an untired engine." I do not know how you feel, but I want to take by the hand this woman who has spoken so nobly to us, this sweet-faced and sweet-voiced English woman, Mrs. Laura Ormiston Chant, who, last night when all of us were asleep, went out into the holiness of moonlight and saw that our capital was not so bad as London; this woman who went to see the little girl that had n't been taught and had n't been helped, and who came from her country home and was getting entangled in the meshes of this great Babylon. God bless you, Mrs. Chant, you are welcome to America. I thought, while you were speaking, of what our Whittier said of our two countries: "Unknown to other rivalries than of the mild humanities and gracious interchange of good."

We women are clasping hands. We do not know how much it means. I have sought this woman from over the water. I wanted her to come here with her large experience in work. I have not seen so many sorrowful girls as she has, and don't know how to reach them, only in a general way; and I have asked her if she will stay and teach us, and she says she will. Are you not glad? So understand that the National Woman's Christian Temperance Union is going to keep Mrs. Chant here and send her about with her sweet evangelism. Now I think, dear friends, that we have certainly this morning boxed the compass of the woman movement, for we have talked purely and sacredly together of the White Cross and the White Shield.

No department of work was ever developed so rapidly as this. The women's hearts were ready for it. White Cross and White Shield pledges and literature, leaflets for mothers' meetings, indeed, for every phase of the Social Purity work, are ordered in constantly increasing numbers. The White Shield work is especially for women. Industrial homes for women are being founded by the state in response to our petitions, and a movement is now on foot to establish homes for adults who are physically, mentally or morally incapable, by reason of irremediable defects. We believe that the harm this large class (including hereditary drunkards) does to society makes it an unquestionable economy to detain them in institutions for the purpose, and render them self-supporting. "Do thyself no harm" would then be a motto alike applicable to these unfortunates and to the state.

It is hoped that this cause will be presented carefully and

wisely to all bodies of Christian, educational, and philanthropic workers in every part of the land. This will best be done under the auspices of the state or local superintendent of the department in person or by letter; or often, better still, by some delegate who has a right to the floor and will present and support a suitable resolution of sympathy and coöperation.

White Cross work contemplates a direct appeal to the chivalry of men: that they shall join this holy crusade by a personal pledge of purity and helpfulness: that boys shall early learn the sacred meaning of the White Cross and that the generous knights of this newest and most noble chivalry shall lead Humanity's sweet and solemn song.

> "In the beauty of the lilies
> Christ was born across the sea,
> With a glory in His bosom
> That transfigures you and me.
> As He died to make men holy,
> Let us live to make men free,
> While God is marching on."

CHAPTER VI.

THE WORLD'S W. C. T. U.

White light includes all the prismatic colors, so the white ribbon stands for all phases of reform, and there is no phase which the drink curse has not rendered necessary. Our emblem holds within itself the colors of all nations and stands for universal purity and patriotism, universal prohibition and philanthropy, and universal peace. For "hearts are near, though hands are far," and women's hands and hearts all round the world will be united by our snowy badge ere another generation passes out of sight. There is now no speech or language where its voice is not heard.

One secret of the success that has from the first attended our great society, is that it always goes on "lengthening its cords and strengthening its stakes."

When I was organizing on the Pacific Coast in 1883, I saw the opium curse in San Francisco alongside the alcoholic curse, introduced the W. C. T. U. into British Columbia, was urged to visit the Sandwich Islands, go to Japan and China, and was so impressed by the outreaching of other nations toward our society and their need of us, that I proposed in my annual address at Detroit, "the appointment of a commission to report the next year plans for the organization of a World's W. C. T. U." This was done, and the general officers of our national society have from that time to the present been leaders in this enterprise. We proceeded at once to send out Mrs. Mary Clement Leavitt, who started a work in the Sandwich Islands which promises to revolutionize sentiment, and make that country in favor of our principles and methods. Mrs. Dr. Whitney, of Honolulu, is president of the white ribbon societies there.

Mrs. Leavitt was supplied with money for her voyage to Australia by the temperance friends at the Sandwich Islands, and left for New Zealand in January, 1884. She there traversed a territory as great as from Maine to Florida, and from the Alleghany Mountains to the sea, forming ten good, strong unions, with Mrs. Judge Ward, of Christchurch, at their head. She then crossed one thousand one hundred and thirty miles of sea to reach the continent of Australia, where she steadily worked on in the Provinces of Queensland, New South Wales, Victoria, and Tasmania (formerly called Van Diemen's Land), and remained until the next autumn, when she started for Japan.

We must remember that Australia is one half as large as South America, being about two thousand, six hundred miles long, by two thousand in width. Like New Zealand, it is settled by English people, and governed partly by officers sent to represent the British Crown, partly by local legislatures. It is a strange and beautiful country, with climate, flora and fauna unlike those of any other part of the world. It seems like the best kind of a fairy story that our W. C. T. U. should be acclimated there, for Mrs. Leavitt writes, "These people are thorough; when they take the white ribbon, they take it to *keep* and to *wear*."

Perhaps they might teach us a lesson in this silent preaching of temperance by the "little badge of snow." Mrs. Leavitt's letters in *The Union Signal* have kept our great constituency informed of all her movements.

In Japan her success was so great that a leading missionary wrote home to his church paper, declaring that what Commodore Perry's visit was to the commerce, Mrs. Leavitt's has been to the women of Japan. She thoroughly established the W. C. T. U. in that bright morning-land of enthusiasm and hope; worked to the same end in the less fertile soil of China and of India; traversed Ceylon, which has, thus far, sent more names to the World's petition than any other country; was received in Madagascar with enthusiasm, and has now plunged into Africa. She is our white ribbon Stanley, not one whit less persistent and valorous than the great explorer. In one more year this intrepid Boston woman will have reached the golden number, seven, in her triumphal march, and will, I trust, receive such a reception as has not yet been accorded to a returning traveler—not even to a successful politician! We have never heard a criticism on her conduct, methods, or words, since she went forth, empty-handed and alone. Her world-wide mission has been largely self-supporting, and her success has led to the sending out of Miss J. A. Ackerman, of California, to follow the route so patiently laid down for all future comers. Miss Charlotte Gray has also visited Switzerland and is now organizing for us in Norway. Mrs. Mary B. Willard is superintendent of our Press Department. Mrs. Hannah Whitall Smith, of Bible Readings; Mrs. Mary H. Hunt, of Scientific Temperance; Mrs. Bishop Newman, of American Petitions; Mrs. Josephine R. Nichols, of World's Expositions. Mrs. Nichols was brilliantly successful in representing us at the New Orleans Expositions, hence her embassy to Paris in the spring of 1889 is full of promise for our cause.

But the two most powerful auxiliaries of the World's W. C. T. U., aside from our own beloved "National," the mother of them all (as the Crusade was our mother), have not yet been named.

As I have recently become President of the World's W. C. T. U., let me epitomize the history of these sister societies from official reports and personal knowledge:

The British Women's Temperance Association was founded in 1876, at Newcastle-on-Tyne, and was the outcome of an inspiration caught by Mrs. Margaret Parker, from the American "Crusaders." The secretary thus sketches its origin: "One of the first aggressive movements was in the town of Dundee, Scotland. A number of earnest women resolved to petition the magistrate to reduce the number of public houses for the sale of intoxicating drinks. Their petition was in the name of the wives, mothers, and sisters, and was signed by upwards of nine thousand of them. * * * The result was that next day not a single new license was given, and many were withdrawn. Thus commenced the first Women's Temperance Prayer Union; and first one town and village and then another followed the example of Dundee in establishing Women's Temperance Unions, until nearly every town was doing something, and many Friendly Inns or British Workman's Public Houses were planted.

"Still there was no attempt at national organization, although it had been a cherished thought in many hearts. Mrs. Margaret Parker, who had been foremost in the Dundee deputation, was

A WORLD'S W. C. T. U. GROUP.

MRS LETITIA YOUMANS,
CANADA.

MARGARET BRIGHT LUCAS,
PRES'T BRITISH WOMAN'S TEMP. ASS'N.

HANNAH WHITALL SMITH,
ENGLAND.

FRANCES E. WILLARD,
PRESIDENT.

MRS. SASAKI TOYOJU,
JAPAN.

MRS. MARY CLEMENT LEAVITT,
ROUND THE WORLD MISSIONARY.

PUNDITA RAMABAI,
INDIA.

in America afterward, and saw the efficient Woman's Christian Temperance Union there, and feeling assured that the time had come for a similar union in Great Britain, she ventured to issue a call, which was nobly responded to. A conference of about one hundred and fifty ladies, including influential delegates from various parts of the Kingdom, assembled in the Central Hall, Newcastle-on-Tyne, on Friday morning, April 21, 1876. On the motion of Mrs. Lucas, Mrs. Parker, of Dundee, was called to the chair. After singing, reading the Scripture and prayer, Mrs. Parker, in opening the proceedings, said: "In accordance with the earnestly expressed wish of the Woman's Christian Temperance Union of America, and the firm conviction in our own minds that God has already prepared the hearts of Christian women throughout the land to do a great work for Him in the cause of temperance, this convention has been called. * * * We believe that there is such a power in the influence of women as, if it were exerted aright, would shake the kingdom to its center on this important subject, and the country is in perishing need of it!" From this time the society has gone straight on, and now has a large number of auxiliaries.

Mrs. Margaret Bright Lucas, who for years has stood at the head of this society, is, with Mrs. Mary B. Willard and Miss Charlotte Gray, of Antwerp, a member of the International Temperance Association of men and women, organized in August, 1885. By my request, the commission of the World's W. C. T. U. chose Mrs. Lucas as first president of that society, it being desired to show all honor to the mother country in this new enterprise, and to enlist our British cousins to the utmost as its active friends.

This gifted gentlewoman is the youngest child of Honorable Jacob Bright, and sister of John Bright, the great English Commoner. Although over seventy years of age, with her children long ago settled in life, Mrs. Lucas travels and organizes constantly, enlisting her countrywomen wherever she goes.

We have also a bright young ally across the border—the Dominion W. C. T. U., with provincial auxiliaries in British Columbia, Ontario, Quebec, New Brunswick and Nova Scotia.

Its history is one of heroism. Our delegates to Cincinnati W. C. T. U. Convention in 1875, met there Mrs. Letitia Youmans, the earliest white ribbon pioneer in Canada. She came to learn our methods and we were in turn astonished and delighted by her power upon the platform. Her "Haman's License" and "Nehemiah Building the Walls" are addresses known throughout the country as unrivaled Bible expositions of great reform.

The British temperance women publish an official organ, *The British Women's Temperance Journal*, and the Canadians have one also. Both exchange with *The Union Signal*, whose readers skim the cream of the temperance world each week. Canada's paper is *The Women's Journal*, and is edited by Mrs. Addie Chisholm, of Ottawa, President W. C. T. U. of Ontario, and one of the ablest women in our ranks anywhere. Canada women fearlessly take advance positions. The Scott Act is covering their land with prohibition; municipal suffrage for women is helping solve the problem of their great cities.

In Toronto a temperance mayor was elected by seventeen hundred majority, thanks to the combined votes of the women and the workingmen. We must look well to our laurels, or our allies of the maple leaf will be first at the goal of prohibition.

Let us clasp hands in the wide sisterhood of the World's W. C. T. U., learning its motto—"*For God, and Home, and Every Land*," wearing our knots of white ribbon, observing the noontide hour of prayer, working steadily for the overthrow of the use and sale of alcoholics and narcotics the world around, and remembering the watch-words, *Prevention*, *Education*, *Evangelization*, *Purification*, *Prohibition*.

Let us also circulate from house to house this the World's Petition to all nations:

Honored Rulers, Representatives and Brothers:

We, your petitioners, although belonging to the physically weaker sex, are strong of heart to love our Homes, our Native Land and the world's family of Nations. We know that when the brain of man is clear, his heart is kind, his home is happy, his country prosperous, and the world grows friendly. But we know that alcoholic stimulants and opium, which craze and cloud the brain, make misery for men and all the world, and most of all for us and for our children. We know these stimulants and opiates are forced by treaty upon populations either ignorant or unwilling, and sold under legal guarantees which make the governments partners in the traffic by accepting as revenue a portion of its profits. We have no power to prevent this great iniquity beneath which the whole world groans and staggers, but you have the power to cleanse the flags of every clime from the stain of their complicity with this unmingled curse. We, therefore, come to you with the united voices of representative women from every civilized nation under the sun, beseeching you to strip away the safeguard and sanctions of the law from the drink traffic and the opium trade, and to protect our homes by the *total prohibition* of this twofold curse of civilization throughout all the territory over which your government extends.

Names of Women. *Nationality.*

Mrs. Mary A. Woodbridge, Ravenna, Ohio, is American Secretary of the World's W. C. T. U., and is doing earnest work for the petition, which will not be presented until we have two million signatures gathered up from all nations of the world.

It is translated into the language of every civilized nation, and is to be circulated in every country. The entire list of names secured will be presented to each government. Thus the American Congress will be petitioned to abolish the liquor traffic in America by women in Great Britain, Australia, Japan, etc. The same will be true of the Dominion of Canada. The British Parliament will, in like manner, be petitioned to abolish the alcohol traffic and the opium trade by women from America, and all over the world. Indeed, the first thought of this petition came to the president of the Woman's Christian Temperance Union of the United States, when reading an English book about the opium trade in India and China. To carry out this idea, an organized movement seemed necessary, that the *women of the whole world*, immeasurably cursed as they are by the results of these gigantic evils, might unitedly appeal to the men of the world, convened in all its great legislative Assemblies, and represented by its Potentates, to protect and deliver them.

There is a vast amount of righteous sentiment on the subjects of temperance and social purity that is scattered, and is, therefore, comparatively powerless. It needs a standard around which to rally ; a focus for its scattered rays ; and the great petition supplies this need. Besides all this, the reflex influence of the petition as an educational force upon the people will be of immeasurable value. It will create or confirm the arrest of thought in a million heads, and the arrest of conviction in a million hearts. It will be, in effect, a muster-roll for our army, and those who circulate it will be virtually recruiting officers in everybody's war. Their words of sweet reasonableness uttered in a million ears will mightily augment the sum total of moral influence. The Gatling gun of pulpit, press and platform, sending out our many-sided arguments and loving pleas, will gain incalculably in directness of aim and force of impression from the clear-cut issue furnished by the great petition. Nor will our work prove to have been "love's labor lost," in the great councils to which it is addressed. Nothing within the scope of our possibilities could be so influential and commanding. What two million of the most intelligent and forceful adults on this planet ask for, over their own signatures, will not long be disregarded or denied by their representatives. This petition will be the beginning of the end. Many years will be required in which to work it up, and it is believed that in no way can the same amount of effort be turned to better account in the interest of unifying and forwarding the reforms which are of equal importance to all the nations of the earth.

Far-sighted philanthropists are looking toward a time in the distant future, when, in the words of the poet—

> "The war drums throb no longer, and the battle flags are furled,
> In the Parliament of Man, the Federation of the World."

All modern thought and effort are tending toward this universal federation, which it is hoped will one day control the world's forces in the interests of peace and of every right reform.

CHAPTER VII.

THE GREATEST PARTY.

The contradiction and malignity of political debate have long since ceased to mar the tranquility of my spirit. I will do what I can do to mitigate the asperities of politics, believing them to be altogether needless, and unnatural, but for myself I have entered the region of calms and "none of these things move me." If this work be of God, it can not be overthrown; if it be not, then the sooner it comes to naught, the better for humanity.

The year 1888 will always rank as having been, up to its date, the most remarkable in the history of the Temperance Reform. Being the year of a Presidential campaign, it was, for sufficiently apparent reasons, the one in which politicians of the old school would do least for prohibition; but the presence of the new school in politics and of women as an active power in public affairs to a degree before undreamed of, mark it as a sort of moral watershed. In England the Primrose League of women antagonizing Gladstone's policy, and the Women's Liberal League presided over by that great statesman's wife, counting among its officers, Jane Cobden (Richard's daughter), and devoted to Home Rule, had already demonstrated the power of women in politics. Meanwhile, the Prohibition party had enjoyed since 1881, the active cooperation of the white ribbon women, and its vote had risen from ten thousand for Gen. Neal Dow, of Maine, as President (in 1880), to over one hundred and fifty-one thousand for ex-Governor St. John, of Kansas, in 1884. The Democratic party, led by President Cleveland, projected the tariff issue squarely across the path of the campaign; Republicans took it up eagerly, distorted the revision of the tariff, which was the actual issue, into the abolition of the tariff, to which the traditions of the money-getting Yankee nation were totally opposed, and won the battle of the ballot-box by making good temperance people believe that they must save their country, just once more, within the old lines of political warfare, by unblushing bribery, and by secretly assuring the liquor element that its interests would be as safe in Republican as in Democratic hands. In this campaign, Mrs. J. Ellen Foster, of Iowa, went before the Republican Convention with representatives of the anti-saloon association, and asked for a temperance plank. The report of the Committee on Resolutions contained no reference to this subject, and its reaffirmation of its previous platform served to leave the infamous "Raster Resolution" in full force. Subsequently, on the night of the adjournment, the following resolution was hurried through under circumstances proving to fair-minded lookers-on that it was but a sop in the form of a subterfuge to the prohibition Cerberus:

Resolved, That the first concern of all good government is the virtue and sobriety of the people and the purity of the home. The Republican party cordially sympathizes with all wise and well-directed efforts for the promotion of temperance and morality.

Concerning this resolution, the liquor men's leaders and newspapers declared that it was "no stronger than the brewers themselves had adopted;" was no hindrance to their remaining in the Republican fold, since it was agreed to by their chiefs at the convention before being offered, and was declared by the doughty Sheridan Shook, a notable New York liquor politician, to be only a little harmless catnip tea for the temperance element. But upon this basis, as well as because of their supposed devotion to "the heart side of the tariff question,"—whatever that may be—Mrs. Foster called upon the women of the nation to rally to "the party of great moral ideas." She was elected by the Republican National Campaign Committee, Chairman of the Women's National Republican Committee, which, like the former, had its headquarters in New York City, and sent out literature in which the tariff, not temperance, had the right of way. Though in other years an advocate of prohibition and denouncer of high-license, she vigorously championed the high-license campaign of Hon. Warner Miller, in New York state, and fought the Prohibition party with a vehemence worthy a better cause. This was the first time that women had ever been recognized as helpers by either of the great parties, and shows the gathering force of the great woman movement in America as everywhere. No doubt the attitude of the Prohibition party, which had from the first recognized women as integral forces in its organization and which had for many years given them a place upon its National Committee, and invited them as delegates to all of its conventions, did much to pioneer the way for this surprising new departure.

The success of Mrs. Foster's effort to organize Republican Clubs of women was not conspicuous, but, chiefly through her efforts, no doubt, some clubs were formed, women participated in the campaign as speakers,—notably Anna Dickinson and Mrs. Foster, women escorted speakers, paraded on foot in processions, and in several instances occupied the ancient and honorable place always heretofore accorded to the brass band.

Democratic women were hardly heard from, except as occasional wearers of the "red, red rose" or wavers of the bright bandana. Women appeared before every one of the national conventions where a president was to be nominated, and asked that an equal suffrage plank be placed in their platforms. This was done by the Prohibition and by one wing of the Labor party, an educational test being attached to the prohibition plank. It goes without saying, that women were out in force at the Prohibition party convention, held May 30, at Indianapolis in Tomlinson Hall. Over a thousand delegates were present, of whom about one hundred were of the steadfast sex.

Every state, except South Carolina and Louisiana, and all the territories but four—Arizona, Nevada, Idaho, and Wyoming—were represented. It was a gathering of the home-folk, but included nearly every leading nationality.

Not a taint of tobacco smoke was in the corridors; not a breath betrayed the fumes of alcohol. Clear-eyed, kind-faced, well-dressed, these men and women were familiar with the inside of the school-house, the church, the home, but not with that of the saloon.

Promptly at 10:00 o'clock A. M., the manly form of Samuel Dickie, chairman of the National Committee, was seen upon the elegantly decorated platform, and he called the other members of the committee and the National Officers of the Woman's Christian

Temperance Union to the front, amid great applause. Then James Black, of Pennsylvania, the party's first candidate for president, John Russell, of Michigan, its founder, John P. St. John, its last candidate, and Neal Dow, the father of prohibition, stood in line on the platform, amid the hurrahs of the convention. "America" was sung, and Rev. Sam Small, of Georgia, led in prayer. In a brief, but happy speech, Professor Dickie congratulated the party on its steady growth, proposing that it should make a coffin of ballot-boxes, weave a shroud from ballots, and bury the saloon in the "bloody chasm." Rev. Mr. Delano, of Connecticut, was made temporary chairman. He said the Democratic party was an interrogation point, "What are you going to do about it?" The Republican was an exclamation point, "A tear on the end of its nose," "Alas! Oh!" But the Prohibition party was a period, "We'll put a stop to it."

Gen. Clinton B. Fisk, of New York, was nominated for the presidency, amid great enthusiasm, and Rev. Dr. John A. Brooks, the great temperance leader of Missouri, was nominated for vice-president. Col. George W. Bain, of Kentucky, and Rev. Sam Small, of Georgia, were also nominated by several delegations for vice-president, but insisted upon withdrawing their names. Thirty thousand dollars were subscribed for campaign purposes.

The convention was an immense success every way. Rev. Dr. John Bascom, ex-president of Wisconsin University, was a delegate; also Father Mahoney, a Catholic priest of Minnesota, Professor Scomp of Oxford University, Georgia, with Bishop Turner, of Georgia, Rev. Mr. Hector, of California, and Rev. Mr. Grandison, of Georgia—three wonderfully gifted colored men.

A resolution urging scientific temperance instruction in the public schools was adopted, also one insisting on the rights of the colored man. The latter was introduced by Mr. Grandison, a representative of Clark University, Atlanta, seconded by Rev. Sam Small, and adopted unanimously.

Prof. Samuel Dickie was re-elected chairman.

A committee of ten, with Chairman Dickie at their head, was chosen to bear the formal announcement of the convention's action to General Fisk. This committee included two ladies—Mrs. Hoffman, of Missouri, and myself, and was another of the great convention's new departures. There was fine music by the

Silver Lake Quartette, Herbert Quartette, Nebraska Quartette (ladies), and the "Jinglers" (mellow-voiced colored men), who invariably brought down the house. The gavel used by ex-Governor St. John was presented by the Kansas delegation, and was made from a bit of the telegraph pole on which he was hung in effigy in Topeka, where for two terms he had been governor, applauded and beloved. At eleven o'clock on the second night the great convention closed with the doxology and prayer.

There was a rare memorial exercise on Decoration Day, five hundred soldiers of the Blue and Gray being assembled. There was also an oratorical contest for the Demorest prize medal (prohibition speeches required), and an intercollegiate contest arranged by Mr. Mills, with original speeches on the same great theme. Thus every opportunity was utilized for awakening public sentiment.

At every session, the hall, holding five thousand people, was crowded. The convention outran the expectations of its friends and followers. It was wonderfully earnest, eloquent, devout, and it marks a new epoch in Christian civilization.

At this memorable convention a small minority, led by Walter Thomas Mills, did its utmost to defeat the equal suffrage plank, on the plea that "two issues" could not be carried at a time, that this plank alienated the South, in general, and conservatives at the North, in particular, with other minor objections. This minority had agitated the subject vigorously for a year or more, and had thus put leaders, as well as rank and file, so thoroughly on guard, that when the vote came, only about sixty voted to drop the plank which had been in from the first nominating convention of the party in 1872.

Although we had a very large majority in the Committee on Resolutions, of which I was a member, our desire to hear all sides and reach a settlement as amicable as possible caused a long debate, in which Rev. Sam Small, of Georgia, gallantly declared at last his willingness to let the resolution pass, because, as he said, "The majority has been so magnanimous that I can not do less than bow my neck to the yoke."

James Black, of Pennsylvania, the Prohibition party's first nominee for president, was chairman of the Committee on Resolutions. He is a man of noble countenance, and every way impressive presence. When our sub-committee, to whom the controverted resolution was submitted (North and South, conservative and progressive, all being represented in that small midnight group of seven), had agreed upon the form, from the deep heart of this saintly man came the solemn words, "Thank God," and he bowed his head in prayer. The resolution was his own; he had carried one, almost identical in language, through the first convention of the Prohibition party and, but a few weeks earlier, through that of his own state.

When our committee filed into the great hall next day, the gentlemen and ladies that composed it marching arm in arm upon the platform, all felt that the hour was come when the manhood of this rising power in American politics was to declare decisively not only in favor of prohibition by law and prohibition by politics, but prohibition by woman's ballot, as the final consummation of the war upon King Alcohol, the most relentless foe of womanhood and home.

I believe history will not forget that scene. Governor St. John, the hero of the Kansas fight for Constitutional Amendment, was the central figure of the platform group, his keen, but kindly face and military bearing being well suited to the duty we had laid on his broad shoulders as the convention's chairman. Around him were men and women known throughout the nation as leaders for many a year of the Prohibition host in every contest made and every victory won.

This was the Prohibition party's platform in 1888, upon which there is reason to believe that in spite of defection, misrepresentation, bribery and the stolen mailing lists of the New York *Voice*, three hundred thousand men took their position. In it, the word Christian occurs perhaps for the first time in American politics:

PLATFORM.

The Prohibition party, in national convention assembled, acknowledging Almighty God as the source of all power in government, do hereby declare:

1. That the manufacture, importation, exportation, transportation, and sale of alcoholic beverages should be made public crimes, and prohibited as such.

2. That such prohibition must be secured through amendments of our national and state constitutions, enforced by adequate laws adequately supported by administrative authority; and to this end the organization of the Prohibition party is imperatively demanded in state and nation.

3. That any form of license, taxation, or regulation of the liquor traffic is contrary to good government; that any party which supports regulation, license, or tax enters into alliance with such traffic, and becomes the actual foe of the state's welfare; and that we arraign the Republican and Democratic parties for their persistent attitude in favor of the licensed iniquity, whereby they oppose the demand of the people for prohibition, and, through open complicity with the liquor crime, defeat the enforcement of law.

4. For the immediate abolition of the internal revenue system whereby our national government is deriving support from our greatest national vice.

5. That, an adequate public revenue being necessary, it may properly be raised by import duties, and by an equitable assessment upon the property and legitimate business of the country, but import duties should be so reduced that no surplus shall be accumulated in the treasury, and that the burdens of taxation shall be removed from foods, clothing, and other comforts and necessaries of life.

6. That the right of suffrage rests on no mere accident of race, color, sex, or nationality, and that where, from any cause, it has been withheld from citizens who are of suitable age and mentally and morally qualified for the exercise of an intelligent ballot, it should be restored by the people through the legislatures of the several states, on such educational basis as they may deem wise.

7. That civil service appointments for all civil offices chiefly clerical in their duties, should be based upon moral, intellectual, and physical qualifications, and not upon party service or party necessity.

8. For the abolition of polygamy and the establishment of uniform laws governing marriage and divorce.

9. For prohibiting all combinations of capital to control and to increase the cost of products for popular consumption.

10. For the preservation and defense of the Sabbath as a civil institution, without oppressing any who religiously observe the same on any other day than the first day of the week.

11. That arbitration is the Christian, wise, and economic method of settling national differences, and that the same method should, by judicious legislation, be applied to the settlement of disputes between large bodies of employés and employers. That the abolition of the saloon would remove burdens, moral, physical, pecuniary, and social, which now oppress labor and rob it of its earnings, and would prove to be the wise and successful way of promoting labor reform, and that we invite labor and capital to unite with us for the accomplishment thereof. That monopoly in land is a wrong to the people, and that the public land should be reserved to actual settlers, and that men and women should receive equal wages for equal work.

12. That our immigration laws should be so enforced as to prevent the introduction into our country of all convicts, inmates of other dependent institutions, and all others physically incapacitated for self-support, and that no person should have the ballot in any state who is not a citizen of the United States.

Recognizing and declaring that prohibition of the liquor traffic has become the dominant issue in national politics, we invite to full party fellowship all those who, on this one dominant issue, are with us agreed, in the full belief that this party can and will remove sectional differences, promote national unity, and insure the best welfare of our entire land.

The opening resolution was listened to with devout seriousness, and was adopted by a rising vote, without debate.

The prohibition resolution was received with hearty but not prolonged applause. We were there as the sequel of its foregone conclusions.

The resolution declaring in favor of women's receiving "equal wages for equal work," evoked enthusiasm; it was rapturously cheered; all felt that it was like the drops that precede the plentiful shower. Toward the close came the crucial test in the famous "sixth resolution." Its reading "brought down the house" with roars of applause and brought up the house again, hundreds rising to their feet with cheer upon cheer of approbation. It was then voted to debate the question two hours, and the clear voice of Professor Dickie, chairman of the National Committee, was heard suggesting that leaders should be chosen on either side to make the arguments. Nobody doubted where he stood whose pure life had delivered him from the worship of physical force; whose first vote and every ballot since then had been cast for the Prohibition candidates, and who, in the call issued for this very convention, had stated that "a fair representation of women delegates was desirable." But the rank and file desired to whack for themselves the ball now set in motion; hence Professor Dickie's plan was voted down, and free lances were tilted with great vigor from floor and platform, scores at a time seeking to obtain the floor up to the final vote. A minority of one, in the person of John M. Olin, of Wisconsin, reported against the resolution. This gentlemen spoke ably from his point of view, as did Walter Thomas Mills, T. C. Richmond and our good Neal Dow. All of them were believers in equal suffrage but thought this was not the time to declare for it, General Dow saying, "After we secure prohibition, we will give the ballot to our faithful allies." But it fell to my lot to remind these good brothers that though Maine had rejoiced in prohibition for over forty years, it last winter voted down a proposition to enfranchise women; that we have what we take the most pains for, and unless we take especial pains to secure the ballot for woman, she will never be armed and equipped as the law directs, for the home protection fight where "the guns are ballots and the bullets are ideas." With some such points as these, I closed the debate, and Sam Small came forward, took my hand and spoke in his eloquent way, saying, in effect, that "as we had added the educational test, he would stand with us." The South had been most generous from the beginning, showing a spirit of forbearance and good-will for which the women of that convention can never be too grateful. If its delegates had not with practical unanimity favored our cause, I fear we might have lost it on that most eventful day ever known to woman's annals of enfranchisement. George W. Bain made one of his most brilliant speeches, in our favor, and other gifted Southerners proved that with them the chivalry of justice outranked that of compliment. "Who would be free, himself must strike the blow," is a truth that received new confirmation in this memorable debate, where not one woman's voice or vote was given against the famous resolution.

When the count came, Secretary Cranfill announced less than thirty negatives, but Walter Thomas Mills claimed sixty, and Chairman St. John, in his humorous way, said, "Let it be as he says." Then came the climax of the convention, when flags waved, wooden "cranks" humorously creaked when turned by live ones, state delegations hoisted aloft their banners, women's white handkerchiefs were like a wind-blown argosy, and with shouts of hallelujah, men pointed to the significant motto above the platform, where the loyal white ribboners of Indiana had flung their pennon forth, "*No sex in citizenship.*" They knew the Supreme Court had said there was none, but they knew also that those cannot really be citizens who have no voice in making the laws they must obey.

At the close of this session, I received what is called in popular American parlance, "an ovation"; with half a score of strong men's hands stretched toward me at a time, I hardly knew which one to grasp, while their kind voices said over and over again, "You ought to be a happy woman;" "This is the Gospel's triumph;" "I wish your old mother had seen this;" "Hurrah for our side!" and other exclamations of rejoicing.

Now and then I would say, "My brother, what led you to vote for us?" The answers were all tributes to home's steadfast influence: "Oh, I was born a suffragist," said one; "Women must help us save the nation if it's ever saved"; "My wife educated me up to this"; and repeatedly young voters answered, "Why should n't we? I don't forget that my mother is a woman!"

Slipping away with those good sisters, Anna Gordon and Anna Shaw, who shared with me Mrs. May Wright Sewall's hospitalities, I could but think, as we walked on in silence, of that other day in Dixon, Ill., in the year 1875, at the second session of the Illinois W. C. T. U., when I was in the second year of my temperance work. I remembered writing a declaration to this effect: "*Resolved*, That since woman is the greatest sufferer from the rum curse, she ought to have power to close the dram-shop door over against her home." I remembered kneeling in prayer with my friend and room-mate, Mrs. Louise S. Rounds, who agreed to support me in this first attempt; then going over to the convention and getting this resolution offered, I seemed to hear once more the quiet emphasis of the presiding officer, as she said, "What will you do with this woman suffrage resolution?" and the decisive tones of the treasurer as she said, "I move we lay it on the table." I almost felt once more the painful heartbeats of suspense, and the joyful surprise when no one seconded the motion; then the debate, when a brave voice—I wish I could know whose—broke the stillness with, "I move it be adopted." I remembered the broken words in which I thereupon asked the women of the prairies that if they did not speak out, who would? Surely not the conservative East, the silent South, the unorganized Northwest. We all knew that woman was the liquor traffic's natural enemy. In Illinois the law said the municipal officers might license or not "in their discretion"; men were not discreet in this matter, as was proved by saloons on every hand, but women would be. Why not let them help good men elect officers who would truly represent the majority, and not saddle the saloon upon our people with its outcome of three thousand lunatics let loose each day upon defenseless homes? I told them that I had no home in that word's highest and most sacred sense, and never should have in this world, though I hoped to in a better, and that if I could brave an adverse public opinion for the sake of other women's homes, surely they could do so for the sake of their own. These words I could hardly speak for the ache in heart and throat, and I saw tears in many a gentle woman's eyes as I made my simple plea. When the vote came I think there was not one dissenting voice—if there were such I can not now recall them.

And thus the good ship Illinois swung from her moorings and put out to sea for a long and stormy voyage.

I thought, too, on that blessed day at Indianapolis, of the ringing words of Mrs. Lide Meriwether, of Tennessee:

> "She is launched on the wave, the good ship Prohibition!
> The wave of humanity, boundless and free."

I had been invited by Chairman Dickie to make a Decoration Day speech before the "Army of Blue and Gray," as represented at this Convention. Here follows the substance of this address:

THE GREATEST PARTY.

Here side by side sit the Blue and Gray. No other than the Prohibition party ever dared to be so great as to ordain a scene like this. I speak the words of truth and—soberness.

What a circle we have here! Sweep the compasses of thought through its circumference. Prohibition, first of all, the fixed point whence we calculate all others. The Blue and the Gray, the workingmen, the women. Inclosed and shielded by this circle is the home—that goes without saying; and beyond its shining curve is the saloon, out-matched, out-witted, and out-voted, which, in a republic, is best of all. For the fiat of the greatest party has gone forth, and we are here simply to set our seals to it; no saloon in politics or law, no sectionalism in law or politics, no sex in citizenship, but liberty, equality, fraternity in politics and law, now and for evermore.

This is our platform in a nutshell, and it is a platform of four ideas, at least.

When, in all history, were such matchless issues espoused by such magnanimous men?

There are two other parties; big, but not great; multitudinous, not masterful. Their tissue is adipose, not muscular. The issues of the one are made literally out of whole cloth, of all-wool tariff, warranted to wash in yet one more campaign, and the ensanguined shirt warranted never to be washed at all. Those of the other are spoils and Bourbonism. They will soon rally their respective clans to their stereotyped, old-fashioned conventions in Chicago and St. Louis, prepared to fight, bleed, and die for their country and its offices once more. Not a woman will be in their delegations. A woman might displace some man. Not a word about the home. No decisive utterance as to the greatest of our national perils.

Probably women would not attend these conventions, even were their presence sought. They certainly could not hold their own at the bar of the saloon, while in the greatest party they are only required to hold their own at the bar of public opinion.

Meanwhile, as if to set before these brethren a loftier example, the greatest party welcomes here the home-folks to equal opportunities and honors, and rallies here a remnant of the noble veterans who have learned that it is good to forgive, best to forget, attesting by this splendid and fraternal object-lesson that one party spells "nation" with the tallest kind of a capital "N" —one that indeed includes "the *people* of these United States"—and that the Blue and the Gray are to us emblems of nothing less than the blue sky that bends its tender arch above us all, and the gray ocean that enfolds one country and one flag.

"Angels look downward from the skies
Upon no holier ground,
Than where defeated valor lies
By generous foemen crowned."

How Grant would have rejoiced to look upon a scene like this—he whose most memorable words were, "Let us have peace!" by whose sick-bed sat General Buckner of the Confederate army, and to whose recent birthday celebration rallied Fitz Hugh Lee and other Southern braves!

The leaders of the party that was great when great Lincoln was its chief, are pleased in these days of its fatal degeneracy to call us the "St. Johnites." He is our patron saint—Heaven bless him!—who laid himself upon the altar of our sacred cause, and in the flame of partisan wrath that followed the defeat of 1884 proved to be a whole burnt-offering, yet I present him to you here to-night, one of the most gallant Union soldiers, "without the smell of fire upon his garments."

That party dare not gather Blue and Gray at its convention lest they should spoil its ammunition and tip one chief plank of its platform into the last ditch. What would it do if thus ruthlessly deprived of that time-worn utterance about "a free ballot and a fair count," which in its long years of supremacy it has proved itself impotent to secure, while the greatest party, by dividing the white vote into two hostile camps on the prohibition issue, is opening a straight path for the black man to the polls?

The women who uniformed their sons in Southern gray, and said, like the Spartan mother of old, "Come ye as conquerors or come ye no more," are here to-night with those other women who belted Northern swords upon their boys in blue, with words as pitiful, as brave. The women who embroidered stars and stripes upon the blessed flag that symbolized their love and faith, to-day have only gentle words for those who decked their "bonny flag of stars and bars" with tenderness as true and faith as fervent. The greatest party seats these women side by side to-night, and we all wear our snowy badge of peace above the hearts that hate no more, while we clasp hands in a compact never to be broken, and solemnly declare, before high Heaven, our equal hatred of the rum power and our equal loyalty to God and home and native land.

What hath God wrought? Surely a winsome thing is the human heart. It went against the grain for us to hate each other, did it not, dear Southern friends and allies? Never in history was there a war involving so little personal animosity. The French by nature hate the English, and speak about "perfidious Albion," and we know that "lands intersected by a narrow frith abhor each other," but our great unsevered continent was meant for an unsevered people, and "man breaks not the medal when God cuts the die." One Anglo-Saxon race, having one heritage of a queenly language and a heroic history of hardships mutually borne—it was hard for us to hate each other. The soldiers learned this first, brave and chivalric fellows, and they helped to teach us stay-at-homes the gracious lesson of fraternity. How often was the rude wreath of leaves placed on the grave of a Confederate by the Union soldier who had killed and yet who had wept over him! The fury of the non-combatant was almost the only fury that survived Grant's brotherly words to Lee at Appomattox.

Devoted to the stars and stripes, the sentiment of patriotism having been, from childhood, like a fire in the bones with me, I have wept over the flag for love of which great Stonewall Jackson and gallant Albert Sidney Johnston died. Nor do I envy the Northern patriot who can read without a tugging of the heart that wondrous poem by Father Ryan, the Southern Catholic priest, about "The Sword of Lee," and I can hardly trust myself to repeat his requiem of the Southern flag:

"Fold that banner, for 'tis weary;
Round its staff 'tis floating dreary,
Furl it, fold it: it is best;
For there's not a man to wave it,
And there's not a sword to save it,
And there's not one left to lave it
In the blood that heroes gave it,
And its foes now scorn and brave it;
Furl it, hide it, let it rest.

"Furl that banner, furl it sadly;
Once ten thousands hailed it gladly,
And ten thousands wildly, madly
Swore it should forever wave;
Swore that foeman's sword should never
Hearts like theirs entwined dissever,
Till that flag should float forever
O'er their freedom or their grave.

"Furl that banner, softly, slowly;
Treat it gently, it is holy,
For it droops above the dead.
Touch it not, unfold it never,
Let it droop there, furled forever,
For its people's hopes are dead."

Not that I loved that flag. No, brothers. I loved the slave too well not to desire its downfall; but then, so many brave hearts bled for it, so many gentle women wept, that I could be sincerely sorry for their grief, and yet be loyal to an emancipated race and my own glorious North. When the troops were mustered out in 1865, we little dreamed that less than ten years later the home guards of the land would be mustered in to the war of the crusade. God bless the crusade state, the veteran of our army!

As the sequel of that mighty movement, God's pentecost of power upon the nations, behold the women who, only a year ago, went to the polls to persuade men to cast their ballot for prohibition in Oregon and Texas, in Michigan and Tennessee. If the voters of the greatest party are true to us as we have been and will be true to them, ten years hence we will help those who were beaten in four states that stood for constitutional prohibition in 1885, with our guns that are ballots, as we are now helping with our bullets that are ideas.

I never expected to speak with pride about the Solid South as such, but surely I may do this now that it is becoming solid for the "dry ticket," and you who dwell there may be glad that the Northern heart is fired once more, this time with the same war-cry as that which fires the Southern, and it is "protection for our homes." That is the spell to conjure by. That is the rallying cry of North and South, Protestant and Catholic, of white and black, of men and women equally. Bourbon Democrat and Radical Republican will seek in vain to stifle that swift-swelling chorus, that "chorus of the Union," for which great Lincoln vainly prayed in his first inaugural. Do you not recall this marvelous concluding sentence (I quote from memory): "The mystic chords of memory, stretching from many a sacred hearth and patriot's grave, all over this broad land, shall once more swell the chorus of the Union when again touched, as surely they will be, by the better angel of our nature." The angel is the temperance reform, and the fulfillment of that prophecy we have lived to see.

The greatest party stands for nationalism as against sectionalism; it stands for the noblest aims and aspirations of the wage-worker as against monopolies that dare to profane that holy word, "trust"; it stands for the future in politics as against the past, the home vote with an educational test against the saloon vote with a beer-breath as its credentials; and, best of all, it stands for the everlasting and absolute prohibition of sin as against any alliance between sin and the government. For while the greatest party will never hesitate to be the champions of these causes good and great, so closely linked with its own central purposes, neither must it fail to put prohibition by law and prohibition by politics so far in the lead that no candid man can for a moment question the august supremacy of these overmastering issues. We are firmly persuaded that the separation of the people into two distinct armies, one voting for men who will outlaw the poison curse, and the other for men who will legalize it, must come, and that such separation can not come too soon. We are not here to speak harsh words of armies rallied under other ensigns, but simply to declare that in this great emergency we can not depend upon them. Party machinery and the ambition of party leaders to-day stand between the people and their opportunity. We would clear the track for prohibition. We are bound to do it. For that were we born, and for that came we into this world.

When I think of Lexington and Paul Revere; when I think of Bunker

Hill and the dark redoubt where General Warren died; when I think of Washington, that greatest of Southerners, upon his knees in prayer at Valley Forge; when I think of Stonewall Jackson praying before he fought; of Robert Lee's and Sidney Johnston's stainless shields; when I remember Sheridan's ride, and Sherman's march to the sea with the boys in blue behind him, and Grant fighting the battle out and on to the glorious triumph of our Northern arms, then my heart prophesies with all a patriot's gratitude, America will win in her bloodless war against the awful tyranny of King Alcohol and King Gambrinus, and proud am I to have a part in it, for, thank God, "I—I, too, am an American."

Bound together by our mutual faith in Mary T. Lathrap, of Michigan and Sallie F. Chapin, of South Carolina; cemented by the martyr blood of Iowa's George B. Haddock and Mississippi's Roderick Dhu Gambrell; made one by the pride we feel in these grand old pioneers, John Russell, the father of our party; James Black, its earliest presidential candidate; Gideon T. Stewart and H. W. Thompson, St. John and Daniels, the heroes of a later day and a more dreadful crisis; Green Clay Smith and Samuel Dickie, Hopkins and Brooks, Clinton B. Fisk and George W. Bain, and glorious old Neal Dow, the father of prohibition for the world, surely temperance people of the North and South may well say each to other, "Whither thou goest I will go; where thou lodgest, I will lodge: thy people shall be my people, and thy God my God. The Lord do so to me, and more, also, if aught but death part thee and me."

Here, upon Indiana's genial soil, midway between the sections that shall erelong be sections no more, but part of the greatest party's family circle, gracious and great, let us say unitedly to the fire-eaters of the South on the one side and the chasm-diggers of the North on the other:

"Oh, meaner folks of narrower souls,
    Heirs of ignoble thought,
Stir not the camp-fire's blackened coals,
    Blood-drenched by those who fought,
Lest out of Heaven a fire shall yet
    Bear God's own vengeance forth
On those who once again would set
    Discord 'twixt South and North."

In the spring of 1863, two great armies were encamped on either side of the Rappahannock river, one dressed in blue and one in gray.

As twilight fell, the bands of music on the Union side began to play the martial strains, "Star-Spangled Banner" and "Rally 'Round the Flag," and this musical challenge was taken up by those on the other side, who responded with the "Bonnie Blue Flag" and "Away Down South in Dixie." But after awhile it was borne in upon the soul of a single soldier in one of those bands of music to begin a sweeter and more tender air, and slowly as he played it, they joined with all the instruments on the Union side, until finally a great and mighty chorus swelled up and down our army, "Home, Sweet Home." When they had finished there was no challenge over yonder, and every Confederate band had taken up that lovely air, so attuned to all that is holiest and dearest, and one great chorus of the two great hosts went up to God; and when they had finished came from the boys in gray a challenge, "Three cheers for home," and as these cheers went resounding through the skies from both sides of the river "something upon the soldier's cheek washed off the stain of powder."

Fellow soldiers in the fight for a clear brain, I am proud to belong to an army which makes kindred of those who once stood in arms against each other. Let us cherish North Carolina's motto from Isaiah's words: "Fear not, I am with thee; I will bring thy seed from the east and gather them from the west; I will say to the North, *give up*, and to the South, *keep not back;* bring my sons from afar, and my daughters from the ends of the earth." I am glad of these good times, and I think we women are in them, equal members of the greatest party, as we have been since the day of its birth.

> "It shall shine more and more
> Till its glory like noontide shall be.
> It shall shine more and more
> Till the home from the dram-shop is free.
> It shall shine more and more
> Till the nation Christ's glory shall see."

While the Democratic National Convention was in session at St. Louis in 1888, the papers had much to say of the Thurman bandana and the red, red rose, as the symbol of simon-pure Democracy. I had also noted the primrose as the emblem of the Conservative women of England, and it occurred to me that our Prohibitionists ought to have a floral badge. What then more beautiful than the white rose to match the white ribbon? So I telephoned the suggestion to *The Union Signal*, wrote about it to our leaders, who officially indorsed it, and when our committee appointed to notify General Fisk of his nomination, assembled for that purpose in the Metropolitan Opera House, New York, June 22, 1888, I asked my faithful friend, Mrs. Frances J. Barnes, of that city, to see that those who sat on the platform were all provided with white roses. This she did. The suggestion was cordially adopted by the gentlemen, who were present in larger number than the ladies, and I had the honor of fastening a white rose to the lapel of our newly-created Bishop Fitzgerald of my own church, a devoted party Prohibitionist, who made the opening prayer on this occasion. A celluloid rose was brought out by our Woman's Temperance Publication Association, in Chicago, and has been sold by tens of thousands, so that we may conclude the white rose is acclimated as the political badge of those who would overthrow the dram-shop and protect the home.

So far as I know, my advocacy of the Prohibition party has not personally alienated a friend, though it has seriously interfered with what friends called a "rising popularity," and has grieved and wounded many who are dear to me and who as honestly believe that I am wrong in my working hypothesis of prohibition as I believe that they are wrong in theirs. How good people can be so deceived by high-license as to see in it anything other than the Trojan horse smuggled into our temperance camp on false pretenses, I expect to discover on the day when I learn how you can elect prohibitionists to power by not voting for them. To me, high-license is the devil's counterfeit for the pure gold of prohibition. And thus believing, I have, in every state and territory of the Republic, declared high-license a high crime, and in the name of boyhood bewildered and manhood betrayed, in the name of woman broken-hearted and home broken down, I have solemnly pronounced upon it the anathema of the American home. This was not what one would have chosen to say who well knew that but for Christian people high-license could never have been for a moment tolerated by the reputable class, who knew that Christian ministers all over the land were voting for it and that some of them were discounting the speaker's wits even while she tried to talk!

CHAPTER VIII.

THE NEW YORK CONVENTION.

(1888).

The New York Convention caused more comment than all the others put together. Held in the great metropolis, in one of the five largest audience rooms of the world; on the eve of a Presidential election and in the most doubtful and determinative of Commonwealths; attended by four hundred and twelve elected delegates from almost every state and territory; filling five days; with a printed program containing fourteen pages and one hundred and eighty-two specifications, with forty departments of work passing in review, over fifty officers to be elected, a dozen memorials and counter-memorials to be replied to; with dress reform and cooking lectures, sermons, flag presentations, introductions, welcomes, White Ribbon Quartette, and a great deal besides, and all listened to by an audience five thousand strong, the great convention was not inaptly described by one who said it was a "Moral Jumbo." Its reports and addresses were highly complimented by onlookers during its progress, and I was many times made to wonder anew if the wrath of man is not going to be made to praise the Lord on this wise: while our brothers handicap themselves with the alcohol and tobacco habits, we women, like the tortoise outdoing the hare, will pass, or, at least, overtake them, on the splendid highway of intellectual evolution. Woman's capacity at branching out was here abundantly illustrated; in proof, note the daring of Mrs. Mary T. Burt, who engaged the costly Metropolitan Opera House and served a free lunch every day to the entire convention, paying the expenses by sales of opera boxes and seats; note the enterprise of Mrs. Dr. Buchanan, walking New York streets to seek entertainment for the throng, and succeeding where missionary and other women's societies had well-nigh failed in Gotham, because the quiet little Scotch Presbyterian woman acted on a Scotch motto, that she perhaps has never heard, "It's dogged as does it." When I knew that we four (disavowed) but duly accredited women delegates to General Conference were not invited to Methodist homes in the metropolis, I supposed it was because they were "too far back,"—as we in the West say of conservatives—but when I heard one of the most noted and conservative Methodist women in the nation mention that she was never yet invited to a Methodist home in New York City, I had my thoughts. Suffice it that at our convention, all received entertainment who wished for it, the expenses of our secretaries and treasurer being paid by the National W. C. T. U. at hotels near by.

An elegant reception was given us by Madame Demorest, at which we met Clara Barton, Jennie June (Mrs. Croly), and other noted leaders in the world of to-day. The courage of Madame Demorest in assuming all expenses of the decorations was in keeping with her enterprising spirit, and last, but not least, the courage of the general officers in taking the convention to New York when almost no white ribboner save the state president gave them hope of its success, deserves to go on record.

Promptly at nine o'clock on the opening morning, Mrs. S. M. I. Henry, of Illinois, began the prayer-meeting, and at ten the convention came to order, with Anna Gordon's bannerets flying at the mast-head, so to speak, of every delegation, the platform brilliant with white ribbon ensigns, national and state, the whole great auditorium decked with the red, white and blue, mingled with the escutcheons of every Commonwealth, and before us, in that huge parquette, four hundred women with white ribbons on their breasts, while from floor to dome the place was packed with people, and the famous temple of Art had become for the time being a famous temple of Temperance. In fourteen years the Hillsboro praying band had gathered around it in this country a direct following of men, women and children, amounting to not less than half a million, and its publishing house had sent out in this year more than sixty million pages, or one for every inhabitant of the United States.

"What hath God wrought?" must have been the grateful

exclamation in every mind, as the Crusade leader, our beloved Mrs. Judge Thompson, of Hillsboro, Ohio, the fragile-looking, sweet-voiced old lady, stood by my side, the Convention rose, and from the big Hillsboro Bible, loaned us for the purpose by the Presbyterian Church there, we read responsively the Crusade Psalm. Then all voices joined in singing the Crusade Hymn, "Give to the winds thy fears," the White Ribbon Quartette from Maine leading, with their golden cornets, and Mrs. Barker, of Dakota, led us in prayer. The Executive Committee had been in session for two days, also the Board of Superintendents, and the report of the former was read and accepted.

It was perfectly well known that the Iowa W. C. T. U. had a memorial protest to present in opposition to the attitude of friendliness toward the Prohibition party, maintained since 1882 by the National W. C. T. U. This state had from the first led the protesting minority and now presented a protest in its own name. Of its nature all were well informed, for it had been given to the public by the Republican press of the country and had become, virtually, a campaign document. Its general terms were the same as those of the protests written by Mrs. Foster for the minority at Philadelphia, Minneapolis and Nashville. Strict constructionists claimed that this memorial should not have been given to the public until presented to the convention, and the hypocritical statements of the Republican press to the effect that the convention "smothered" what the said press had for weeks industriously circulated from Maine to California, were, to say the least, eminently characteristic of its policy through the entire campaign of 1888.

The Illinois W. C. T. U. also had a "protest," but theirs had not seen the light. They had very properly kept it for the tribunal to which it was addressed. This protest called in question the wisdom of the National W. C. T. U. in permitting its members publicly to antagonize the Prohibition party, to which it had promised to "lend its influence." While no attempt was to be made to control the personal opinions of members, this protest held that they should not be at liberty publicly to antagonize the action of the National W. C. T. U. As Mrs. Foster was the only one who had conspicuously done this, the memorial seemed to be aimed at her. Besides this memorial, there were four from

OHIO
For God and HOME and NATIVE LAND
W.C.T.U.
NAT'L PRIZE BANNER
Woman's Christian Temperance Union State of New York
For God and
WORLDS

NATIVE LAND
W.C.T.U.

Evanston
Loyal Temperance Legion

Tremble King Alcohol
We shall grow up.

Company A 4th Division

Humanity

That our daughters may be as corner-stones polished after the similitude of a palace.

Y.W.C.T.U.

TEMPERANCE UNION
ND NATIVE LAND.

the minority in Iowa who disagreed with Mrs. Foster's views, in which they asked the help of the National W. C. T. U., declaring that the parliamentary machinery of the State W. C. T. U. was being used to rule them out; that on purely partisan grounds they were deprived of representation; that the literature of the National W. C. T. U. was not permitted to be circulated, and that they could not hold their own unless assistance was soon furnished them, and one of the protests distinctly called for the discontinuance of Mrs. Foster as a vice-president of the national society, because of her antagonistic attitude toward the W. C. T. U.

In view of all these facts, it was thought best by certain of the leaders, that these memorials should not be read in the National Convention until first considered by the Executive Committee, which, so far from being a "Star Chamber," as some of our "non-partisan" sisters have called it, is made up of the presidents of all the states and territories, and the District of Columbia, or forty-eight women, representing every section of the country, besides the five general officers of the society. Several of these protests were addressed to the Executive Committee, and were already in our hands, but it was felt by some that by having all of them so referred, the whole subject could be more temperately and fairly passed in review than if it were launched without such preliminary consideration upon the surging waves of the great convention. Besides, by this method, the program could first be gone through, giving to the public an adequate idea of our many-sided work, and forestalling the false impression already created by the Republican press, that the National W. C. T. U. was simply a "political annex" to the Prohibition party. Hence, the motion of Mrs. Henrietta Monroe, president of the Ohio W. C. T. U., that "memorials and protests be referred to the Executive Committee without reading." In the handling of this motion there was no possible motive for doing any one injustice, and none whatever was intended by the presiding officer.

The largest vote mustered by the minority was thirty-one; the convention was heartily in favor of the motion to refer, and it promptly prevailed. These are the facts concerning an action relative to which the misapprehensions—to call them by no harsher name—of a partisan press have been more widely circulated than has anything helpful to our movement, since the Crusade.

If we could have had the same use of Republican newspapers for an argument exhibiting the falseness of their high-license theory, constitutional prohibition would have received the greatest "boom" in all its history.

The memorial breeze having blown over, the convention held itself steadily to its work. Under the heads of Preventive, Educational, Evangelistic, Social, and Legal, we had, with the Department of Organization, and including Sunday afternoon, which was devoted to the Department of Social Purity, three days filled with the reports of forty leaders, earnest, intelligent women of the church, the home, and school, who came forward and without manuscript, compressed into a few minutes of always attractive and often eloquent speech, the steadfast work of a year.

Our annual sermon was preached, as usual, by a woman, Miss Elizabeth Greenwood, of Brooklyn, whose perfect equipoise in the pulpit, breadth of thought, elegance of diction, and deep spirituality, place her in the front rank of pulpit orators. She was chosen national superintendent of our Evangelistic Department, and with Dean Wright, of Cambridge, is working to place it on a basis of real Christian scholarship.

Bishop Fallows gave us a remarkable sermon on "The Ecclesiastical Emancipation of Woman," choosing his text, as did Miss Greenwood, from the Crusade Bible, which lay on the table throughout the convention, and was a constant comfort and inspiration to us all.

It seemed like that rarest thing on earth, poetic justice, to hear a woman preach and a Bishop declare that women ought to be freely permitted so to do, on the same platform where, but a few months before, women had been ruled out of a great ecclesiastical convention. And when Rev. Dr. J. M. Buckley, woman's redoubtable opponent in her broader fields and pastures new, was introduced, and handsomely received by the white ribboners, the amenities of civilization could no farther go.

General Neal Dow came, by my urgent request, glorious old man, erect and vigorous in his eighty-sixth year, wearing his frosty, but kindly age like an imperial crown. I wanted our blessed white ribboners to have the joy of seeing the immortal "Father of Prohibition." And Governor St. John was there, the hero of journalistic abuse, on which he has grown constantly more gentle-hearted and beloved. Whenever he appeared the women's handkerchiefs were in the air. Gen. Clinton B. Fisk is a great favorite, personally, being one of the most genial and gifted of men, while as "our candidate" he carried off the white ribbon honors. Joseph Cook, that oratorical cyclone, swept all away with him in his magnificent enthusiasm for "whatsoever things are pure, lovely, and of good report." Gentle Clara Barton was received as a grand elder sister might have been; Mary A. Livermore, with the love we give our very own.

Chairman Dickie, on being introduced, suggested playfully that the convention indorse the action that had just occurred, by which I was made a counseling member of the Executive Committee of the Prohibition party, and this was done, in my absence, in our own Executive meeting, in the same vein, as I supposed, until the hostile press made much of it. Mayor Abram S. Hewitt gave us an address of welcome in the midst of his candidacy for re-election, quite in line with his well known reputation for mental shrewdness and square dealing. Elizabeth Thompson, the philanthropist, presented us, not in person, but through the happy intervention of Rev. Anna Shaw, with a "woman's flag," bordered with the flags of all nations, and symbolic of that international peace for which she works so earnestly and well. Madame Demorest had a reception in our honor, as elegant as New York's luxurious facilities could furnish, and this enumeration but hints at the handsome pageant of our fifteenth convention.

On the last afternoon came the report of the Committee on Resolutions, Mrs. Governor Wallace, chairman, Miss Helen L. Hood, secretary. For two years this report had been printed beforehand, as nearly all our documents are, for the convenience of delegates, and in both cases unfortunate misapprehensions have resulted from the reporters' not unnatural supposition that all that was printed was indorsed. The following resolution adopted from that of Rhode Island W. C. T. U. was passed with no dissent except from Iowa, a part of Pennsylvania, and a few other scattering votes:

Resolved, That we re-affirm our allegiance to that party which makes its dominant issue the suppression of the liquor traffic, declares its belief in Almighty God as the source of all power in Government, defends the sanctity of the Christian Sabbath, recognizes equal suffrage and equal wages for women, demands the abolition of polygamy and uniform laws governing marriage and divorce, and aims to remove sectional differences, promote national unity, and insure the best welfare of our land.

Woman's ballot was thus dealt with :

Resolved, That the right of citizens to vote should not be abridged or denied on account of sex ; we therefore urge an amendment to the National Constitution granting women the franchise.

Another resolution read as follows :

" WHEREAS, Individual membership in the W. C. T. U. has never been, and is not based upon the holding of certain political views ; and whereas, the individual member is accorded perfect freedom of private opinion and private utterance of the same, we nevertheless recognize the fact, that the action of the National W. C. T. U. in promising "to lend its influence to that party, by whatever name called, which would give the best embodiment of Prohibition principles, and would most surely protect the home," gives to our organization a policy which each member is in honor bound to respect.

Resolved, That it is the sense of the National W. C. T. U. that no member should speak from the public platform to antagonize our policy toward the party to which our influence is pledged, and that any member thus antagonizing our policy is hereby declared disloyal to our organization.

When this was read, Mrs. Benjamin, our superintendent of Parliamentary Usage, to whom all points of difference under that head were referred throughout the convention, said, "I object." The chair asked, as in duty bound, "Is the objection sustained?" And by an overwhelming majority this was done ;—yet it went out to the country that we "had passed a gag-law for the express purpose of persecuting Mrs. Foster."

The general course of *The Union Signal* was sustained, as it certainly ought to have been, the following resolution being adopted :

Resolved, That we extend to Mary Allen West, the able editor of *The Union Signal*, our hearty thanks for the manner in which she has conducted our national organ, and that we hereby indorse the position she has taken in the exercise of editorial prerogatives on the political as well as any other questions which concern our organization, and in testimony of this we express our appreciation of her labors and our determination to stand by her in her difficult and trying position.

George W. Bain, the orator-in-chief of the American temperance movement, was introduced amid vociferous applause ; among other good things he said :

Having traveled this country from ocean to ocean, and from the Lakes to the Gulf, I have found our prisons filled with men, our saloons filled with men, and the school-houses, or rather the high schools, graduating more girls than boys, our Sabbath schools and churches filled with women,—and I believe I serve my country, its homes, and heaven, when I pledge myself that I will henceforth do everything in my power to bring more directly to bear upon the political life of this Republic, the virtuous, intellectual offices of womanhood. When the church gets into trouble, it returns at once to the Preachers' Aid Society of women, and when the youth of this country is being blocked by vices, I apprehend it won't be very long till our country will be in such a condition that it will have to turn to its womanhood for salvation.

Every action of the New York convention showed a liberality of spirit for which, I dare assert, no parallel can be found in the history of associated effort among men or women.

The closing hours of the convention, extending to midnight of the fourth day, were occupied with the consideration of the six memorials and the replies. To Iowa's objections to our recognition of the Prohibition party, a general demurrer was entered, the specific points involved having been taken up when they were first brought forward in 1885. To Illinois' urgent request that women who antagonize our policy should be declared disloyal, the reply was that to do this would be out of harmony with our present safety and past policy. To the Iowa W. C. T. U. minority the following, among other messages, was sent:

We have lamented with you, and more deeply than you have been aware, the hardships you have suffered.

But the National W. C. T. U. makes two constitutional requirements of its members—and two only; signing the pledge of total abstinence, and paying annual dues.

It has always been with us a cardinal doctrine that each state should be left free in all things except these.

The debate was spirited, but kindly, and at midnight the convention rose, the members stood hand in hand to sing, "God be with you till we meet again," our beloved "Deborah" Wallace prayed, Rev. Dr. C. H. Payne pronounced the benediction, and the National W. C. T. U. Convention of 1888 was duly adjourned.

Meanwhile, our publishing interests constantly increase in volume; the devotion of white ribboners grows stronger; the honest, outspoken position of the society in saying just what it means and being really a coadjutor of the Prohibition party, rather than an ally of Republicanism, but professedly "non-partisan," compels respect, and we move forward to a victory, slow but sure, which shall bring in the day of national prohibition, woman's enfranchisement, alcohol's downfall, and home's supreme dominion in America and over all the world.

But that any considerable advance in legislation will be achieved by the party whose cause we have espoused, while it retains its present name, I for one, do not expect.

While we maintain the "courage of our convictions," politically, our other departments of work have never "called a halt." At the Minneapolis convention in 1886, at Nashville in 1887, and at New York in 1888, our official organ was published daily, with a stenographic report of the proceedings. The minutes of our St. Louis convention (debates are never reported) covered two hundred and sixty-three pages of a large pamphlet; those of Philadelphia, three hundred and ninety; those of Minneapolis, four hundred and eleven; of Nashville, four hundred and fifty-three. Every important document that comes before the convention, from the president's address to the ballots, is in printed form, the printed program covering several pages. A large book would be required to furnish even an outline history of the W. C. T. U. movement by means of which the children, from primer to high-school grade, in thirty-six states and territories, are now studying the laws of health, "with special reference to the effects of alcoholic drinks and narcotics upon the human system," this study being required by law, and teachers being obliged to pass examination therein, before securing a certificate. Not fewer than ten millions of names have been gathered for our petitions on this subject, and the first temperance legislation ever granted by Congress was in this interest. Still the good work goes on, and will go on until every state is under this wholesome law. Meanwhile, the Sandwich Islands, Australia and Japan are adopting the same temperance text-books indorsed by our society. I hope that Mrs. Mary H. Hunt, of Boston, superintendent of this department, may, ere-long, write the thrilling story of which she is the heroine; also that Miss Lucia Kimball, whose temperance work in Sunday-schools has culminated in the Quarterly Lesson now provided in the International Lesson Series, may tell how that mighty field was won.

From my annual address at the New York Convention, I select the following as touching on advanced phases of our work:

The new movement for the study of the Bible, as the finest of English classics, introducing it into colleges and seminaries of the highest grade, is full of possibilities for Christian progress and development. The marvel is that Christian scholars should ever have permitted the heathen classics to outrank the psalms of David, the visions of Isaiah, and the wonderful philosophy of the four Gospels. But something else needs to be done on the same line, and must become universal before we can fairly call ourselves other than a practically pagan republic. This is the teaching of those principles of ethics that are found in the Scriptures and questioned by no sane mind, whether Jew or Gentile, Catholic or Protestant. No general movement toward making our great public school system an ethical system has yet been inaugurated, except by the Woman's Christian Temperance Union, and this kingdom of heaven has come to the children of the land, as its wont is, "not by observation," but so quietly that our people hardly know the good thing that has happened to them.

The effort of good women everywhere should be to secure the introduction of a text-book of right living; one that should teach the reasons for the social code of good manners, every particular of which is based on the Golden Rule, and those refinements of behavior which involve the utmost kindness to the animal creation, including the organization of Bands of Mercy in all our public schools. All this is sure to come, and that right speedily, as a consequence of the awakened interest of women everywhere in the subject of education, and their increasing power along these lines. The time will come when it will be told as a relic of our primitive barbarism that children were taught the list of prepositions and the names of the rivers of Thibet, but were not taught the wonderful laws on which their own bodily happiness is based, and the humanities by which they could live in peace and good will with those about them. The time will come when, whatever we do not teach, we shall teach ethics as the foundation of every form of culture, and the "faith that makes faithful" in every relation of life will become a thing of knowledge to the child of the then truly Christian republic. For we can never teach these things and leave out Christ as the central figure, and His philosophy as the central fact of our system of education. At the same time our teaching must be as far removed from anything sectarian or involving the statement of a creed, as the North Star is from the Southern Cross. There will be no trouble in those days about opening school with such extracts from the Bible as have been agreed upon by men and women of all faiths, and the repetition of the Lord's Prayer with its universal benignities will be a matter of course. It is for the Woman's Christian Temperance Union to work on quietly to this end, without haste, without rest.

THE ECCLESIASTICAL EMANCIPATION OF WOMEN.

By a strange and grievous paradox, the Church of Christ, although first to recognize and nurture woman's spiritual powers, is one of the most difficult centers to reach with the sense of justice toward her, under the improved conditions of her present development and opportunity. The sense of authority is here so strong, and woman's capacities for reverence and humility are still so great, that, while we can not fail to deprecate, we need not wonder at the present situation. Here, as elsewhere, enlightened womanhood will come with the magic open sesame which shall ere-long prevail even against these gates so sedulously barred: *Woman, like man, should be freely permitted to do whatever she can do well.*

Who that is reasonable doubts that if we had in every church a voice in all its circles of power, it would be better for the church, making it more homelike and attractive, more endeared to the people, and hence more effective in its great mission of brotherly and sisterly love? By what righteous principle of law or logic are we excluded from church councils when we so largely make up the church's membership? Who that did not know it beforehand would believe that good men actually desire to keep us out? Antecedently I would have made my affidavit that nothing could have pleased them so much as to have us come in and share with them the power and honor, as we do the burdens and responsibilities, of the church home. Indeed, I can not help thinking that it might be said of us, "O fools, and slow of heart to believe all that the prophets have spoken!" We have not ourselves rightly understood the liberty wherewith Christ hath made woman free by introducing a religion that removes the world from a war footing to a peace basis, thus rendering science possible, with invention as its consequence, from all of which comes a civilization having as its choicest blossom the material comforts and contrivances of the modern home. We have not seen that old-time duties have been taken from our hands that we might enter upon higher ones, and that to make the whole world homelike is the province of one half the race. But as these truths take possession of our inmost hearts we shall go gently to our brothers, asking them to open to us every opportunity and to share with us every prerogative within the Church of Christ. In the United States, the generous spirit of whose manhood has nowhere been excelled, we have a vantage-ground in any effort that may be quietly and unitedly put forth for the opening of closed doors, ecclesiastical or otherwise. I have long thought that the spectacle of well-nigh a hundred thousand church edifices closed, except at brief intervals when meetings were in progress, was a travesty of the warm-hearted gospel of our Lord, and I rejoice to see that just as woman's influence grows stronger in the church, those doors stay open longer, that industrial schools, Bands of Hope, church kindergartens, reading-rooms, and the like, may open up their founts of healing, and put "a light in the window for thee, brother."

The time will come when these gates of Gospel Grace shall stand open night and day, while woman's heavenly ministries shall find their central home within God's house, the natural shrine of human brotherhood in action, as well as human brotherhood in theory.

"Stay in the church and help reform it," says one. "No, that is impossible; old churches and old parties are equally crystallized," comes the reply. "Let the W. C. T. U. organize a church, and we will join it, every man of us," is the declaration of an influential group of earnest men. "No, we have too many churches already," objects a listener, "let the wheat and tares grow together until the harvest." Meanwhile, many letters and consultations with men and women high in church circles develop on the part of some a plan like this:

An organization to be formed, called the "Church Union," made up of those who are unwilling longer to leave inoperative the protest of their souls against a government of the church by its minority; this Church Union to be open to any and all who will subscribe to the Apostles' Creed, and the triple pledge of total abstinence, anti-tobacco, and social purity; none of the members obliged to leave a church to which they now belong in order to join this; men and women to be on terms of perfect equality, and women to be regularly licensed and ordained. The special work of this Church Union would be among the masses of the people, still, alas, so generally ungospeled, and in foreign lands, especially among the women. In this country, buildings now devoted to amusements to be utilized rather than new ones erected, and everywhere the steadfast effort made to go, not send, and to go rather than to stay at home and say "Come" to the great humanity that beats its life along the stony streets.

But for myself, I love my mother-church so well and recognize so thoroughly that the base and body of the great pyramid she forms are broader than its apex, that I would fain give her a little time in which to deal justly by the great household of her loving, loyal, and devoted daughters. I would wait four years longer, in fervent hope and prayer that the great body of her ministers and of her membership may make it manifest to all the world that the church of Lady Huntington, Barbara Heck, and Phebe Palmer, does not hesitate to march with the progressive age it has done so much to educate, nor fear to carry to their logical sequence its life-long teachings as to woman's equality within the house of God. I say this frankly, from my present outlook, though so often urged, and not a little tempted, and sometimes quite determined to take a new departure. The time will come, however, and not many years from now, when, if representation is still denied us, it will be our solemn duty to raise once more the cry, "Here I stand, I can do no other," and step out into the larger liberty of a religious movement where majorities and not minorities shall determine the fitness of women as delegates, and where the laying on of hands in consecration, as was undoubtedly done in the early church, shall be decreed on a basis of "gifts, graces and usefulness," irrespective of sex.

W. C. T. U. DEACONESSES.

I wish that we might here state with all considerateness, but with fearless honesty, our position on the question of women in the church. But, as I have already said, women are, if possible, even more to blame than men that they are so discounted in church as well as state at this late day. A majority of men in this country and age have so far outgrown the ignorant notion of their divine right to rule over women, that if we had but the courage of conviction, and that sense of dignity that ought to mark us as daughters of the Lord Almighty, men would within a twelvemonth, seat us beside themselves upon the thrones of government in church and state, ruling the world jointly, as He meant we should, when, as the Bible says, "He gave to *them* dominion."

Truly we have what we take the most pains for, and women must be up and doing if they expect the co-operation and fealty of men in politics, ecclesiastical or secular. It also seems to me we should, at this convention, provide for White Ribbon deaconesses to be trained in our Evangelistic Department, taught to be skilled nurses at our National Temperance Hospital, and employed by our local unions in preaching, teaching and visiting the sick and poor. I am confident that there are men of the best standing in the pulpit, who will not hesitate to set them apart to this sacred office and ministry in accordance with the custom of the early church. There are thousands of women, young and old, whose hearts the Lord hath touched and who would rejoice to find a vocation so sacred and so full of help within the sheltering fold of the W. C. T. U.

> "She spoke of justice, truth and love,
> How soft her words distilled;
> She spoke of God, and all the place
> Was with His presence filled."

Of how many a sweet soul within our borders those words are true? What hindereth that they be set apart with every guarantee and safeguard that can emphasize their gospel ministry? Of them how long has it been said, as of Christ's early servants, "the people magnify them," and "the common people hear them gladly."

Rev. Dr. Black, of Mississippi, says in his new book:

"The offices of deaconesses formed a part of the machinery of the Church for many centuries. The deaconess received ordination by the imposition of hands. The ordination ritual is given in the Apostolical Constitutions, from which we extract the following prayer of the officiating bishop:

"'Eternal God, Father of our Lord Jesus Christ, Creator of man and of woman, thou who didst fill with thy spirit Miriam, Deborah, Hannah, and Huldah, thou who didst vouchsafe to a woman the birth of the only begotten Son, thou who didst in the tabernacle, and in the temple, place female keepers of thy holy gates, look down now also upon this thy handmaid, and bestow on her the Holy Ghost, that she may worthily perform the work committed to her to thy honor and the glory of Christ.'"

What a practical element the deaconesses would introduce into religion. Doubtless, in early days, when the conflict was between idolatry and the worship of God, "divine service" may have rightly consisted largely in sermon, song, and prayer, but to call that "service" now, as is universally done, seems to me a mockery. That is a delight, a coveted and blessed means of growth; but "service" now is to our fellow-men, and he whose purse and work are not invested there knows nothing about "divine service," and might well name his place of Sunday lounging and æsthetics the "Church of the Divine Emptiness," or the "Church of the Celestial Sugar Plum."

What the world most needs is mothering, and most of all in the spirit's natural home, the church, and on the Sabbath day. It needs the tender sweetness of the alto voice, the jubilant good-will of the soprano, in sermon as in psalm; tenor and bass become monotonous at last, and the full diapason of power and inspiration is impossible except we listen to the full chorus of humanity. God hasten that great chorus, in church and state alike, with its deep-hearted love and its celestial hope!

* * * * * * * * * * *

The *sine qua non* of our success is mutual faith and fellowship. We must "have fervent charity among ourselves."

It is not uncharitable to judge an act as good or bad, but we should be very slow to judge the actor bad. Only by rising to the sublime sense of our sacred sisterhood with every woman that breathes, be she good or bad, foreign or native, bond or free, shall we find our individual pettiness covered and flooded out of sight by the most inexorable force of all the universe, the force of Love.

If I could have my wish for all of us, it would be that in our measure we might merit what was said of that seraphic woman, Elizabeth Barrett Browning. It is an ideal that we shall all delight to share:

> "Persons were never her theme, unless public characters were under discussion, or friends were to be praised, which kind office she frequently took upon herself. One never dreamed of frivolities in her presence, and gossip felt itself out of place. Books and humanity, great deeds, and, above all, politics, which include all the grand questions of the day, were foremost in her thoughts, and therefore, oftenest on her lips. I speak not of religion, for with her everything was religion. Her Christianity was not confined to the church and rubric; it meant civilization."

Envy and jealousy light the intensest fires that ever burn in human hearts; gossip and scandal are the smoke emitted by them. If, as has been said, these passions could, like some modern chimneys, be consumers of their own smoke, a purer and a better atmosphere would then prevail.

In all the battle of opinion that rages, and must rage until a better equilibrium is reached in this great nation, be it ours, beloved sisters, to remember that "when either side grows warm in argument, the wiser man gives over first."

Good-breeding has been called "the apotheosis of self-restraint." But the higher evolution is not to need restraining, but to have that inward quietness which, when God giveth it, "who then *can* make trouble?" All strife in manner, word and deed, grows out of worldliness, and to this there is but just one antidote, and that is, OTHER WORLDLINESS.

One look into the silent heavens, and all our earthly jargons seem unworthy; one deep tone of the forest's mystical æolian, and our deeper hearts respond in tenderness; one solemn strain out of the sea's unutterable anthem, and the soul hears in it that "something greater" that speaks to the heart alone.

All true souls know that this is true. "Let my soul calm itself, O God, in Thee," sings the stormy spirit of St. Augustine. "Live without father and mother, but not without God," cries Count Tolstoi from Russia, that center of the world's unrest.

"We should fill the hours with the sweetest things,
If we had but a day.
We should drink alone at the purest springs,
In our upward way,
We should love with a life-time's love in an hour
If the hours were but few,"

are the sweet lines of our own Mary Lowe Dickinson.

And these are the words of a great but unnamed saint: "The strongest Christians are those who, from daily habit, hasten with everything to God."

METROPOLITAN OPERA HOUSE.

CHAPTER IX.

AIMS AND METHODS OF THE W. C. T. U.

Thus have I tried to set forth the sequel of that modern Pentecost called the "Woman's Crusade." That women should thus dare was the wonder after they had so long endured, while the manner of their doing left us who looked on, bewildered between laughter and tears. Woman-like, they took their knitting, their zephyr work or their embroidery, and simply swarmed into the drink-shops, seated themselves, and watched the proceedings. Usually they came in a long procession from their rendezvous at some church where they had held morning prayer-meeting; entered the saloon with kind faces, and the sweet songs of church and home upon their lips, while some Madonna-like leader with the Gospel in her looks, took her stand beside the bar, and gently asked if she might read God's word and offer prayer.

Women gave of their best during the two months of that wonderful uprising. All other engagements were laid aside; elegant women of society walked beside quiet women of home, school and shop, in the strange processions that soon lined the chief streets, not only of nearly every town and village in the state that was its birthplace, but of leading cities there and elsewhere; and voices trained in Paris and Berlin sang "Rock of Ages, cleft for me," in the malodorous air of liquor-rooms and beer-halls. Meanwhile, where were the men who patronized these places? Thousands of them signed the pledge these women brought, and accepted their invitation to go back with them to the churches, whose doors, for once, stood open all day long; others slunk out of sight, and a few cursed the women openly; but even of these it might be said, that those who came to curse remained to pray. Soon the saloon-keepers surrendered in large numbers, the statement being made by a well-known observer that the liquor traffic was temporarily driven out of two hundred and fifty towns and villages in Ohio and the adjoining states, to which the Temperance Crusade extended. There are photographs extant representing the stirring scenes when, amid the ringing of church-bells, the contents of every barrel, cask and bottle in a saloon were sent gurgling into the gutter, the owner insisting that women's hands alone should do this work, perhaps with some dim thought in his muddled head of the poetic justice due to the Nemesis he thus invoked. And so it came about that soft and often jeweled hands grasped axe and hammer, while the whole town assembled to rejoice in this new fashion of exorcising the evil spirits. In Cincinnati, a city long dominated by the liquor trade, a procession of women, including the wives of leading pastors, was arrested and locked up in jail; in Cleveland, dogs were set on the crusaders, and in a single instance, a blunderbuss was pointed at them, while in several places, they were smoked out, or had the hose turned on them. But the arrested women marched through the streets singing, and held a temperance meeting in the prison; the one assailed by dogs laid her hands upon their heads and prayed; and the group menaced by a gun marched up to its mouth singing, "Never be afraid to work for Jesus." The annals of heroism have few pages so bright as the annals of that strange crusade, spreading as if by magic, through all the Northern States, across the sea and to the Orient itself. Everywhere it went, the attendance at church increased incalculably, and the crime record was in like manner shortened. Men say there was a spirit in the air such as they never knew before; a sense of God and of human brotherhood.

But after fifty days or more, all this seemed to pass away. The women could not keep up such work; it took them too much from their homes; saloons re-opened; men gathered as before behind their sheltering screens, and swore "those silly women had done more harm than good," while with ribald words they drank the health of "the defunct crusade."

Perhaps the most significant outcome of this movement was the knowledge of their own power gained by the conservative women of the churches. They had never even seen a "woman's rights convention," and had been held aloof from the "suffragists" by fears as to their orthodoxy; but now there were women prominent in all church cares and duties eager to clasp hands for a more aggressive work than such women had ever before dreamed of undertaking.

Nothing is more suggestive in all the national gatherings of the Woman's Christian Temperance Union, that sober second thought of the crusade, than the wide difference between these meetings and any held by men. The beauty of decoration is specially noticeable; banners of silk, satin and velvet, usually made by the women themselves, adorn the wall; the handsome shields of states; the great vases bearing aloft grains, fruits and flowers; the moss-covered well with its old bucket; or the setting of a platform to present an interior as cozy and delightful as a parlor could afford, are features of the pleasant scene. The rapidity of movement with which business is conducted, the spontaneity of manner, the originality of plan, the perpetual freshness and ingenuity of the convention, its thousand unexpectednesses, its quips and turns, its wit and pathos, its impromptu eloquence and its perpetual good nature — all these elements, brought into condensed view in the National Conventions, are an object-lesson of the new force and unique method that womanhood has contributed to the consideration of the greatest reform in Christendom. It is really the crusade over again; the home going forth into the world. Its manner is not that of the street, the court, the mart, or office; it is the manner of the home. Men take one line, and travel onward to success; with them discursiveness is at a discount. But women in the home must be mistresses, as well as maids of all work; they have learned well the lesson of unity in diversity; hence by inheritance and by environment, women are varied in their methods; they are born to be "branchers-out." Men have been in the organized temperance work not less than eighty years—women not quite fifteen. Men pursued it at first along the line of temperance, then total abstinence; license, then prohibition; while women have already over forty distinct departments of work, classified under the heads of preventive, educational, evangelistic, social, and legal. Women think in the concrete. The crusade showed them the drinking man, and they began upon him directly, to get him to sign the pledge and seek "the Lord behind the pledge." The crusade showed them the selling man, and they prayed over him and persuaded him to give up his bad business, often buying him out, and setting him up in the better occupation of baker, grocer, or keeper of the reading-room into which they converted his saloon after converting him from the error of his ways.

But oftentimes the drinking man went back to his cups, and the selling man fell from his grace; the first one declaring, "I can't break the habit I formed when a boy," and the last averring, "Somebody's bound to sell, and I might as well make the profit." Upon this the women, still with their concrete ways of thinking, said, "To be sure, we must train our boys, and not ours only, but everybody's; what institution reaches all?—the Public Schools." How well they wrought, under the leadership of Mrs. Mary H. Hunt, has been told on earlier pages.

To the inane excuse of the seller that he might as well do it since somebody would, the quick and practical reply was, "To be sure; but suppose the people could be persuaded not to let anybody sell? why, then that would be God's answer to our crusade prayers." So they began with petitions to municipalities, to Legislatures and to Congress, laboriously gathering up, doubtless, not fewer than ten million names in the great aggregate, and through the fourteen years. Thus the Woman's Christian Temperance Union stands as the strongest bulwark of prohibition, state and national, by constitutional amendment and by statute. Meanwhile, it was inevitable that their motherly hearts should devise other methods for the protection of their homes. Knowing the terrors and the blessings of inheritance, they set about the systematic study of heredity, founding a journal for that purpose. Learning the relation of diet to the drink habit, they arranged to study hygiene also; desiring children to know that the Bible is on the side of total abstinence, they induced the International Sunday-school Convention to prepare a plan for lessons on this subject; perceiving the limitless power of the Press, they did their best to subsidize it by sending out their bulletins of temperance facts and news items, thick as the leaves of Vallambrosa, and incorporated a publishing company of women.

It is curious to watch the development of the women who entered the saloons in 1874 as a gentle, well-dressed, and altogether peaceable mob. They have become an army, drilled and disciplined. They have a method of organization, the simplest yet the most substantial known to temperance annals. It is the same for the smallest local union as for the national society with its ten thousand auxiliaries. Committees have been abolished, except the executive, made up of the general officers, and "superintendencies" substituted, making each woman responsible for a single line of work in the local, state and national society. This puts a premium upon personality, develops a negative into a positive with the least loss of time, and increases beyond all computation the aggregate of work accomplished. Women with specialties have thus been multiplied by tens of thousands, and the temperance reform introduced into strongholds of power hitherto neglected or unthought of. Is an exposition to be held, or a state or county fair? there is a woman in the locality who knows it is her business to see that the W. C. T. U. has an attractive booth with temperance literature and temperance drinks; and that, besides all this, it is her duty to secure laws and by-laws requiring the teetotal absence of intoxicants from grounds and buildings. Is there an institution for the dependent or delinquent classes? there is a woman in the locality who knows it is her duty to see that temperance literature is circulated, temperance talking and singing done, and that flowers with appropriate sentiments attached are sent the inmates by young ladies banded for that purpose. Is there a convocation of ministers, doctors, teachers, editors, voters, or any other class of opinion-manufacturers announced to meet in any town or city? there is a woman thereabouts who knows it is her business to secure, through some one of the delegates to these influential gatherings, a resolution favoring the temperance movement, and pledging it support along the line of work then and there represented. Is there a Legislature anywhere about to meet, or is Congress in session? there is a woman near at hand who knows it is her business to make the air heavy with the white, hovering wings of petitions gathered up from everywhere asking for prohibition, for the better protection of women and girls, for the preventing of the sale of tobacco to minors, for the enforcement of the Sabbath, or for the enfranchisement of women.

Thus have the manifold relationships of the mighty temperance movement been studied out by women in the training-school afforded by the real work and daily object-lessons of the W. C. T. U. Its aim is everywhere to bring woman and temperance in contact with the problem of humanity's heart-break and sin; to protect the home by prohibiting the saloon, and to police the state with men and women voters committed to the enforcement of righteous law. The women saw, as years passed on, that not one, but three curses were pronounced upon their sons by the nineteenth century civilization: the curse of the narcotic poisons, alcohol and nicotine; the curse of gambling; the curse of social sin, deadlier than all, and that these three are part and parcel of each other. And so, "distinct like the billows, but one like the sea," is their unwearied warfare against each and all. They have learned, by the logic of defeat, that the mother-heart must be enthroned in all places of power before its edicts will be heeded. For this reason they have been educated up to the level of the equal suffrage movement. For the first time in history, the women of the South have clasped hands with their Northern sisters in faith and fealty, wearing the white ribbon emblem of patriotism, purity and peace, and inscribing on their banners the motto of the organized crusade. "For God and Home and Native Land."

"No sectarianism in religion," "no sectionalism in politics," "no sex in citizenship"—these are the battle-cries of this relentless but peaceful warfare. We believe that woman will bless and brighten every place she enters, and that she will enter every place on the round earth. We believe in prohibition by law, prohibition by politics, and prohibition by woman's ballot. After ten years' experience, the women of the crusade became convinced that until the people of this country divide at the ballot-box on the foregoing issue, America can never be nationally delivered from the dram-shop. They therefore publicly announced their devotion to the Prohibition party, and promised to lend it their influence and prayers, which, with the exception of a very small minority, they have since most sedulously done. Since then they have not ceased beseeching voters to cast their ballots first of all to help elect an issue, rather than a man. For this they have been vilified as if it were a crime; but they have gone on their way, kindly as sunshine, steadfast as gravitation, and persistent as a hero's faith. While their enemy has brewed beer, they have brewed public opinion; while he distilled whisky, they distilled sentiment; while he rectified spirits, they rectified the spirit that is in man. They have had good words of cheer alike for North and South, for Catholic and Protestant, for home and foreign born, for white and black, but gave words of criticism for the liquor traffic and the parties that it dominates as its servants and allies.

While the specific aims of the white ribbon women everywhere are directed against the manufacture, sale and use of alcholic beverages, it is sufficiently apparent that the indirect line of their progress is, perhaps, equally rapid, and involves social, governmental, and ecclesiastical equality between women and men. By this is meant such financial independence on the part of women as will enable them to hold men to the same high standards of personal purity in the habitudes of life as they have required of women, such a participation in the affairs of government as shall renovate politics and make home questions the paramount issue of the state, and such equality in all church relations as shall fulfill the gospel declaration, "There is neither male nor female, but ye are all one in Christ Jesus."

The cultivation of specialties, and the development of *esprit de corps* among women, all predict the day when, through this mighty conserving force of motherhood introduced into every department of human activity, the common weal shall be the individual care; war shall rank among the lost arts; nationality shall mean what Edward Bellamy's wonderful book, entitled "Looking Backward," sets before us as the fulfillment of man's highest earthly dream; and Brotherhood shall become the talismanic word and realized estate of all humanity.

In concluding this portion of my book, I can not better express my view of what we have been and what we may be, than by the following quotation from my address before the Women's Congress, at its meeting in Des Moines, Iowa, 1885:

Humanly speaking, such success as we have attained has resulted from the following policy and methods:

1. *The simplicity and unity of the organization.* The local union is a miniature of the National, having similar officiary and plan of work. It is a military company carefully mustered, officered and drilled. The county union is but an aggregation of the locals, and the district, of the counties,

while each state is a regiment, and the National itself is womanhood's "Grand Army of the Republic."

2. *Individual responsibility is everywhere urged.* "Committees" are obsolete with us, and each distinct line of work has one person, called a superintendent, who is responsible for its success in the local, and another in the state, and a third in the National union. She may secure such lieutenants as she likes, but the union looks to her for results and holds her accountable for failures.

3. *The quick and cordial recognition of talent* is another secret of W. C. T. U. success. Women, young or old, who can speak, write, conduct meetings, organize, keep accounts, interest children, talk with the drinking man, get up entertainments, or carry flowers to the sick or imprisoned, are all pressed into the service.

There has been also in our work an immense amount of digging in the earth to find one's own buried talent, to rub off the rust and to put it out at interest. Perhaps that is, after all, its most significant feature, considered as a movement.

4. *Subordination of the financial phase* has helped, not hindered us. Lack of funds has not barred out even the poorest from our sisterhood. A penny per week is our basis of membership, of which a fraction goes to the state, and ten cents to the National W. C. T. U.

Money has been, and I hope may be, a consideration altogether secondary. Of wealth we have had incomputable stores; indeed, I question if America has a richer corporation to-day than ours: wealth of faith, of enthusiasm, of experience, of brain, of speech, of common sense—this is a capital stock that can never depreciate, needs no insurance, requires no combination lock or bonded custodian, and puts us under no temptation to tack our course or trim our sails.

5. Nothing has helped us more than the *entire freedom of our society from the influence or dictation of capitalists, politicians, or corporations of any sort whatever.* This can not be too strongly emphasized as one of the best elements of power. Indeed, it may be truly said that this vast and systematic work has been in nowise guided, moulded or controlled by men. It has not even occurred to them to offer advice until within a year! and to accept advice has never occurred to us, and I hope never will. While a great many noble men are "honorary members," and in one or two sporadic instances men have acted temporarily as presidents of local unions at the South, I am confident our grand constituency of temperance brothers rejoice almost as much as we do in the fact that we women have from the beginning gone our own gait and acted according to our own sweet will. They would bear witness, I am sure, to the fact that we have never done this flippantly or in a spirit of bravado, but with great seriousness, asking the help of God. I can say, personally, what I believe our leaders would also state as their experience, that so strongly do good men seem to be impressed that the call coming to Christian women in the Crusade was of God, and not of man, that in the eleven years of my almost uninterrupted connection with the National W. C. T. U., I have hardly received a letter of advice or a ver-

bal exhortation from minister or layman, and I would mildly but firmly say that I have not sought their counsel. The hierarchies of the land will be ransacked in vain for the letter-heads of the W. C. T. U. We have sought, it is true, the help of almost every influential society in the nation, both religious and secular; we have realized how greatly this help was needed by us, and grandly has it been accorded, but what we asked for was an indorsement of plans *already made* and work *already done.* Thus may we always be a society "of the women, by the women," but for humanity.

6. *The freedom from red-tape and the keeping out of ruts* is another element of power. We practice a certain amount of parliamentary usage, and strongly urge the study of it as a part of the routine of local unions. We have good, strong "constitutions" and by-laws to match; blanks for reports; rolls for membership; pledges in various styles of art; badges, ribbons and banners, and hand-books of our work are all to be had at "national headquarters," but we will not come under a yoke of bondage to the paraphernalia of the movement. We are always moving on. "Time can not dull nor custom stale our infinite variety." We are exceedingly apt to break out in a new phase. Here we lop off an old department and there we add two new ones. Our "new departures" are frequent and oftentimes most unexpected. Indeed, we exhibit the characteristics of an army on the march, rather than an army in camp or hospital.

The marked esprit de corps is to be included among the secrets of success. The W. C. T. U. has invented a phrase to express this, and it is "comradeship among women." So generous and so cherished has this comradeship become, that ours is often called a "mutual admiration society." We believe in each other, stand by each other, and have plenty of emulation without envy. Sometimes a state or an individual says to another, "The laurels of Miltiades will not suffer me to sleep," but there is no staying awake to belittle success; we do not detract from any worker's rightful meed of praise. So much for the "hidings of power" in the W. C. T. U.

There are two indirect results of this organized work among women, concerning which I wish to speak:

First. It is a strong *nationalizing* influence. Its method and spirit differ very little, whether you study them on the border of Puget Sound or the Gulf of Mexico. In San Francisco and Baltimore white ribbon women speak the same vernacular; tell of their gospel meetings and petitions; discuss *The Union Signal* editorials, and wonder "what will be the action of our next national convention."

Almost all other groups of women workers who dot the continent, are circumscribed by denominational lines and act largely under the advice of ecclesiastical leaders. The W. C. T. U. feels no such limitation. North and South are strictly separate in the women's missionary work of the churches, but Mississippi and Maine, Texas and Oregon, Massachusetts and Georgia, sit side by side around the yearly camp-fires of the W. C. T. U. The Southern women have learned to love us of the North and our hearts are true to them; while to us all who fight in peaceful ranks unbroken, "For God and

Home and Native Land," the Nation is a sacred name spelled with a capital N.

Second. Our W. C. T. U. is *a school,* not founded in that thought, or for that purpose, but sure to fit us for the sacred duties of patriots in the realm that lies just beyond the horizon of the coming century.

Here we try our wings that yonder our flight may be strong and steady. Here we prove our capacity for great deeds; there we shall perform them. Here we make our experience and pass our novitiate that yonder we may calmly take our places and prove to the world that what it needed most was "two heads in counsel," as well as "two beside the hearth." When that day comes, the nation shall no longer miss as now the influence of half its wisdom, more than half its purity and nearly all its gentleness, in courts of justice and halls of legislation. Then shall one code of morals—and that the highest—govern both men and women, then shall the Sabbath be respected, the rights of the poor be recognized, the liquor traffic banished, and the home protected from all its foes.

Born of such a visitation of God's Spirit as the world has not known since tongues of fire sat upon the wondering group at Pentecost, cradled in a faith high as the hope of a saint, and deep as the depths of a drunkard's despair, and baptized in the beauty of holiness, the Crusade determined the ultimate goal of its teachable child, the W. C. T. U., which has one steadfast aim, and that none other than the regnancy of Christ, not in form, but in fact; not in substance, but in essence; not ecclesiastically, but truly in the hearts of men. To this end its methods are varied, changing, manifold, but its unwavering faith, these words express: "Not by might, nor by power, but by my spirit, saith the Lord of Hosts."

BOURBON JUG WATER COOLER (NEW ORLEANS EXPOSITION.)

CHAPTER X.

MISCELLANEOUS INCIDENTS OF TEMPERANCE WORK.

How threadbare, because so frequent, is the reiteration of the excuse among moderate drinkers, "I can take a glass of beer, or I can let it alone." A stalwart young Scotchman came to Evanston. He was of good family, fine, athletic figure, handsome face expressive of strength and resolution. He took the University course with credit to himself, afterward graduated from the Law Department and began to practice in Evanston. Years passed by, twelve of them, I think, when this man entered the Gospel Temperance meeting addressed by me one Sunday afternoon in Evanston, and when the speech was over came to the front, and turning toward the audience, largely made up that day of University students, he raised his trembling hand, and with a face more marred and marked by dissipation than any language can depict, he cried out in his deep voice, full of tears, "Boys, don't drink, don't drink! I was a student just as you are, with prospects just as bright; held my own well in the University all through the scholastic and professional courses, but said from time to time as I took a glass of beer, 'This can never master a man so masterful as I.' And here I stand to-day and you see how it is. I am the slave of that little glass of beer. Let me say it once again and don't forget it while you live, 'Boys, don't drink, *don't drink!*'"

Another man in the same town, a blacksmith, a Scotchman by birth, or at least by heritage, after having been known in Evanston as a pronounced inebriate, resolved one Thanksgiving Day, nine years or more ago, that he would never touch liquor again.

He has faithfully kept his word, is a pillar in the temperance work in Evanston, no man being more respected or relied upon. I am glad to count him among the friends of our family, and to invite him with his family whenever we have a reception. What pride he takes on these occasions, going to the railroad magnates, getting them to lend great engine head-lights to make the grounds bright, both in front and on the lawn behind the house. He trims up the place with festoons of evergreens, and is our chief standby throughout the enterprise. I remember when he was going away after mother's eightieth birthday festival, when four hundred guests had passed through our home, from the Governor of the state to the humblest of our reformed men, with their families, and every clergyman, including the pastor of the colored church, so that our own pastor said that if ever he saw a gospel feast this was the one—this good man said to me as he left our door, nearly all the guests having gone, "I suppose it did n't mean so very much to most of them that live in nice houses and have everything they want, but I tell you it was a mighty epoch in my life, and will make me a better man." It was this same kind friend who placed in front of Rest Cottage, and of my sister's annex adjoining it, a beautiful standing vase which he fills every year with flowers. It is to him and his family that we are glad to send remembrances from time to time, and to him that the ladies of our society gave a nice arm-chair one Christmas, in token of their appreciation of all that he had done, suffered and survived.

At one well-remembered meeting in the town of S., Mr. C———, who was from an excellent family, and had been a leading merchant, but was now a confirmed drunkard, came forward to sign the pledge. Something in his face interested me, the more so as I noticed a look of positive distress on the faces of some of the white ribbon women. This was so contrary to the usual cordial reception given by our workers to any one—no matter how degraded—who wishes to enter on a new life, that I asked an explanation afterward and they said, "He has signed it so many times and broken it so often that he is bringing the pledge into positive disrepute. Some saloon-keeper will offer him a drink if he will let him have his pledge card and they will nail it up behind the bar." I could not wonder that the ladies were jealous for their cause, but somehow I believed that this time he would stand firm. I resolved to go and see his wife, and the next morning did so. She was a stony-faced and broken-hearted woman. I could not get the least intimation of hope. Finally I asked her to kneel with me in prayer, which she did, I think out of courtesy more than from any interest in the exercises. And as I left, after urging her to cheer him up all she could, she replied, without a particle of light in her face, "I will agree to this much, I won't hinder him the least bit in the world." If her manner was as inspiring to him as it was to me, I think that he must have had to get a good deal of it before he could extract any appreciable amount of enthusiasm. A year passed and I returned to the same village, and spoke in the same church once more. Standing in the pulpit, I read my audience, pew by pew, as one would read a book line by line, to find the countenance of this gray-haired, kindly man. He was not there. No one had spoken to me of him and I began to fear it was because they did not like to disappoint me. I sought his home again. A lady, smiling and affable, came out of the door as I approached, and met me at the gate. I did not know her, but she introduced herself as the same woman whose stony face I had carried in my memory throughout the year. "Come around into the garden, he is sitting on the bench under his favorite apple-tree," she said. So I went, and he rose and came forward to meet me, his face full of a new hope, his whole appearance instinct with self-respect. I thought to say a pleasant word to him and so remarked, "Why were you not at my meeting last evening, Mr. ——— ? I counted on you more than on any one except my cousin." At this came a look of pain and a quick glance at his wife, as he exclaimed, "There now, we have got to tell her, and we did n't mean to." Then he said : "You have n't heard a word from me this year, although you have written me several times, and I have got those letters, every one of them, put away carefully, and I have read the newspapers you sent, and appreciated your kindness just as much as if you had heard from me. And I have said to my wife often when she would ask me why I did n't write, 'Anyhow, I am doing what she wants me to.' But the fact is that I have n't been outside my gate since you was here before, and I am ashamed to have you know about it, but it is an honest fact—I have n't dared to. The only way for me, even with God's grace, to keep true to what I promised was to stay right close at home. I tell you that woman there has been kind to me, my daughter and all the folks, the best they know. And I have hoed these garden beds, don't you see how fresh and nice they are?—and asked God to take the weeds out of my heart as I do the weeds that get among the flowers, and to take care of the posies, if I have got any, just as I try to take care of these. But now I want to tell you," he went on, as we all seated ourselves on the bench under the apple-tree, "you can go up and down throughout the country just where you have a mind, for you don't carry any ball and chain. Now, make a speech for me every time you stand before the people and tell them how it is with me. Tell them that good men come along past my gate and lean their elbows on it, look at me as kind as can be, and say, 'You are doing first-rate, ———, keep right at it,' and that very minute their breaths are so full of beer or something even stronger that I must get speedily to windward, and am as tempted as I can well be. Then they came along here on election day, leaned their elbows on my gate and said, 'I tell you, you are making a good fight of it. You will show them how it is done this time,' and they walk right on down to the ballot-box and put in little pieces of paper with the names of men on them that they know favor the liquor traffic and will license it to set its trap here in this town, so that I dare not go outside my gate. Now, when I think of this, it makes their words of cheer sound sort of empty; I think they might have helped me more by their example and their vote. You talk a good deal about the arrest of thought, I wish you could screw it into the heads of the men in my own village."

Among the invitations that I have most prized is the following from that most cultured of all Indian races, the Cherokee, and signed by the famous Chief, Bushyhead:

EXECUTIVE DEPARTMENT, CHEROKEE NATION, I. T.,
TAHLEQUAH, May 18, 1881.

MRS. L. I. STAPLER:—In expectation of a visit to the Nation from Miss Frances E. Willard, president of the Christian Temperance Union, about the twelfth instant, I respectfully request you, in connection with Mrs. French, Miss Carrie Armstrong, Rev. A. C. Bacone, Rev. Daniel Rogers and W. W. Ross, Esq., to act as a committee, on behalf of the Nation, to welcome Miss Willard to the capital when she arrives, and, jointly and severally, to devise such means as may seem to you best, to make her visit to the Nation pleasant and agreeable to herself, and profitable to our people. Miss Willard comes highly recommended as a lecturer and laborer in the cause of temperance and humanity. Very respectfully,

D. W. BUSHYHEAD,
Principal Chief Cherokee Nation.

My first extended temperance trip was in the state of Ohio, in the month of May, 1876, two years after the Crusade. The saloons were all back again, flourishing as usual. I asked men and women the question, "What good do you think the Crusade accomplished?" One woman answered: "Until we went out praying on the street I never knew where the saloons were, or how they looked. Of course, I had passed by them, but I had the impression that those second-rate looking places were barber-shops. The Crusade taught me that they are places where men get shaved, not of their beards, but of their honor." Another made this explanation: "Until the Crusade I never taught my children especially about temperance, but now they have had it dinned into ear and mind, until, this morning, when I was going down town with my little boy, hardly six years of age, I felt his hands grasping my own more closely than usual, and noticed that his step was quicker. 'What is the matter, my son? Why do you hurry mamma along?' I asked, and I shall never forget how he rolled up his bright eyes to my face, and said, 'Why, mamma, don't you want to hurry? Don't you know we are passing a saloon?'" A movement that can point out to women that there are saloons, and what they are like, and can inspire in children a wholesome dread of such institutions, will bear fruit far beyond the hopes of those whose heroism set it going.

Naturally enough, I was desirous of seeing Mrs. Judge Thompson, leader of the first praying band in the Crusade, and I went for that purpose to speak in Hillsboro. I found a little town that thinks well of itself, not a great ways from the Kentucky line, the former home of Governor Trimble, who was a great temperance man and the father of this same Mrs. Thompson. I found the beautiful home he had built for her, a fine house, with every comfort and convenience, large, shady grounds about it, and at the door, as I entered, was the sweetest woman, of medium height, slight figure. with the remains of striking beauty in her face, golden-brown, curly hair, kind eyes and rare, winsome smile. Her voice was low and sweet as she welcomed me, almost as my own mother might have done, to her delightful home. She told me all the story, and in her own room, where she first read the Crusade hymn, we read it once again together and knelt in prayer. Then I said to myself, "What if this woman had not dared? What if her noble coadjutors had shrunk from the undertaking? Many a time had Dr. Dio Lewis in his lectures urged the women to go forth into the saloons and pray. What if these women, like so many others, had declined?"

I spoke in the Presbyterian church from which the noble band marched two by two and there I heard Mrs. Thompson read the Crusade psalm once more out of the Bible that is now our Magna Charta of the Crusade. On the tenth anniversary of the movement, I went again to Hillsboro, staying with Mrs. Thompson, and speaking in the hall where Dr. Dio Lewis spoke. Going from Hillsboro, the cradle, to Washington Court-house, the crown of the Crusade, I spent Christmas of 1883 in the home of Mrs. Ustick, who with Mrs. George Carpenter made up the Crusade duet of leaders in that famous town. Mrs. Carpenter was the wife of the Presbyterian minister, and the success of the movement in Washington Court-house so far outranked that of Hillsboro, that the good people, naturally enough, have always felt that justice was not done them when the muse of history represented Hillsboro as the vital historical center of the greatest Pentecost of modern times. This was manifest on the evening when I addressed them in their Temperance Hall, and it grieved me to the heart that they must always think so, and, perhaps, blame me a little that at first I had accounted Hillsboro the starting point—which it was by the space of twenty-four hours. But surely all temperance people will love and cherish the memory of that splendid beacon-light flung out by the brave women of Washington Court-house, from which it shone to every corner of the Buckeye State, and thence throughout the nation, and thence throughout the world.

Every public speaker must endure the contradiction of sinners and of saints as well. This should be taken into account beforehand, and should not be looked upon with disgust, ill-temper or surprise. For instance, the ladies of Elmira W. C. T. U. had written me to be present at the Annual Fair, and I went, knowing simply what I have stated. At the entrance of the fair grounds my carriage was met by a band of music, of which I had no previous knowledge; but the statement went all over the country, north and south, east and west, that I had become so strong-minded that I traveled with a brass band, and came to the entrance of the Exposition Building where United States Senator Hiscock was speaking, breaking up his address, and going on the platform with the statement that the time was mine and I proposed to use it. None of my acquaintances would believe this, but what of the public in general? No one can ever track down a lie like that. The facts were, that as we drove up to the hall, preceded by the band, Senator Hiscock was speaking, at the hour assigned to the ladies for their meeting, and, no doubt, was disturbed by the music. I entered the hall with other ladies, took my seat and listened to what he had to say, which was a panegyric on tobacco-raising, a theme not specially congenial to the audience that had gathered to hear a temperance speech, and was largely made up of thorough-going temperance people. At the close of the speech I went upon the stand, expressed to him my regret that he should have been incommoded, and we proceeded with our meeting.

I had spoken before an afternoon audience of ladies in a village of Delaware. It was in my earlier work, and I probably did not make my points as clear as I ought, for a nice old lady to whom the membership card was handed by one of my assistants who sought her signature, looked at the card, poised the proffered pencil in her honest hand, and mused audibly as follows: "She wants me to join this society, and I have no idea in the world what they intend to do. But I suppose it will be a good deal as it is when I take my lantern of a dark night to go to prayer-meeting—I can see but one step ahead, and I take that, and when I have done so the lantern is there and I am there, and we can just go on and take another." So her honored name went down upon the card, and she handed it back, saying still to herself, "If the Lord has got any temperance work for me to do, He's going to give me light to do it by."

In a town in Virginia, a group of lovely women gathered

about to hear what I wanted them to do, and when I proposed an organization, the loveliest of them said to me, in a low, sweet voice, "Because my own home has never known this curse, but my husband and sons are pure and true, I will join the society from a simple sense of gratitude and loyalty."

In Griffin, Georgia, at a similar meeting, going down the aisle for signatures, I passed a sweet young lady who shook her head when the membership card was offered her. A few moments later I came back up the same aisle, when she laid her hand upon my arm, saying, "I think I'll change my mind." Of course, I recognized her ancient, inalienable right to do just that, and as she wrote her graceful autograph, I said in a low voice, "Would you mind telling me, my dear, how you came to change your mind?" And with flushed cheeks, she answered, earnestly, "I am in the senior class at the High School, and very busy, but when I came to think it over, I could not go home and say I had declined to help you form this society – I did not dare to do that, for my only brother spends all his evenings out!"

In Virginia City, Nevada, there was a charming old lady in our audience whom I especially coveted for the society, but I did not observe when the cards were passed whether she gave her name or not. At the close of the meeting she came forward to greet me, and I said, "Dear lady, I coveted you with a 'righteous coveting'; did you give us your name?" She answered, presenting her little grandson Neddie to me, "He sat by my side during your address. I kept saying to myself, 'I am a member of the Episcopal Church, and that is vow enough; I don't propose to take another, nor do I think it is required of me.' But when the paper was passed around, he drew his little stub-pencil from his pocket, and reaching his hand for the pledge, printed his name, never yet dishonored, in the proper place, and turning to me with a smile in his blue eyes, he said, 'Here, grandma, put your name right down under Neddie's.' Of course I did just what the boy desired."

Among our pleasant convention episodes, should be named our visit to President Arthur, whose home was then in a stone house on Capitol Hill. Anything more elegant than his manner of receiving us I have not seen. At my suggestion, the delegates stood in groups according to their states and territories. The

President entered on the arm of Senator Blair, and on being presented I said to him, "We will not take your time, Mr. President, to shake hands with every one of these ladies, but have arranged that each delegation shall be presented to you by its president, and she alone will claim the honor of a personal recognition." His handsome face lighted up with a genial smile as he replied, "Please permit me the pleasure of grasping every lady's hand," and this he insisted on doing, making some pleasant remark to each of the leaders and presenting a magnificent rose to almost every lady present, although some cross-looking politicians seated on the sofas around the great reception room looked disgusted that a "parcel of women" should take up so much time, and some of them had so little grace as to make some such observation within hearing of the delegates. President Arthur did not reply to my little speech, save with the eloquence of his rarely attractive smile.

We went down to Mt. Vernon on the day after the Washington Convention closed; we planted there a tree near the tomb of the great chief, each delegate throwing on a bit of earth, Miss Narcissa White (now Mrs. Kinney) making an offhand speech and all of us singing, "My country, 'tis of thee."

In Philadelphia the convention visited the grave of Dr. Benjamin Rush, the first American writer on the evils of intemperance, who, in 1785, sent out his famous essay, from which returned to him the loud echoes of Lyman Beecher's sermons and the organization of the first temperance society, at Moreau, in Saratoga County, New York, in 1808; bread cast upon the waters to be found after many, many days. Beside this honored grave a tree was planted and a marble tablet placed, with the record of our visit, Edward S. Morris, the well known Quaker philanthropist, helping us with this enterprise and bearing the expense thereof.

From Louisville most of the delegates went to the Mammoth Cave, where we began the building of a white ribbon cairn, each of us gathering a stone for the fast-rising heap, and leaving instructions that all of like faith with us should follow that example, and so place an object-lesson of temperance before all visitors in that weird sanctuary. Our little "golden cornetist" from the state of Maine, Mrs. F. A. Bent, a niece of our beloved Mrs. Stevens, woke the echoes of the cave while we sang our favorite hymns.

At Nashville the convention visited Mrs. President Polk, the widow of James K. Polk, whose grave is in the grounds in front of her stately home. In 1881 I had suggested that the po - trait of this accomplished lady of the old régime ought to adorn the White House, and had started the subscription for that purpose after my first visit to the South. The enterprise was successful, and, so far as I know, this is the first united work of Northern and Southern women in our day. Mrs. Polk has been a dear, kind friend to me, and she received our delegates with the utmost cordiality, although in her eighty-seventh year.

Among the pleasant tokens of a growing spirit of tolerance, I would like to record that we have had public meetings under the auspices of the W. C. T. U., especially in the South, where besides the usual varieties of religion represented by the Protestant clergy, we have had on the platform the Catholic priest and the Jewish rabbi, all meeting in harmony and evincing the sincerest interest in the work of the white ribboners.

I have spoken repeatedly in Episcopal churches, but never as yet stood in one of their pulpits. I was invited to speak in a Catholic church on Saturday night, with the explicit statement that as it was new and not to be dedicated until the next day, my speaking would not be a desecration ! This invitation I declined.

My good friend, John Campbell, a Catholic lawyer in Philadelphia, invited me to speak before the Total Abstinence Society of his church in the Cathedral Hall, not the Cathedral itself, on Sunday afternoon. I went with my friend and hostess, Mrs. J. R. Jones, president of our local auxiliary. We were invited to seats upon the platform. When the priest entered every person in the hall rose. I was sorry to feel that the good father's response to the introduction to me was not specially cordial, although courteous. After speaking half an hour I was obliged to leave, on account of an engagement to meet a local assembly of the Knights of Labor, when, behold ! as I took my departure, every mortal stood up, as he had done for the priest. And they all Catholics, and I a Methodist sister !

In St. George's Hall, Philadelphia, where in 1885 we celebrated the one hundredth year since the publication of Dr. Rush's essay, this same John Campbell presided at the meeting when the work of the churches in the temperance reform was the subject, and it was curious indeed to hear him call a distinguished doctor to the stand to report for the Presbyterians, and other eminent ministers for the Baptist, Methodist and the various Protestant societies. At the close of this meeting, Father Cleary, a Catholic priest, who devotes himself to the temperance work, was, at my request, called upon to pronounce the benediction. I do not know of any other cause that would so have melted away the prejudice of centuries; temperance is indeed the Greatheart among reforms.

I have been asked to speak before the Presbyterian Social Union of my own city, which was certainly a liberal-minded thing for those good conservatives to do, also before the Congregational Club in New York City, where Dr. Buckley and I appeared on opposite sides of the great question of woman's ballot, and Rev. Leonard Bacon fired his brilliant sky-rockets in opposition to the W. C. T. U. and the prohibition movement.

The young men of Beloit College, which, sorrowful to relate, does not admit women, were gracious enough to invite me to speak at Commencement, in 1878, before the Archæan Society, of which my brother was a leading member away back in 1859. I thought this a hopeful token, and my ears are always intent to hear that the girls have been admitted to this, and to all other colleges throughout the nation.

One summer I went to Redding Ridge, Conn., some miles off the railroad, expecting to have a week in the country, busy, indeed, with my pen, but entirely free from interruption or the necessity of public speaking. On the very first evening, as I sat contentedly on the piazza listening to the fascinating chorus of the forest, a bright boy of twelve leaned against the post in front of me and said, "Don't you make speeches, sometimes?" "Yes, my lad," I answered, "but I came up here to get away from seeing people." "But I think you ought to speak," he said; "don't you notice how many orchards there are, and a good deal of cider is made up here, and the people who drink it get very cross. I think it is as ugly a drink as ever was made." It occurred to me that I would see if he was really in earnest, so I replied:

"When a boy asks me to speak it is hard for me to decline, more so than it would be for almost any other sort of a person, because I think boys have so many temptations, and I am so glad when they are friends of temperance. But would you not rather have me speak on the pyramids? I traveled in Egypt some years ago, and climbed that tallest pyramid of all, named Cheops, nearly five hundred feet high. On the top of it I gathered some bits of mortar, older than Abraham, and I have pictures and diagrams with which I can illustrate my lecture. Don't you think that would be more entertaining to the people?" Ned's bright eyes danced at the thought of such an evening. I said, "Don't you expect some day to see the pyramids?" "Oh, yes," he answered, "I expect to see all there is to be seen one of these days. And since I am a temperance boy it would be right for me to hear that lecture, but then I think about our people, and how much they need to have you talk of temperance, so temperance let it be." Of course there was nothing else to do, and Ned rode up and down, over hills and through valleys, drumming up an audience, so that on Sunday afternoon the old church was packed with people who came, some of them in wagons, some in great loads with a hay rack to enlarge the wagon, now and then some in carriages, others in carts, many on foot, and I wondered if we should not see some man rolling his children along in a wheelbarrow. It was a very interesting and unusual audience. I talked as best I could, pleading for total abstinence, and at the close brought out the muster roll of the temperance army, the total abstinence pledge, and asked how many would enroll their names. A grand response was given, and at the close whom should I see coming demurely along the aisle but little Bessie, a sweet child of six years old, who was under my care at the time for a short outing. I can see her yet in her white dress and blue ribbons and little white shoes as she stood before me. I laid my hand on her young head and said, "I did n't ask you to come, because I thought your mamma would think you were too young to put your name down on the pledge. Do you understand what it means, my child?" And I shall never forget how her little face lighted up with the words, "I sign not for myself so much, but at home I have a little brother, Artie, he is only four years old, and when he grows to be a man you said that folks would ask him to go into the saloon and drink, and I thought maybe if he knew I signed the pledge it would help him, so I want to sign for an example." Could a better reason have been given?

I was to speak in the Congregational church in Hartford, that had rejoiced in the preaching of that wonderful man, Dr. Horace Bushnell, for many years. The present pastor was himself a genius, Dr. Nathaniel Burton, son-in-law of Isabella Beecher Hooker. Meeting him in his study just before the service, I said, "Doctor, I am a great admirer of Horace Bushnell and have read everything he wrote. My reverence for his memory is such that every leaf on the pathway of Bushnell Park seems to me worthy to be preserved in an herbarium. I have visited his home, been received with the utmost courtesy by his accomplished wife, reverently entered his study where he wrote that marvel among books, 'Nature and the Supernatural,' and glanced out of the window upon the beautiful scenes that soothed his mind while he devoted himself to his gigantic tasks. His book, on the 'Reform against Nature, opposing woman's ballot, has, of course, afflicted me, and though it seems an impertinence, I thought I should be glad to speak of woman's suffrage as a means of home-protection from the saloon curse, in this very pulpit, from which Dr. Bushnell used to fling his varied thunder-bolts."

"Do so by all means," was the Doctor's answer.

"But I would not if it would in anywise embarrass you," I said; "your people might not like it."

"Like it," he answered, "I don't care a continental whether they do or not. If they don't like it, that is the very best reason in the world why they should hear you tell what makes you differ from them." So we went into the church, ascended the elegant pulpit, and I saw over at my right a bust of the philosopher whose mighty spirit seemed to brood in the very atmosphere. Dr. Burton was a mischievous man, and he whispered to me softly, "Mrs. Horace Bushnell sits well up toward the front." Under these interesting circumstances I gave my argument, nor can I say that I felt any special embarrassment, for I believed in my cause.

After a long, dusty ride on a summer's day, I arrived in a famous Hudson river town, which shall be nameless, and was taken to the elegant home of an Episcopal lady who had volunteered to entertain me. No sooner had I reached my beautiful and quiet room, than the hostess, who had greeted me at the door, came in, saying earnestly, "Will you not allow me to send you up a glass of wine? You must be very tired after your journey." The blood flushed in cheek and brow as I said to her, "Madam, 200,000 women would lose somewhat of their faith in humanity if I should drink a drop of wine." And I pointed to my white ribbon, saying, "This is the sign between us." The lady's eyes filled with tears and she impressively begged my pardon, and begged me to understand that in her home wine was not used as a beverage, beat a hasty retreat from my room, and with her family showed me the utmost kindness and consideration throughout my stay. It was difficult for me to understand how she came to ask such a question of me. I know that the popular belief is that temperance men who speak are not always invulnerable, but I am confident this is a libel on these men and largely originates in the saloon. Evidently this lady lived in a world so different from my own that it did not occur to her that a temperance woman was a total abstainer!

A party of fashionable young gentlemen and ladies came into the Palmer House restaurant from Mc Vicker's Theatre one night, and sat down at the table next to that at which Mr. and Mrs. Barnes and I were taking an oyster stew, after a temperance meeting. The young people ordered supper. One of the young men spoke to the head waiter, who disappeared and soon returned with a long-necked wine bottle, whereupon the handsomest of the elegant trio of American girls said quickly, "I am sure, gentlemen, you will respect our wishes not to have wine. We belong to the Young Women's Temperance League of Cleveland." "Yes, let us have lemonade instead," said the gentle young lady beside her. "Very well, it shall be as you wish," assented the gentleman courteously, and they were soon discussing the play over a thoroughly temperance repast. My heart smote me, for I had said to myself, "These young theatre-goers naturally enough take wine," when behold, they were as staunch as the most strenuous church-goer in all the land.

Silhouettes.

"Not by the page, word painted,
Let life be banned or sainted.
Deeper than written scroll
The colors of the soul.

Sweeter than any sung
My songs that found no tongue.
Nobler than any fact
My wish that failed of act."

—*Whittier.*

WHAT I HAVE DONE AND SUFFERED AS A PEN-HOLDER.

I was early encouraged by my parents to keep a daily record, not of events only, but of commentary as well. A short time previous to entering the Woman's College in Milwaukee (1857), I began to branch out in this direction largely, and continued to do so right on through my student and teacher years, writing so steadily during the nearly two years and a half that I spent abroad, that I have about twenty volumes of note-books filled out during that period. It is a token of my good health that I was able to do this writing anywhere, on the cars, on steamers, and on horseback, besides constantly contributing to papers at home.

I was taught by my mother to read out of a tiny juvenile paper, no longer than a postal card, entitled, "The Slave's Friend." The little bound copy lies before me now, marked at my favorite articles. There are two childish pencil strokes at the following, and as I read it over I smile at its current value—something above all else dear to the journalistic mind—if only the word "slavery" be changed to "temperance."

LITTLE DANIEL.

DANIEL.—Mr. W. is going to give a lecture this evening, papa, in the school-house, on slavery. May n't I go hear him?

MR. TRACY.—Go to hear him! No, indeed, you shall not. I am glad they would not let him have the meeting-house.

D.—I am told, father, that he is a very good man, and a very interesting lecturer. May I ask *why* you will not permit me to hear him?

MR. T.—Why? Because he is a fanatic, an incendiary, a brawler, a cut-throat, a fool. I hate him.

D.—O papa! When he published his report on manual labor schools, don't you remember that you said it was the most sensible pamphlet you had ever read, and that the author was one of the wisest and best young men in this country?

MR. T.—Did I? Well, I had forgotten that I ever said so. But he is doing more hurt than he ever did good.

D.—They say he is a temperance man, a peace-maker, a friend to liberty, and you have said he was a wise and good man ; how then can he be a fool, or a fanatic, or a cut-throat, or an incendiary, father?

MR. T.—Wherever he goes there are mobs ; and there will be one here, or I am mistaken. I have said so a dozen times to-day.

D.—Is not that the way, sir, to get up a mob? and how is Mr. W. to blame if people will stir up mobs instead of going to hear him lecture?

MR. T.-Go to bed, Daniel ; you are too young to talk about such things ; if you don't take care you will be just such a fanatic as this Mr. W. before you are much older.

D.—Good night, papa ; but you have forgotten you once told me, after Mr. W. had made an address in our Sabbath-school, that you hoped to see me just such a man.

Mr. T.—Did I? But you need not remember everything I say.

D.—No, father! I will not if it displeases you.

Early impressions are made on a memory that is "wax to receive and marble to retain," so I may justly say that I owe to journalism in the shape of that little anti-slavery paper, my earliest impulse to philanthropy and much of the fearlessness as a reformer that has surprised me no less than my friends. I liked nothing so well as to go away alone and read this little book, the bound volume having been given me by Mary Thome, daughter of the well-known Oberlin professor. I often vexed my playmates because I preferred it to doll, doll-dishes or doll-clothes. But my mother's favorite paper was *The Mother's Assistant*, published in Boston, and filled with hints and helps for the Christian nurture of children, so I read that at a tender age. My father's paper was *The Oberlin Evangelist*, and as I looked up to him as the greatest of men, I pried into its pages, determined to know what he found there that held his steady gaze so long. President Charles G. Finney's sermons seemed to be the main thing, and my little mind had many a fright and untold "horror of great darkness," as I read the tremendous terrors of the law therein set forth. My older brother had for his own, *The Youth's Cabinet*, the chief, if not the only, juvenile paper, that was to a generation ago what *St. Nicholas* and *The Youth's Companion* are to this. There I learned a love for natural science, outdoor sports, and story reading. The first time that I was ever mentioned in a paper was when about four years old, and it was not in a fashion calculated to excite my vanity or my dear mother's, either, for we were therein held up not as an example, but as a warning.

The article was by Prof. George Whipple, of Oberlin College, and published in *The Mother's Assistant.* His wife had been to see us, and my mother, after the immemorial manner of our maternal relatives, told her something I had said, then changed the subject. Whereupon I left my play, drew my little cricket to mother's feet, seated myself with elbows on her knee, and piped out with intense interest, "Oh, mother, tell the lady something more that I've done!" I think it was a good lesson, for my mother was not given to that defect in training thereafter; I mean, not "before company," for she always praised us immensely in private for every good thing we tried to do, and when we were not good, her chief weapon with which to restore us to our right minds was, "I wonder where my nice little girl has gone? She was so helpful and polite, but this scowling little thing must have been left here by a peddler or a witch."

When I was in my seventh year, we removed to Wisconsin overland, in "prairie schooners," going ten years ahead of the railroad. But to our isolated farm, came *The Morning Star* and *The Myrtle* from our life-long friend, the wife of David Marks, that famous "Boy Preacher" of the Free Will Baptist Church; the *National Era* in which, when eleven years of age, I read and wept over "Uncle Tom's Cabin;" *The Ladies' Repository*, then edited by Rev. Dr. B. F. Tefft, whose historical story, "The Shoulder Knot," fascinated my brother and me, who were never permitted to read novels; and the *Horticulturist* of that artist in landscape gardening, A. J. Downing, whose death by a steamboat accident upon the Hudson River smote us almost like a personal bereavement. We had also *The Agriculturist* and *The Prairie Farmer.* Later on, we had *Putnam's Magazine* and *Harper's Monthly*, besides our own church papers, *The New York* and *Northwestern Christian Advocates.* All these we children were encouraged to read, but "father's political papers" were by him declared to be to us unlawful. He kept them out of sight so far as possible, and asserted with strong emphasis that he "did n't want his family, and, above all, his women folks, to know about anything so utterly detestable as politics." Meanwhile, he was a good Democrat, an active politician, and a man of the highest honor and integrity. Therefore, I reasoned that politics could n't possibly be so bad or else he would n't so greatly relish being in them, and the one particular in which I disobeyed my father was in getting and reading those papers with the utmost particularity on every practicable occasion. I found myself to be indeed "a chip of the old block," for these political papers were more attractive to me than any others. *The Democratic Standard*, its politics and candidates, were subjects of great interest, and, later on, S. M. Booth's *Milwaukee Free Press* was more to me than any partisan paper has been since, until the era of the New York *Voice*. John P. Hale and George W. Julian visited the neighboring town of Janesville and my mother would go to hear them speak, Oliver acting as her escort; returning late at night from her unexampled adventure she found us all up and waiting "to hear the arguments." My father forsook the Democrats, erelong, and joined the "Barn burners," Free-soilers and Republicans, all parts of one tremendous whole.

I read Benton's "Thirty Years in the United States Senate," and the great Missouri Senator made a strong impression on my mind, but we were all Frémonters, and my brother's first vote was cast for the hero of the day, the fearless "Pathfinder." It was journalism that tracked us into the wilderness, kept us company in our isolation, poured into our minds the brightest thoughts of the best thinkers, and made us a family of rural cosmopolites. It was journalism that developed in us the passion of patriotism and the insight into politics as the arena of loftiest philanthropic achievement. Our college-bred neighbor, Professor Hodge, who came west ten years later than ourselves, was a devotee of the New York *Tribune*, and we had the reading of that paper in Horace Greeley's day, when it was the friend of human freedom, and not flung from a tall tower, wherein,

> "The spirit above is a spirit of sin,
> And the spirit below is the spirit of gin."

What wonder that to us, upon our prairie farm, one mile from any neighbor and several miles from anywhere, the white wings of the press flying in, so broad, so free and manifold, seemed like kind visitants from some great fairyland that we were bent on seeing and living in, ourselves, in the sweet "sometime" of our expectant dreams!

My brother Oliver had decided literary talent and early declared his purpose and desire to be an editor. I remember an

The first composition
ever written by me age
ten and a half

The Kitten

F. N.

There was once a little kitten the pride & idol of its mother & of the children in the neighborhood in which it resided & indeed it was worthy of their warmest love & care for with its soft silken fur & beautiful eyes it was certainly very attractive But one sad fate befell it one evening in the form of a great big cat dog almost hourly [illegible] against the poor little fellow had no means of defence so it strove to bear the insults of tommy as best it might knowing that as soon as its friends heard of its pitiful condition they would hasten to its relief & in this he was not mistaken for in a few hours down came a troop of friends & after held a sort of council & it was determined that unless the actions of tommy were [illegible] he should pay the forfeit of his head for his crimes But some how or other it got to tommy's ears & his dog relations [illegible] at once & it is hoped that they [illegible] be [illegible] But time will [illegible]

FIRST COMPOSITION. (*Fac Simile.*)

article he wrote for the college magazine when he was about twenty-one, and how much my emulation was stirred by its opening sentence, which was as follows: "I believe in metempsychosis, yet I am not a Hindu, nor a worshiper of the sacred ibis." "Oh," I thought, "if I could only roll out words after that manner!" But it was not for women; so far as I then knew, no woman had ever dared aspire to such a thing. Sarah Josepha Hale had done so, beginning as far back as 1828, but we were oblivious of one who, however gifted, had got no farther than to edit "a woman's fashion paper."

I do not remember trying to reduce my ideas to writing until I was about eleven years old, at which time Miss Burdick, the first teacher that I ever had, herself a young lady under twenty years, told me that I must write a composition once in two weeks in the little school of six or eight pupils that used to assemble around a big table made for us by father, in what was afterwards the parlor of our home. I had run wild out-of-doors, and had written so little that it was a formidable undertaking, not so much to think as to write down my thoughts. I had an unlimited enthusiasm for pets, and just then was making a live doll out of my pet kitten, so I thought it would be the easiest thing to write upon a subject with which I was acquainted, and which had fascinations for me. This famous production is given here, for I feel sure the actual experience of that first composition may bring a waft of cheer to some white ribboner, boy or girl, by whom pen and paper are as little loved as they were by me at that age.

At our farm, named by us "Forest Home," we established a paper called *The Tribune*, with three columns to the page, nicely ruled off for us by mother, and filled in with exceedingly "fine work" in the way of penmanship, not forgetting an occasional drawing that would have been more satisfactory if labeled. Mother contributed poetry, my brother wrote the "solid articles," and I did the "literary part," the specimen that has survived being a natural curiosity, of which the less said the better.

When about fourteen years old, I first ventured to send a "contribution" to an educational paper in Janesville, the "organ" of a classical school long ago extinct. "Rustic Musings" was the uncooked title of my exceedingly raw composition. Life had no charms for me during the interval between the secret sending in of this manuscript by one of our hired men, and the next issue of that paper. My name I had not given. This was the first thing I saw about myself "in print," after that wretched checking up that mother and I received in *The Mother's Assistant* aforesaid:

"Zoe's 'Rustic Musings' have some good points, but we can hardly use the article. Besides, we don't believe a lady wrote it. '*Ex pede Herculem.*'"

I asked father what that Latin quotation meant, and he replied, "Hercules is known by his foot." I confided to mother what I had done, and asked her what that Latin meant to me. "Oh," she said, "it means that the writing is like a man's. Your father set most of your copies when you learned, don't you remember? Try again, my child; some time you will succeed." Soon after, Grace Greenwood's *Little Pilgrim* was sent us, and I resolved to get up a club, for she said all who did that would have their names printed in a list, and I, so distant and obscure, found a fascination in the thought that my name would be put in type, away in Philadelphia, where the Independence Bell had rung out long ago! So I went on horseback, near and far, to get the names, when, lo, my own appeared! but, as so often since, it had an "i" where "e" ought to have been; whereat I lost my temper, and querulously complained to mother that "The first editor said I wrote like a man, and the second spelled my name like a boy, and I guessed they did n't think a girl could come to anything in this world, anyhow."

Not long after, mother said to my brother and me one winter evening, "See who will write the best composition in twenty minutes by the clock." We chose the fresh and charming subject, "Falling Leaves." I got the verdict, it being one of those rare decisions in favor of the weak. Encouraged by this victory, I sent my "piece" to the *Prairie Farmer*, in Chicago, where it appeared the next week, as follows:

An autumn zephyr came sighing through the branches of a noble elm, which stood like a protecting giant over my cottage home. It shook, half regretfully, I thought, one tiny bough; and down through the gnarled branches of the grand old tree, fell one, two, three, dark crimson leaves.

The sight, though insignificant, was a sad one to me, then. It reminded me of the similitude existing between leaves and mortals. Both wake to being in a bright, beautiful world; both live their appointed season, enjoy their allotted share of happiness, die their inevitable death, and are, alike, forgotten. This is the epitome, the simple story, of everything that ever existed, save the Eternal God. We all begin life with bright hopes and eager expectancy. In time we leave the stage of action with one conviction—that all is vanity.

We all build our splendid air castles; alas! how often have we seen the anticipated consummation of the cherished plans of some bright being suddenly dashed to the ground, and instead of the fruition of those gay dreams, we have seen "The sable hearse move slowly on, as if reluctantly it bore the young, unwearied form to that cold couch which age and sorrow render sweet to man;" and all of hope and joy and happiness for that peerless creation has passed away.

We have our individual hopes and fears; joys and sorrows; loves and hates. These feelings we may not if we would, impart to any living thing. They are our own, peculiarly our own.

We go on through life. Our eyes lose the brilliancy of youth; our frames cease to be erect and powerful; our steps become slow and spiritless; our intellects lose their vigor. Yet we still cling fondly to our cherished schemes; we hope that *we*, at least, notwithstanding the thousands that have been unfortunate, may be successful. Still we plan and endeavor.

We become older, feebler, sadder. Still we try. The cold autumn of our lives sets in. We tremble before its relentless power. Yet we hope on. Colder grow the nights, more cheerless the days. Death, like the zephyr, though not unwillingly nor sadly, sweeps with icy breath across the now tender, yielding cord of our lives; he snaps it rudely, and we launch forth into the vast, unfathomable—Unknown.

How like our fate to that of the falling leaves! Sad, mournful, dirge-like, everything seems murmuring—"Falling Leaves."

No literary distinction, not even being solicited to write for *The Atlantic*—which, I fear, will never "transpire"—could give me such a thrill of joy as that small leverage imparted then.

Just here I will say, though it is not usual to reveal one's highest literary ambition, especially when one has failed to attain it, that I am willing to admit that mine has been during the last thirty years to write for the *Atlantic Monthly! The Century*, *Harper's*, *Scribner's*, etc., are all very well, but when I began writing for the press the *Atlantic* was the nectar and ambrosia of literary people as well as of those who aspired to be literary, and early loves last longest. I have written for *Harper's* and had a letter in the *Century*, but I have never yet dared offer one to the *Atlantic*. Once I went so far as to send its admired editor, Thomas Bailey Aldrich, a printed article that I thought tolerably good, that is for me, asking him if he believed I could write anything the *Atlantic* would accept. I received in reply a courteous note with the enigmatical statement that he was unable to say from the article forwarded whether I could or not! The question in my mind is now and ever shall be, "Is that a compliment to the article?" This point I have never been able clearly to settle for myself, but one thing is certain, I have not yet recovered sufficiently from the shock to make any other venture *Atlantic*-ward. But I give the cultured editor notice that though I may never be lifted to the Olympian heights of his pages, I intend so to live that somebody who is, shall yet write of me between those magic yellow covers of the Queen of Monthlies!

Next came, in the same friendly columns that opened to me first, an offer of a premium from the Illinois Agricultural Society, to consist of silver cup and medal, for the best essay "On the Embellishment of a Country Home." Our farm had taken the prize at county fairs; it was a beauty, with such a flower garden as careful study of A. J. Downing had helped my tasteful father to create. I "wrote it up," won the prize, and danced about the house like a kitten with a ball.

Of "poems" I wrote many, of which, happily, almost none have seen the light. My "Epic" was begun at nineteen.

This poem I had the grace to bestow upon the flames some years ago. It was nothing less aspiring than an account of the creation of the universe. I suppose most young writers would begin at this point; it was my familiar theme for many a year. To this I added an account of the pre-historic history of my heroine, who was the central figure of the drama. The only vestige which remains of this exploded stellar system is the following:

> Up above thee smiles no planet,
> Far beyond it gleams no star;
> Whizzes there no fiery comet;
> Thou'st not known in ages far.

Going away to school soon after, I was made editor of the college paper, and some poetic effusions long since forgotten and forgiven, appeared in the *Home Journal*, edited by John F. Eberhart, then superintendent of Cook county schools, with headquarters in Chicago. Soon after, this same gentleman gave me my first certificate to teach (in 1860), and the ferule replaced the pen in a wild prairie school at Harlem (near Oak Park), west of Chicago.

Teaching was now for many years not the goal of my ambition, but the necessary ally of my financial independence. If I had my life to live over again, I would do differently. I cannot too strongly counsel any ardent young spirit who feels, as I did, that to express with pen or voice her deepest thought, her ruling love and purpose, is to her more than all else, not to be diverted from that path except by absolute necessity. No such necessity was laid on me. My father was well off, ours was a comfortable home, we had now moved to Evanston, seat of the Northwestern University, and the best minds in that choice literary circle were my friends. Books without limit were at my command, and sweet, shy paths, wild groves, and the anthem of Lake Michigan, were all to be had for the asking. My father begged me to remain at home. He "did n't believe that women were called on to earn money; he would take care of me gladly—indeed, should feel compromised if I set out to care for myself."

But I was a "free born" nature, hence was determined upon independence. My father believed in the one-purse theory and I felt that only money of my own could give me self-determining power. Hence it was that, having graduated at nineteen, when I was twenty I proceeded, without leave or license, to bind myself to teach the hardest school in the county, and my literary paradise forever closed its doors on one who had loved it, no words may say how well. But the ruling passion was still strong, although in death. Editors were kind to me and gave me books to review, in return for which I got the books; *Emery's Journal of Agriculture* sent me flower-seeds and Webster's Unabridged; I read a great deal, wrote for *The Ladies' Repository* once in awhile, and for Mr. Sewell's *Little Corporal*, even had an article in that most exigent of Western papers, the *Chicago Tribune*. In the "Centennial Year of Methodism" (1866), as corresponding secretary of the American Methodist Ladies' Centenary Association, I bombarded our own church press with paragraphs and circulars, making the acquaintance of *Zion's Herald*, I think, at that date.

When our good Bishop Wiley edited the *Repository*, I ventured to send him my first story. It was along a new line—so I fancied—was entitled "Jenny and John;" had held me amazingly in the writing, and I said to myself, "If this only succeeds, I'll give up independence, go home and be a writer without, rather than a teacher with, money." Joy to the world! a letter of acceptance promptly came with complimentary allusions. Then I watched; going to the postoffice, and when the magazine came cutting the index page impatiently and enduring the heart-tattoo that every untried aspirant for literary honors knows so well, as I searched for my story. Twelve months passed and no story appeared. I wrote Dr. Wiley, asking him why this was thus and urging the manuscript's return. He replied curtly that they did n't undertake to keep track of everybody's manuscript, evidently having forgotten that he had once accepted my poor little novelette. I had no copy, and in my discouragement I reasoned thus: "If it had been really good he would n't have forgotten; he is a great man and I am nobody, as yet; he has, unwittingly, given me a final judgment; it is not for me to be a literary woman; it is too high, I cannot attain unto it."

So I turned aside once more to teaching, but at Pittsburgh Female College and Genesee Wesleyan Seminary, wrote essays for our church press and for the society papers of my girls; one address on "Woman's Lesser Duties," was my first "publication" "by order of the society." What an epoch was that, my countrymen! I was twenty-four, but the sight of that pretty, crisp, new pamphlet, with my name on the cover, filled me with delight.

Going abroad in May of 1868, and remaining until the autumn of 1870, I sent letters home to the Chicago *Republican*, then edited by the celebrated Charles A. Dana, author of the Cyclopedia, and now proprietor of the New York *Sun*. Returning, I had an article in *Harper's Magazine*, wrote for the New York *Independent* and our church papers, also for our Chicago magazine, *The Lakeside Monthly*, edited by F. F. Browne, and later on for *The Christian Union*, *Sunday School Times*, *The Forum* and a score of lesser lights.

Meanwhile, all along the years, I have been a writer of paragraphs and items in which a few lines would set forth an opinion. The aggregate of these would make volumes, but nearly all appeared impersonally. When in the summer of 1874, Henry W. Adams, of New York, started *The Morning*, his sunny, sweet-spirited paper, that earliest incarnated the Woman's Crusade, I had a hand in it as chief contributor. It was my first pen-work for temperance.

When our W. C. T. U. launched its organ, *Our Union*, in 1875, with no subscribers and much faith, I again "put pen to paper" with new-found zeal, trying my "'prentice hand," strange to say, at a story once more. It was entitled "Margaret's Victory," but was declared, after twelve chapters, "too woman's rightsy" and withdrawn "by order of the management." I also wrote (in 1875) my "Hints and Helps," the first hand-book for white ribboners. Indeed, since the Crusade I have always been writing my uppermost thought in railway stations, Pullman cars, on convention platforms and anywhere, glad when it was chronicled, and never on the lookout to ascertain whether it went into the paper or the basket. But our editors have had loving and sisterly consideration for me always. *The Union Signal*, into which *Our Union* was merged at the Louisville National Convention in 1882, has now fifty thousand subscribers, and is rapidly climbing up to one hundred thousand. My sister-in-law was the first and Miss Mary Allen West is its present editor; I have had more articles in its columns than I was entitled to expect or they, perhaps, were wise to set before the public.

As already stated, my brother, who had for years been editor of a daily paper in Chicago, passed away suddenly, in 1878, leaving the Chicago *Evening Post* without a chief, and his gifted wife, Mrs. Mary Bannister Willard, had the heroism to undertake to save the paper; it was in the crisis of reconstruction when my brother died, and was left in a position so critical that no man would try to stem the tide. I agreed to stand by her, and we accordingly became the forlorn hope of an enterprise that was running behind at the rate of several hundred dollars a week, and for about three months, without fee or reward, we tried to hold our own. Though briefly mentioned before, I may be permitted here to give further details concerning this, the most novel experience of all my life; I found myself at the head of a corps of twelve editors and reporters, all of them inured to journalism, of which I knew practically nothing, and to which I came from the ardors and hap-hazard of a popular temperance campaign, into the sorrowful inheritance of my brother's desk, chair, and dingy city offices. My editorial associates, Collins Shackelford, James C. Ambrose, Henry Ten Eyck White, Alanson Appleton, and others, were most considerate toward me. They had loved my gifted, genial brother and were loyal to the women who tried to take up the herculean task that bore him down. Foreman, proof-readers, compositors, and all the force of sixty persons or more, stood by us to the last.

Coming and going, Evanston still my home, mother my home-maker, Anna Gordon with me at the office, helping in all the ways I could invent, with evening engagements to speak on temperance, as my only source of income, I felt the great world-wave strike hard against my life ship, as it does far out at sea.

But there was so much of home solace and spiritual renewing that, though practically submerged, I do not remember ever being sleepless over the strange, new work or the impending doom. We had acted in good faith and done our best. Why should we make ourselves sick in the bargain? for health and good heart, with faith in God, these were our capital. This was not the first time that the inheritance of being one of the "seven sleepers," has carried me through.

My sister acted as publisher, for figures—other than those of speech—have been foreign to me always. She had helped my brother with book reviews and editorial writing, for which she has especial gift, but in this emergency her hand was on the monetary helm.

In our card to the public, May, 1878, I declared our purpose as follows:

"*The Post* will be more than a buyer and seller in the news mart. It will aim so to outline the story of the world's doings to-day that the reading thereof will tend to make the world better to-morrow. It will address itself to a constituency located not in bar-rooms and billiard halls, but in business offices and homes. It will warmly advocate all causes that tend to ennoble human nature, and will strive always to express itself in words which a woman might hear and speak.

As heretofore, *The Post* will be a political paper, independent and fearless, lending its influence to such measures only as are calculated to hasten the time when all men's weal shall be each man's care."

I soon had occasion to define our idea of how to behave as editors:

"*The Post* wishes to say here and now and once and for all, that its notion of journalistic courtesy involves the same principles that govern well-bred persons in the intercourse of society. Any word that may creep into these columns not in keeping with this statement, is hereby disavowed beforehand, for all possible measures will be employed to forestall such mistakes."

We found on coming into our thrice mortgaged heritage that there were contracts for advertisement of liquors, proprietary medicines, etc., such as we could not approve, but as we had no money and these were unexpired, we could not discontinue them. Meanwhile, liberal offers of advertising flowed in from liquor dealers, which my sister, of course, instantly declined. In face of these facts, we had little relish for the "moralettes" that came to us in every day's mail to this effect:

"Dear Ladies: I have had high esteem for you, but certainly the advertisement (inclosed) that you persist in flaunting before the public, lifts you very little above the lowest journalistic level. I am at a loss to account for such flagrant inconsistency."

[Signed] ANONYMOUS.

Or this: "You will please stop my paper. I subscribed supposing it marked a new era in journalism, but evidently (see advt.), 'the dog returns to his,' etc.

"X. Y. Z."

I verily believe we had more letters of warning and exhortation, than of subscription and good cheer, during that most trying ordeal of my life. I used to say to myself, "Is it possible that I was once a happy, care-free, temperance worker, skimming contentedly along the sea of life? Alas, I am now fathoms deep in the wilderness of waters and well nigh suffocated," but not enough to lose my sleep!

In the financial extremity that tightened around us every day, some leading business men of the city showed us great kindness and our creditors were remarkably considerate. But this terribly unequal strife of plus with minus could not long continue. I consulted with my sister and my hopes, and then went to New York and laid our case before Elizabeth Thompson, the well-known philanthropist, with whom I had a most agreeable acquaintance. To obtain an audience with this lovely and loving-hearted woman is extremely difficult, but through the intercessions of my loyal hostess, Mrs. M. P. Hascall, I succeeded in seeing her. So I laid our case before Sister Elizabeth, who listened most kindly, with pitiful face, and said: "My dear friend, if you had asked me to help you in almost anything else, I would have done so, but I dread journalism as a burnt child dreads the fire. Putting money into a paper is like pouring water into a sieve. Drop that enterprise before it beggars you all. Drop it, I implore you. It was heroic, as you say, for your sister to try; but no *man* would have tried." So our last hope was like our first, forlorn! As I went down the stairs, after a kindly leave-taking, Mrs. Thompson leaned over the railing and called out:

"Give my love to your sister and tell her to *drop that paper* before she is a day older." And I told her. Our valedictory came out within a fortnight, and the paper, franchise and all, was sold at auction to the *Daily News*, owned by Victor A. Lawson and Melville E. Stone.

This is the only paper for which I ever personally stood sponsor, and among the score of different positions to which I have been chosen since my first official relation to the public, (when, at eighteen, I taught our district school near Forest Home) it is the only one in which I might not freely have continued had I chosen so to do. But the mandate of an empty exchequer drove me from this, and there is no other fate quite so impressive or inexorable. I thought of all this for my consolation as I packed up my few literary effects and turned away forever from "No. 88 Dearborn street," to resume the work that I had learned to love the best.

My resolution then taken remains unchanged. I will never again be the responsible head of any journalistic venture, nor be in any wise financially accountable to any, save as a contributor of money or of articles. I have freely allowed my name to be used in this way, as a matter of course. When women asked for it, on the list of almost any temperance or philanthropic paper, and when Joseph Cook, that grand defender of every faith sacred to humanity, did me the honor to request my name for his magazine, *Our Day*, what could I say but "Yes"? In like manner, when Rev. Dr. Theodore L. Flood, founder of *The Chautauquan* and a firm friend of woman's wider opportunity, asked me to contribute, I told him that if Anna Gordon would make herself responsible for me and would "see that I wrote," he would be sure to hear from me. Out of that contract came "How to Win." When Alice Stone Blackwell of *The Woman's Journal*, asked me to be an occasional contributor, I was glad. When Alice M. Guernsey wished me to write for our W. C. T. U. juvenile paper, *The Young Crusader*, I gathered up the dropped threads of a story begun in *The Little Corporal* away back in 1865 at the instance of my friend, Alfred L. Sewell, and unceremoniously cut short at the third chapter through some misunderstanding between us, and carried it on through fifty-two numbers, written "en route," and picturing out the twelve years during which "We, Us & Company" lived on a farm. When a Hartford publisher, persistent as the forces of gravitation, persecuted me with petitions to write "Woman and Temperance" (his own elected title), and appeared upon the scene for personal interviews until I saw there was but one alternative, and that was to get it ready, I took refuge in the home of my staunch sister and ally, Mrs. Hannah Whitall Smith, of Philadelphia, and there in the space of three weeks had "carpentered and joinered" a rough strong-box which has the single merit of enshrining some of the newly-mined jewels of fact, which the stately historian of the temperance reform can polish at his leisure.

When the National Convention of 1887 asked me to signalize my approaching semi-centennial (1889) by a volume of personal reminiscences and speeches, I sat me down to evolve the same as best I could from my "internal consciousness," clearing a little space on my workshop table by pushing aside so much that I ought to do, that I bring to my present task a mind sadly divided. Few have learned more thoroughly than I, from the things that they have suffered, that the paths of true literature are shady and silent; as leisurely as the slow lap of wavelets when the lake is still; as secret as the mossy nooks in the valleys of my old Forest Home. "Far from the madding crowd" lies the pastoral path of the life I longed for most, and treading whose piney wood aisles I might perhaps have thought out consolations for the fierce fighters of the plain; but with the battle on and my own place chosen for me at the front, I shall never get beyond "Notes from the Saddle," at least not until too old or too deeply wounded by the fray. A lifetime ago, one who had wished me well and hoped much from my future wrote me thus: "You always write with your left hand; I think when reading after you, 'How much better this would be if she could take more time.'" How well I knew this was the truth and that the unhasting pen alone creates the works that do not haste to die!

Aside from my little hand-book of "Hints and Helps," written in 1875 for the W. C. T. U., the only book not asked of me, but freely written out of hand and out of heart, is "Nineteen Beautiful Years," published by Harper & Brothers in 1864, reprinted by the Woman's Temperance Publication Association of Chicago, to which I gave the electrotype plates in 1885, and brought out in England, thanks to the influence of Mrs. Hannah Whitall Smith, by Morgan & Scott, of London, publishers of *The Christian*. That little book said itself—both my sister's part, so unconsciously furnished when she wrote her girlish journal seen only by us two, and mine—out of a heart that spoke aloud its strange, new grief.

It was one year after she left us, and in the home where all of us were last together; "Swampscott" we called it, on Church Street, Evanston, the grounds but not the house being those now owned by William Deering. I was there alone with mother in the summer of 1863, my brother having married and gone to Denver, Col., my father being in the city all day.

"To us the silence in the house,
To her the choral singing."

Never in this world could we all be again what my dear brother had once called us: "A family unbroken by death, discord, or distance."

Alone in my desolate room, so lately brightened by her sunny presence, I prepared the little volume which would have been larger by half had all I wrote gone in. My father, who was of reticent nature, disapproved the undertaking; he hated publicity for women, and most of all for his "two forest nymphs," as he used laughingly to call us. But for myself I liked the world, believed it friendly, and could see no reason why I might not confide in it. Besides, it was more than I could brook that she should live and die and make no sign—she who was so wise, so sweet and good. I had a chivalric impulse to pass along the taper that she lighted at the shrine of Truth, even though her weary little hand had dropped it early at the tomb.

And so, when my manuscript was ready, I went to Mr. E. Haskin, who was then the leading business man of my own church, borrowed a hundred dollars and started for New York, under escort of T. C. Hoag, one of our nearest friends. It was my first real outing, and zestful beyond telling. Mr. Hoag never knew how grateful I was for his kindness in stopping over a day at Buffalo that I might go out to see Niagara Falls. The wonder of that revelation roused all the recklessness for which I had been famed at Forest Home and which had been toned down by later years. The fascination of the Falls drew me to the ragged edge of every cliff and set me running down steep banks, so that Mr. Hoag soon supervened and took me into custody. Somehow, the sense of God was with me on those heights and with that wraith-like form and thunder-voice smiting my ear. It gives me satisfaction that, young and ardent as I was, and with the desire ever innate in me to "wreak myself upon expression," I did not drop into poetry, nor yet into prose, in presence of that gleaming mystery.

The scenery of the Susquehanna and Chemung was simply fascinating in its autumnal garniture. We reached New York at dark, took a coach for the St. Nicholas Hotel, and as we rolled along Broadway I was far more dazed than by anything in all my life before, except Niagara! Mr. Hoag, though a merchant on a business trip, told me to make a list of what I wished to see and he would "help me through with it." It was Saturday night. I chose Grace Church, Dr. Cheever's and Dr. E. H. Chapin's, the first for its fame, the second for its reformatory spirit, the third for its pastor's eloquence. On Monday we climbed Trinity steeple, went to the Battery and Castle Garden, Barnum's, and Wall Street. Here Mr. Hoag had to stay awhile, and he put me into a Broadway stage, telling the driver to stop at the St. Nicholas. It did not occur to my kind friend that I had never in my life been anywhere alone, nor to me that my pocket-book was locked up in my trunk at the hotel. "Ting-a-ling" went the driver's bell. I sat in sweet unconsciousness, studying the pageant of the street.

"Ting-a-ling-a-ling," with vigorous vexation. I gave no heed. "Hand up that fare!" he shouted through an aperture; the passengers looked at each other; my face turned crimson. "I have n't any money," I whispered confidentially, in my great fright and desperation, to a big Jew with diamond shirt front and forbidding countenance. "What can I do?"

"Oh, Miss," he answered kindly, "it's of no consequence, just let me hand up the fare and there's an end of it!" At that moment his countenance seemed fairly angelic. "You are so kind," I faltered almost with tears. "Indeed, it is an honor; don't mention it," he said. Forever and a day that act of his made me think better of mankind, trust more in human nature. I thanked him again as the 'bus pulled up for me at the St. Nicholas; he lifted his hat and was gone, the great, beak-nosed, unmistakable Jew. I went up to my room and cried at remembrance of his kindness.

That night we went to Wallack's Theatre. It was the first and last time in all my life that I ever attended the theatre in my own land. I said to myself: "This is the most respectable one there is; 'Rosedale, or the Rifle Ball' is a reputable play and Lester Wallack is at his best in it; no one knows me and no harm will be done." This I then stated to my father's friend, and he agreed, both of us being good Christians and church-members. We went—it was an evening of wonder and delight, but I forbear to state who of our Western friends and fellow church-members we then and there beheld, who had gone from the same motives that actuated me!

All my life I have read the "Amusement column" of the daily paper and often greatly enjoyed it. For the stage I have strong natural liking. In England I saw Sothern as David Garrick, and it lifted up my spirit as a sermon might. But in this age, with my purposes and its demoralization, the stage is not for me. Sometime, somewhere, it may have the harm taken out of it, but where or when, this generation, and many more to follow this, will ask, I fear, in vain.

A week or so later, my good father came on to take me to New England, having decided, perhaps, that my embassy was not so foolish as he had thought at first. Together we went up the Hudson to Sing-Sing, where Rev. Dr. Randolph S. Foster (now Bishop) was pastor of the M. E. Church. This noble man had been President of the University at Evanston, and I wanted his opinion and influence in my new enterprise. Cornelius J. Walsh's family had driven in their elegant carriage from Newark to visit Dr. Foster. I remember my palpitations of heart as they all assembled to hear me read my manuscript. Annie, the Doctor's gifted daughter, was the one I feared and loved the most; upon her verdict hung my hopes. I read the whole little book at one sitting, and when I finished they all sat crying—it was a circle of white handkerchiefs, and nobody said a word.

How I loved them for their sympathy and thanked God for raising up such friends for Mary and for me!

Dr. Foster took the manuscript to the city next day. Harper & Brothers were his friends; most of them had been his parishioners. They accepted it at once, asked the Doctor to write an Introduction, which he did, and so the life of my sister, playmate, and comrade came to the world.

What a delight were my beautiful proof-sheets, the first I ever saw; what a marvel the letters that accompanied them from Thomas Glenn, the long-time proof-reader of Harpers, whose penmanship seemed to me vastly plainer than print! What a comfort to dedicate the little book to my beloved parents! Dear father said very little about it, but five years after, when he had passed away, we found a copy locked up with Mary's photograph in a secret drawer of his desk. And what a rude assault was the *Round Table* criticism! Up to that time all had been plain sailing; the press, so far as I could learn, had dealt gently with the record that was so sacred in my eyes. But one day a friend drew from his pocket a copy of the New York *Round Table*, and proceeded to read what Gail Hamilton afterward called "A bludgeon criticism."

It was my first heavy blow from a "reviewer," and it struck so deeply home that I can not forget it in any world. In these years, when to be "taken to task" is a matter of course, and to be bitterly blamed, or even cruelly maligned, is not uncommon, I have learned a calm philosophy that neutralizes the virus and takes the harm out of the wound. But in those days such blows bewildered me, more from their manner than their matter, for criticism I expected, and had been bred to believe that it was wholesome, which I do now believe with more intelligence than I could bring to bear upon the subject then.

Being in need of money at one time, I wrote my publishers that if they would give me a hundred copies I would forego the ten per cent royalty on which we had agreed. This they did, and that is all that ever came to me, except that in later years I gave away a hundred or more copies furnished without charge by them. In 1885 I bought the plates and presented them to our own temperance publishing house in Chicago. This is a fair sample of the financial side of my pen-holder work.

Each new book is to me a new impoverishment; I give them away freely, never having been able to keep a book of any sort, least of all, my own, any more than I can an umbrella or a section of the atmosphere. All of my ventures combined have not netted me one thousand dollars.

From England I have encouraging accounts of the little book's success, and I have had no more welcome greeting than from those who, wherever I go, speak gently to me of the good that Mary's life has done them. So the sweet young soul lives on in minds made better by her presence, and still in artless language tries to "tell everybody to be good."

Messrs. Morgan & Scott, publishers of the English edition, courteously allowed me a royalty amounting now to about two hundred dollars.

As years go by I find that my jottings gain wider hospitality, my last two magazine articles having been for two monthlies most unlike — *The Homiletic* and *The Forum*. My article for the first has been printed in full as a book entitled, "Woman in the Pulpit," by D. Lothrop & Co., Boston.

And now, to sum up what I have learned by the things sought, suffered and succeeded in, along my pathway, pen in hand, let me urge every young woman whose best vehicle of expression is the written word, not to be driven from her kingdom by impatience as was I.

1. If you can have a roof over your head, a table prepared before you and clothes to wear, let them be furnished by your "natural protectors," and do you study and practice with your pen. Read Robert Louis Stevenson's revelations of how he came to be a master of style; he worked and waited for it, that is all.

EDITORS OF "OUR DAY."

W. F. CRAFTS, ANTHONY COMSTOCK, EDMUND JAMES, L. T. TOWNSEND,

2. If you must be self-supporting, learn the printer's trade in a newspaper office. The atmosphere will be congenial; you will find yourself next door to the great world; if you have "faculty," the inky powers will find it out and your vocation will take you into fellowship.

3. The next best outlook is the teacher's desk. A majority of our most celebrated women writers were teachers once. The life is intellectual and, though one of routine is not most favorable to the freedom that a writer should enjoy, it conduces to surroundings that enhance, rather than deteriorate, the mental powers. But imagination, that angel of mind, is a shy spirit and breaks not readily to harness; while Pegasus in the tread-mill sawing up the fire-wood of necessity is the sorriest spectacle alive.

But journalism will be a larger field to-morrow than it is to-day, and nine tenths of our literary aspirants, if they have the divine call of adaptation and enthusiasm, will enter there.

Newspapers need women more than women need newspapers. Fewer tobacco cobwebs in air and brain and a less alcoholic ink are the prime necessities of the current newspaper. Mixed with the miraculous good of journalism note the random statements given to-day only that they may be taken back to-morrow. Note the hyperbolism of heads not level, the sensationalism, the low details not lawful to be uttered, the savagery of the pugilist and baseball columns, the beery mental flavor, the bitter gall dipped from the editorial inkstand and spattered on political opponents. In brief, note that newspaperdom is a camp and not a family circle — a half sphere not a whole one.

But the journalistic temperament is almost the finest in the world — keen, kind, progressive, and humanitarian. Take away the hallucination of nicotine and the craze of alcoholic dreams, and you would have remaining an incomparable set of brother-hearted men, whose glimpses of God would be not at all infrequent. Anchor alongside these chivalric-natured experts, women as gifted as themselves, and free from drug delusions; then, in one quarter century, you will have driven pugilists and saloon-keepers, ward politicians and Jezebels from the sacred temple of journalism, and the people's daily open letter from the great world shall be pure as a letter from home.

Until the bitter controversy about the Prohibition party's

relation to politics, I have been treated almost universally with kind consideration by the editorial fraternity. I attribute this to my brother's membership therein and to my own participation in journalism, also to a certain kindliness that I believe belongs to the journalistic temperament. There is much of the dramatic in these editorial brethren and the theory on which I account for the oceans of abuse that they seem to dip up out of their inkstands, is that each in thought separates his own genial personality from the dreadful pen-and-ink dragon who writes the perfunctory editorials and paragraphs.

It seems to me this is a great evil, doing incalculable harm to their own nature and character, and greatly diminishing the sum total of the world's good will. If the politics of the future can not be more reasonable, if men and women can not discuss great questions without using abusive epithets, then the true civilization is a long way off. I confidently believe that all of this sanguinary style of writing is but an unconscious reminiscence in the editorial brain of the cruel bloodshed of his ancestors when they matched spear with spear instead of fighting at the pen's point alone. Surely this will wear away and we shall learn to think and speak with the utmost personal kindliness concerning our opponents in the field of politics.

PEOPLE I HAVE MET.

I console myself as regards many famous personages that I have tried to give them a little peace of their lives. Attracted by great characters far more than by any other magnet in this world, I have visited their haunts on both sides of the sea at every opportunity; have gone scores of miles out of my way to stand beside De Quincey's grave, and Coleridge's and Wordsworth's, but have not intruded upon the living objects of my admiration, for the mere purpose of the sight, save in a single instance, which I have felt guilty over ever since; to Longfellow, at my request, my friend Elizabeth Stuart Phelps gave me a note of introduction, saying to him and me, "I think she has earned it by her honest, hard work for temperance."

It has been my good fortune, however, to have had many a glimpse of those the world calls great. I have seen the motherly Queen of England graciously distributing prizes to the peasantry at Windsor Castle; the dignified Emperor Napoleon III. driving in state along the Champs Elysées; the martial Emperor William saluting the enthusiastic crowd from his box at the Imperial Opera House in Berlin; the handsome Pope of Rome pronouncing benedictions at St. Peter's; the ponderous Sultan of Turkey riding to the Mosque of Santa Sophia, and several Presidents of the United States in the parlors of the White House.

But my most cherished memories are not of those whose heads were crowned by virtue of rights not in the least divine. Only the world's true aristocracy, its kings and queens in the better realms of literature, art, science and humanity, have held sway over my loyal heart. In seeking to pay them worthy tribute, I have found that such reminiscences alone would fill a volume. Within the limits allotted here, I can sketch but a few out of the scores by whose presence, as well as by their grand words and lives, my life and character have been enriched.

HANNAH WHITALL SMITH.

Among the friends who have been most helpful to me is Mrs. Hannah Whitall Smith, wife of Robert Pearsall Smith, of Philadelphia. Mrs. Smith is the author of "The Christian's Secret of a Happy Life," a book that has reached numerous editions and been translated into eight languages; a book from which I had already derived great advantage in my spiritual life before ever meeting her who has long been to me like "the shadow of a great rock in a weary land."

The first time I ever saw this noble woman was when I spoke for the first time in the city of Philadelphia, and was informed by those having the meeting in charge that she was to conduct the devotional exercises. I was not a little impressed by the honor and pleasure of having her associated with me, and when a tall woman of strong physique, not stout, but far from thin, walked up the steps into the pulpit with a business-like air, her fine, beaming countenance, motherly tones, and warm grasp of the hand made me at ease with her at once. From that hour we have been warm friends, and her home seems like my own, so often has she said to me, "When thee comes to my house thee is to do just exactly as thee likes, and while thee is here the house and all we have is thine." This most hospitable mansion at Germantown, in the suburbs of Philadelphia, has been a refuge to me many a time, more so than any other of the thousand homes that have so kindly opened their doors to me, except "Rest Cottage," and "Weary Woman's Rest," as I call the beloved Auburndale home of Anna Gordon.

I did myself the pleasure to sketch "H. W. S." at length in "Woman and Temperance," but a large volume would hardly suffice to show the many-sided amplitude of character with which this woman, a thorough American type and one of our choicest, is endowed. Her sunny spirit has hardly its peer for sustained cheerfulness in all the shining ranks of the W. C. T. U., with which she has been associated almost from the beginning. The Bible readings given by her at our National Conventions are the most unique religious meetings I have ever attended. Her Expository Leaflets on "Chariots," the "Crusade Psalm," and other subjects, have had an immense sale among our local unions where they are reproduced to the great advantage of all who hear them. Once a month, for many years, Mrs. Smith has furnished us one of these inimitable readings.

Their eldest daughter, Mary Whitall Costelloe, having married an English barrister, the family now reside in London, but wherever they are, their noble character, varied accomplishments, and great wealth are consecrated to the cause of "God and home and every land."

MARY A. LATHBURY.

Some twelve summers ago I was in that great literary caravansary called the Methodist Book Rooms, Broadway, New York. Passing the editorial doors, a soft voice called me from within, and a timid hand touched my arm, as Mary A. Lathbury, whom I then saw for the first time, said to me, "Won't you come in and let me talk to you a little?" She had just been chosen assistant editor of the *Sunday-School Advocate;* a position of an unrecognized sort, in which a woman has an opportunity to do a vast deal of hard work without anybody being any the wiser as to her individuality. This will be considered a crabbed remark, but it always seemed to me that a woman, as well as a man, should have the happiness of an honest recognition for the good she does and the help she brings to any enterprise. My own immediate corps of lieutenants in the office amuse themselves at my expense because I insist on devising some responsible name that shall belong to each of them, preferring not to bunch them all under the general name of clerks, but naming one, office secretary, another, department secretary, etc., and yet I believe they like it, all the same, and recognize, as I do, that it is simply just that those who do the work should have the pleasure of forming the wider circle of friends naturally belonging to those who work in a wide field. I also think it an advantage to the work itself, from the added individuality and enthusiasm of those who give themselves, body, soul, and spirit, to the enterprise, whatever it may be.

Mary A. Lathbury is one of the most delicate, crocus-natured women that I know. She takes strong hold of the nutritive powers of the universe, so that no amount of cold above the ground can make her less hardy, and yet she is as fragile as a harebell to look upon, and as shrinking as a mimosa. We were at once acquainted and our *rapport* has been well-nigh perfect ever since. She had planned her pretty Bay-Window Department and asked me many questions that I could not answer, about ingenious ways of interesting children and young people. I told her all I knew and more besides, which did not take long, and went my way, enriched by the knowledge of one more beautiful soul. As I am somewhat of a questioner, I then and there learned from her much of her history and aspirations. She came from a quiet New York village; was converted early, and as she knelt in consecration, knowing that she had some special gifts of brain and hand, she there specifically dedicated them to the worship of the Master whom she loved and the humanity for whose sweet sake He gave Himself to sorrow and to death. I think she told me that just then flashed on her fancy a series of pictures, since embodied in a beautiful book entitled "Out of Darkness Into Light," where the progress of a human spirit is typified in the life of a young man. She has gone on her shining way, with light always falling on her pencil from the celestial country toward which her course is steadfast. As we had no money, I early asked her to design for us a picture for our children's pledge card, and a seal for our National Society, so we call sweet Mary Lathbury our "special artist." She has also written for us beautiful hymns, and shares with Rev. Dr. Rankin, the celebrated author of some of the choicest contributions to our modern hymnals, the title of our poet laureate. In the Centennial year Miss Lathbury wrote what seems to me the finest hymn of that epoch, beginning,

"Lift up, lift up thy voice with singing,
Dear land, with strength, lift up thy voice!
The kingdoms of the earth are bringing
Their treasures to thy gates, rejoice!"

Music and words were never more rarely suited to each other than the lamented William P. Sherwin's and Miss Lathbury's in that celestial song. Another of her hymns written for white ribboners begins thus:

"Room for the truth, make room before us,
For truth and righteousness to stand!
And plant the blessed banner o'er us,
For God and Home and Native Land!"

Miss Mary Van Marter succeeded to Miss Lathbury's place when the latter's gracious and growing fame led her into the pathways of artistic book-making, and the two women have set up their rest together in New York where a handsome little nephew of Miss L. furnishes a model for many of her fairy faces, and is bound to grow up, under the hallowed influences of this pure home, to be one of the new-fashioned men that shall help bring about the new-fashioned world of men and women.

REV. DR. JOHN HALL.

Some years ago, when the Presbyterian General Assembly was held in Madison, Wis., I attended with Mrs. Elizabeth Hibben and Mrs. Hinckley, who were at that time respectively presidents of the W. C. T. U. of Illinois and of Wisconsin. We wished to bring a knowledge of our methods to these good, conservative men, leaders of a great religious sect. But as we knew we should not be admitted to their sanhedrim, we arranged for a meeting in a church near by at an hour when they were not in session and the local union of Madison sent a tasteful ticket of invitation to each member. There was a good attendance, and among others the massive form and kindly face of Rev. Dr. John Hall, of New York City, dignified the audience. He was courteously invited to open the meeting with prayer, but said he would prefer to witness the proceedings first, so the Rev. Dr. Stryker, who is not afraid of the white ribboners, prayed for us, and then we three women spoke as we were moved. Coming down from the pulpit I met Dr. Hall for the first time, who spoke to me most gently from his tall height, and asked if he could have an interview with me next day. We arranged one in the Capitol building, where the Presbyterian Assembly held its sessions. I invited my two partners in distress to accompany me, and for an hour or more we had a talk that was to me surprising. In substance Dr. Hall said that he had been convinced I had a mission as a public speaker; he wished to tell me this and to beg me to confine my speeches wholly to the members of my own sex. He said the Bible clearly taught this, and he believed it to be his duty kindly to urge this truth upon my attention. He also spoke about the sacerdotal line, and that while we might accomplish good, he very much questioned if, on the whole, we had not already done still more harm; preaching was the work of men set apart to do it, and there were now so many going about with Bagster Bibles under their arms who could imitate Mr. Moody in nothing save that action, that he feared the sanctity of the clerical office and its high prerogatives were not so clearly defined in the popular mind as they would otherwise be. Mrs. Hinckley was visibly hurt by his words and rose to leave, saying, "With such a curse on hand in this country as the drink habit and the liquor traffic, I wonder that any man dares to speak as you have done to a woman like our president. To me it seems that you would frustrate the grace of God. You say that woman's place is in the home. I grant it, and if you will discover a way by which you can protect our homes and our boys from the wolves that howl upon their track, I will gladly stay at home with my four little boys for the remainder of my days to sew on buttons and make the kettle boil." The great man inclined his head slightly, saying, "Indeed, madam, I hope your boys may grow up good and happy." His entire stress was laid upon the personal conversion of drinking men, and so far as he could seem to see there was nothing beyond this in the temperance reform. I told him of our work among the children: that the mother-hearts of the land were working along the line of prevention, rather than spending all their time on reformation. We talked to him of prohibition, but met with small response. He was very kind and thoughtful, but spoke to us out of one world and we answered him out of another. One of us said to him, "Is it not possible, Doctor, that in your church, the most costly in the United States, surrounded by millionaires as you are, you may not have as broad a view of this great question as we whose lives are spent among the people?" "Indeed," he answered, "the best members of my church are servant-girls." "But servant-girls do not set the key-note of public opinion in your church," was the response. He assured us that he never tasted wine, no matter at whose table he might be, which we were very glad and grateful to find out. On the whole, the interview was rather unsatisfactory to all concerned, and as we left him I remember saying, "It is impossible for you, Dr. Hall, born and reared in Ireland and in the Presbyterian fold, to have any conception of the outlook of an American woman, of all that stirs in her brain and heart. Some day when we get home to heaven, I expect to see you high up among the shining ones and from a very low place close by the door, if I am so happy as to attain so much, I expect to look up at you with an inquiring glance, recalling to you this interview, and that you will then glance down toward me and the look will mean, 'Sister, away yonder in the little planet Earth, when I reproved you for speaking of a pure life to my brother-men, I was egregiously mistaken.' "

FRANCIS MURPHY.

I first met Francis Murphy at Old Orchard Beach, finding him a whole-hearted, genial man. I invited him to come to Chicago; he did so, and held meetings for several nights. I engaged Brunswick Billiard Hall for him, and my brother, through his paper, did all he could to help the movement on, but for some reason his first visit was not successful, though subsequently he has had great audiences and good results. I was in Pittsburgh when thirty different churches in the city and suburbs were packed each night with Murphy meetings and he was conveyed in a carriage from one to another of the principal audiences, sometimes being admitted through a window because the aisles were as thoroughly packed as the pews. I was myself at a meeting where this occurred, in the United Presbyterian Church, where they sang psalms, and such a breaking up of formality as this was for staid old Pittsburgh can not be described. I also spoke on that occasion, in the Episcopal Church, packed after the same manner, and as I stood inside the chancel rail, I could hardly believe my eyes as the motley throng rolled in out of the human tides along the street. Had Brother Murphy's constructive plans been equal to his magnetism, he would have excelled any reformer of our time, and I am constrained to say that if he had adhered to prohibition and kept along side by side with the W. C. T. U., his influence would have been incomparably greater, but a high-license advocate can not under any circumstances be acceptable to the white ribboners. Prohibition is our watch-word and our guiding star. We shall follow where it leads, though it be to prisons and to death.

DR. WM. H. HOLCOMBE.

Mrs. Judge Merrick, of New Orleans, introduced me in that city to Mrs. Anna Y. Waugh, a Boston woman of great accomplishments, who had lived in many foreign countries; known more remarkable people than almost any one I ever met and was a seer in her own right. This lady took me to see Dr. William

H. Holcombe, a Northern gentleman for many years resident in the Crescent City, and its leading homeopathic physician. Many years before I had read this gentleman's curious book, "In Both Worlds," an account of the supposed whereabouts of Lazarus during his absence from the body, as determined by Swedenborgian standards. I had also read many of his religious articles and his ingenious putting of the Christian Scientists' philosophy. That the doctor has a wide and lofty soul, and one totally fearless, no one can disbelieve who thinks his thoughts after him. What was my surprise, not knowing that he had cognizance of me, to hear him say as my name was announced, "Oh, I know about you, and I regard you as a man-spirit sent into this sphere of being to help the women up—they are too passive, they're like sheep, they've been dogged so long that they'll never rally without a man-spirit to go before them, shepherd-fashion." Not a little taken aback by this greeting, I said, "But, Doctor, I'm a woman, and it is my greatest glory to be one."

"O yes, I know you are 'for the present distress' and to fulfill your ambassadorship, but all the same, what I tell you is the truth, and you'll find it out some day," was his final affirmation, for I speedily dismissed the subject and talked to him of the psychical themes in which he has long been a specialist.

MRS. ELIZABETH RODGERS.

When the Knights of Labor held their great convention at Richmond, Va., a score of women appeared and were heartily received as delegates. Chief among these was Mrs. Elizabeth Rodgers, Master Workman of District No. 24, Chicago. Always desirous of meeting remarkable women, I ascertained her address, asked an interview, and received a cordial invitation.

So I went; in an unfamiliar, but reputable part of the city, where the street-car patrons are evidently wage-workers, I was welcomed to a small, but comfortable, modern house by a woman who came to the door with sleeves rolled up and babe in arms. She was the presiding officer over all the Knights of Labor in Chicago and the suburbs, except the Stock Yards division. Her orders came directly from "Brother Powderly" (as she calls him), and were by her promulgated to the local societies, including fifty thousand or more working men and women. She presided once a fortnight over a meeting of three hundred, who represent the mass; and when I asked her "if she studied Cushing's Manual" she replied, "Indeed, I do; for these men are very wide-awake, and on the watch to see if I make mistakes." Probably no parallel instance of leadership in a woman's hands, conferred by such peers, can be cited in this country, if indeed in any other.

Mrs. Rodgers is about forty years of age; height medium; figure neither stout nor fragile; complexion fair, clear, and healthful; eye an honest gray; mouth sweet and smiling; nose a handsome, masterful Roman; head square and full; profile strong and benignant. I was glad to note her fair, unpunctured ear—a proof of wholesome instincts. She has been the mother of twelve children, ten of whom are now living. The youngest was but twelve days old when her mother started for the Richmond Convention, where the baby was made "Delegate No. 800," and presented by the Knights with a silver cup and spoon, and the mother with a handsome Knights of Labor gold watch.

"My husband always believed that women should do anything they liked that was good and which they could do well," said Mrs. Rodgers, proudly; "but for him, I never could have got on so well as a Master Workman. I was the first woman in Chicago to join the Knights. They offered us the chance, and I said to myself, 'There must be a first one, and so I'll go forward.'"

"How do you speak to them?" I asked.

"Oh, just as I do here to my children at home," she answered, simply. "I have no time to get anything ready to say, for I do, and always have done, all my own work, but I just talk as well as I can at the time."

And that is well enough, for Mrs. Rodgers is ready of utterance, with a round, clear voice, gentle and womanly, and that concise and pointed method of expression which shows her mental faculties to be thoroughly well in hand.

"Our leaders are all in favor of temperance and the woman's ballot, and every other thing that's good," she said, "and will bring the rank and file up to these things as soon as they can."

"Some people object to you because of your secrets," I said.

"Oh, we are not a regular secret society," she answered, "we have no such ways as the Masons; no oath in such a sense as they have. We are like the Good Templars, with a 'grip,' that we may know each other, and a 'password,' that strangers may not get in, and that's about all."

"Then your only secret is that you have n't any?" I inquired, glad to learn this because opposed, by nature and by nurture, to close corporations.

"That's about it," she smilingly returned.

Mrs. Rodgers got her training as the chief officer of a local board of the Knights of Labor, which office she held four years, and by the death of the District Master Workman became the chief for our great city.

"We take no saloon-keepers," she said, "not even a saloon-keeper's wife. We will have nothing to do with men who have capital invested in a business which is the greatest curse the poor have ever known; but wage-workers connected with the liquor business are not forbidden to join us." I told her I hoped the pledge of total abstinence might be made a test of membership, and she heartily acquiesced in the plan. I spoke of the White Cross movement, and my desire to enlist the Knights in its favor, leaving with her some of the literature and the petitions for the protection of women and the prohibition of the liquor traffic. She seemed to me a sincere Christian, and warmly seconded my statement that "Mr. Powderly must have the help of God, or he could not speak and act so wisely."

"The Socialists are our greatest trouble," she said. "All they are good for is to agitate mischief and misrepresent us to the public. I do wish good and earnest people would join us, and hold the balance of power; then we could be a great blessing to this country."

That is the key to the position. Out of this workingwoman's pure and motherly heart comes the appeal to all good people, and I pass it along, that we may, instead of standing off to find fault, come near to help this blind Hercules of labor in its mighty struggle toward a better day.

I told her of my warm sympathy with the labor movement along the lines of coöperation, arbitration and the ballot box; of my advocacy of the eight-hour law, the prohibition of child labor, and the ownership by Government (that is by the people) of all railway and telegraph lines; of my belief that the Sunday law is our chief bulwark of the workingman's liberty and that the New Testament is our best treatise on political economy and Christ the only being whose life, law and love can bring in universal brotherhood so that humanity will become one great Republic. Her fine face glowed with spiritual beauty while we talked—ourselves a prophecy of all we prayed for—the Irish and the Yankee woman, the Catholic and Methodist. "If such as you would only come and help us!" she repeated; "if the educated and earnest would lend a hand, instead of standing off to criticise and blame us! We do the best we can, but we've not had the chance to learn, and you folks could just set us on our feet and put down the few loud-mouthed anarchists if you would only join us."

I told her I would like to do so and to get all our temperance leaders to make common cause with them, but when I tried this afterward, found it could not be done. Still it remains true that the Local Assembly in every town and village draws young men away from the saloon, its debates help to make them better citizens, and that the mighty Labor movement has, by outlawing the saloon socially, done more for temperance than we who devote our lives to its propaganda have been able to achieve in the same period.

GLADSTONE.

Westminster Palace is by far the noblest pile of governmental buildings that Europe furnishes. It is an eye-filling and a heart-satisfying portion. So stately, yet so sturdy, so solid, yet so gracious, that when one thinks of all it means touching the royal English race, there is a spell on every thoughtful traveler who stands before the Parliament Buildings at Westminster.

Once, when doing this, oblivious of all around me, I noticed the gathering crowd at last, and some one said, "There is Gladstone!" He was not in 1870 so much my hero as he is now, but as I looked upon that tall and stalwart form, a temple in itself, that noble head, bright countenance, on which goodness is stamped, no less plainly than learning, and where the eyes are indeed the windows of a wonderful soul, I could but feel that in this, the greatest leader of the century, England had a human offset to Westminster; for what one is among buildings, the other is among men.

HENRY F. DURANT.

Henry F. Durant, founder of Wellesley College, was one of the most agreeable men whom I have met, as well as one of the handsomest, with his tall, perfectly proportioned figure, his noble head and brow, his hair, fine as silk and white as snow, parted in the middle, yet without any sign of effeminacy as the result, his piercing black eye, classic nose and radiant smile. His wife is hardly less agreeable than he was, devoted, unworldly, living the life of her Lord, literally going about doing good to the lowest and the most forsaken of God's creatures.

There are hundreds of the outcast in the city of Boston, who, if they knew enough, would say,

"The blessings of her quiet life fell on me like the dew,
And good thoughts, where her footsteps passed, like fairy blossoms grew."

When I went East in my early temperance pilgrimage, I first met Mr. Durant at Old Orchard, and he said to me, "I have built a college as perfect and beautiful as any palace and I have dedicated it to the girls of the nation. It is my firm resolve to have only women in the faculty. You are a believer in the emancipation of women. I ask you to become a member of my faculty when I have searched this country as with a lighted candle to find the women whom I can trust, but you deliberately decline. Come and see the college and it will give you everlasting regrets, to say the least of it." So I went out to Wellesley and saw its beauty, comparing favorably with the finest buildings that one finds abroad. We lingered longest in the library, which was Mr. Durant's delight, a perfect gem, as everybody truly said, and he asked me again if this college were not my fitting place. But I had turned my face forever from the only educational institution in all the world to which I was devotedly attached, and nothing that I could see anywhere after that could ever give me regret or hope.

MARY MORTIMER.

The first woman of remarkable gifts and reputation whom I recall is Miss Mary Mortimer, for many years President of Milwaukee Female College. She was a special friend of Catherine Beecher, who brought her to the West when the college was founded. I remember the day she came to our quiet farm-house when I was about fourteen years of age. She was a small, plump woman, with an astonishingly impressive head, so high, so ample and satisfying in its curves and arches. Her face was kindly, but not specially impressive. Her conversation was more like that of Margaret Fuller than any other to which I have yet listened. She was philosophic, humanitarian, prophetic in every utterance; incapable of commonplace, smitten by the sense of God, of duty and of immortality, and devoted to the unfolding of woman's mental capabilities. Miss Mortimer was a figure that thirty years later would have become central in the pantheon of American women. To have heard her talk is an inspiration that remains with me unto this day.

ELIZABETH STUART PHELPS.

By invitation of Elizabeth Stuart Phelps (now Mrs. Ward), I have repeatedly visited Gloucester, Mass., her summer home, and had the honor and pleasure of being her guest, hearing her conversation, and driving about with her through the old-fashioned streets, where, whether she stops at the blacksmith's shop, the market or the humble home of some reformed man, she is greeted with a reverence that I have almost never seen manifested toward any other person. Probably her hidden life, delicate face and figure, the knowledge of her physical suffering and the great love she has shown to these poor people, chiefly account for this agreeable phenomenon.

JOHN SWINTON.

One man of splendid powers in New York City is John Swinton, whom we saw in company with Mrs. Celia B. Whitehead, the bright little "dress reformer," whose articles attracted so much attention in the *Cloak and Dress Review*. He left the New York *Sun* and a salary of twelve thousand dollars per year, to devote himself to the cause of working men and women. He is a man fifty-five, who, by reason of hair prematurely white, is often thought to be much older. He wears a black silk cap, his face is worn with years of night work, and his black eyes are inscrutable. In his little office in Park Row, with less of elbow-room than any journalist with whom I am acquainted, he writes *John Swinton's Paper*, and his sweet-voiced wife opposite answers letters and works at the subscription list. She is constantly with him, and their mutual devotion is good to see. He asked us of our work, and I gave him a brief outline as did Mrs. Barnes of her own beautiful mission for boys "up town." Then we told him we wanted to know his views—as much as could be told in a few minutes. At this he began, and such a cylopean talk as he gave us I never heard. It was Carlyle and Mazzini in one. Words were fairly dynamited from his lips. They roared and rang, they scorched and hissed. Something of the primal energy of nature was in the man. He brushed aside our favorite plans as if they had been butterfly wings in the lurid flame of Chicago's conflagration. He rolled from that deep bass chest his *anathema maranatha* against our trifling expedients, our straws to stay Niagara! He volleyed statistics of the increase of pauperism and crime in New York, "a city that gives ten millions a year in charity"; he tore down our scaffolds for building and uprooted our levers for lifting, until—as a face may be so ugly as to seem positively handsome by the positiveness of its quality—his pessimism approached the sublime. History was ransacked from Constantine onward to show that the year '89 in any century is the year of fate.

The fifth of Nehemiah was quoted as appropriate reading for the epoch. It had been lately read at a workingmen's union and they had no idea what book it came out of! He told us to go, as he had done last Sunday, to a district in New York, which he described, where seven hundred thousand people are flung into the chaos of poverty and crime; to watch the women and little children at work for a crust, as desperately as a drowning man works for a breath, and he said, 'Anybody who can look at them, knowing the horror of their slime and sin, and not cut his own throat, is a scoundrel." I forebore to remind him that he had thus looked, and still lived on! He summarized the horrors of our present situation thus: Aggregation of the masses into great cities; aggregation of the money into monopolies; working of women and children like beasts of burden; "and last of all, nearest the devil of all, is this danger (his voice was full of sulphurous portent here), this workingman, this Titan, this monster of the mud-sills, who in other crises has been but the bond-slave of wealth and power, this giant with the basal brain and hairy hands, this Caliban has found his Cadmus; he begins to think; *he has learned how to read—and he is reading the Police Gazette!*"

When he was a New York boy, he said, but fifteen thousand papers were issued daily to one million five hundred thousand now. Then, the shipping news was the staple article, arousing such questions as "Where is Hong-Kong?" "Where is Rio de Janeiro?" Now the news was of bursting bombs and monster strikes, and the question, "How can I get my hands upon the throat of the man who is richer than I and choke him to death?" He shook his great head and paused a moment in the tornado of his speech. I lifted a copy of *John Swinton's Paper* from his desk and said, "But here, my friend, is something better than the *Police Gazette*. You at least would help these men to a better road, and, little as you think of me, I would cool their brains from the alcohol delirium." He dropped the splendid jeremiad, smiled a radiant glance upon our quiet trio, said, "I was tired; I did not sleep last night. Am charmed to meet you ladies; delighted by much that you have told me," and we shook hands with him and his gentle monitor, and went on our way believing that all of us, after our fashion, are trying to help solve the problem of poor old Humanity's bewilderment and heartache.

NELSON SIZER.

A most antithetical character to burly John Swinton is Nelson Sizer, for thirty years the head examiner of Fowler & Wells. Anna Gordon had a fancy that I should let him know who I was when we dropped in one day to look at the collection of casts, whereupon he proceeded to give me the benefit of his life-long studies of the "bumps." I told him that mother always had a kind side for phrenology, one of her earliest and most oft-repeated remarks to me having been this: "You have combativeness largely developed, my child." After a fashion as cheery as John Swinton seemed sad, Nelson Sizer is the talker among ten thousand. He seems to be endowed with the balanced, or "tempered temperament," as Henry Tuckerman, the essayist, used to call it. His vocabulary is boundless, its pictorial quality exhaustless, and his anecdotes many and apt. A skilled stenographer with a little stenographic type-writing machine sat near him; and as he walked back and forth, between making his cranial observations, Mr. Sizer had only to speak his mind and the swift click of the machine did all the rest. When I told him of the tens of thousands of letters received and written at Rest Cottage, he said, "And do you people waste yourselves on that eternal scratching? It is the poorest of economy. You could quadruple your efficiency by dictation." I asked him if he thought I could after a life-time of thinking along a pen-holder learn to work in this easier harness, and he said, "My own experience is that twenty days of this new liberty will make you quit the other method forever and a day."

FRANCES FOLSOM CLEVELAND.

During the Cleveland administration I attended a reception given at the White House to the Woman's International Council, and thought the President seemed somewhat taken back by the invasion of such an army of representative women, although he was all that one could wish in the way of cordiality, and Mrs. Cleveland wore her usual charming smile. I had seen her when she was a school-girl at Wells College, where I went to speak by invitation of the lady principal, Miss Smith, a life-long friend of my sister-in-law, Mary B. Willard. My niece, Katharine Willard, who was a student there, was one of Mrs. Cleveland's special friends, and has received from her at the White House many tokens of her loyal remembrance and affection. I spoke to the young ladies at Wells College on the duty that girls owe to their country as well as themselves and the homes of the future, urging upon them the motto, "*Noblesse oblige*," and I remember that my niece and Miss Folsom accompanied me in the omnibus to the railway train, and seemed entirely sympathetic with what I had said. Mrs. Cleveland has written me letters showing her devotion as a Christian woman to what she believes to be right, and assuring me of her steadfast total abstinence principles. I hold her in the highest honor and regard, and believe that no woman of her age has ever had it in her power and in her heart to do more for the sacred cause of temperance. The position of a total abstainer in the White House is, of necessity, a difficult one, because of the inevitable contact with the representatives of other nations whose temperance ideas are even less advanced than those of our own high officials.

THE BEECHER FAMILY.

When but a school-girl, the sense of the worshipful in me bowed down before the first member of this magnificent family that my eyes had yet beheld; the woman who had built her whole life into the rising temple of woman's work and worth. I looked for "somebody wonderful to behold."

Catherine Beecher was really the first distinguished woman that I met. On one of her trips to visit and inspect her favorite college at Milwaukee, she came to Evanston and was the guest of my friend and benefactress, Mrs. Dr. Kidder. I entered the room where I was told she was, with a feeling of appropriate awe, which was, however, soon dispelled by the wholly unconventional manner of the sturdy little woman who was putting on her rubbers preparatory to a walk. She seemed to me essentially Beecherish, like a lump of ore out of the mine, not smelted in the mill of custom nor hammered into shape on the anvil of prejudice. To me the Beecher family has always lived in a Valhalla of its own, and been an original force, strong and refreshing as Nature herself. My parents were never done talking about them and holding them up as examples. I have improved every unforced opportunity to meet the different members, and have had personal acquaintance with eight out of the twelve.

At Elmira, where I had the pleasure of being a guest in the well-known water-cure conducted by the Gleason family, I met Thomas K. and Mrs. Beecher in their own home, and in their church at an evening sociable. Brother Thomas was so genial that I said to his wife, "He is one of the most affable men I ever saw, and yet I had been told he was a man of moods." "Ah, well," she answered in her cheery tones, "you have seen my bear when his coat was stroked the right way, and I'm glad of it."

Henry Ward Beecher was always my mother's hero beyond all other men. His sermons were her Sunday reading in the *Independent* and the *Christian Union* for many a year. She never saw him until in one of his last trips West he came to Evanston to speak, and it grieved me that in my absence she failed to meet him personally, for he never had a warmer friend or one more true and steadfast in the night of his great calamity. She would not hear a word against him, and her sturdy strength, when almost every one around her wavered, gave me a new sense of her native force of character.

Mr. Beecher was more than any other man, a grown-up boy. It was seen in his whole manner. The very way in which he would take off that broad felt hat and tuck it under the chair or pulpit as he sat down; the way in which he would push back his hair and drum with his fingers on the chair arm; the curious forgetfulness that frequently led him to wear his rubbers into the pulpit and stand up in them to preach, showed the unpremeditated character of his words and thoughts. His "Lectures to Young Men" was one of the first books read by my brother and me. His papers on Pomology were special pets with my father, who was as fond of horticulture as Beecher himself.

In 1876, by invitation of Mary A. Livermore, I was her guest for a day at the Twin Mountain House, New Hampshire. Mr. and Mrs. Beecher were there as usual. I sat at the same table, but not near enough to speak beyond the mere acknowledgment of the introductions with which I was then for the first time honored.

Next morning, the guests of the hotel all gathered in the parlors, as the custom was, and Mr. Beecher conducted family prayers. In my pocket testament I find these notes, penciled at the time:

TWIN MOUNTAIN HOUSE, August 18, 1876.

As usual Mr. Beecher conducted morning prayers. Hon. William Wheeler, a worthy candidate for vice-president, was present, also Mrs. Beecher and Mrs. Livermore. The exposition of Romans xiv. and the prayer of Mr. Beecher were memorable and beautiful and helpful to my soul. There was in them so much of breadth, of strength and gentleness. In a word, they had the Christ-like spirit. He desired us to ask questions, and mine was on the twenty-first verse, "It is good neither to eat flesh nor to drink wine."

Mr. Beecher was very earnest in his reply. "It is just like this," he said: "Suppose there is a precipice out by a school-house where many children are assembled. Suppose that half way down that precipice there is a spring I specially enjoy, and, strong man that I am, I can go down there safely, by a narrow path, dangerous to many, but not to me. Suppose that the children are determined to go down there after me and won't believe the path is dangerous since they see that I tread it with impunity. Some of them that try it fall and break their necks and others are lamed for life. Now what sort of a man, much more, what sort of a Christian should I be, if, under these circumstances, I persisted in going down that dangerous path? Nay verily, if I have one particle of magnanimity of soul, if I have been at all taught of Christ, I shall put a good, strong fence across that path and never tread it any more. That's my position on the total abstinence question; that's why I am, myself, a total abstainer and shall always be unless I take alcoholic drinks by a physician's prescription. For why should I insist on drinking wine, even if I were fond of it? which I am not. It would do me no special good, and what I gain in character by the habit of studying the good of others is an incalculable and an eternal gain."

Mr. Beecher then went on to say that relative to the question of going to the theater he held the same position. "I would like to see Edwin Booth," he said; "I would like to see Ristori and greatly would it have delighted me to watch Rachel, but I was never in a theater in my life, and on precisely the same basis that I never drink wine." He also testified strongly against the use of tobacco in any form. I asked him about speaking in a criticising way of people, and his answer was most noble; I wish in these notes I could but do it justice, the gist of it was this: have no rule about it, but keep your own heart so full of loving kindness that the words that brim over will take care of themselves.

At the great meeting arranged for me in Plymouth Church by the Brooklyn Woman's Christian Temperance Union, he presided, saying, just before I came forward, "Pardon me, if I leave the platform to sit beside my wife—I almost never get the chance to do so in this church, you see;" and after I had finished he walked up the steps, smiling, and pointing toward me as he came, then turning to the audience, he said in his dramatic way, "And yet—she can not vote! Are n't you ashamed, men, that this should be?"

I was grateful indeed to him for thus clearly taking sides with the sacred cause of women's enfranchisement—but then, he was President of the "American Woman Suffrage Association" away back in 1870. I had spoken as strongly as I was able in favor of prohibition as the best method of dealing with the liquor traffic, and he said distinctly, "Not a word has been uttered, but that we all know to be just and true and right." This too seemed natural, for was not his very first temperance speech, when he was an Amherst collegian, in favor of a law against the liquor traffic?

After these two sermons in a sentence, he proceeded to make such a "collection speech" as outdid all I ever heard elsewhere for wit and wisdom. Of course everybody "stayed through" and the baskets came back actually full — I have never seen them thus except on that occasion.

I believe him to have been in hearty accord with us of the white ribbon movement, except as he was led away by the "high-license" theory, like many another good, but deceived man in New York, Brooklyn and elsewhere.

The last time I ever saw him was in 1886 as he descended from his pulpit after the sermon. Having heard in later days that he had abjured his total abstinence principles, I went to him and said:

"Mr. Beecher, I am denying what the papers say about your drinking wine and ale — that is what you expect of me I hope?"

He smiled, shook hands cordially and answered as the throng pressed upon him, "Yes, you are right—I stand where I always did, but I have no harsh word for my brethren in the ministry who do not see as I do." This was his testimony the last time I ever heard his kindly voice and it outweighs all testimony uttered against him.

I did not agree with his theology, but all the same I bought and read his "Sermons on Evolution" and extracted any amount of spiritual nutriment therefrom for my soul's growth. By the same token I do not live upon theology, but "by the faith of the Son of God," and while I glory in the great men who, in the name of exact science, defend that formulation of the faith which my orthodox home cherished, in which I was trained and from which I shall never depart, I can cherish Henry Ward Beecher too, and it would be the joy of my life if I were sure that I loved Christ as well as he did.

Mr. Beecher had a most inconvenient capacity for seeing both sides—hence, men of electrotyped nature called him inconsistent. He was not "all of a piece" like certain accurate and exact minds, hence whoever sentenced him on the evidence of any single sentence he had uttered was sure to do him wrong. Perhaps the most salient instance of this is that one about "Bread and water" so often and so absurdly quoted to prove him an aristocrat and the enemy of wage-workers. But to reason thus is to make a pyramid stand on its apex, for the whole body of divinity that his character and words have given to the world is one that glorifies work as a sacrament and makes "the reign of the common people" essential to the world's redemption.

"He had his faults"; yes, so he had—like all the greatest and best souls—of whom he was one of the best and greatest; but, somehow, like my dear old mother, I dearly love to praise him—he has been blamed so much!

Genius would rather go and tell its story to the whole world than to an individual. There is no stronger proof of its universality than this. Poets and heroes always take the human race into their confidence—and to the everlasting credit of the race let it be said, that confidence is not abused! "The great, but sceptered sovereigns who still rule our spirits from their urns," the mighty men of whom "the world talks while they sleep," have loved the world, bemoaned it and believed in it. Henry Ward Beecher was one of these.

An æolian harp is in my study window as I write. It seems to me the fittest emblem of him who has gone to live elsewhere and left our world in some sense lonely. The compass of its diapason is vast as the scope of his mind; its tenderness deep as his heart; its pathos thrilling as his sympathy; its aspiration triumphant as his faith. Like him it is attuned to every faintest breath of the great world-life, and like his, its voice searches out the innermost places of the human spirit. Jean Paul says of the æolian harp, that it is, like nature, "passive before a divine breath" and in him who has gone from us there was this elemental receptivity of God. Other natures have doubtless developed that God-consciousness which is the sum of all perfections, to a degree as wonderful as Mr. Beecher did, but what other, in our time, at least, has been *en rapport* so perfect with those about him that they could share with him this blissful consciousness to a degree as great? John Henry Newman says, "To God must be ascribed the *radiation* of genius." No great character of whom I can think illustrates that most unique and felicitous phrase so clearly as Henry Ward Beecher. His was the great, radiating spirit of our nation and our age. For fifty years his face shone, his tones vibrated, his pen was electric with the sense of a divine presence, not for his home only, not for his church or his nation, but for Christendom. He radiated all that he absorbed and his capacious nature was the reservoir of all that is best in books, art, and life. But as fuel turns to fire, and oil to light, so in the laboratory of his brain, the raw materials of history, poetry and science were wrought over into radiant and radiating forces which warmed and illumined human souls. Plymouth Church was the most home-like place that could be named; its pulpit a glowing fireside ever ready to cheer the despondent and warm those hearts the world had chilled. No man ever spoke so often or wrote so much whose classic, historic, and poetical allusions were so few, but the potency of every good thing ever learned by him who was an insatiable student of nature and an omnivorous reader of books, was all wrought, in the alembic of his memory, into new forms and combinations. He intersphered so perfectly with the minds and hearts about him, that he seemed to them a veritable possession. The interpenetrative character of his mind has not been matched, for the reason that he was that doubly dowered phenomenon—a great brain mated to a heart as great. This royal gift of sympathy enabled him to make all lives his own; hence, he so understood as to have charity for all. As Sir James Mackintosh has said, "If we knew each other better, it would not be to love each other less." It was because, in human measure, our great friend "knew what was in man" that men so loved him.

> "What I aspired to be
> And was not, comforts me,"

is the sweet song in minor key that every heart has sometime sung. Our friend knew these aspirations better than any other preacher of his time, and spoke out frankly of them to his brother men. Since Terence uttered the words, no life has echoed them so roundly as this life now transplanted to the skies, "I am human and whatever touches humanity touches me." For this reason he was born a patriot, a philanthropist and a reformer. We read of "epoch-making books," but here was an epoch-making character.

Goethe said that when any one did a great deed, the world at once formed a conspiracy to prevent him from ever doing another. The demands of a personal nature that come to every person of the least achievement—demands for "inflooence," as the lamented Nasby taught us to say; for letters, autographs, and "situations," were what this greatest of the Germans meant. Emerson says in tones of pathos, "Why should we desecrate noble and beautiful souls by intruding on them?" Why should we, indeed? If we will but leave them free, they will last longer and accomplish more in those great lines of thought and action that they and we both have at heart. I was sorry that Charles Sumner said to Julia Ward Howe—if indeed he did so say, as was reported—when she came to him for help in the care of a poor negro, "Madam, I am trying to lift up a race, do not ask me to take my time for individuals." I do not think that Henry Ward Beecher would ever have said that, but we can ourselves defend the magnanimous souls who like him seem to have no weapons of self-defense from those constant interruptions and personal demands which yield but little in the way of valuable results, and thus leave them free to live their own lives and work out their own great destinies, helped by our prayers, our love for them, our faith in their sincerity and their success. How often have I said this in my heart of some among my elect circle of heroes and heroines, with the inspiration of this one thought more: "If ever I reach your level in this or any world, I shall find myself face to face with you by the law of spiritual gravitation, and shall need no note of introduction."

HARRIET BEECHER STOWE.

It is stated by those who are informed, that except the Bible no book ever written has had a circulation so boundless as "Uncle Tom's Cabin." Translated into a score of languages, issued in a hundred different editions, scattered as far as printer's ink has ever gone, that mother-hearted book has been one of Christ's evangels to humanity.

On our return (October 22, 1887) from the Connecticut W. C. T. U. Convention, at Bridgeport, Anna Gordon and I availed ourselves of the opportunity received through the kindness of Mrs. J. G. Parsons, of Hartford, to grasp the hand that wrote the matchless book. We drove to her pleasant home on Farmington street, in the elegant city of Hartford. Mark Twain's home is within a stone's throw, so is Charles Dudley Warner's; while Judge John Hooker and Isabella Beecher Hooker, his wife, are but a few blocks distant.

An autumnal chromo in maple stood before the door of a tasteful, lilac-colored wooden house of medium size, with porch over the front, and old-fashioned hallway through the centre. Three well-to-do cats, one yellow, one tortoise, one black, and all handsome, had dignified positions on the walk, the porch, and the rug before the door.

The bell was promptly answered by a plump colored maid who evinced uncertainty as to the whereabouts of her mistress. A voice from upstairs called out, "I am at home—I *am* at home," and we were shown into a pleasant study with book-cases, easy-chairs, writing-table, and many photographs, the largest being of Henry Ward Beecher, evidently taken just before his last illness, the hair snow-white.

A little woman entered, seventy-five years old, decidedly undersized, and weighing less than a hundred pounds. She was very simply attired in a dress of black and white check, with linen collar and small brooch, her hair, which had once been brown, hung fluffily upon a broad brow and was bound by a black ribbon in front and gathered in a low knot behind. Her nose is long and straight, her eyes are dimmed by years, her mouth is large, and with the long, Beecher lip, full of the pathos of humanity's mystical estate.

This is what Time has left of the immortal Harriet Beecher Stowe. She greeted us with cordial hand and voice and smile.

"On a Wisconsin farm, away back in the fifties, I read Uncle Tom, and have always dreamed that some day I should see its author," was my inane remark.

"Nobody is so much surprised about Uncle Tom as I am," she replied. "I first intended to write two or three numbers, and when I got going could not stop."

"The world now knows that your pen was divinely guided," I said. "Do you not believe that pens and voices are constrained from on high?"

She smiled, nodded her head, and made a most dulcet remark to the following effect:

"You have written a very valuable book yourself, 'How to Win.' I have it on my mantel-shelf upstairs, I want all our girls to read it."

"I little thought that anything ever done by me would win such words of praise from the most distinguished of my country-women," was my grateful reply, at which she smiled and said:

"Oh! you are doing and saying more valuable things than you know."

Her praise was sweet, but I had grace given me to change the subject.

"It does me good to hear that you are a remarkable pedestrian," I said. Her glance kindled.

"Indeed, I am, I learned that long ago at a water-cure," she answered; "I go out in the morning and again in the afternoon, making from five to seven miles daily. If I am not feeling well I can usually walk it off, or if not, I sleep it off, going to bed by eight o'clock."

"Do you go walking alone?" I said, admitting that "for my part, I wanted 'a friend in my retreat to whom I might whisper solitude is sweet.'"

"But I can not have it so, and though I would prefer company, I go alone," she answered, adding, in reply to Mrs. Parsons' query, that she "was in excellent health, never better."

Speaking of her brother Henry's pictures, she said, "That profile is like him—it has his uplift glance. The full-faced one I do not like. I think the photographer must have been flattering him, hoping to get a good impression, and nothing made him so cross as that."

She told us that her "twin daughters kept the house and would not let her do a thing, which was as well, since they knew how she wanted everything done." She showed us a charming photograph of her grandson, saying, "He is so handsome that he is not vain, and the way of it is this: he has heard himself called handsome since his earliest recollection and thinks it is some quality belonging to all boys."

"Well," I said, "you have told us that 'whatever ought to happen will happen' and as everybody ought to be beautiful, doubtless some day everybody will be."

"We can not dictate to God," she answered earnestly, "but we know He desires that we shall all have the beauty of holiness."

I told her of my dear old mother, "Saint Courageous," to whom she sent her love, adding, "I love everybody; as I walk alone in the fields and along the streets, meeting many who speak a friendly word to me, I rejoice to think how much I love them, and every creature that God has made."

I repeated this verse from one of her poems:

> "It lies around us like a cloud,
> A world we do not see;
> Yet the sweet closing of an eye
> May bring us there to be,"

and told her how in hours of grief the poem had comforted my heart. At this she took me by the hand, saying earnestly, "God help you, God be with you." I kissed the dear, old, wrinkled hand that in its strength had written "Uncle Tom's Cabin"; she gave a kind good-by to each of us, and we went our ways—to meet "some sweet day, by and by," in heaven.

DEACON WILLARD.

When working in the revival with Mr. Moody in Chicago, January, 1877, I met for the first time Deacon L. A. Willard, a well-known leader for many years of the Y. M. C. A. My witty Irish friend, Mrs. Kate McGowan, spoke to me of him first, and said, "If you wish to be forever a favorite of this lovely old gentleman, you must respond to the question he will be sure to ask, namely, What single passage of Scripture contains within it the whole plan of salvation? you must speak up brightly and say, 'Acts x: 43,' and there is nothing that he will not do for you from that time forth."

He was one of the loveliest old men in face, manner and spirit that I ever saw. His whole soul was absorbed in his own method of presenting the plan of salvation, which he did with remarkable clearness and efficiency. He has doubtless been the means of the conversion of more persons than the entire membership of an average church can show for all its work in any given year, perhaps in several years. At this time I was intensely stirred by the desire and purpose that my brother should be converted over again, for although at twelve years of age he had started in the Christian life, had graduated in theology at twenty-five, and become Presiding Elder of the Denver District, Colorado, at twenty-seven, he had some years after that seemed to fall away from his allegiance, and the dearest wish of our hearts was that he should return to the Shepherd and Bishop of his soul, and of all our souls. I had told Mr. Moody of this, and urged his help, but he answered, "I am so preoccupied that I can not see individual cases, but I will pray for you and you must work and pray." Just then I made the acquaintance of this dear patriarch, Deacon Willard, and told him all my heart about my brother, begging him not to go at first on a religious mission, but to call upon him as a friend and a possible relative. My brother, like my father, was exceedingly interested in the annals of his family, and delighted to read the Willard Memoir, the History of Dublin, N. H., with which his great-grandfather, Rev. Elijah Willard, was so long connected, the History of Marlborough, N. H., and indeed every scrap that he could learn touching his lineage was sedulously treasured. On the contrary, Deacon Willard seemed to care very little about all this, but, as he said, he had "learned to angle skillfully for souls." Going to my brother's editorial sanctum at a time when I told him he would be most likely not to be preoccupied, the Deacon talked up ancestry with great spirit, told my brother he believed they were related, that he had no son himself and as my brother had not long since lost his father, he proposed they should "club together and make believe father and son." So with much bright and genial talk, he threw his arm over my brother's broad shoulders and said, "Let us go to lunch, Willard, and talk this matter over more at length." So it began and the rest of the story is told in the priceless letter which I preserve in my dear old friend's handwriting. We learned that we were really cousins at two removes, but I am sure we shall be nearer of kin than that when we meet in the Celestial Mansion, to which, as I believe, that gentle old hand was God's instrument to open the way for one we loved so well.

WALT WHITMAN.

One Christmas I was in the home of Mrs. Hannah Whitall Smith, where I have met many most interesting literary people at her "hobby parties," which are a witty invention of her gifted husband, herself or her ingenious children, I do not know which, the plan being to have some person of distinction in a particular line of literary, moral or religious activity, as the central figure of the evening. Each of these persons brings out his or her hobby, and paces it up and down before the group, after which any other person has a right to ride upon it, if so disposed. This results in a really charming and informal conversation, following the brief special disquisition, and is the most enjoyable home entertainment I ever attended.

Finally the suggestion was made, "Why not ask Walt Whitman, who lives just across here in Camden? let us see him for ourselves;" and the invitation went. In due process of time, there appeared on the scene a man about seventy years of age, attired in gray, from his soft gray overcoat to his old-fashioned gray mittens, with sparse gray hair, kind, twinkling gray eyes, and russet apple cheeks, the mildest, most modest and simple-hearted man I ever saw. It almost seemed as if a grand old oak had opened suddenly and turned the good, gray poet loose upon the world. He is the farthest possible from being leonine in aspect or intent. He has no ends to serve, no place to hold in conversation, nothing to gain or lose. He is the soul of geniality and seems never better pleased than when others are talking and he is seated in a large arm-chair gazing reflectively into the glowing grate. But if you talk of Nature and her shy ways, he is at home. I remember his look of amused surprise when some-one mentioned the title of one of his books, "The Wake Robin," and he told us John Burroughs, who seems to me to be a sort of spiritual son to Whitman, had suggested it. I said, "I did not know what a Wake Robin was, unless it was a bird—they used to wake me early at Forest Home in olden days"—when, behold, the mild old man informed me gently that it was a flower! He did not like to talk about his books and seemed to me as a hunting hound lying at full length on the rug before the fire, content and quiet, until some reference is made to horses, hunting-horns and guns, when it rises up, intent, alert, electrified with activity. So the common hum and talk seemed quieting to Father Walt, but when Thoreau or Burroughs were referred to, or a quotation given from Wordsworth, Thomson, or some dear Nature-lover, the kindly eyes beamed upon us with joy, and some pithy sentence, clean-cut enough to be a proverb, fell from his lips. What he really is I do not know. I only tell about him as he was to me, and his sense of God, Nature and Human Brotherhood struck me as having been raised to such a power, and fused in such a white heat of devotion, that they made the man a genius.

CAPTAIN PRATT AND THE CARLISLE INDIAN SCHOOL.

Captain Pratt is a man six feet in height, and every inch a soldier. His great, well-balanced head, dauntless profile, and kindly smile predict the qualities of a born leader. A native of New York state, reared in Logansport, Ind., of Methodist parentage and training, but a Presbyterian by reason of his wife's preference, he has the root of the matter in him as a muscular Christian of the nineteenth century. Joining the Union forces as a volunteer at the outbreak of the war, he was appointed lieutenant in the regular army in 1867, and assigned to a post in the far West. From that time he studied the Indian question at first hand, and he has become an expert, not excelled in all the nation. Later on, when his pre-eminent ability as an Indian civilizer came to be known, he was put in charge of the captured "hostiles" in Florida, where he remained three years, and was then sent to Carlisle, Pa., to found and conduct an Indian school there. His "views" are best expressed in his own words:

"There are about two hundred and sixty thousand Indians in the United States, and there are twenty-seven hundred counties. I would divide them up, in the proportion of about nine Indians to a county, and find them homes and work among our people; that would solve the knotty problem in three years' time, and there would be no more an "Indian Question." It is folly to handle them at arms-length; we should absorb them into our national life for their own good and ours. It is wicked to stand them up as targets for sharp-shooters. The Indians are just like other men, only minus their environment. Take a new-born baby from the arms of a cultivated white woman, and give it to the nurture of a Zulu woman in Africa; take the Zulu's baby away from her and give it to the cultivated white woman. Twenty-five years later you would have a white savage in Africa, and a black scholar, gentleman, and Christian in America. This sharply illustrates what I mean. We can, by planting the Indians among us, make educated and industrious citizens of them in the briefest time and at the least expense. I would teach them trades and turn them loose.

"The Indians are naturally religious, an infidel is to them an unknown quantity. All you have to do is to familiarize their reverent minds with the truths of the New Testament. Our Sunday-school and prayer-meeting are the best proof of their readiness to take on Christianity; their testimonies are full of earnestness and genuine religious fervor. If I have a strong point as their friend, it is my intense confidence in the holiness of hard work; the sanitary and ethical power of a useful occupation. Indians, as other people, like to be independent, and to do this they must earn money.

"How do your scholars stand upon the temperance and tobacco question?" was my natural query.

"We are a section of the millennium, as I can prove," replied the Captain with pardonable pride. "In my nine years upon this hill I have had thirteen hundred pupils—eight hundred of them young men. Intoxicating liquors and tobacco from the first are represented to them as unhealthful, uncleanly, and wasteful, and they are expected and required to give them up. Except once at a county fair, where whisky-sellers tempted my boys to go behind the cattle-sheds and drink, and where three of them yielded, I have not in nine years had a single case of drunkenness among them. Considering the utter lack of training and the universal tobacco heredity, I consider this remarkable. We furnish them very simple food, insist upon strict personal cleanliness, and our young people readily fall in with the prevailing usages."

"We keep them moving," said the Captain as we passed from shop to shop, in this great, humming hive of industry," and they have no time for homesickness, none for mischief, none for regret."

"Are the girls as smart as the boys?" was my ever-recurring question.

"Every bit, rather quicker-witted on the whole," was Captain Pratt's reply.

"The history of the Indians as set forth in books is a bundle of falsehoods," he said. "They are like other people, and, unprovoked by outrage and injustice, behave far more peaceably than they get credit for."

"Better to capture them by love, uniform them in blue, and kill them with kindness than to send out our own boys in blue to be killed by them," was my grateful commentary. Anna and I both talked to them of temperance, and they applauded heartily.

When Prohibitionists come into power they will, if they do not get dizzy on the heights, do the Indians a sovereign favor by making Captain Pratt Secretary of the Interior.

THE DEN — REST COTTAGE.

JOSEPH COOK.

The nineteenth century has its kings—not the puppets of a succession, dressed in a little brief authority, but monarchs ruling in their own right, and defenders of the faith by force of intellect, variety of knowledge, and unswerving devotion to Him whose motto is, Come, let us reason together, and whose symbol is the lighted torch of truth passing from hand to hand.

First among these to-day stands Joseph Cook, of Boston. The record he has made in the last few years has no parallel in history. When the W. C. T. U. held its second annual meeting in Cincinnati, in November of 1875, probably there was not a delegate among us all who had ever heard of him. He began his residence in Boston the year of the crusade, as pastor of a small Congregational church. In the winter of 1875 he was invited by the Y. M. C. A. of that city, to speak briefly, on Monday of each week, at its noon prayer-meeting. This is the day when most denominations hold ministers' meetings, and the ministers of Boston and its suburbs were wont to adjourn in time for this noon meeting. In them this Christian scholar had audience fit but few. They were no less delighted than astonished by his art of putting things. The results of the latest German, English, and American scholarship on the more important and difficult topics concerning the relation of religion and science were the things he put, and precisely those concerning which they most desired to hear. Soon the audience was so large that it removed to Tremont Temple, and now, during the "Monday Lecture Course," "the busiest hour of the busiest day of the week, the seats and standing-room of that immense auditorium are fully occupied."

But what has this man of royal intellect and profound learning set himself to prove? Meeting the skepticism of science with its own "scientific method," he proves that if a man die he shall live again; that God was in Christ, reconciling the world unto Himself; "that whosoever believeth in him shall not perish, but have everlasting life"; and that those who ultimately persist in sin shall be shut out "from the presence of the Lord, and from the glory of his power."

These matchless themes Joseph Cook handles with a logic unequaled save by his pathos, and a wit unmatched save by his rhetoric. But he does not stop here. Even as pure mathematics must be the basis of mathematics applied, so must pure Christian doctrine be the basis of Christianity applied, and that application has never been made more forcibly than in the famous "Preludes" wherein he considers practical questions of philanthropy. How we ought to handle the Chinese, the Mormon, the Temperance, the Woman and the Labor questions, has never been more ably shown than by this master of theologic controversy.

Mr. Cook was born at Ticonderoga, N. Y., January 26, 1838, and retains so much affection for his old home that he has established his summer headquarters there, at "Cliff Seat."

It is needless to say that the man who has accomplished such mental prodigies, has never squandered his vital forces upon alcohol or tobacco. Joseph Cook is the uncompromising foe of these two abominations. His genuineness of character, sturdy integrity, and purity of life set the seal to his profession of Christianity. He is not one of those deadly enemies of Christ's church who preach cream and practice skim-milk.

The quality of his education is shown in this statement from one of his nearest friends:

"Mr. Cook's favorite teachers and authors are Professor Park, Julius Müller and Jonathan Edwards, in theology; and in philosophy Sir William Hamilton, Rudolf Hermann Lotze, Leibnitz, and Kant."

Doubtless it is no small factor in Joseph Cook's solved problem of success that his heart is not a stranger to the "supreme affection" of which he so eloquently discoursed in his lectures on Marriage. Mrs. Joseph Cook, a New Haven lady whom he first met in his Yale College days, has shared his life and honors since the summer of 1877. She is his counselor as well as his companion, and constantly aids him in his correspondence and researches, the two being omnivorous and insatiable students.

But any record that fails to bring out his earnest advocacy of the temperance reform, by word as well as by example, does Mr. Cook injustice. A note from one cognizant of his early history reads as follows:

"When he was but nineteen years old, Joseph Cook gave a course of six lectures on temperance in his native town. During the progress of these lectures a poor woman, living in the village, died from the effects of injuries inflicted by her drunken husband.

The material for her shroud was procured at the same store where her husband obtained the liquor that "stole away his brain." Her sad death made a profound impression on the community, and when, at the close of the last lecture, Mr. Cook gave a picture of what rum will do, and produced a piece of the identical shroud-cloth, with a lock of the woman's hair pinned to it, and suspended it from the desk, the audience was in deep excitement; most of the women were in tears, and the faces of the men were white with indignation."

Concerning the home-protection movement and work, Mr. Cook has spoken plainly. "Woman's vote would be to municipal politics depending on saloons, what the lightning is to the oak. God send us that lightning."

JOHN GREENLEAF WHITTIER.

Whittier was the household poet of our abolition family. We knew more of him by heart, in all senses of that phrase, than of any other singer, living or dead. As a teacher, I gave his shorter pieces to my pupils, even as mother had once given them to me. So when, in 1880, I was speaking all about in Massachusetts, and Amesbury was on my list of towns, I asked at once of my hostess, "Is he at home?" "I do not know," she said, "but we will call and see." He was absent, but his genial friends met us most kindly, and showed us the simple, comfortable house that has for years divided with Danvers, a few miles distant, the honor of being called home by the greatest home poet of the age. The desk at which he wrote and the picture of his beloved sister so exquisitely described in "Snow Bound,"—that most perfect picture of the old-fashioned New England homestead,—impressed me most of all. That afternoon I met various ladies of the village, and as my mission at this time was to induce them to use the school ballot in the interest of scientific temperance instruction, I asked if this were their intention, and was much impressed by the reply that came to me repeatedly, "Oh, yes; we women vote in Amesbury—*Mr. Whittier wishes it.*"

This unconscious testimony to the silent, pervasive power of that great nature, impressed me more than all the praise of which their talk was full. Toward evening the poet returned, and was so graciously considerate as to send for me. I called a few minutes on my way to the hall where I was to speak. Nothing could be more modest, mild and winsome than his manner. He spoke of our home protection movement, then at its height in Illinois, where the women had voted on the saloon question in Rockford, Keithburg and elsewhere, under special ordinances, and always solidly against license.

I said I was surprised that he had heard of me, whereupon he replied in his deep low voice and with a sun-bright smile in the great, Websterian eyes, "But thee must know thee is becoming a figure quite conspicuous yonder on thy prairies!"

For such an utterance from him one well might work a life-time, so thought I, and said, "What a matchless power do those possess who by an utterance can thus gild life with imperishable halos!"

Not long after, the generous poet wrote me that he was giving copies of "Nineteen Beautiful Years," my sister's life, to his young friends, and for the later and English editions he wrote a lovely introduction. There is just one thing that I have desired of this great soul and failed to get—a temperance home protection song for the children of our half million white ribbon and white rose prohibitionists. He says he is too old, but I can not bear to have him pass away from us until these fresh upspringing voices shall bear across the continent his heavenly thoughts of a pure life.

Whittier's birthplace, the old log-house near Haverhill, Mass., immortalized in his fireside epic, "Snow Bound," is more to the home hearts of America than any other national shrine. I visited this place long years ago, and have long hoped it might become the property of the Whittier Club in Haverhill. But a wealthy citizen of that town who owns the old farm declines to sell, but declares his purpose to preserve and keep it open, under proper regulations, to the public. What Ayr's world-famous cottage is to Scotland, Whittier's birthplace will become to America; for to paraphrase his own words,

"Blow high, blow low, not all Time's snow
Can quench *that* hearth-fire's ruddy glow."

In 1877 the poet Whittier's Boston publishers gave him a birthday banquet to which only the male contributors to the

Atlantic Monthly were invited. Apropos of this I sent the following to the *Boston Advertiser:*

THE ATLANTIC WHITTIER DINNER—A WOMAN'S THOUGHTS THEREOF.

To the Editor of the *Boston Daily Advertiser:*

Some of us feel as if our own mothers had received a slight; a few of us have cried, and many stormed, but I alone am left to tell thee. In the Republic of Letters, if nowhere else, woman is a citizen. Parnassus seats gods and goddesses on the same throne; the Muses are feminine, the entire nine of them! Alongside facts like these, set the Brunswick banqueting table, with a guest at its head accustomed to see women honored equally in his Quaker home and church, and down the sides of the groaning board, among the "contributors to the Atlantic" see the brilliant women of that guild conspicuous only for their absence!

"Astræa at the capital," forsooth! Dear Bard of Freedom, what did you think about Astræa's absence from your birthday fête?

"Assuredly," we thought, glancing along the columns radiant with the wit and wisdom of the feast, "there will be letters of regret showing that all the leading contributors were at least invited," but the hope proved vain. "Then, most assuredly," we gasped, "the publishers or editors will give some explanation of all this, some recognition of services so splendid, some brief phrase, at least, to redeem the very dome of American brain from the charge of an obliviousness not explainable by any law of mind yet ascertained?" But no! from generous publishers and genial editors to grotesque humorist, all combined in "expressive silence." The only reference to the gentler sex that anywhere creeps in is this: "When the after-dinner speaking began, the women who were staying in the hotel entered and were favored with seats."

Indeed! but who had *earned* a seat at Whittier's own right hand? Who but Harriet Beecher Stowe, one of the chief contributors to the *Atlantic?* and Harriet Prescott Spofford, Rebecca Harding Davis, Gail Hamilton, Elizabeth Stuart Phelps, Mrs. Whitney, and Louisa M. Alcott—were they not "to the manner born"? Among the sweet singers, ought Rose Terry and Lucy Larcom, Celia Thaxter, Florence Percy, and H. H., to have been overlooked? And Mrs. S. M. B. Piatt, why should she not have had an invitation, and sent a poem as well as John?

Yet this is Boston that sat on her three hills and ruled the world! And these are the Bostonians—so broad, so liberal and just!

And Colonel Higginson was there, and he forgot us, too! Ah me! this is the most unkindest cut of all!

Hopeless as seems the task, we must still seek an explanation of this uncomely state of things. Was it because "women are angels" that the contributors belonging to that celestial class were not invited to a banquet (nor mentioned at it) in honor of a total abstainer before whom were set (in delicate compliment, of course) eight kinds of wine? Was it because of Eve's being "first in transgression" (as tempter-in-chief at the first dinner), her sons determined she should never more sit down beside them at the convivial board? Or was it that the *prestige* of sex is not yet offset by the chivalry of justice, even among the liberals?

If it were not Boston we should say, "I wot it is through ignorance ye did it." But as it is, we dismiss the subject with the mild reproof, in sorrow not in anger, "My brethren, these things ought not so to be!"

A *Few* AMONG MANY.

Parnassusville, Dec. 18, 1877.

OLIVER WENDELL HOLMES.

No book ever fascinated me more than the "Autocrat of the Breakfast Table"; indeed, everything that Dr. Holmes has written, I have eagerly absorbed. It has always been one of my chief regrets, when in Boston, as I so often am, that I had no right to the rare privilege of seeing him.

One day in 1877, on a crowded Boston street, I met the famous autocrat. He was not pointed out to me, but I knew him from his photograph and from a certain sixth sense. He passed me so that we were for a moment face to face. I could not be mistaken in that upright, well-knit figure, alert bearing, and remarkable face with its keenness of perception and geniality of heart. I wheeled about instinctively and followed, for some distance, the little man who is so great, hardly knowing that I did so. This is the only time I ever saw him, or, probably, ever shall.

SARAH K. BOLTON.

Mrs. Sarah Knowles Bolton, of Cleveland, Ohio, was Assistant Corresponding Secretary of the National W. C. T. U. in 1876. She was a leader in our work in Ohio, and that she made a most capable officer goes without saying. Probably no woman in America has a style more telling and compact. She excels in seizing upon the salient points in a character, and her word-pictures, though but outline sketches, are complete revelations of men, manners, and times. What Samuel Smiles and James Parton are as biographers of men, that Mrs. Bolton is as the chief woman biographer of our times, and popular as her work has been from the beginning, her best days are now, and in the smiling future of her literary history.

JOHN B. GOUGH.

Almost the only temperance lecture that I ever heard in my life, previous to entering the field myself, was by John B. Gough. It was in 1863, when I was a teacher in the Pittsburgh Female College. There was such a mob of good people waiting for the doors of the great hall to open, that when at last they did so, I was carried off my feet and borne along on the crest of this wave of humanity, half frightened out of my wits. It was the only time that I ever thoroughly lost my equipoise, save when I was thrown from my horse in Palestine, my donkey in Switzerland, and my tricycle in Evanston. How I marveled at the first great orator to whom, save Bishop Simpson, I had ever listened at that time. Indeed, he then impressed me as an actor rather than an orator. That lithe form was always in motion up and down the immense platform; that sallow, bearded face, framed in a shock of iron-gray hair, was of protean aspect, now personating the drunkard, then the hypocrite, anon the saint. Those restless, eager hands, supple as India-rubber, were always busy, flinging the hair forward in one character, back in another, or standing it straight up in a third; crushing the drink fiend, pointing to the angel in human nature, or doubling up the long coat-tails in the most grotesque climaxes of gesticulation when, with a "hop, skip, and jump," he proceeded to bring down the house. Dickens says of one of his humorous characters that "his very knees winked," but there was a variety and astonishment of expression in every movement of Mr. Gough that literally beggars description. He had all weapons at command; but argument, pathos, wit and mimicry were the four elements which, entering almost equally into every speech I ever heard from him, made Mr. Gough the most completely equipped and many-sided orator of his time. Others have equaled him in any one of these gifts of persuasion: a few, possibly, have excelled him in each, but none approach his rank as a combination of all the elements of power in public speech. More than any one else, he kept his audience on the *qui vive.* We never knew what to expect next, his antitheses were so startling, his transitions as an actor so abrupt. "From grave to gay, from lively to severe," he ranged, "all things by turns and nothing long."

His voice was in complete harmony with the make-up I have

described. It sounded the whole diapason of human joy and sorrow; at one breath it thundered and the next was soft and cooing as a dove; now it was rich with laughter, then deluged with tears; now hot with hate, then balmy with tenderness; now vibrant with command, or sibilant with scorn, then full of coaxing and caress. The voice was the man's completest instrument and exponent; he was its perfect master, and hence with it could master all who heard. I think his theme that night was "Eloquence and Orators," anyhow, it was not temperance, but the impression I brought away was that I had been under an enchanter's spell and in a "temperance meeting." I remember he told how, years before, he had, in speaking, brought down his hand with so much force upon a marble-topped table as to break a finger bone, but was so intent upon his subject that he never knew it until the address was ended.

How little I dreamed of approaching the great orator that night. The distance between us seemed like an abyss; and so, while others, in no wise entitled to do so, intruded upon him in his weariness, I went home through the mud and darkness, a loyal but silent worshiper at his shrine, saying to myself, "It is the sublimest thing in all the world to lift humanity to nobler levels through the gift of speech, but to women the world does not permit such blessedness." How little did I dream that in the unfolding of God's great fairy story, entitled "Life," twenty years should not elapse before that chief leader of the world's greatest reform would say of the W. C. T. U. with its two hundred women speakers in the field, "Your society is doing more to advance the cause of temperance than all other agencies combined."

I heard him but four times. The next was in 1877, when, by Mr. Moody's invitation, and during his three months' meeting in Boston, I spoke in the great Tabernacle on the same day with Messrs. Gough, John Wanamaker, and Stephen H. Tyng. Then, for the first time, I met him personally, and found the modest, self-distrustful, brotherly man, who professed to be in doubt about his speech, and seemed as appreciative as a boy when told how splendidly he had succeeded. He was the same magician as of old, but I could feel the change that had come over the drunkards' outlook under the influence of "Gospel Temperance," for the wonderful personation of delirium tremens brought an expression full of pain to Mr. Moody's face, and he did not smile when the antics of the half-tipsy man were imitated. There is a compassion felt for the wives and families of the inebriate, now that we know so much more about them, which shrinks in sympathetic pain from such delineations, and the only criticism I ever heard on Mr. Gough's lectures was at this point, nor was that made until the Crusade period.

The next time I met him was in Chicago when he lectured for the Central W. C. T. U., and by Mrs. Carse's request I introduced him to nine thousand people in Moody's Tabernacle. Though suffering from a severe throat trouble, and distressed by the fear that he could not be heard, he was his old self, and fully measured up to the height of his great reputation. When he had finished and was dropping into a seat, exhausted to a pitiful degree, an "autograph fiend" pounced upon him, and he scrawled his name, his hand being so bathed in perspiration that the whole page was defaced. The marvel is that he lived so long, he who gave himself so completely to his work that at the close of every lecture his clothes were literally wringing wet, and hours of attention were necessary so to soothe .and recuperate him with food and baths that, long after midnight, he could sleep. For this purpose some friend always went with him, usually his wife, that strong, brave, faithful "Mary," in whose praise he could never say enough. On the evening of this tremendous effort in the great Chicago Tabernacle, she sat upon the platform, a little in the background, knitting, with a proud and happy smile upon her face. We paid Mr. Gough five hundred dollars for that lecture, but made seven hundred dollars clear of all expenses. Many have criticised Mr. Gough for accepting such large sums, but he earned them if ever mortal did, and he was one of the most generous men that ever lived. His gifts were private and most unostentatious, but the young men and women he sent to school and college, the friends he helped, the families he supported, would make up a list of princely benefactions. Money passing into his hands was always transmuted into blessing.

On the day after the lecture I went about noon to see Mr. and Mrs. Gough at the Sherman House. Mrs. Gough was ill in bed with a throat difficulty. It was delightful to witness the tender thoughtfulness toward his wife of this man who had been so praised and loved by the people of two continents that if he had not possessed a really great nature he would surely have been spoiled. In all his practical affairs she was evidently his guide, as well as his philosopher and friend in their home life. I have never met a woman less injured by prosperity than Mrs. Gough, or possessing a more affluent endowment of good common sense.

The next time I met our orator was at the Saratoga Temperance Convention of 1880, where I had the high honor to stand once more on the same platform, Mr. Gough and Rev. Dr. J. O. Peck being the other speakers. How little did I think then, as the Wizard of Worcester wrought his spell afresh upon an audience, that I should see the wondrous sight no more! I remember with what inimitable force he said, "While I can talk against the drink I'll talk, and when I can only whisper, I'll do that, and when I can't whisper any longer, faith, *I'll make motions*—they say I'm good at that!" How prophetic were the words. He talked right on against the drink evil until he lacked but six months of being seventy years of age, speaking nearly nine thousand times, to at least nine millions of people, and traveling four hundred and fifty thousand miles to reach them. His last words were to the public in the great audience, and his last motion was to raise his hands to heaven for temperance, throw back his head, and pass beyond our human ken forever.

Twice I have visited the home of John B. Gough, on a quiet farm, six miles from Worcester, Mass. Once I went in his absence, with my cousin, Rev. Dr. A. Hastings Ross, of the Congregational Church, then his pastor at West Boylston, a couple of miles from his residence. Probably his location at Hillside, in a place so secluded, was for a twofold reason: his wife's old home was near here, and only by living in the country could a man so celebrated enjoy the seclusion and secure the quiet for work and recuperation that were essential to his health and usefulness. One of the penalties paid by all who have that "large following" which is essential to a reformer's success, is loss of invaluable time through constant interruption, and failure to rest adequately because of the local interests of the movement with which they are connected. Probably Mr. Gough solved this problem in the only way possible to a nature so genial; he literally "tore himself away"; he followed the highest possible example and injunction, "Come ye apart into a desert (ed) place, and rest awhile."

His home was the shrine of natural beauty, good sense and good taste. A quiet farm-house, it was sheltering, ample, and the very incarnation of comfort. Rare pictures and engravings, books, souvenirs, and testimonials were in every room.

The last time that I saw him was in 1883, when, by invitation of Mr. and Mrs. Gough, Anna Gordon and I spent a day and night at Hillside where his wife and his accomplished nieces graciously ministered to our comfort, and we had a memorably delightful time.

He was, as usual, full of anecdote and personation. He showed us with pride an elegant and complete set of Spurgeon's works, recently sent him with a beautiful letter from that great preacher, and told how on hearing that Mrs. Spurgeon, who has been an invalid, confined to her house for years, was lamenting that she "never should hear Gough," he said to Mr. Spurgeon, "She shall hear me if she wants to," and he actually went to her sick-room, stood up before her, and for one hour exhausted all the resources of his genius and experience to impress that saintly woman with the merits of the temperance reform! This incident reveals a volume relative to the simple, kindly nature of this man with a child's heart.

He told us, playfully, that, being received by processions, bands of music, etc., when he landed at Liverpool, and having had such a wonderful experience in England, speaking one hundred nights in succession to packed audiences in Exeter Hall, and having reached people of all grades, from the nobility down, as no American had ever done (he did not say all this, but I knew it), he was a little nervous on approaching New York Harbor, as his return had been cabled and he did not know what demonstration might be made. But behold, "Brother Jonathan" held on the even tenor of his way; there was none so poor to do the returning hero reverence; and greatly relieved he took a hack and drove to a hotel, newly enlightened as to American characteristics and more profoundly impressed than ever that "this is a great country."

At this visit Mr. Gough urged me to go to England for a

year, and proffered his influence to introduce me under the most favorable auspices, giving me a survey of the situation, and declaring that the outlook for woman's work in England was unequaled, and the temperance reform certain to win. He spoke with especial affection of Robert Rae, the accomplished secretary of the British Temperance League, who had been so helpful to him in all his work for the mother country. Subsequently he wrote me repeatedly on this subject, and but for my unwillingness, at her advanced age, to put the sea between my mother and myself, I would have gone.

It was a privilege, indeed, to kneel with Mr. Gough and his family at their fireside altar and join in the simple, fervent prayer he offered for God's guidance. The last communication I had from him was a note accompanying a beautiful *solitaire* tea-set for dear mother's eightieth birthday. He was a guest in Mary B. Willard's home in 1884, having lectured in our W. C. T. U. course at Evanston, while I was absent. It was just after the great election, and quite a sensation was produced when Mr. Gough spoke in this wise:

"I had to face a difficult question, recently. Forty years a temperance worker and advocate of prohibition, the temperance people's prayer denied and no recognition of this principle in any national platform but one, what was my duty as a Christian and a patriot? I considered the matter seriously and talked it over with my wife. 'John, there is but one thing you can do,' she said, and I thought just the same, so I voted for St. John and Daniels."

He has left us a clear testimony that, in all the changing, evolving phases of the great movement which he did more to advance than any other man of his time, he kept step to the music and fought upon the picket line of progress. No words ever spoken to the young men of America have greater significance than the last uttered by this man whose pitiful past haunted him like a perpetual nightmare; words that seemed to come to them out of eternity, because with his last conscious breath, "*Young men keep your records clean.*"

Good friend, great heart, gallant leader, hail and farewell; we shall not look upon thy like again.

PUNDITA RAMABAI.

I am bound to say that this gentle Hindu woman showed extreme reluctance to being "written up," permitting it only at my earnest solicitation, and adding at last, "Do as you will with me, only help my college for women all you can."

So here she stands before us—a young woman of medium height and ninety-eight pounds weight; not thin, but small-boned, muscular, lithe, straight as an arrow, with action quick and graceful. Her simple dress of gray silk, guiltless of occidental humps and trains and furbelows, and her native "chuddar"—the white wrap of the East—attest her freedom from the bondage of mantua-maker and milliner. The spirited pose of her head, when the chuddar is removed, gives fullest revelation of her character. The close-cut, blue-black hair clearly shows those noble outlines where perception, conscience, benevolence, and indomitable purpose hold their lofty thrones. She has dark gray eyes full of light, a straight nose with a tiny tattoo between the eyebrows, high cheek bones, mobile lips, and perfect white teeth. She can trace her Brahmin ancestry a thousand years; they were all strict vegetarians and never tasted wine, nor does she know the alcoholic flavor (except through the communion), although "for others' sake" she signed the pledge. She has broken her caste in many minor ways, such as eating with Christians, but the Pundita can not abide the taste of animal flesh—or anything "cooked in grease," and marvels much how persons of refinement can tolerate it in their houses. Her food is of cereals, vegetables, and fruit. But so unobtrusive is she, in all these peculiarities so beautiful, to my thinking, at least, and in the habitude of immaculate cleanliness, that except as she is closely questioned, one would hardly note her mode of life as peculiar.

She is delightful to have about; content if she has books, pen and ink, and peace. She seems a sort of human-like gazelle; incarnate gentleness, combined with such celerity of apprehension, such swiftness of mental pace, adroitness of logic, and equipoise of intention as make her a delightful mental problem. She is impervious to praise, and can be captured only by affection, to which, when genuine and delicate, her response is like that of the rock to Moses' rod. She is full of archness and repartee, handling our English tongue with a precision attained by few of us who are to the manner born. But I must repeat that her gentleness exceeds any other manifestation of that exquisite quality that I have yet seen. This seems to be her motto: "Has any wronged thee? Be bravely avenged: slight it, and the work's begun; forgive it, and 'tis finished."

When we recited verses at family prayers, she could not, on the instant, think of one, and my mother told her to repeat some Sanskrit precept, which she did, with a quick translation, saying, "Madam, you have a broad and generous spirit." She knew her poets were usually spoken of as "heathen," and not to be for one moment tolerated at a Christian fireside. When she spoke in our Sunday gospel meeting of the W. C. T. U. at Evanston, I asked her what hymn she preferred, and in her clear, earnest voice she instantly replied,

"I heard the voice of Jesus say,
Come unto me and rest."

The Pundita is a woman-lover, not as the antithesis of a man-hater, for she is too great-natured not to love all humanity with equal mother-heartedness, but because women need special help, her zeal for them is like a quenchless fire.

My mother wrote thus of her in her "Diary":

"The Pundita Ramabai is a marvelous creation. She has a surprisingly comprehensive intellect and is as open to receive truth as the daisy to the sun. With face uplifted she marches straight into its effulgence, caring for nothing so she find the eternal truth of the eternal God—not anxious what that truth may be."

Ramabai is the daughter of a Marathi priest. In his youth he saw his preceptor teaching Sanskrit to a royal princess and resolved that he would thus teach his own wife. But their kindred on both sides looked upon this as hardly less than insanity. They doubtless said, as did a Hindu who was criticising the missionaries, "Having determined to teach the women, we shall next find you going with your primer to the cows." There was no peace in the house and our liberal-minded Marathi priest gave up the unequal contest. But a few years after, his wife died, and on one of his pilgrimages he met at a sacred river, a learned Brahmin whose lovely little girl he married and being three times her age, he found it more easy to do as he would about her education. She was very bright, and glad to learn, but after awhile his strange course excited so much comment that he resolved to retire from the world and carry out his ideas without further molestation. He accordingly sought a home in the forest of Gangamul on the Western Ghats in Hindustan, and here on the 23d of April, 1858, Ramabai was born. She lived in entire seclusion, and the consequent enjoyment of outdoor air and exercise; she was taught by the mighty ministries of Mother Nature, who has stamped her sanctities on this impressionable soul. Her earliest recollections are of the birds singing in the morning twilight, at which time her mother (busy during the day with household cares, as she had several other children and step-children) was wont to take little Ramabai in her arms to teach her the Sanskrit language. In this way and as they walked, later on, thousands of miles on pilgrimages to sacred shrines, Ramabai learned twenty thousand verses from the poets and sayings of the philosophers.

Before she was sixteen this gifted girl was left an orphan; she traveled several years with her brother, a noble young man who sympathized with her in the determination she had made to devote herself to the elevation of her countrywomen. The genius, learning, and devotion that she evinced, gained for her a wide celebrity. She was never a member of the Brahmo Somaj, but perceiving its theism to be higher and better than her Hinduism, she became a convert to its ideas and broke her caste, for which she received the anathemas of her people. But she had one of the bravest souls ever enshrined in clay, and so went on her widening way, unperturbed by the criticisms of her people. She lost her brother, and was once more sorrowful, but kept steadily to her work of traveling, lecturing, and writing in the interest of Hindu women. The English admired and trusted her. Before their high commissions her word was taken as authority concerning the needs of those for whom she labored with unselfish devotion. She urged that native women should be trained as physicians and taught to teach. Measures were introduced having these ends in view, and as a sequel to the society formed by her among leading Brahmin ladies of Poonah, that city now has not only primary schools for girls, but high schools; while Bombay has several high schools, and Calcutta the "Victoria" school, conducting to the university.

In the latter city, learned pundits (professors in the university) proceeded carefully to examine into her acquirements, and as a result, conferred upon her the degree of Sarasvati—equivalent to "the Hindu Minerva." This made a stir throughout the empire, as no woman had ever received such a degree up to that time. Soon after, Ramabai married a Bengalese gentleman, a lawyer, whom she freely chose, this being an instance almost without precedent. He did not belong to her caste and she suffered much criticism on this account. She taught him Sanskrit and he gave her English lessons. She called him by his first name which was a dreadful thing in the opinion of the women round about. (They lived in Cachar, Assam.) She did not especially wait upon him, but took her meals at the same time, which was another mortal sin. She had already determined to go to England and study medicine, and he agreed to help her all he could. But he died suddenly of cholera, when they had been but two years married, leaving her a widow with an eight months' baby when she was only twenty-four years old. But, though her protection and support were thus suddenly cut off, Ramabai did not despair. She sold their little home, paid off the debts, wrote a book which brought her money enough for the journey, and sixteen months after her husband's death set off across the unknown seas for England. This was in 1883. She found that a slight deafness, the result of scarlet fever, would prevent her from studying medicine. Professor Max Müller and other learned men took up her cause. She was made Professor of Sanskrit in Cheltenham College, where she remained until 1886, when Dr. Joshee, who was her cousin, a lady of high caste, was to graduate from the Woman's Medical College, of Philadelphia, and the Pundita came over to see her and to study our educational methods. The death of Dr. Joshee soon after she returned to India, was a heavy blow to Pundita and to the women's cause in Hindustan.

Ramabai has thoroughly studied the kindergarten system; has lectured in our principal cities, and has written a remarkable book entitled "The High Caste Hindu Woman," in the eighteen months of her stay in America. Dr. Rachel Bodley,* Dean of the Woman's Medical College, Philadelphia, in an introduction to this book, which can not fail to enlist every reader, says that she

*Now deceased.

never read one more remarkable. It tells of women whose only and unpardonable crime is having been born at all, and who are all their lives accursed in the eyes of their kinsfolk because death took away the boys to whom they were betrothed in infancy, and they are held to be the ones who caused this loss and grief in their prospective husbands' homes. It tells with tender pathos of their bondage from which suicide and shame are the only sources of deliverance and it tells in burning words of Pundita Ramabai's undying purpose to work out their deliverance by means of a Christian education. For the great question is now and has always been: "Ought women to learn the alphabet?" After that all else is easy and no man may fix the limit of their "sphere."

Pundita Ramabai became an avowed Christian while in England, was baptized, and declared her acceptance of the Apostle's Creed, and her belief in Christ as the Master and Redeemer. But her acute mind finds it difficult to choose among the sects, so she announces herself as being in harmony with all, and has joined none. But every Christian grace blooms in her life, communion with God seems her most natural habit, and love to Him and all that He has made, her atmosphere. She wishes to found in India a school for high-caste Hindu widows, and asks good people of every name to help her. But she is not under any "auspices"; no denominational missionary board can consistently take up her enterprise, nor does she wish it. Were she more worldly-wise, she would avoid this hindrance by attaching herself to one of them and accepting their counsel and their money together.

But, earnest Christian though she is, the Pundita is a woman of "views" and will defend them to the last. She believes there is room for this new agency; and that through the plans formulated by a Christian Hindu widow who knows the inner workings of that class, its members may best be reached.

I can not help cherishing the earnest hope that, under Pundita Ramabai's Christian sway, women never yet reached by the usual missionary appliances of the church may be loosed from the prison house of ignorance, lifted out of the habitations of cruelty, and led from their darkness into the marvelous light of that gospel that elevates women, and with her lifts the world toward heaven.

DISTINGUISHED SOUTHERNERS—CHIEFLY LITERARY MEN AND WOMEN.

"We know your authors, but you don't know ours," was a frequent observation of my Southern entertainers, and, as I eagerly noted every allusion to the household favorites whose genius was indigenous to their own soil, the exclamation was not infrequent, "Tell your friends about our writers, when you go home." Hence these brief notes, gathered up by the way.

Almira Lincoln Phelps, the sister of Emma Willard, though not a native, was an acclimated Southerner. The Patapsco Institute, near Baltimore, was most successful under her management; and, when I saw her in 1881, she took a hearty interest in the later phases of that irrepressible "Woman Question" with whose evolution she and her famous sister had as much to do as its more pronounced advocates. In her stately home, on Eutaw Place, Baltimore, I visited the genial and accomplished octogenarian (since deceased), who manifested lively pleasure in the declaration that her "Botany" was one of my most cherished companions on a Wisconsin farm; but shook her long finger ominously at me as she expressed her dissent from my "views" of woman's relations to the manufacture of public sentiment and its crystallization into beneficent law. She smiled, however, at the soft impeachment that our present work in manifold forms of intellectual and philanthropic endeavor is but the logical sequence of the higher education, and when she gave me a nice picture of herself in the gracious days of her prime, I felt assured her opposition was not fundamental. In this opinion she confirmed me by calling attention to a large swinging book-case, within reach from her easy-chair, and crowded with the best results of modern, as well as ancient thought—the Bible having evidently the first place in her study and affection. Mrs. Phelps shared her home with her son, Gen. Charles E. Phelps, the gifted orator who was chosen to give the memorial address at Baltimore's magnificent sesqui-centennial in September, 1880.

At Johns-Hopkins University I had the rare pleasure of hearing Sidney Lanier, who almost up to the time of his death was lecturer on literature in that marvelous institution, which has risen at one bound to the very first rank, by reason of its wealth and the statesman-like qualities of its president and board of trustees, who, taking as their motto from the beginning, "Get the Best," have attracted a coterie of rarely gifted and accomplished professors, and by their post-graduate studies a quality of students altogether superior to the average of American colleges. Indeed, "the liberal education" in Max Müller's sense, which leaves the student at liberty to give large scope to elective affinities in scholarship, and to become at once a man of culture and a specialist, has wide illustration here. My only regret was that the genial Quaker whose name the institution bears did not pay sufficient respect to his schooling in the grand Society of Friends (whose object-lesson in equality of right between the sexes is its chief glory) to ordain co-education as its crowning feature. It is humiliating to know that Carey Thomas, a young Quakeress, the daughter of Dr. James Carey Thomas, a leading trustee, was refused admission and pursued in the University of Leipsic, Germany, the post-graduate studies denied at her own door. To-day she is the best educated woman in America and Dean of Bryn Mawr College. But there is a strong co-education sentiment among the powers that be, and its realization is but a question of time that shall prove brief. What Sidney Lanier thought on this weighty subject I did not learn; but, surely, the preponderance of ladies, grave and gay, at his superb lectures must have given him food for a generalization thereupon. Taine made the study of environment enter largely into his philosophy of literature, but Lanier's root principle is the *development of personality*. This he traces from its embryo, among the Greeks, wherein the state is everything and the individual nothing, to its consummate blossom in Shakspeare and George Eliot. It was refreshing to listen to a professor of literature who was something more than a *raconteur* and something different from a bibliophile, who had, indeed, risen to the level of generalization and employed the method of a philosopher. Georgia is proud of Sidney Lanier, whose birthplace and early home was Griffin, and whose services in the Confederate army are added to his fame as a poet. He will be remembered as author of the "Centennial Ode" of that Centennial year wherein the arts of peace did more than has been generally understood to bind the broken sections in new bonds of amity and emulation. He also wrote a charming novel of Southern life, entitled "Tiger Lilies," published in 1867. Several of his best productions have appeared in *Scribner's Magazine* and in *The Independent*. His brother, Clifford, is also a man of talent, having published a novel, "Thorn-Fruit" in 1867. Sidney had varied fortunes. He was once a teacher; then being a fine musician was attached to Theodore Thomas's concert troupe. Later he found fit audience at the great university until his death.

He had a theory of the art of rhyme and rhythm set forth at length in a volume on the subject. Many have compared his shorter poems with some of Emerson's least comprehensible efforts—"The Red Slayer," for instance; but the more carefully one studies his unique effusions, the more of strength and genius and that "personality" which is the key-note of his creations and criticisms alike is felt and seen. In personal appearance Sidney Lanier was of medium height, exceedingly slight figure, closely buttoned in a black suit; face very pale and delicate, with finely chiseled features, dark, clustering hair, parted in the middle, and beard after the manner of the Italian school of art. Altogether, he had a countenance rare and pleasing as his verse. He sat not very reposefully in his professional arm-chair and read from dainty slips of MS. in a clear, penetrating voice, full of subtlest comprehension, but painfully and often interrupted by a cough, which proved that the fell disease of our New England climate had fastened on this gifted son of the South. As we met for a moment, when the lecture was over, he spoke kindly of my work and Southern mission, evincing that sympathy of the scholar with the work of progressive philanthropy which our grand Wendell Phillips declared to be pathetically rare. "We are all striving for one end," said Lanier, with genial, hopeful smile; "and that is to develop and ennoble the humanity of which we form a part."

Paul H. Hayne was, *par excellence*, the poet of the South—"their Longfellow," as I often heard Southerners say, although they claim a share in the love and reverence that we feel for ours. He was in 1881, the only literary man in the South who relied on the labor of his pen in poetry for his living. Through the leading magazines of the North he drew the remuneration for his literary labors—meager enough, at best. He was devoted to his art, working, doubtless, far beyond his strength; for his health was very delicate. He lived in almost absolute seclusion at Berzelia, near Augusta, Ga., ministered to by his devoted wife and only child, William, a young man who shares his father's genius. Hayne was quite the ideal poet in physique, with dark hair and eyes, mobile and kindly features, cast in heroic mould. His home was plainer than that of any among his brother singers at the North, one room being papered from floor to ceiling by his wife's ingenuity, with a mosaic of wood engravings, but it was a most attractive place, lighted up by their two beautiful souls, and their welcome to us was the soul of refinement and cordiality. The beloved Southern laureate has now passed on to heaven.

Hayne was a descendant of him against whom Daniel Webster directed the reply that added so largely to his fame. He was a South Carolinian by birth, a voluminous writer and his verse is of exquisite finish, delicate, melodious, brilliant in imagery, but marred by occasional affectations of obsolete phraseology and strained quaintness of expression. At his best he was strictly a lyrical poet, a sky-lark, flying from the grass with a throat full of song, not the matchless eagle whose pinions bear him out of human sight, up toward the sun. The South is justly proud of this lovable man and true literary artist and points fearlessly to his works when its literary development is sneered at by the thoughtless or malicious.

The press of the South is far above the grade usually assigned by the vanity and ignorance of our Northern popular opinion. It is in the large cities exceptionally independent and allies itself with religion and philanthropy. Perhaps its temptations are less than ours at the North. Certainly it does not cater to the ignorant and base. It has no fear of "the German vote" before its eyes, and speaks with fairness of the temperance cause, often with undisguised friendliness. As yet, it has not joined in the "conspiracy of silence," by which Northern journals, while they give full reports of the meetings of brewers and distillers, are often "so crowded" that, "much as they would like to, you know," they find it "impossible" to furnish to the temperance people that larger audience which hears with its eyes and might understand with its heart and be converted, had the greatest of reforms the help of this greatest of allies.

At Mobile I met Augusta Evans Wilson, the famous author of "Beulah" and other well-known novels. She could not be induced to speak of her writings, but showed me her superb collection of azalias and her costly Jersey cows, in both of which curious creations she is a connoisseur.

In Memphis, I made the acquaintance of Mrs. Jefferson Davis, one of the best talkers imaginable, a queenly looking woman of cosmopolitan culture and broad progressive views. She spoke with pride of her New England tutor, and attributed to him a determining impulse toward books, philosophies and art. Her daughter Winifred, I met at a New Orleans kettledrum, where Mrs. Judge Merrick introduced us, and I have rarely seen a nobler type of educated American womanhood. Her talents as a writer promise to lead her to a literary career.

At a reception given me by Mrs. Merrick, in the Crescent City, I met Mrs. Nicholson, owner of the New Orleans *Picayune*, and Mrs. Field ("Catharine Cole") of the New Orleans *Times-Democrat*, literary women and also charming society women.

Joel Chandler Harris is a fine critic and paragraphist, and writes almost equally well in verse and prose. He is set down by Southern literary authorities with whom I talked as their best humorist. He was educated at the printer's case, is a native of Georgia, and about thirty-five years of age; but his fame rests on the well-known collection of (colored) folk-lore entitled "Uncle Remus." It is not easy to make his acquaintance, by reason of a shyness easily accounted for when one remembers that he has "a brilliant mind encased in a homely and unprepossessing body," as a friend of his expressed it. Not knowing this beforehand, I made this entry in my note-book on the day of my interview with him: "The creator of 'Uncle Remus' is a most unexpected-looking man; but a good woman has condoned the fault, and in his pleasant home, Harris is writing out his wealth of wisdom concerning the legends and traditions of the slaves." He told me that "Uncle Remus" is a veritable character, the favorite companion and friend of his boyhood, and that these stories which were the delight of all the children for miles around had been traced upon his youthful memory in outlines so clear and deep, he could not forget them, if he would. Learned men in Europe and America will gladly know that in the mine he has been working with so much skill there are treasures not yet brought to light, for which he will not delve in vain.

James R. Randall is, perhaps, the most graceful and scholarly writer of the Southern press. He edits the *Chronicle and Constitutionalist* of Augusta, Ga., and gives to his editorials all the advantages of a pure literary style and a rich and flowing diction. His descriptions of President Garfield's inauguration are the most picturesque on record, and his spirit toward the North, like that of all the leading journalists of his section, is liberal and conciliatory; yet his fame is founded on the ringing war-lyric, "Maryland, My Maryland," in which

"Huzza! she'll spurn the Northern scum"

is a well-remembered line. Mr. Randall is a large, fine-looking man, with full, dark eyes, ample forehead, and delightful manners. When I asked him if

"Hark to a wandering son's appeal"

was the correct version of a familiar line in his famous song, he replied, promptly: "No. It should be 'exiled son'; for, as a native of Maryland, I felt my change of residence as, indeed, an exile in that crisis."

"And another line. Does it read

"'His foot is at thy temple door,'

or 'his touch,' as in some versions?"

"Oh! 'his touch,' by all means," said Mr. Randall, laughingly. "That more clearly involves the idea of profanation!"

But the war-songs do not exhibit Mr. Randall at his best. He has the true fire of genius, the *divine afflatus*, in abundance and of the purest quality.

But why is it that "Maryland, My Maryland," "Father Ryan's Conquered Banner," his "Sword of Lee," and other Southern favorites are unmatched in fire and pathos by our Northern verse of that unequaled period? The answer is not far to seek. With us the war was at arms-length; with them an awful grapple for life or death. Our homes, at least, were safe; theirs might any day be food for fire-brands. Our fields still smiled! theirs were trampled by the ruthless hoof of war. Hence the wild fervor of their best martial strains.

One Sunday afternoon in 1881, I gave a temperance talk at Franconia, N. H. In the audience, as I afterward learned, were Mr. George W. Cable and his wife and daughter. It pleased me not a little to hear him say that, going home from the meeting, this bright young girl, after a long reverie, said to her mother, "I intend to be a total abstainer always after this, and sometime a temperance talker with a white ribbon on my breast."

For one I have not been greatly encouraged by the applause or commendation of my auditors—indeed, have said an hundred times that if I judged by their lack of demonstration I would immediately quit the field, but one pure girl's approbation thus unconventionally expressed, helped me onward more than the genial man and great author who took the trouble to report it will ever know—unless, as is unlikely, he reads these grateful lines.

Among other exceptionally gifted Southerners whose names I string as pearls on the rosary of friendship, are Sallie F. Chapin, author of "Fitzhugh St. Clair: the Rebel Boy of South Carolina"; Georgia Hulse McLeod, of Baltimore, Fannie Casseday Duncan, the Louisville journalist, and her saintly sister Jennie; Mrs. James Leech, who carried off the parliamentary prize at the Chautauqua Examination; Col. George W. Bain and family, of Lexington; Mrs. Jenny Morton, the poetess of Frankfort, Ky.; Mrs. Lide Meriwether, of Tennessee, who wrote, "She Sails by the Stars"; Laura C. Holloway, the popular author, now of Brooklyn, N. Y.; Rev. Dr. Atticus G. Haygood, who declined to be a bishop, and who wrote "Our Brother in Black"; Judge East, whom I call "the Abe Lincoln of Tennessee"; Sam Jones, the out-yankee-ing Yankee of the South; Judge Watson, of Mississippi, once a Confederate Senator and always a Virginia gentleman of the old school; Dr. Charles Marshall, of Vicksburg, Judge Tourgee, of North Carolina, and Mrs. H. B. Kells, the white ribbon editor of Mississippi.

The South is moving steadily up toward its rightful place as one born to the purple of literary power, and that its women are in the van of the march to the throne-room of this highest aristocracy, gives their Northern sisters special encouragement and pleasure.

WOMEN SPEAKERS.

The first woman I ever heard speak was the first woman I ever had a chance to hear. Her name was Abby Kelley Foster; she was refined, inspired, but so far ahead of her age that she was a potion too strong for the mental digestion of the average man. She was a woman speaking in public and that was not to be tolerated. She spoke against the then cherished institution of slavery and for that she was to be mobbed. In the International Council at Washington, in 1888, I heard some of her former associates say that she went to church one Sunday in a certain town where she had spoken the night before, and the minister took as his text, "That woman Jezebel which calleth herself a prophetess," and rained oratorical fire and brimstone on the poor little reformer throughout the morning service. Let us remember this, for there are those who are abused nowadays by short-sighted mortals whose children will be very likely to build the sepulchers of those whom their fathers traduced.

I was a little girl when I heard Abby Kelley, for it was before we left Oberlin, so that my impressions are not as definite as I could wish.

The next one was a woman whose name I do not recall. I think she was a spiritualist, and she spoke in a little out-of-the-way hall in Milwaukee, when I was a student there in 1857. I had to coax my Aunt Sarah for some time before she would consent to let me go, but she finally did so as a concession to what she called my "everlasting curiosity," sending me in charge of a city friend. The woman was perched in some queer fashion midway between the floor and ceiling. I think she had short hair. I know she looked very queer and very pitiful, and I felt sorry, for my intuitions told me that a woman ought to be at least as good a speaker as a man, and quite as popular. Nothing of all she said remains with me, except one sentence, which I half believe is a fragment from some poet: "I love to think about a central peace subsisting at the heart of endless agitation."

The next woman I heard was Anna Dickinson in the handsome Crosby Opera House, Chicago, during the war. The auditorium was packed; the stage occupied by the most distinguished gentlemen of the city, no ladies being allowed on its select precincts save one, a young woman hardly past twenty, who came forward with poised, elastic tread, took her seat modestly and smiled her thanks as thunders of applause woke the echoes of the great pavilion. Her dark, curly hair was flung back from her handsome brow, her gray eyes, of which a gifted man had said, "They make one believe in immortality," glanced around upon us with a look of inspiration. What she said I do not know, but it set vibrating within my spirit the sacred chord of patriotism, for Anna Dickinson was queen of patriots. Going home that night I could not sleep, for I heard as clearly as I had done in the audience the cadence of that wondrous voice, its courage, its martial ring, and its unmeasured pathos. Beyond all men and women to whom I have yet listened, Anna Dickinson has been to me an inspiration. In 1875 I met her first when I was President of the Chicago W. C. T. U. and she came to the city to lecture. Her agent wished her to speak in Evanston, and I think I never had more pleasure than in using my influence to secure our church for her and entertaining her in my own home. According to her custom, she refrained from eating till the lecture had been delivered; then we had supper in our little dining-room and I sought to have it to her liking. We remained at the table until two o'clock at night, for we were all so much delighted with her conversation that my dear mother, for the first time, forgot her early hours and sat there until after midnight. We talked of things past, present, and to come. If we had known each other always we could not have had more *abandon*. My mother said to her, "What do you think of Christ?" She paused as if she had been smitten with a blow, then changed the subject skillfully, but made no answer. When I showed Anna to her room, she put her arm about me saying, "The question was so sudden that I hardly understood your grand old mother's meaning. What do I think of Christ?" And then for several minutes she spoke of him with an eloquence and tenderness that I have never heard excelled and rarely equaled in the pulpit.

Later on I saw her many times, for she spent weeks at the Palmer House writing her plays. The National Temperance Society had a great convention in Farwell Hall during her stay. I remember Vice-president Wilson spoke and other distinguished men and women, among them all who were leaders of the National W. C. T. U. I had prevailed on Anna to be present at one of these meetings when the question of equal suffrage was to be debated. Miss Lavina Goodell, a lawyer from Madison, Wis., daughter of William Goodell the noted antislavery reformer, moved, at my suggestion, that Miss Anna Dickinson be invited to speak, and at once the house manifested both excitement and applause. The friends of the pending resolution wanted her help, the foes dreaded her voice. But the motion prevailed by a large majority, and as she came along the aisle and ascended the platform, I could think of nothing except Joan of Arc. Indeed I suppose she has reminded everybody of that great character more than any other woman could. As she stood there in the prime and plenitude of her magnificent powers, simply attired in a tasteful walking suit of gray, her great eyes flashing, her eloquent lips tremulous at the thought of what was pending, she was a figure long to be remembered. Often as I have heard her speak, it seems to me that day crowned all. It was not so much her words, as I read them in cold type when the meeting was reported, but it was the mighty spirit that moved upon the hearts and consciences of those who heard. She seemed an avenging angel as she depicted the injustice that fastens saloons upon this nation, and gives women in the home no remedy and no redress, although they and their children must endure its awful cruelty and shame. Our resolutions carried and that was the first gun of the ever thickening campaign, in the midst of which we now are, and whose final result will be woman regnant in the state, an outlawed liquor traffic and a protected home.

How earnestly I pleaded with Anna Dickinson to come with us in the temperance work! Sometimes she seemed half persuaded, but the brilliant friends around her were patrons of the drama; she felt her power, and I am one of those who believe she was entitled by her gifts to make a magnificent success upon the stage. Earnest and tender were the letters I sent her and eloquent of hope the bouquets of flowers. Indeed, for some months I was conscious that my spirit was polarized toward this splendid specimen of womanhood. When she was writing her last book "A Paying Investment," I saw her almost daily. She said to me, with her inimitable smile, showing me the chapter in which a capital argument was made in favor of the temperance work, "See, Missy, I wrote that for you.'

One evening I took Elizabeth Comstock, the dear old Quaker philanthropist with me to the hotel, and we made a combined assault upon Anna to devote her gifts to the temperance reform. She took a hand of each in her strong, warm palms, and said, "Kind hands, gentle hands, and sisterly, fitted to the deeds you do, and to the burdens that you carry. Go your own sweet way and do your work, but leave me to do mine in my own fashion. Your souls are calm and steadfast, while mine is wild and stormy. Let me go my way!" Her voice trembled and tears were in her eyes. After that I knew the case was hopeless, but my love and prayers have followed her all the years, and I have been grieved, as words may not relate, in all the griefs and losses that have come to her.

Everybody agrees that our present queen of the platform is Mrs. Mary A. Livermore, than whom no American woman has a better record for patriotism and philanthropy. We women of a later time were fortunate in having for forerunners the two remarkably endowed women I have named, and we should be forever grateful to that statesman-like speaker and chief-reformer, Susan B. Anthony; to Elizabeth Cady Stanton, the philosopher, and Lucy Stone, the heroic pioneer, who still earlier bore the brunt of battle for us, and whose names millions of loyal hearts will cherish. As a speaker, Julia Ward Howe has a rare niche of her own among the most cultured women of her century, and surely our gratitude to her will not be less, who has laid fame and fortune on the altar of a sacred cause in circles the most difficult to reach and win. The platform is already a conquered field for woman; so is the pulpit in all senses save the sacerdotal, and here our progress is steady and sure. God bless the generous-hearted men who from the first have fought valiantly for the fulfillment of that blessed prophecy, "The Lord gave the word, the women that publish the tidings are a great host."

HOW I CAME TO BE A PUBLIC SPEAKER.

One day when I was doing house-work at Rest Cottage, the winter my mother, my friend Kate and I decided to have no stranger intermeddle with our lot, either in kitchen or parlor, a gray-haired gentleman, the scrupulously elegant style of whose toilet made an impression even upon me who gives but little attention to such subjects, rang our door-bell and inquired if this was the home of Frances E. Willard. Being affirmatively answered, he entered, with much mingled dignity and urbanity, and addressed his remarks about equally to my mother and myself as we were all seated in the little south parlor. He discoursed somewhat on this wise: "I have been present at several of the meetings of the Women's Foreign Missionary Society before which you have been speaking within the last few weeks concerning your observations in Egypt and the Holy Land. It seems to me you have the art of putting things, the self-possession and many other of the necessary requisites of a good speaker. And I said to myself, I will go and see that lady; she is a good Methodist, as I am, and I will invite her to lecture in Centenary Church, of which I am trustee, making this agreement, that if she will work up a good, popular lecture, I will work up a good, popular audience, will pay her a fair price for her effort, and will see that it is well represented by the press of Chicago. It occurs to me that as the result, if all goes as well as I believe it will, she will have no more difficulty in making her livelihood and broadening her opportunities of usefulness."

The pleasant-faced gentleman looked to me very much like a combination of Santa Claus and a horn-of-plenty as he uttered these words. Mother seemed equally delighted, and we told him that he was the kindest of men to have thought of me with so much interest; that I had returned from Europe a few months before, earnestly desirous of employing my time to the best advantage for the support of my mother and myself, and for the good of those among whom I might labor; that what he had promised would suit me to a dot, as I had all my life felt a strong inclination to speak in public and had only been withheld from doing so before, because of the somewhat conservative atmosphere of the educational institutions in which I had spent the last few years and my own sensitiveness to appearing in public.

Declaring that he had no claim upon our gratitude, the pleasant gentleman went his way, and for the next three weeks he invested a good share of his time in interviewing influential persons and in working up with all the ingenuity of which he was a consummate master, an interest in me and in the lecture that was to be.

For myself, I spent those three weeks in the closest kind of study, writing and committing to memory a lecture about one hour and a half long entitled, "The New Chivalry."

On the evening of March 21, 1871, I appeared with my friends, Rev. Dr. Reid, editor of the *Northwestern Christian Advocate*, and his daughter Annie, at the luxurious home of the kind gentleman, where we took tea, and then went over to the handsome city church, where I was presented at the door with an elegant card, the first ticket that I had ever seen about a lecture of my own. It read as follows:

MISS FRANCES E. WILLARD WILL GIVE HER LECTURE,

"THE NEW CHIVALRY."

In the Centenary (Dr. Fowler's) Church.

Tuesday Evening, March 21, 1871, at 7:30 P.M.

TICKETS - - - - - TWENTY-FIVE CENTS.

The pleasant-faced gentleman said, as he reached his kindly hand to me, "Turn the crank skillfully at your end of the church, and I will do so here," for, behold, he was gathering up the tickets himself! I was gracefully introduced by Dr. Fowler, the pastor of the church, and spoke my piece, making no reference whatever to my manuscript which lay concealed in a modest portfolio that had been previously carried in and placed upon the pulpit. My audience consisted of the *élite* of the West Side, with many from the North and South Sides, and they cheered me far beyond my merits. At the close the pleasant gentleman introduced me to a semicircle of well-known journalists of the city, whom he had as good as coerced into being present, and in my private opinion, he had caused to be written up at his dictation the very nice notices that the young débutante upon the platform was so fortunate to win from the Chicago press. Need I say that I have always gratefully remembered him, perhaps more gratefully than he or his have been aware, and here I write, with affectionate memory of one who has passed beyond our sight, above our ken, the name of Albro E. Bishop.

ABOUT SPEAKERS.

Always, in presence of an audience I am saying to myself at one time or another, "How dare I stand here, taking at least a thousand hours of time, and focalizing the attention of a thousand immortal human spirits? Who am I, that so great possibilities of influence should have fallen to my lot? And I must remember that there is a stenographer always present, the stenographer of memory, and that in the white light of the world to come, not only what I utter here, but every thought I think, will stand out plain as the sun in the heavens,—for every soul shall give account of himself to God.

There is something unspeakably pathetic about the life of one to whom must frequently recur the unmatched responsibility of meeting public audiences. His is a joy and sorrow with which none intermeddleth. A ring at the bell may dissipate a thought he was just catching on his pencil's tip in the preparation of a speech; a rap at the door may put to flight the outline of an address; the constant coming and going of people who really must see him, break into staccato snatches the speech that might have been flowing, deep and bright. His riches, what he has, are like Sojourner Truth's—"in his idees," yet they are scattered right and left, as if they were of the smallest consequence, because they are impalpable, invisible, unheard. He grieves for the thousand children of the brain that might have come to light, had they not been throttled in their birth. He knows the meaning of the words, "travail of soul." Then he must put aside a thousand pleasant things in nature, music, books, society, for he has a certain speech to make at a certain time, and, like an engine on the track, he must go forward toward that time. True as this is on a great scale of the great speakers, it is also pathetically true of us who are the lesser lights

THE NEW CHIVALRY;

OR, THE SCHOOL-MISTRESS ABROAD.

[Here follows my first public lecture, which is chiefly made up of observations upon women in Europe—whose sorrowful estate, as I studied it twenty years ago, had much to do with giving me the courage to become a public speaker.]

Bayard Taylor, Paul du Chaillu and Dr. Hayes picture for us the inhospitable climes in whose exploration they hazarded their lives; Emily Faithful comes across seas to tell us of her work among the toiling masses of Great Britain; the Sage of Concord, founder of our lecture system, comes from his meditations to tell us what he heard a voice saying unto him, "Write."

A humbler duty lies upon my heart. I have no poem to recite, no marvelous discovery to herald. I come to you in the modest character of the school-mistress abroad; in the capacity of friend-in-general to our girls.

Gail Hamilton, in that most racy of her essays, entitled "Men and Women," exclaims with a burst of enthusiasm: "I love women, I adore them!" But, by way of compensation, she declares in the next sentence that "There's nothing so splendid as a splendid man."

Now I have no disposition to deny either of Gail's statements, but I would repeat and emphasize the first.

And by "women," be it distinctly understood, I always and invariably mean girls. The largest part of my life, thus far, has been spent in their service. I claim to have coaxed and reproved, caressed and scolded, corrected the compositions and read the love-letters of more girls than almost any other school-ma'am in the Northwest. I began with them before I was eighteen, in my "Forest Home" on the banks of a Wisconsin river, the noblest river in the world to me, though since last I floated on its breast I have wandered as far as the Volga, the Jordan, and the Nile.

In district schools, academies, and ladies' colleges, both East and West, I have pursued their fortunes; in schools where they were marshalled, two by two, when taking daily exercise, and when it was my happy lot to be their guardian on shopping expeditions; and anon, in easy-going schools, where in the recitation rooms black coats were numerous as basques, and opposite each demure young lady at the dinner table sat a being with a bass voice and hair parted on one side. Then I wandered away from the merry-faced girls of America, and for two years and a half studied their sisters in Europe and the East. Coming home full of new thoughts and more earnest purposes, I gathered them around me once again—the fortunate daughters of the dear Home Land—and understood, as I could not have done before, what maketh them to differ from the sad-faced multitudes beyond the seas.

Let me, then, invoke your patience while together we review the argument from real life which has placed me on the affirmative side of the tremendous "Woman Question"—while we consider the lot of woman beyond the seas, and then contrast this with her position, present and prospective, here in America, and while we seek the reasons of this amazing difference. Or, as I like better to express it, let me try to picture the position taken by the *New Chivalry* of our native land in contrast with that of the Old Chivalry in the old world. And by this term, "The Chivalry," for I do not use it as a dictionary word, I mean to denote (sometimes sincerely, and sometimes sarcastically) the sex now dominant upon this planet.

I shall ask you, first of all, to take a glance with me at the saddest of destinies in whose presence I have deduced conclusions, the destiny of an Egyptian woman. It is a June day in the month of February. We are floating lazily along the balmy Nile, reclining on the crimson cushions of our gay dahabeah. As we gaze upon the plumy palm trees and away over the desert's yellow sands, a tall, slight form comes between us and the dreamy horizon, and passes rapidly along the bank, looking weird and strange in its flowing robe of black. If we come near enough, the sight of that dusky face, into which the misery of centuries seems crowded, will smite us like a blow; and as the child shares always in the mother's degradation (as in her joy), we shall find the baby on this sad woman's shoulder the most wretched little being ever victimized into existence. This woman is perhaps seventeen years old, and has already passed the noonday of her strength. Into this fate of marriage was she sold before the age of ten, by her own father's hand. If she should prove unfaithful to its vow, *honor* would call upon him, with imperious voice, to cut her into pieces and consign her to the Nile. The history of this silent, uncomplaining woman is a brief one. She asserts her "rights" in no "convention"; she flings no gauntlet of defiance in the face of her "manifest destiny." She is the zero-mark upon the scale of being, and her symbol is a tear. But upon a fate so dire as this, I will not ask you to look longer. Let us turn our eyes westward—the Star of Bethlehem moves thither evermore, and the next illustration of old-world Chivalry, though sad enough, will be far less painful than the last.

La Signora Sopranzi is a Roman matron of the period, with all Italia's romance stifled in her heart. She was once celebrated for her beauty, but she is already thirty-four years old. Her hair is gray, her gentle eyes are dim, and of the glory long ago departed, only those "traces" remain on which the novelist lingers with so much pathos. Her father was a Roman lawyer, but he was also Garibaldi's friend, and so the Pope shut him up in the ample dungeons of St. Angelo. Her husband, the veriest ne'er-do-weel who ever joined the beauty of Adonis to the wiles of Mephistopheles, has gallantly left her to solve the problem of a maintenance for himself, herself, and her little ones. The only "genteel" avocations suited to her "sphere," are to keep a fashionable boarding-house and give Italian lessons. I have reason to congratulate myself upon the remarkable enterprise she thus displayed, for in her capacity of hostess and instructor, she introduced me to an extensive circle of acquaintances among the more intelligent of her countrywomen, and all I learned of them gave me a stronger purpose of helpfulness toward women. They were not innovators, I promise you! They had never heard about a "College Education"; no taint of the new world's unrest had ever reached their placid souls. Indeed, their average wisdom as to the Great Republic, is well illustrated by this question, propounded gravely to me on more than one occasion:

"When our Cristoforo Colombo discovered your America, did he find many Indians there as light-complexioned as yourself?" They knew they were not very wise, poor things! and often said, shrugging their shoulders most expressively:

"We marry so early, you know, there's really very little need that we should study much. Indeed, in Italy, it *hurts a woman's prospects* to be *troppo istrutta* ('too well instructed'), and you see this is a point we cannot guard too carefully, for out of marriage, there is no place for us, except the cloister."

My landlady's daughter, Bianca, was the most beautiful girl in Rome, chief city of fair women. Although but twelve years old, she was a woman in her words and ways. I was very fond of her, and used often to wish I could lift her out of that lifeless atmosphere—breathed by so many generations that almost all the oxygen is gone—and electrify her with the air that blows across our Illinois prairies. In one of our frequent conversations she thus stated her ideas upon a theme to which she had evidently given no casual thought. Remember I give her precise language–that of a young lady of twelve (for my practice when abroad illustrated that line of Burns', "a chiel's amang ye takin' notes"):

"We are too tender-hearted, we women of Italia. Why, I have a cousin who is dying of grief because her lover seems cold of late. I laugh at her, and say, 'Ah, *bella Margherita*, you are a little idiot! You should not waste yourself thus, upon that silly Antonio.' You shall see how I'll behave! I will never marry in this world. I have seen too much unhappiness among these husbands and wives. And yet, you see, 'twill not be easy for me to escape (she said with charming *naiveté*). Why, the other evening I went to see the sunset from the Pincian hill with my naughty, handsome papa, and a foolish boy, not so tall as I am, a mere child, indeed, but dressed up like a young gentleman, with white vest, gold chain, and carrying a silly little cane, whispered to me, while papa smoked his cigar upon the terrace and I sat near the fountain, that he should come this very night and play the mandolino under my window. But I turned my face away, and when he persisted, I scowled at him from under my black eye-brows and just *dared* him to come! I tell you, Signorina, that I will not fall in love for a long, long time yet, if ever, for in our country it kills women or else it drives them mad. I'm going to give Italian lessons like my poor mamma, and in character I'm going to be a real *Americana*—calm as the broad Campagna, cold as the catacombs. For I am very sad over the women of my country. Life begins with them at twelve, and at twenty-five they are already old; the lights are out—the play is over."

And yet when I have sung the praises of my native land to beautiful Bianca, her eyes have gleamed with a new splendor as she stood erect and said: "Ah! but I am a Roman, and still to be a *Roman* were greater than a king." (But, mind you, some bright American had taught the little magpie that!)

Somewhat to the same purpose as dark-eyed Bianca's words, were those her pale-faced mother had spoken to me that very morning:

"Men cannot be as good as we are," she said in her voice most musical, most melancholy. "I'm sure that they are not so dear to God. We suffer so—our lives call down the pity of all the Saints in Heaven. Life gives us just one choice—to be wives or to be nuns, and society sneers at us so cruelly if we neither wear the marriage-ring nor the consecrating crucifix, that we are never happy unless we are miserable—and so we marry! You of the North have a thousand defenses," she continued, mournfully, "the intellect yields you so many pleasures, and your manner of life renders you brave—so that you are seldom at the mercy of your hearts. Sometimes I think there must be a sort of magic, though, about it all, and I have asked many of your country-women to let me have their talisman, for my poor daughter's sake."

One of my nicest little friends in Rome was Greca Caveri, of Genoa, who had come with her father to witness the opening of the Æcumenical Council. She was seventeen years old, and evinced so much delight when I offered to give her English lessons, that, struck with her youth, I asked why she did not go to school. She looked at me in surprise, saying,— "Does not the Signorina know that I am superior in education to my countrywomen generally? My father is one of King Victor Emmanuel's lawyers, and a learned man. Moreover, he has very advanced ideas about what a lady should be permitted to know, and so he placed me in the best school for girls at Turin. I completed my education there on my sixteenth birthday, one year ago. This is what has kept me unsettled until I am so old. But then I have learned music, French, drawing and dancing—not to speak of the Catechism and the lives of the Saints."

She went on to tell me that her dear mamma, whose loss her dear papa so much deplored, had been three years married, at her age, and then it dawned on my dull wits that she was one among that vast and noble army of martyrs who, with sad face and lifted glance, await the Coming Man.

Poor Greca's sad dilemma gave me long, long thoughts about a brave young country far away, whose institutions each year more generously endeavor to take sides with homely women in the tug of life, and to compensate thus for nature's wayward negligence. I tried to talk of this to sweet-voiced Greca, and she listened with a flush of pleased surprise, but soon relapsed into her normal way of thinking, saying as she shook her little head: "But then, dear friend, you know we women have but one vocation—there's no denying it."

A few days later, on New Year's morning, she ran to my room, saying:

"Now, I'm going to try a sign! As I go to the Vatican with papa, on this first day of the year 1870, I'm going to notice whom I meet first. If it's a *giovinotto* (young man) I shall surely be married this year; if it's a *priest*, why I shall die, and there will be an end of it; but *misericordia!* if it should be an old man, I must *restare in casa* another year still."

"What's that?" I asked; the idiom was new; literally translated, it meant, "Stay in the house."

"Why, don't you understand?" the girl explained; "in my country, if a girl isn't married, she *stays in the house*, and, oh! I do so long to get *out into the world!*"

"You say, Signorina, that the women are so crazy as to set up for doctors in your country? It is a folly and a crime. I wonder that the priests don't interfere. Whatever will become of the buttons and the general house-work?"

Thus spake an elderly Italian dame, the thinning ranks of

whose own buttons I was even then contemplating with a somewhat startled glance!

"And you tell me there are fifty thousand lady teachers in the United States? It is alarming! What will you come to, at last, in a country where women are permitted thus to usurp authority over the men?"

I told her what a wag has called "the horrible statistics." How that two millions of men had been killed in our late war, and that hence there were in many of our states thousands more women than men; that in England there are three millions of unmarried women, of whom two millions have a choice different from the fair Italians—namely, to be their own bread-winners, or starve. Indeed, my figures grew conclusive, whereupon she stopped her ears and exclaimed, with a charming grimace, "For love of Heaven, don't go up any higher! Don't you know that I can't add more figures than I have fingers on this hand?"

I should regret to weary you with my Italians, but am tempted to give you a glimpse into the life of a Roman old maid; because I fancy I have here that single aspect of human life in Rome which neither poet nor historian has ever treated—and because the reverse of the medal has a lesson for us also.

She was a *rara avis.* I did not see another of her species in all Italy, and if she had not been a little unbeliever in all such shams as Pope and priest, she would long ago have sought the shelter of a convent, and borrowed the name of some woman-saint, since she could not otherwise get rid of her own. And yet, hers was a pretty one, I thought—Alessandrina Paradisi. She was one of those against whom Nature seems to have a pique, yet often, as I looked at her puny, hump-backed figure and heavy features, it seemed to me that, after all, Nature had treated her very much as legend tells us Jupiter did the Poet, who came to him complaining that to Tellus had been assigned the earth, and to Neptune the sea, while to him nothing whatever had been offered, whereupon Jupiter said: "For thee, O Poet, I have reserved the key of Heaven, that thou mayst come and go at will, and be my guest." For a spirit looked from the intense, dark eyes of Alessandrina, which had no peer among her sisters; an eloquent voice kept silence behind those mournful lips; a brain that harbored noble thoughts, was lying half-asleep under that mass of shadowy hair.

Permit this record of an evening's talk with my favorite little Italian:

Jan. 10, 1870. She has been to see me again, "*la povera piccola sorella*" ("the poor little sister") as they all call her. It is really marvelous, the faculty this small creature has of making me understand the rich, soft utterance of her mother-tongue. To-night she gave me, without intending it, perhaps, a peep into a place I had greatly wished but dared not hope to see—*her heart.* It was on this wise. She was describing a representation she had witnessed, recently, at the theatre in Naples. As the climax approached she became animated. It was, as it ought to be always, the triumph of virtue and punishment of vice, or, to employ her words,—"So, at last, the husband confessed his fault to his forgiving wife, and they lived in peace ever after, while the hateful woman who had caused the mischief, was sent off to parts unknown." And here the little narrator clapped her hands, saying,—"Don't you see, *cara amica*, that it was a beautiful play?" When I asked if, after witnessing the pageants of the stage, every day life did not seem doubly tame, she scowled, shrugged her poor shoulders, and, *presto*, came my peep at hearts:—

"Yes, Signorina, what you say is true. But look at me! Life cannot yield me much at best. Indeed, it is so sombre, that it does n't matter if these brilliant contrasts the theatre affords, make that look a shade darker, which is always dark. I frankly tell you that if the good God had asked me I would have begged Him not to thrust me into this world. But he did not, and here I am, and there is nothing left me but to make the best of it. I am twenty-nine years old, and by this time, you see, I am accustomed to my lot. I quarreled with it, sadly, though, when I was younger. Ah, I have passed some bitter years! But I've grown wiser now, and try to bring what happiness I can to others, and to forget myself. Only I dread lest I must grow old, with nobody to take care of me. But I try to keep a young heart, and so I give my thoughts to God's fair world, and to hopes of a future life. Is not God kind, who gives me sweet sleep, always, and dreams more fair than anything that I have ever seen in any play or read in any poem? And He lets me sleep ten hours in every twenty-four, and dream right through them all! I would never dare to care for any one, you know, and nobody could be expected to find any charm in me—besides, in Italy, people like me never go into society. And so Rome, my native city, has the love I might have given in ties more tender. Ah, shall I live, I wonder, to see Rome free? What would I not do for her, if I dared?"

But here her tone changed to the mocking spirit that is more pitiful than tears: "Women are nothing in Italy, you know. Think of it! I am twenty-nine years old! my brother Romana is eighteen, but on my father's death, this boy became my guardian, and I take from his hand whatever he chooses to give me from the estate for my support, and do not murmur. For him there is that independence which I count one of the noblest elements of character; for him there is brave work to do; for me there is—*to twirl my thumbs* and wait to see if the *next life can possibly atone for this.*"

Poor child! Let me hasten to deliver her from the limbo to which by some she may have been consigned. She had never heard about a college education and a wider work with better pay for women who must earn their bread, and those frightful words, "strong minded," have never been translated into her sweet, Italian tongue.

In our quest for illustrations of what chivalry has wrought beyond the seas, the most ancient and the most poetic civilizations have yielded us their lessons—let us pass on to interrogate the most luxurious. We shall soon see how differently they do these things in France. In Egypt, as we have observed, the husband buys his wife; in Paris, by strange contradiction, it is the wife who buys her husband, and he knows his value, be assured! In proof of this, let me give a conversation I chanced to have with an intelligent Parisian lady, who, starting out in life without sufficient capital, had made no matrimonial investment up to the ripe age of forty-four.

"I am much concerned," she said, "for my friend, Madame D., who is just now doing her best to marry off her daughter; and it is high time, too, for the girl is already eighteen. But it will not be an easy task, I fear, for she has not a tempting dowry, and but few personal charms."

. . . . .

"How will they begin their operations?" I inquired.

"Oh, the parents will say *tout franchement* (quite frankly) to their friends, 'Find me a husband for my daughter,' and the friends (knowing that one good turn deserves another) will beat up for recruits, and will, perhaps, find a young man who is deemed suitable and who is willing 'to consider the project,' at least. Then, as if by chance, for we are a people of quite too much delicacy to give a business air to proceedings of this nature"—she explained with true French vivacity, "then, as if by chance, the parties meet in the picture gallery of the Luxembourg, or at an open-air concert in the *Champs Elysées.* The young people are now introduced, while the old ones look on sharply, to witness the effect. After several minutes of casual conversation, they separate. The young man says to his friends, 'She pleases me,' or 'She pleases me not,' and upon this turns the decision."

"But what about the girl?" I pursued innocently.

"Oh, the girl? She is charmingly submissive. She simpers and makes a courtesy, and says: 'As you please, dear parents; you know what is for my good far better than I';—so glad is she to marry upon any terms, it is *such a release.*" The lady then went on to say, "If the girl has been so fortunate as to 'please' the young man, and if his friends pronounce her dowry adequate, the necessary papers are made out; she receives half a dozen calls from her *fiancé* in the presence of her mother; he sends her a huge bouquet daily for about three weeks, and so the courtship merges into the wedding day."

Will you believe it? I was stupid enough (but then it was because of the interest I take in girls) after all this to ask: "*And what about love?*" How she laughed! that "lady of a certain age" as the French say, avoiding harsher epithets.

"Dear Mademoiselle," was her voluble reply, "that question tells the whole story! You are *Américaine*, you have read those pretty fictions of Miss Dinah Mulock, and you have not lived very long abroad."

Then she explained to me how, established in her new home, the young wife tastes her first liberty. Her husband goes his way to theatre and club, and she goes hers—often learning what love is (since you insist), from another than he. Her children she puts away from her at an early age; the girls in a convent, the boys in a Lycée, and when they emerge from there, they repeat the scenes of their parents' courtship and marriage—the sons, after several years of profligate life; the daughters, after a brief period of espionage at home. And so the drama goes from age to age.

In good old Fatherland the relations of men and women are hardly less irrational than in France. Young gentlemen never visit young ladies, and the latter are rigidly prohibited from all social intercourse with them except in presence of their parents and guardians, and at the public balls. How they ever arrive at an engagement is one of the mysteries that the uninitiated desire to look into, but, strange to say, that stupendous crisis does at last occur. Whereupon the friends of the parties are promptly notified, and it is customary to call upon the fortunate maiden who has staked her all upon a throw, and won. With the young gentleman — a gallant Knight of the Old Chivalry! — it is quite a different matter. His good fortune consists principally in the amount of very hard cash that rewards the sacrifice of his liberty. He has paid the sex a great compliment in the person of his betrothed, which she will appropriately acknowledge on her own and their behalf. Not that he means to be exacting—oh, no! He is a down-right good-natured fellow, and will require in return nothing more than—unconditional surrender to his will from this time forth until death do them part.

A friend, long resident in Berlin, writes me as follows:

"In Germany a girl exists so exclusively for marriage, that the linen for her bridal *trousseau* is collected from the time she is born. At family Christmas festivals contributions to this outfit form the prominent feature of the gifts to girls, and being questioned they will reply without the least embarrassment: 'Oh, that's for my *aussteuer*—wedding outfit.' German girls marry principally for greater social freedom. Those of the upper classes care less for this, and are slower to change their estate in life."

In "merrie England" there is far more freedom, but Thackeray's incomparable satires, which denounce "more in sadness than in anger" the customs that preside over marriages in high life, are as true to-day as when he wrote them. To my delight I found Thackeray reverenced in England as we reverence Bryant, and loved as we love Whittier, but to my grief they told me the shades in his sad pictures are not dark enough. You remember the episode in that noblest of his books, "The Newcomes," about the queenly Ethel, whose aristocratic grandmamma is bound to marry her to Lord Farintosh, in spite of her repugnance and her protestations, and how Ethel is made to pursue the noble lord through every lane of life, until he lays his coronet before her? You remember how this compromised young woman, visiting an Art Collection and seeing a green card with the word "Sold" attached to a picture there, slyly carries it off, fastens it in front of her white muslin frock, and thus appears at dinner. When asked what this queer fancy means, she makes the old dowager a profound courtesy, saying "Why, grandmamma, I am a *tableau vivant*—living picture." "Whereupon," says Thackeray, "the old lady, jumping up on her crooked stick with immense agility, tore the card out of Ethel's bosom, and very likely would have boxed her ears, but that just then the Marquis of Farintosh, himself, came in. 'But after his departure there was, I promise you, a pretty row in the building,' relates Ethel afterward."

Going to Hyde Park at the fashionable hour, one sees many a poor Ethel who needs no green ticket on her breast to tell the story of her barter. One's heart aches at the thoughts of "sweet bells jangled," whose music might have filled so many lives with soothing melody. For Hyde Park is the scene—as an English gentleman expresses it in language that grates harshly on our ears—"of the richest and most shameful marriage markets in the world." "Men stand by the rails," he says, "criticising with perfect impartiality and equal freedom, while women drive slowly past, *for sale in marriage*, with their careful mothers at their side, to reckon the value of biddings and prevent the lots from going off below the reserved price. Instinctively you listen for the auctioneer with his 'going—going—gone!'"

Listen to the moral drawn by the same Christian Englishman under his frightful picture:

"Such is the pitch at which we have arrived by teaching women *that marriage is their whole duty*."

I turn with grateful pride from these sad pictures of the Old

World, to the glowing colors of the New. The difference between them has been often figured to my fancy by that between the mystic, melancholy sunsets behind Rome's sad Campagna, and their brilliant pageantry as they light up the west from the prairies of my own Illinois. I see what is noblest in the manhood of America rallying like St. George of old, to fight the Dragon, while firm and brave rings out their manly war cry, claiming "Fair play for the weaker" in life's solemn fight. Do you wonder if this contrast set me thinking about the New World's Chivalry? or if, the more I studied the movements of this matchless age, the more clearly I saw that it can give a Roland for an Oliver, till History calls off its last heroic name?

The Knights of the Old Chivalry gave woman the empty husk of flattery; those of the New, offer instead, the wholesome kernel of just criticism; the Knights of the Old Chivalry drank our health in flowing bumpers; those of the New invite us to sit down beside them at the banquet of truth.

"By my lady's bright eyes," was the watch-word of the Old; "Fair play for the weaker," is the manly war cry of the New! Talk about the Chivalry of Ancient Days! Go to, ye medieval ages, and learn what that word meaneth! Behold the sunny afternoon of this nineteenth century of grace, wherein we have the spectacle, not of lances tilted to defend the *prestige* of my "lady's beauty," by swaggering knights who could not write their names, but of the noblest men of the world's foremost race, placing upon the brows of those most dear to them, above the wreath of Venus, the helmet of Minerva, and leading into broader paths of knowledge and achievement, the fair divinities who preside over their homes.

No picture dawns upon me so refulgent as this Home that yet shall be the gift of this Better Age to the New America, in which a *three-fold tie* shall bind the husband to his wife, the father to his daughter, the mother to her son. Religion and affection—as heretofore in all true homes—shall form two of the strands in this magic three-fold tie; the third *this* age is weaving, and it is *intellectual sympathy*, than which no purer or more enduring bond survived the curse of Eden!

Whoever has not thought thus far, has failed to fathom the profoundest significance, or to rise to the height of the noblest inspiration, which our new ideas of woman's privilege infallibly involve.

Those far-off lands of which I told you, made me very sad. I had not known what a wide world it is, and how *full* of misery. Walking in the market-place of proud Berlin, where dogs and women were fastened side by side to carts laden with country merchandise; riding along unfrequented Italian roads where I encountered at one end of the plow a cow and a woman yoked together, while at the other a man presided, whip in hand; or watching from the car window as we whirled along from Alexandria to Cairo, women building railway embankments under the overseer's lash, how often have tears blurred these grievous scenes, as I felt how helpless one frail arm must be to right such wrongs. Sometimes it seemed sweetly mysterious to me, but I understand it now, that always when my heart was aching over the measureless woes of women in almost every land beyond the seas, a voice would whisper to me: "Not to these, but to the dear girls of your home shall you be sent, and some day the broader channels of their lives shall send streams of healing even to these far-off shores."

Do not think my purpose idle, in sketching sombre scenes from lands afar, or evoking in your hearing the jangle of sweet bells, for the foundation of the faith that is within me rests on no theory of "rights" or "wrongs," but is a plain deduction from my contrast of woman's lot in the Old world and the New. Shall we not learn a lesson of unutterable gratitude from this contrast of our affluent lives with those which, under sunnier skies than ours, and in more genial climes, are yet so shadowed and dwarfed? Thinking of them and us, how often do I murmur to myself an adaptation of the Laureate's noble lines that has sung itself out of my own heart and brain:

Ring out the grief that saps the mind,
  Whose thralldom dates from days of yore;
  Ring out false laws from shore to shore,
Ring in redress to all mankind!

Ring out the contest of the twain
  Whom thou for noblest love didst make,
  Ring in the day that shall awake
Their life-harp to a sweeter strain!

THE NATIONAL COUNCIL OF WOMEN.

The greatest movement ever undertaken by women is the outgrowth of that unparalleled International Council held in Washington, March 25 to April 1, 1888, of which Susan B. Anthony was the central figure. By her invitation I made five speeches there, and through her generous partiality was chosen president of this national federation of women, when the office would naturally have gone to her. A more unique and wonderful book has not been published in America than the stenographic story of that Washington meeting. Send 90 cents to *Woman's Journal Office*, Boston, for a copy to *read and lend.*

The purpose of the National Council is thus stated in its constitution:

> We, women of the United States, sincerely believing that the best good of our homes and nation will be advanced by our own greater unity of thought, sympathy, and purpose, and that an organized movement of women will best conserve the highest good of the family and the state, do hereby band ourselves together in a confederation of workers committed to the overthrow of all forms of ignorance and injustice, and to the application of the golden rule to society, custom and law.

We have just sent out our first call to the organized womanhood of the land, hoping to enlist them in this effort for solidarity among women workers as a preliminary to the universal solidarity sought by the International Council of which Mrs. Millicent Fawcett, of England, is the leader.

We should have our representatives constantly at the state capitals and ask unitedly for the things that have heretofore been asked for only by separate societies. Laws for the better protection of women; for the teaching of hygiene in all grades of the public schools, with especial reference to alcoholics and other narcotics; for compulsory education; also for appropriations in aid of industrial schools for girls, and other institutions to which our philanthropic women are devoted—we must together strive for these.

Locally, a Woman's League should, in the interest of that "mothering" which is the central idea of our new movement, seek to secure for women admission to all school committees, library associations, and boards intrusted with the care of defective, dependent and delinquent classes; all professional and business associations; all colleges and professional schools that have not yet set before us an open door of ingress; and each local league should have the power to call in the united influence of its own state league, or of the National Council, if its own influence did not suffice.

In the development of this movement I am confident that it will impart to women such a sense of strength and courage that their corporate self-respect will so increase that such theatrical bills as we now see displayed will not be permitted for an hour, without our potent protest; and the exhibition of women's forms and faces in the saloons and cigar stores, which women's self-respect will never let them enter, and the disgraceful literature now for sale on so many public news stands, will not be tolerated by the womanhood of any town or city.

An "anatomical museum" that I often pass, bears the words, "Gentlemen only admitted." Why do women tolerate this flaunting assumption that men are expected to derive pleasure from beholding objects that they would not for a moment permit their wives to see? Some day women will not, and then these base exhibitions will cease, for women will purify every place they enter, and they will enter every place on the round earth. To develop this great quality of corporate, as well as individual, self-respect, I believe no single study would do more than that of Frances Power Cobbe's noble book on "The Duties of Women." It ought to be in the hands of every woman who has taken for her motto, "Heart within, and God o'erhead," and surely it ought to be in the hands of every one who has not this high aim, while I am certain that every man who lives would be a nobler husband, son, and citizen of the great world, if he would give this book his thoughtful study.

The following extracts from my addresses at the wonderful meeting in Washington will show the trend of thought on some of the subjects presented:

We only wish to turn all the bullets into printers' type; we only wish the war to be a war of words, for words are wings; they are full of lightning. Every brain the open furrow, every word the seed cast in, and you have humanity brought to a different plane; but you can't do it alone; you can't do it unless you come along together; it is easier to climb up taking hold of hands.

Somebody who has studied these things a great deal said to me: "You can tell a harmonious and organizing nature, because the involuntary position of the hands will be like that" (folded together).

See a little, lonesome, stray snowflake come down through the air; it falls and melts and is no more. Now see others come along talking in that noiseless, gossiping way together, and as they come down more and more they have evidently got something on their minds. After awhile these are joined by others, and, their organized attack will make a drift thirty feet high that will stop a fifty-ton engine.

Now, women are the snowflakes. And the organized attack is against this old, hoary-headed, materialistic, conservative way of doing things. And the mighty breeze that shall set them flying is the new sense of sisterhood, and it will bring in all that is good, and true and pure. It has been the curse of humanity in the past that half the wisdom, more than half the purity, and more than half the gentleness did not find any organic expression. Now it is getting expression, and we are here not only to see it and sit by, twirling our thumbs and watching it come, but we are here to put in all our mighty force to make it come. Each woman that has just sat here and lent a kind attention has helped it. Each one who has gone away and spoken a kind word has helped it. Each one that has lifted an aspiration toward the great Heart that holds the world has helped it.

The highest power of organization for women is that it brings them out; it translates them from the passive into the active voice; the dear, modest, clinging things didn't think they could do anything, and, lo and behold! they found out they could. They come to you with a quiver of the lip, and look at you so hopeful and expectant, and wonder if they could do something; and a year or two after, you hear them with a deep voice and perfect equipose telling their dearest thought to a great audience, or you see them in the silent charities, carrying out their noblest purpose toward humanity.

* * * * * * * * * * * *

I will tell you how it is with me: I go like a bee into the gardens of thought; I love to listen to all the voices, and I go buzzing around under the bonnets of the prettiest flowers and the most fragrant, just like this bee, and when it is a lovely life and a sweet life, like the lives of those who have spoken to us to-day, it seems to me I get a lot of honey; but I have a won-

OFFICERS OF (Permanent) NATIONAL COUNCIL OF WOMEN, U. S. A.

MAY WRIGHT SEWELL. FRANCES E. WILLARD,

derful bee-line fashion of carrying it all home to my own Methodist hive. I couldn't do any other way. I am made that fashion; it is part of me. It is worked into the woof and warp of my spirit, the result of the sweet old ways in which I was brought up. I should have to deny myself in my inmost heart, if I didn't believe what mother had taught me at her knee, if I didn't, above all the teachings and all the voices, reverence the voice that calls to me from the pages of the Bible; if I didn't, above all things and always, in my mentality and spirituality, translate God into terms of Jesus Christ. I cannot rest except there. And so I frankly tell you how it is with me this sweet Easter day. The inmost voice, deep down in my heart, says: "Lord Jesus, receive my spirit! Receive it as I sit here listening to women whom I love and revere and honor for their loyalty to what they believe is the highest and best. Receive it as I go forth into the crowded ways of life with so many voices calling me on every hand. Receive my spirit!" It will be the last thought that this brain will think, it will be the last quiver of this heart that has ached and rejoiced, "Lord Jesus, receive my spirit!"

* * * * * * * * * * * * *

I don't know that it will make me stand any better with the ladies of the audience, and certainly it won't with the gentlemen, I suppose, but, honestly, I always thought that, next to a wish I had to be a saint some day, I really would like to be a politician.

Now, I was a farmer's daughter, and got this idea of politics through father's and mother's talks together, as much as from the newspapers. I remember so well sitting by and listening to their talk, and mother was a very motherly woman, and a tremendously potential politician, though I don't think she ever knew it, and I only discovered it within the last fourteen years. I never knew quite what was the matter with her, but in these days I believe she was born to be a Senator, and never got there. * * * Then my brother came to be twenty-one, and we had gone around the pastures and prairies together; we had kept along in our ideas and ambitions; we had studied the same books and had the same general purposes. But lo and behold! there came a day when there was a separation. I saw that voting made it, and it seemed to me the line was artificial and should be broken down. Then I said to myself: "My politics is sacred; there isn't anything about it with which a pure heart, serving its kind, wouldn't like to have to do. But it is a kind of poor man that went down to Jericho. Now, can't we get politics out of the company of thieves into which it has fallen? Cannot we get it out from among the beasts of Ephesus? Are we going to pass by on the other side or are we going to come, like the good Samaritan, and to make politics a home question, something that women care for and are greatly interested in?

If to all this our brothers answer, "It is not because you women are inferior that we don't want you to vote, but because you are too good and nice and pure to come into politics," then I say to you: "My friend, we don't expect to leave political affairs as we find them; not at all. You, our brothers, all alone by yourselves and no women with you, have constructed this "filthy pool" that you talk about so much, and that you don't admire, and you can't make it any worse. You know that into the witch's broth they pour all the ingredients together. Now, you have all the ingredients there are, except women's votes. Turn them in; it may be the branch of sweetness that it needs; and certainly it can't be any worse." So I want to say to my brothers, that we are coming in, as we believe, just as we should go into a bachelor's hall. We should take along broom and dust-brushes and dust-pans, open the windows and ventilate the place, and try to have a general "clarin" out, and that is exactly what we want to do in Old Aunt Columbia's kitchen. Brother Jonathan hasn't kept house there in an orderly and cleanly manner, and if ever a place needed "clarin" out we think it is the kitchen of Uncle Sam. So we have made up our minds and you will see us coming in, and nothing on this universal earth will keep us out of it. It seems to me just the difference between the smoking-car and the parlor-car; in the smoking-car there are men alone, and in the parlor-car men and women together. And how nice and wholesome it is in the parlor-car; and how everything but wholesome and nice it is in the smoking-car. It seems to us women that every great thought must be incarnated, that disembodied principles and disembodied spirits fare about equally well in this work-a-day world; that every principle seeks a hand that can cast its ballot into the urn, where a republic manufactures its own destiny. And so we believe that into this magnificent scene we may well enter, because the weapons are not carnal, but spiritual. We believe that when coal in the mine and not in the grate will warm you; when flour in the barrel and not in the loaf will feed you; when wool on the sheep's back, and not woven into cloth will clothe you, then public sentiment that is lying around loose and not gathered up through the electric battery of the ballot-box, or sent tingling along the wires of law, will change the ways of men.

God made woman with her faculties, her traits, her way of looking at all great questions from the highest to the lowest, and he made her to be a helpmeet for man, and he made man to be a helpmeet for her; he made them to stand side by side, sun-crowned; he made them to stand in a republic, as I believe, bearing equally its magnificent burdens. I like to see how men are grandly meeting the uprising of womanhood. I recognize, and all of us here do, that it was our big brother man who said, Come and sit down beside me at the banquet of Minerva. I recognize, and so do we all, that it was a man that encouraged us when we made our first ventures; that it is not with any special purpose to keep us down that men do not let us enter into politics, but that they are sort of considering it; they are waiting for us to be a little more anxious. They are waiting themselves to get wonted to the notion, and they are growing rapidly. The time is not distant, and every man knows it who hears me.

But I do not forget that if we come, you and you only must open the door!

* * * * * * * * * * * * *

You are told that public opinion seems to demand the saloon, and as a White-Ribboner I ask, "Whose public opinion? That of the home?" "Oh, no; the home is solidly against it." "Whose public opinion? That of the church?" "Oh, no; two-thirds of the church is made up of women." "Whose public opinion?" That of men who drink and men who sell, and men in professional, business and political life, who don't like to get the ill-will of those who drink and sell. Thus, as the outcome of deliberate choice, based upon motives wholly selfish, these men have saddled the liquor traffic on this nation. But the nation has great guns of power pointing sublimely up into vacancy. We want to bring them to the level of our use, and send their shot banging into the eyes of the foe. It is this purpose of arming women with the ballot that makes me so perfectly at home on a platform like the present. It is this which brings me to do homage to these grand pioneers, just as you do, and no one can pay them too much gratitude and honor.

Let us be grateful that our horizon is widening. We women have learned to reason from effect to cause. It is considered a fine sign of a thinker to be able to reason from cause to effect. But we, in fourteen years' march, have learned to go from the drunkard in the gutter, who was the object lesson we first saw, back to the children, as you will hear to-night; back to the idea of preventive, educational, evangelistic, social, and legal work for temperance; back to the basis of the saloon itself. We have found that the liquor traffic is joined hand in hand with the very sources of the National Government. And we have come to the place where we want prohibition, first, last, and all the time. While the brewer talks about his "vested interests," I lend my voice to the motherhood of the nation that has gone down into the valley of unutterable pain and in the shadow of death, with the dews of eternity upon the mother's brow, given birth and being to the sons who are the "vested interests" of America's homes.

We offset the demand of the brewer and distiller, that you shall protect their ill-gotten gains, with the thought of these most sacred treasures, dear to the hearts that you, our brothers, honor—dear to the hearts that you love best. I bring to you this thought to-night, that you shall vote to represent us, and hasten the time when we can represent ourselves.

I believe that we are going out into this work, being schooled and inspired for greater things than we have dreamed, and that the *esprit de corps* of women will prove the grandest sisterhood the world has ever known. As I have seen the love and kindness and good-will of women who differed so widely from us politically and religiously, and yet have found away down in the depths of their hearts the utmost love and affection, I have said, what kind of a world will this be when all women are as fond of each other as we strong-minded women are?

So, friends, as I think of the new America, the good time coming, when He who is the best friend that women ever knew, the Christ of God, shall rule in our hearts and lives, not outwardly, but by His Spirit—as I think of it all I say, to myself, I am glad I am alive, I am glad I was not alive till this last part of the nineteenth century, I am glad I shall be alive when the golden hinges turn and roll wide open the door of the twentieth century that shall let the women in; when this big-hearted brotherhood of broad-shouldered men who have made it possible for us to have such a council as this, who listen to us and are more pleased with us than we are with ourselves—and that is saying a great deal—and who, if we write a book that is interesting, or a song, or make a speech, are sure to say, "That is good; go on, and do better next time; we will buy your books and listen to your speeches,"—when these men shall see that it was not to the harm of the home, but for its good, that we were working for temperance and for the ballot.

Home is the citadel of everything that is good and pure on earth; nothing must enter there to defile, neither anything which loveth or maketh a lie. And it shall be found that all society needed to make it altogether homelike was the home-folks; that all government needed to make it altogether pure from the fumes of tobacco and the debasing effects of strong drink, was the home-folks; that wherever you put a woman who has the atmosphere of home about her, she brings in the good time of pleasant and friendly relationship and points with the finger of hope and the eye of faith always to something better—always it is better farther on. As I look around and see the heavy cloud of apathy under which so many still are stifled, who take no interest in these things, I just think they do not half mean the hard words that they sometimes speak to us, or they would n't if they knew; and, after awhile, they will have the same views I have, spell them with a capital V, and all be harmonious, like Barnum's happy family, a splendid menagerie of the whole human race — clear-eyed, kind and victorious!

MY OPINION OF MEN.

"I've heard of unkind words, kind deeds
With deeds unkind returning;
Alas! the gratitude of men
Has oftener left me mourning."

Men know where their true interests lie, and women whom men love and trust and honor are always motherly at heart.

If there is a spectacle more odious and distasteful than a man who hates women, it is a woman who hates men. If I am glad of anything it is that, while I have my playful quips and passing sallies anent them in my own inner home circle, when some passing injustice of the old régime quickens my pulses, the life-long tenor of my pen and voice and work has been not more for "Peace on earth" than for "Good will to men." This frank utterance may surely be permitted to one now entered on her fiftieth year, and who thanks God with unspeakable tenderness for all the pleasant land on which she can look back from the high chronologic vantage-ground she has attained. If this had not been so, surely the royal wives and mothers who in all these working years have rallied around me, would rightfully have refused my leadership.

From this time on, the world will have in it no active, vital force so strong for its uplifting as its organized mother-hearts. I do not say all mothers, because all women who are technically mothers are not mother-hearted, while many a woman is so, from whom the criss-cross currents of the world have withheld her holiest crown.

In my own quiet refuge at Evanston, where we are wont to talk of these things, I once said to Susan B. Anthony, that noblest Roman of them all:

"Bravely as you have trodden it, and glorious as has been your *via solitaria*, have you not always felt a sense of loss?"

She answered in the gentle, thoughtful voice that we all love:

"Could I be really the woman that I am and fail to feel that under happier conditions I might have known a more sacred companionship than has ever come to me, and that this companion could not have been a woman?"

But that she also felt God's call, under the unhappy conditions that exist, to go her own victorious way alone, is proved by her reply to a good man who once said to her:

"Miss Anthony, with your great head and heart, you, of all women I have met, ought to have been a wife and mother."

Our noble pioneer answered him after this fashion:

"I thank you, sir, for what I take to be the highest compliment, but sweeter even than to have had the joy of caring for children of my own has it been to me to help bring about a better state of things for mothers generally, so that their unborn little ones could not be willed away from them."

And now, concerning my opinion of men, let me give a few scenes in which they have been chief actors and I "a chiel amang ye takin' notes":

I was coming from New Orleans alone after attending the Louisiana W. C. T. U. Convention in that city in 1881. Mrs. Judge Merrick, my generous hostess, had provided me with such a lunch as rarely falls to mortal lot. As usual, I had a section which I hardly left during the trip, and as has happened several times in my experience, I was the only lady in the car. The porter provided me with a table and I had open my well-worn traveling bag, "Old Faithful," and was writing letters and articles uninterruptedly. By some mischance, I do not now remember what, we were side-tracked twelve hours and no food could be had. In traveling, my constant preoccupation makes me peculiarly uncommunicative. I have gone from Chicago to Boston without speaking to any one except the porter, indeed almost without seeing any one. But as the day wore on and our car stood there motionless, my thoughts went out to those stalwart men about me, those hungry travelers. After much reflection and some quiet observation, I selected a man in whom by intuition I believed, and catching his eye, beckoned him to come to my side. I had spread out my tempting lunch in all its fascinating forms and colors and I said, "Will you do me the favor to divide this among my fellow-travelers?" Those words were a magic spell! The glow of gratitude upon his face was worth doing without one's meals twenty-four hours to enjoy. The grace and courtesy with which he acknowledged my thoughtfulness, the gathered group of men who came to take away a fragment of the feast, the doffing of hats, and charm of manner were worthy of any drawing-room. Poor fellows! they had been trying to get themselves some coffee and had gone to the engine for hot water. I had sugar and cream, which they had not, but my coffee was cold and such an ado as they made to see that it was heated, and such solicitude lest I should not keep refreshments enough for my own needs!

My chosen spokesman said, "I am from Illinois and my wife belongs to the W. C. T. U." Another echoed, "I am from Massachusetts; have heard you speak in my own town," and a third chimed in, "I was in your audience two nights ago at New Orleans." Of course I think well of those men; the little incident did me good for many a day and I rejoice to hope that those men think well of me!

Early in my work it became necessary for me to go across the country in Michigan on a freight train, the trip involving a whole day's ride in a caboose. Although my secretary is almost always with me, on this occasion she was not. I seated myself opposite the stove on a rough bench, and began reading and writing, as is my custom, now so confirmed that while hours and days flit by I do not find travel wearisome, and often think I have but fairly begun work when I find a half day is gone and we are at the lunch station. But on this occasion there slowly stole over my senses a dull perception of something strange, and then of something most unpleasant, and then of something deadly. It was the foul emanations from the pipes and mouths of six or seven freight train "hands," sitting at a short distance from me. I hurriedly rose, went out of the rear door and stood in the cold and snow upon the platform, filled my mouth with snow and tried in every way to take my mind off from the intolerable misery of the situation. But I could not long remain outside, the cold was too extreme. I re-entered the car and was soon enveloped in a tobacco cloud, the nausea becoming so violent that a manifest exhibition thereof in a form recalling "Neptune's tribute," soon occurred. I suppose my face was very white, for the men all came toward me in consternation, cursing at one another and each separately cursing himself with oaths, not loud but deep. They flung open the doors, they established me on the long wooden settle, bringing their coats and fitting the place up for me, folding one or two for a pillow, which they placed under my head with as much gentleness as my own mother could have done, asking my pardon over and over again, saying, "Our hides are so rough and so thick we did not have sense enough to know how this smoke would strike a lady." Indeed, their penitence was of such a poignant type that in my efforts to assuage it I quite forgot my sad condition. They brought me some nice apples, and after a little I was able to resume my work. But there was no more tobacco smoke about that car, and there was very earnest consideration for my comfort, they often asking me if the ventilation was right, and if the fire was warm enough. These men always remain in my mind as one more proof of what I steadfastly believe, that if there are remainders of evil there are also great, noble conceptions of good in every human breast. And of these men, in spite of their tobacco smoke, I can but have a good opinion.

In 1884, just after the presidential election, when politics ran high, I received a letter postmarked ——, Wisconsin, guiltless of punctuation, and as to its orthography, gone quite astray. Opening it curiously, and finding it voluminous, I read in the initial lines the gist of the communication. It was from Mike, our man-of-all-work on the farm, one of the best-hearted and brightest of Irishmen, whom it had been our good fortune to indoctrinate into the mysteries of reading, writing, and, perhaps, a little arithmetic. He had evidently retained a kindly remembrance, for what I read was to this purpose:

DEAR MISS — It is long since I seen you and you will be glad to hear that now I am a farmer mesilf and not working out. I have three sons, one studying at the Wisconsin University, another at a Catholic school in Milwaukee, and a third is minded to be a lawyer. We are all Dimocrats but I have read in the papers that St. John and Daniel were your candidates, and

I said to my boys, "That lady and her folks was good to me when I was a lonesome broth of a boy just over from the Old Country, and now the lady has n't a vote to bless herself with, but we can put in four and let 'em all count on her side." So I and me boys went to the poles and did just that, and I thought I'd wright and tell ye.

With respect,

MIKE CAREY.

Of course, a letter written after this manner helped to give me a good opinion of men.

In Scranton, Pa., I spoke in the Opera House one Sunday evening and at the close went home particularly wearied, for to hold steady a large audience and a six-horse team are, perhaps, somewhat analogous mental proceedings. Going at once to my room, as is my invariable custom, with the statement to my friends that I owe it to the next audience to do so, I was, as I hoped, to be out of sight and hearing until eight o'clock next morning, when a hesitating rap on the door recalled me to my duty, and my hostess said, "I was very sorry to come after you, but a young man in the parlor insists that he has something you must hear." So preparing myself I went down to see him, lifting up my heart for patience, for I find no other talisman but prayer suffices to hold a temper naturally so quick as mine under control. A young fellow rose as I entered, and said, "Perhaps you think all the people who sell liquor are opposed to you, but I came to tell you that they are not by any means. Probably one reason is you don't abuse that class, but you admit, what everybody knows to be true, that they are by no means alone responsible for all the mischief they have caused. If you had not said that, I should not be here to-night, for I am a saloon-keeper's son. I wanted you to know that my mother has always been bitterly opposed to father's business, and I have refused to engage in it and am learning the printer's trade, and hope to become a successful man in the true sense of that term and a reputable citizen." I was delighted with his words, and his honest, kindly face. "Why does your father go on selling?" was my natural question. "Not because he likes the business, but he knows no other. It is an easy way to make a living and all he has in the world is invested in his saloon." "Have you sisters?" I inquired. "Yes, two of the nicest girls you can find anywhere." "What do they think about your father's way of getting a living?" I asked. "They are grieved to the heart about it, just as mother is. They are never received in the kind of society where they naturally belong, and of course it embitters their lives. In fact, I assure you it is not pleasant to be a saloon-keeper's wife, daughter or son in these days. It puts a ban upon us and hard as it is to bear, I thought I ought to come and tell you for your encouragement. That's all." He reached out an honest hand to me, said "God bless you," and was gone. Of course this incident was calculated to make me think well of men.

I had been invited to speak in the Central Congregational Church, Boston, where for many years Rev. Dr. Nehemiah Adams had preached, he who was known in his prime as the Washington Irving of the American pulpit. But word had come to me that Sarah Smiley had at one time spoken in that same pulpit, when the good doctor was absent on a trip, and that he was so shocked to think that a woman had trodden its sacred planks and precincts that, not being in good health, he fell into a spasm. I therefore sent word to him that I would on no account speak if it would cause him discomfort. But the years had come and gone since then, "the ripe, round, mellow years," as Gail Hamilton has called them, and the good doctor sent me this message: "Go on, my child, speak as you will, I shall be glad to have you do so, and I hereby send you my benediction."

I thought well of that man, beyond a doubt!

In 1875, when without salary I was serving the National W. C. T. U. as its corresponding secretary, Mrs. Wittenmeyer, knowing my embarrassment, mentioned to Eliphalet Remington, of the well-known firm of Remington Bros., that she would be very glad to have him give me the encouragement of some financial aid. Forthwith there came a beautiful letter, full of the most brotherly sympathy, and inclosing a check for five hundred with the modest remark that he hoped she would pardon him for sending so little, as the calls were just then more numerous than usual!

This noble man is the founder of the New York *Witness*, a fact not generally known, perhaps. He had seen the Canada *Witness* and been impressed with its value as a promoter of morality and of our Christian faith. So without taking counsel other than of his own keen conscience, he went to Montreal and induced the good and great John Dougall, editor of the *Witness*, to come to New York City, assuring him of sufficient help to establish a paper just as able as the one he was then editing. This generation has hardly been fed from purer springs than those of the two papers—the Montreal *Witness*, and its comrade namesake in New York.

My acquaintance with Eliphalet Remington, not alone because he gave me money when I needed it, but because he belongs to the nobility of character, helped me to a noble estimate of men. So did my father and my brother—one, the soul of uprightness, the other, of geniality; so do the hundreds of my Christian brothers in Evanston where I have lived these thirty years, and so do uncounted thousands in the great and kindly continent that I have traversed, who have shown true magnanimity of soul toward modern movements among women, and who are White Cross heroes illustrating the last beatitude of man, as man is yet to become, that high and holy virtue—chastity. Nothing to-day makes woman so regnant over the thoughts and imaginations of men as this great quality. But it took centuries for Christianity to work it into the warp and woof of her character, and Hebrew women, as a class, are foremost in its illustration, and have always been.

At first, courage was the greatest virtue of man; he must smite the beast of the field and ride forth to the wars; he must subdue the savage earth, while woman, the fountain at which life was to be replenished, must be kept pure, else the race would perish in the long lesson and fierce battle of its uplift and development. But now the savage world is under foot, and man lifts his strong hand up toward woman, who stands above him on the hard-won heights of purity that she may lead him upward into freedom from the drink dominion and the tobacco habit, and that he may learn that highest of all human dignities—a chastity as steadfast as her own. Meanwhile, she must learn of him that noble, masterly grace, physical courage, and that other manly virtue, intellectual hardihood, while she imparts to him more of her own courage of conviction. Into what mutual greatness they shall yet grow! We have never seen the royal men and women who are to illustrate God's ideal when He set apart a peculiar people and taught them first of all that letter in His alphabet of centuries that meant one Supreme Spirit rather than many monstrous materialistic objects of worship; then followed up this great lesson with others, all of which grew out of it. The old time exclusiveness of the Jews is not in harmony with Christianity, but *it had to be* to make them conservators of that monotheistic religion which was to lift future generations up into the light, and it had to be to conserve in savage ages the purity of woman. The same is true of many other things hard to be understood — and only a part of which is dimly apprehended by us.

The only wise way is for us to declare, "I will wait; what God does I know not now, but I shall know hereafter; he has promised this, and it must be that *faith* is to be the final beatitude of character, or he would not require its exercise. Nay. He does not arbitrarily *require* it, but my present infancy of being involves it as a part of the nature of things."

Mr. Moody says, "I might as well try to impart my plans to a fly, as for my Heavenly Father to impart His to me." Let us, then,

> "Still achieving, still pursuing,
> Learn to labor and to wait."

MAN IN THE HOME.

Home has already done more for man than for any other member of its favored constituency. It is his special humanizer; the garden where his choicest virtues grow. Man's heart is lonesome often and the feeling does him honor, for his lonesomeness is always for the home that was, but is not, or else that is not, but ought to be or to have been.

He sits alone, when he knows that it was in his power to have sat beside his other, gentler self in the calm content of a completed life. He warms himself beside other men's hearthstones when he knows that for him one might have glowed, a guiding light, through all the darksome years. He hears the gleeful shout of boyhood and knows that the tenderness of a father's love might have rejoiced and purified his breast. In this sorrowful period of his existence Bayard Taylor uttered what most men's pride would have left unexpressed :

> "I look upon the stormy wild,
> I have no wife, I have no child ;
> For me there gleams no household hearth,
> I've none to love me on the earth."

Never has woman bemoaned the fact that she, too, had missed life's crowning joy, in sadder language than man's strong hand has penned, with a stormy and sorrowful heart behind the words. If his wounds have seemed sooner to heal, it was because his life was fuller of distractions. If he sought less sedulously to found a home, it was because there were so many other things for him to do outside of that—even as for her there is now so much else to do and will be from this time forth.

Indeed, in the present transition period, when woman, deprived of her earlier interests and occupations, and not yet adjusted to her new opportunities, is found in an anomalous position, it may be questioned if man does not love home even better than his partner. How many women are content to vegetate in a boarding-house because they can support more "style" and avoid more care than they could in a home ! How many women who are idle all day long, will urge their husbands out to the theater or card party at night when the weary benedicts would fain toast their feet on the fender and enjoy some book or magazine instead ! How many women leave their minds untilled and bring no wit or brightness, no fresh thought or noble impulse into the evening's converse, because they are worn out with shopping, or a daily round of calls and other fashionable occupations !

The charm of any home is its individuality. Coleridge said that Art is man added to Nature. In like manner home is man and woman added to a house. If it is to be really a home, it must be a mirror repeating their united thought, sentiment, purpose and taste. How much Whittier tells in that one most poetic phrase where he speaks of his home, "No step is on the *conscious* floor." That is it ; a home, as contradistinguished from a house or an upholstered model, is a place conscious of wise, benignant personality ; instinct with lives that are noble and beloved ; differentiated as thoroughly from other homes as its founders are dissimilar in character, education, and inmost intent from other people.

To such a home in the evolution of our time, the bass voice will bring a tone as true, as sweet, as needful as the soprano; and upon it man's individuality will reflect as much significance as woman's. Indeed, his change of occupation has changed home more than hers. When he spent his life in war, home was a castle; when he pioneered, it was a cabin; but now when he begins to "settle down," ceases to be a nomadic, or a partially wild animal, and becomes domesticated, home takes on a docile, cozy, feather-lined aspect and condition.

To judge man in the home at his right valuation, we have but to compare him with his fellows in the club, the camp, the ship, the pinery. That is, we have but to estimate the dignity and value of the normal over the abnormal, of the complete as against the fractional. Nor does it matter whether his home be a "dug-out" in Dakota, or a brown-stone front in Boston. The man with the one woman that he loves, and who loves him, standing in the relation of true yoke-fellow to all his plans and toil, with happy children at his knee, and an unselfish purpose in his soul, is as far removed from his self-centered, squandering, dissatisfied brethren as is the light-house keeper from the shipwrecked crew.

All the world knows that it must look to married men for its types of the ideal in manhood. They have a delicacy, a brotherly considerateness, a homelikeness of character and manner, quite unmistakable. It is the outcome of their nurture; it could not be other than it is, because like causes lead to like results. All women think that if all men were but like some married men whom they could name, the world would reach its acme. But no man can be like these model men except by passing through the flower-wreathed gate-way of the home.

The man who, in his uncompanioned estate, yet carries steadily from year to year the "lily of a stainless life," would oftentimes command our reverence if we but knew why he so resolutely walks that shadowed pathway. Perhaps like our own beloved Washington Irving, he is keeping faith with some sweet woman long since dead. Perhaps, like Longfellow in those years of his pathetic widowerhood, life seems a blank to him, which he tries to fill by singing the song of an uncomplaining, but sorely smitten heart.

This world of halfness and mirage has many, doubtless, who thus go uncompanioned, buffeting the waves of temptation "like some strong swimmer in his agony," and for them heaven must twine its brightest amaranths, and angels plan their sweet surprises.

"He who wrote home's sweetest song, ne'er had one of his own." So sang Will Carleton of gentle John Howard Payne. "*Heimweh*," or "home-ache," that stronger, tenderer word for "homesick," coined by the Germans, was indubitably coined by men. "Blessed are the homesick for they shall go home" was a holy thought smitten from a man's and not a woman's heart. I undertake to say that the dearest and most disinterested lovers of home upon this earth are men. A thousand motives, prejudices, and conventions hedge women into homes, but men, with all the world to choose from, *choose* the home. It is the noblest and most redeeming fact in their long annals, and predicts their perfectibility as nothing else can. This innate tenderness makes every man, cultured as well as ignorant, respond with a thrill of the heart to the simple, but famous lines:

> "One little hut among the bushes,
> One that I love,
> Still fondly to my memory rushes,
> No matter where I rove."

That very "roving" has much to do with it, for contrasts alone educate the soul into a knowledge of values. Tempest-tossed and battle-worn, deceived and buffeted, the manly heart loves the sacred refuge of its home.

It was said of a French soldier, whose well-nigh fatal wound near the heart was being probed, after the battle of Waterloo, that he whispered to the surgeon, "If you go much deeper, Sir, you'll find the Emperor." I believe that if every normal heart of man were probed, its deepest, sweetest, and most cherished image would be home. Those who have none of their own are well described in Grace Greenwood's lines:

> "Thus was his soul tempestuous,
> As the ocean on the beach
> Moans for the inland quiet
> Its waves can never reach.

Man needs home, if possible, more than woman does; though without it, either, is at best, but a jewel torn from its setting. He is in more danger without its anchorage than she, for the centripetal forces of her nature will always draw her strongly toward the light, even though its beacon shine from some happier woman's fireside, while the centrifugal forces of his nature will drive him afar off into darkness. Women who go their way alone are not, in this kindly age, so lonely as men who do the same. Almost always such women make for themselves a niche in some home sanctuary, are sheltered by its walls and warmed by its genial glow, but an isolated man finds this solace impracticable. "In the long run," God's compensations balance destinies once cruelly unequal, and to-day, in America at least, the term "old maid" has in it as little of reproach and almost less of pathos than "old bachelor."

But does any one suppose we have found out what man might be in the home? He has been thus far an embryonic figure there, a mere sketch or outline, dim and shadowy. Nor is it yet apparent what he will be, but we may catch some glimpse of that new and magnificent creation by a study of the evolution of home. This is the most attractive theme in sociology, and the silence of philosophers concerning it seems unexplainable. The locomotive has in sixty years been developed from a speed of six, to one of sixty miles an hour, and the car from a lumbering stage-coach propelled by steam, to a luxurious and palatial "Pullman"; the plow has grown from a wooden board to a glittering, steam-driven monarch of the sod; the public school has advanced from hornbooks to the methods of Pestalozzi and of Froebel—and meanwhile the home has kept pace with these other forms of growth which are but its caterers and its conservers.

No greater change has been witnessed in material surroundings than that between the log-house of the pioneer and the palace of his grandson, for the embellishment of which every country has been ransacked and where every device of invention has been exhausted upon the comfort and convenience of the family. This outward progress does but symbolize the development of its interior spirit and advancing life. At the present rate of improvement, two generations will not have passed before the outgrowth of invention will have reduced to a minimum housewifely cares, and the wholesale will have supplanted the retail method in household economics. This is a perfectly fair inference from what has been already wrought by the transformation of the simplest home duties into great industries carried forward by machinery. Thus set free from accustomed occupations the average woman will enter more largely into her husband's pursuits and share more constantly her children's studies and recreations. The desideratum will be found when the house becomes a unit, not by such extinguishment as makes "husband and wife one and that one the husband," but by such recognition as makes one-half the property the wife's in fee simple, and associates the husband with her as equal partner in the rearing of their children.

A brilliant, but irreverent writer began an article on home-training with the words, "Show us the father and it sufficeth us." The New York *Independent* in a description of the Knights of Labor convention in Richmond, Va., brings the father forward in a new and, perhaps, prophetic role. These are its words:

"On the first day of the session there was in attendance Mrs. Elizabeth Rodgers, of Chicago, with her twelfth babe in her arms, that day two weeks old. Mrs. Rodgers is District Master Workman of District 24 in that city and was accompanied by her husband, both being delegates. She is a woman thirty-nine years old; tall, large and noble-looking, with a pleasant face and fine features. She and her child received very general and kindly consideration. A gold watch and chain were purchased and presented to Mrs. Rodgers on the platform, the father standing and holding the child; and the group was a very pretty and touching sight."

Doubtless this honest workman, cradling in his strong arms his little one, felt no sense of degradation, but rather was proud of his place and honored by his fellows. That this could be in the rank of life to which he belonged, is a vivid proof that we have moved a long way onward in this Christian republic from the Indian who loads his wife with the rations given out at a Western fort, or the peasant of Berlin who fastens wife and dog together to the cart of vegetables.

Man in the home will have a larger place in the proportion that woman, in the constantly more homelike world, gains larger standing-room. Motherhood will not be less, but fatherhood a hundred-fold more magnified. To say this is to declare the approaching beatitude of men. For when to the splendor of their intellectual powers and the magnificence of their courage shall be added the unselfish devotion that comes of "childward care," we shall see characters more Christ-like than the world has known save in its calendar of saints.

Immeasurable has been the loss to men that in the age of force, of war, and pioneering, they were so much shut out from the holy ministries of home's inmost sanctuary, where Madonna and Child are evermore enshrined.

Our environments are so largely answerable for our virtues or defects, that the quality of character we would produce must have its promise and its potency in the recurring experiences of our daily lives. When the hand that rules the world shall also rock the cradle, the millennium will no longer be far off. When the father builds his life and thought into his daughter as the mother has hitherto built hers into her son, the world will see her grandest women and her kindliest men. The manhood of strength and gentleness can only come as a result of the ministry of gentleness and strength, and home will be its training school.

"What is home without a father?" shall then become a question as natural and as genuinely full of pathos as is now its maternal correlate. The capacity of the human mind to resist knowledge is nowhere more painfully illustrated than in the postulate laid down by average minds that home is always to be just what it is now—forgetting that in no two consecutive generations has it remained the same; and the other postulate that man's relation to the home can never change—forgetting that the one constant quantity in his evanescent relations to every sublunary object has been change itself.

Already the word "obey" has been expunged from woman's marriage vow; already her relation of inferior to her husband is changed to that of comrade; already the time-worn phrase, "no home can hold two purses," is regarded with contempt by the best men, and the relation of financial equality before the law hastens to replace that of "coverture" which had its value in a warlike age but hastens to its exit from the age of peace; already woman as an individual, standing beside man as her equal partner in life, love, and opportunity, is the ideal of the typical young American, both male and female, so that man in the home is becoming a new factor under conditions that make him joint high-priest of that holiest temple made with hands.

The nearer he approaches to the cradle and the more frequently, the happier for him and for his home and for the state. Habits of impurity will seem more loathsome in that presence than anywhere else upon the earth. The loftiest chivalry of which the strongest can be capable comes as a sequel of their service to the weakest.

When the White Cross gospel shall have been embosomed in young manhood's life for one blessed generation, the sanctities of fatherhood shall be seen to exceed all others to which a manly spirit can attain in this state of existence, and the malarious dream of wicked self-indulgence shall slowly but surely give place to the sacred self-restraint which waits to crown with all good fairies' gifts the little life which noble love alone may dare invoke.

IS MARRIAGE A FAILURE?

With all its faults, and they are many, I believe the present marriage system to be the greatest triumph of Christianity, and that it has created and conserves more happy homes than the world has ever before known. Any law that renders less binding the mutual, life-long loyalty of one man and one woman to each other, which is the central idea of every home, is an unmitigated curse to that man and woman, to that home and to humanity. Around this union, which alone renders possible a pure society and a permanent state, the law should build its utmost safeguards, and upon this union the Gospel should pronounce its most sacred benedictions. But, while I hold these truths to be self-evident, I believe that a constant evolution is going forward in the home as in every other place, and that we have but dimly dreamed the good in store for those whom God for holiest love hath made. In the nature of the case, the most that even Christianity itself could do at first, though it is the strongest force ever let loose upon the planet, was to separate one man and woman from the common herd into each home, telling the woman to remain therein with grateful quietness, while the man stood at the door to defend its sacred shrine with fist and spear, to insist upon its rights of property, and to stand for it in the state.

Thus, under the conditions of a civilization crude and material, grew up that well-worn maxim of the common law: "Husband and wife are one, and that one is the husband." But this supreme power brought to the man supreme temptations. By the laws of mind he legislated first for himself and afterward for the physically weaker one within "his" home. The *femme couverte* is not a character appropriate to our peaceful, homelike communities, although she may have been and doubtless was a necessary figure in the days when women were safe only as they were shut up in castles and when they were the booty chiefly sought in war.

To-day a woman may circumnavigate the world alone and yet be unmolested. Twenty years ago when I was traveling in Palestine, a lady of wealth made the trip, tenting by herself and escorted only by a dragoman, as was our own party of ten men and three women. A recent book, the name of which I have forgotten, gives a piquant account of the journey made by a party of American ladies in Africa, and nothing is more common than the European rambles of newly-fledged collegians of the gentler sex. Our marriage laws and customs are changing to meet these new conditions. It will not do to give the husband of the modern woman power to whip his wife, provided that the stick he uses must not be larger than his finger; to give him the right to will away her unborn child; to have control over her property; and, in the state, to make all the laws under which she is to live, adjudicate all her penalties, try her before juries of men, conduct her to prison under the care of men, cast the ballot for her, and in general hold her in the estate of a perpetual minor. It will not do to let the modern man determine the "age of consent," settle the penalties that men shall suffer whose indignities and outrages toward women are worse to their victims than death, and by his exclusive power to make all laws and choose all officers, judicial and executive, to have his own case wholly in his own hands. To continue this method is to make it as hard as possible for men to do right, and as easy as possible for them to do wrong, the magnificent possibilities of manly character being best prophesied from the fact that under such a system so many men are good and gracious.

My theory of marriage in its relation to society would give this postulate: Husband and wife are one, and that one is—husband and wife. I believe they will never come to the heights of purity, of power and peace, for which they were designed in heaven, until this better law prevails:

"Two heads in council, two beside the hearth,
Two in the tangled business of the world,
Two in the liberal offices of life;
Two plummets dropt for one to sound the abyss
Of science and the secrets of the mind."

Poets are prophets, and the greatest poet of our time has set humanity's great goal before us, only to be gained

"When reign the world's great bridals, chaste and calm."

One-half the world for the wife—an undivided half apiece for wife and husband; co-education to mate them on the plane of mind, equal property rights to make her God's own free woman, not coerced into marriage for the sake of a support, nor a bond-slave after she is married, who asks her master for the price of a paper of pins and gives him back the change, or, if a petted favorite, owing her lease of purse wholly to his will and never to her right; free to go her honored and self-respecting way as a maiden *in perpetuo* rather than marry a man whose deterioration through the alcohol and nicotine habits is a menace to herself and the descendants that such a marriage must have invoked—these are the outlooks of the future that shall make the marriage system, never a failure since it became monogamic, an assured, a permanent, a paradisiacal success.

In that day the wife shall surrender at marriage no right not equally surrendered by the husband—not even her own name. Emile Girardin, that keen-sighted writer of France, says that it is so much easier, for obvious reasons, to trace ancestry along the mother's line, that historic records have incalculably suffered by the arbitrary relinquishment of her name. Probably the French have hit upon the best expedient, the union of the two. Thus I recall that in Paris my home was with an accomplished lady whose maiden name was Farjon, and whose husband's was Perrot, her visiting-card bearing the inscription, "Madame Eglantine Perrot-Farjon." The growing custom, in this country at least, to give the mother's name to a son or daughter indicates the increasing, though perhaps unconscious, recognition of woman as an equal partner in the marriage sacrament and compact. But the tendency, even among men of intelligence, to sign themselves

"John Jones, wife, child and nurse," as we see it in the registers of fashionable hotels, is a frequent reminder of the pit from which wives are slowly being digged. The man who writes "Mr. John and Mrs. Jane Jones," may be regarded as well on the road to a successful evolution! although "Mr. and Mrs. John Jones" is about the correct thing up to this date. The time will come when the mother's custody of children will constructively be preferred in law to that of the father, on the ground that in a Christian civilization it is safer and more consonant with natural laws.

Last of all and chiefest, the *magnum opus* of Christianity, and Science, which is its handmaid, the wife will have undoubted custody of herself, and, as in all the lower ranges of the animal creation, she will determine the frequency of the investiture of life with form and of love with immortality. My library groans under accumulations of books written by men to teach women the immeasurable iniquity of arresting development in the genesis of a new life, but not one of these volumes contains the remotest suggestion that this responsibility should be at least equally divided between *himself* and *herself*. The untold horrors of this injustice dwarf all others out of sight, and the most hopeless feature of it is the utter unconsciousness with which it is committed. But better days are dawning; the study by women of heredity and prenatal influences is flooding with light the *Via Dolorosa* of the past; and the White Cross army with its equal standard of purity for men and women is moving to its rightful place of leadership among the hosts of men. I believe in uniform national marriage laws, in divorce for one cause only, in legal separation on account of drunkenness, but I would elevate and guard the marriage tie by every guarantee that could make it at the top of society, the most coveted estate of the largest-natured and most endowed, rather than at the bottom, the necessary refuge of the smallest-natured and most dependent woman. Besides all this, in the interest of men, *i. e.*, that their incentives to the best life may be raised to the highest power, I would make women so independent of marriage that men who, by bad habits and niggardly estate, whether physical, mental, or moral, were least adapted to help build a race of human angels, should find the facility with which they now enter its hallowed precincts reduced to the lowest minimum.

THE LAW OF KINDNESS.

I am proud to belong to the Universal Peace Union, and the Massachusetts Society for the Prevention of Cruelty to Animals, and to echo every word uttered by Frances Power Cobbe of England, and George T. Angell of America, those brave defenders of the gentle faith that "Nothing is inexorable but love," and that we are

> "Never to blend our pleasure or our pride
> With sorrow of the meanest thing that feels."

My shepherd collie, "Prohibition" ("Hibbie," for short, and "Hib," for shorter), is a perpetual gospel to me as he reaches out his shaggy paw with a wise look in his eyes that seem to say, "Have patience with me and it shall grow to be a hand."

MY EXPERIENCE WITH GENERAL CONFERENCES.

I have seen three of these courts. The first was in Chicago in 1868, when, dressed in my spick-and-span new traveling suit for Europe, I glanced in through the crowded door of Clark Street Church, where a tremendous debate was going on about lay delegation; but it was nearly time for my train to New York, and this glance was all I had.

The next was in 1880 in Pike's Opera House at Cincinnati. Our National W. C. T. U. had sent a message that year to all the leading ecclesiastical assemblages, respectfully asking for a friendly word from them, and suggesting that they appoint representatives who should attend our National Convention to see what we were doing and bring us words of cheer. In our simplicity, we thought it the most natural thing imaginable thus to bring the work we loved back to the church that had nurtured us and given us our inspiration, and we thoroughly believe that history will declare not only that our purpose was true and good, but that our plan was altogether reasonable. One would have thought, however, that something revolutionary had been proposed, when it was known that my friend, Miss F. Jennie Duty, of Cleveland, and myself were in the Opera House desirous of presenting this message! Grave, dignified clergymen who had always been my friends, looked curiously upon me as if I were, somehow, a little daft. "We have no precedent," they said. "How could you have?" was my answer, "the Crusade was, like the Day of Pentecost, unprecedented. The case is a new one, and your Methodist sisters earnestly believe that you will meet it on its merits."

I will not write here the names of the good Bishops, almost as dear to me as my own brothers, who passed by on the other side, not wishing to commit themselves, also not wishing to hurt my feelings at this crisis. We sought in vain for their advice. Somehow, they were always busy, and never could be seen. Meantime the buzzing went on. Poor Anna Oliver, who was trying to gain recognition as a preacher, seemed hardly more of a black sheep than we two white ribbon women with our harmless little message.

The Temperance Committee, however, treated us well, invited us in to its session, and incorporated in its report a resolution that we desired about communion wine, also made kindly allusion, though not by name, to the W. C. T. U. My noble friend, Bishop Foster, consented to preside at a temperance meeting addressed by me, and stood his ground valiantly, at much cost, I have no doubt, to his prejudices. Some liberal-minded delegates, Dr. Payne, Dr. Theodore L. Flood, and Philip Gillette, a lay delegate from Illinois, flung down the gauntlet for me by introducing a resolution that I should have ten minutes in which to speak before the Conference. And now began the war of words, the opposition being headed, as a matter of course, by Dr. Buckley, who, with his faithful ally, Dr. Daniel Curry, dealt sledge-hammer blows against a man of straw. Two hours or more were expended in the debate, when the call of ayes and noes demanded by Dr. Buckley, showed that two thirds of the Conference favored giving the ten minutes. Dilatory tactics were now resorted to by the conservatives, and adjournment was secured, it being a little after noon. In the interval, I saw that my brave friends were weakening, and they suggested that I send a note saying I would not speak, for as the matter now stood, I had the right to do so, but Dr. Buckley had declared that he would exhaust parliamentary resources to prevent it. I told them that personally I thought it would be wiser to let the question settle itself, and I was neither afraid nor ashamed to stand in my lot and place as a disturber of the peace for the sake of all that I believed was involved in the decision, but seeing that my champions strongly preferred to settle the question peaceably, I compromised the matter and wrote the following:

TUESDAY MORNING, May 18, 1880.

To The General Conference:

HONORED BRETHREN—It is the judgment of many of your members who championed the cause of woman in yesterday's debate (in which judgment I concur), that I would better state to you, with my hearty thanks for the final vote, that I decline to use the hard-earned ten minutes allotted me. Suffer me, however, to explain that, having been sent here as a fraternal visitor by our Woman's National Society, and, moreover, having so often spoken before ecclesiastical bodies upon their earnest invitation, and never having attended a General Conference before, I had no idea of the strong opposition that would be manifested, or I would not have listened to the generous friends who urged the matter on your attention.

Your sister in Christian work,

FRANCES E. WILLARD.

In October, 1887, Anna Gordon and I were at Binghamton, attending the W. C. T. U. Convention of New York State. It was a grand occasion, so many delegates being present that the large church was filled with them. We were entertained in the home of Mrs. Mather, granddaughter of Jonathan Edwards, and while sitting at the breakfast table in her pleasant home, I opened a telegram there handed to me, and read these words:

CHICAGO.

I suppose you know that the Rock River Conference has chosen you one of its lay delegates to the General Conference.

S. A. KEAN.

The tears sprang to my eyes, and turning to my dignified hostess I said: "You can hardly imagine how much this means to me. The dear old Rock River Conference of which my brother was once a member, and many of whose ministers I have known from girlhood, selects me as one of its two lay delegates, and my father's business partner of twenty years ago kindly telegraphs the pleasant news. Why should I not think well of men when they can do things so magnanimous? Every one who voted for me would have given his eye teeth to have gone in my stead, yet they set to work and sent me, just out of brotherly good-will."

Much more after this sort I poured out, in my gratitude and gladness, to the quiet old lady, whose face lighted up as she "rejoiced in my joy."

No one had ever named to me the possibility of such an honor, save that Miss Phebe and Mrs. Franc Elliott (daughter and daughter-in-law of Rev. Dr. Charles Elliott, former editor of the *Central Christian Advocate*, but now deceased) had sent me a letter stating that they thought women should go to the General Conference, as they had for years helped to elect those who did go as lay delegates, and had themselves been chosen alternates, and their names placed without question on General Conference lists. I had always thought that no fair-minded person could have a doubt of their inherent right to go, since women constitute at least two thirds of the church membership, bear more than one half its burdens, and have patiently conceded to the brethren, during all generations, its emoluments and honors.

No more was known to me until, on returning West, I heard that certain lawyers of the contrary part (*i. e.*, well-known opponents of woman's larger recognition in these modern days) had said that I would never be allowed to take my seat. But my friends declared, what I fully believed, that the Discipline was so explicit, that "the wayfaring man, though a fool," could not fail to find its meaning friendly.

In the midst of the contention that came up later on in the papers of my church, I gave myself no anxiety about the subject; indeed, I hold that word, "anxiety," to be altogether atheistic, and have endeavored to weed it out of my vocabulary. "Careful for nothing, and in *everything* a giver of thanks," is what the commonest sort of a Christian is sacredly bound to be, or to become. My invitation was duly sent, my name was on all the published lists of delegates; the author of "Representative Methodists" (containing sketches and portraits of delegates), to be brought out by our official Methodist publishing house, wrote to obtain the necessary data; my Methodist friends in New York not inviting me, I had accepted the assignment to the Oriental Hotel, suggested by Gen. Clinton B. Fisk, and I went to New York a few days before the great Conference was to begin its quadrennial session as the Supreme Court of our church, representing over two millions of Methodists. By this time, Dr. Buckley had taken his position against the admission of women, the tintinnabulation of tongues had set in, and the pent-up pendulosity of pens had fairly burst forth.

I arrived in New York on the Friday previous to the Conference, and wishing to know just what was the best course for me to pursue, I went over to the Opera House where the Conference was to hold its session and inquired for General Fisk, finding him already conferring with grave dignitaries of the church and busy with his duties as chairman of the Committee of Arrangements. He went with Mrs. Carse and me into the Opera House and we took our seats on the platform with the great yawning auditorium before us, empty and dark. He told me there was going to be a vigorous fight, but he thought the women would get in. I asked his advice about sitting with my delegation, assuring him that I would on no account take a wrong attitude toward the controversy. He replied, "Your moral right, there is none to dispute, and if you are ruled out it will be on a pure technicality and not upon the merits of the case. This being true, I advise you to be on hand bright and early the morning that the Conference opens, and if you like, I shall be glad to escort you along the aisle to your place with your Rock River brethren." But there had come to me that morning a disquieting telegram from home; my dear mother had not been well for two or three weeks, but I had received repeated notes in her usual hand and as I knew her cheery spirit and great desire that I should be a member of the Conference, I had gone on with my engagements, knowing that she was in the very best of care, and believing that I should be able to enter on my novel duties. However, on receiving the morning telegram that mother was not very well and Anna Gordon would perhaps better go to her, I telegraphed at once, "Would it not be better for me to go?" That this made it almost a foregone conclusion that I should return to my home, I knew, for my faithful secretaries there would hardly take the risk of telling me not to come when I had so plainly expressed the thought and purpose of doing so. Therefore, I was prepared for the response that soon arrived, "Do not be anxious, but come." And so on Saturday night I took the limited express, for the first time in my life deliberately setting out on a Sabbath day's journey. A few times, chiefly during my travels abroad, I have been under circumstances that seemed to me to justify taking a train on Sunday, but while I would not conceal any such action I should wish to go on record as having the totality of my life opposed to Sunday travel. The way was long and dreary, but closely filled in with reading and writing, the unfailing solace of all my years since childhood. It was on this trip, however, that for the first time in my life of travel I had a downright ill-mannered *vis-a-vis*.

My kindest of neighbors in the "annex," as we call the cottage that my sister built joining our own, were at the depot in Chicago. Helen L. Hood, that staunch white ribboner of Illinois, reached out her strong hand to me before I left the platform of the car, and said, "Your mother is better." I think no words were ever sweeter of all that I have heard. Now followed a month in which I exchanged the busy and constantly varied activities of a temperance reformer for the sacred quiet of my mother's sick-room. I had never seen her so ill, but she was, as always, entirely self-possessed. We had a council of physicians and she went through the diagnosis with even smiling cheerfulness, saying, "I think I shall get well, but I am not at all afraid to die." Little by little she crept up again under the skillful care of that noble woman, Dr. Mary McCrillis, who by day and night was with us in our trouble.

Anna Gordon arrived in New York the day I left, and remained, at my request, until the great question was decided, sending me constant bulletins from the Opera House box where General Fisk, with his customary thoughtfulness, had assigned her a seat. Nothing could exceed my surprise when I learned that our good bench of Bishops had prejudged the entire case in their opening address. Only the cold type of the Associated Press dispatch, giving their language, could have made me believe this possible. Anna Gordon pictured the scene dramatically, catching on the wing many of the bright turns and arguments of the debaters, and seeming full of expectation that the women would carry the day. She wrote that there was unrivaled commotion, that our side felt confident, that friends were urgent for my return and strongly counseled it, but without saying anything to my mother, who is so self-sacrificing that I knew she would tell me, "By all means go back, my child," I fully determined that I would have nothing to do with the controversy, directly or indirectly, and so in great quietness of spirit awaited the result. When the morning *Inter Ocean* was thrown on the steps, I would refrain for some time from going after it, and mother asked no questions. But when I read that the lay delegates gave a majority against the admission of women, and remembered that the vote of women, as they well knew, at the time of the debate on the eligibility of the laity to the General Conference, had forced open its doors to the laymen who now deliberately voted to exclude women, I had no more spirit in me. Once more it was a case of "Thou, too, Brutus!" That the Bishops should have "left us lamenting," grieved me, but when the lay delegates did the same, I said in my heart, "Once more the action of my fellow mortals weans me from love of life, and by so doing they have doubtless helped me more than their generosity of action could possibly have done." However, I lost no sleep and wasted no tears over the curious transaction, and I confidently predict that we five women, whose election was thus disavowed, will have more enviable places in history than any who opposed us on those memorable days. Of them it will be written, while doubtless they did not so intend, that they committed an injustice; of us, only that in silence we endured it.

The champions of equality made a splendid record, of which they will be prouder with each added year. They are forerunners of that grander, because more equitable, polity that shall yet glorify our Methodism when in her law, as in Christ's gospel, there shall be "Neither male nor female."

SOCIETIES OF CHRISTIAN ENDEAVOR.

The wonder to me has long been why ministers don't strike! They are, beyond all others, the burdened brain-workers of the world. Like the work of women, theirs is never done. At everybody's beck and call for the greatest variety of counsel that human ingenuity can devise or prodigious power supply, the ministers are so well entitled to complain, that the fact of their not doing so is proof positive of their superhuman grace. More unreasonable than all the other demands upon them in these enlightened days is, to my thinking, the demand for a Sunday-evening sermon. When books were few and guiding intellects were fewer, when the present affluence of home-life was unknown, it may have been, and very likely was, essential to require the pastor to serve up two sermons weekly. But, surely, under modern conditions it is cruel as well as inconsistent to make such a requisition. What shall we substitute? is the problem now before us. To this, it seems to me, the Christian Endeavor Societies afford an admirable solution. The elders do not, as a rule, largely make up an evening audience, and the younger ones may here find a field for the exercise of their constantly increasing experience and zeal. Missionary meetings, home and foreign, for which the Endeavor Society is held responsible, at stated intervals; temperance meetings ditto; Bible readings, praise services, Sunday-school concerts—may not these be the beginning of a new outlook for the overworked pastors and a blessedly increased activity of the pews?

GOD AND MY HEART.

It was one night in June, 1859. I was nineteen years old and was lying on my bed in my home at Evanston, Ill., ill with typhoid fever. The doctor had said that the crisis would soon arrive, and I had overheard his words. Mother was watching in the next room. My whole soul was intent, as two voices seemed to speak within me, one of them saying, "My child, give me thy heart. I called thee long by joy, I call thee now by chastisement; but I have called thee always and only because I love thee with an everlasting love."

The other said, "Surely you who are so resolute and strong will not break down now because of physical feebleness. You are a reasoner, and never yet were you convinced of the reasonableness of Christianity. Hold out now and you will feel when you get well just as you used to feel."

One presence was to me warm, sunny, safe, with an impression as of snowy wings; the other cold, dismal, dark, with the flutter of a bat. The controversy did not seem brief; in my weakness such a strain would doubtless appear longer than it was. But at last, solemnly, and with my whole heart, I said, not in spoken words, but in the deeper language of consciousness,

"If God lets me get well I'll try to be a Christian girl." But this resolve did not bring peace. "You must at once declare this resolution," said the inward voice.

Strange as it seems, and complete as had always been my frankness toward my dear mother, far beyond what is usual even between mother and child, it cost me a greater humbling of my pride to tell her than the resolution had cost of self-surrender, or than any other utterance of my whole life has involved. After a hard battle, in which I lifted up my soul to God for strength, I faintly called her from the next room, and said,

"Mother, I wish to tell you that if God lets me get well I'll try to be a Christian girl."

She took my hand, knelt beside my bed, and softly wept, and prayed. I then turned my face to the wall and sweetly slept.

That winter we had revival services in the old Methodist church at Evanston. Doctor (now Bishop) Foster was president of the university, and his sermons, with those of Doctors Dempster, Bannister, and others, deeply stirred my heart. I had convalesced slowly and spent several weeks at Forest Home, so these meetings seemed to be my first public opportunity of declaring my new allegiance. The very earliest invitation to go forward, kneel at the altar and be prayed for, was heeded by me. Waiting for no one, counseling with no one, I went alone along the aisle with my heart beating so loud that I thought I could see as well as hear it beat, as I moved forward. One of the most timid, shrinking, and sensitive of natures, what it meant to me to go forward thus, with my student friends gazing upon me, can never be told. I had been known as "skeptical," and prayers (of which I then spoke lightly) had been asked for me in the church the year before. For fourteen nights in succession I thus knelt at the altar, expecting some utter transformation—some portion of heaven to be placed in my inmost heart, as I have seen the box of valuables placed in the corner-stone of a building and firmly set, plastered over and fixed in its place for ever. This is what I had determined must be done, and was loath to give it up. I prayed and agonized, but what I sought did not occur.

One night when I returned to my room baffled, weary and discouraged, and knelt beside my bed, it came to me quietly that this was not the way; that my "conversion," my "turning about," my religious experience (*re-ligare*, to bind again), had reached its crisis on that summer night when I said "yes," to God. A quiet certitude of this pervaded my consciousness, and the next night I told the public congregation so, gave my name to the church as a probationer, and after holding this relation for a year — waiting for my sister Mary, who joined later, to pass her six months' probation, I was baptized and joined the church, May 5, 1861, "in full connection." Meanwhile I had regularly led, since that memorable June, a prayerful life — which I had not done for some months previous to that time; studied my Bible, and, as I believe, evinced by my daily life that I was taking counsel of the heavenly powers. Prayer-meeting, class-meeting (in which Rev. Dr. Hemenway was my beloved leader), and church services were most pleasant to me, and I became an active worker, seeking to lead others to Christ. I had learned to think of and believe in God in terms of Jesus Christ. This had always been my difficulty, as I believe it is that of so many. It seems to me that by nature all spiritually-disposed people (and with the exception of about six months of my life, I was always strongly that) are Unitarians, and my chief mental difficulty has always been, and is to-day, after all these years, to adjust myself to the idea of "Three in one" and "One in three." But, while I will not judge others, there is for me no final rest, except as I translate the concept of God into the nomenclature and personality of the New Testament. What Paul says of Christ, is what I say; the love John felt, it is my dearest wish to cherish.

Five years passed by, during which I grew to love more and more the house of God and the fellowship of the blessed Christian people who were my brothers and sisters in the church. The first bereavement of my life came to me about three years after I was a Christian, in the loss of my only sister, Mary, whose life-long companionship had been to me a living epistle of conscientiousness and spirituality. In her death she talked of Christ as "one who held her by the hand," and she left us with a smile fresh from the upper glory. A great spiritual uplift came to me then, and her last message, "Sister, I want you to tell everybody to be good," was like a perfume and a prophecy within my soul. This was in 1862. In 1866 Mrs. Bishop Hamline came to our

PICTURESQUE EVANSTON.

village and we were closely associated in the work of the "American Methodist Ladies' Centennial Association" that built Heck Hall. This saintly woman placed in my hands the "Life of Hester Ann Rogers," "Life of Carvosso," "Life of Mrs. Fletcher," Wesley's "Sermons on Christian Perfection," and Mrs. Palmer's "Guide to Holiness." I had never seen any of these books before, but had read Peck's "Central Idea of Christianity" and been greatly interested in it. I had also heard saintly testimony in prayer-meeting, and, in a general way, believed in the doctrine of holiness. But my reading of these books, my talks and prayers with Mrs. Hamline, that modern Mrs. Fletcher, deeply impressed me. I began to desire and pray for holiness of heart. Soon after this, Dr. and Mrs. Phebe Palmer came to Evanston as guests of Mrs. Hamline, and for weeks they held meetings in our church. This was in the winter of 1866; the precise date I can not give. One evening, early in their meetings, when Mrs. Palmer had spoken with marvelous clearness and power, and at the close, those desirous of entering into the higher Christian life had been asked to kneel at the altar, another crisis came to me. It was not so tremendous as the first, but it was one that solemnly impressed my spirit. My dear father and a friend whom we all loved and honored, sat between me and the aisle—both Christian men and greatly reverenced by me. My mother sat beyond me. None of them moved. At last I turned to my mother (who was converted and joined the church when she was only twelve years old) and whispered, "Will you go with me to the altar?" She did not hesitate a moment, and the two gentlemen moved out of the pew to let us pass, but did not go themselves.* Kneeling in utter self-abandonment, I consecrated myself anew to God.

My chief besetments were, as I thought, a speculative mind, a hasty temper, a too ready tongue, and the purpose to be a celebrated person. But in that hour of sincere self-examination I felt humiliated to find that the simple bits of jewelry I wore, gold buttons, rings and pin, all of them plain and "quiet" in their style, came up to me as the separating causes between my spirit and my Saviour. All this seemed so unworthy of that sacred

*A little later my father did publicly ask prayers, though an officer in the church and a Christian from early manhood. His remarkable experience, and triumphant death in 1868 I have described in "The Guide to Holiness."

hour that I thought at first it was a mere temptation. But the sense of it remained so strong that I unconditionally yielded my pretty little jewels and great peace came to my soul. I can not describe the deep welling up of joy that gradually possessed me. I was utterly free from care. I was blithe as a bird that is good for nothing except to sing. I did not ask myself, "Is this my duty?" but just intuitively *knew* what I was called upon to do. The conscious, emotional presence of Christ through the Holy Spirit held me. I ran about upon His errands "just for love." Life was a halcyon day. All my friends knew and noticed the change, and I would not like to write down the lovely things some of them said to me; but they did me no harm, for I was shut in with the Lord. And yet, just then, there came, all unintended and unlooked for, an experience of what I did not then call sin, which I now believe to have been wrong. My own realization of it was, however, so imperfect that it did not mar my loyalty to Christ. In this holy, happy state, I engaged to go from Evanston to Lima, New York, and become preceptress of Genesee Wesleyan Seminary. Just before leaving, my honored friend, Dr. ———, who was visiting Governor Evans, said to me one evening:

"Sister Frank, there is a strange state of things at Lima. The Free Methodists have done great harm in Western New York by their excesses in the doctrine and experience of holiness. You know I believe thoroughly in and profess it, but just now our church has suffered so much from the 'Nazarites,' as they are called, that I fear if you speak and act in this cause as zealously at Lima as you do here it may make trouble. Hold to the experience, but be very careful in statement."

So I went to Lima with these thoughts, and there, quite soon, in a prayer-meeting in the old Seminary Chapel, my good friend, Professor ———, whose subsequent experience has been such a blessed heritage to Christians, replied to a student who rose to inquire about holiness: "It is a subject we do not mention here."

Young and docile-minded as I was, and revering those two great and true men, I "kept still" until I soon found I had nothing in particular to keep still about. The experience left me. But I think my pupils of that year will bear me witness that for their conversion and spiritual upbuilding I was constantly at work.

Since then I have sat at the feet of every teacher of holiness whom I could reach; have read their books and compared their views. I love and reverence and am greatly drawn toward all, and never feel out of harmony with their spirit. Wonderful uplifts come to me as I pass on, clearer views of the life of God in the soul of man. Indeed, it is the *only life*, and all my being sets toward it as the rivers toward the sea. Celestial things grow dearer to me; the love of God is steadfast in my soul; the habitudes of a disciple sit more easily upon me; tenderness toward humanity and the lower orders of being increases with the years. In the temperance, labor and woman questions I see the stirring of Christ's heart; in the comradeship of Christian work my spirit takes delight, and prayer has become my atmosphere. But that sweet pervasiveness, that heaven in the soul, of which I came to know in Mrs. Palmer's meeting, I do not feel. I love too well the good words of the good concerning what I do; I have not the control of tongue and temper that I ought to have, I do not answer to a good conscience in the matter of taking sufficient physical exercise and the sweet south wind of love has not yet thawed out the ice-cake of selfishness from my breast. But God knows that I constantly lift up my heart for conquest over all these evils, and my life is calm and peaceful. Just as frankly as I "think them over," have I here written down the outline phenomena of my spiritual life, hoping that it may do good and not evil to those who read. I am a strictly loyal and orthodox Methodist, but I find great good in all religions and in the writings of those lofty and beautiful moralists who are building better than they know, and all of whose precepts blossom from the rich soil of the New Testament. No word of faith in God or love toward man is alien to my sympathy. The classic ethics of Marcus Aurelius are dear to me, and I have carried in my traveling outfit not only à Kempis and Havergal but Epictetus and Plato. The mysticism of Fénelon and Guyon, the sermons of Henry Drummond and Beecher, the lofty precepts of Ralph Waldo Emerson, all help me up and onward. I am an eclectic in religious reading, friendship and inspiration. My wide relationships and constant journeyings would have made me so had I not had the natural hospitality of mind that leads to this estate. But, like the bee that gathers from many fragrant gardens, but flies home with his varied gains to the same friendly and familiar hive, so I fly home to the sweetness and sanctity of the old faith that has been my shelter and solace so long.

"Lord Jesus, receive my spirit," is the deepest voice out of my soul. Receive it every instant, voluntarily given back to Thyself, and receive it in the hour when I drop this earthly mantle that I wear to-day, and pass onward to the world invisible, but doubtless not far off.

All my life I have heard of the old stone church—the church of my ancestors—founded in 1815, two miles north of Churchville, my place of birth, which is fifteen miles west of Rochester, N. Y. In 1854 I had seen it when my sister and I came from Wisconsin, as "prairie girls," to visit the old-fashioned home-nest; I had then entered the antiquated auditorium, that with its galleries could hardly seat three hundred persons. Much had I wondered at its pulpit perched on high, and a solemn awe had struck my heart as my Grandfather Hill, revered and venerable, gave his testimony on the Sabbath day, and my tall, gentle Uncle James, his son, extolled the grace of Christ. Ever since I began to speak in public, eighteen years ago, I had greatly wished to declare within those hallowed and historic walls, my loyalty to Him. But not until April, 1888, did my time come. At my request, dear mother penciled her recollections a few days earlier for my reference; they read as follows:

The people that came from Vermont and founded what was then called "Gilman settlement," brought their religion with them.

Our family came in the spring of 1816, and meetings were held in the block-house which was our home, as well as in other private houses in the winter and in barns during the summer. Sometimes, service was held in the "log school-house," in the "stone school-house," and in the "Bishop school-house." Elder Jonathan Hinkley was our first pastor, and the old stone church was built in 1832. John Hill, my father, J. F. Willard, your father, James Hill, your uncle, and many others, were those who, after consultation, decided to build this house of worship, and it was not long before it was completed. In that church the last tribute has been paid and the final eulogy pronounced over the dearly loved and tenderly revered, when I was far away; tears have fallen that I could not witness, and hearts have been wrung with grief in which I participated at a distance and alone. Here I have heard my father's voice in prayer and praise, and I remember to have heard my dear mother in monthly meeting with much emotion bear testimony to her love to Christ, and my brother James with impressive earnestness, speak of his firm conviction that there is no "other name either in Heaven or among men" whereby we must be saved. Many others have I here heard speak of their earnest, abiding, uplifting trust in the world's Redeemer. All of my father's family and nearly all of your grandfather Willard's, belonged to that old church, and it is the sacred shrine of our two households and of many others.

My mother does not here record what she has often told me, that in 1829 my father, then a handsome, popular young man, who, while he was noted for good morals, had never manifested any interest in Christianity, had gone to the neighborhood prayer-meeting in the "stone school-house," now demolished, and rising in his place had asked for prayers. But so set back were the people that for a moment nobody moved, whereupon he fell on his knees in the midst of the group and poured out his soul with strong crying and tears. This was in the midst of "harvest time," that busiest season of the Western New York farmer, but so great was the resulting interest that a "reformation" broke out, involving more than thirty heads of families. Almost without exception, the older households of Willard and Hill, my father's and mother's kindred, were already members, and from that time on, the younger were strong adherents of the faith. It was a non-sectarian denomination, gathered from Presbyterian, Baptist, Methodist and Unitarian, and called by the broadest possible name, "The Church of God in Ogden." The neighborhood was of the best; a profane word would have marked a man as "below the pauper line," in brain and social status. A drunkard was unknown. My father's only brother, Zophar Willard, now seventy-nine years old, for sixty years a leader in the community, assures me that he never saw a drunken man until he was seventeen, and that one was an importation. My uncle says of Grandfather Hill: "He was a wonderful exhorter and when imbued with the Holy Spirit, the tears would run down his cheeks and a holy unction inspired his very tones. He was never satisfied except when thus broken down by the Spirit. Once he felt that he was not as helpful in the meetings as he wished to be and he went home. That night the power of God rested so mightily upon him that his whole household, wife and eight children, joined with him in a most memorable prayer-meeting. He was a marvelous man in prayer. His wife was one of the Lord's saints. She was goodness itself and a mighty power in talking." She was so spiritually-minded that she would talk out loud to herself about God's beautiful world, for she seemed to hear Him breathing in all His works. Her son James was herself over again, and his daughter Morilla was so spiritual that she seemed not to belong to this world and when she died she was perfectly aware of the presence of angels in her room. My gentle Grandfather, Oliver A. Willard, was the first, Uncle James Hill, second, and Cousin Henry Dusinbury, third and last clerk, of the Old Stone Church. Uncle Zophar Willard, Uncle Ward Hall, Cousins John and Sheldon Hill were all officially connected with it.

The 16th of April, 1888, was calm and sunshiny. Uncle Willard's beautiful home on the hill in the suburbs of Churchville gave us, as so often, its quiet shelter, and though we missed the loving smile, the wit and brightness of dear Aunt Caroline, his widowed sister, and so long his home-maker, we were thoroughly content in the care of the noble, genial uncle, who had done us good and not evil all the days of our lives. In the morning we went with him to the Congregational church in the village, of which he has so long been the leading spirit, and listened to the gifted young minister in whom his heart rejoiced. After dinner we drove "up North," where we had delightful calls in the pleasant, well-to-do homes of Aunt Sarah Hill Hall and Cousin Sarah Gilman Dusinbury. At three o'clock we all gathered at the church, a quaint old structure standing at the foot of a long, graceful slope on the top of which is the picturesque Willard homestead of auld lang syne. The present residents of the home, Mr. and Mrs. Way, with Cousin Sarah, had brightened and beautified the old sanctuary with an improvised setting for the platform, of carpet, easy chairs and potted plants. All the relatives and neighbors who yet remain, with many new ones, besides youth and maiden, boy and girl, not of our circle, packed the little church, and, Uncle Willard presiding, we sang the old hymns so often echoed by those walls from voices long since silent. "How firm a foundation, ye saints of the Lord," "Guide me, O Thou great Jehovah," and "There is a land of pure delight," seemed to me tenderly to invoke the spirit of the sacred past. Then in rich tones full of pathos, my Cousin Sarah read the ninetieth Psalm, "Lord, thou hast been our dwelling place in all generations," and the Churchville minister, Rev. Mr. McConnell, led in prayer with a brother's sympathy for all that the hour signified to us. After that I frankly told the kind people all my heart, taking, "The Master is come and calleth for thee," as a text, and setting what I tried to say to the key of

"We are traveling home to God,
In the way our fathers trod."

I told them what Christianity meant to my heart, and what I believed it meant to custom and law, to society and government. It stirred my spirit deeply as I realized in some small measure what it signified to testify as one of the cloud of witnesses who belonged to the same household of faith with those who within these walls had found and taught the unsearchable riches of Christ. Born of a Christian race, bred in a Christian home, I dedicated myself anew in the Old Stone Church that day to Christ and to His Gospel, vowing that by His grace I would be in this and every world where I might live, a woman whom the Lord could trust.

THE GOSPEL OF HEALTH.

It was my remarkably good fortune to be born of parents who were clean from the alcohol and tobacco taint, and, so far as I can trace my ancestry through several generations, there was but one intemperate person in the ranks, and he was a distant relative out of the direct line. It was also my unspeakable privilege, being "only a girl," to enjoy the utmost freedom from fashionable restraints up to my seventeenth year. Clad during three fourths of the year in flannel suits, not unlike those worn at "gymnastics" now by young lady collegians, and spending most of my time in the open air, the companion in work as well as in sport of my only brother, I knew much more about handling rake and hoe than I did of frying-pan and needle; knew the name and use of every implement used by carpenter and joiner; could chase the sheep all day and never tire; had a good knowledge of farming, gardening, and the like; was an enthusiastic poultry raiser, and by means of this natural, outdoor life, eight or nine hours' sleep in twenty-four, a sensible manner of dress, and the plain fare of bread and butter, vegetables, eggs, milk, fruit and fowl, was enabled to "store up electricity" for the time to come.

My parents lived five years at Oberlin before I was seven years of age, at the time when "Grahamites" were popular, and they became indoctrinated with many of the ideas of Dr. Jennings, whose "Water Cure" book my father was fond of reading. As a result, the three children were each promised a library, to cost $100, if we would not touch tea or coffee until we became of age. Subsequently I used both for years, very moderately, but have now almost discarded them. A physician was an unknown visitant to our home in early days. I have no recollection of such a personage being called for me before I was fourteen, and although my mother says that, when an infant, I was the feeblest of her children, I have outlived all the family except herself. My father died in his sixty-third year, and my mother is now in her eighty-fifth, her grandmother having lived to be nearly ninety-seven, and the ancestors on both sides being remarkable for their longevity.

I never saw the inside of a school-house until near my teens, but was encouraged to read and study somewhat at home, and always lived in an intellectual atmosphere, my parents and our few friends and neighbors being persons of education and earnestness of purpose. Although my first school was in a country district, the teacher was a graduate of Yale, and had been for years a classical tutor in Oberlin College. My parents were of Puritanical training as to Sabbath observance, and I count its rhythmic period of rest, as well as the late beginning of my school days, an element in the health antecedents here enumerated. I have written thus in detail of what might be popularly termed the "indirect reasons" for my life-long good health, because my study of the temperance question teaches me that heredity and early training are the most direct "procuring causes" of physical soundness.

I am now in my fiftieth year, and though, since sharing the great and varied disabilities of a more conventional life, I have had two acute illnesses and several slight ones, my health is so uniform that I have often laughingly told my friends I had composed the first line of my "great epic," and it is this:

"Painless, in a world of pain."

The chief wonder of my life is that I dare to have so good a time, both physically, mentally and religiously. I have swung like a pendulum through my years, "without haste, without rest." What it would be to have an idle hour I find it hard to fancy. With no headache, why should I not think "right straight ahead"? My whole life has been spent in intellectual activities, having begun to teach when about twenty years of age, and having pursued that difficult avocation with no set-back or breakdown until I dedicated myself to the Temperance Reform in 1874. (I should except about two years and a half of hard study, writing and travel in Europe and the East between 1868 and 1870.) In the last twelve years I have been perpetually "on the road," going 15,000 to 20,000 miles per year, visiting in 1883 every state and territory in the Union and holding a meeting once per day on an average throughout the entire period. It has been my custom to write articles and letters and plan work, all day long on the cars, being thus constantly employed, and then to give an address at night.

Now, I am aware that this is not a hygienic mode of procedure, and that to breathe car-air and audience-atmosphere, year in and year out, is not conducive to the best development. But it was the only way for me to reach the one thousand towns set as my "stint" (a farm fashion we had, this of "doing our stint," persisted in as an inherited tendency), and feeling so adequate to the day's doings, I went steadily on, taking the opportunity to recline in the quiet of my apartment, between the meetings, stating to my friends that visiting was impossible to me, and making it an invariable rule to go directly from the platform to my room. Here a cup of bread and milk, a cracker, or a few spoonfuls of beef-tea were taken in order to set up a counteraction to the movements of the brain, and I went to sleep a few minutes after going to my room, usually getting eight hours, in every twenty-four, of "tired nature's sweet restorer." A bright Chicago woman said to me when I told her this, "You acted according to the proverb, 'He who fights and runs away, may live to fight another day,' for I interpret that to mean, 'He who runs away promptly at nightfall from the day's warfare will live to plunge into the fight next morning, and so on from year to year, and will be a victor always.'"

My rising hour has long been from seven to half-past (I wish it were earlier) and retiring anywhere from half-past seven to half-past nine, but when traveling it has been about ten. I regard that hour as the dead line of recuperation, vigor and sustained mental activity. Eight hours of writing and study, all of them between breakfast and tea, has been my rule. After the evening meal at six o'clock I will not work — lecturing, of course, excepted. In this field I have studied the non-dramatic style, because it is less wearing and fully as well adapted to purposes of information and conviction. Illustrations can be used that involve but little acting, thus keeping the circulation normal, avoiding the exposures that attend perspiration, and the reaction resulting from undue fatigue.

My manner of life has recently been changed from peripatetic to stationary, and my purpose is, for the next ten years at least, should God spare my life so long, to live in my quiet cottage home at Evanston, in the suburbs of Chicago, with my mother and a dozen secretaries, and help to spread the temperance propaganda by pen instead of voice. I expect, as a rule, to sit at my desk from 8:30 or 9:00 A. M., until 6:00 P. M., daily, with a half-hour's interval from 12:30 to 1:00 o'clock, with the exception of an outing of about half an hour. The tricycle for open air purposes and Dr. Dio Lewis's home exerciser within doors, are my basis of gymnastic operations. Walking I delighted in when I could go unimpeded; but from the sorrowful day when my hair was first twisted up and long skirt twisted down, I have never enjoyed that noble form of exercise, and I have met very few women in this country who really walk at all. Wrigglers, hobblers, amblers, and gliders I am familiar with among the ways of women, but walking is an art hereditarily lost to our sex.

"'Tis true, 'tis pity, and pity 'tis, 'tis true!"

I never touch the pen after tea, and ten o'clock finds our house dark as a pocket, silent as a tomb, and restful as a cradle. To this single fact more than all others, excepting fortunate inheritance, I attribute my life-long good health and cheery spirits.

I have not jotted down these personal items because I think my methods specially noteworthy or by any means faultless. Hoping that we may learn the health decalogue of our Heavenly Father so thoroughly, and be so loyal to it that we shall all become as hearty and as happy as, I am sure by the analogies of Nature and the teachings of grace, He meant us to be, I hereby declare myself willing to live a century and work right on.

But I must confess that after my long day's task with the pen, I say to myself often, "If I could put on a hat, button a coat around me, and step off freely, how delightful a walk would be." But no; there are intricate preliminaries before a woman can do anything so simple as take a constitutional. In my own case, the easy wrapper that I wear at my work must be changed for a street dress, with its long, heavy skirt; the slippers, for shoes to be buttoned up; a bonnet affording no protection from light, wind, or observation, must be "tastefully" put on; tight-fitting gloves drawn to their places, and then only, with skirts to be lifted at every step until one's knees grow weary, the airing may begin. A man would have two things to do—put on his coat and crowd a hat over his eyes; a woman has three articles to take off (wrapper and slippers), dress to draw on, collar and cuffs to adjust and pin, shoes to button, wrap to fasten, bonnet to tie, and then all of their burdens and constrictions to endure.

So, for the thousandth time, I return to my room, actually too tired to "get ready" and then "get over the ground," though Lake Michigan's splendid expanse stretches away to the east, and there are cool, shady nooks, and tempting by-ways all about me. I recognize joyfully the progress we have made since I was a student, when no girl was really "stylish" who wore less than eight white skirts trailing on the ground after her; but how slowly we move when women of refinement will wear bustles, lace themselves as of old, pinch hands and feet, bare their heads to the blast that their tufts of bonnets may be "like the rest," and simper their criticisms on "dress reform." Near me on the walls of my study hang Annie Jenness-Miller's picture and engravings of her new costumes. I look up at them with a prayerful heart, saying, "How long, O Lord, how long?"

Instead of the walk I would like to take, had I the old-time conditions—the modest, simple, short dress, loose jacket, and broad-rimmed hat of auld lang syne—I pen this jeremiad, and bid God-speed to the earnest-hearted woman who, in roaring Gotham, plans for us women a costume that hints at better days.

"PROVE ALL THINGS."

I am often asked what I think about the mental method, mind-cure, Christian science, or whatever may be the most appropriate term, and I have been warned repeatedly against it by excellent and trusted friends. However, I cannot see in it the danger that many do. We live in a strangely materialistic age, when thought is declared to be a secretion of the brain, and revelation looked upon as nothing but a myth. Thousands of well intentioned persons had come to the end of the rope and were beating their heads against a stone wall, finding no mode of egress into the upper air of spirituality and faith. It seems to me that just because the world had gone so far, and had so largely become a victim to the theory that only seeing is believing, the Heavenly Powers brought in this great reaction, which declared that the invisible is all and in all, that thoughts are the real things and things are but effervescent shadows; that there is no escape from what is infinitely good and infinitely immanent in everything created; that evil is a negation and must pass away; that to be carnally minded is death, but to be spiritually minded is life and peace. I have never studied the question seriously, because I have not had the time, but from conversation with experts in this study, who are also among the best men and women I have ever known, I have certainly felt that it would be disloyalty to God and to humanity for me to speak against this new era. That some who have entered upon it are not genuine; that some cases of cure are not actual, must necessarily be, in so great a movement; there must be a counterfeit beside the real, but I am confident that if Christians will take what is good in this new evangel and eschew what is evil, it may become a mighty power for the triumph of Him who said: "My words are spirit and they are life."

Something analogous to this seems to be true of theosophy, and the occult studies that have come to us from those wonderful religions of the East, that furnished the soil out of which grew the tree of life—Christianity. "God hath not left Himself without a witness" anywhere. A philosophy that takes immortality as its major premise must conduct toward a good life, as opposed to the materialism that says, "I was not—I lived and loved—I am not"—the saddest epitaph ever penned.

COMPANIONSHIPS.

If I have a virtue in the world, it is loyalty to old memories and old friends, and nothing rejoices me so much as to have this trait believed in by those who walk with me the path of life. One dear lady who had been my teacher thirty years before, died in 1886, and her son wrote me that she had mentioned to him in her last days, her belief that I would gladly write the notice for our church paper. The request came to me with a sense of solid satisfaction that she had so believed in me when we had hardly once met since I was her scholar in the little district school near Forest Home. It did my heart good to turn aside from my pressing cares to write the *In Memoriam* she had desired.

With my naturally adventurous disposition I fear that but for a strenuously guarded girlhood I might have wandered into hopeless unbelief. But I recall only one reckless friend in all my life, and I was with her but a single term at school. Christian women have been my constant and intimate associates throughout my pilgrimage and Christian men have been like loyal brothers to me always. Beyond every other influence outside my home, I reckon that of a circle within which I have moved for well-nigh fifty years, made up of persons who were chaste, totally abstinent, truth-telling, philanthropic and devout.

"Tell me with whom thou goest and I'll tell thee what thou doest." No precept was ever more frequently repeated and enforced by my parents than this. In guarding Mary and me from illiterate and harmful associations my father evinced a solicitude that many of his friends considered morbid. But he would smile and say, "These are 'Two forest nymphs that dwell in the depth of the woodland shade,' and I propose to keep them *innocent.*" So we never went anywhere except with our parents until I was sixteen, and almost never, after that, until fully fledged and flown. Even my brother was eighteen years of age before he ever spent an evening away from home. Around the fireside we were always busy with books, pencils and plans until the early hour of bed-time came. We were literally never left alone with children or work people ;* there was always quiet but careful supervision. "Heredity may count for much, but environment is next of kin to destiny ;" these are my mother's words at eighty-four, the outcome of her observant and reflective life. Who, then, have entered the inner circle of my confidence in fifty years? I ask myself and answer with deep thankfulness: All who have done so meant to be good, sought after goodness, lifted their eyes toward the heights rather than lowered them to the level of the depths. Only two persons, one of them a child and one a girl in her early teens, ever said to me things that were calculated to mar the purity of my thoughts in the formative years of my life, and these were neither of them persons who had influence with me or the ability to determine my actions or opinions. To their everlasting honor be it said that the many men and women who worked in our home and on our farm, never tried in word or deed to lead us astray. But I have always felt that he who is forewarned is best forearmed, and wished that my first ideas concerning the mysteries of being had come early to my observant spirit from my dear mother's lips, which were closed by her reticent New England habitudes.

Meanwhile, there was the heart, the ardent, impulsive heart of childhood and of youth, with its perpetual instinct of bestowment, what did it do? I remember with pleasant pain how early, how vigorously and often that truant heart went forth, seeking rest and finding none! I was hardly six years old when the flame of the ideal burned in my breast for a sweet girl of sixteen, Maria Hill by name, daughter of "Secretary Hill," an English gentleman who was a central figure in the College Board at Oberlin. Her coming meant a new world, her going shrouded my little life in gloom, but she never dreamed of this—she only saw an impetuous child whose papa had (as was the custom in those days of the hygienic revival) induced the little one not to eat butter, and paid her a penny a week for such sacrifice, and who was so determined "to give her pennies to Miss Hill" that when the young lady declared that she could on no account accept them, the child flung them after her retreating form upon

*Margaret Ryan, an Irish girl that lived with us for years, was an exception to this rule, but then she was as refined as she was good "and her uncle was Bishop of Limerick!"

the gravel walk and burst out crying. That was my first "heart affair," and I have had fifty since as surely as I had that one. I have had the subtle sense of an affinity for persons of all ages and conditions, for man and woman, youth and maiden, boy and girl. The solar system has for a season seemed to revolve around each one of these beloved objects and for each of them I have endured all stages of the divine disease that was meant, as I believe, to acclimate us to heaven. They pass me now in bright array, my choice procession of immortals; how can I "express unblamed" so much of sweetness and of nobility as they in turn enshrined for me? After Maria Hill the hiatus was long. Nature became my one dear love and for many a youthful year I knew no other, needed none.

Then came the vision of my cousin Mary G., several years my senior, self-poised and gracious, little dreaming of the commotion that her presence stirred in the wayward heart of her Western cousin then in her fifteenth year, who coming back to the old home at the East, met for the first time since infancy a troop of relatives unknown before except by name. My boy cousins I liked, my other girl cousins I loved, but for my cousin Mary I felt nothing less than worship. She had such royal dignity and she knew books and she was good—so I said to myself a thousand times over, but she thought not of my devotion and I was far too shy to tell her. That soft, white hand on mine seemed to complete the circuit that brought me into harmony with the electric tides of God's great universe; life was full to the brim and its rich draught I drank with solemn joy. But in two weeks we came away and the star I would have followed faded to a spent meteor within a year. Next came the sweet-faced blind girl, Carrie, with her gift of music, sending my blithe spirit up to heaven's gate, but soon she went away; then Anna C., the superintendent's daughter, but she liked my sister Mary best and my budding hopes were swiftly nipped; then my blind music teacher, a young married man of beautiful nature, who was wont to make his way alone down to our house, which was a mile from his, and I was wont to watch for him at the gate and go to meet him up the road. But so did sister Mary. and never in the world by voice or sign had he reason to believe that the elder sister's greeting had more back of it than the child-like good cheer of the younger's. Carefully as I had been reared, I had no special sense of sin in dreaming of this young man's loveliness. I knew that he would never be the wiser nor would the woman he loved be grieved; she was my friend and I was hidden utterly from both of them in my eye-and-ear-proof armor woven of mingled cheerfulness and pride. Erelong he, too, went away, and the next enshrined ideal of my life was Marion, "whose soul was like a star and dwelt apart," the high-bred girl with whom in 1857 I contested the palm for scholarship in Milwaukee Female College; then Susie B., the rich merchant's daughter in that same city, who was a very Saint Cecilia to my ardent fancy; and then Maggie H., of early Evanston fame, the "wild girl" of the school, whom I followed to the extent of being a "law unto myself" as to the rules, but from whom I recoiled with absolute rage when without any hint to me she arranged for us to take a surreptitious moonlight horseback ride with Hart, a certain gay Lothario of the University, and his friend Will. Ignorantly I entered into her plot enough to walk out in the College grounds while all the teachers were at prayer-meeting—a thing we had no right to do. But when, in the most shadowed part, two young men rose before us, I dropped her arm and fled back to the college building like a startled fawn. For this affront I refrained from speaking to my *inamorata* for three weeks, but finally made up our difficulty when she admitted that I was right in saying that no "self-respecting girl would ever make a clandestine appointment of any kind with a young man." It was my mother's fear lest this young woman, who was most attractive, would get a stronger hold on me, that led her, after I told the whole story on going back to Forest Home, to determine that she would give my father no rest until he left the farm and came to Evanston to live. Here I met Mary B., for whom my attachment was so great that when she very properly preferred my brother, although I had devotedly desired their union, the loss of her was nothing less than a bereavement, a piteous sorrow for a year and more, as my journals testify, one of the keenest of my life, to which the death of my only sister Mary put a sudden, and as I have always thought, a well-nigh miraculous end, while our sisterly affection has remained intact. Other attachments followed, so much less restful than friendships, that I can not fairly call them by that consoling name. Their objects were good women all, thank God! and the only trouble was not that we loved unwisely, but too well. They are all written in the records of those days. One of them, dating from 1864, led to my trip abroad with all its riches of observation, study, and acquaintance. A more loyal heart never beat than that of Kate A. Jackson, who, though a rich man's daughter, went with me to Lima as a teacher when I was (in 1867) preceptress of Genesee Wesleyan Seminary, and afterward took the French professor's place in Northwestern University, leaving there when I did, in 1874. Her father was founder of the New Jersey Locomotive Works, at Paterson, a sturdy-natured, generous-hearted man, who freely adopted his daughter's suggestion that she and I make a long tour together, for

> "We determinèd *to go abroad,*
> *To go abroad*, strange countries for to see."

We stayed over two years, since which time Kate has spent six years more in foreign lands, but has come home at last, living, with her accomplished sister, Mrs. Dr. Whitely, and that lady's two charming young people, next door to us. There are several other good and gifted women whom I might name as having belonged to my inner circle of affection at some time in my life; but in Anna A. Gordon, a lovely Boston girl, whom I met when conducting revival meetings with Mr. Moody, in 1877, I found the rarest of my intimate friends. For twelve years she has been at once a solace and support in all my undertakings. I call her "Little Heart's-ease," for, as she knows, I have struggled through the depths and come out on their Beulah side; have voyaged through roaring storms to emerge at last in the region of perpetual calm; and as I am so much her senior she seems quite sure to be my loved and *last*.

The loves of women for each other grow more numerous each day, and I have pondered much why these things were. That so little should be said about them surprises me, for they are everywhere. Perhaps the "Maids of Llangollen," (in Wales) afford the most conspicuous example; two women, young and fair, with money and position, who ran away together, refusing all offers to return, and spent their happy days in each other's calm companionship within the home they there proceeded to establish. Tourists visit the spot where they once dwelt, to praise their constancy and sigh for the peace that they enjoyed. In these days, when any capable and careful woman can honorably earn her own support, there is no village that has not its examples of "two heads in counsel," both of which are feminine. Oftentimes these joint-proprietors have been unfortunately married, and so have failed to "better their condition" until, thus clasping hands, they have taken each other "for better or for worse." These are the tokens of a transition age. Drink and tobacco are to-day the great separatists between women and men. Once they used these things together, but woman's evolution has carried her beyond them; man will climb to the same level some day, but meanwhile he thinks he must have his dinners from which woman is excluded and his club-house with whose delights she intermeddleth not. Indeed, the fact that he permits himself fleshly indulgences that he would deprecate in her, makes their planes different, giving him a sense of larger liberty and her an instinct of revulsion. This has gone so far on man's part that a learned writer has a treatise to prove the existence of organic reasons why men were made to drink and smoke, but women not! This opinion sets up a standard that influences the minds of men who do not use these poisons, and thus extends the domain of the most harmful separating force that to-day alienates so many men and women. It is safe to claim that among the leading advocates of woman's advancement, and of an equal standard of chastity for both sexes, we do not find tobacco users or drinkers of beer and wine.

The friendships of women are beautiful and blessed; the loves of women ought not to be, and will not be, when the sacred purposes of the temperance, the labor, and the woman movements are wrought out into the customs of society and the laws of the land. For the highest earthly good that can come to any individual, or home, or state, or to humanity, is told in the poet Thomson's lines:

> "Oh happy they, the happiest of our race,
> Whom gentle stars unite and in one fate,
> Their lives, their fortunes, and their beings blend."

With a belief so orthodox, why did I miss life's crowning joy? Surely a serene heart, now closed forever (on the planet Earth) to love's delirium or delight, may tell its secret for the help of those less way-wise? One of my early friends was wont to call me "Opal," because that jewel has an edge of snow and heart of flame. When I told my dear mother, going home from my first term at Evanston, that I had written thus to Maggie: "I love you more than life, better than God, more than I dread damnation!" that great philosopher exclaimed, "Oh, Frank! pray Heaven you may never love a man!"

But her prayer was not answered — for I have been so fortunate as to fancy, at least, that I loved a man, — nay, more than one.

When I was but fourteen, a brilliant young scientist came on a brief visit to our family. Of course he never knew it, elegant fellow that he was, but for many a day I dreamed dreams and saw visions of which he was the central figure. No one supposed this, not my own mother, even; though I have always claimed that she knew my every thought — however, this was not a thought — only the most occult of dreams! We lived so much alone that I was almost nineteen before the slightest token of interest came to me from beyond the mystic line that a virtuous woman's glances may not cross. This epoch in my history took the form of a carefully written note, sent through the post-office, inviting me to go to a student's entertainment, and the missive came soon after we removed to Evanston. It was passed around as a rare curiosity, and the wisdom of the family was combined in my discreet affirmative reply. I took the young man's arm with feelings akin to terror, for it was the first time in my life. At the evening's close I noticed that he and I were almost the only ones remaining. He said reluctantly, "I beg your pardon, but is it not time for me to take you home?" Alas! the wise ones of the family circle had not supposed it necessary to tell me I must give the signal to return, and I was morbidly afraid of seeming "forward"!

At this distance I understand the situation—I only felt it then. Of a forceful mind and an imperious will, it was not natural for me to fall into a passive attitude toward anybody. Having so long had great Nature for my teacher, and country freedom as my atmosphere, the sudden conventionalities of society set heavily upon me. Without knowing it, I felt that her code did not deal with me justly. Her dictum was that no well-bred, delicate-natured woman would ever let any man living know she had a gentle thought of him until he gave the sign. And I had said in my inmost spirit, not in so many words, but by just such a vow, "You heartless old tyrant of custom, since you have dared thus basely to decree, hazarding the holiest interests of two lives on the perceptions of the one less finely organized, you shall have full measure of obedience," and no actor, no detective, no *alias* ever schooled himself more sedulously to carry out his part, than I did to be utterly impassive, to treat all men alike, with universal calm, with casual good-will, and that alone.

And have men dared, when all these stern defenses were set in array, to speak their potent word to one like me? Yes, but under such conditions it "stands to reason" that most of the messages received must have been perfunctory, the queries coming by letter and being answered by my secretaries with the official statement that I had no time for other than business correspondence. But so high has always been my admiration and respect for any good and true man that never, when I could avoid it, did I permit one of them to pay me the ineffable compliment of an expressed personal preference, unless my heart felt the potentiality, at least, of a response. My mother strictly taught her daughters to do by other women's brothers as they would have them do by theirs, *i. e.*, never through look or word to lead any young man to an avowal of regard that was not mutual. The ingenuities by which our handsome Mary "moved the previous question," that the impending one might be avoided, were far beyond what her plainer sister ever needed to employ, and proved the generosity of Mary's heart—for what tribute to a woman's charms and goodness equals that of the true man who says to her, "It would be the highest happiness this world could yield if I might spend my life with you"? Only the noblest, best instructed natures among women are willing to forego the music of such words.

Per contra, the man who permits himself even the most delicate approach in deeds unaccompanied by the honest, self-committing *words* that honest women always expect to hear in such connection, is not the soul of honor, and his familiarity, however small, should be resented on the instant. "Hands off" is the golden maxim for every genuine girl and for each true gentleman.

All this I say out of a heart that suffered once and to help those as yet untried.

A gifted man (who has made two women happy since) once wrote me on this wise: "Dear friend, methinks your heart deceives you, for when we meet, though you speak kindly, you hardly look at me, and I take this as a token." I replied: "Dear Brother: This is the explanation. I had a clear and direct gaze until much study weakened my eyes, and I protect them now by studying the carpet."

Another, true and loyal, had heard through a near friend of mine that I was supposed to have a special admiration for him, whereupon he wrote a frank letter implying the truth of that hypothesis. My answer was, "Dear Friend: You have had the misfortune to begin at the wrong end of life's most intricate equation; you have assumed the value of the unknown quantity — a sin that hath not forgiveness in this life; no, nor in that which is to come." He sent me back a royal letter, saying he "would never have dared write what he did, but for the encouragement of my friend's words, and he would like to know why I of all women might not help a man out of such a fearful quandary;" indeed, he went farther, and declared that "there was no reason in nature, grace or anything but *sin*, why a woman must stifle her heart, and a man wear his upon his sleeve." But the sphinx that I have always been had spoken once, and there the drama ended and the curtain fell.

In 1861–62, for three-quarters of a year I wore a ring and acknowledged an allegiance based on the supposition that an intellectual comradeship was sure to deepen into unity of heart. How grieved I was over the discovery of my mistake the journals of that epoch could reveal. Of the real romance of my life, unguessed save by a trio of close friends, these pages may not tell. When I have passed from sight I would be glad to have it known, for I believe it might contribute to a better understanding between good men and women. For the rest, I have been blessed with friendships rich, rare, and varied, all lying within the temperate zone of a great heart's geography, which has been called "cold" simply because no Stanley had explored its tropic climate, and set down as "wholly inland" because no adventurous Balboa had viewed its wide Pacific Sea.

DEMERITS.

I wonder if we really know ourselves in respect of discount as well as we do in respect of advantage? It seems equally important that we should, else our undertakings will be out of all proportion to our powers, and failure a foregone conclusion. I have always believed that in a nobler state of society we should help each other by frank and kindly criticism, coupled with equally frank praise, and have held, in the face of steady contradiction from my friends, that Christian people ought thus to help each other here and now.

Probably the most haunting disability of my youth was a hot temper. If, as a child, I stubbed my toe, it was instinctive with me to turn back and administer a vigorous stroke to the object, animate or inanimate, that had caused the accident. A blow for a blow was my invariable rule, but my temper was a swift electric flash, not the slow burning anthracite of sullenness. Indeed, the sulks and blues are both foreign to my natural habitudes. My sister, though vastly more amiable than her older brother and sister, was somewhat inclined to brood, or "mump," as we graceless young ones called it.

I well remember the last time that I ever "struck out," and am ashamed to say it occurred in the first years of my student life at Evanston. My father had a queer way of buying the dresses, bonnets, indeed, almost the entire outfit of his laughters, and continued it until we were well nigh grown up. One winter he brought me home a red worsted hood that I declared I hated with "a hatred and a half," but all the same I had to wear it. We two sisters were wont to dress alike, and while the bright color set off Mary's dark blue eyes and ruddy cheeks, it simply extinguished what little "looks" I had, and some of my school-mates made fun of my appearance. One, in particular, a handsome girl belonging to a family that was well at the front socially, hectored me unmercifully. I gave her fair warning that "if she did not stop she would be sorry," but this only added zest to her attack. We were all at the entrance to the chapel, school was out, and no teacher left in sight. I began putting on the hated hood and the "hectoring" also began. My anger burned so fiercely against my handsome tormentor that, though she was much taller than I, the vigor of my attack was such that she was flung in a crumpled heap between the benches, face foremost on the floor. Nobody spoke—the deed was so sudden that it took their breath away; I finished tying on that red hood and walked home. The handsome girl never retaliated, never referred to the subject again, and we have been the best of friends from that day to this.

Dear mother says she does not know when in well-nigh thirty years she has seen me angry, and beyond a momentary flash that I am glad to see and say grows more infrequent every year, that inborn energy is slain. I have only written of it here because I want the picture truthful, and hope my failings may help others, handicapped as I have been, to "rise on the stepping stones of their dead selves to higher things."

A tendency to exaggeration is the next enemy that I have tried to fight. When traveling in Europe, my friend, Kate Jackson, would see the same landscape or city, picture or celebrity, and in the midst of my enthusiastic efforts to describe them she would often interrupt with the words, "Why, Frank, you don't mean to say that we saw *all that?*" While I would break in on her efforts at description, with the words, "You didn't half tell it." Neither had meant to give a wrong impression, but the personal equation needed in both cases to be taken into the account. "You see double," has been said of me when I had delineated a friend whom I admired, but if so it was with one real and one idealizing eye. It comforts me to know that in the habit of accurate recital I have gained greatly with the years, and to know also that I have n't a near friend who does not deem me fairly accurate and scrupulously truthful so far as my intention goes.

As to money, a five-cent silver coin sewed into each tiny toe of a pair of stockings knit by the tireless hands of my father's mother and sent to the far West when I was about ten years old, was the first (except my "butter pennies") of my financial possessions. Money was something far off, unnecessary, except for the convenience of those who dwelt in cities. On the farm, having formed an alliance with generous old Dame Nature, we were abundantly able to take care of ourselves without it. This was about the view I held in childhood.

When in Milwaukee, at seventeen, attending school, good

Irish Mike, one of our farm hands, sent fifty cents apiece to Mary and to me, all the spending money we had for three whole months. After a careful consultation with my wise aunt Sarah, I invested mine in a ticket to the menagerie (not the present circus, by a long moral distance), a blank book for my historical and other charts, and five cents' worth of peppermint candy. When away at school in Evanston, we had no spending money either; it was never named or thought of as necessary. My father furnished us with all needful stationery and postage, and paid all bills. "What would you more?" he used to ask. But I wrote an article for the Prairie Farmer, and received two dollars for it at two different times; whereupon I invited my friends to a feast, also treated my favorite Maggie to a buggy ride, and for the first time looked upon myself as a moneyed proprietor. From that day to this I have been, by pen and voice, an earner of money. My first solid possession was a little gold stud for my sister and myself, then a pair of sleeve buttons, then an engraving of Longfellow's "Evangeline," then a handsome gilt-edged book for my sister's journal and a photograph album for each of us, then the photographs of mother, Mary and myself, but for which we should have had no picture of the dearest girl that ever died. In all those earlier years I kept accounts, but was careless about adding them up; and as for a "balance sheet," I have never even seen an object so distasteful. When tottering out uncertainly into the world of bread-winners (for while I lived near home my father generally clothed me, and my own small earnings went for "extras"), I was, for a brief period, somewhat given to borrowing in a small way; but the concurrent testimony of all who know me best is that the money has been scrupulously returned. I am one who, while she never lays up money, keeps the finances in a snug, thrifty way, and is careful to meet all obligations of a financial sort.

For this good reputation the chief credit should be given to those good women who, ever since the unspeakable loneliness of my sister's going from me, have been what she was to me, "guide, philosopher and friend." A thousand times they hear my "don't forget," whether it is to pay the insurance or to return a borrowed slate pencil, and with punctilious care they see it done. This care-taking about rendering even-handed justice in financial accounts was a prime trait with my parents and in both their families. My mother gives no rest to herself or to us while a debt, no matter how small, hangs over us. Though I have earned tens of thousands of dollars, I have nothing except Rest Cottage, the joint inheritance of mother and myself, and finally to revert, after a tenure of "life use," to the National W. C. T. U., to be employed by that association for the purpose of training boys and girls to habits of physical purity, with especial reference to personal chastity and the non-use, in any form, of alcoholics and narcotics. For I have felt, as the great Agassiz declared of his, that one of my vocation "could not afford to make money." Living comfortably, but with entire simplicity, and not keeping horse or cow, we barely succeed in making both ends of the year meet, after giving away from a fifth to a fourth of our income. Until 1886 I was not salaried by the National W. C. T. U., and for three years before that, generous friends sent money to mother to keep the home intact. I hold that a reformer cannot advantageously lay up money--at least I cannot. The leverage lost in public confidence is too great an off-set; the demands are too varied, constant and imperious. Some years ago I set out to receive no more than $25 per lecture, and though offered $50, $75 and $100, I have steadily declined to advance my figures. My friends have talked severely to me about this, but I am convinced my course was Christian, and along financial lines more in harmony with that day of brotherhood toward which we hasten than any other one thing of all that I have tried to do. For I believe that "the love of money is the root of all evil;" that it has warped and minified more lives, turned more homes into small compacts of perdition, and defeated the Gospel's blessed purpose, more than all other curses that ever crazed the human heart. May the slow, steady lift of Christian justice hasten us to the grander height where stand already, with clear heads and helping hands, some of the noblest thinkers of the world.

MY HOLIDAYS.

The holidays of fifty years! Seven weeks apiece of Christmas, New Year, and the Fourth of July, with Washington's Birthday and one's own, as milestones on life's pathway—surely that ought to be a toothsome theme, redolent of savory dinners and fragrant with good will.

My seventh is the first birthday I recall. We were in the isolated Wisconsin farm-house, newly built and unplastered, not to say unpainted. But mother had made me a big rag-doll, fastening the historic curls, described before, upon its head, and father had painted its face, drawing thereon the most surprising pair of eyes it has ever been my lot to see. Doll Anna was attired in a Turkey red calico gown, made from one of my mother's old aprons, and I was permitted to hold her all day, except when I put her to sleep on the pillow on mother's high, four-posted bed. Later on, my sister fell heir to this doll and its hair, and last of all, my brother's children played with its remnants in their infancy. On the day that mother, in the midst of all her farm-work, gave me this memorable and beloved image, she made me a birthday cake, and permitted me to wear her gold pencil,—a souvenir of her teaching years, and the one article of jewelry that she possessed. Happy as a queen, I little knew, what now I know so well, that the spell wrapped around me that day, and every other, was spun from my mother's happy thoughts.

The Fourth of July was a high day in our Zion, for patriotism was the most attractive form of religion that my reckless childhood knew. Thanksgiving was passed lightly over, in that new country where there were no absent members of the family to come home. Christmas made us hang up our stockings and find but little there, next morning; New Year hardly counted at all. Birthdays cut no great figure, even Washington's going for almost nothing. But the Fourth of July!—*that* came in, went on, and passed out, in a blaze of patriotic glory. This does not mean powder, though, and a big noise, for never a cracker nor torpedo snapped off our Yankee Doodle "sentiments" on the old farm in all the years. We had no money to spend, and if we had, it would n't have been allowed to pass away in smoke. Nor had we any fire-works. Not so much as a single "rocket" ever shot toward the stars above the close-set trees that sheltered

Forest Home. From the steeple on the barn we watched with wonder the fiery serpents and Roman candles "up at Janesville," three miles away, and shuddered in the summer dark at thought of what it would be to fall down the steep roof beneath us, as father had so nearly done once, when painting a favorite ornament upon the Gothic gable. But Forest Home patriotism rose all the higher, perhaps, because it lacked the fizz and buzz and sputter of the regulation Fourth of July "break-down."

Mother had talked to us so much about America that from earliest recollection we had spelled nation with a capital N. To us our native land was a cherishing mother, like our own in gentleness and strength, only having so many more children, grateful and glad, under her thoughtful care. We loved to give her praises, and half believed that sometime, when we grew big enough, and got out into the wide, wide world, we should find her and kneel to offer her our loving service and to ask her blessing.

The "Annual Agricultural and Mechanics' Fair of Rock County" was another notable holiday, perhaps the most pronounced of all the year. Of later Christmas-tides, there was one in Paris, and my Roman Christmas was noteworthy. New Year's calls did not begin for me until my twentieth year. We had lived in the country twelve years, where no such novelty was known, and it was with not a little perturbation that we arrayed ourselves "to receive with mamma." Evanston was a wee bit of a village, but the University newly planted there had attracted a really cultured group of men and women, while the students were a very "likely" class of young people. My fears—for the others had none—lest we might not know just what to say or do were put to flight by the advent at nine A. M. of a quartette of boys hardly more than half my age, with whose pleasant talk of outdoor sports I was in perfect sympathy, and when the grown-ups came they were in groups so large and so intent on seeing "who could make the most calls," that conversation was impossible, and the business-like spirit of the day was so thoroughly Chicagoesque that I forgot my fears, and concerned myself chiefly with "counting up" how many calls we had. From that day on, the custom has seemed to me to be one best honored in the breach, though a few of our friends who still drop in find those of us who are left sincerely glad to see them. But the convivial feature alone gave cohesion to the custom of New Year's calls, and it has already fallen into disuse. The only day thus employed that I ever really enjoyed was in 1875, when the Chicago W. C. T. U. received its friends.

Among the touching incidents of the day was a call from a young German, who came in, arm in arm with his wife. He signed the pledge while she wept tears of joy. He gave her the witnessed pledge-card, and she took it as if it had been a wedge of gold. He clasped her hand and kissed her, and we all knelt in prayer. He looked up as I pointed to our beautiful motto above the pledge-table, "Trust in God," and promised me he would, and they went away weeping. Yet they understood no word that I had spoken,—it was wholly an "affair of the heart"; but how sacred and how true!

But mother's eightieth birthday (1885) was the greatest holiday that our house ever saw. Twenty-five hundred invitations were sent out to our old friends and the white ribboners, in the name of Mrs. Mary B. Willard and myself. Evergreens came from her native town, Danville, Vt., from our former home on Pleasant street, Oberlin, Ohio, from the Wisconsin farm, with products of "the old place," kindly furnished by the present owners; gifts in great variety were sent from everywhere; reformed men with their families decorated and lighted up the grounds; old neighbors at Janesville, Wis., united in a testimonial; Whittier and John B. Gough, Neal Dow and Marietta Holley, with hundreds of others, sent letters and remembrances. Kinsley served the feast, with eighty candles gleaming around the birthday cake. Mamie Willard, her youngest grandchild, recited this as she gave her an album:

Dear grandmamma, I'm only ten,
While you have passed four score;
But every day I live with you
I'm sure I love you more.
And I do hope, when I'm as old,
That I'll be kind like you,
And make the children care for me
When I am eighty, too!

I pray that God will let you stay
Here ten more years at least;

And when your ninetieth birthday comes,
  Then *I* will make the feast.
And with this wish, and loving kiss,
  Because you are so dear,
I want to give you, for your own
  This birthday souvenir.

A group of lovely children brought a basket with eighty roses, repeating Anna Gordon's happy lines:

Now, last of all, your *little* friends
  Have just a word or two;
We can't imagine how 'twould seem
  To be as old as you.
But then you have so young a heart,
  And are so good and kind,
If we could all grow old like you,
  We think we should n't mind.
We bring you eighty roses fair,
  One for each fragrant year;
Accept them with a blessing, please,
  From little hearts sincere.

Anna also wrote a song of which space permits only a single stanza. It was rendered by voices sweet as the song's significance, to the tune of "Auld Lang Syne":

We join to-night to honor one
  Whose crown of eighty years
Reflects a faith that's born of love,
  A hope that conquers fears:
A life enriched by blessed deeds
  All through its busy days;
A soul that e'en in darkest hours
  Still sings its song of praise.

Down upon the sweet scene looked the portraits of our trio beloved who had passed onward. Dear mother was her own unchanging, sunny self, and after receiving from eight until eleven, was up bright and early next morning, going to "Love Feast" and to "Quarterly Meeting" at the church.

Mother's reply to the birthday greetings was as follows:

I have no language in which to respond appropriately to the kindly sentiments just expressed in such polished phrase. This is my eighty-first birthday. Eighty years is a long time, longer than any one now present can remember. I did not expect to live so long, I wonder that I have. And so my friends have come to congratulate me upon my continued life and health. I appreciate your kindness, and the honor you do me; coming, as it does, from persons of exceptional excellence of life and character, and of rare discrimination and attainment, it will lend a halo to the sunset of my life. But I am aware that it is to an ideal that you show this loving courtesy and unfeigned respect. I, too, have had ideals from my girlhood, and I still pay homage to the creations of my imagination, just as others do. It does no harm when our friends put an overestimate upon us; it stimulates us to endeavor to be such persons as our friends charitably think we are.

I have a prayer in my heart for you all, that your lives may be prolonged and that your influence in the cause of God and humanity may be extended and multiplied until time shall not be measured by the flight of years.

Accept my sincere and grateful thanks for this expression of your kind regard.

MOTHER.

Concerning my mother, I wish to say that for mingled strength and tenderness, "sweetness and light," I have never met her superior. The word "dauntless" best expresses the attitude of her mind; the word "loving," that of her heart. She has such equipoise of character, such anchorage in God, that no storm surprises or is able to make shipwreck of her sovereignty and faith.

My father and mother both had marked gifts with voice and pen, and a colloquial quaintness that kept our home in perpetual merriment. My brother and sister had a rich inheritance of humor from this double source of drollery and fun. It did not take the form of far-fetched puns or thrice-told anecdotes, but bubbled up perpetually in original phrases and felicities of playfulness that enlivened their conversation like the play of lightning upon a summer cloud. But beyond all of "My Four" best and nearest ones, she ranks, whose supreme gift of motherliness reached, in her children's estimation, the height of actual genius.

My mother was a school-teacher not far from Rochester, in the prime of her youth, beginning at the age of fifteen. An elegant gentleman entering her school-house one day, asked if he might make a temperance speech. It was Gen. Riley, of Rochester, who lived to be nearly one hundred years old, and talked temperance all his life, being a man of wealth and going out at his own expense to speak. This lecture that he gave in mother's school-house was the first she ever heard, and she signed the pledge then and there for the first time. One of her friends, a young man, learned of this later, and thought it so purely fanatical that he said with warmth to her, "I hope, just to pay you for doing that, you will never be able to get married." This is an interesting side-light on the popular thought of that day,

When mother was seventy years old she became President of the Woman's Temperance Union of Evanston. I am very glad that she, though in the evening of her life, may be reckoned not only a white ribboner, but as one who has served in the army as captain of a company recruited in her own village, and which still holds on its way, one of the best, most level-headed Unions in the whole ten thousand.

Mother says that at family worship in her home, they were wont to sing together, "How firm a foundation, ye saints of the Lord," and her parents used to say "it would never wear out, because it was so full of scripture." When mother came back to us, after being confined in her room six weeks, we sang that hymn for her, Anna and I, at family prayers, and she broke in at the verse about "hoary hairs," and said, "How I enjoyed that from my old grandmother, who lived to be ninety-seven, and then I enjoyed it from my dear father, who was eighty-six when he passed away, and now my daughter enjoys it for me, who am eighty-four, and perhaps she will live on to be as old as I, when I feel sure she will have friends who will enjoy it just as tenderly for her." I said, "The hymn is memorable in connection with the St. Louis Convention, where we sang it just before we entered on the great political debate, and I was wonderfully borne up by the words beginning,

> "The soul that on Jesus hath leaned for repose,
> I will not, I will not desert to its foes."

But above all other hymns, mother's favorite seems to be, in these days:

> "Lead, kindly light, amid the encircling gloom,
> Lead thou me on."

On the 26th anniversary of our Mary's funeral day, June 10th, 1888, when she was slowly recovering from her long illness, my mother said, coming into the "Den" where I was writing, and standing near the door, with her beautiful hands raised and clasped as her frequent custom is, "When I slip away before long, as I shall, you must be consoled by remembering how long you have had your mother; how much of our pilgrimage we have walked together, and that you are already over the roughest of the road.

THE PARLOR — REST COTTAGE

for you are well-nigh fifty and I am in my eighty-fourth year. Then you must be glad and grateful that I was not a clog or hindrance to you, but kept my health so long and retained my spirit of good cheer and tried to make your home a real and happy one. And then you must be glad that you are able to keep up such a home, one that grows more beautiful and pleasant every year, and is hallowed by so many sweet and sacred memories. Few daughters could have done for their mothers what you have done for me. From the other side, I can help you more, perhaps, while I leave you untrammeled, for I cannot bear to be an invalid on the hands of one whose life is so greatly and growingly burdened. I have never been a hindrance to you in anything, and you do not know how it would grieve me to become one now. If I were not here you would be likely to spend your winters South, and your throat seems to require it as you grow older, and the organic trouble so increases. But I can never live anywhere but here. I am a sort of snail and Rest Cottage is my shell.

"They are nearly all gone now, our five, of whom we used to talk so much together, and I shall slip quietly away from you and follow them. Don't allow yourself to grieve, my child, for the time will fly so much faster than you think until you too are gathered home, and so we shall all be 'forever with the Lord.'" The same day, I think, she said to me at dinner, "You have always been asking your friends to tell you your faults. For myself, I do not care to hear about mine. At my age there is no help for them. Rather let me say with Whittier,

> 'Suffice it if—my good and ill unreckoned—
> I find myself, by hands familiar, beckoned
> Unto my fitting place.'"

When she was seventy-five years old I took her back to her birthplace in Danville, Vt., which she had not seen since her eleventh year, and she found the location of the old home and school house with unerring eye, though not the faintest remnant of either yet remained. It did my heart good to have her visit New York and Boston, and to look out over "old ocean's gray and melancholy waste," which she had never thought to see. She has also attended the National W. C. T. U. conventions at Washington and Minneapolis, going as a delegate.

Life is a joy to her among the hundred papers and magazines coming to us each week; she looks over her favorites, examines many books sent me for review, and gives me her opinion, for I can seldom find time to read them; she goes to church once in awhile, but mainly stays in her own room, except when our kind neighbors take her out to ride. The presence of her grand-children, Robert and Kate, Frank and Mary, who were with us last summer, brightened her days greatly; in her grandson, Robert, she seems to live anew his father's youthful days, and from her illness of last year she seems to have recovered altogether.

In the earlier years of my temperance touring, mother always said to me, "Go, my daughter, your work is mine—I will stay at home and pray for your safe return." So I left her with our good Hannah and usually a student in the house, my brother and his family living in Evanston, and some of them seeing her daily. After his death we were all together, as my sister built an annex to Rest Cottage, and in the latest years my secretaries have been with her, and our kind and capable Swede girl, Eda. It pained me not a little to find one day in mother's portfolio these lines, composed after she was seventy years of age:

ALONE IN THE HOUSE.

Alone in the house! Who would dream it,
Or think that it ever could be;
When my babes thrilled the soft air with love notes
That had meaning for no one but me?
Alone in the house! Who would dream it,
Or think that it ever could be,
When they came from their small garden-castle,
Down under their dear maple tree:
Or from graves of their pets and their kittens
With grief it would pain you to see.
Then with brows looking weary from lessons,
Pored over with earnestness rare,
And then from a thoughtful retirement,
With solitude's first blanch of care.
A house of stark silence and stillness
Is this, where I think of the rush
Of childhood's swift feet at the portal,
And of childhood's sweet spirit of trust.
All alone in the house, all alone.

On this generous festival day.
O where have my girls gone this New Year's,
Who made the home merry as May?
One went to the call of Death's angel,
And one, duty called her away.
O how will it be in the future?
I wonder so how it will be,
When we all meet together in Heaven,
Husband, son, gentle daughters and me?
Who will bring us together in glory,
When the long separation is done?
'Tis the Friend who will never forsake us,
And who never has left us alone.
Then fearless I'll enter to-morrow,
'Twill be one day nearer our home.
But when shall we reach there, I wonder?
Where father, brother and sister now rest,
To dwell with the Christ who redeemed us,
In the beautiful land of the blest?
Shut in from life's strange contradictions,
These questionings, these heart-aches and tears,
Never more shall I sigh for the absent,
Throughout all eternity's years!

My dear mother was an admirable home-maker as well as housekeeper. The literature of her good housekeeping was enshrined in two volumes that always lay upon her dressing bureau, Catherine Beecher's "Domestic Economy," and the "Domestic Receipts," by the same author. She was immaculately neat, though we never felt oppressed by it. There was a wholesomeness about our way of living, a comfortable abundance without any approach to display, and an inviting table, with mother's cooking, the flavor of which remains with me as one of the most pleasant of my childish memories. Indeed, since then, it seems to me, I have cared very little about the pleasures of the table. I remember the samp she used to make and what a luxury we children thought it with the fresh sweet milk from our own cows, and the hulled corn that she often had "doing" on the back of the stove for our especial delectation.

One of her pet books was, "The Mother at Home." Nothing seemed to fascinate her so much as the few volumes that were at her command relative to the proper training of children. I think there must be twenty now where there was one in her day.

When she was eighty-four, my mother said to me one day in her reminiscent tone : " I sometimes wonder, as I think it over, that I minded it so little when you were away almost all the time for so many years, and I lived here in this house. It is well for you that neither of your parents took on unnecessary care. Your father never worried, he never laid awake or tossed upon his pillow. He often said to me that he did not lose sleep through care. He had a philosophical way of looking at everything, indeed, we both had, and you inherit it. The Thompson generosity, the Willard delicacy, the Hill purpose and steadfastness, the French element coming from the Lewis family, make up an unique human amalgam."

Mother was fond of music, and on the farm she taught herself to play on the melodeon. She was always studious to acquire, and we felt, although she did not say it, that she had a purpose to keep along with her children, so that they should not look upon her as antiquated, or come to acquirements themselves that made her a less congenial comrade. In this she surely showed the subtlest wisdom.

I think the key to mother's long and tranquil life is to be found in the conscientious care with which she required herself to sleep. Many an evening, so many that it became a proverb in the family, she would take her leave of us before the circle around the evening lamp was broken, saying, "I must go to bed and to sleep, for my children's sake, that I may still be young-hearted when I'm old." Of course, this made us think that sleep had magic in it, and the habit was sedulously followed by my sister and myself, and, so far as I know, by my brother.

One of my mother's most frequent stories when she was taken to task for not initiating her daughters early into the routine of daily domestic cares, was this : " I once read about two Arabs entering on a competition between their favorite steeds. They flew over the ground as by magic, and for a long time were neck and neck, as if their horses had been paired ; then one shot a short distance ahead of his rival, and he who was left behind called out, 'Did your horse ever do a day's plowing?' 'Yes,' was the answer, 'just one day.' 'Then I will win the race,' proudly exclaimed the Arab whose horse had been left a little behind, 'for the steed I ride has lived a free life always, and never knew a plow.' He urged him forward with every token of affection and of confidence, outstripped the Arab who had thought to gain the race and came in with grand strides to the goal far in advance of him."

My mother's theory was not that girls should not do housework, but that if they distinctively evinced other tastes that were good and noble, they should be allowed to follow these to their conclusion, and that in doing so they would gain most happiness and growth themselves, and would most truly help forward the progress of the world.

Mother dictates this account of her occupations between seventy and eighty-four:

A capable Swede girl named Hannah Swanson was with us the best part of ten years. She was very desirous to learn, and having leisure much of the time, I enjoyed teaching her, she was so earnest and appreciative. She took lessons in the simple rules of arithmetic, read history and paid some attention to the principles of English grammar; she was quick to reckon and I could send her to the bank or to pay any bills and found her always accurate. I taught her a little of everything. She was prominent in the Swedish Sunday-school and in church work in her own church. She is now happily married, has a comfortable home of her own. While she was with us one summer. I remember I thought it would be pleasant for her to have her friends, the other girls who worked in the neighborhood, come in and take lessons in English. So I gave them an afternoon each week, I think it was Thursday. They were bright, improved rapidly, and seemed very happy; I had a class of five such girls for years, and to me it is a very pleasant memory. Since I gave up the active cares of the family, I have amused myself one year (my eighty-fourth) by keeping a journal; writing in it every day things that seemed to me to be of interest, and choice sayings of the good and gifted. I have also occupied myself by clipping from the newspapers, of which we have a hundred or two each week, such things as I considered to have superior merit, or on some favorite topic, and have preserved them in scrap-books, of which I have a voluminous collection, which I think will be of interest to the younger members of the family in years to come. Though fond of the society of my friends, I have found pleasant pastimes in these occupations in my own home. I have preferred that other people should come to see me, rather than that I should go to see them. I do not find life less enjoyable as I grow older and the cares fall off. I have a world full of people to sympathize with; many to love; many to deplore; and on the whole, sufficent to interest and keep the sympathies of my heart alive. I have none but kindly feelings for any human being; and there is no person whom I would not gladly comfort if I could; and so "my days go on, go on," without haste and without rest, while the ideal future lends inspiration to my buoyant hopes.

I have but one fault to find with mother: she strenuously *insists* on my drinking a weak decoction of tea and coffee in opposition to my declared purpose, and I think it right to state the fact publicly, inasmuch as she is proud of it, and I have publicly given in good faith the impression that tea and coffee were banished from my bill of fare.

Miss Mary Allen West, editor of *The Union Signal*, and one of my mother's chief admirers, asked her to pencil some of her views on the training of children, which she did in these words:

I have been asked to write some of the thoughts suggested by my experience in training my own children. We lived in Oberlin, Ohio, when my children were in their infancy. There were mothers' meetings at stated times; I felt my utter inefficiency to train these young immortals; I was almost always present at the meetings. I hoped they would tell me just what to do, so that having the approved formula, or program, I might make no mistake. But new conditions were constantly arising, and in my despair I said to a wise friend, "I don't learn anything from those meetings! I don't know what to do." He said, "They are making an impression upon you all the time." It gave me a little comfort to think that perhaps down deeper than my consciousness I was gaining a gleam of light.

And now, first of all, I would insist, teach your children to be truthful; by all the incentives that occur to your prayerful thought, keep their love and confidence so that they will be open to you as the day. Then I would recommend the do-everything method, according to the varying needs of your priceless charge. If the nerves are startled, quiet them in the best way you can. Don't put your child into a dark room and let it cry itself to sleep. It would be more motherly to hang it to the limb of a tree, like an Indian baby, where it would see the light and feel the gentle motion of the breeze. Don't regard it as a mere animal, only to be fed and clothed. It needs sympathy very early; it smiles back your love when only a few weeks old. Never punish a child when it can think you are in anger or about to take its life. It will be so frightened as to lose all self-control. You may think it obstinacy when the little creature is in a frenzy inspired by one in whose power it is utterly helpless. Mothers should try to keep their health, so as to be bright, agreeable company for the older children, and to be patient with the little ones. I know this is easier said than done, especially if the mother is sick or overborne with care; but the attempt, if partially unsuccessful, will not fail of its reward. The habit of unselfishness and kindness can not be too early impressed. The mother should be in spirit and manner, or should aim to be, such as she desires the child to become. I would not recommend over indulgence, but genuine tenderness and love can hardly go to an extreme, especially in the early helpless years. If complications arise between the children, do not let them accumulate. Don't let the little ones lie awake all night dreading a punishment in the morning. Deal with each case at once upon its own merits without referring it to any umpire but yourself. When they are old enough to commence study, do not be indifferent to the trials they meet with in the effort to solve the, to them, difficult problems, but solve them often yourself; don't be so fearful about weakening their self-reliance and desire for high achievement as to the future. On no account allow them to be discouraged at the outset. Should a child show a strong bias toward any laudable line of life that promises self-support and easy independence I would encourage this tendency with all my power. Try to cultivate a tender conscience, a delicate sensitiveness to right and wrong. I would place the acquisition of character infinitely before that of wealth, desirable as is a moderate share of the latter. Wealth ends with life, character is immortal, and toward perfection all our efforts should tend. I must not forget my pet idea to be more careful to praise children for doing well, than to chide them for doing ill. When the children are young and in the mother's care more directly, there may be a feeling of comparative safety, but when they bloom into young men and women, and begin to assume personal responsibility, it is the hour of doom which threatens to make or mar all your careful handiwork. Who is wise enough to counsel then? Silence seems safest, but silence would be treason; the mother must have the heart of her loved ones in keeping in this hour of destiny; no one can be consulted with such safety as she, and she will need the electric light of Deity to guide her in this supreme emergency. Who can arrest the flying hours? What issues hang upon the decision of a moment! She can find refuge only in Him who has said, "If ye ask anything in my name I will do it." Here she may anchor in a sublime faith that the young, inexperienced, and adventurous feet may, through infinite riches of grace, be led into paths of safety, usefulness, and to a lasting peace.

MOTHER'S RETROSPECT AT SEVENTY-SIX.

My daughter wishes me to sketch some incidents of past years in our Wisconsin home. But who can picture the changing skies or the currents in the ocean? Lives are experienced not written. Young life came to me with odors wafted from eternity. Feelings, perceptions, fancies were mingled in a kind of chaos. Then the prospect widened, every aspect became more clearly defined, more serious, more grave. Then came a very hopeful, but solemn womanhood, wifehood, and who can write it—the story of my motherhood? My life would not have been more changed if some white-robed messenger from the skies had come to me and said, "I will send five spiritual beings into your arms and home. Two I shall soon recall, three may remain. It is a momentous charge, potent for good or ill, but I will help you, do not fear." Who would attempt to explain the change that comes to the home where such mysterious questions are entertained? The material care demanded by helpless infancy; the boundless welcome bursting from parental hearts, the feeling of a new and measureless responsibility, the unspeakable tenderness of parental love, the painful consciousness of limited powers in the presence of an infinite need. We can not stay it, habits are begun, character is forming, destiny is being determined. Here are wise little faces looking up to you, as to an oracle, every nerve of the soul thrilling to your slightest touch, divining by a strange intuition your tone and spirit, with the certainty of a seraph. Mother, step softly, you shall be the accepted creed of these young immortals; in all the coming years these unwritten lives shall herald your example and counsels when you are resting from your labors.

To the parent as to the child, there is something strangely pathetic in the first efforts to practice its infant wings, the first struggles to solve the mysteries of its being. "Where is Christ?" Frances once inquired of her father, "I can not see Him, I do not feel His arms around me." And then how inspiring to mark the change when the soul grasps the mystery of the atonement, and proves by the development of childhood into maturity, that the spirit searcheth all things, even the deep things of God. Oliver, when writing his first letter to his grandmother, was told he could improve it by rewriting; he did so, and was encouraged by being told he had bettered it, and was then asked to copy it again. I can not forget, after nearly forty years, how despairingly he looked up and said, "I can not write any better with my present amount of knowledge." I saw him in a very few years with plumed wings, ascending to a high intellectual life, beyond the realm of my thoughts. The quiet happenings in our farm-life, remote from town, were so different from the noisy tumult of a large city that the spirit there was a direct contrast to what my children later learned. The education of the children was more the result of circumstances than of any definite plan, except the living in the country; there was special solicitude in regard to their intellectual wants. For their moral training, living remote from the excitements of the town, and depending for the most part on older persons for society, the conditions were not unfavorable.

Of their physical education there is not much to be said. They lived largely in the outdoor air. Their lives were free from restraint; their plans seldom or never opposed if harmless and at all practicable.

I remember once, when tired and weary of care, I went to my room and had determined on a restful and quiet hour, but Frances came with her hands full of children's papers, *The Myrtle* and *Youth's Cabinet*. "I came, my dear, to be alone and to think my own thoughts," I said. She seated herself upon the carpet, and with perfect *nonchalance*, remarked, "It is natural that I should want to be with my mother, and I mean to be," then proceeded to read her papers, to which there was no further objection made.

Oh! these little girls and boys that come to our homes and play with their pets, and are so conscious of safety if by our side, then reaching maturity, assume bravely life's duties, and stand erect under its mountain-load of care! or dying fold the Redeemer to their hearts, saying, as did our dearly beloved Mary who, when being asked by her mother in her last sickness "what she could do for her," said, "Put your arms around me and press your cheek to mine, that is all I want." Thus one of the loveliest beings that ever visited this world of mystery, lovely in person as in character, beautiful as good, and good as beautiful, passed from our stricken hearts and home to holy regions out of sight.

Motherhood is life's richest and most delicious romance, and sitting in sunshine calm and sweet, with all my precious ones upon the other side, save the daughter who so faithfully cherishes me here, I thank God most of all that he ever said to me, "Bring up this child for me in the love of humanity and in the expectation of immortal life."

FATHER.

Mother's description of my father is as follows:

Of fine personal appearance, tall, rather slight, a well-poised head, dark blue eyes, square forehead and strong chin, a firm mouth, dark, full, and ornamental hair and beard.

Mr. Willard was select and true in his friendships; devout in religion; honorable and exact in business relations; proud of his children, though undemonstrative; versatile in affairs; analytical in his judgments of persons and principles; reserved and dignified to outsiders; easily accessible to only a few; fond of nature and books, to which he was especially drawn in all matters pertaining to horticulture.

He was an amateur artist, and most appreciative student of the writings of A. J. Downing. He had towering aspirations and a consciousness of reserved power, and was a marked and positive character, who achieved honorable distinction both in business and public positions.

Relative to his unique utterances, Dr. Bonbright, one of his most valued friends, once said to me, "Your father was the most audacious man in speech, and the most conservative in action, that I have ever known." He was thoroughly intellectual, and an insatiate reader, a life-long habit of the house being that we all went to bed early except father, who would sit up after the rest, saying he was going to read mother to sleep, a feat speedily accomplished, after which he sat alone for hours, poring over his books.

He had exceedingly fine taste, but I always thought he made a mistake in directing everything not only about the farm and the beautiful garden and grounds, but also the minutest expense within doors. This was not because mother was extravagant, for she was a thrifty though never a niggardly housekeeper, and she had excellent capacity in buying whatever goods were needed for the family, but father fell into the habit of buying everything himself. Indeed, he selected nearly all our dresses and bonnets, mother saying nothing about it, though I think she would have been glad to have had it different. Very likely this resulted from his being almost every day in town, where all these things were to be had, while mother stayed with the children, because it was a solemn compact between them that both of them should never leave us at a time. My mother's abounding good health must have had to do with her always cheery spirits and equable temper. My father was a life-long invalid, though so brave and forceful that he said very little about it, but his lungs were greatly weakened and he not only had several hemorrhages, but suffered from their frequently threatened recurrence. All this, of course, affected his disposition and made him more irritable than he otherwise would have been, though I would not on any account represent him as other than a kind man in his home, for he certainly was so in intention, and usually in action. He was very loyal to all the ties that he had formed in life, to kindred, neighbors, associates in church and business, yet he disdained anything frivolous, was a Cromwellian sort of man in his loyalty, and in his convictions of duty.

Every home in which my father lived has memorials of him in the way of beautiful evergreens. He planted more trees and loved them better than any other person I ever knew. Rest Cottage was built by him on a large area of ground that was simply a marsh, considered perhaps as undesirable a lot as there was in Evanston, except for its location on the principal street, about a block and a half from the University campus. Now there is not a handsomer row of elms in the beautiful college town than the double row that stands in front of our home, shown in the picture entitled "Picturesque Evanston," and known by us as "Father's Monument."

My Uncle Zophar says there was nothing so pitiful in father's long illness during which he was with us at the home of this dear uncle, as his lamentation, sometimes with tears, when he would tell the story of the Irishman who died away from home, and who, grieving in his homesickness, would repeat over and over again that he should see his "beautiful Belle Valley no more." My father said to his brother that his greatest sorrow was that he should no more see Rest Cottage, which his loving skill had translated from a swamp into a charm.

In 1848, father was one of thirteen Free-soilers in the Madison legislature who held the balance of power to such a degree th· excellent law was secured through their instrumentality ·gh they belonged to a third party, the Democrats and ·higs being the two great parties, and fully convinced that wisd· would die with them.

It interests me not a little that Hon. Samuel D. Hastings, who was a fellow-member of the Legislature with my father, and a valued friend of his, should now be treasurer of the Prohibition party and one of my most valued associates and friends in that p· Executive Committee. If such a suggestion had then ·en made to either of these men, they would have said that no w·man would ever hold such a relation to politics unless chaos and old night had settled down upon the world, whereas the facts are that order and the rising day are the fitting emblems of the change that makes this possible.

For one year my father's feeble frame endured that most terrible disease, consumption. It crept upon him slowly, allowing him a daily respite at first, attacking him with great violence in the early months of summer, pursuing him when he left his home on the lake-shore as the chilly winds of autumn began to blow, and went to his friends at the East, hoping much from change of air and scene; confining him constantly to his bed for four months, wasting him to a mere skeleton, and finally, in untold suffering, wresting away his last faint breath. This is the earthly side; not so stands the record, thank God, upon the heavenly side. Almost from the first, he thought it would be his last illness, and quietly, diligently, and wisely proceeded to arrange his earthly affairs. No item, however minute, seemed to escape him. Whatever was of the least importance to his family, whatever friendship, or acquaintance, or any of his relations in life demanded or suggested, ever so faintly, was done by him.

Much that he said has been preserved, and dimly shadows the delightful visions by which the sick-room was made sacred. Extracts from these memoranda show the experience of his last days on earth:

Once when a dear friend sat beside him, while his cheek wore the hectic flush, he said: "If Christ sat here, as you do, by my side, and said to me, 'My dear brother, what can I do for you, in any way that I have not already done?' I should say, 'Nothing, beloved Lord!'"

Speaking of that wondrous verse, "And ye are Christ's, and Christ is God's," he said:

"What a stupendous meaning is in those words! Think them over for yourself! Ah, as one nears the border of that plane which breaks off suddenly, these things grow clearer to the mind."

September 19.—I was writing up his brief diary and he said:

"I did not mention it, but you might put it in every day, 'Peace, great peace in God.'"

September 22.—He talked long and in a most interesting way about faith—always his favorite theme—concluding with these striking words:

"'Trust me and I'll take care of you'; that's what Christ says. That's religion and that's good for something! Walk right out on this plank into the dark eternity; when you come to the end of the plank, Christ will be there to catch you."

November 23.—Referring to a plan he had feebly sketched in pencil of the family burial lots in Rose Hill Cemetery, he said:

"I drew this with as much pleasure as I ever planned a garden. How God can change men's minds! I never used to think about our cemetery lots, but now I very often do, and love to call them our family home—our blessed family home!" (Uttering these words with tears.)

November 24.—"I have often thought of late how much richer I am than any Emperor. An Emperor has this world to back him, to be sure, but think of me! I have God and His universe on my side, because of the child-like faith which I, a poor, trembling, dying man, repose in my Redeemer! This is a high truth—a wonderfully inspiring thought. People who are well don't know anything about my feelings in these crisis hours. Ah! I've rested my case with the eternal God!"

December 2.—Rev. J. N. Simkins (whose kind attentions were a great comfort to him) called. Father said to him, very naturally, "I have been dictating letters, having business papers filed, etc. It's a good deal of work, getting ready for so long a journey. You know there are so many 'last things' to be regulated!"

"The doctrine of sanctification by faith in Christ, preceded by entire self-surrender to Him, is unspeakably dear to me. It should be fearlessly preached from our pulpits and earnestly sought by our people. How little does one know of his powers of submission until the Holy Spirit helps and teaches him! How God can humble and chasten a strong, self-reliant man, until he lies in His hand like a simple, loving, teachable child! The hour in which he does this is life's holiest, truest hour."

Extracts from a dictated letter:

MY DEAR SISTER BRAGDON—Your poor friend lies helpless in the arms of Jesus, waiting to depart. I often think of you and of your little family gathered up there in your cozy home so near that dear home of mine which I had hoped longer to enjoy, but which I have given up, though not without many a bitter pang. But it was one of the sacrifices of this life which I must make before going to my glorious home in heaven. I expect we shall be again settled near each other in a better world. I'm going soon, to take possession of my mansion, and perhaps I shall see, marked with golden letters, the name of my Sister Bragdon upon the one adjoining, the one awaiting her. I expect to find Brother Bragdon quite at home and able to lead me by the hand to pleasant pathways and delightful contemplation of the marvels of that world which he has now for several years enjoyed.

I praise God for our prospects, and believe the day is not far distant when your family and mine and all our dear friends will be spending our years unitedly in heaven.

January 21.—I sang his favorite verse:

"Take my poor heart and let it be
Forever closed to all but Thee."

He said, "Oh, my child, that is my prayer for you—perhaps the last I shall ever breathe, but it is enough. For saint or sinner, it does not matter who, that is the most elevated purpose of which a human mind can be possessed."

"Brush up the evergreens in the garden and let them stand—emblems as they are of an immortal life—mementos of my last work on earth. You will want a crocus bed in our garden next spring—don't forget that. Go to the greenhouse at Rose Hill for plants of all kinds that you need. Remember how fond I was of flowers, and do as I would have done if I had lived. I expect you will observe nature more than ever when I am gone."

January 22.—His sister, Mrs. Robinson, said to him: "Josiah, we do not know how to spare you—there are not many of us now." He answered cheerfully: "You spared me when I was a boy of sixteen, to go from home; later in life you spared me to go West and live for many years; the time that you will have to spare me now won't be so long as those times in the past."

"As I waked up just now and consciousness came over me, this question flashed over my mind: 'Is it possible that there is any unsafety—any unsafety for me anywhere in God's universe?' My child! That is a startling thought to one just going into the unknown world. But in a moment I settled down again quietly, saying to myself: 'No, I'm safe in any event! I am safe by the mercy of my Lord and Saviour Jesus Christ.' If I have one strong wish which is not a heavenly aspiration, it is that I may die with a clear intellect; that I may be able to look God in the face as I go into His presence, and into the eternal world.

"I look forward to a scene like that when our dear Mary went to heaven, as a pleasant scene,—the pleasantest of all my history here on earth. But I shall be unconscious in that final hour, perhaps, notwithstanding my desire. May it be just as God wills."

God willed to take him one cold winter night, January 24, 1868, in storm and darkness, to take him in an hour when consciousness was clouded and the power of speech was gone.

A little while before his death we caught these words, among the last indistinct utterances of his receding spirit:

"*Jesus—take me—take me to Thyself.*"

BITS FROM MY NOTE-BOOK.

CONCERNING TABLE-D'HOTE.

This is a subject so rich in humor and philosophy that the silence of travelers concerning it is without other explanation than that afforded by the homely old proverb, "A burned child dreads the fire"; to the average tourist, fresh from an unconventional American home, the ordeal of an English *table-d'hote*—usually the form of this phenomenon that first presents itself—is sufficiently trying to make upon a sensitive epidermis, impressions of a lasting character.

But be it ours to rise superior to this weakness, and to offer ourselves as martyrs to the promulgation of some notions touching the mighty Juggernaut of the European hotel system.

Call we then to mind our first solemn down-sitting before "the table of the host." It was at the Lakes of Killarney—"Royal Victoria" Hotel. There was such a land-and-waterscape outside the windows as rarely meets the eye; but something close at hand obscured it—namely, one dozen dinner-plates; for there was an officious young clergymen, in white cravat and claw-hammer coat, who, aided and abetted by the whole senior class of a theological seminary, seemed to have an eye single to despoiling us of our trenchers at intervals so frequent that our plate of soup was hastier than General Scott's, and our salmon melted away like the fabled draught from the lips of mythologic Tantalus. So unequal, indeed, was our game of knife-and-fork to his brilliant maneuvers of spoliation, that we soon resigned ourselves in desperation to our fate, while this thought flashed cheerfully athwart the chaos of consciousness: "Who says we can't have tea and toast upstairs, in spite of these theologues, when this horrid farce is over?" Words are inadequate to measure the degree of awe that the chief of these young men inspired.

Such a sense of helplessness and ignorance of the world as his very glance created, can only be compared to the emotions which Steerforth's "man" aroused in the gentle breast of David Copperfield; for he was thoroughly master of the situation—and the situation was so frightfully new to us! Indeed, I shall always believe he racked his brain on this occasion to impale me upon dilemmas whose horns were never before brandished, and at junctures the most unexpected. His unctuous voice, using faultless French, glided over lists of unimagined delicacies, and his pause was as the silence of fate, while I made election of "the last" with a presence of mind that astonishes me as I contemplate it. Nor was this all. Eight English dames and seven bald-headed gentlemen, written all over with the marks of the most unmistakable gentility, surrounded this aristocratic board. A hush was in the air, suggesting to my feverish fancy that a ghost was at the banquet; while the decorum of each movement, the measured rhythm of those noble jaws, and the geometric precision of those mouthfuls of roast beef, recalled that period in history when dining was a ceremony of religion. Nor was this all. Opposite sat Viscount Fitz-Noodle. To see this scion of a noble race recruit exhausted nature was my despair. What a perfect *connoisseur* was he in all culinary things! how thorough was his mastery of the mystic Art of Dining! It haunts me still, that high-bred face, that Cupid's bow of a moustache, that faultless hand with fairy wine-glass poised between the first and second of its taper fingers, regardless of so commonplace a grasper as the thumb. Less pleasing was the merciless glass screwed beneath a patronizing eyebrow, in the long intervals of the repast, and the anatomizing glance across the table at his *vis-a-vis*. But never mind—bread and cheese came at last, and then the *Charlotte Russe* and the signal that the ceremonies were concluded, from Lady Weazened, at the table's head.

Thus ended my initiation into that vast and highly respectable company who learn by what they suffer at *table-d'hote;* for be it mildly intimated to all "intending tourists," that he who declines to avail himself of this means of grace falls at once to zero upon the social scale and takes his modest steak or slice of beef, as he can catch it, after the elect, at a dollar or two per head, are served.

Upon the continent this service is often really enjoyable. It is far less formal than in England, everybody talking freely with his neighbor, so that the grinding of one's own molars is not all the sound one hears. Besides, the requisitions of the toilet are not so rigid, the time occupied is less, and when one's initiation is well over, *table-d'hote* is rather agreeable as a study of customs and character. A racy book would that be which Mark Twain might write on "*The Table-d'hote of Different Nations,*" since the most prosy traveler's "Notes" yield material varied and amusing. For example: In Denmark they bring one's "portion" of tea to the table in a small silver box, with a curious contrivance—a combination of furnace and tea-pot—in which one prepares it as he best can. In Sweden, before sitting down, the gentlemen, at a side-table, take off or put on the edge to their appetites—we could never exactly determine which—over sandwiches, sardines, and gin. In Russia, also, one learns to relish a slice of lemon in one's tea, though travelers seldom fall into the custom of drinking it from tumblers, *à la* Muscovite; and in a Moscow restaurant, where ladies lean back in their chairs, enjoying cigarettes, the waiter brings you with the bill of fare, a list of tunes from which you select what you will listen to as you take an ice, whereupon a huge hand-organ grinds it out for your æsthetic delectation. Coming up the Danube on the elegant steamer Orient, a grim old Turk sat opposite our party, and it was something other than amusing to see him eat dried herring, tail and all. Germany and Egypt have one heathenish custom in common—that of supplying the tables with candles which are lighted during dessert, and are a signal and means for igniting the gentlemen's cigars, which soon emit smoke enough to drive any but a very strong-diaphragmed lady from the table.

Going up the Nile we had a droll *table-d'hote:*

> It was the steamship Behera that sailed the Nile's broad sea,
> And fifty hungry tourists that formed the company.

We were divided into two parties and dined fore and aft, according as we had or had not "come out" with Thomas Cook, "Tourist Manager," from London. Being, happily and unhappily, among the "had nots," we were classed with those who occupied the sailors' cabin instead of the saloon; and one of our companions — a nice old English tea-merchant — used to watch the dishes as they came up from below, or rather down from above (though they had none of manna's gracious qualities), and report the unfairness with which the dainties (?) were dealt out.

At Suez we were served with Red Sea fish and mountain honey, by tall, handsome waiters from Hindustan, in the tight-fitting linen garments of their country. Their only English words were "Tank you"; and they repeated these in their soft tones even when berated by irate English colonels. At Damascus, solemn Syrians in Turkish costume were our waiters; and at Moscow, Tartars with inconvenient paucity of expression and close-cropped hair. In Constantinople, on Greek Easter Sunday, two "Paschal Lambs" flanked by plates of red eggs formed a leading feature of our *table-d'hote*. Odd enough they looked, with a lemon apiece squeezed between their herbivorous jaws, double rosettes of white paper garnishing their tails, and lettuce leaves fastened to their sides with silver spikes. But our Jerusalem *table-d'hote* was the most unique. Nobody could here object that he was n't at his ease. We used to go to the "cupboard" and help ourselves, under the very eyes of the dark-skinned proprietor. One day a gentleman of our party happened to upset his coffee-cup on the already copper-colored cloth. Mine host looked so seriously afflicted at this that we tried to console him by suggesting that a napkin be laid over the offending stain, adding — as conclusive authority for such a device — "That's the way they do at Paris." He raised his hand in energetic deprecation, exclaiming, "You may think so, lady, and the people may do so if they like in Paris, but I can tell you it won't answer for Jerusalem!" Next day we had a spotless damask cloth — the only clean feature the table could boast.

***

In the autumn and winter of 1869 and '70 we were in Rome, studying Italian, and studying also the wonderful palimpsest of that enchanting city. Most of all I delighted to spend my days in the gallery of the Vatican where Raphael's Transfiguration, and the Greek statue of the Minerva Medici were my favorite studies. To write about the Transfiguration were an impertinence, and of the Minerva I have only to say that she seemed to me the embodiment of perfect equipoise of regal strength, and the most soothing and womanlike helpfulness. Perceiving it to be my favorite of all the marvels we had seen in all the galleries, my friend, Kate Jackson, had the head cut for me on a cameo by Tignani, the finest cameo artist in Rome, and ever since this has been my preferred and almost my only ornament.

FOR THE CHILDREN.

In looking over "books for big folks," as the children say, I used in my own childhood to wish that somewhere between the covers they had remembered my own small self, and put in a picture or a word that I could claim. So when I found that some bright-tinted pages were provided for, I fell to thinking of one for the little folks. Our kind business manager favored my views, so you have a picture in colors of four of my special treasures, joined with the blue ribbon that so many earnest men have worn upon their breasts in their heroic fight for a clear brain. The traveling bag, "Old Faithful," that I have carried to every state and territory of our blessed Republic and to one thousand of its towns and cities; out of which from the cars, which are my customary workshop, tens of thousands of articles, paragraphs, letters and postals have gone forth on their home-protection errands; out of which have come the "Documents" that have led to founding local unions from Victoria on Puget Sound to San Antonio, Texas; to say nothing of gospel temperance speeches—for I make no other—on prohibition, woman's ballot, philanthropic politics, and all the rest of it. My ten-cent New Testament, carried in almost all these campaigns, explains, I hope and pray, what the traveling bag is for. My silver cup and medal for a prize essay are described on page 69, and the cameo representing the Minerva of the Vatican is mentioned above. The most interesting relic on the page is Father Mathew's medal, given by his own hand to Mrs. Kate Crossley McGowan, of Youghal, Ireland, when she was a child, and bestowed on me by that gifted Christian worker, in Chicago, in 1878. The entire page gives to thoughtful mothers many a text on that curious, hopeful, twofold theme, *Woman and Temperance*. What the flowers are I have been unable to make out, so I submit the question to the children as a botanical conundrum.

FAMILY IDIOMS.

Every household has its own vernacular and it would be a most interesting study to make a list of the words and expressions that are peculiar to different homes.

The study of family idioms is often more curious and self-revelatory than that of national idioms, for the field is smaller and the generalization not so difficult to make. I think the philological society should send out its circular for a list of family idioms, as the psychological society has sent out its request for a list of family spooks.

Our family had its full share of these peculiar phrases. When we would become somewhat rampant in our sense of self-sufficiency, my father would raise his heavy eyebrows, gaze upon us with a queer grimace, and ask in his significant, sarcastic tones, "Who dug you up and set you going?" When he wished to express the ultimate of distrust concerning any individual he would say, "I would not set him with the dogs of my flock."

Once when I spoke to him quite flippantly, he remarked, "Do you know that what you are saying is simply the puling of an inanity?" I did not proceed with my observation.

One of my father's most frequent phrases was, "Have you got the victory in you?" also this, "If it's in it's in, and will come out, but what's wanting can't be numbered."

We always spoke of yeast as "emptin's." We children were quite apt to become boisterous in our fun when lessons were over in the evening; my father, when he could bear it no longer, would rap on the table and say, "This is nothing but running emptin's, you young ones must go straight to bed."

INVITATIONS.

Anna Gordon says that often in the letters, which she looks over first, giving me only those that are important for me to read, occur such words as these, coupled with, perhaps, a thrice-repeated invitation to speak in a given town: "It is evident she does not care to come to us, for we have asked her often." It afflicts me that my friends should write in this way, for if they knew the actual situation they would see how impossible it is for me to go. I have spent ten years chiefly upon railroad trains, going to little and large towns alike, but now when my dear mother is so old I can not do as I would otherwise. Besides, Anna says I have at least fifteen thousand invitations already unaccepted. Long ago I should have made the trip around the world, to which I have been invited many times, but for mother. Indeed, I tell her often that she is my only anchorage. If she were gone I should no more have a home or place of refuge on the planet earth.

NAMESAKES.

May I say to all my namesakes, boys and girls, of whom Anna Gordon, who carefully keeps the records, says she has account of over one hundred, that if I do not send them each a silver cup it is not because I would not like to do so, but I am sure the parents who do me an honor so high and sacred as to name their children for me, would far rather any money I may have should go into the work than to make any other disposition of it. My New Year card will be sent them regularly (unless Uncle Sam's messengers should fail me), my affectionate regard will follow them, and if I can ever be of service in their future lives they will not call upon me in vain. Perhaps, indeed, in my old age it may fall to my lot to call on some of them, instead.

ON THE DOLL QUESTION.

(*From* BABYHOOD, *October*, *1888.*)

To the Guardians and Inhabitants of Babyland:

Can I come in? Or will the dolls roll their eyes, shake their heads, and whack away at me with their wax hands? I had always fondly supposed myself a loyal friend of little folks, but now I am held up as a warning, and burned in effigy, figuratively speaking, with dolls to light the fagots.

Please let me tell you how it came about that I was thus grievously misapprehended. Having been asked to write a leaflet on the assigned topic, "Dress and Vice," I was trying to show how the French doll may unduly foster that love of finery which is one of woman's greatest temptations. Against the simple, modest, "old-fashioned" doll I did not mean to say a word, for my dear old doll "Anna" was a favorite plaything of my childish years. But I did not guard my point as carefully as

I would now, after the terrible hair-pulling that has fallen to my lot, or as I will in future editions of my harmless little leaflet.

Let me, then, here and now, declare my faith more definitely: I believe that boys and girls should be trained very much alike and have the same toys. This will give the girls abundant out-door exercise, fit them out with that physical equipoise that we call health, which means wholeness, which means happiness. It will also develop their observing faculties, now so much less brought out than those of boys. Perhaps the fact that a doll is so early placed in the girl's arms may help to account for her dulled curiosity, her greater passivity, her inferior enterprise, bravery and courage. Perhaps the doll may help to shut out the world of wonder and surprise in which she was meant to dwell. The ever-present doll may close her mind to studies and observations which would develop inventors among women. I have always believed the lack of mechanical inventions as the fruit of woman's brain, was superinduced by a false training, and that possibly doll-nurture had somewhat to do with it. Perhaps because my own early years were spent upon a farm, I have thought that live dolls, that is, pets, were nobler, as they are certainly far more frolicsome and responsive companions for children than the wax imitations that form the "regulation pattern" toy of girls.

The excessive altruism of women is one of the greatest wrongs to men, and defrauds men of a thousand opportunities for forming noble character. The doll may have much to do with this much-to-be-regretted outcome. I repudiate the notion that any girl of normal constitution needs a doll to develop or to cultivate a mother-heart. God has been before us all in this, and the central motive power of every woman's heart is mother-love. It has a thousand ways to show itself, and makes women, not a few, take the part of foster-mother to thousands of human beings that are worse than motherless.

There are cogent reasons why the fatherly instinct is less strong in boys than is the motherly in girls, and nothing more beneficent could happen to men or to the world than that they should have this sacred, home-conserving instinct more strongly accentuated in heart and life. If either is to play chiefly with dolls, by all means let it be the boy.

This is my heresy in full, and I do not believe it to be monstrous or in any wise unreasonable. Let me, then, humbly commend it to the kind, thoughtful, and charitable attention of all who share the sacred cares and joys of babyland—I mean all but the dolls.

ERRORS.

Typographical errors are the despair of pen-holders. Here follow a few of those from which I have suffered:

I said of Joseph Cook that, of certain evils named, he was the "uncompromising foe"; the types re-christened him "uncompromising *Joe*"; of a lovely white ribbon friend who had gone to the Better Country, I wrote, "Some of us are like comets, but she was a steady shining star"; the types said, "Some of us are like *camels*"; in a mild quotation I wrote, "'Tis only strength makes gentleness sublime"; the types said, "'Tis only strength makes *gentlemen divine*"; again, this was written, "The souls of some sit on the ends of their nerves"; typo declared that the "souls of some sit on the ends of their *fingers*"; a friendly journalist in Boston declared of me that I was "a believer in Immortality"; but typo echoed, "*immorality*"; and so on and on and the end is not yet. Be it understood that, solid as they are, the types refract the light of truth and often make out of an unoffending human creature a Specter of the Brocken.

A SPELLING SCHOOL.

When I was president of the Chicago W. C. T. U., the mania for spelling-schools was at its height and we arranged for one, working it up with great care and trying to enlist the chief men and women of the city, sixteen on a side, to help us out by spelling up or down, as the case might be. Emory Storrs, the brilliant lawyer and reformed man (for so he was at that time), consented to act as pedagogue, and did his best to enlist distinguished friends. He showed me several answers, or, rather, declinations, that piled in upon him. I remember, in particular, one from Robert Collyer, who took an entire sheet of foolscap and wrote at the top "Dear E."; in the middle, "It can not be," and at the bottom, "R. C."

But we had a fair showing, in spite of all. My genial friend, the Rev. Dr. W. H. Thomas, agreed to be the head one of the boys' side, and I took that place on the girls', and my coadjutors and myself appeared with hair braided down the back, and wearing old-fashioned, high, white aprons. Emory Storrs had an unconscionably tall collar, swallow-tail coat, and a ferule at least six feet long. He was also fitted out with the biggest kind of a big dictionary. Clark Street Church was packed, at twenty-five cents apiece, a ticket after the following pattern having been very generally sold beforehand:

"AWL FUR TEMPURUNCE.

SPELIN' SKULE.

FUST METHUDDIS'

KORNER KLARK & WASHUNTUN STREATS.

8T APERILE, THORS DAY."

25 - - - - - SENTS.

"Come, Henry, stand straight and toe the line," were the pedagogue's instructions to the tall and somewhat attenuated Doctor. "Frances, no giggling, attend strictly to business," and he rapped the ferule with vigor and rolled his eyes in the most threatening manner. After various other preliminaries, he began, "Henry, spell abscess," and Henry was left to spell it without the preliminary *s* of the three that adorn its physiognomy. Fortunately profiting by his mistake, I got in the *s* and brought down the house, while Henry sank back discomfited at the very first attack. "Aspergeoire" was the word that came to my friend, Kate Jackson, who sacrificed herself to the cause on this occasion. Mr. Storrs was not an adept at pronouncing French, and Miss Jackson, who was, attacked him and at the same time gave him a lesson then and there on the correct method. An appeal was taken to the house, which voted that all those who had lost their places through his bad pronounciation should be allowed once more to return to the attack. And so the fun went on until a savage word that I have forgotten, "downed" us all at last.

It occurs to me that we should do well as temperance people to utilize more than we have yet done, the love of amusement that is in young people, and put money in the purse of the reform by

THE CHILDRENS PAGE.

bidding for the presence of the amusement-loving public in the villages and towns during the long winter evenings. Our new department of entertainments will, I believe, do much to supply in a perfectly legitimate way the natural demands that young people make upon the ingenuity of their elders in this regard.

METHODS OF COMPOSITION.

Everybody's method of composing is his own. For myself there is much to be done on such occasions in the way of mental preliminary, and a great deal to clear my mind of; it is like a pail of water that has just been drawn from a spring and it must settle. Or, to use a more familiar figure, which I have quoted a hundred times, I am like a hen that is about to settle herself for a three weeks' incubation. She goes fluttering about with every feather porcupine-fashion, scratches the ground, gets sort of cross and blusters this way and that; finally, with great care, she settles herself, but even then her bill is at work, pulling a straw here and throwing one out of the nest there, until she gets it just to her mind, and then she begins to do some execution, and she keeps at it until the end she has in view is reached. But you must let the hen have her own way, or she will never set at all and you will never get your chickens.

I would like exceedingly to know if other people who write, perhaps not more, but better, have similar experiences. Indeed, I think an interchange of the internal methods and operations of "composing minds" would be a study of great interest.

In preparing for the National Convention, I begin for the next year before leaving the platform of this year. I have memorandum-books and papers and scraps on which are jotted notes of any deficiency in the arrangements, so that they may be avoided the next time, and bright points suggested to me by ingenious women, or read about in temperance papers or women's missionary or suffrage papers, for I wish our convention to be made up of every creature's best. All these items are kept in a series of pigeon-holes, labeled with the date of the year to come, and later they are taken out, classified in books, and acted upon so far as possible.

The manner of preparing my annual address is analogous to that already described. Whenever any topic occurs to me, a memorandum is made, and when I am writing the address, these are taken up and classified in the best order that I can contrive, though of late years the address has been written in from four to seven days, and with so many other cares dragging my thoughts away on every side, that I have the misfortune of being judged most widely by that to which I pay the least attention, for the special occupation of my mind is the National W. C. T. U. itself, with the World's W. C. T. U. and the Woman's National Council. Plans for the advancement of all these are with me when I wake. I can not truthfully say when I sleep, also, for I am, as a rule, a dreamless sleeper, but often in the morning so many thoughts come to me before rising that I have the room peopled with mnemonic figures lest I should fail to recall the good-fairy plans that seem to have been given me in my sleep.

REQUESTS.

A sadder feature, even, than the loss of what one might imagine himself capable of achieving for humanity if unhindered, is the revelation of humanity's weakness and distress, of its helpless outreaching to grasp in the darkness a human hand almost as helpless as its own, when, if it would but take a firm grip upon the Hand that holds the world, it would swing itself forward into the tides of power.

If I could epitomize here the letters asking for a position as private secretary, office secretary, stenographer, type-writer, housekeeper at Rest Cottage, care-taker of my dear mother, not to mention the suggestions that new departments be formed in the National W. C. T. U., the requests that we enlarge the force of the W. T. P. A., or send out new organizers and speakers in the World's or the National W. C. T. U., or the Woman's National Council, the list would reveal the mighty unrest of women's hearts, and such a striving earnestly for the best gifts as would make gainsayers laugh and good hearts cry.

Why any one should think that a temperance worker without fortune is a proper person to apply to in case of need, will evermore remain to me a mystery. But strange to tell I have, among the constant applications extending over fifteen years, the following that I recall as specimens:

A woman traveled from Puget Sound to Evanston, telling me

that she felt called to take up the work of temperance and came to offer herself to me. She had no credentials that were sufficient to identify her, no fitness for the work that I could see, and when I gently remonstrated with her, she took such an "excess of nerves," as the French say, as was harrowing to behold, crying so loudly at the boarding-house in which I placed her, and where I paid her expenses for some time, that the people thought she was likely to do herself harm.

A merchant in good standing, and a bright man, desired me to prevent his wife from securing a divorce.

A young minister was confirmed in the conviction that I alone, of all people on this continent, would direct him to the right woman as partner of his joys and sorrows.

A miner in Idaho, who confessed himself to have been one of the worst of men, but was now thoroughly reformed, and sent references to people altogether creditable, wanted me to forward to him from our Chicago Anchorage Home for degraded women, one who had reformed, whom he promised to marry and be faithful to, saying, with a sense of justice too infrequent, that he was well aware she was the only sort of person fit for him.

A woman desired me to send her a hired girl away out to Colorado.

Another asked me to secure for her a patent on a new style of rolling-pin.

A man wished me to arrange for the manufacture of his new carpet-sweeper, and would give me half the proceeds.

A woman said if I would get her husband the appointment to be postmaster in their village, she would pay me twenty-five dollars.

A woman whose daughter had evinced elocutionary talent, said if I would write her a speech, she could quite likely support the family by rehearsing it in California.

A young man wished me to write his part in a debate, that was to occur in a certain college, on the Prohibition question.

Another wrote: "You wod doe us a grate favor if you Could Send us a mishineary to this Place."

One who "was born a prohibitionist," after detailing her husband's financial losses, asked if "I would be so kind as to present her with a dolman or some other wrap, and a dress that would be nice enough to go into company of any kind."

Another good friend—a perfect stranger—who was in debt, inclosed two bills in the letter, and asked me to pray over them, and then pay them.

Another was sure I would gladly aid in the circulation of a book she had written concerning myself.

The following is from a poem dedicated to the W. C. T. U., and placed in my hands at one of our National Conventions:

To you Who Comes With Hearts So Brave
Mounted the Stage like tidel waves
Like a Statue to Behold
White as marbel Pure as Gold

With Words of truth From throbing Heart
Your Misels like a piercing dart
Turned the key of Pandors Box
And threw the Rubish ore your Flock

Revealed to light the dark conclave
And Sent them out like tidal waves
Of Polyticks and Royal Kings
O My What Joy to Hearts it Brings

But not with you By Power of might
But your the Sword of truth and Right
you Shield is Faith Sword is prair
On this platform you need not feare

For He Who claved the Red Sea
Will Stand For you and liberty
Will carry you ore to cannens land
And then will Shout a Happy Band

A HELPFUL BOOK.

No single book has helped me more in these last years than the little French treatise translated by Hannah Whitall Smith, entitled, "Practice of the Presence of God." Brother Lawrence, a Franciscan friar, who did the cooking for his monastery, is the hero of the narrative and I do not believe it possible for any well-intentioned person to read the contents of this little volume once a month throughout a single year without being lifted above the mists and vapors of his every-day environment into the sweet, clear air of that spiritual world which is always with us if we only knew it, and in which we may perpetually dwell if we only try, or rather, if without trying we just *accept* its presence and its hallowed communion.

***

In all the harvest there was nothing sweeter to us than the sense of independence and security that came from feeling that the old farm could supply our wants ; could garner up for us and all the hundreds of four-footed and two-winged creatures that were our fellow-beings and our friends, enough to keep us safe and sound in all the winter's cold. We liked to watch our mother's wonderful butter, that smelt of clover blooms. We rejoiced in her pickles and preserves, her wild plums, and "rare ripe" peaches, and it seemed to us that people who buy everything at the store, live at a poor dying rate, and take everything second-hand—finding life a sort of hash of things left over.

Happy this harvest home of the honest-handed farmer, who knows and loves the good creatures of God too well to turn into crazy drinks what a bountiful Creator has given him for food. As "Old Rye" said :

"Make me up into loaves, and your children are fed ;
Make me up into drinks, I will starve them instead ;
So mind what I tell you, my strength I'll employ,
If eaten, to strengthen, if drunk, to destroy."

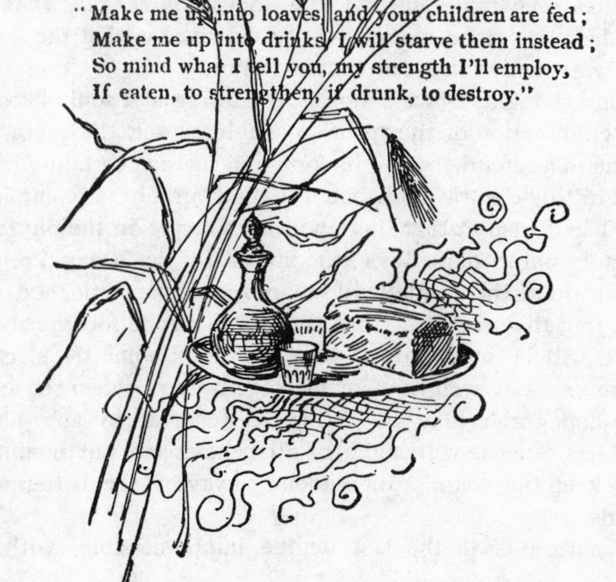

INTROSPECTIVE.

What mind I have is intuitional. The processes of calculation are altogether foreign to me, and old school-mates will testify without dissent that while I stood at the head of my classes in all other things, I hobbled along with a crutch in "higher algebra." It consoled me not a little to read in some of General Grant's biographies, that when officers galloped up to him in battle bringing bad news and asking his commands, he never commented on the disaster, consulted nobody, but as swiftly as the words could be uttered, told just what he wanted done. This trait that he showed as a great chieftain I have had always on my own small field, that is, I have never been discouraged, but ready on the instant with my decision, and rejoicing in nothing so much as the taking of initiatives. Such facilities as I have are always on hand. What I do must be done quickly. Perhaps it is the possession of this very quality that by the law of opposites renders a reflective life, the *otium cum dignitate* of which I have never for one moment tasted since we left the farm, supremely attractive to me in contemplation.

To my thought, conversation is the filling and soul of social life, the culmination of the spirit's possible power, the giving of a life-time in an hour, though its form and method certainly have changed in this electric age when the phonograph has come into being. I half suspect that there will be a strike in the physical manufactory one of these days ; the muscles of the face will refuse to do their duty, the tongue will make believe paralytic, and the lips will join the rebellion. But there is this good fortune about it, people will be more careful how they talk when the electric waves are secret as well as open message-bearers, when the concealed phonograph may be acting as reporter in any place they enter. Science will make us all behave and put us under bonds to keep the peace. Its outcome always is the betterment of mortals.

My nature is to the last degree impressionable, without

strong personal antipathies, and though ready with some remark for any one into whose company I happen to be thrown, nothing short of a congenial atmosphere can "bring me out." A human being, like a cathedral organ, has many pipes and stops and banks of keys; the sort of music that you get depends upon the kind of player that you are. Oliver Wendell Holmes never wrote a subtler thing than that he likes people not so much for what they say, as for what they make him say! Judged by this standard, I do not believe that six persons have ever heard me talk, and not more than three ever in private converse heard my *vox humana*, simply because they were not skilled musicians. There is no egotism in this statement, it is so universal. All of us have been so happy as to meet a few persons who made us blossom out. We did n't dream ourselves half so great, so noble, so lovable as they proved us to ourselves to be. "Is it possible that I can talk like that?" I have said to myself in such companionship. The intoxication of it is the soul's true wine. There are a few fortunate and elect spirits who have expanded under such sunny skies into flowers whose fragrance was the rarest fame,—perhaps all might; in some world let us hope all will! For myself, I know so little of it, that only as a foretaste of heaven's companionships do I think of such beatitude at all.

I shall never forget how like a flash it came to me one winter day, when I was preceptress of Genesee Wesleyan Seminary at Lima, N. Y., in 1866, as I was seated in my large, pleasant sitting-room, with as many of my pupils gathered around me, chiefly sitting on the floor, as the room could possibly accommodate, and while we were planning something good, I do not recall what, in which we were all greatly interested, that just what was happening then in the way of aroused enthusiasm, unified purpose, and magnificent *esprit de corps*, might just as well happen on a scale involving thousands instead of scores.

I did not then determine that it should, but only with swift intuition and sudden pain felt that I might have filled a larger place. I have been called ambitious, and so I am, if to have had from childhood the sense of being born to a fate is an element of ambition. For I never knew what it was not to aspire, and not to believe myself capable of heroism. I always wanted to react upon the world about me to my utmost ounce of power; to be widely known, loved and believed in—the more widely the better. Every life has its master passion; this has been mine. Very few things waken my contempt, but this couplet in the hymn book did:

> "Make me little and unknown,
> Loved and prized by God alone."

Its supreme absurdity angered rather than amused me, for who could be "loved and prized" by the Great Spirit and yet despised by the lesser spirits made in His image? Who could deliberately desire to be "little and unknown"—of small value and narrow circle in a world so hungry for help and strength and uplift—yet be "loved and prized" by God? No, I wanted to be now and in all worlds, my very utmost. I fully purposed to be one whom multitudes would love, lean on, and bless. Lying on the prairie grass and lifting my hands toward the sweet sky I used to say in my inmost spirit, "What is it—what is it that I am to be, O God?" I did not wish to climb by others' overthrow and I laid no schemes to undermine them, but I meant that the evolution of my own powers should do for me all that it would. But a woman, and most of all a woman shy and sensitive, could not determine on a "career" except as a writer of books, when I was young, and I was too impatient of the utter dependence that results from having no money of one's own, to take that doubtful path, though it had supreme attractions for me in my loftiest hours. During the war I begged my dear father to let me offer my services to the Sanitary Commission, but he scouted the idea for "a girl just out of school." I then pleaded with him to let me go and teach the freedmen, but he was more careful of his daughters than any other father I ever knew, and shook his head saying, "Stay at home—that is your natural and proper place until you have a home of your own; I am able to take care of you."

My mother would have let me do any good thing that I liked; it was her method always to encourage our self-activity along the line of strongest impulse, only that impulse must be beneficent. But she, too, liked us to be at home and would not antagonize "the head of the family" in this respect.

If to have some innate sense of a confidential relationship

with humanity at large, so that it was always pleasant to be known and recognized, is to be ambitious, then I plead guilty, for I never liked to be impersonal, and chose a *nom de plume* for a few earlier journalistic ventures only; then not because I did n't like the dear public, but because I did n't like my own dear family to know what I was doing. Somehow I always felt that "faith in folks" of which I speak so often, and wanted them to know about me as I about them. I believed we were all made of one blood and there was no need of this ado about "impersonality." To my notion, personality was the grandest production of the ages ; it came into fuller perspective by reaction on the world of matter and of spirit according to one's power ; let it carry us as far as we would. Besides, I felt that a woman owed it to all other women to live as bravely, as helpfully, and as grandly as she could, and to let the world know it, for so many other women would thus gain a vantage-ground, and I used to sing with this thought, sometimes, the hymn beginning :

"A cloud of witnesses around
Hold thee in full survey,
Forget the steps already trod
And onward urge thy way."

I once heard the Jubilee singers render an old plantation melody with this refrain :

"May the Lord He will be glad of me,
May the Lord He will be glad of me,
May the Lord He will be glad of me,
In the heaven He'll rejoice."

The words and music touched a chord very far down in my heart and I have hummed the strange old snatch of pathos to myself times without number at twilight on the cars, after a hard day's work with book and pen.

If it be ambitious to have no fear of failure in any undertaking, to that I must plead guilty. Fools rush in where angels fear to tread, and this may help explain it, but I frankly own that no position I have ever attained gave me a single perturbed or wakeful thought, nor could any that I would accept. No one could induce me to become a professor of mathematics or of domestic economy, but outside these and what they imply, I can think of no helpful calling that I would not undertake, and there is none that would render me anxious. But with all this hardihood I have not sought advancement. So far as I can recall, except when at twenty years old I secretly applied for a district school, and two years later for the public school in my own village, the positions that I have held have all sought me, and as for writing such poor books as I do, it is at the point of the bayonet they have been ground out—all save Mary's "Nineteen Beautiful Years." If I had been a man the pulpit and politics would have been my field in case I was early driven from the Eden of literature by the desire for financial independence. But a woman who did n't purpose "to make a spectacle of herself" had to walk softly in the years when I suddenly emerged from nature's boundless hospitality, into custom's pinched arena, away back in '57.

Not to be jealous of others who come at rattling pace along the track, speeding onward neck and neck, or else distancing one's self altogether, is a difficult grace. I do not profess to have attained it, but am grateful that its outward expression has not yet aroused my self-contempt, and I will own that, so far as I recall, I have never seen myself outdone without *making* myself secretly say to God, "I thank thee for this other one's beautiful gifts; may they grow and abundantly flourish;" and (if it were a speaker who left me behind, and especially a woman speaker) I have also prayed, "May she have more power this time than she has ever had before."

Still, with it all, I have odious little "inwardnesses" of discomfort when distanced, as one must be so often, and my only consolation at such times, is that I loathe these selfish symptoms and have in their presence the instinct of prayer.

People little know the good or harm they do us by a word.

Edward Eggleston once lived in Evanston, was superintendent of our Sunday-school and a brother to us all. After he became famous he once said to me, "I do not believe there is another young woman in America of your ability, who is content to move about in the small circle of a girl's school." And when I visited his family in Adelphi Street, Brooklyn, he said, when I apologized for some remark, "My child, don't make your manners to me—you're never impolite; in fact, you *could n't do a rude thing*." The happy tears sprang from their out-of-sight fountains; I ordered them back and he never saw them. Great generous soul, but what words may measure the encouragement to me to have made such an impression upon one like him! So when I saw Whittier and he said, "I am glad of thy work; thee is becoming a quite conspicuous figure yonder on thy prairies," I was more than ever determined that I would be one. The letters of Bishop Simpson, Frances Power Cobbe, Elizabeth Stuart Phelps, Gilbert Haven, and a score besides of the best men and women of our time, how can I do them justice for the spur that they have been to my ambition? The dictionary tells us that this word comes from the Latin "*ambitio*," a going *around*,—especially of candidates for office in Rome, to solicit votes. As my self-respect has always protected me from this, I conclude that what I have is aspiration; *i. e.*, "ardent desire" for the achievements herein confessed as having been "the top of life" to me.

A friend, greatly revered, said to me in my youth: "Do things because they are in themselves pure, lovely and harmonious, without regard to whether anybody knows that you do them or not."

But every nature has its limitation, and mine was here precisely: I wanted some one else to know!

"How sweet, how passing sweet is solitude;
Yet graut me still a friend in my retreat
Whom I may whisper, 'Solitude is sweet!'"

Whether for weal or woe, I had to care about that other one, about his *knowing*, too, and take the consequences. That same friend said to me in my youth, "Be true to your ideals, hold fast to them, what e'er betide." And so I have: but to be widely known, widely helpful and beloved, *was* my ideal. That same friend said, "You are nothing if not frank," and used the words, I thought, reproachfully, But I was "Frank," how could I help it? and, having the faults of my qualities, have had to pay their penalty. A sweet white ribbon woman once said to me as simply as a child: "I would like a window in my heart that all might see my love for them; there is nothing that I wish to hide."

Often have I wished I could afford to be equally transparent—perhaps in heaven I shall be so. But this consoles me: if all could see the keen regrets, the self-contempt, the wistful purpose, the ever new outreaching toward a higher life; if all could know the instant prayer, "God pity, God forgive!" such sight and knowledge would go far to prove the selfishness a distemper, certain to be healed some day. Long, long ago, a friend gave me a pretty journal with morocco cover, and wrote on the first page these words:

"DEAR F.: Record here your inner life as freely as you think it, as carefully as you speak it, as genially as you live it and as bravely as you meet it day by day."

I have tried to do so in this chapter, chiefly written at my own expense.

By nature I am progressive in my thought. As Paul said of himself, "I was free born." For a great sum do they purchase this freedom who have it not by heritage. A life of patient study and research, with steadfast effort to hold the soul open to "skyey influence" will hardly send one along the adventurous path of progress if he was not born with a soul hospitable toward new ideas. Being a woman, I have grown, inside the shell of such environment, all that one of my sensitive nature could, toward God's pian for our souls—so different from that of man. Under the mould of conservative action I have been most radical in thought. Christianity has held me as the firm bridle steadies the champing steed. Early embracing my father's and mother's faith, it has mellowed my nature and made me "true to the kindred points of heaven and home." But I do not recall the time when my inmost spirit did not perceive the injustice done to woman; did not revolt against the purely artificial limitations which hedge her from free and full participation in every avocation and profession to which her gifts incline her, and when I did not appreciate to some extent the state's irreparable loss in losing from halls of legislation and courts of justice the woman's judgment and the mother's heart. The first sharp and painful consciousness of humiliation that came to me was from the English-bred boy who, when I was a girl of four or five years, called me a "Tom-boy" and dared me to play with my brother—the two being together in our door-yard. Angered by his interference, and encouraged by my brother's more tolerant spirit, I declared I would play and nobody should hinder me, whereupon the English boy held up his broad-bladed pocket-knife, in striking at which I received a wound, the scar of which is with me to this day. My cries brought mother to the rescue, who chased the foreign invader from our soil and, instead of telling me that little girls must "stay in the house," declared that I should play just where and when I liked and no bad boy should interfere with me. The next hard lesson—and well-nigh unendurable—was when I was required to wear my hair long and wadded on my cerebellum, instead of short, evenly distributed, and leaving every motion of the head easy and free. But my cup was more than full, and brimmed over in bitterest tears when the light, unimpeded gait and easy spring over fences and up into trees was forever debarred by the entanglements of numberless white skirts and a long dress. At this I felt a sense of personal rights invaded, and freedom outraged, such as no language may express, and a contempt for "society" and its false standards from which I have never recovered. But I quietly accepted the inevitable; "conformed" down to the smallest particular in wardrobe, conduct and general surroundings, confident that I could thus more completely work out my destiny in the midst of a crooked and perverse generation, having always for my motto, "To *re*form one must first one's self *con*form."

Dedicating my life to the uplift of humanity, I entered the lists at the first open place I found and have fought on as best I could, not blaming any one as having of set purpose caused the conditions, which I so entirely reprobate, in the customs that immeasurably hamper and handicap the development of women, but thoroughly convinced that these conditions are the necessary outcome of the Age of Force, so long in its duration, but certain to be slowly followed by the age of spiritual power when the gentler sex shall take its rightful place in humanity's great family.

Holding these opinions I have the purpose to help forward progressive movements even in my latest hours, and hence hereby decree that the earthly mantle which I shall drop erelong, when my real self passes onward into the world unseen, shall be swiftly enfolded in flames and rendered powerless harmfully to affect the health of the living. Let no friend of mine say aught to prevent the cremation of my cast-off body. The fact that the popular mind has not come to this decision renders it all the more my duty, who have seen the light, to stand for it in death as I have sincerely meant in life, to stand by the great cause of poor, oppressed humanity. There must be explorers along all pathways; scouts in all armies. This has been my "call" from the beginning, by nature and by nurture; let me be true to its inspiriting and cheery mandate even "unto this last."

FINALLY.

The foregoing book has been written, revised and the proofs corrected, in about three months, largely in enforced seclusion, away from books of reference and to a great degree from memory. It does not then claim to be absolutely accurate, and it is quite likely that in respect to some minor dates there may be a discrepancy between the book and the series of journals beginning when I was about twelve years old and ending when I returned from Europe in 1870.

"Seen through memory's sunset air,"

the far away Delectable Mountains of my youth may have a halo around them greater even than when with eager feet I climbed their summits. My mother says that I have idealized her character, and friends have always accused me of seeing them in colors more glowing than the cold light of day revealed.

All that I claim is that in this book, from cover to cover, I believe I have been loyal to the higher law of truth, if not to the common law of fact, and my purpose, from first to last, has been to tell the story as it was told to me by the higher faculties of my nature. I have had the happiness of illustrating in a small way the result of American institutions upon individual and family life, in the hope that good might come of it to some who are now in the formative period of their career; and with the purpose to applaud whatsoever things are true and lovely and of good report, frankly bemoaning those things that are not, in myself especially.

Nothing in this book is meant to give the impression that its author undervalues the household arts or household saints.

If anybody living is beholden to them, I surely am. A well-ordered home is the beginning of wisdom and of virtue and, I have always dwelt in such a home, made wholesome and delightful by other hands than mine. Most girls take kindly to the spelling-book of home's beautiful literature of action as exemplified in the needle, broom and kneading-trough, but I had not this happy gift, never having got beyond the A B C of sampler, dust-brush and cake-making in my home education. Lack of natural facility should have condoned the offense whose inexorable penalties I have been, under the present régime, obliged to pay as the years brought in their bills. All that I plead for is freedom for girls, as well as boys, in the exercise of their special gifts and preferences of brain and hand. It is also my belief that the law of development will at no distant day, so largely relegate the household arts to the realm of invention and coöperation that unless this larger liberty of woman is fully recognized she will, during the transition period, at least, prove less useful to society than she was meant to be and must be for her own highest happiness.

This is the sum total of my creed concerning household economics, and if it be treason I mean to make the most of it, for I expect to see the day when hot water and steam-heated air will be supplied to every house as gas is now from common reservoirs ; when we shall have a public laundry system, so complete as to drive the washtub out of every kitchen, banishing forever the reign of steamy, sudsy, indigo-blue Monday ; and a caterer's system so complete as to send the cooking-stove into perpetual exile. If men had these problems on hand, complicated with the unspeakable servant-girl problem, they would have solved them by a syndicate long before this, putting no end of money in their purses and no end of misery outside of home's four walls.

I often think, when rejoicing in the homelike amenities of a vestibule train, with its day coach, dining-car, and sleeper, that if George M. Pullman could be induced by a council of women to give five years of his wonderful brain to this problem of household comfort off the rails, counseling with the housekeepers, as he would be wise enough to do, he might crown his life by carrying into the average home the same wholesale comforts and elegancies with which he now regales the traveling public. Only in that case we must petition him to spare us the diffusive atmosphere of that horrible smokers' annex!

To preserve the individuality, the privacy, and sanctity of home, while diminishing its cost and friction, is the problem that women in council must set themselves to solve. Notable home-makers, ready for the next thing, and not afraid of it because it is the next and not the last, should be organized into a standing committee on this subject.

But with these varied cares and perpetual annoyances removed, how will the home-maker of the well-to-do classes employ her time? In the care of her children, the companionship of her husband, and in works of philanthropy, by which will be hastened forward the coming epoch when there shall be no classes that are not well-to-do.

There will always remain abundant territory to be possessed in home's illimitable realm. Women in council working to improve that sanctuary of their hearts will find grievous inequalities in the laws that relate to the control of children and of property as between husband and wife; they will find that in most of the states a wife can not bring a civil suit for damages against her husband; that as a rule, the crime of despoiling a woman of her honor is not punished so heavily as the crime of stealing a cow; that in general, the protection of the person ranks far behind protection of the purse.

A great new world looms into sight, like some splendid ship long-waited-for—the world of heredity, of prenatal influence, of infantile environment; the greatest right of which we can conceive, the right of the child to be well born, is being slowly, surely recognized. Poor, old Humanity, so tugged by fortune and weary with disaster, turns to the Cradle at last and perceives that it has been the Pandora's box of every ill and the Fortunatus casket of every joy that life has known. When the mother learns the divine secrets of her power, when she selects in the partner of her life the father of her child, and for its sacred sake rejects the man of unclean lips because of the alcohol and the tobacco taint, and shuns as she would a leper the man who has been false to any other woman, no matter how depraved; when he who seeks life's highest sanctities in the relationships of husband and father, shuns as he would if thoughtful of his future son the woman with wasp-waist that renders motherhood a torture and dwarfs the possibilities of childhood, French heels that throw the vital organs out of their normal place, and sacred charms revealed by dresses décolleté, insisting on a wife who has good health and a strong physique as the only sure foundation of his home-hopes,—then shall the blessed prophecy of the world's peace come true; the conquered lion of lust shall lie down at the feet of the white lamb of purity and a little child shall lead them.

Forces of infinite variety conspire to bring in the kingdom to which poets, orators, philosophers, philanthropists and statesmen have looked with longing eyes since humanity set forth on its mystical career. If this true story of my life has any force at all, I pray that it may help to hasten the coming of Christ's Kingdom, whose visible token is universal brotherhood; the blessed time drawing nearer to us every day, when in the most practical sense and by the very constitution of society and government, "all men's weal shall be each man's care."

APPENDIX.

Ancestry.

My good friends, S. Millett Thompson, of Providence, R. I., and Mrs. Jane Eggleston Zimmerman, of Evanston, Ill. have prepared the data for this chapter.—F. E. W.

ANCESTRY.

In the suburbs of the classic town of Concord, Mass., on a granite bowlder by the roadside, is the inscription given in the picture on the preceding page.

Major Simon Willard came from Horsmonden, Kent county, England, in 1634, aged thirty-one. The name has been known on English soil for eight hundred years, being five times recorded in the Doomsday book. All the American Willards are his descendants. The family memoir, written by Joseph Willard, of Boston, says:

The will of Richard Willard, of Horsmonden, father of Simon, shows him to have been a man of very good landed estate. The wording of the will shows that he designed this son, not his eldest, but an issue of his second marriage, to succeed him as the principal landholder in the family. His designs were defeated, however, by the removal of his son to New England.

Simon Willard, born in the early part of 1605, became in his manhood a very thorough Puritan. New England offered the only asylum where he could enjoy his religious opinions undisturbed and unquestioned, and thither he determined to proceed with his family.

Various restrictions upon emigration were rigidly enforced during the greater part of the time from 1630 until the power of the king began to sink, and that of Parliament to rise upon its ruins. Persons intending to remove to New England were not allowed to embark until they had obtained from the local authorities certificates of uniformity to the orders and discipline of the Church of England, and of having taken the oaths of allegiance and supremacy. Other vexatious restraints were in like manner imposed. * * * Winthrop tells us, under date of July, 1634, that "it appeared by many private letters that the departure of so many of the best, both ministers and Christians, had bred sad thoughts in those behind, of the Lord's intentions in this work, and an apprehension of some evil days to come upon England. Then it began to be apprehended by the archbishops and others of the council as a matter of state, so as they sent out warrants to stay the ships, and to call in our patent; but upon petition of the shipmasters (attesting how beneficial this plantation was to England) in regard of the Newfoundland fishing, which they took on their way homeward, the ships were at that time released." Simon Willard probably came over in this fleet.

His wife, Mary Sharpe, born at Horsmonden, in 1614, daughter of Henry Sharpe and Jane Feylde, was twenty years old when she accompanied her husband to America. Simon Willard established himself on one hundred acres on the Brighton side of Charles River, at Cambridge.

The following year, 1635, in company with Rev. Peter Bulkely, a man of great learning and large heart, of noble family, and distinguished as a divine, who had lately come from England, Simon Willard and twelve others. with their families, obtained a grant of "six miles square upon the river" at a place called Musketaquid, where they, amid great hardships and difficulties, established the town of Concord. Immediately upon the organization of the town, Simon Willard was appointed "Clerk of the Writs," and continued in that office, by annual election, for nineteen years. His military service was continuous for forty years, until his death. At the earliest election made by the town (1636) he was chosen as deputy to the General Court, and was re-elected every year, with three exceptions, till 1654, a term of eighteen years. He also held the office of commissioner for three years, and was associated with Apostle Eliot and Major Gookin in their friendly missions with the Indians. The court appointed him, under the title of Lieutenant Willard, with John Holeman and Richard Collecott, to form a company for trading with the Indians, forbidding all others, except such as they should choose, to trade in furs or wampum with the native tribes.

The early history of Massachusetts is full of allusions to the many and varied services of Major Willard in an official capacity, all reflecting high honor upon his character as a man of integrity, ability and energy. His name also appears among those of the members of the General Court who so steadily resisted the commissioners sent out by Charles II. to look into the affairs of the colonies, whose attitude of loyalty was seriously questioned. The commissioners were baffled at every point, the General Court resisting every infringement of their patent, indeed, hardly stopping at that, being determined to maintain every right they had hitherto enjoyed.

At the outbreak of King Philip's war, we find Major Willard, a man of seventy years, in active service, filling important posts of duty, and enduring hardships which might well have been the death of many a younger man. Although past the age of legal military service, having, as we have seen, done his full share of public duty for the infant colony, and suffered also his full share of privation and exposure, he seems to have undertaken all the military duty falling to a soldier of his prominence, giving his inestimable services freely and unstintingly. Major Willard was looking forward to a further term of service in civil life as an assistant adjutant, and in military life to continued exertion in the field against an enemy still active and destructive. But, in this last year, an unusual load of care, with its train of anxieties, added to the hazards of an intense winter, to which he was so often exposed on the journey or on the march in long continued absences from his cherished home, must have rendered him easily accessible to the attacks of active disease. It so happened in the spring-time of this year, in the order of Providence, that there was an unusual amount of sickness. Scarcely a hearthstone in New England escaped the visitation. * * * The disease was an epidemic cold of a very malignant type, and to this disease, after a short illness, Major Willard fell a victim at Charlestown, on Monday, the 24th day of April (corresponding to May 4, new style), 1676, in the seventy-second year of his age. * * * Increase Mather, in lamenting over the widespread desolation caused by this pestilence, occurring as it did during the gloomy period of a war in which some six hundred persons had fallen a sacrifice, remarks: "There have been many sick and weak, and many have fallen asleep; yea, eminent and useful instruments hath the Lord removed. * * * This colony of Massachusetts hath been bereaved of two, viz., Major Willard and Mr. Russell. who for many years had approved themselves faithful in the magistracy, and the death of a few such is as much as if thousands had fallen."

The memoir further says:

Early called into the public service, disciplined by the teachings of toil, deprivation, and varied experience, with his character and capacity well understood and valued, it was a natural sequence that he should retain his hold upon the confidence and affection of an enlightened community throughout all the emergencies of a new state, in important trusts as legislator, judge and military commander until his death. This, as we have seen, was no light or easy service. It engrossed, doubtless, a large part of his time and attention; certainly so after he was called to the Council in 1654, and thence until his death in 1676. It took him away from his family, from the cultivation of his estate, and from special attention to his private interests. He must be present at every session of the General Court, every meeting of the Governor and Council, at the terms of the Court of Assistants and of the County Court. From 1634-1636 the sessions of the General Court were quarterly, and afterward semi-annually. The meetings of the Governor and Council were to be held monthly, according to the provision of the charter. As a judicial tribunal, their terms were quarterly. The Major attended the County Court in Middlesex, probably between seventy and eighty terms. * * * Add to this, the numerous meetings of committees, in and out of legislative sessions; and in military matters, the time necessarily occupied in attending to the minute and detailed provisions of the laws in the organization, equipment, discipline and mustering — first, of his company and afterward of his regiment — for a period of forty years.

Again we quote the memoir:

Fathers are often said, and truly, to live again in their children; and traits of character descend through several generations, distinctly brought out in many instances, and in others still somewhat prominent, but modified by circumstances. Thus we may suppose that Samuel, the most distinguished son of his father, inherited that mildness, as well as firmness and noble independence which universal testimony concedes to him. I may add, that so far as my observation extends, and so far as we can predicate any quality of an entire genus, this temperament belongs to the present generation of the family.

Major Willard lived in Lancaster and Groton, Mass., as well as in Concord. Among his immediate descendants are two presidents of Harvard University, also Rev. Samuel Willard, pastor of the Old South Church, Boston, who opposed the hanging of the witches; and Solomon Willard, of Quincy, Mass., the architect of Bunker Hill Monument, who refused to accept pay for his services, and of whom Edward Everett said that "his chief characteristic was that he wanted to do everything for everybody for nothing." Rev. Samuel and Solomon were brothers of Deacon Cephas Willard, of Petersham, Mass., who died at ninety-three years old, having served the Unitarian church there as deacon fifty-six years.

My own line of descent is from Henry, fourth son of the major, whose mother was Mary Dunster, sister of President Dunster of Harvard University. The order is as follows:

[1]Simon, [2]Henry, [3]Henry, [4]Abram, [5]Elijah, [6]Oliver Atherton, [7]Josiah Flint, [8]Frances Elizabeth.

As the derivation of family names is largely fanciful, I have chosen to think of mine as meaning "One who wills"; Joseph Cook makes it signify, "will-hard"—and either definition is acceptable. My great great-grandfather, Abram Willard (great-grandson of Simon), died in the American army during the French war. His home was Harvard, Mass., where my great-grandfather, Elijah Willard, was born, March, 1751. Elijah died at Dublin, N. H., August 19, 1839, six weeks before my birth. He was forty years a Baptist minister in Dublin, and even at the advanced age of eighty-eight, only four weeks previous to his departure from this world, he preached a funeral sermon. He was three times married, his first wife, Mary Atherton, being the mother of my grandfather, Oliver Atherton. He served in the Revolutionary war. His ministry at Dublin, near Keene, N. H., was faithful and long.

The following droll story is told of his powers as a peace-maker. A member of his church had called another "an old skinflint," whereupon accusation was brought by the offended party. When the authorities of the church were sitting in council on this grave piece of indecorum, Elder Willard suggested, in his character of presiding officer, that they should look in the dictionary and see what a skinflint was. This met with great favor. But lo, and behold! there was no such word in the book referred to. The elder then said, that inasmuch as there was no definition there given, he would appeal to the brother who had used the word to give the definition. This was done, the brother replying: "Why, Elder, what I meant was that Brother Blank is a downright clever sort of a man." At this they shook hands, and the church quarrel was at an end. It is shrewdly suspected by some that Elder Willard cooked up this reconciliation, dictionary and all.

My grandfather, Oliver Atherton Willard, married Catherine Lewis, one of the twelve children of Captain Lewis, who fought in the Revolutionary war and whose wife was Martha Collins, of Southboro', Mass., where she married James Lewis, September 5, 1753, and remained there until 1771, when they removed to Marlboro, N. H. Immediately after their marriage Oliver A. Willard and Catherine Lewis went with other pioneers to Wheelock, Vt., where my father, Josiah Flint Willard, named for a maternal uncle, was born, November 7, 1805. His mother was a woman of great force of character, piquant and entertaining; the finest singer in the county. The family lived within a few miles of my mother's but never met until both went on runners across the snow to Ogden, Monroe county, N. Y. (two miles from Churchville), in 1816, where they were neighbors and friends, the Willard brothers, Josiah and Zophar, marrying two of Deacon John Hill's daughters, Mary (my mother) and Abigail. Grandmother Willard became an invalid in middle life and died at the age of seventy-seven.

My mother's line of ancestry is more difficult to trace, the names involved being those of much larger families.

Her grandparents were Samuel Hill, born in Lee, N. H., October 6, 1720, and Abigail Huchins, born in Lee, February 20, 1733. Samuel died in Danville, Vt., and Abigail in Ogden, N. Y., in 1829. Mother's father was John Hill, of Lee, N. H.

Traditions concerning the great bodily strength, agility and intense energy of some of the members of the family at Durham still exist, and notably of Samuel Hill, who was quite a giant in his way; and the family generally are represented as excelling in those brave, manly and strong qualities which make successful pioneers in a new country; while their generally great longevity stands as proof positive of their good habits in temperance, peacefulness and moderation. They were ready to defend their homes and honor, however, at all hazards; quite an extended list of their names appears in the early Colonial military roster, and I still have in my possession the signatures of three of the Hills of Durham and Lee—Nathaniel, Robert and John—all three probably the sons, or grandsons, of Nathaniel. They joined a volunteer organization of patriot minute-men in Durham, June 29, 1775.

As a rule, the Hills were well-to-do, had a fondness for mills, machinery and mechanical pursuits, most of them owning and cultivating large or good-sized farms. Many of them removed early and settled in the interior of New Hampshire and Vermont.

My great-grandfather Hill was a man of most self-sacrificing integrity. When, rather early in his career, he had become security for a friend, who failed, men of good conscience came to him urging that a man's family was "a preferred creditor" in all business relations, and that he should refuse to give up all he had to satisfy another man's creditors. But he was a man of clean hands — swearing to his own hurt and changing not. He only answered, "It is the nature of a bondsman when the principal fails to stand in the gap." And so he stood in the gap, losing all his fortune rather than fail to be true to the implied promise of his bond.

This good man's wife, Abigail Huchins, was a woman of strong character, and firm of will and action. It is related of her, that when a young girl, she was alone in the house one day just as a storm was coming up. A man somewhat off his mental balance came to the door and exclaimed, "I am the author of this storm!" "If you are, then you are the Prince of the Power of the Air," said the young girl, "and you sha'n't stay in this house," and she resolutely drove him off.

Concerning these ancestors, notable in character, mother writes:

My grandfather Hill was a man of meditative habit of mind, almost morbidly conscientious, with intense spiritual convictions, and strong religious faith. He prayed incessantly for his children, until he received the evidence that they would all be saved. He died before my remembrance.

My grandmother Hill who lived with my parents till I was a young lady in the twenties, and died at the age of ninety-seven years, was a woman of sanguine temperament, strong every way, strong of heart, strong of mind, strong in moral and religious convictions—a Whitefield Congregationalist.

My father was like his mother, a sort of Hercules. When a child I had no idea there was a power in the universe that could attack him successfully. I felt safe in the thunderstorm if he were near. He was very fond of his children and we felt that he stood between us and all trouble. He was a zealous and active Christian of the Freewill Baptist church. I can do no justice to my mother's character, it was such a rare combination of excellencies—religious, devotional, cheerful, industrious, frugal, hopeful, buoyant, mirthful at times, loving and lovable always; my father's heart did safely trust in her, so did her children and friends. She was a member of the Freewill Baptist church.

A sister of my father married Uncle Clements, and one of my most valued cousins was Rev. Dr. Jonathan Clements, at one time Principal of Phillips Academy, at Andover. He was an uncle of Rev Dr. Phillips Brooks and a teacher of Dr. Oliver Wendell Phillips.

The Thompsons were from Scotland, and tradition says from the County of Cromarty. The name is patronymic from Thom, the head of a Norse family, and, though widespread, stands only twenty-first in the list of common names. The line runs thus: David Thompson, Gent., a Scotchman who settled on Thompson's Island, so named for himself, in Boston Harbor, in May, 1619, a year and a half before the Pilgrims landed at Plymouth, thus being, as the Dorchester Historical Society affirms, "The first recorded permanent white resident of Boston Harbor." David died in 1628, leaving an infant son, John Thompson, of Piscataqua. His son, John Thompson, Sr., of Durham, died in 1734. His son, John Thompson, Jr., of Durham, died in 1727. Next comes his son, my mother's maternal grandfather, Nathanael Thompson (or Nathaniel) of Durham, N. H., baptized by Rev. Hugh Adams, May 29, 1726, an "infant." He was a trader, millwright and shipwright; settled in Holderness, now Ashland, N. H., (after living at Portsmouth, N. H.), where he was an importer. He lost his property and was killed in the launching of a ship. He married Elizabeth Stevens, of Newburyport, Mass.

He was once at a dinner where everybody was a Tory and drank the health of the tyrant whom Americans were fighting, and said, as they clinked their glasses, "King George's health, *and it shall go round*," whereupon Grandfather Thompson cried out, "Washington's health, and *it* shall go round!" But the disloyal Tories struck him, drove him from the room, and even threatened his life.

The best testimony to this man's character is found in the following extracts from his will. Being wounded and unable to reach home, three days before his death he dictated the following:

"Letter of Nathaniel Thompson to Elizabeth Thompson, his wife, dated Durham, N. H., June 24, 1785: Three days since, I now conclude, I received my mortal wound; and expecting soon to take my final and long farewell of Time, I now send you my affectionate, dying care. I feel the most tender sympathy for the disconsolate situation in which you are to be left, as a bereaved widow, with a number of young children. I exhort you to put your trust in God, who is the God of the widow in his holy habitation. And it is now my last prayer and earnest request that you may teach them to love and fear the King of glory, and bring them up in the nurture and admonition of the Lord. And in my name, I request you to exhort my two eldest sons, in particular, by no means to frequent evil company, or follow trading in horses, which, I conceive, is attended with many temptations ruinous to the souls and bodies of youth. And it is my dying request they would exercise all possible kindness to their mother in her bereaved state and manifest all friendly, brotherly affection toward my other children. And above everything which can be named, O that my children may remember their Creator in the days of their youth! and often recollect and observe the counsels and advice of their kind father while he was with them."

These were the last words of a man mortally wounded, and they are full of Christian faith and fortitude.

Of her mother, Polly Thompson, daughter of the heroic Nathaniel, my mother has always spoken in terms that surprised me by their delineation of a character almost angelic. My cousin, Sarah Dusinbury, from the old homestead, sends me the following peep into the home life of these revered grandparents:

About that spinning wheel of your grandmother Hill's that you found in our garret and carried away, I asked Aunt Sarah if she could furnish interesting facts. She said that all she knew was that it was brought by your grandmother from Vermont, and that she used always on winter evenings to draw it up by the fireplace and spin a "run of flax" before retiring; and that grandfather at the same time read aloud from the large Bible placed on a small stand at the other corner of the hearth, the low hum of her wheel not disturbing his reading or his after conversation on the Scripture which he had read. "Hum, hum, hum, hum," as easily and almost as noiselessly as one would ply the knitting needles, she spun the whole evening through; for women must work in those days, early and late, or their families would suffer. Ah! what do we not owe to the patient, toiling, pious grandmother! I wonder if my grandchildren will ever know aught of me so worthy of their admiration? Probably not; such timber as our grandparents were made of is scarce in these days. My mother has always told me that there was Irish blood in my veins from my adorable maternal grandmother.

John Hill and Polly Thompson were married February 4, 1796, and removed to Danville, Vt., where my mother, Mary Thompson Hill, was born January 3, 1805. My father was born in Wheelock, Vt., November 7, 1805, and they were married in Ogden (near Churchville,) N. Y., November 4, 1831.